Marketing Management for the Hospitality Industry

Marketing Management for the Hospitality Industry

A Strategic Approach

Allen Z. Reich
Virginia Polytechnic Institute and State University

John Wiley & Sons, Inc.
New York · Chichester · Weinheim · Brisbane · Toronto · Singapore

Library of Congress Cataloging-in-Publication Data:
Reich, Allen Z.
    Marketing management for the hospitality industry : a strategic
approach / Allen Z. Reich.
        p.   cm.
    Includes bibliographical references.
    ISBN 0-471-31012-3 (acid-free paper)
    1. Hospitality industry—Marketing.   I. Title.
TX911.3.M3R43   1995
647.94′068′8—dc20   94-47535

Printed in the United States of America
10 9 8 7 6 5 4 3 2

This book is dedicated to my grandmother, Pola Ribak; to my parents, Harold and Clara; and to my wife, Jennifer.

Contents

Preface

The past several decades have seen unparalleled changes in the competitive land-scape of the world. The trend from mass markets to target markets and even micro- and individual markets is moving faster than ever. With the introduction of the information superhighway, dining and lodging habits are certain to change; Europe will soon be a unified common market; the Far East is experiencing one of the largest economic expansions in history; China's economy is expanding at three to four times that of the healthiest industrial giants; Eastern Europe and the Middle East represent major potential markets for consumer goods and services; and through NAFTA, Mexico, Canada, and the United States will have most major trade barriers removed. At the same time, American corporations have been downsizing, realizing that heavy bureaucracies could not be supported in a fiercely competitive marketplace. As corporations have begun searching for new niches in their respective markets, operators are finding themselves embattled by giant, more nimble, foes, with huge budgets and a strong instinct for survival.

Every year, as the pace of change quickens, the abilities required of business operators to deal with new situational factors become more diverse and complex. The time when an operator could run a hospitality business with a friendly smile and a strong work ethic is virtually gone. Managing in today's environment requires a strong and constant focus on a broad range of issues and factors that will impact the firm's success. Those prepared for the change will stand the best chance for survival. Those who ignore it until it has battered their firm's image and income statements will find themselves wondering what happened (or perhaps find employment with their more astute counterparts). As the market changes, so must the business, and change is most effective when it is well thought out through an effective plan.

Marketing Management for the Hospitality Industry: A Strategic Approach presents a strategic approach to the management of the marketing function. This means that the book will cover marketing strategies, in the traditional departmental sense, in-cluding the preparation of internal and environmental analyses, objectives, strate-gies, action plans, and controls. But it will also describe how marketing interacts (or should interact) with the business's strategic plan and other functional departments to produce effective organizational change. Marketing is not a stand-alone function, but a set of principles that directs the company in deciding what must be done to satisfy the customer. This will require businesses of the future to remove barriers between functional departments and will require that their primary objectives be customer driven, rather than departmentally driven. Ninety percent of the book focuses on marketing strategies. The degree of focus on strategic planning and other functional areas is optional and could be increased or decreased based on individual instructor needs or course requirements. The problem with ignoring the business's strategic plans and related functional areas is that, without at least a reasonable understanding of the relationships, the creation and implementation of successful marketing strategies will be all but impossible. The only change in content is a minimal focus on the strategic or grand strategies and the related management and financial strategies necessary to carry out the marketing strategies.

AUDIENCE FOR THIS BOOK

Marketing Management for the Hospitality Industry: A Strategic Approach is designed to be used as a means of learning marketing strategies for any type of hospitality business. The book's target market consists of professionals who want to improve their firm's competitive position, and college and university educators who want to provide their students with a cutting-edge knowledge of marketing management and strategy development. To expedite comprehension, each chapter is an actual component of the strategic marketing model. To expedite reading, each chapter includes only essential information. Therefore, chapter lengths will vary. Additionally, within each chapter are two brief examples of strategic marketing plans—one for a hotel and one for a restaurant. To further help clarify the process, there is an annotated strategic marketing plan in the end-of-book Appendix.

Industry Professionals

The competitive environment is changing, and each executive must make sure that his/her business's plan parallels or, preferably, leads that change. This book can be used as a guide to the development and preparation of most planning needs of any hospitality business. It covers the major aspects of business planning, from strategic or long-term planning, to functional strategies and tactical execution. The strategic marketing model itself has built-in marketing information and control systems. These systems function continuously to make sure that current plans are not derailed and that future opportunities are noticed before the broad market has already taken advantage of them. The major focus is on marketing strategies, because these decisions provide the major focus of the business's efforts to compete. Other functional areas are discussed based on their required support of marketing strategies. Since the book is essentially a course in how to compete in the hospitality business, it can provide many insights into gaining a competitive advantage in any market segment. It can also be used for professional development courses.

College Courses

The vast majority of all college and university hospitality programs have at least one course in marketing. In this first course, the student should learn the principles and practices of marketing, essentially becoming familiar with many of the terms and concepts necessary to put together a marketing plan. While this book is designed to be used for a second marketing course, one that teaches students how to set marketing strategies, it could also serve as a more rigorous first-year marketing text. At the *undergraduate* level, *Marketing Strategies for the Hospitality Industry* is most suitable for seniors, preferably during their last semester. If the college had two marketing courses, placement should be at the end of the student's degree plan, based on tying all marketing and other functional area coursework together. Likewise, in *graduate* curricula, the best timing would be during the last semester. Marketing strategies could also be taught at *two-year institutions* that focus on the preparation of managerial candidates. Since the book teaches cross-functional planning and decision-making, it could also be used as a *capstone* or *strategic management course* for any hospitality management program. Since the book includes a brief review of the essentials of marketing, it could be used for two semesters of marketing: the first focusing on principles and practices with some marketing planning (a departmental or functional perspective); the second focusing on designing strategies (a strategic or cross-functional perspective).

STRATEGIC RESPONSIBILITIES OF HOSPITALITY COLLEGES

One of the key responsibilities of educators is to provide the hospitality industry with graduates who can help their businesses compete. Some could argue that most first jobs will be with large chains, where strategic decisions are made only at top corporate levels. To a certain extent that is true; but not every graduate will be content to stay at that entry level position, and not every graduate will be going to work for a large firm (DeFranco & Reich, 1995).

In small to average-sized firms, and even many larger proactive firms, key decisions affecting all functional areas are being made at progressively lower levels on the organizational chart. In fact, in many organizations, the traditional organizational chart has been replaced with a customized version that recognizes the decision-making importance of all employees. *Empowerment* and *decentralized decision-making* are not uncommon terms today. Most restaurants and hotels expect new graduates to assist in making strategic decisions, especially if the company is paying them $5000 to $15,000 more per year than those without a formal hospitality education. Also, one of the fastest growing management practices today is the use of cross-functional teams to solve problems and develop strategies (sometimes referred to as the *horizontal* or *circular organization*). With a cutting-edge understanding of how cross-functional strategies are set, graduates will be prepared to take active roles in strategy-making—one based on an understanding of the facts, issues, and a problem-solving process, rather than naive enthusiasm.

Allen Z. Reich

Blacksburg, Virginia
May 1996

Acknowledgments

I would like to acknowledge Gus Katsigris of El Centro College, whose enthusiastic devotion to hospitality education helped guide me toward my career as an educator and writer; Linda Hayes of the University of Houston's Marketing Department and Ken McCleary of Virginia Polytechnic Institute and State University, for their insightful suggestions and graduate marketing strategies courses that presented innovative methods of dealing with marketing issues; K. S. (Kaye) Chon of the Conrad N. Hilton College, for his invaluable feedback and clarification of marketing issues and theories; and Cathleen Baird, Director and Archivist of the Conrad N. Hilton Archive and Library, for her support and assistance in gathering critical research information.

Marketing Management for the Hospitality Industry

Introduction to Strategic Market Management

Unless we admit that rules of thumb, the limited experience of the executives in each individual business, and the general sentiment of the street are the sole possible guides for executive decisions of major importance, it is pertinent to inquire how the representative practices of business men generally may be made available as a broader foundation for such decisions, and how a proper theory of business is to be obtained. The theory of business, to meet the need, must develop to such a point that the executive, who will make the necessary effort, may learn effectively from the experiences of others in the past what to avoid and how to act under the conditions of the present. Otherwise, business will continue unsystematic, haphazard, and for many men a pathetic gamble, with the failure of each serious business depression made up largely of the best moral risks.

No amount of theory can be a substitute for energy, enthusiasm, initiative, creative ability, and personality, nor will it take the place of technical knowledge. Now, however, all of these personal qualities may be coupled with an adequate technical equipment, and yet the executive of wide experience may fail through our inability to grasp the broad underlying forces controlling business, a knowledge of which would give a sound basis for judgment. It is a serious criticism of our business structure that it so long lacked an adequate method by which these broad forces may be appraised, their probable course charted, and their applications to individual executive problems made reasonably clear.*   Wallace B. Donham, *Harvard Business Review*, October 1922

The above quote is the introduction from the first article in the inaugural issue of *Harvard Business Review*. The key frustration of Mr. Donham was that there was an absence of a systematic process to assist with business decisions, not only for questions about the present, but also for the future. He proposed the legal system as the starting point for a scientific approach to business. Early law was written to provide precedents so that legal scholars could go about their tasks in a systematic manner without having to start from square one for each new case (Donham, 1922). Strategic marketing planning is hopefully the scientific and systematic process for which Mr. Donham was searching—a process with precedents that could be duplicated to minimize mistakes.

HISTORICAL PROGRESSION OF BUSINESS PLANNING

Management planning systems began around 1900 with *budgeting and controls.* The internal focus was on controlling deviation from the budget; externally, it assumed that the past would repeat itself. The 1950s brought *long-range planning,* with a similar external assumption, the exception being that the future could be forecasted based on an analysis of trends (trend extrapolation), such as the economy, technology, costs, and business cycles. The planning task was primarily to prepare the business for growth or contraction of sales based on those trends. In the 1960s, *strategic planning* assumed that simple trend analyses based on extrapolations of the past were inadequate. It considered forecasts of the future but also included forecasts of changes in the marketing environment (primarily that of customers and competitors). The goal was to anticipate change. Like its predecessors, this planning system was periodic, generally completed on an annual basis (Mintzberg, 1994).

Strategic market management was popularized in the 1970s by the need for a planning system that was more responsive to a rapidly changing market than annual planning cycles. Its foundation is a continuous scanning of the environment and internal abilities to give the firm the information necessary to develop quick responses to sudden changes (Aaker, 1988). Strategic market management is a comprehensive approach that integrates all planning requirements for the management of a business's market. Today, when managers refer to strategic planning or strategic management, they are generally referring to what is technically strategic market management.

OVERVIEW OF THE STRATEGIC APPROACH TO MARKET MANAGEMENT

Marketing strategies (or competitive strategies) could be approached exclusively from a functional level (the marketing department alone) or from a strategic level (all functional departments necessary to create and support the marketing strategies). The current trend is to approach marketing strategies from a strategic or long-term viewpoint.

The American Marketing Association has defined marketing as "the process of planning and executing the conception, pricing, promotion, and distribution of ideas, goods, and services to create exchanges that satisfy individual and organizational objectives" (Cravens, 1994, p. 25). This definition focuses on the functional processes required of the marketing department. No marketing department can be successful unless it accomplishes these tasks. This is why a student of marketing must first learn the basics of marketing, as detailed in this definition, before attempting to set strategies. However, management of the marketing function requires much more than an isolated effort. It requires all the various actions of the organization necessary to achieve customer satisfaction (Cravens, 1994). This is the reason this book focuses on a strategic approach to marketing management in the hospitality business.

A *strategic marketing plan* may be defined as the joint preparation of a strategic (long-term) plan with supportive functional plans, to assure a compatible and continuous fit between the organization's goals and capabilities and its competitive environment (Porter, 1980; Pearce & Robinson, 1988; Kotler, 1991; Reich, 1994).

There are three important parts to this definition:

1. *Joint Preparation of a Strategic Marketing Plan with Supportive Functional Plans.* Strategic marketing plans consider the broad decisions surrounding existing and new products and markets (customers and geographic markets). From a theoretical perspective, strategic decisions affect a company's ability to generate cash and profits; influence the business's long-term success; are generally approved by top management; commit major amounts of physical, financial, or human resources; and affect most areas of the business (Hahn, 1991; Pearce & Robinson, 1991). Various definitions for the term *strategic* will be discussed later in this chapter.

The concept of planning is now and always will be in a constant state of evolution. Every year a large number of quality researchers introduce concepts that assist practitioners in dealing with a competitive marketplace that zigs and zags with greater frequency. Traditionally, strategic planning has been the domain of management theorists, with responsibility of implementation primarily that of administrative executives. However, the current trend is toward a heavy focus on cross-functional integration of the planning process and marketing as the key planning function of the business (Peters & Townsend, 1986). Even if the ultimate responsibility lies with people outside the marketing department, the focus of planning, especially long-term planning, is marketing—"What is our product, and who is our market?" Consequently, the terminology used in this book will be that of *strategic market management*. Whatever theorists and business people wish to call the long-term planning function of a business is up to them. Who in the business takes credit for its preparation or what the plan is called is of little significance (Reich, 1994a).

Another view of strategic marketing is that it can be prepared in conjunction with a management-focused strategic plan as long as it is compatible and supportive of it. The marketing department would simply use its expertise to further define the product and market decisions made in the strategic management plan.

The annual functional plans must flow directly from strategic plans. The strategic decisions will normally provide general guidelines for the planning needs of the functional departments. For example, if a new customer market is going to be targeted, various functional departments will develop plans to attract the new market.

In addition to the need for coordination between the strategic plan and functional plans, there is a need for the various functional departments to work together. If the plans are prepared in concert, a coherent and logical plan is much more likely than if the plans are developed in isolation or by bureaucratic fiefdoms. The choice is between joint preparation or disjointed preparation.

Independent or isolated study of functional strategies—such as marketing, management, and finance courses—is important, and students receive this information in basic courses. But without a cross-functional or comprehensive approach to strategy development and execution, few strategies will succeed. Annual functional or departmental plans in this book primarily concern marketing but also include such areas as operations (food and beverage, purchasing, rooms, housekeeping), human resources, finance, and accounting.

In the past, marketing plans have been the primary planning instrument for most hospitality businesses. Management and financial planning was given minimal attention. Generally, the status quo of previous strategies or policies was honored (located in policy manuals) or perhaps addressed in the marketing plan—usually through some type of operational or financial support of the marketing plan. With strategic marketing, all key functional areas of business—operations, human resources, marketing, and financial —and their individual planning needs can be developed systematically with mutual support.

It would be all but impossible to develop effective marketing strategies without being aware of all the influences on the development and implementation of those strategies. It is commonly said that decisions in any one functional area of a business are not made in a vacuum, but too often marketing plans are prepared with little consideration of the means to carry them out. Often, individual departments prepare plans that, on their own, appear professional and well thought out, but when matched against the firm's strengths and weaknesses, its opportunities and threats, or the plans of other departments, their inadequacies become apparent. For this reason, the creation of marketing strategies must be viewed from a broader perspective than a customer or competitor analysis and the 4 P's (product, price, place, and promotion).

For example, traditionally in marketing the key strategies focus on the marketing mix variables or 4 P's. The problem is that the most wonderful and ingenious marketing strategies ever imagined would not be worth the paper they were written on without cooperation from the operations department, which will carry out many of the strategies; the human resources department, which will supply employees with appropriate skills; and the finance department, which will set budgets and control costs.

The strategic marketing plan requires the cooperative efforts of all functional areas of the business. Unfortunately, many hotels and restaurants have viewed planning as isolated exercises, basing rewards exclusively on meeting departmental rather than organizational objectives. Consequently, this has diminished the likelihood of cross-functional planning efforts: the marketing department prepares its plan, while operations, human resources, and finance each prepare their own, without adequate consideration of the possible cross-functional impact they will have.

For example, a marketing decision to upgrade the decor may increase the overhead, forcing an increase in menu prices or room rates. An ill-conceived new decor could also be viewed as negative by the target customer. If the marketing department decides that a value menu should be developed, then operations, purchasing, and financial managers must be a part of the discussion. How can a hotel ad (marketing) promote friendly, efficient service, when front desk personnel (operations) have not been properly trained? If marketing strategies are set without adequate consideration of the ability of other functional departments, they are doomed to fail. The term for this current trend in cross-functional planning and implementation is the *horizontal* or *circular organization*. This is essentially organizing departments based on the needs of the customer and business, rather than the needs of the department.

Historically, most planning models were based on sequential decisions. The marketing department conceives of the product, operations designs the product and decides on production requirements and logistics, and then the sales department decides on the best way to sell it. With cross-functional cooperation, or simultaneous development (also called parallel development), time from conception to market is reduced, with far fewer mistakes, a lower cost, and less fear of the unknown (Knorr & Thiede, 1991).

There is a movement in the hospitality business to get different groups of employees to *work together* to provide the best possible product, but for this effort to be maximized, there needs to be an effort on *planning together* to create an environment conducive to the task.

The functional departments in a business should work together somewhat like the musicians in a symphony orchestra, each on the same page and supportive of the end result, without personal gain or recognition being sought. The challenge is to help the marketing, management (operations, human resources, etc.), and finance departments realize the importance of collaborative planning efforts. The potential benefits are tremendous. How much more effective and efficient will operations, purchasing, finance, and other departments be if strategies are developed in conjunction with the marketing department and vice versa? Strategic marketing planning may complicate business planning initially, and cause varying degrees of anxiety, but once participants see the benefits of their cooperation, support and adoption become ingrained.

Since participation in decisions is a necessary part of developing strategies and policies, strategic market management forces a cooperative style of leadership that helps motivate and gain the commitment of subordinates. This may initially necessitate additional time in planning, but the results will be worth the effort. An added benefit of the planning process is that it opens up lines of communication that may not have existed before (Hahn, 1991).

2. *Assurance of a Compatible and Continuous Fit.* Long-term profit is determined by a series of short-term profits. Unfortunately, short-term profit is often maximized at the expense of long-term profit. For example, saving money by reducing maintenance, training, or research and development expenses will increase short-term profit but reduce long-term profit. Marketing planners, through habit, have predominantly limited themselves to a one-year time horizon, neglecting long-term opportuni-

ties and ignoring future threats. One-year plans have tended to be minimal revisions of the previous year's plan. When the time horizon is extended, trends (both long- and short-term) are noticed, analyzed, and, as appropriate, incorporated into short-term planning efforts. This historical short-term bias has led to an operational focus on short-term goals and rewards, precipitating diminished long-term growth and profit potential for the company, its employees, and the society in which it operates.

3. *Compatible and Continuous Fit Between the Organization's Goals and Capabilities and Its Competitive Environment.* Actions must be based on realistic, achievable goals and should extract the greatest advantage from the environment. Without a thorough analysis of the strengths and weaknesses of the business, and the opportunities and threats in the environment, it is unlikely that a business will maximize its potential.

With an ever-increasing pace of change in markets, how can a plan prepared on an annual basis help on a daily basis? This question (and implied complaint) is based on a misunderstanding of the strategic marketing planning process. The core of the process is a system of strategic and operational controls. Strategic controls consist of monitoring (1) changes in the capability of the business and (2) critical events taking place in the environment—primarily the business's customers and competitors. Operational controls consist of determining whether the firm is achieving its objectives: if not, why? As changes in any area dictate the need or opportunity to modify or redirect current strategies or tactics, then the appropriate action can be taken. (This is discussed further in Chapter 11, Institutionalization and Controls.)

STRATEGIC MARKETING CONCEPT

The *marketing concept* has been defined by many and basically consists of determining the needs of customers and then satisfying those needs better than competitors (Kotler & Armstrong, 1990; Peter & Donnelly, 1991). The *strategic marketing concept* can be defined as focusing all planning and implementational activities on the primary goal of long-term customer satisfaction at a profit. Satisfaction of the customer over the long term requires continuous monitoring of the environment, incorporating findings into long- and short-term plans, achieving a sustainable competitive advantage, and enlisting the cooperation of employees to support the firm's mission. Firms that work according to the strategic marketing concept use various types of marketing plans as decision-making models. These models help guide the company toward its goals through the logical analysis of relevant information and formulation of well-conceived strategies. Managing according to the strategic marketing concept is simply the most efficient means (strategies, policies, and action plans) to an end (goals/mission). The underpinnings of the strategic marketing concept can be understood by answering the following questions (Drucker, 1974; Porter, 1980):

1. What is the firm's current strategy and position in the market? How does the firm's current abilities match up to future strategic requirements? Are there minor or major problems?

2. What is happening in the environment now and how might that be expected to change in the future (the primary concerns being customers and competitors)?
3. What should the firm's short- and long-term strategy be in light of the analysis? Are radical or moderate changes in existing strategies required to meet current and future customer needs?

Marketing Management for the Hospitality Industry: A Strategic Approach will show the benefits of strategic market management, including how joint preparation of strategic and functional plans can improve the efficiency and effectiveness of management's and employees' efforts, and how decisions can be made that more accurately reflect the company's capabilities and environment. Additionally, this book will show how the majority of the information needed for the plan can be integrated into an ongoing information system, thereby shortening and simplifying the process for future plans, and hastening the recognition of strengths, weaknesses, opportunities, and threats. Preparation guidelines and examples of the strategic marketing plan are included to help clarify the process.

STRATEGIC MARKETING MODEL

This section provides a brief review of the components of the strategic marketing plan and the strategic marketing model (Figure 1.1). The traditional marketing plan model is also presented (Figure 1.2). The primary differences between the two models are that the strategic marketing model includes long-term objectives and grand strategies, plus the analysis and setting of strategies for various functional departments.

MISSION STATEMENT   This is basically the firm's overall purpose: the products, services, markets, goals, and philosophies of the firm. The mission is also referred to as the vision of top management.

INTERNAL ANALYSIS   This in-depth analysis of the performance of each key functional area of the company aims to expose the company's strengths and weaknesses. All functional departments essentially fall within the headings of marketing, management (general usage), and finance. Marketing would include all marketing responsibilities, including planning, advertising, promotions, sales, and perhaps reservations. Management will generally include personnel or human resources, purchasing, business management (that coordinates all functional departments and assumes responsibility for the success of the business), and operations (that covers any production-oriented functions, such as food and beverage, rooms, or maintenance). Finance includes financial and accounting functions.

ENVIRONMENTAL ANALYSIS   This analysis covers (1) the remote environment, where the firm will have minimal control—political regulations, the economy, societal trends, and technology (PEST is the acronym for the remote environment), and (2) the operating environment, where the firm will have varying degrees of control—

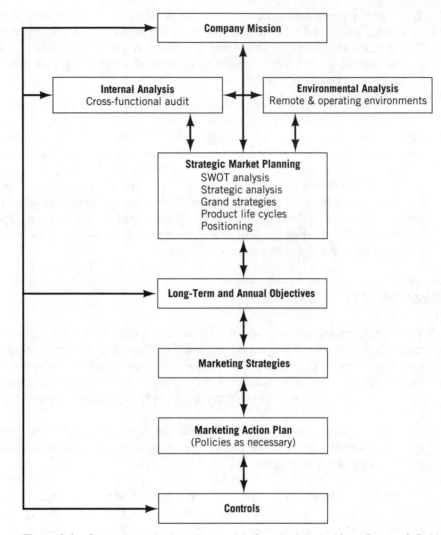

Figure 1.1   Strategic marketing plan model. *Source:* Adapted from Pearce & Robinson (1991), *Formulation, Implementation, and Control of Competitive Strategy.* Homewood, Illinois, p. 12.

personnel, ecology, customers, competitors, and suppliers (PECCS is the acronym for the operating environment, pronounced *pecks*). (Together, the internal and environmental analyses are referred to as the situational analysis.)

STRATEGIC MARKETING   This is a series of planning decisions concerning the long-term or broad focus of the firm related to grand strategies, the chosen product, and market segments. The firm must first create a *SWOT analysis* or summary of the firm's situational factors. Then, through *strategic analysis*, it determines the most critical factors influencing the firm's future and develops optional strategies to address

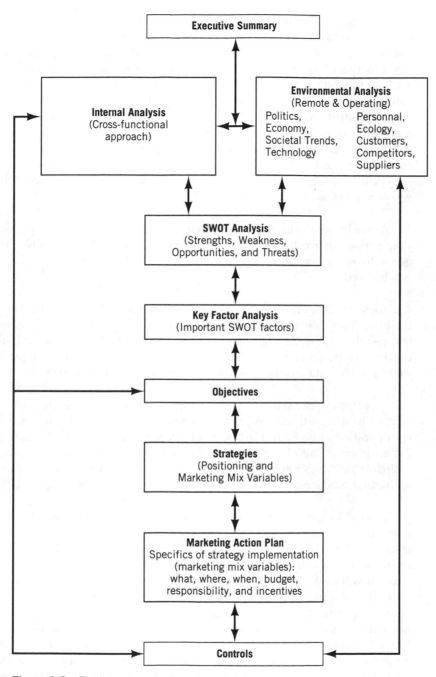

Figure 1.2 Traditional marketing plan model.

these factors. The primary decisions here are the degree of emphasis on concentration (current products and markets), product development, and market development. Market development refers to the addition of new consumer or organizational (business) markets and expansion into new geographic markets. Concurrently with the setting of grand strategies, the firm should examine the extent to which *generic strategies* (e.g., differentiation, lowering costs, focusing, and preemption), *product life cycles* (i.e., introduction, growth, maturity, and decline), *portfolio analysis* (for multiple-business corporations), and factors related to its *industry position* (leader, challenger, nicher) should be incorporated into the grand strategies. Finally, based on the grand strategies and other strategic considerations, such as generic strategies and product life cycles, the firm would decide on its desired *position* in the market (how the firm wants to be viewed, relative to competitors).

LONG-TERM OBJECTIVES   These are internally developed objectives for a multi-year period—normally three to five years. In some instances, industry *benchmarks*, generally recognized industry standards (those of high-achieving or excellent firms), will be used.

ANNUAL OBJECTIVES   These are the objectives of the firm for the first year of the plan. They flow primarily from the long-term objectives but will be more specific because they focus on what needs to be accomplished in the immediate future. As desired, daypart (i.e., lunch), daily, weekly, monthly, or quarterly objectives could be set to expedite monitoring and achievement of the annual objective.

FUNCTIONAL STRATEGIES   These express how the marketing mix variables will be used to achieve the firm's grand strategies. Other functional strategies, such as for the operations, human resources, and finance departments, that will impact marketing efforts must also be addressed. As shown in this introductory chapter and the entire text, setting strategies in any one functional area without adequate coordination with other functional areas is not an effective means of planning or implementation.

ACTION PLANS AND POLICIES   Action plans are temporary actions (sometimes referred to as *tactics*) necessary to carry out the strategies. They are generally associated with the marketing function, being the specifics of carrying out the marketing strategies (what will be done, when, and where; who will be responsible; and how much it will cost). An additional consideration in the action plan is referred to as *institutionalization.* This concerns the ingraining of the plan in the firm. The focus is on making sure that the appropriate organizational structure, management, corporate culture, and rewards are in place to carry out the strategies (Pearce & Robinson, 1991). Temporary or interim plans for any functional unit could also be included here if they were known at the time of the plan's preparation. *Policies,* as necessary, are the relatively permanent and recurring day-to-day tasks or actions necessary to carry out the strategies. Most of a firm's policies are recorded in manuals for the various functional areas—operations, personnel (human resources), purchasing, marketing, or cash and financial management.

There are innumerable ways of dividing the use of the marketing mix variables between the marketing strategies and action plan. For this reason, the overall use of marketing mix variables will be discussed in Chapter 10, along with implementational details.

This explanation is made because in various marketing textbooks, the marketing mix variables are described as *either* strategies or tactics or as *both* strategies and tactics. Each of these uses is correct based on the author's interpretation. What is critical is not what they are called or in what section of the plan they are addressed, but how they are used to increase the effectiveness of the firm's planning efforts. The essential feature is that all implementational details for the current planning period show up in the action plan. If not, no one will be assigned responsibility for their accomplishment.

CONTROLS   These consist of the ongoing monitoring and measuring of the actual performance of the firm compared with its proposed objectives. Additionally, the general abilities of the firm and the marketing environment must be monitored.

KEY TERMS USED IN STRATEGIC MARKET MANAGEMENT

To fully understand the theory of strategic marketing management, it is necessary to comprehend certain terms and concepts:

STRATEGY   Strategy refers to the plan for achieving a goal or objective. *Webster's* definition for strategy (a noun) is: (1) the science of planning and directing large-scale military operations, specifically (as distinguished from tactics), of maneuvering forces into the most advantageous position prior to actual engagement with the enemy; (2) a plan or action based on this; (3) skill in managing or planning, especially by using strategem (a plan for deceiving an enemy) (Guralnik, 1986).

Another definition of strategy is: "something an organization needs or uses in order to 'win' or establish its 'legitimacy' in a world of competitive rivalry and numerous challenges to managerial autonomy." Rumelt's (1979) definition stressed that strategy was what a firm used "to create and maintain an 'asymmetric' advantage in its product markets" (cited in Thomas, 1993, p. 3). Miles and Snow (1978) and Mintzberg (1978) agreed with the widely held view that "strategy reflects a pattern in a stream of conscious managerial decisions, aimed at ensuring organizational adaptation" (cited in Thomas, 1993, p. 4).

TACTIC   A term closely related to strategy is "tactic"—a specific action or means for accomplishing a strategy. In this book, tactics are the policies (the relatively permanent day-to-day specifics of carrying out marketing, management, and financial strategies) and action plans (the temporary specific actions necessary to carry out marketing strategies and, less frequently, other functional strategies). In business, the word can have other meanings depending on the person using it or the context, such as when a five-year plan is discussed as the strategy and the first year of the plan as a tactic. The most common usage is for short-term actions of a firm.

STRATEGIC   The term *strategic* (an adjective) lends itself to various interpretations. It evolved from the Greek word *strategia* and historically has referred to a military maneuver designed to deceive or surprise the enemy (Robert, 1991).

In business, the term *strategic* has the general connotation of "something important" and can be utilized in many different, but related, contexts, such as the following:

STRATEGIC MARKETING PLAN   A long-term plan to enhance the firm's competitive position or a plan that encompasses the firm's primary strategies, especially those related to its product or services and market. In the context of this book, and in the opinion of many modern marketing theorists, it also refers to the fact that it is an all-inclusive plan covering all functional departments of the firm, along with implementation and control procedures (Boyd & Walker, 1990; Peter & Donnelly, 1992; Cravens, 1994).

STRATEGIC SKILLS   Abilities critically important to the success of the firm, such as the offering of quality products and services, consistency over the long term, effective promotions, holding down costs, clean well-maintained facilities, and management's decision-making ability or overall performance.

STRATEGIC ASSETS OR RESOURCES   Both tangible and intangible assets of the firm that are essential to its success. Examples are good locations, attractive buildings, strong customer base, well-received concept, popular menu, inexpensive building, low general overhead, equipment that impacts key areas of performance, positive image, and a secure financial position. Often, strategic assets are the result of strategic skills, as when a hotel's or restaurant's image and its customer base are the result of high-quality products and services.

STRATEGIC ISSUES OR CONCERNS   Anything considered important to the long-term success of the firm. Strategic assets and skills are strategic concerns, as are related major strengths and weaknesses of the company, and opportunities and threats in the environment. Ansoff and King describe strategic issues as "emerging developments, trends or events that have the potential to affect organizational performance" (cited in Dutton, 1993). A dirty or worn carpet in a hotel could be a strategic issue if it negatively influenced customer satisfaction and deterred long-term growth and profit. If this single hotel's problem was addressed in the context of a chain of hotels, it would likely not be considered strategic, unless the carpet problem was systemic. The concept here is that, while everything the firm does is important, each level of management, in this case unit management and corporate management, will have different priorities and responsibilities.

STRATEGIC THINKING   Not jumping to conclusions, seeing the "big picture," thinking through each possible factor that could influence important decisions, especially those that can impact the long-term success of the business. A manager would not use strategic thinking to get a busser to take water to a table; but it would be used to figure out why this situation happens too frequently. Perhaps the problem could be traced to inadequate hiring policies, insufficient training, ineffective supervision, or low morale. Strategic thinking could mean spending 100 hours on a problem, or 10 seconds, as long as is necessary in each case for vital implications to be considered before action is taken. In foodservice terms, each important action should be "fully cooked" before being implemented. For example, Manager A, upon hearing customers ask for fish, adds it to the menu immediately without considering how it could affect the operation or image of the business. This is not always a terrible decision. Sometimes there is a place for impetuous action, but, at the minimum, the potential outcomes must be factored into the decision. Manager B, on the other hand, knows something about strategic market management and decides to "think strategically." Manager B might ask the following questions:

1. How many (or what percentage) of the customers are asking for fish?
2. How often do customers requesting fish eat at the restaurant?
3. How much are these customers willing to pay for fish?
4. How much do these customers normally spend at the restaurant?
5. What kinds of fish do they want?
6. Are those varieties available, and if so, on a regular basis?
7. Should the restaurant use fresh or frozen, off-shore or aquaculture, products?
8. Should the restaurant cut its own fish, or order it precut to the desired portion size?
9. What size portions are desirable?
10. How do customers want the fish prepared?
11. Will other items need to be added to inventory, such as Worcestershire sauce, pickle relish, or horseradish for sauces, and buttermilk, eggs, and cracker crumbs for frying?
12. Is there room for the fish and the ancillary items in the refrigerated and dry storage? Will odor transfer from the fish be a problem?
13. Does the restaurant have the right plates? Are platters necessary?
14. Will the new plates or platters affect the number of entrees that will fit on the pass-through shelf or on serving trays?
15. Should plastic, ceramic, or stainless steel ramekins be used for sauces?
16. How many new plates and ramekins would be needed?
17. Who is going to decide on the recipes? Will they be tested on customers?
18. What preparation methods should be offered for each type of fish?
19. Will different types of preparation overload the broiler or sauté station during a busy period?
20. Where will the fish be stored on the front line?
21. What type of ice is available for the fish? If the only ice machine produces cubed ice, should a flaker be purchased?

22. How will the fish be inventoried—daily with a variance for tight control, or the same as other inventoried items?
23. Do cooks have the ability to prepare the fish according to the restaurant's standards and recipes?
24. What are the current prices, the seasonal highs and lows, and the average annual prices of the varieties of fish being considered?
25. Should the fish be priced at market, or have a set menu price?
26. Does the restaurant have the right equipment? If not, what is the best equipment to prepare fish in the manner desired by customers?
27. If a focus on seafood is considered, should the decor be changed in any way to complement the new items—more airy ambiance, nautical artifacts, a fish tank?
28. How will the new item be promoted to regular customers and to other potential customers in the trade area, other potential customers living in the city, and to those visiting the city?
29. Will advertising or sales promotion be considered? If so, what media will be used?
    • Print media—newspapers, magazines, flyers, or direct mail (with or without discount or some other type of sales promotion)
    • Display media—billboards and signs
    • Broadcast media—radio, TV, and computer
30. How should suggestive selling be used? Could personal selling to neighborhood businesses help?
31. Should a publicity release or promotional event (charity fundraiser with special fish dinner) be considered?
32. Should the introduction of fish be accompanied by some type of merchandizing, such as table tents, an iced display case with fresh fish, menu clip-ons, or blackboards?
33. Would sales promotions, such as discounts, specials, or dinners for two, be appropriate?

This list could go on, but hopefully it conveys an initial understanding of the importance of strategic thinking.

A common remark is that "strategic thinking or planning takes too long!" Manager B would still have at least two options with which to approach the decision. First, strategically think through the implications or process; then, if reasonably assured that no major problems could result, decide to try a minimal number of fish entrees, perhaps as specials on a slow night. Manager A's approach might be similar, but problems could arise if key factors were not considered.

Second, an experienced restaurant operator could develop in-depth answers to each of the questions in the above list in a very short time. Would it be worth waiting a few days before making a final decision to avoid a potential error that could negatively affect sales and potentially ruin the business? One might ask, "How could a little decision like adding fish have a major impact on a business or cause it to fail?" Consider the potential outcome if the fish were added, and any of the following were true:

- The type of fish offered was not what the customers wanted.
- The prices were too high.
- It was not prepared the way customers wanted it.
- The quality of preparation was subpar.
- The new kitchen requirements slowed down ticket times.
- The fish was dry—from overcooking or sitting too long in the pass-through window.
- Food cost escalated due to errors in pricing or various types of waste.
- Fish was spoiling from poor purchasing systems and storage controls.
- Some less-than-fresh fish is served to customers.
- The cooks like to eat fish (cooks can eat an extraordinary amount of fish because it can be eaten quickly and is not as filling as beef or chicken).
- The restaurant, once known for good food, becomes known as a place where customers say, "Whatever you do, don't order fish!"

MULTI-UNIT STRATEGIC THINKING   Additionally, if decisions such as those above were made for multi-unit businesses, the ramifications are exponentially greater. For example, using the above scenario, if problems were to occur when fish was added to a chain of five restaurants, because of logistics—the larger number of people, different processes, and the various locations—correcting the problems would be more than five times more difficult than correcting problems at a single restaurant.

Strategic thinking does not tell managers how to think. It just increases the effectiveness and efficiency of the decision-making process by giving its practitioners a conscious and subconscious framework within which to process information. Each decision a manager makes offers the potential for a large or small success or failure. Often, 15 minutes of strategic thinking will avert problems and reveal the best action to take. Why use trial-and-error on customers when strategic thinking improves the chances of success? As shown in the busser example, it is not used to solve every problem or to find an answer to every question. It is used to help management think through situations to find the most intelligent solution. In an article entitled, "Acting Versus Thinking: A Debate Between Tom Peters and Michael Porter," Reimann and Ramanujam (1992) concede that "an unthinking, random flurry of action and experimentation is as unlikely to lead to success in today's fast moving global business environment as is an excessive preoccupation with the process of strategic thinking and planning." While there will always be a need for experimentation, the chances for success are increased with organized thought. However, planning time should be held to a reasonable limit.

IMPORTANCE OF STRATEGIC MARKET MANAGEMENT

Historically, before strategic marketing, firms assumed that whatever occurred in the past would continue in the future. A stable environment significantly reduced the need for analysis of future trends. Radical changes in the competitive status quo of most industries were rare, occurring perhaps every 20 years or so. Often, this was a safe supposition. Until World War II, most companies in the United States promoted their products or services to mass markets. During the war, production focused on defense, so many consumer products were either unavailable or were rationed. After the war, pent-up demand propelled one of the quickest and largest economic expansions in American history. Not only was almost everything selling, but because of the international exposure of millions of soldiers, new products were being demanded. The next great push to consumerism came when television began bringing commercials into a majority of America's homes. The Vietnam era produced the next major shift in consumer activity. This polarization of America led to the questioning of authority and then to the desire to be different.

It has been said that Americans find alternatives to entrenched ways of doing things. The historical freedom of a capitalistic society, an entrepreneurial spirit, effective communications channels, multiple social classes, and materialism have helped fuel the search for new products and services and, hence, the division of markets. In countries where there are limited channels of communication and few alternative products available, there will generally be fewer social classes and, therefore, fewer market segments. This occurs partially because people are less motivated by status and are not bombarded by ads trying to convince them that they need a certain product or service. The greater a country's industrial development, political freedom, and education, the greater its chances of diversity of social classes and target markets.

As U.S. tastes and trends became economically and racially more diverse, market segments became smaller, and customers became more enlightened and astute in their purchases. This segmentation of consumer markets subsequently caused competition to intensify, requiring operators to develop the ability to adapt to serve the smaller target groups. This adaptation required the ability to forecast future wants of targeted markets, hence the need for research—gathering, recording, and analysis of information—and for planning for the future—strategic market management. Businesses quickly found that the standardized process of updating last year's plan and turning it in for supervisory approval was no longer sufficient.

Generally, most successful companies achieve their industry positions by some means of planning. In the short term, many hospitality management decisions are made in the heat of the battle and are based on what is deemed best for the customer and company. This is a necessary activity, since the customization of the hospitality product offering does not always allow the luxury of time to comprehensively analyze various factors and the preparation of a detailed plan. As these situations were repeated, management would develop a plan for dealing with it by writing an appropriate policy. On the other hand, decisions regarding the future of a company, whether it be for several months, one year, or five years, not only allow adequate time to plan but also demand it.

One of the advantages of a formal planning system is that it forces management to routinely analyze critical aspects of the firm's competitive environment, consequently reducing the number of strategic decisions made without a strategic plan or strategic thinking.

Change and adaptation in modern business are good, but change without structured thinking can be perilous. Voltaire's statement that "no problem can stand the assault of sustained thinking" is almost correct. What is missing is that without an "organized process" for the "sustained thinking," results will be less than desirable.

Unfortunately, the importance of strategic planning in many firms is realized only after a crisis (Aram & Cowen, 1991). Many of the requests for hospitality consulting services come from companies that reached this point of crisis without a plan. Unfortunately, as the story often goes, "it's usually too late." There are many cliches about planning, among them, "Plan your work and work your plan," "Poor planning yields poor results," "Proper planning prevents poor performance," and "If you fail to plan, you plan to fail." There will always be exceptions to these generally accepted maxims, but in the majority of cases, the better the plan, the greater the success.

JAPANESE PLANNING HABITS   One of the major managerial or strategic advantages the Japanese have over Americans is their adherence to the importance of taking adequate time to plan. The Japanese are amazed at how little time Americans devote to planning. A Japanese executive commented that, in America, managers will meet for a short time to decide what actions should be taken, then begin working on their project. Thorough planning is looked upon as a waste of time. In Japan, managers meet until it is felt that a thorough analysis has been made of the situation, and each individual is confident that actions proposed are based on supported facts, not opinions. An additional motivation is that increased time in planning results in a shorter time in execution; essentially "lining up our ducks" before implementation. It has frequently been said that each hour of planning saves four in execution. During planning, Japanese marketers will observe customers as they use their own and competitors' products. This is a critical piece of planning information. It is referred to as "getting closer to the customer" (Gemmell, 1991), something too few U.S. firms have done.

EXPONENTIAL BENEFITS   Often a small, insignificant additional amount of time spent in planning sessions will yield exponential results. What new opportunities could turn up from a survey? Possibly, customers want a faster lunch. How valuable could the addition of a previously neglected market segment for a hotel or restaurant be? Metaphorically speaking, "a relatively small number and amount of ingredients can spell the difference between a highly satisfying entree and a mediocre meal" (Aram & Cowen, 1991).

LITTLE QUESTIONS   Before major decisions and consequent actions are taken, the following question should be asked: "What additional information do I need before deciding on a strategy?" Bill Gates of Microsoft fame, while in planning sessions for new products, is said to be constantly asking, "What about this?" Since all companies, both successful and unsuccessful, perform at least a minimum amount of planning, the key to increasing effectiveness is to direct the process by means of a well-thought-out, strategic marketing planning model. Incomplete or abbreviated plans rarely yield satisfactory results. It is imperative that the plan selected focuses on relevant issues in the firm's environment and provides the means to translate the plan into action (Aram & Cowen, 1991).

EFFECTIVE ANALYSIS   There will always be arguments over the value of planning (Campbell, 1991), but for the majority of firms, factually based critical thinking will generally win out over shoot-from-the-hip intuition. Since research will not always expose the most suitable strategy, intuition will play a part in the decision-making process; but its impact and reliance should usually be guided by effective analysis.

Though the cause of most corporate failures or setbacks can broadly be attributed to poor planning, specific origins are as follows (adapted from Makridakis, 1991):

- *Failure as a Natural Process.* Most firms eventually vanish through bankruptcy, liquidation, or being taken over.
- *Analysis Paralysis.* Decisions are not made for fear of not having the complete picture.
- *Indecisiveness.* Decisions are not made for fear of making the wrong decision, or inability to take responsibility for a decision.
- *Denial Related to Errors in Judgment.* Unwillingness to admit to making a mistake; consequently, problems uncorrected or opportunities are missed.
- *Overaggressive Innovation.* Leading the field with the wrong product or the right product at the wrong time.
- *Excessive Debt.* Assuming that optimistic sales projections will cover debt.
- *Not Recognizing Personal Flaws.* Frequently, people in business, especially those with either money or the ability to solicit funds from others, do not see their limitations. No one is an expert in everything.
- *Inability or Refusal to Hire Competent Workers.* Some people with various psychologically related complexes feel inferior when surrounded by skilled performers.
- *Ignoring or Underestimating the Competition.* Either through inflated egos or ignorance, a primary or secondary competitor is allowed to siphon off customers.
- *Preoccupation with Short-Term Profits.* Funds are not reinvested in maintenance, training, or upgrading of facilities.

Examples of companies that have benefited from effective planning abound.

- *Taco Bell,* through its recognition of the demand for value and nutrition, dramatically increased its sales and operating profit. Their goal is to expand into 200,000 distribution points by the year 2000. In addition to restaurants, this includes retail items in grocery stores and kiosks in airports, businesses, and convenience stores.
- *Wendy's* "Value Menu," upgraded sandwiches, and creative commercials have helped it recapture lost market share. (In the mid-1980s, Wendy's "Where's the Beef?" commercials increased sales by 35%.)
- *Choice International* has expanded quickly by their multi-segment expansion approach. Knowing that mass marketing is out, the firm focuses on bringing in individual concepts that offer multiple levels of lodging service. This way, when people call their reservation system, Choice can supply nearly any type of lodging product requested.
- *Marriott Corporation* has similarly diversified its portfolio of hotels but has carried it a step further by adding retirement communities, such as Brighton Gardens, and contract food service.

- *Radisson Hotels* are recognizing the trend toward a globalized market by seriously looking for locations in many of the world's developing countries. The chain is considering expansion in China, where there are over 200 cities with populations over one million.
- *Hyatt Hotels* introduced Camp Hyatt to accommodate the increased number of children traveling with parents on business and vacations. The service includes reduced rates for children, special menus, a welcoming packet for each child as they check in, a variety of games that can be borrowed from the front desk, and an 800 number for children that features educational facts and information about traveling and Camp Hyatt.

BENEFITS AND RISKS

Strategic market management allows administrative management to consider various strategies in the most objective setting possible; that is, each strategy must be supported by factual research. Furthermore, it helps management devise new strategies and appropriate policies through a systematic process rather than relying primarily on speculation and intuition. Traditionally, we have forecasted the future based on the past. With the strategic marketing model, and strategic planning in general, management can come nearer the true goal of planning—preparing for the future, based on the future.

Obviously, no one can look into a crystal ball and tell with utmost certainty what will occur. The goal is to increase the accuracy of projections and consequent actions, and to provide the most effective direction for the hospitality firm. It must also be recognized that specific strategies for any company cannot be looked up in a book. Answers to strategic questions must be developed from an analysis of the company and its environment. The strategic marketing model provides the basis for identifying and selecting strategies and objectives that are compatible with projected environmental trends and the organization's capabilities. Subsequently, it carries the process through to policies, a marketing action plan, institutionalization, and the control process.

Additional Benefits of Strategic Marketing Management

- It promotes group decision-making, thereby increasing the chance of the best options being addressed, and helps promote the unification of the organization behind common goals.
- It improves acceptance through pride of authorship.
- It reduces planning gaps: the firm can be reasonably assured that most necessary details have been considered.
- It reduces overlaps: redundant efforts are minimized through cross-functional analysis of work.
- It promotes effective resource allocation.
- It provides an organized means of analyzing the environment to locate potential opportunities and threats.
- It gives the firm a means of quickly addressing environmental changes.

- It sets reasonable and relevant objectives.
- It provides a control system to monitor progress toward objectives.
- It allows the firm to become better at planning by utilizing the same planning process each year. The longer or more frequently it is practiced, the more effective the outcomes will be.

Risks of Strategic Marketing Management

- It can take away time from functional responsibilities: to some managers, planning is more enjoyable than routine work.
- An inordinate amount of time can be spent on various levels of analysis (analysis paralysis).
- Cross-functional cooperation can lead to groupthink—the withholding of information or different views in order to appear in agreement.
- Often, the plan is accepted as "The Book," discouraging deviations or questioning of superiors' opinions.
- Objectives can be set too high.
- If rewards are offered, it must be determined if they will be effective and productive.

DECISION-MAKING AND THE TRADITIONAL PLANNING MODEL

Most decision-making or planning models (also referred to as problem-solving models) are essentially the same. Each will generally cover identification of a situation or problem, the gathering of information, developing optional solutions, deciding on the best solution, implementation of the solution, and some type of control mechanism to verify that the original problem was actually solved. The traditional six-step planning model follows, along with its related component of the strategic marketing plan (SMP):

Step 1. Identify current problems or situation.
 SMP—Situational Analysis
Step 2. Gather information.
 SMP—Situational Analysis
Step 3. Seek possible solutions.
 SMP—SWOT Analysis and Strategic Analysis and Selection
Step 4. Decide on the best solution.
 SMP—Objectives, Strategies, Policies, and Action Plans
Step 5. Implement the best solution.
 SMP—Policies, Action Plans, and Institutionalization
Step 6. Have a control mechanism in place to monitor results of implementation and make modifications as necessary.
 SMP—Controls

The time allotted for planning and problem-solving will vary according to the situation. Problems such as employees not working according to standards must be solved immediately. Even though the decision will be made quickly, each step in the planning process will be followed to some degree. If this is the symptom of a larger problem, such as insufficient policies or a lack of them, then more time will be necessary. One of the key advantages of strategic market management is that it reduces the number and frequency of managerial decisions by establishing policies or standards that support the overall mission of the firm as well as its objectives and strategies. Any business will be substantially better off if its managers can spend more time dealing with customers rather than putting out fires caused by improper planning.

LEVELS OF STRATEGY DECISIONS

There are three levels of organizational strategies (decisions)—corporate, business, and functional levels. Decisions made at each level will vary in magnitude, specificity, and degree of centralization. Some companies will make most decisions at the highest level possible—*top–down decision-making,* while others will enlist input from the lower levels of the company—*bottom–up decision-making.* The following is a review of the various decisions and activities at the three primary levels of strategy-making authority.

CORPORATE-LEVEL STRATEGIES   Corporate-level strategies are made by the top management of a company. These decisions are normally associated with multi-business corporations, but they must also be made by single-business corporations with many locations or those with a single location (see Figure 1.3). These decision-

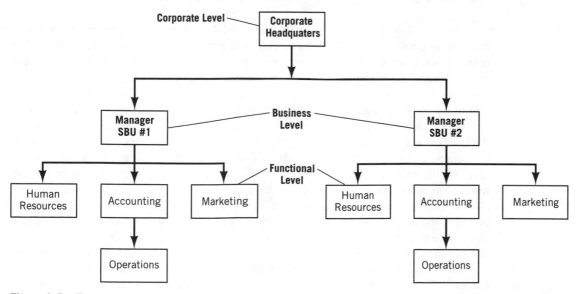

Figure 1.3   The three levels of decision-making.

makers will have titles such as chairman of the board, chief executive officer (CEO), and chief financial officer (CFO). The types of decisions made at the corporate level for each company will vary, but the majority of these concern the following:

- The corporation's public and internal image.
- The degree of social responsibility desired.
- Major resource allocations, for example, basic strategy decisions of whether to:
  Grow, that is, invest in the business with hopes of future profits.
  Hold or milk, that is, keep the business at its present operating and financial level while investing profits in other business units.
  Harvest, that is, skim off most profits while reinvesting only enough to keep the business solvent.
  Divest, that is, sell the business.
- With what businesses the corporation should be involved.
- Financing of possible expansion internally through existing businesses or through debt or equity funding.
- Selection of managers/presidents for business units.
- Setting of strategic parameters and key objectives for business units: the corporate level will prepare the corporate mission statement and assist in writing the mission statement for the individual businesses.

The importance of each of the above decisions and the degree of centralization will vary from one corporation to another. For example, the chairman, president, and other top management personnel of Pepsico, the parent company of Pepsi, Taco Bell, Pizza Hut, Frito-Lay, and KFC, must decide which businesses are slated for rapid or moderate growth, what the image of each business should be, and whether any new businesses should be added. The research for this decision is normally prepared by means of some type of portfolio analysis. (This is discussed in Chapter 7.)

BUSINESS-LEVEL STRATEGIES   Business-level strategies are concerned with how the business will compete in its particular industry. These decisions will focus on the firm's product mix, customer and geographic markets served, exploitation of the firm's specific competencies (major strengths), and achievement of one or more sustainable competitive advantages (Olsen, Tse, & West, 1992). Business- and corporate-level strategies are the long-term portion of the strategic marketing plan.

Business-level strategies are made at what is often called the *strategic business unit* (SBU). This is a single business (or group of closely related businesses within a multi-firm corporation) with different products and markets that will require unique strategies. A SBU could have thousands of locations or only one. It may be part of a larger multi-firm corporation—as Taco Bell, Pizza Hut, and KFC are a part of the restaurant SBU of Pepsico—or it could be a single firm, such as La Quinta Inns. When there is one SBU in a corporation, both corporate- and business-level strategies would generally be the responsibility of the president or general manager. When there are several SBUs, the corporate level will often assist in preparation of each SBU's mission statement and then review the balance of the plan before it is finalized and implemented. The current trend is for each general manager of an individual business within the SBU to also prepare his/her own strategic plan. In this situation, the general manager would set long-term strategies that are both supportive of the SBU's strategies and helpful in guiding the future of the individual unit (the individual hotel or restaurant within the SBU).

FUNCTIONAL-LEVEL STRATEGIES   These are made by the managers and employees of various functional departments. Often, the primary responsibility of general managers of individual hotels and restaurants will be the coordination of the planning efforts of the managers of functional departments. Departments traditional to the hospitality industry, such as the kitchen, dining room, bar, front desk, housekeeping, and maintenance, as well as marketing, human resource management, and finance, can be considered functional areas. Functional-level strategies are primarily concerned with the preparation and implementation of policies and action plans that support the objectives and strategies set by the corporate- and business-level managers. Participation in the setting of policies and action plans is often quite limited. Ideally, those who carry out the strategies should participate in the setting of objectives, strategies, policies, and action plans. Functional-level managers—for example, chefs, dining room managers, front desk managers, reservations and rooms division managers, finance and accounting heads, executive housekeepers, and directors of marketing—should be allowed to help their general manager set annual objectives and functional strategies and be responsible for carrying them out. Functional participation was earlier referred to as bottom–up strategic development—that is, soliciting ideas from those who will be responsible for carrying out the strategy.

DECISION-MAKING SKILLS

There are few circumstances in business that will allow the exact same decision to be made twice. The volatility of change in the competitive environment requires managers to develop their own personal methods of seeking solutions to an unlimited variety of situations. This is especially true of high-contact service businesses as found in the hospitality industry. Generally, developing an internalized plan of action, such as the problem-solving model, will help, but more is needed. There are four basic managerial skills that must be present for an effective decision: data and information gathering, technical expertise, conceptual skills, and inferential skills.

DATA AND INFORMATION GATHERING   There is an old saying, "I made the best decision I could with the information I had." Simply put, the better the information, the better the decision. With adequate supportive data and information, specific issues and the overall competitive environment can be analyzed to see how one factor affects another, and to uncover important facts that would never have been considered (data are raw facts, while information is usable facts). Decisions made strictly on intuition without adequate supportive information will rarely be as effective as those reinforced with adequate information. Additionally, continuous monitoring of the environment provides the firm with the first signs of potential opportunities and threats. For example, in the early 1990s there was a controversy over fresh fish because the FDA (U.S. Food and Drug Administration) did not have a mandatory inspection program. When reports surfaced about contamination, the public became alarmed and reduced their purchases of fresh seafood products and, especially, of raw fish, such as sashimi. Foodservice operators with effective information-gathering systems proactively countered this scare by being the first to let customers know that they were using only reputable sources, and that they personally inspected and guaranteed the freshness of their seafood. There was another problem when several women were raped in hotels. Most hotels immediately increased security, while some, unaware of the problem, wondered why occupancies were dropping. (Unfortunately, some promoted an increased security effort without following through, casting a stigma over the entire industry.) (Data and information are discussed further in Chapter 3.)

TECHNICAL EXPERTISE   A manager without a reasonably in-depth background and understanding in any pertinent field is not likely to make the best possible decisions. There are too many nuances in hospitality operations for an outsider, or inexperienced insider, to make major decisions based on conventional logic. It might be appropriate for someone with related experiences to have input into the decision-making process or even to help guide the planning process, but technical expertise is a necessary component for effective hospitality-related planning decisions. It will be possible for someone with general business experience to play a major role in strategic market management, but most functional decisions should be made by those with technical experience.

The length of time required to approach competency in strategic market management for the hospitality industry will vary, based on the intricacy of the concept. In most cases, the time will coincide with the time it takes to become a unit manager. For example, it will take about one year, possibly two, to gain the knowledge required to take responsibility for a restaurant, and about three to five years for even a fast tracker to progress to general manager of a large hotel. Some small or low-volume fast-food restaurants or budget hotels will develop managers in less time, but their responsibilities are normally limited and compatible with their experience.

CONCEPTUAL SKILLS   The ability to see how all parts of the business fit together to form the whole is a necessary skill for decision-makers. Most issues and problems in business are not one dimensional. Externally, management must be able to recognize the advantages of competing firms and determine if those advantages should be incorporated into their business; if they can be, management must then decide what procedures are necessary for implementation. Internally, if there is a problem with food cost, for example, there are many areas that could have an impact on the problem. The fault could lie with people, equipment, or logistics—such as the buyer, the prep cook, the line cook, the server, the cashier, general management, too many sales promotions, ineffective pricing policies, inadequate or poorly maintained equipment, thefts during receiving, theft or spoilage during storage, the number of menu items, and all procedures associated with the food from the time it is received until it is consumed. Assessing why check-outs are going slowly is considerably more complicated than assuming that employees are not working fast enough. Outdated property management systems, ineffective scheduling, unusual problems or volume of checkouts, new employees, inadequate training, and low morale are possible starting points for locating the cause of the problem. Recognizing the symptom without being able to track down the various possible causes will lead to ineffective planning and decision-making.

INFERENTIAL SKILLS   This is the ability to identify relevant issues and recognize the degree of their importance (Boone & Kurtz, 1987). This statement is the essence of strategic market management, and decision-making in general. Few questions that arise in business automatically lead to explicit answers. There are clearly too many variables that must be considered to make business decisions easy, especially those concerning the long-term direction of the firm. The ability to analyze thousands of pieces of information and to decide which will have the greatest impact on a business is necessary if one hopes to achieve a higher-than-average degree of success. For example, inferential thinking brought us Domino's Pizza and delivery, Embassy Suites and the all-suites hotels, and Subway Sandwich Shops, which saw the need for a highly recognized sandwich shop franchise. A manager's track record in intuitive thinking can greatly improve decision results.

SUSTAINABLE COMPETITIVE ADVANTAGE

In the hospitality industry or any business venture, one of the primary goals is expressed as achievement of a sustainable competitive advantage (SCA). This is an advantage in a strategic area of an industry that can withstand the assault of competitors. The keys to deciding on whether or not a strategy can become an SCA are as follows: (1) there must be enough customer demand to make the SCA profitable; (2) the strategy represents an advantage over competitors; and (3) the advantage should represent a degree of exclusivity for a minimum of approximately one year. There will be some instances where a SCA will last only a few months, but because it gives the firm such a large short-term competitive advantage, the benefits of being recognized as first in an area prevail for a much longer period of time. For example, if Hotel A in a certain market was the first to have a professional workout facility, a free quality breakfast buffet, or a special frequent-guest bonus, then even when competitors copy the strategy, Hotel A will have a continued benefit of being first. What could happen in this situation is that a certain number of customers would switch their business to Hotel A; then, when competing hotels add the strategy, hopefully a lesser number of customers will switch back. In the ideal situation, customers will be willing to pay a surplus for the benefits of the SCA, but this is not mandatory.

Quantity or quality of locations, brand recognition, strong customer base, high relative perceived product or service quality (RPPQ) for any particular attribute, high customer satisfaction index (CSI), high relative perceived value (RPV), and technical superiority are examples of sustainable competitive advantages. SCAs are difficult to attain and even more difficult keep; that is why the term is often abbreviated to *competitive advantage*.

SCAs are generally used in discussions of large companies but can be applied to smaller firms. McDonald's has several sustainable competitive advantages, for example, being the first major fast-food hamburger restaurant, name recognition, sign recognition, brand loyalty of millions of people (especially children), economies of scale, and excellent locations. Smaller hospitality firms, because of their size and limited assets, will generally find it more difficult to establish sustainable competitive advantages. A common means of achieving a SCA is to find a market that is not being adequately served—a *niche*. This could be a new geographic market, a new consumer market, or consumer demand within an existing market. A *geographic market* into which major competitors have not expanded—and hopefully will not expand in the near future—may represent a profitable niche. With the economizing trend in some firms, there may be a *consumer market* segment that will demand less expensive midscale hotels. These hotels would be able to charge less because they would offer a smaller room and fewer amenities. In most markets, there is a substantial *consumer demand* for hotels and restaurants that offer superior-quality products and services at a reasonable value.

The strategy for taking advantage of the niche would then be to meet that demand in some manner, such as developing an acceptable concept, or to be known as the quality leader in that market. When La Quinta opened its first hotel in the late 1960s, it saw an unmet need for an inexpensive business-class hotel. Likewise, hotel concepts such as all-suites (extended stay or residence hotels) and microtels (economy hotels with small rooms and almost no amenities) have found niches in the hotel market. Many independent restaurants achieve their success by selecting geographic or consumer markets where they will not be competing directly with major corporations—a niche in the market where current demand is not being met. Possibly, the most effective means of establishing a niche for smaller operations is being the quality product or service leader in a specific trade area.

For any size firm, the greatest competitive advantage is achieved when strategies, based on a thorough analysis of internal and external factors, are developed and implemented. This, of course, will not develop into a SCA unless those successful strategies are maintained year after year. For example, a restaurant that has great food or a hotel with exceptional service that is maintained over the long term will develop a SCA based on these factors. It is often said of the Disney Corporation that one of their SCAs is the fact that they execute the basics better than anyone.

The strongest SCA, a patent, which is commonly available to many businesses, is generally not available to the hospitality industry. But with recent court decisions, "trade dress," or the combination of unique appearance and operating procedures of a business, has been coming under increased legal protection. Figure 1.4 shows an sample of an SCA.

One of the key factors in long-term success is the location and development of sustainable competitive advantages. There are three basic requirements for this: (1) there must be enough customer demand to make the advantage viable and profitable; (2) the advantage must represent an "edge" over the competition; and (3) the "edge" must be sustainable for approximately one year or more. The Bluzz Room will meet the requirements necessary for a sustainable competitive advantage.

ADEQUATE CONSUMER DEMAND

Consumer demand will be sustained through the increase in demand for blues music and the delivery of a product and service quality that will be unmatched in each market. Increase in the demand for blues music has been documented at over 900% in the past few years. The Bluzz Room will manifest itself as the leader for blues music in the Houston area.

Consumers will also enjoy being able to visit a restaurant that creates a fun and positive environment and that meets the needs and concerns of today's society. The environment, children, and racial harmony are all issues with which society is greatly concerned, and they are resolved inside the doors of The Bluzz Room.

EDGE OVER COMPETITION

The Bluzz Room will become an icon in the industry through its variety of profit- and socially oriented strategies. The fact that The Bluzz Room has a variety of food, live music, a retail store, folk art, and recording studios will differentiate the business, allowing it to remain a major player in each market it enters. With a serious commitment to these goals, the benefits should be sustainable for several years.

The relationship with Mirage/Maxxam and a noncompete clause in our contract will give us "first-right-of-refusal" for new ventures with similar strategies that desire to locate in the entertainment complex. This will create a substantial barrier to entry for potential competitors.

Finally, The Bluzz Room Foundation (a charitable organization) will provide a major vehicle for continuous public relations.

SUSTAINABILITY

The product will be sustainable through its location and public relations efforts. The customer loyalty garnered will be worth more than any amount of advertising. The downtown location will provide a consistent flow of lunch and dinner customers during the week because of its closeness to the largest collection of businesses in the area. The casino will be an enticement for people to stay a little late one night a week or so, to try their luck. These people will need someplace to eat, and, after their sojourn in the casino, they may be in the mood for a drink and some great music to pick them up. The location should also stimulate weekend consumers, especially after downtown renovation. The Richmond location, if selected, has also established itself as a hotspot for activity, with a growing number of restaurants and clubs locating in that area.

The club will attempt to create a loyal customer base by making guests feel that the club is there for them, concerned about the environment, committed to and excited about Houston, and concerned about raising the quality of society through educational and environmental programs.

Figure 1.4   Sample of a strategic plan for SCAs for The Bluzz Room.

STRATEGIC AGGRESSION

There are five basic divisions of organizational persona or strategic aggression: proactive, reactive, passive, adaptive, and discordant. Being proactive at the appropriate time is a primary goal and benefit of strategic market management, as opposed to a traditional marketing plan. Because marketing plans do not usually include exhaustive studies of the environment and the related internal abilities of the firm, they tend to focus on repeating past strategies. Some will address trends in the current environment, but few discuss how the long-term impact of the trend may influence present and future planning decisions.

Proactive can be defined as assessing future opportunities and threats; deciding which could provide avenues or hindrances to growth and profit; then acting on the assessment before competitors. A proactive stance can come from the development of an entirely new or innovative strategy (Drucker, 1985; Ross, 1985), from capitalizing on an existing trend by incorporating more of its elements into the business than competitors (Quinn, 1985), from seeking incremental innovation through improvements in existing practices (Brown, 1991; Stalk, Evans, & Shulman, 1992), or from reviving a strategy from the past. Normally, being proactive is associated with the future. The key yardstick of proactiveness is actually being first. By the time Hyatt Hotels implemented their strategy of offering rooms with a wide array of business services, all of these services had been available for many years. They were simply the first to promote them as a package.

In the ideal case, early innovators will accrue advantages of increased sales, profit, and improvements in image that can lead to sustainable competitive advantages (Makridakis, 1991). Proactive firms such as McDonald's, the first national fast-food franchise; Taco Bell, the first major fast-food Mexican food franchise; Domino's, the first major pizza delivery franchise; Holiday Inn, the first major midpriced hotel chain; and Motel 6, the first major budget hotel chain, attest to the fact that being first with something desired, but not currently offered, can be quite beneficial.

Important to the selection of proactive strategies is the firm's ability to carry out the strategies (Covin, 1991; Feltenstein, 1986). The need for an accurate assessment of the firm's ability increases with the degree of risk involved. Also critical to the proactiveness decision are the cross-functional cooperation of the firm's different functional departments and the timing and aggressiveness of the new product announcement. Empirical research by Olson, Walker, & Ruekert (1995) shows that highly innovative strategies are best implemented by cross-functional teams, where less innovative strategies, such as product improvements, are more effectively directed by the individual functional department closest to the products production.

New product announcements (NPAs) obviously serve the purpose of informing customers, with the ultimate objective being to increase sales. However, they also let competitors know about the introduction. There are two options to decreasing or reducing competitor reaction. One is to keep the introduction secret until the new product is available for purchase. If this is a new location, secrecy may be a problem. If it is a major menu introduction, then this strategy may be a reasonable option. The second option for NPAs is to limit the aggressiveness with which the announcement is made. An announcement that proposes a major change in product offerings or one that is heavily focused on comparisons will often bring a quicker and stronger response from primary competitors (Green, Barclay, & Ryans, 1995; Robertson, Eliashberg, & Tymon, 1995).

A key to earning the designation of being a proactive firm is the speed with which a new product is brought to market. Time lapses can dilute potential impact, allowing competitors to either catch up or beat the firm to market. A study by Arthur D. Little (cited in Topfer, 1995) shows that increases in research and development costs associated with speeding product introduction resulted in only minimal reductions in revenue as compared to delays in introduction.

An example of proactive posturing would be the trend toward reduced fat. A company could easily recognize that in most markets the sale of foods that are high in fat is decreasing. Additionally, the U.S. government is attempting to lower the average American's consumption of fat from about 40% of total calories to 30%. In most marketing plans, the analysis of this topic would be made based on forecasts for the current year. A proactive marketer would attempt to recognize where this trend will be headed for the next several years, then position its product offering between that of competitors attempting to meet the current year's demand and the forecasted demand for the following several years. This proactive stance would allow the company to be recognized as a leader in the market, rather than a follower. This action could also lead to a sustainable competitive advantage. Being first to adopt a certain plan of action is known as a preemptive strategy (discussed later in Chapter 7, in the Generic Strategies section). This is also known as pioneering a concept and can occasionally produce disastrous results. Care must be taken not to offer products that will not be accepted in the current market.

One of the reasons that entrepreneurial firms frequently outperform conservative firms is because of an increased propensity toward risk. They are usually smaller, less bureaucratic, and in need of strategies that help differentiate themselves from larger competitors. This allows the entrepreneurial firm to assume a more proactive stance when it comes to taking advantage of potential opportunities. Conservative firms, on the other hand, tend to be risk-averse, noninnovative, and reactive (Covin, 1991).

Probably the largest number of hospitality organizations choose to adopt a *reactive* posture. There are firms that react to, or pursue, proactive firms' strategies with a positive outcome. The primary benefits of being reactive are that strategic mistakes are generally minimized and there is an above-average degree of stability in functional areas. For example, earnings for reactors are generally stable, as are management tenure, operational performance, and customer loyalty. The problem is that, because of being just a little late in recognizing the trend, the firm's full potential was not realized. The quicker a business can identify and begin posturing toward an opportunity-producing trend, the greater its lead time, the stronger its applicable skills, and therefore the greater its competitive advantage over rivals. Also, being known as a firm that utilizes "copy-cat strategies," rather than "innovative strategies," does little for a business's image. Conservative firms tend to take the reactive position of quickly following innovators—after it has been established that the new product or service is viable and profitable.

Passive firms simply do what they have been doing with little or no focus on changes in their competitive environment. Instead, efficiencies through standardized, high-volume products and services, and cost minimization in all functional areas are the focus of strategic efforts. Proactiveness and even reactiveness are discouraged, because this would be counterproductive to the firm's abilities and philosophies. Passive firms may follow the lead of reactive firms, but only after the success of the strategic change is unquestionably evident and sales have shown a significant downward trend (Miller, 1986). Occasionally, there will be a market for passive firms. When, for example, the elderly constitute a firm's primary market, the business can often successfully pursue passivity, because this is what its market expects.

The penalties of not acting or acting too late include lost market share, reduced customer base, and an outdated image. The following prose describes what happens to firms that attempt to stay with outdated strategies:

> Upon the plains of hesitation, bleached the bones of countless millions who, on the threshold of victory, sat down to wait, and waiting they died.   *Source:* Unknown

An example of a company that pursued a passive posture can be seen in the 1980s failure of Steak And Ale to recognize major changes in its environment. Depending on one's viewpoint, they had at least four marketing problems:

1. The decor was out of touch with current tastes. The dark woods contrasted with red were quite acceptable and even proactive in the 1970s during the heyday of theme restaurants, but they became dated during the 1980s.
2. Quality declined during a time when customers were demanding better quality.
3. Steak And Ale did not foresee the diminishing middle market for red meat. Throughout the 1980s, the overall market for steaks was declining, while selected concepts that offered steak to selected market segments were doing quite well. For example, Ryan's Family Steak Houses (cafeteria/buffet) and Ruth's Chris (an upscale steakhouse chain) have been very successful in spite of the decline in the number of restaurants specializing in steak. The middle market that Steak And Ale served consisted primarily of the baby boomers, who were shifting to chicken and fish. (In the mid-1990s, midscale or casual dining steak concepts are reemerging, but the overall shift away from red meat continues.)
4. The name Steak And Ale, while being quite recognizable, had a stodgy image and obviously focused on red meat. Perhaps a name change or a slogan communicating other food items (coupled with other strategies) could have helped to avert decreasing sales.

Under new management in 1994, Steak And Ale is going through major changes and reassessments, including better targeted promotional campaigns, improved quality of products and services, and the possible reconcepting of some units. Though Steak And Ale will likely not regain its previous position as an industry leader, it is possible that with new strategic initiatives it will emerge as a viable concept for the future.

Adaptive firms choose to be flexible to allow them to adapt to their relatively stable environment. Sometimes this level of strategic aggression is chosen when management wants to continue with its current highly or reasonably successful strategies, but remain open to appropriate changes if the right opportunity presents itself. This works because the firm has acquired the image of a market leader and can rest on its current reputation until it is ready to pursue a more aggressive strategy or market demand for its current product/service mix begins to weaken. This does not mean that the firm ignores the environment; it simply chooses to be opportunistic about its strategic moves. In some cases, rather than make major strategy decisions during their annual planning meetings, adaptive firms will make minor strategy decisions throughout the year. Firms in less attractive positions may select this strategy because they are satisfied that their current position is probably as high as their concept, management, or finances can take them.

The adaptive level of strategic aggression differs from the reactive level because the firm is not aggressively following proactive firms' actions. It is instead searching for the most suitable strategy for its specific circumstance. This new strategy could be proactive or reactive, but it could also have the purpose of simply keeping the firm in its present desired position. The adaptive level differs from the passive level in that the firm is actively monitoring its market in pursuit of potential strategies; it simply has not found an appropriate choice.

The *discordant* firm will usually be poorly positioned, has had problems with past strategic decisions, and is unsure about how to deal with its current position, particularly deciding where its best opportunities lie. This strategy is not usually selected, but acquired through poor performance. The causes vary, but include disagreements between management personnel, doing too many things at once, misperceptions about the environment, preconceived (personal) strategic agendas, and analysis paralysis (fear of action). Discordant firms are generally in need of a turnaround but, unfortunately, may not realize it until it is too late.

STRATEGIC MARKET MANAGEMENT PROCESS

There is considerable variation in the marketing management process, the personnel involved, and the timing of the process. The process can be divided into four primary activities: (1) the gathering and analysis of information, (2) the actual planning meetings where the plan is prepared, (3) implementation, and (4) controls. Companies with sales in the several-hundred-million-dollar range and above may have a separate strategic marketing planning staff that gathers information for the plan throughout the year. Strategic planners would then update management before strategic planning meetings. For medium-sized and smaller companies, the planning process is usually overseen by the marketing department or the business's president or general manager and accomplished with the assistance of key managers and employees. Participating personnel would gather information during their routine activities, then forward it to someone responsible for compiling it (see Chapter 3).

To be successful, the process should be carefully organized, otherwise time will be wasted and morale will suffer (Bungay & Goold, 1991). The actual gathering of information is the key time constraint. For this reason, it must be an ongoing process. If the gathering of information and its compilation for the strategic plan are kept up-to-date, then the actual planning process is greatly simplified. With proper advanced preparation, most companies will produce a strategic marketing plan in about five working days. The following is a basic schedule for strategic market management meetings (subsequent chapters will cover each topic in detail):

- Organize information contained in the situational analysis—internal aspects of the company and environmental factors (external). During the year, information should be gathered by various departments and individuals, then accumulated in a computerized database or a manual file system. Pertinent general or specific information can be gathered in a "fact book."
- A company mission should be developed or updated to help guide the general direction of the planning process. Normally, the situational analysis is first discussed from the perspective of what will happen in the next five years or so. A long-term SWOT analysis may be prepared. All key areas of the business and its environment must be thoroughly discussed and debated to help clarify issues, resolve conflicts, and, ideally, achieve a consensus (Brooker, 1991). This will help managers write the mission statement and, later, guide decisions on the importance of pertinent factors in the situational analysis.
- Review information in the situational analysis to decide what the critical SWOT factors are for the coming year—for example, details of the firm's strengths and weaknesses, and the opportunities and threats in the environment. These will be used to help set objectives and strategies.
- Develop general objectives and strategic options. Brainstorming is encouraged to help decide on general objectives and generate a broad selection of strategic options.
- Decide on specific long-term and annual objectives, grand strategies, and functional strategies that the company can profitably and capably pursue. It is generally best to decide first on marketing-related strategies and their corresponding marketing-mix variables—the four P's—and second on strategies that will support marketing strategies, such as those for operations, personnel, finance, and accounting (Brooker, 1991).
- Develop appropriate policies and action plans for functional areas. These will serve to communicate how the plan will be implemented—how the work will be accomplished.
- Decide how the plan will be institutionalized into the firm. These are critical elements of the company that will influence the implementation of the plan. Implementation without institutionalization will result in problems. Factors to consider will be the ability of management, the organizational structure, the corporate culture of managers, and the employees who will implement the strategies, and whether or not rewards of some type will be offered to help motivate personnel.
- A control system must be developed, detailing how the implementation of the plan or progress toward objectives will be monitored, and how necessary corrections will be made.

The above schedule will be modified by (1) the natural progression of discussions about which direction the company should take, (2) the particular importance of various factors or components of the process, (3) management's subjective or experiential inclination to focus on areas of personal interest, (4) management's experience with strategic planning, and (5) the degree of strategic change necessary. Some companies may need one to two weeks of meetings; others may need only one or two days. If a company is satisfied that its present strategic course is acceptable, or if the strategic market planning process has been in use and is ingrained in the organization, then relatively little time may be required.

The following are key components of a successful planning process:

- Follow and earnestly complete all applicable portions of the strategic marketing model.
- Objectives for each meeting should be set and adhered to. Meetings should conclude with an action plan for the next meeting, including an agenda, tasks, and individual assignments (Aram & Cowen, 1991).
- To ensure that interruptions will be held to a minimum, planning meetings should be held at an external site (Brooker, 1991). Having all participants arrive at the meeting on time and remain until the end of the scheduled time will also reduce diversions. When personnel leave early, an unintended message may be sent that there are other things that are more important (Feltenstein, 1992).
- The process requires teamwork and open communication among all levels of the organization.
- It is most important that complacency in the process be eliminated. Careless errors can be costly and detrimental to the company's future. Often, the difference between a reasonable and an exceptional profit is a few hours of concerted effort on the part of participants. Everyone participating in the process must be aware of the seriousness of their task.

TIME HORIZON

The strategic marketing plan has two time horizons: One is the long-term or strategic portion, normally about three to five years for the hospitality industry; the other is the short-term (one year or less) or functional portion. Even though the strategic portion is for longer than one year, it is generally updated each year, sometimes, referred to as a rolling five-year plan. The reason for the annual update is that since internal and environmental factors will change, the firm will know more about the long-term future one year from now than it does today. The functional plans, or annual portions of the strategic marketing plan—those that will be accomplished this year—will be written each year but updated hourly if needed. For example, in the case where a hotel competing in the midscale market came up against another hotel in the trade area that had downgraded from upper-midscale to midscale, a more aggressive marketing effort would be needed, requiring a modification of the existing annual plan. If a restaurant manager realized that there was a great potential for specialized catering during a major convention, then either the annual plan would be amended or a separate brief plan would be written. Because the world does not stop revolving, the strategic marketing plan is never completed. Everything is subject to change at any time, so those in decision-making positions must keep one eye on their functional activities and the other on their competitive environment.

GENERAL RULES FOR STRATEGIC MARKET MANAGEMENT

The following are practices that will simplify the preparation of the plan and help to reduce major errors:

RULE 1   *Put it someplace.* When in doubt about where to place any particular fact or piece of information, put it someplace. It is much better that a fact be recorded in the wrong place than not recorded at all. If a company is successful, it matters little if its objectives or strategies were technically or theoretically incorrect. For example, pricing or room rates would normally be included as competitive position objectives. If they were instead included as profitability objectives, the net effect would be the same. Also, each company differs slightly on how it manages all functional aspects. In one business, the chef is solely responsible for menu development; in another, someone from the marketing department is responsible.

The more experience individuals have with strategic planning, the faster they will be in developing plans. Since some may be frustrated by details, recording information in the most logical place will help minimize any initial frustration. Placement, though potentially important from an organizational or procedural perspective, is secondary to inclusion.

RULE 2   *If it does not end up in the policies or action plan sections, it will not get done.* A 300-page strategic plan costing $100,000 can be prepared, but if desired actions are not specified and communicated to individuals in the company with the responsibility and authority to carry them out, they will not get done. By functional planning standards, strategic market management is a long and detailed process. There may be dozens of grand strategies and hundreds of functional strategies set forth in the plan. Each grand strategy must have supporting functional strategies; while each functional strategy must likewise have a supporting policy or action plan detailing how the strategy will be implemented: basically, how, when, and where it will done, who will be responsible, and how much it will cost. In each case, the supporting strategies or policies must be of sufficient detail to assure attainment.

RULE 3   *Let the facts speak for themselves.* Obviously one cannot blindly follow the results of research, but at the minimum, serious consideration must be given. Too often, excellent, well-thought-out strategic alternatives are ignored because they do not support the top executive's personal philosophy—based on experience, comfort level, or private agenda. Once the "right" answer is found, alternatives are either not sought or are given second billing (Campbell, 1991). In any particular situation, if power and politics have helped bring the firm to its present level of success, some recognition must be given to their role. But when power and politics stand in the way of prudent thinking, someone must force a reality check. What is right must always take precedent over *who* is right. If thorough, reliable, and relevant research indicates that customers want greater value, better service, or specific services, then the results should be approached without personal prejudice.

RULE 4   *Does the strategy represent strategic thinking?* Strategic thinking dictates a thorough analysis of all factors that influence long- and short-term actions and outcomes for the firm. Reading a few articles, going to a seminar on future trends, or asking the opinion of a few friends in the business does not represent strategic thinking. Management must make a commitment to accepting the strategic market management process as a decision-making model that will guide all major actions of the firm. Care must be taken to avoid shoot-from-the-hip decisions (or mentality) and overanalysis (analysis paralysis). Each decision should be given an appropriate and realistic amount of consideration before a strategy is selected. The goal, of course, is to make a decision or select a strategy that takes into account most, if not all, possible influences and outcomes. A strategy to expand without a thorough analysis of the projected market could prove fatal. A strategy offering the wrong product or service to customers could hurt the hotel or restaurant's image and affect costs. For various reasons, some political and some justified, younger managers with less experience in the field will need solid, verifiable research to support their strategic ideas.

Consider the following example. At a meeting of the marketing staff of a hotel, a sales manager says that he thinks it would be a good idea to deliver a copy of the *Wall Street Journal* to each guest in the morning. The options for making the decision could range from an immediate decision by the director of marketing, such as "Good idea, let's start it next week," to utilizing strategic thinking as follows: Do guests want it? How many guests want it? Are any competitors offering it? How long have they been offering it? Do they think it is a good idea? Do they plan on keeping it? If we offer it will competitors do the same, thereby lessening its uniqueness? Will it make a difference to our guests? Will it increase a guest's frequency or duration of visits? How much will it cost? (Surprisingly, considering the cost of labor and the cost of the newspaper, an average hotel could spend $20,000 to $30,000 or more per year for this amenity.) Will there be future increases in the price of the *Wall Street Journal*? Are its benefits worth the cost? What logistics problems will be encountered if the policy is adopted? Will unwanted papers in the hall become an eyesore? Will housekeepers have enough room in their trash bags for the tossed papers? If delivery of the *Wall Street Journal* is stopped, will some guests become upset? How will the hotel deal with those guests? Is a less expensive alternative available, such as free delivery upon request? Would it be more efficient and appreciated to offer it free upon request?

The foregoing analytical process would usually be the responsibility of the sales manager and would take no more than an hour or two of time to prepare—well worth the avoidance of a $30,000 error and the possible ire of guests.

After employing strategic thinking, and if the company is satisfied that the best possible decision has been made, there must be some relatively standardized means of testing it. Generally, the best method of testing a potential action is to try it on a small targeted group of customers. However, it is wise to limit and closely monitor the test so that mistakes will not affect the firm's image.

RULE 5   *The strategic plan is like a road map: there are many different routes to the same destination, and travel conditions are constantly changing.* It is up to the driver and others along for the ride to decide which paths will produce the best outcome. If it could be guaranteed that all factors in the competitive environment would not change, the same route could be followed each year. Since the environment and the abilities of the firm are changing by the minute, planners and decision-makers must adapt by altering their plans to meet the new circumstances.

The vast array of successful strategies and concepts also tells us that there are many different strategies that will lead to the same result. If one of the objectives for a particular company was a 15% return on sales, there could be hundreds of different strategies that would successfully achieve it. The key, of course, is that the strategy be within the capabilities of the firm, compatible with the environment, and effectively executed.

RULE 6   *There will never be enough time to prepare a complete strategic plan or to thoroughly analyze every issue.* How many articles and books have been written in the last few years relating to topics on environmental analysis? Certainly hundreds of thousands. How many different surveys could be taken to analyze and cross-analyze significant samples from a firm's customer base? Managers must do their best within an appropriate and reasonable amount of time. Research must be balanced with action. Hotels and foodservice establishments make money by providing services for customers, not by performing research. The most critical pieces of information must be gathered from the millions that exist; then a decision must be made. Analysis paralysis must be avoided at all costs.

RULE 7   *The apparent redundancy in the planning process has its purpose.* It must be recognized that there will be some redundancy in the strategic market management process. This is a necessary and purposeful part of strategic market planning. Once it is decided that an issue is critical, it will be noted in the grand strategies. Subsequently, related long- and short-term objectives will be written that, if attained, will assure the firm takes advantage of the issue, defends against it, or corrects it. Then functional strategies to accomplish the objectives will be prepared, followed by policies and action plans to detail how the strategy will be achieved and to assign specific responsibility. Finally, some means of controlling its accomplishment is required. This consideration at all levels of decision-making will require some repetition.

THE BRYAN HOUSE AND CITY GRILL STRATEGIC MARKETING MODELS

A detailed explanation of each integral component of the strategic marketing model for the hospitality industry will now be presented. To clarify preparation, plans for two hypothetical businesses—a casual dining restaurant, City Grill, and a hotel, The Bryan House—are included at the end of each chapter, except Chapter 3. This chapter on research reviews methods of gathering data for the internal and environmental analyses. For further explanation, an annotated plan for a food and beverage facility that increases the nutritional content of the facility's menu is provided in the Appendix at the back of the book. Even though this book focuses on hotels and restaurants, a strategic marketing plan can be developed for any hospitality concern or any business where a comprehensive strategic vision is desired.

Executive Summary

Any business report that is longer than two pages should be accompanied by an executive summary, a brief statement reviewing the report's highlights. The length of the summary should be in proportion to the length of the report: about one sentence per page, but rarely more than one page long.

While there is no strict format to follow, the executive summary usually begins with a brief statement about the business's current position; then it reviews the main objectives and presents the key strategies used to reach those objectives. It should create a feeling of excitement, or at least optimism. Although it will be the first page of text in the plan, it is the last section to be written.

The Bryan House

EXECUTIVE SUMMARY

While the past few years have been difficult for the hotel industry, the future appears to be a steady progression in a positive direction. The Bryan House is positioning itself to move with this current trend. The primary product strategies for the upcoming year include the addition of a business center, concierge, and workout facility. We will hold the line on our current room rates so that we will be in line with competitors. For promotions, the JAGUAR feature (a video display) of SABREvision will be added. Also, an increased focus will be placed on keeping in closer contact with present accounts, creating a system for increasing referrals, and upselling reservations and walk-ins; in addition, a new weekend package will be added. A property management system will be purchased to improve our check-in and check-out timing. Employees at all levels will be brought into the decision-making process and empowered to do whatever is reasonably necessary to please our guests.

It is hoped that with these changes The Bryan House can become a leader in profits and quality of operations in the downtown area market.

City Grill

EXECUTIVE SUMMARY

The past year saw a continued improvement in sales and profit. New menu items and increased operational efficiency were thought to be the primary reason. Because of competitive pressure, we feel our current 15% return on sales to be an appropriate long-term and annual objective. Food and labor cost objectives, respectively, have been set at 25% and 32%. To continue this level of financial and operational performance during the coming year, we will add a bakery and new seafood entrees, and will experiment with vegetarian entrees.

QUESTIONS AND PROJECTS

1. Bring two articles from periodicals, one showing how proper planning helped a hospitality company succeed and one showing how poor planning caused a company to fail or lose money. (All actions or strategies are based on some type of planning, or the lack of it.) Each student will present a summary of his/her article(s) and lead a class discussion on them. The discussion will center on what the company did right or wrong, what the company might have been thinking when they decided on the strategy, and, for unsuccessful strategies, what they could have done differently.
2. What do you feel are relevant benefits and risks of planning for any particular type of hospitality business?
3. Write down a common customer complaint for a hotel or restaurant; then record the possible number of causes.
4. What is the definition of "strategic"? How is the word used to describe several different tangible and intangible components of the business?
5. What is the definition of "tactic" and which components of the strategic plan are considered to be tactics?
6. Using strategic thinking, analyze the possibility of adding 24-hour room service for a Holiday Inn located in a business district.
7. Use strategic thinking to analyze the addition of a curried chicken salad sandwich to a casual dining concept's menu (e.g., Chili's, Friday's, or Bennigan's).
8. What new elements of strategic thinking could be added to the fish example when investigating each possible implication?
9. In your own words, define strategic marketing planning and discuss how it relates to marketing strategies.
10. What are some of the benefits and risks of planning?
11. Describe the traditional six-step problem-solving model. How do various components of the strategic model relate to the problem-solving model?

12. List and define the decision-making skills necessary for effective strategic market management.
13. What is a sustainable competitive advantage, and why is it important?
14. Define the terms *proactive, reactive, passive, adaptive,* and *discordant.* Which do you feel is the safest business posture?
15. Discuss the seven basic rules for strategic market management.

CHAPTER 2

Mission Statement

Over the past ten years, the popularity of the mission statement has rapidly increased. The primary reason is elementary. Firms with operationalized mission statements have generally outperformed those without operationalized mission statements. In a study of the Business Week 1000 (the 1000 largest businesses in America), firms with mission statements had an average return on stockholder's equity of 16.6%, while the return for those without mission statements was 9.7% (Rarick & Vitton, 1995). There would obviously be other variables that influenced these results, primarily the fact that the firms with mission statements are more likely to be vigilant planners and operate the firm according to the principles proclaimed in the mission (Campbell, 1992). But the 71.1% disparity between the two groups of firms is large enough to substantiate the value of having and utilizing a mission statement (16.6 − 9.7 = 6.9; 6.9 ÷ 9.7 = 71.1). Preparing a mission statement is not difficult, but preparing and implementing one that is worthwhile requires a major managerial commitment. Some firms will spend more time developing their mission statement than their entire strategic plan. This time is often justified by the enormous benefits, primarily those of providing the firm with a moral compass for employees and management; being an explicit guide for the business's planning and implementational activities; and providing a tool to communicate the firm's philosophies to the general public.

The mission statement can be defined as a broad statement of characteristics (product and market), goals (profit and growth), and philosophies of a business (Pearce & Robinson, 1991); or simply its purpose and philosophies (Byars, 1984). It is also referred to as the company mission, mission, vision, and creed or credo. The mission statement is frequently thought of as being a nonsensical bundle of platitudes, and for companies with little sense of direction, this is true. But the mere putting down on paper of what general direction the company should take is essential, even if it does sound like every other company mission. You've got to start somewhere! A company that has not organized its thought process enough to know what it is, where it's going, and what it stands for, is charting treacherous waters. Two excellent quotes that point up the importance of the mission statement follow.

Only a clear definition of the mission and purpose of the business makes possible clear and realistic business objectives. It is the foundation for priorities, strategies, plans, and work assignments. It is the starting point for the design of managerial jobs and, above all, for the design of managerial structures. Structure follows strategy. Strategy determines what the key activities are in a given business. And strategy requires knowing "what our business is and what it should be." (Drucker, 1974, p. 75)

Effective strategic leadership starts with a concept of what the organization should and should not do and a vision of where the organization needs to be headed. (Thompson & Strickland, 1992)

THE PLACE OF THE MISSION STATEMENT IN THE PLANNING PROCESS

For most firms, the mission statement is the first thing addressed in a strategic planning session. This is possible because, prior to the session, participants have reviewed a copy or detailed summary of the situational analysis. During the year, internal and environmental data are gathered, so that when the planning process begins, necessary research information is available. For companies in development or formation, the first step in the strategic planning process would be to prepare the situational analysis, rather than the mission statement. Essentially, this means an analysis of the current and future competitive market and its receptiveness to potential products and services. The mission statement would be prepared from this information.

THE NEED TO PUT THE MISSION STATEMENT IN WRITING

Historically, most businesses had an implicit vision for the future, but until the increased popularity of strategic planning, few companies committed it to writing. In one survey, 70% of the respondents with mission statements had prepared them within the last four years (Klemm, Sanderson, & Luffman, 1991). In the past, one or a few people at the top made the majority of the important decisions for the company, negating the need for lower-level employees to be aware of specific goals. People simply did as they were told. As authority and responsibility were decentralized, managers and employees at all levels began making decisions that influenced the firm's success and strategic direction. Without a central vision or goal, decision-makers will by nature do what they think is in the best interest of the firm or themselves (Drucker, 1974). Obviously, there is still a great need for job descriptions, guidelines, policies, and procedures, but the fact is that not everything can be put into writing. This realization has fueled the drive to provide employees with increased empowerment to do, within defined parameters, what they think is best, as long as it supports the company's mission.

Because today's mode of business can rapidly become obsolete, a set of principles, practices, and foundations are necessary to serve as a starting point for change. If a firm's philosophies are understood by management, then the firm will have a built-in mechanism to control the selection of new strategies. At most proactive companies, the only sacred cow is their philosophy of doing business: anything else can be challenged. The measure of this stance is the quality and success of these firms' strategies and the consistent ethical treatment of people.

PURPOSE

The mission statement's specific and primary purpose is to articulate top management's desires concerning their vision for the firm's future, and to communicate those desires to the people who will prepare the strategic plan and be responsible for carrying it out. For this reason, it is viewed as the first step in writing the strategic marketing plan (Campbell & Yeung, 1991). It must be recognized that without a reasonable amount of research in the form of a situational analysis, an effective mission statement cannot be written. The secondary purpose is for use in external public relations and to motivate management and employees of the firm (Klemm, Sanderson, & Luffman, 1991). This recognition of the mission's purpose and importance produces the following benefits.

1. It reduces political infighting by setting a general course for the firm. As strategies are considered and objectives formulated, planners will review the mission statement to be sure that top management's priorities are being adhered to. If a strategy will not be supportive of the mission, then it must be either rescinded or approved by the keeper of the mission—the CEO, president, owner, or top executive. If the mission statement stresses new product development, then this should be a critical point of analysis and subsequent strategies. If, after specific research, middle management feels that it would not be wise to add new products at this time, then their reasoning can be presented to top management for review. Figure 2.1 shows the relationship among the mission statement, objectives, and strategies.

MISSION STATEMENT	OBJECTIVES	STRATEGIES
Profitability	Reach a 10% profit.	Promote lower-cost food items.
Social responsibility	(1) Host fundraiser for deserving charity. (2) Recycle all plastic beginning June 1, 19xx.	(1) Host fundraiser for Women's Crisis Center. (2) Kitchen manager is responsible for recycling objectives.
Personal growth for employees	(1) Hiring from within beginning May 1, 19xx. (2) Training program beginning May 1, 19xx.	(1) All functional managers must be hired from within. (2) Each functional manager will prepare training manuals for all positions.

Figure 2.1   Mission statement, objective, and strategy sequence.

2. It communicates an explicit goal for all employees and management personnel. Many companies take critical excerpts of the mission statement to be used as a credo—a statement of principles—sometimes known as the silver bullet mission statement. For example, McDonald's credo of QSC&V (Quality, Service, Cleanliness, and Value) is known by all within the company and serves as their employees' unifying purpose and personal mission. A corporate credo or vision can be likened to a good battle cry: as George Bernard Shaw once said, "A good battle cry is half the battle." All employees of the firm should either know the company credo or at least be able to express the company's vision (Hinterhuber & Popp, 1992).

3. It tells the local community and general public what the company considers to be important and what its basic goals are. One of the reasons the mission statement is becoming more important is that it is being used for various forms of corporate communications, from brochures in the marketing department to annual reports. An effective mission statement should give readers a "warm, fuzzy feeling" about the company, making them feel that the primary motivator is not greed but the general good of all those affected by the firm. This is often critically important for multinational firms, especially those that operate in third-world countries.

COMPONENTS OF THE MISSION STATEMENT

The mission statement's primary components consist of characteristics, goals, and philosophies (Pearce & Robinson, 1991).

Characteristics

This section should include broad descriptions of products (product mix and type of business) and services (service mix, style of service, and services offered), and the customers or markets served. Here is where the answer to "What should our business be?" will be expressed.

PRODUCTS AND SERVICES   This description need not be extensive, but it should be adequate to guide those involved in setting functional strategies. For example, consider the following description:

> We sell high-quality hamburgers and sandwiches, served on breads we bake daily in each restaurant. Portions are larger than any competitor's and all foods are cooked to order. New products that are desired by customers, which can be prepared to our standards and are compatible with our concept, should be sought and considered. Our service style is an upgrade from traditional self-service restaurants in that we deliver the meal to the customer's table. The atmosphere is characteristic of 1920 art deco restaurants.

Other unique features could be mentioned if readers of the mission statement will benefit from the additional information. The purpose here is only to set a course for the company and those who will prepare the strategic plan. Specific additions or modifications to the menu or services and other detailed information will be presented later in the plan. It must be recognized that, although today's product offering may be quite successful, it may not garner the same prosperity next year. In five years, will consumers be eating hamburgers made primarily with beef, or will turkey be increasing in popularity? Will fast-food restaurants require fewer seats? Will less expensive hotels with smaller rooms be preferred over larger, more expensive facilities? An analytical view of the environment will help management ponder these questions.

There is a trend to broaden the scope and creative horizons of hospitality businesses by defining their characteristics in less confining terms. Casual or fine dining restaurants, for example, could be thought of as being in the dining and entertainment business, while fast-food concepts belong in the convenience dining business. Hotels, as viewed by managers at the Hilton Corporation, should be considered as being in the "travel business."

With a broadened scope may come new opportunities that were not previously acknowledged. For example, viewing themselves as being in the convenience dining business has helped fast-food restaurants focus on and develop new means of making it easier to get something to eat—quicker takeout service and a greater focus on delivery. Also, many casual and upscale restaurants consider themselves to be in the entertainment business. This has directed the focus on a complete dining experience, rather than simply offering a good meal. It has also created points of differentiation for aggressive concepts. Romano's Macaroni Grill's two exhibition kitchens, with ingredients displayed in deli cases, helps set their concept apart from primary competitors.

Precaution must be taken when considering a broad view of the firm's business. Negative results may surface if management strays too far from its base of experience or area of greatest opportunities. A hotel without experience in organizing tours may hurt its reputation by expanding its horizons too far. Each business must decide how broad or narrow its scope of operations should be. Since the hospitality industry is highly dynamic and creative, a broad definition of the business scope should be considered.

THE TARGET MARKET   Who are the primary customers of the firm? (A *customer* is an individual or company that purchases a product or service. A *market* is defined as the actual and potential users and purchasers of a product or service—basically a group of actual and potential customers. Hence, a customer is an individual within a *target market.*) The number of primary target markets for hotels and restaurants generally has an inverse relationship to the degree of service offered. Fast-food restaurants and budget hotels will normally have a much more diverse target customer base than fine dining restaurants and luxury hotels. A fast-food restaurant could have four or five targeted market segments, while a fine dining restaurant may have only one target market. As in the broad interpretation of the product, the market is generally referred to in its broadest context. The mission statement for a fast-food restaurant would not go into detail in describing the market segmentation variables but would simply express the core need of the business, perhaps "Serving the needs of people with little time to eat," or "Offering quality food to those with a limited budget." A luxury hotel could describe its market as "Serving the traveling needs of those with discriminating taste." If applicable, the discussion on the business's markets could include important geographic or location characteristics. A business that wants to add locations might include a statement such as, "We will penetrate the California market before expanding out of state."

Goals

The goals of the company are generally stated in terms of profitability and growth. Generally, no specific numbers are included in the mission statement. These are calculated and expressed later, in the objectives section. They are based on a thorough analysis of the firm's abilities and the opportunities and threats existing in the environment. Profit is the result of what the firm will do, based on its mission (Thompson and Strickland, 1992). The importance of profit to the firm is usually expressed by describing its general uses—growth, dividends, helping the community—and employee opportunities, such as advancement, security, and benefits. Even though the firm will not generally state a specific profit goal for the mission statement, it could commit to divide its profits according to a predetermined formula, as shown in the following:

DIVISION OF PROFITS
- Five percent of the profit before taxes will go to charitable, educational, and cultural organizations.
- Fifteen percent of the profit before taxes will be for employee bonuses.
- Ten percent of the profit before taxes will be for management bonuses.
- Twenty-five percent of the profit after taxes will be declared as dividends.
- Forty-five percent of the profit after taxes will be reinvested in the business.

Source: Adapted from Hinterhuber & Popp (1992). Are you a strategist or just a manager? *Harvard Business Review*, Jan.–Feb., p. 106.

Since the mission statement may be presented to the public, a socially responsible philosophy toward profit could serve as a public relations tool.

Growth can be indicated by stressing no expansion, slow or rapid expansion, or, if times are difficult, contraction of units. The expansion could also be expressed as penetrating the current market, moving to new customer or geographic markets with the existing business, or diversifying into new businesses. If a change in financial management of growth is required, the method of financing could also be included, for example, "Seventy-five percent of growth will be financed from internal sources," or "The debt-to-equity ratio will be kept below 50%." Survival is generally included only if there is concern over past or potential losses, or during times of economic downturns.*

---

*There is no rule set in concrete regarding the use of the terms "goals" and "objectives." In this text, goals refer to the broad aims of a business, while objectives are detailed and measurable specifications that lead to the attainment of the goal. In application, it is not critical which term management uses, as long as the meaning is understood. An objective of 10 percent profit or a goal of 10 percent profit will have little bearing on its attainment.

Philosophies

Appropriate philosophies of management should be expounded in the company mission to communicate its values and how it intends to consummate its transaction with stakeholders (defined below). The most important aspect of the firm's philosophy is that it communicates standards, beliefs, and values that management and employees see as practical, worthwhile, and elevating. The goal is to turn the mission statement into a "sense of mission." (The integration of the mission and strategic actions into the corporate culture is discussed in Chapter 11.) British Airway's promotional slogan, "Putting People First," had an obvious commercial purpose but also a moral one—life would be better for all of us if we took better care of each other (Campbell & Young, 1991). McDonald's open-door policy reveals to all levels of management and employees that the company is concerned about the need for personal expression. Most philosophical aspects of the mission statement tend to sound the same, and there is really nothing wrong with this as long as they express the honest feelings and actions of management. After all, how many ways are there of saying "We care about people, our community, and sound management policies"?

STAKEHOLDER APPROACH TO COMPANY RESPONSIBILITY   The mission statement is generally addressed to the stakeholders of the company—those people or groups that have the most to gain or lose based on the firm's performance (Pearce & Robinson, 1991). The stakeholders for most companies would include management, employees, owners, stockholders, customers, suppliers, creditors, competitors, the local community, society in general, supported charities, and local, state, and national governments and their agencies. The purpose of directing the mission statement to the stakeholders is that these parties all have a mutual concern that the company should:

- Seek to do business in an honorable manner.
- Have a foundation set on sound principles.
- Have philosophically prudent goals.
- Prosper adequately to supply applicable parties with a return on their investment, prompt payment for supplies, or donations.

In defining or redefining the company mission, strategic managers must recognize the legitimate rights of the firm's stakeholders. The basic steps in this process are as follows:

1. *Identify the stakeholders.* Some firms may have to contend only with investors, managers, employees, suppliers, and customers. For other businesses, the list may be much more extensive. (See Figures 2.2 and 2.3.)
2. *Understand their specific claims with the firm.* Because of human nature, each claimant will have different agendas, priorities, and requirements. These must be scrutinized carefully; a misinterpretation or lack of understanding can lead to dire results and missed opportunities (e.g., demonstrations in front of a business location by a local environmental group whose needs were not satisfied).
3. *Reconcile those claims and assign priorities.* Who has the greatest effect on the firm?

Internal Stakeholders		External Stakeholders
Proprietors and Stockholders Board of Directors Management Employees	**Versus**	Customers Suppliers Creditors Competitors Governments Local Community General Public

Figure 2.2   Internal and external stakeholders in a company. *Source:* Adapted with permission from Pearce & Robinson (1991), *Formulation, Implementation, and Control of Competitive Strategy.* Homewood, Illinois, p. 68.

STAKEHOLDER	KEY CONCERNS
Executive officers and board of directors	Competitive compensation, challenges, company growth, stock value, and a reputation for management excellence and social responsibility
Stockholders	Profits, value of stock, voting rights, election of board of directors, preemptive rights, freedom to sell stock, and stability in profits, management, and company growth
Employees	Livable wage, secure employment, potential for personal growth, pension, insurance, and a safe and pleasant work environment
Customers	A product that satisfies a need, value, consistency in management and products, and cleanliness and sanitation; to be treated with respect and fairness in all dealings; and credit
Suppliers	Timely payment of bills, regular source of business, and professional relationship
Creditors	Payments on interest and principal, security of pledged assets, stable management, and financial flexibility
Governments	Various types of taxes (income, property, sales, business/corporate, etc.); operation of business in accordance with pertinent laws—primarily those for labor, health, and safety—and the Americans with Disabilities Act (ADA)
Competitors	Honesty in competitive practices, and participation in industry organizations
Local community and general public	Personal and monetary support for community and charitable organizations, stable source of employment, commitment to improve product quality, fair prices, and purchase of a reasonable amount of goods from other local businesses.

Figure 2.3   A stakeholder view of company responsibility. *Source:* Adapted from Pearce & Robinson (1991), *Formulation and Control of Competitive Strategy.* Homewood, IL: Richard D. Irwin, p. 67.

What are the potential impacts derived from expenditures of capital or human resources? What are the monetary, personnel, and image costs of various decisions?

4. *Coordinate the claims with other elements of the company mission.* How can the firm satisfy its claimants and at the same time optimize its success in the marketplace? No firm can make everyone 100% happy, so compromises must be made. A trend that appears to be spreading is the inclusion of outside stakeholders on corporate boards. A major supplier that is key to the success of the business could provide the board with critical information about prices, future availability, and viable substitutes.

A simple categorization of expectations by stakeholders is that internal stakeholders, those with a vested interest—executive officers, board of directors, stockholders, and employees—are concerned primarily with operating the company to yield the greatest reasonable profit, good pay, and appropriate benefits, satisfactory working conditions, and a respectable image. External stakeholders are primarily concerned that the company operate for the good of society. Since there are few companies that can completely satisfy all claims, compromises must be advanced and priorities established. The first priority of any company must be to assure long-term profit growth. This must be balanced with the knowledge that without a strong societal structure and markets for products and services, opportunities for long-term profit will be substantially diminished. Therefore, companies must adopt a philosophy that balances the drive for success and profit with the attempt to be a contributing member of the local community and the general public.

DRUCKER'S QUESTIONING SEQUENCE

Peter Drucker (1974), in his seminal work, *Management: Tasks, Responsibilities, Practices,* stressed the importance of answering three questions during the process of preparing the firm's mission:

What is our business?
What will our business be?
What should our business be?

These questions, though seemingly simplistic, cannot and should not be answered without considerable debate. The outcome of the decision will place the entire organization—both capital and people—at great risk and will consequently establish the basis for setting new objectives, strategies, and policies and, perhaps, for making changes in the organization's structure or corporate culture. That business purpose and business mission are so rarely given adequate thought is perhaps the single most important cause of business frustration and business failure (Drucker, 1974). Participants in the decision will inevitably see the existing business and its future according to personal experiences and conceptual and inferential judgments. What seems right to one may seem incredibly wrong to another. Disagreements must be openly encouraged and discord aired so that all possible alternative choices are considered. For this exchange to be productive, it is important that each member of the mission panel have a detailed knowledge of the firm and its environment. This will help minimize opinions based on either no research or unreliable research.

"What is our business?" This must be defined based on the customer's perception; it is essentially the objective positioning of the firm—the image of the business in the minds of its customers (Drucker, 1974). For example, "Benny's is a casual restaurant providing quality seafood at reasonable prices." The reason for this question is that a business must find out what it is doing right so that it can continue those activities that fulfill customers' wants, discontinue those activities that are not needed, and be in a position to seek out customers' desires that are not currently being met. Parallel with this question one must ask, "What are the key satisfactions (also values) derived from purchasing our product or service?" Basically, why do target customers purchase the company's products or services? From marketing it is learned that the customer buys the satisfaction of a need—the core benefit. The product itself may be a secondary consideration. Another way of answering this question is to find out what the customer values most about a business. The core benefit for some restaurants will be satisfaction of hunger, for others, status. The actual or formal product or value-enhancing attributes may include quality, large plates of food, unique spices, fresh baked bread, a convenient location, a relaxing atmosphere, courteous service, fast or leisurely service, status, or price. The core benefit for a hotel will be a place to stay, while the actual product will include a room with some desired or appropriate level of quality, a free breakfast when staying at the hotel, a reasonably sized bar of bath soap, thick towels, front desk personnel who address a customer by name, a concierge, safety, recreational activities, food and beverage service, and so on. Answers to these questions can come from customers only through research, such as internal records, surveys, focus groups, or observation.

The answer to "What will our business be?" is central to the creation of a mission statement. Most managers recognize that although today's product offering may be quite successful, it may not elicit the same prosperity next year. In the long term, the business as described today will probably not be the same in the future. Will restaurants change their present menu mix, pricing, promotional, and distribution strategies in the next three to five years? At some point, will consumers begin eating more turkey or vegetable burgers than burgers made with beef? By what percentage will delivery precipitate the need for smaller dining rooms? The hotel industry has undergone dramatic changes over the past five years. Will this trend continue? Will less expensive full-service hotels with smaller rooms be preferred over larger, more expensive facilities? Will smaller motel or hotel chains be able to compete without being part of larger reservation systems? Will changes in the economy, personnel supply or characteristics, societal trends, or technological changes have an effect on managerial decisions for hospitality firms? The answer to each of these questions is a resounding, "Yes!" To remain competitive, every business concept that exists today will be required to change to some extent in the next one, five, or ten years (See Figure 2.2). One of the key factors to consider in answering these questions is what current or

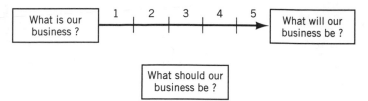

Figure 2.4 Deciding on the business's long-term direction.

future needs of customers are not currently being met? For example, are there certain features that could be added to the business, such as delivery, Internet reservations or advertising, upgraded product quality or services, less fat, more spices, or market penetration in nontraditional locations?

Subsequently, the answer to "What should our business be?" will be guided by the assimilation of those potential changes with the internal capabilities and desires of the firm's management (Schoemaker, 1992). In the past, the decision to change has always carried with it a degree of risk greater than the decision not to change. In the future, this relationship will likely be reversed. Are there forecasted changes in the environment that should be incorporated into the business's current operating philosophy? If there is a perceived opportunity for rapid expansion, should the firm proceed? If 50% of customers say they want something that no competitor is currently offering but the service would require a major change in current operating logistics, should the service be considered? The decision is difficult, but this is what management gets paid to do.

EXAMPLES OF MISSION STATEMENTS

The Ritz-Carlton

Perhaps one of the best examples of a hospitality mission statement is that of the Ritz-Carlton Hotel Company. Their mission statement is included in an employee manual called *The Quality Vision*. Along with the mission statement is a credo—a brief statement of The Ritz-Carlton's desired market position—and "The Quality Vision"—an explanation of the process by which quality is reinforced. The successful implementation of their mission has been recognized with the Malcolm Baldrige National Quality Award for service, given annually to the American firm that best meets stringent standards of the following criteria and values: excellence in leadership, information and analysis, strategic quality planning, human resource development and management, management of process quality, quality and operational results, and customer focus and satisfaction.

THE RITZ-CARLTON®
HOTEL COMPANY, L.L.C.

MISSION STATEMENT

The Ritz-Carlton Hotel Company will be regarded as the quality and market leader
of the hotel industry worldwide.

We are responsible for creating exceptional, profitable results with the investments
entrusted to us by efficiently satisfying customers.

The Ritz-Carlton Hotels will be the clear choice of discriminating business and leisure travelers,
meeting planners, travel industry partners, owners, partners and the travel agent community.

Founded on the principles of providing a high level of genuine, caring, personal service; cleanliness;
beauty; and comfort, we will consistently provide all customers with their ultimate expectation,
a memorable experience and exceptional value. Every employee will be empowered to
provide immediate corrective action should customer problems occur.

Meeting planners will favor The Ritz-Carlton Hotels. Empowered sales staff will know their own product and
will always be familiar with each customer's business. The transition of customer requirements from Sales to
Conference Services will be seamless. Conference Services will be a partner to the meeting planner, with
General Managers showing interest through their presence and participation. Any potential problem will be
solved instantly and with ease for the planner. All billing will be clear, accurate and timely. All of this will create
a memorable, positive experience for the meeting planner and the meeting participants.

Key account customers will receive individualized attention,
products and services in support of their organization's objectives.

All guests and customers will know we fully appreciate their loyalty.

The Ritz-Carlton Hotels will be the first choice for important and social business events
and will be the social centers in each community. Through creativity, detailed planning,
and communication, banquets and conferences will be memorable.

Our restaurants and lounges will be the first choice of
the local community and will be patronized on a regular basis.

The Ritz-Carlton Hotels will be known as positive,
supportive members of their community and will be sensitive to the environment.

The relationships we have with our suppliers will be one of mutual confidence and teamwork.

We will always select employees who share our values. We will strive to meet individual needs because our
success depends on the satisfaction, effort and commitment of each employee. Our leaders will constantly
support and energize all employees to continuously improve productivity and customer satisfaction. This will be
accomplished by creating an environment of genuine care, trust, respect, fairness and teamwork through
training, education, empowerment, participation, recognition, rewards and career opportunities.

Source: Reprinted with permission of the Ritz-Carlton Hotel Company.

The Bryan House

MISSION STATEMENT

The Bryan House will serve the needs of the business traveler and convention market by offering the best quality lodging available in a midscale hotel. Exceeding the customer's expectations will be our overriding goal.

Profits will be increased through a dual focus on customers' and employees' needs. The Bryan House will be the number one hotel to work for in our city.

We will set aside 5% of our profits as donations to charitable organizations, with the goal of making our community a better place to live.

City Grill

MISSION STATEMENT

City Grill is a casual upscale restaurant and bar catering to middle- and upper-middle-income singles and couples who like a lively atmosphere and high-quality, trend-oriented foods and beverages. We will always strive to use the freshest, most nutritious ingredients possible and prepare all menu items from scratch.

We are committed to providing the best possible working conditions and opportunities for employees and attractive earnings for stockholders. To accomplish this, we will strive to maintain our record of long-term profits above industry standards, and a rate of growth matched to our abilities and current economic conditions.

As a responsible member of our community we will actively participate in helping those who are less fortunate.

QUESTIONS AND PROJECTS

1. Write a definition for the "mission statement." Include and define three main components.
2. What is the purpose of having a mission statement? How important do you think it is to have one?
3. Describe what is meant by the "stakeholder approach to company responsibility."
4. What are the pros and cons of attempting to balance the need for profit and social responsibility?
5. What is Peter Drucker's question sequence for the preparation of the mission statement?
6. Prepare a mission statement for any desired or assigned hospitality firm.
7. What opportunities are created by broadening the scope/description of one's business? Answer with an example.
8. Critique examples of mission statements currently being used by hospitality firms.

CHAPTER 3

Marketing Information Systems and Marketing Research

Marketing information systems and the research principles on which they are based are not a specific component of the strategic plan, but they do establish the foundation for all strategic decisions and controls. Preparation of both the internal and environmental analyses is guided by principles of research. The purpose of the marketing information system is to provide marketing decision-makers with an organized and continuous flow of relevant marketing data and information. Marketing research is the process by which the data or information is gathered. Sometimes, the research process will require that a formal research report be prepared, such as when there are problems or when a strategic change is being considered. Most often, it entails the regular and routine gathering of information to keep the marketing information system updated with relevant and actionable data and information.

The aim of this chapter is not to make expert researchers out of readers, but rather to introduce them to the concepts and key terms typically used by researchers, to enable marketers to implement basic research studies, and to improve the effectiveness and efficiency of the marketing planning process.

RESEARCH AND DECISION-MAKING

An effective information and research program will not automatically make the best strategic or tactical choice obvious, but in most instances it will reduce the range of possible alternatives from thousands to some manageable number. A marketing information system and marketing research will bring an organized and logical process to bear on important questions, thereby lessening the number of decisions made by intuition, conjecture, or back-of-the-envelope calculations. Too often firms make decisions that are based on what management assumes the market wants, rather than making the necessary effort to assess the true need. If a hotel chain is considering a weekend package, the marketing department would first need to find out if there was adequate demand for the promotion and then what features would make the offering attractive to the target customer (Steinle, 1992). A short survey of likely weekend customers could help design the package that will best match the customers' demands and therefore increase the chances for the promotion's success. A simple ranking of benefits from the customers' perspective will increase the effectiveness of all promotional efforts.

Often, a hotel will spend millions of dollars on renovations based on what a designer thinks should be done, rather than the customer. A few thousand dollars for a survey to find out what the customers would like to see in their "ideal" hotel would be well spent. The Medallion Hotel in Houston, Texas, took such a survey and found that its target customers wanted warmer colors to help them relax after a hard day's work. The Hotel's research effort paid off handsomely with an occupancy well above the area average.

MONITORING PERFORMANCE

Besides supplying planning information for both the internal and environmental analyses and strategy formulation, research methodology is also used for monitoring current operational performance through employee surveys and various quantitative and qualitative measures of functional area performance: for example, establishing task standards and allowable variances for cooks, servers, housekeepers, bartenders, and so on. Additionally, research serves year-round functional needs, by helping departments keep up with current and future trends, such as the latest POS equipment, key-product pricing, new services or food items, innovative employee incentives, and new ideas for decor. Formal research efforts, such as a customer survey, can also be utilized as a control mechanism to alert the firm if the premise on which decisions were made has changed, and, if so, to allow the firm to determine if there was enough of a change to force a revision of the plan. Research will never replace experience and good judgment, but it does help marketing managers increase their percentage of successful strategic and tactical decisions through a more objective appraisal of the situation (Sandelman & Associates, 1994).

DATA AND INFORMATION

Data, by definition, are not the basis for managerial decision-making. *Data* are only the unconnected pieces of knowledge or facts that may or may not be relevant to the business. When effectively arranged and organized, or characterized as relevant, the data are then classified as *information*—that is, data in a usable form. A business magazine is filled with data. Perhaps some of the data will be considered as information that can be used in the decision-making process. For example, the following individual pieces of data on a primary competitor (hotel or restaurant) may not mean much; but when considered together, they become information that could be used to surmise that the competitor may be expanding soon.*

- A primary competitor implemented a new training program.
- The company had recently negotiated a large loan.
- It is not experiencing financial difficulties.
- It is modifying its menu or service mix.
- The company has hired a new advertising agency.

After managers analyze this information, based on their personal experience and knowledge, it becomes competitive intelligence—one of the major goals of research (Fuld, 1991).

MARKETING INFORMATION SYSTEMS

The *marketing information system* (MKIS) is a combination of people, equipment, and procedures organized for the purpose of supporting the decision-making efforts of marketers. The basic concepts of the system are as follows:

- Various pieces of data are gathered from the environment in which it operates—*marketing intelligence or the environmental analysis,* and from the company itself—the *internal records or internal analysis.*
- It must be determined if primary data are required: if so, a formal research plan should be prepared to acquire it—*marketing research.*
- The data are then analyzed to determine what is useful for decision-makers—*information analysis.*
- Data and information must then be made available in a usable form to decision-makers; if information is critical to any aspect of the business, it must be distributed immediately to the appropriate individuals or departments—*distributing information.*
- Marketers must determine if additional information is necessary before decisions are made—*assessing information needs.*
- The information is then used to make the essential marketing decisions—*planning, execution or implementation, and control* (see Figure 3.1).

Marketing Decision Support Systems

Historically, the MKIS was primarily a manual task. Recently, as with most everything in business, it became more computerized. In fact, some firms are beginning to

---

*The question of labeling of facts about a customer or competitor as data or information is somewhat academic. Most researchers refer to data as that which has been gathered, and information as the data categorized and organized for analysis and decision-making.

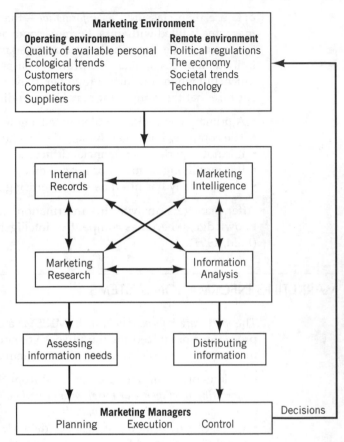

Figure 3.1 Marketing information system (MKIS). *Source:* Adapted with permission from Kotler & Armstrong (1990), *Marketing: An Introduction*, 2nd ed. Upper Saddle River, NJ: Prentice-Hall, p. 81.

use a relatively new process that originated in the decision information sciences: *marketing decision support systems* (MDSS). A *decision support system* (DSS) is defined as "an information-producing system aimed at a particular problem that a manager must solve and decisions that managers must make" (McLeod, 1993). The sophistication of the different types of systems will vary with the complexity of the problem. All decisions are essentially on a continuum between programmed (repetitive and routine decisions) and nonprogrammed (new, unstructured, and of a potentially serious nature). Consequently, a DSS could be used as a tool to gather data, analyze files, prepare reports, estimate decision consequences, propose decisions, or, in the case of highly programmed decisions, make decisions.

The MDSS is made up of four components: a database, reports and displays, models, and analysis capabilities (see Figure 3.2). The database should contain a broad variety of relevant data and be tied to other databases within the firm, and preferably to various outside services such as ABI Inform (a CD-ROM business database). Reports and displays can be qualitative, quantitative, or both. For example, through guided dialogue or prompts, the user would enter certain information, perhaps a competitor, then specify what types of information were desired on that

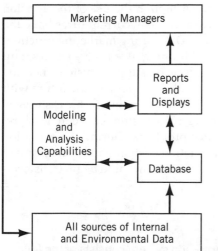

Figure 3.2 Marketing decision support system (MDSS). *Source:* Adapted from Aaker, Kumar, & Day (1995), *Marketing Research.* New York: Wiley.

competitor. The database would then assemble the information in narrative form or into tables or charts. Models are used to test marketing managers' theories about certain actions, answer "what if" questions, and assist in setting more realistic objectives. Analysis capabilities include the ability to relate available data to models, clarify relationships between them, perform statistical functions, and recommend courses of action (Aaker, Kumar, & Day, 1995).

DIFFERENCES BETWEEN THE MKIS AND MDSS   There are two essential differences between the marketing information system (MKIS) and the marketing decision support system (MDSS). The first is that the MDSS has the ability to convert raw data into information that the marketing manager can actually use for making decisions. The extent of the problem of information overload that occurs in many marketing information systems is greatly reduced in the MDSS. The necessary information is simply retrieved and then manipulated to help with the decision—hence the term decision support systems.

An example of how a computer can help make a decision is the use of spreadsheet-based software packages with built-in formulas for marketing and financial analysis. If the marketing department wanted to find out what would happen to profits if they implemented a three-month advertising campaign, they could procure the information from the MDSS. Assume that the campaign has a cost of $30,000. Based on its characteristics and similarities with past campaigns, the program projects sales increases for the first three months of the campaign at $15,000, $18,000, and $22,500. These figures would be entered in the spreadsheet along with the cost of the campaign to determine possible changes in profit, basically its initial viability. Potential residual sales increases for later months could also be entered to determine total estimated increases in profit from the campaign. The differences between current marketing expenditures, sales, and profits and the MDSS projection could be compared and presented in a table or graph format.

The second difference is the cost of the MDSS. Although the use of the decision support system (DSS) concept will increase in the future, few current firms have the financial and human resources necessary to support DSS for the marketing function. Besides requiring additional software packages and training, it is necessary to set up a computerized marketing information center. As decision support systems become more user friendly, their use will increase. What will likely happen in the future with MDSS is essentially what happened during the evolution from electronic cash registers to computerized point-of-sale systems. Lower prices, simpler technology, reduced labor requirements, and fewer maintenance problems. During the evolution from the MKIS to the MDSS, the marketing information system will be the primary source of marketing information. Figure 3.3 details how a firm could begin transforming its MKIS into a MDSS.

Key Tasks of the Marketing Information System

The tasks necessary to support a marketing information system consists of the following: deciding which data are necessary; gathering, storing, and cataloging the data; and analyzing and communicating the data.

ASSESSING WHAT DATA ARE NECESSARY   The first step is to decide what data will be gathered and who will participate in the gathering process. Basic divisions of information needs are *internal* and *environmental*. Management must recognize that while every internal or environmental factor may not be of equal importance, each has the ability to positively or negatively affect the business's future. A diagram of the data needs of the firm, such as the information system charts in this chapter, could be made to help clarify and highlight specific needs (Sandy, 1991).

INTERNAL DATA   Each business should keep reasonably detailed records on what customers have purchased. When possible, it is helpful to be able to identify the customer by demographic or geographic data and, in the case of a hotel, to know how to contact them. To limit the amount of time required for gathering this information, it should be systematically integrated into routine recordkeeping. Internal information could consist of overall sales [occupancy percentage, average daily revenue (ADR), and revenue per available room (REVPAR) for hotels]; sales by day part (11 a.m. to 2 p.m., etc.), day, week, month, and year; individual product or service sales; customer comments (postmeeting or group reports for hotels); and reservations.

ENVIRONMENTAL DATA   Environmental data will include information related to political regulations, the economy, societal trends, technology, personnel, ecology, target customers, competitors, and suppliers and creditors. The key concerns are customers and competitors.

CUSTOMERS   The majority of research in the hospitality industry deals with customers' perceptions and purchase behaviors: essentially, what they have bought in the past, what they are currently buying, what they say they will buy in the future,

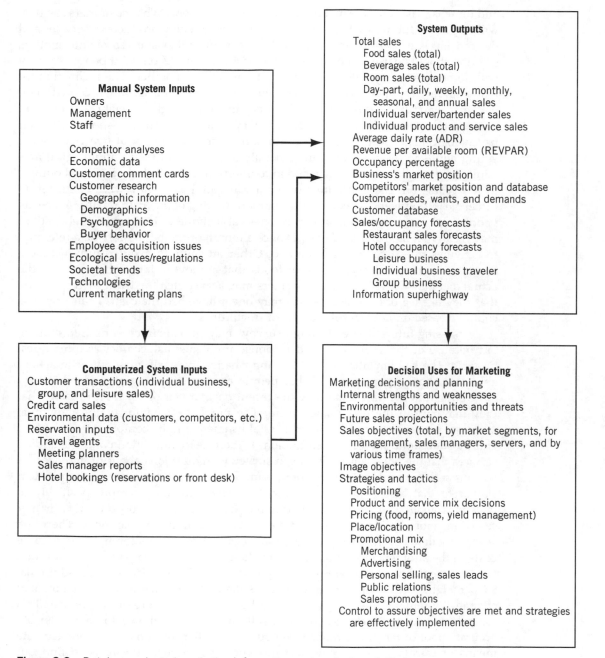

Manual System Inputs
Owners
Management
Staff

Competitor analyses
Economic data
Customer comment cards
Customer research
    Geographic information
    Demographics
    Psychographics
    Buyer behavior
Employee acquisition issues
Ecological issues/regulations
Societal trends
Technologies
Current marketing plans

System Outputs
Total sales
    Food sales (total)
    Beverage sales (total)
    Room sales (total)
    Day-part, daily, weekly, monthly,
        seasonal, and annual sales
    Individual server/bartender sales
    Individual product and service sales
Average daily rate (ADR)
Revenue per available room (REVPAR)
Occupancy percentage
Business's market position
Competitors' market position and database
Customer needs, wants, and demands
Customer database
Sales/occupancy forecasts
    Restaurant sales forecasts
    Hotel occupancy forecasts
        Leisure business
        Individual business traveler
        Group business
Information superhighway

Computerized System Inputs
Customer transactions (individual business,
    group, and leisure sales)
Credit card sales
Environmental data (customers, competitors, etc.)
Reservation inputs
    Travel agents
    Meeting planners
    Sales manager reports
    Hotel bookings (reservations or front desk)

Decision Uses for Marketing
Marketing decisions and planning
    Internal strengths and weaknesses
    Environmental opportunities and threats
    Future sales projections
    Sales objectives (total, by market segments, for
        management, sales managers, servers, and by
        various time frames)
    Image objectives
    Strategies and tactics
        Positioning
        Product and service mix decisions
        Pricing (food, rooms, yield management)
        Place/location
        Promotional mix
            Merchandising
            Advertising
            Personal selling, sales leads
            Public relations
            Sales promotions
    Control to assure objectives are met and strategies
        are effectively implemented

Figure 3.3 Database-oriented marketing information system for hospitality firms.

and on what basis they are making each of these decisions. What customers say they will buy in the future will help management decide on new products or services and desired levels of performance, and will help verify other sources of information. Caution should be used when considering basing strategies on what people *say* they will do because many will often say one thing and do another. The inclination for many survey respondents is to answer questions either in a socially accepted manner, in a way that will psychologically place them in a higher social class, or in an attempt to impress the interviewer. They may also base their response on their psychological age. Teenagers tend to think of themselves as about five years older, young adults in their twenties are generally satisfied with their chronological age, adults between thirty and forty respond to questions as though they were about five to ten years younger, and adults over forty respond as if they were about ten to fifteen years younger. For example, a common twisting of the truth relates to the way people reply to questions about their physical activities. "I stay extremely active" may mean that the respondent bowls once a month or might possibly be a reference to activities from five or ten years ago. Other attempts to avoid reality include a customer saying "I always try to eat foods that are low in fat," when, in fact, the actual diet may not reflect this. Customers may also stretch the truth by responding that they like leg of lamb, when they may never have had the dish. Their response could be based on not wanting to appear uncultured.

Assessing future desires through surveys may provide interesting information, but because of the aforementioned response problems, its accuracy is often questionable. The key limitation is that this information, by itself, may not yield actionable data about future trends. What people are currently buying and what they have bought in the past, especially the recent past, are far better indicators of what they may buy in the immediate future. The purchase behavior of the individual customer for each hotel or foodservice establishment and its competitors is the best and most accurate source of information. If the research question concerns adding services that the hotel is not offering, a survey with questions about preferences for various services could be taken from a sample of current customers. One problem similar to that discussed above is that customers commonly reply positively to questions about their desire for additional services. Most people want a greater selection, more comfort, greater convenience, and additional services. There are several methods of increasing the accuracy of this line of questioning. One is to tie costs to the additional benefits: "How much are you willing to pay for the addition of a continental breakfast with your stay in our hotel?" "Is this worth an additional $5 per night?" Another is to have the respondent prioritize a series of potential changes by ranking them from 1 to 5, or however many there are in the list. This forces them to make choices between alternatives and allows for a reasonably accurate pool of target customer preferences. Another and possibly more accurate means of calculating what new features current customers desire is to find out what they are currently purchasing from various competitors. If a primary competitor increased sales after adding certain products or services, then, depending on intervening circumstances or variables, it may be worthwhile to consider the addition.

Often, there are questions concerning the *geographic base of data*. National or regional syndicated surveys denoting trends should be considered in an analysis, but the closer the information is to the business, the greater its importance in the decision-making process. (Syndicated surveys from private research firms are available in various forms to the general public.) Large chains with a dispersed customer base can make suitable use of major syndicated poll results, such as that of the Gallup, Roper, and Yankelovich organizations. For example, national polls concerning the spending habits of children and teens would be beneficial to national fast-food chains, because they show likely trends in the behavior of their target customers. These same data would be only of passing interest to a local independent fast-food company. While they may provide insight into where societal shifts are occurring, the data are not reliable enough to use exclusively for planning major new strategies on a localized basis. Like the larger chains, the local fast-food operator must have data on the target customers located within its trade area, or at least within its community. The smaller the firm's geographic territory, the greater the requirement that data be gathered from that territory. This reduces the possibility of results that do not mirror the firm's target market.

The U.S. Census Bureau provides an enormous amount of data, but because of the way in which they are gathered, the data are of greater benefit for larger firms. Data are collected on two forms: a short form that goes to all households and includes only basic demographic data, and a long form that goes to a sample of households but is much more detailed. The data are available in both printed and electronic formats. In general, the larger the area being studied, the greater the detail of the Census Bureau's reports. This means that firms focusing on limited trade areas must generally rely on other sources of data. There are various types of analysis for Census reports: demographic and expenditure data; examination of changes over time; differences between cities or areas; and customized reports, such as how increases in various age, occupation, or racial groups affect the overall expenditures for an area (Myers, 1993). (Chapter 5 on the Environmental Analysis provides detailed information on tracking customers' actions.)

COMPETITORS   A business must first determine who the competitors are that most affect its sales, essentially, which businesses in the trade area can be viewed as alternatives by the target customers. These will be known as primary competitors. Strategic groups, secondary competitors, and industry competitors must also be identified and categorized. After the competing firms have been identified, a system must be set up to gain as much information as possible about them. (See Chapter 5 for more information on competitors.)

An effective and thorough research program increases the likelihood of the company taking a proactive rather than a reactive or passive posture in dealing with the future. Past philosophies of planning have emphasized being prepared for change. In modern competition this is not good enough. A proactive response helps the company meet the cutting-edge needs of customers and gives it a time advantage over less astute and aggressive competitors. (See Chapters 1 and 8 for more information on strategic aggression and proactive posturing.)

SECONDARY DATA   Most data are secondary data—data that already exist and were not gathered for the current need. The vast majority of research for the hospitality business will be secondary data. These data are usually the first sought because they are the quickest and least costly to gather. Their value is critical for the hospitality industry. If each time a company needed to do some type of research, the data had to be acquired firsthand, the decision process would quickly be bogged down and become excessively expensive. For example, if, instead of testing a particular service for a hotel, management had found an article detailing how the service was already tried and how successful or unsuccessful it was, much time and effort could be saved.

Secondary data will come from two sources, internal and environmental (or external). Much of the information necessary for the internal analysis of a company can be collected from secondary sources, such as financial statements, operational policies, supplier files, employee records, and manager's meeting notes. Some will need to be collected from primary sources, such as customer surveys (typically, customer comment cards). Environmental data should generally be gathered through industry journals, trade magazines, business magazines and newspapers, local newspapers, competitors' annual reports, and various association and government reference books at the library. If secondary sources do not provide adequate information for the planning process, then a research plan must be prepared for the purpose of gathering primary data. Figure 3.4 graphically depicts the basic process for deciding whether primary data are necessary.

PRIMARY DATA   If data are collected for a specific purpose, they are called primary data. Even the most successful companies must keep up with the current needs of their customers. Business volume may be good today, but consumer tastes can change rapidly. Primary data supply a business with the most current and relevant appraisal of a particular question.

Sources   Common sources of research data include internal records; personal contacts of management and employees; trade journals and magazines; business journals and magazines; restaurant and hotel associations; chambers of commerce; industry experts; electronic databases (CD-ROM); the U.S. Census; marketing research firms; and primary research, such as observation, experiments, and surveys. The vast majority of internal data will come from computerized information systems, such as point-of-sales (POS) systems for restaurants and property management systems (PMS) used in hotels. In addition to keeping track of sales in dollars and products and services sold, these systems can store data on customers, as well as provide operations and inventory controls.

Internal Records   The most critical data should become a component of daily or periodic controls, such as the daily sales report or income statements. These would normally be internal data but could occasionally be environmental data, such as weather conditions, pay day, or other occurrences, such as a convention or sporting event, that caused an increase or decrease in sales. [The daily sales report

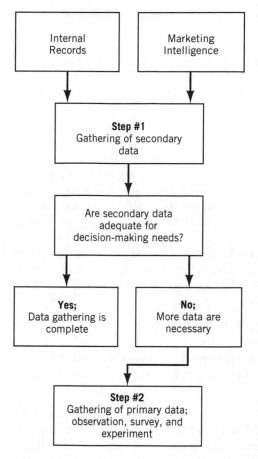

Figure 3.4 Secondary and primary data gathering process.

(DSR) summarizes various sales categories, such as total sales; sales by product category, market segment, or sales personnel; cash over and short count; paid-outs for items purchased with cash; and other key data and information such as reservations, customer comments, weather conditions, conventions, operations or personnel problems.]

INTELLIGENCE GATHERING   Each business should have a research or intelligence gathering system that is executed throughout the year. One of the most important parameters for a firm's research or intelligence gathering system is its consistency. The intelligence function cannot be expected to reach its potential for benefit until a substantial amount of information is accumulated. Granted, a considerable volume of information can be gathered in a week's time, but only a historical record of events coupled with recent happenings will yield the best information and subsequent intelligence. The data search must be intensified during an approximate three-month period prior to making any major changes in the strategic plan. This action serves two purposes. First, it obviously helps to accumulate more current data; and second, it focuses management's conscious and subconscious thoughts on relevant issues in the environment.

Necessitated by their dispersed customer base, hotels must focus on gathering data from the key origination cities supplying them with business. As the number of locations and sales volume increase for both restaurants and hotels, there is a corresponding need to include more information in the analysis, simply because more variables exist.

Ideally, there should be a free flow of environmentally related information—opportunities and threats—from all functional departments of the organization. Those individuals closest to the customer can prove invaluable in deciding on key factors to consider in the environmental analysis and in supplying appropriate information (Perry, 1991). Some hotels give each employee memo pads designed to record specific information about each customer. The information is then recorded in the hotel's database, to be used in the future to allow the hotel to cater to guests' desires without the guests having to ask.

Each member of the management team should be assigned a key data source to review on a regular basis. For example, one manager may be responsible for *Restaurant Business* and the *Wall Street Journal;* another may have *Hotel Business* and *BusinessWeek.* This task has a multiple purpose:

- It helps to gather data for competitive intelligence.
- It is a form of continuing education for managers.
- It improves teamwork because managers will begin to discuss their findings.
- It gives managers a feeling of confidence in their personal ability and knowledge—possibly its greatest benefit.

Each manager should be given an area of responsibility for research that most relates to his/her experience and interest. For example, an older manager could be assigned the elderly target market; someone interested in quantitative data could be assigned the analysis of statistical data, competitors' annual reports, or other sources of financial data; a female manager could be assigned societal trends related to women's dining and travel habits; and a manager with a young family might be assigned the traveling and dining needs of his/her target group.

Management personnel should also be assigned a set of primary and secondary competitors to visit throughout the year. Competitor analysis reports should be prepared on each visit. These visits will help the manager and the business keep a better perspective on what is going on in the industry and on their own company's abilities compared with others competing for the same customer.

Nonmanagement personnel could be given specific assignments, such as to cut out all articles from a particular periodical or newspaper relating to restaurants or hotels, or simple research assignments for the library. For example, on a monthly basis, spend four hours at the library searching for articles concerning primary competitors. Some primary research for nonmanagement personnel should entail reporting on their experiences at local restaurants and, perhaps, hotels while on vacation.

STORAGE AND CATALOGING   The strategic marketing plan should serve as the framework for storage and cataloging marketing information. Essentially, each component of the plan should have a file folder to accumulate applicable data. The data are collected throughout the year and stored in the appropriate file. If possible, someone in the company should be responsible for compiling a manual or computerized database dedicated to internal and environmental data (Fuld, 1991). This person does not need to be from management but must be cognizant of the specific information needs of the firm. If equipment, personnel skills, and time permit, key elements of the data could be entered into a computerized database. Although it is possible to store data on wordprocessing software, database software is preferable. If key data or information is stored in a computerized database, questions of whether a piece of information is important enough to be entered can be simplified if management specifies by circling or highlighting the information.

An option to a file system is to accumulate critical data or information in a *fact book* (Brooker, 1991). Since it may be difficult to take all records to a strategic planning meeting, data and information considered essential could be placed in the fact book and taken to the meeting. There are various options for the fact book. If there is not enough room to store all work in a single book, the book might be kept in sections covering certain topics. Separate fact books could be utilized for internal and environmental information. One could contain articles about each major competitor. Smaller businesses could keep all environmental research in a single fact book.

Since information will be needed both for planning purposes and for routine decisions, it should be organized for the convenience of users. Having information in designated files is helpful, but perhaps further subdividing is necessary. A competitor's signing of a major convention may be hidden in a file unless a system is available to prioritize or cull critical events. Standardized reports or analysis forms can be used to help organize the data for analysis. On a regular basis, individuals can be assigned the task of summarizing data from specific sources. For example, whoever is assigned to gather intelligence on a particular primary competitor could also be responsible for summarizing relevant data on a monthly, quarterly, or semiannual basis.

ANALYSIS AND COMMUNICATION   Without a systematic means of analyzing and communicating the data, much of the effort expended in gathering and cataloging will be wasted (Porter, 1980). Analysis consists of deciding which pieces of data are important and their accumulation in reports, charts, graphs, and statistical forms to allow management to discover any meaning. Even though actual planning meetings are not being held, discussions of key information that may influence strategies should be held on a regular basis. Internal information will obviously be discussed at regular manager's meetings, but environmental data should also be a standard topic at each meeting. Since the majority of planning decisions will be based on the firm's marketing information system, it should be viewed as a vital functional component. In larger firms, management information systems, of which marketing information systems are a vital subset, are being upgraded to functional staff positions. These managers have titles such as director of management information systems (MIS) or vice-president of MIS.

THE MARKETING RESEARCH PROCESS

The American Marketing Association has defined *marketing research* as "the function that links an organization to its market through information. This information is used to identify and define marketing opportunities and problems (weaknesses or threats); generate, refine, and evaluate marketing actions; monitor marketing performance; and improve the understanding of marketing as a process. Marketing research specifies the information required to address these issues; designs the method for collecting information; manages and implements the data-collection process; interprets the results; and communicates the findings and their implications" (Bennett, 1988).

Smaller independent hotels and restaurants may get by with a minimal amount of primary data or formal marketing research information. Their main focus would be on secondary data, such as internal records (statements of income, daily sales reports, and product mix reports), or data gathered by reading a few trade magazines and talking to customers. Most companies will have extensive research requirements, that is, information to increase the company's knowledge of opportunities and threats and to support the conclusions made when selecting objectives and strategies.

As marketers determine that additional data are necessary for decision-making, a proper marketing research project must be planned and implemented. The process provides a systematic approach to research that ensures that the necessary data are gathered, that the data are gathered in a scientific manner, and that the gathered data are relevant to the decision-making process (Aaker, Kumar, & Day, 1995). There are five basic steps in the marketing research process (Figure 3.5): (1) decide on the purpose of the research and set research objectives, (2) design the research plan, (3) collect the data, (4) analyze and interpret the data, and (5) report the research findings.

Research Purpose

Decide the purpose of the research and set research objectives. A clear understanding of the purpose of the research is needed to expedite the remainder of the research process. The purpose will most often be to gather data about critical problems or threats and about significant opportunities faced by the firm. Sometimes, the problem will be obvious, such as the sales of certain menu items being very low. Other times, the actual problem will be somewhat unclear, such as when overall sales are down. The most frequent research problems and opportunities are generally related to sales being less than desired or to the need to know more about customer behavior.

The setting of research objectives (or research questions) helps to further clarify the problem or opportunity, to decide what information is needed by marketers to answer questions about the problem or opportunity, and to determine what type of research design is necessary. Generally, the number of objectives should be limited to

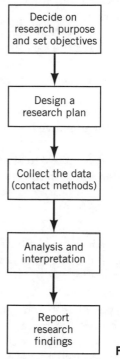

Figure 3.5   The marketing research process.

about six to avoid attempting to answer too many questions with the same research project. An extremely long questionnaire, or one that includes questions on too many different topics, may limit the number of usable responses and consumers willing to complete the survey. Research objectives will usually be of a more general nature than those on the actual questionnaire. The following are typical objective-oriented questions:

1. Why are sales low?
2. Are we missing any major opportunities?
3. What are the main reasons that target customers are eating at the restaurant for lunch/dinner? What are the main reasons that target customers are selecting our hotel?
4. At what other restaurants/hotels are the business's target customers dining/staying?
5. Of the customers in the trade area, which segment is most likely to select a restaurant with a menu similar to ours?
6. What type of ambient sound is most desired by target customers? (Ambient sound is the average noise level of the room.)
7. Which restaurants/hotels have the friendliest employees?
8. When entering the doors of the business, what are the target customers' expectations?

9. How important is speed of service/check-in or check-out for target customers?
10. What is a fair price for a meal/room at our restaurant/hotel?
11. Does the restaurant have an appropriate selection (or portion size) of appetizers, entrees, desserts, and beverages? Does the hotel have the services most desired by our guests?
12. Does the number of telephone sales calls per sales manager affect the number of rooms sold?
13. Which of our three recipes for Italian dressing do customers like most?
14. What effect does the addition of two vegetarian entrees have on the sale of other entrees?
15. What might happen if we raise our corporate rates from $90 to $95?
16. Will a new headline for print ads attract more attention than the one we now use?

Research Plan

Design a research plan for gathering the information. Here, decisions on types of research, research continuity, collection methods, sampling plan, measurement scales, research instruments, and data requirements must be made.

TYPES OF RESEARCH   There are three basic types of research (or research approaches): exploratory, descriptive, and causal. The type of research to be implemented will depend in large part on the nature of the research objective. A decision-making process for establishing the type of research necessary is presented in Figure 3.6.

EXPLORATORY RESEARCH   When it is necessary to better identify a problem, exploratory research is generally implemented. Many times, before research can be undertaken to gather specific data on an issue, information must be gathered to give researchers a clearer understanding of the issue. Answers to questions 1, 2, and 3 above could be viewed as requiring exploratory research. Sometimes exploratory research is thought of as a waste of time because it lengthens the time needed to complete the research project. In practice, exploratory research will shorten the time needed for the research project by increasing the focus of the remainder of the research and, in some cases, will provide insights showing that a formal research project is unnecessary. One useful research design is the two-stage approach, where the researcher first uses exploratory research to learn more about which issues are important, and then proceeds to descriptive research to learn more about the specific issues. Exploratory research is commonly obtained through literature searches, discussions with individuals experienced on the subject, and focus group interviews.

DESCRIPTIVE RESEARCH   The usual purposes of descriptive research are to describe the potential for a product or service, the characteristics of various target markets, and the relationship of different variables. Answers to questions 4 through 12 above would call for descriptive research. Descriptive research could include identifying segmentation characteristics such as geographic, demographic, psy-

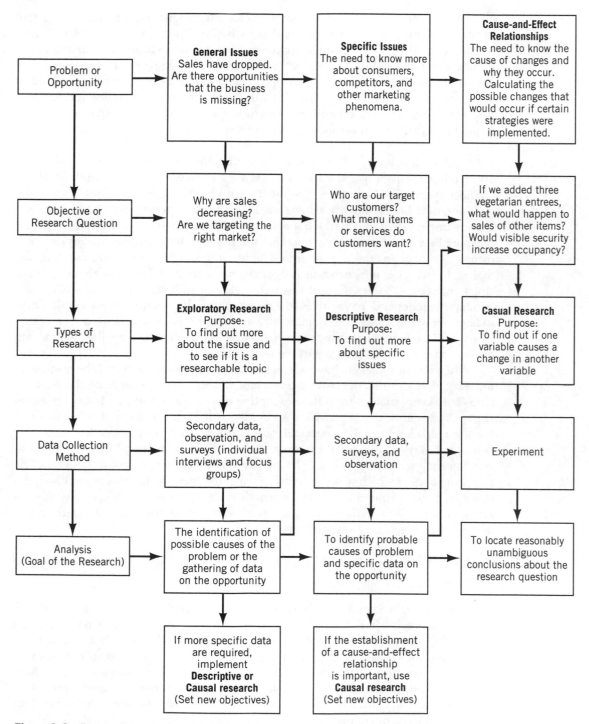

Figure 3.6 Research method decision hierarchy.

chographic, and buying behavior (occasions for use, frequency, attributes sought) of heavy, medium, light, and non-users (see Chapter 5 for a further explanation of segmentation); identifying similar characteristics of competitors' customers; determining the relationship of different variables; and making predictions regarding customers. Descriptive research, as opposed to exploratory research, is aimed at gathering information about a specific issue, problem, or opportunity and has specific objectives. The typical collection method for descriptive research is a survey, though observation and secondary data can also be used.

CAUSAL RESEARCH   This type of research gathers evidence about a cause-and-effect relationship between variables. Answers to questions 13 through 16 above would require causal research. The relationship between the variables is generally considered to be asymmetrical: one variable (the independent variable) causes a change in another variable (the dependent variable). The simplest means of distinguishing between the two is the fact that the independent variable always precedes (causes a change in) the dependent variable. In descriptive research, the decision-maker, based on experience and judgment, must make inferences about relationships between variables. Causal research yields considerably less ambiguous data because the independent variables (the cause), through experiment, are manipulated to show how they affect the dependent variable (the effect). It is used to measure which variables cause a change in what is being predicted, why the relationship exists, and the nature or degree of the relationship.

When decision-makers have adequate experience in research and the hospitality industry, they can use the *implicit causal model*. This entails examining the relationships between variables from the descriptive research for cause-and-effect relationships. While this does not provide clear evidence of a relationship, it is often possible for the marketer to make reasonable assumptions that certain relationships exist (Kinnear & Taylor, 1987). For example, it is normally understood that if a business promotes the fact that prices have been lowered, then customer counts will rise. The problem arises of which was the actual cause of the increase in customers. Was it the discount or the promotion? Causal research is designed to clarify causality. Causal research generally entails conducting an experiment. A less accurate method is a detailed interrogation of respondents through a survey.

RESEARCH CONTINUITY   There are two categories related to continuity or time dimension.

LONGITUDINAL STUDIES   The same respondents (referred to as a *panel*) or different respondents (referred to as *cohort groups*) are questioned at different points in time to find out how their opinions and attitudes have changed. If a restaurant is considering some changes in its menu, management could use a longitudinal study (possibly a survey) to get a "before-and-after" picture of the menu change. Many hotels and restaurants have ongoing surveys (often customer comment cards) that are tabulated every three months or so for a customer satisfaction index (CSI). This allows them to compare present performance with past performance.

CROSS-SECTIONAL STUDIES   These studies are taken at one point in time, representing a snapshot of the opinion of a segment of the applicable population. For example, "What do people currently think of our products or services?," "What menu items or services would customers like to see added?" or "What level of importance do customers place on certain key attributes?" Since longitudinal studies that utilize extensive questionnaires may be expensive, the addition of questions concerning past behavior patterns and future expected patterns can be included in a cross-sectional study. Most firms will do longitudinal studies for general performance measurement and cross-sectional studies when a significant quantity of information is required.

COLLECTION METHODS   There are three primary types of collection methods used in the hospitality industry: observation, survey, and experiment. The decision as to which type to use will be based on the type of research being done, the firm's research skills, and its ability to purchase outside research support.

OBSERVATION   This involves the recording of relevant characteristics or actions of customers. Observation makes it possible to gather data without going through the formality, expense, or time necessary for a survey. The chief advantages of observation are that it can be used to accurately gather data on present behavior (no reliance is made on recall, as is the case for surveys), it takes little time to gather the data, and it is the least expensive method of collecting primary data. The main drawback is that simple observation cannot expose attitudes, motivations, and product knowledge that result in purchase behavior. It basically gathers data related to who, what, when, where, and how much, but it does not expose why the behavior occurred (Kinnear & Taylor, 1987; Aaker, Kumar, & Day, 1995).

Observation methods include the following:

- *Direct Observation.* This consists of passively watching or sometimes mingling with subjects to note or elicit relevant actions and to assess characteristics. It is relatively easy to determine what type of mood customers are in by observing their degree of satisfaction with service during and after check-in or check-out at a hotel, or during and after a meal in a restaurant. Customers' behaviors can also be examined at competitors' businesses. By seeing how customers dress and what types of cars they drive, researchers can assess whether they have white collar or blue collar jobs and, within broad categories, their income. Additionally, estimates can be made of their age or observations can be made of their family circumstances, such as couples, couples with children of a certain age, and single adults.
- *Contrived Observation.* This occurs when the researcher becomes a participant in the relevant actions, such as staying at a competitor's hotel and recording certain aspects of the experience.
- *Content Analysis.* This is an analysis of any marketing phenomenon to categorize important characteristics such as emotions, humor or serious tone, colors, headlines, illustrations, or targeted audiences.
- *Physical Trace Measures.* This includes the examination of actual behaviors. Because

of the time involved and since the behavior may or may not be indicative of typical actions of the subject, it is not a popular method of observation research. Examples of this method including examining the garbage of subjects, walking by their cars to see or hear what radio stations they listen to, and noting wear on a floor to determine traffic patterns. By seeing how often customers finish their beverages and meals or ask for doggie bags, management could form opinions on food quality and portion sizes.

- *Behavior Recording Devices.* These include various types of mechanical devices such as traffic counters, the people meter (used by A.C. Nielsen to record which television channel a subject is watching), video tape recorders, equipment that measures the subject's galvanic response to certain stimuli, eye movement recorders that can determine what portion of a print ad catches a reader's attention, and voice pitch analysis devices to note changes in emotions.

SURVEYS   Surveys gather primary data by asking people questions about their knowledge, attitudes, preferences, motivations, and intended behavior (Kinnear & Taylor, 1987). The primary purpose of the survey is to learn something about the larger population from which the survey sample has been drawn. Sometimes the gathered data are qualitatively analyzed, such as when assumptions are made after talking to individuals or groups. Individual interviews are sometimes termed *depth interviews* and have the purpose of examining the reasons for specific behaviors and attitudes—essentially determining why the respondent has acted in a certain way in the past and how this may or may not change in the future. *Group* or *focus interviews* are designed to gain insight into a situation by stimulating free-flowing exchanges between the interviewer and respondents. If the questions are statistically interpreted, whether by multivariate statistics determining the mean (average) or by (showing how two or more independent variables are related to a dependent variable), the analysis is normally said to be quantitative. This helps explain what is happening and its frequency.

EXPERIMENT   Experimental research designs are based on a cause-and-effect relationship between an independent variable and a dependent variable. Basically, the independent variable, such as advertising, causes a change in the dependent variable, usually sales. In the experiment, the researcher will normally manipulate one independent variable, such as raising prices during a certain time period but not during another, to see what effect the price increase (the independent variable) has on sales, customer counts, or guest nights (the dependent variable). A common problem with experimental research is that there will always be more than one independent variable that is causing a change in the dependent variable. If the experiment focuses on price resistance, the personalities and sales abilities of sales managers will influence customers' reactions, as will competitors' price changes during the experiment's time period. For this reason, careful analysis is necessary before major decisions based on experimental research are made.

There are two basic types of experiments used in business research: the *laboratory experiment,* done in an artificial setting, such as a booth for taste testing or a special hotel room set up specifically for the experiment, and the *field experiment,* where testing is done in a natural setting—the restaurant or hotel.

SAMPLING PLAN   Before data can be gathered, the firm must decide who or what will be the target of the research. This is accomplished by selecting a *sample,* a group of elements (generally individuals) chosen to represent the population that is being studied. The main reason that a sample is selected is that the alternative would be to study the entire population, referred to as taking a *census.* Obviously, this would be too costly and take a considerable amount of time. A surprising reason for using a sample is that it will generally be more accurate than a census. This occurs because the firm would need to hire more interviewers who would likely be less skilled, more supervisors for the interviewers, and more people to enter the data into the chosen research software program. Normally, the greater the number of people involved, the greater the possibility of measurement errors.

The basic process for selecting a sample is as follows:

1. *Identify the target population.* The *population* is the aggregate of all elements in the study. Since the purpose of research is to learn more about a certain population, that population must be identified. If the population is not properly identified, then subsequent data collection and analysis will be of little value to decision-makers. The description of the target population should include the sampling elements, the sampling units, the area of coverage or extent, and a time period.

Sampling elements are objects about which data are being sought. They will most likely be individuals but could also be families, businesses, products or services, time periods, or anything else that researchers desire to learn more about.

The *sampling unit* is the relevant population from which the sample will be drawn. This unit would normally be the customers of a business, who could be further categorized, such as people of a certain age, income, occupation, gender, user status, or purchase behavior. In some cases there would be several *stages* to the selection of a sampling unit. For example, if a hotel desired research data on meeting planners working for Fortune 500 firms that have three or more 400-room-night meetings per year, there would be a three-stage sample: stage 1, Fortune 500 firms; stage 2, three or more major meetings per year; and stage 3, meeting planners. The most critical of the sampling units in this multi-stage progression is the final unit, referred to as the *final sampling unit.*

The *area of coverage or extent (also geographic scope)* concerns the decision of how far-reaching the research study should be. This would include parameters such as in-store, local, state, regional, national, and international. Area of coverage decisions will be based on the specific requirement of the study. If the purpose is to find out what people think about a product or service for one facility, an in-store survey may be adequate. When management wants to know what people in the immediate market think, then a local survey should be taken. For multi-unit chains, state, regional, or national samples must be used. Since hotels have a much broader trade area than that of restaurants, surveys should be taken in each community that supplies a significant percentage of the hotel's business, or, at the minimum, in the hotel from each primary customer segment.

The *time period* would indicate when the study should be made. If data are sought on buyer behavior on Sundays, then this would likely be the best day to gather the data. This might be expressed as May 7, 14, and 21 of 19XX. Other examples of the time period are during May of 19XX and May 1 through July 31, 19XX.

2. *Identify the sampling frame.* The *sampling frame* is a list of sampling units that will be used to acquire the sample. This could consist of telephone books, lists from a marketing company, lists of subscribers to a magazine or newspaper, or lists of registered voters, business owners, and association members. There are few lists that include all members of the population, so the researcher must determine which sampling frame will be most representative of the population. If there is a multi-stage sampling unit, as in the above example of the Fortune 500 firms, then there would need to be a separate sampling frame for each stage.

3. *Determine the relevant sample size.* The central issue in *sample size* is to be reasonably sure that the mean (average) of the sample is representative of the mean of the population. Generally, the question of having a large enough sample size is not a major concern, because most marketing studies contain sample sizes that are more than adequate to represent the population from which they were drawn. The sample size depends on six factors (Kinnear & Taylor, 1987; Aaker, Kumar, & Day, 1995):

1. *Statistical Theory.* For many firms, the size of the sample will be determined by statistical analysis. While the formulas themselves are not complicated, the theoretical knowledge required to use them is beyond the scope of this book. In spite of the availability of statistical determination, the majority of sample size decisions are made based on the remaining five factors.

2. *The Number of Groups and Subgroups in the Sample.* In most studies, there will be several targeted groups, such as seniors, singles, and various income classes, for which the data are being gathered. A rule of thumb is to have a minimum sample size of 100 for the largest target group, with remaining groups sampled proportionately. For example, if a firm's largest primary target group represented 40% of sales, then 100 surveys would be collected for this group. The remaining groups would require 150 surveys, for a total sample size of 250 (100 ÷ .40 = 250, 250 − 100 = 150). If a group represented about 20% of sales, its sample size would be 50 (250 × 0.20 = 50). If there were groups that comprised less than 20% of total sales or customers, then the marketer would first determine if the size of the group warranted specific strategies and tactics and therefore survey information. If the answer is yes, then the sample from the small group would have to be large enough to gather an adequate number of responses. However small the targeted group, fewer than 30 surveys would rarely be adequate.

For studies of a large group whose characteristics were thought to be relatively homogeneous (highly representative of the firm's targeted population), the minimum sampling size of 100 could be applied. If there was a question about how representative they were, the sample size could be increased based on the judgment of the researcher. Some national surveys of representative groups have sample sizes of as little as 500.

3. *Variability of Respondents' Opinions.* One of the most important factors in deciding on the size of the sample is the size of the population variance. If researchers feel that a high percentage of the sampling units think and act similarly, then the size of the sample could be quite small. As the number of different opinions on key issues increases, the sample size should also increase.

4. *Budget Constraints.* If a firm had $5,000 budgeted for the study and the preparation of the questionnaire was $1,500, printing and collection of survey data was expected to cost $10 each, and the quantitative and qualitative analysis of the results were $1,500, then the maximum number of surveys would be 200 ($5,000 − $3,000 = 2,000 ÷ $10 = 200).

5. *Importance of the Study.* If the desired data are critical to the future of the company, then a larger survey may be necessary. For issues of less importance, either a smaller sample size could be used or perhaps simply conducting individual or group interviews with a few people representative of the population would suffice.

6. *Time Constraints.* If a firm is in dire need of the data, then a large study may not be feasible. If the research is part of a marketing plan and has been anticipated, then the question of the size of the sample would be more flexible.

SELECTING THE SAMPLING PROCEDURE   There are two different classes of sampling procedure: probability and nonprobability sampling.

PROBABILITY SAMPLING   In *probability sampling,* the size (or approximate size) of the population is known, the population is clearly defined so that researchers can tell which sampling units belong to the population, and each element of the population has an equal or known chance of being selected. Random selection allows researchers to calculate the nature and extent of any biases in estimates, to estimate the sampling error (difference between the sample and the population), and to use various types of statistics to formulate conclusions about the study's results. The most frequently used methods of probability sampling are simple *random sampling,* in which each element or respondent in the population is selected in some randomized manner (generally from lists); *stratified sampling,* in which the population is divided based on homogeneity within the groups and then elements of the groups are selected randomly (e.g., college students, business professionals, and retirees); and *cluster sampling,* in which the population is divided based on heterogeneity within the groups, one or more of the groups for the study are selected randomly, and then either all elements within a cluster or random samplings of the clusters are selected for the study. One purpose of cluster sampling is to lower the cost of the study by reducing the size of the sample and increasing the proximity of the elements.

NONPROBABILITY SAMPLING   The key difference between probability and nonprobability sampling is that with nonprobability sampling the selection of elements cannot be statistically projected to the population. While probability sampling is technically superior to nonprobability sampling, there are advantages to the latter. First, because of human error, careless implementation, and sampling and nonsampling errors, the goals of probability sampling may not be achieved. Because of these errors, the results of a carefully controlled nonprobability sample will often be as accurate as a probability sample. For example, even though the study is based on a random sample, the respondents themselves choose whether or not to participate. This will invariably introduce some degree of error in the survey results. Perhaps those that respond are people who are trying to be courteous and do not often express negative opinions. Sometimes the opposite is true, as when there is a relationship between those who respond and the negative feelings they have toward the issue. In this instance, every other detail in the research might be technically correct, but the resulting data and conclusions based on the data will likely be inaccurate. Second, if the objective of the research is only to gather data to learn more about a few specific issues, then nonprobability sampling may be suitable. Nonprobability sampling is generally adequate for most exploratory and sometimes descriptive research. Third, when time and cost are issues, nonprobability sampling may be the only alternative (Emory & Cooper, 1991).

The three primary types of nonprobability sampling are (1) *convenience sampling*, in which researchers choose whomever they desire or the most expeditious source of survey participants to be included in the sample; (2) *judgment sampling*, in which sample members are selected based on their knowledge, experience, or perceived value of their opinions on the subject; and (3) *quota sampling*, in which respondents are selected based on various demographic or other segmentation variables such as age, gender, race, income, personality, or group affiliation. Of the nonprobability sampling methods, quota sampling is the one that comes closest to the reliability of probability sampling methods.

MEASUREMENT SCALES   For most research projects, especially major studies, the task of developing measurement scales will normally be assigned to a research specialist. When the task is less critical or will not require statistical interpretation, a marketer with a knowledge of the basic principles of measurement should be able to select a measurement scale. Although the measurement scale developed by a nonresearcher may not be adequate for many statistical inferences, it would likely be adequate for the purposes of the research project. Since the purpose of this book is not to teach statistical applications, only the basics of measurement will be reviewed.

Measurement scaling is the procedure used to assign numbers to measure various attributes possessed by elements such as people, products, events, and businesses. The critical task is to select the most appropriate measurement scale, one that gathers information that will help researchers obtain answers to research questions and achieve their objectives. The categories include nominal, ordinal, interval, and ratio scales. Each successive scale has the characteristics of the previous scale, plus more rigorous properties that can be utilized for additional statistical applications. Even so, the selection of a particular scale will be based on the information needs of the research study, not the ability of researchers to provide numerous statistical inferences (Dillon, Madden, & Firtle, 1987; Emory & Cooper, 1991; Aaker, Kumar, & Day, 1995).

NOMINAL SCALES   These are used to divide one group into mutually exclusively subgroups for the purpose of categorization (e.g., Moslem, Jewish, Protestant,

Catholic). Gender, race, religion, geographic areas, societal groups, occupations, housing status, and marital status are examples (see Figure 3.7). There is no particular order or distance relationship that can be interpreted and there is no arithmetic origin. Because the responses do not indicate the amount of an attribute possessed by the element, the mode (the most frequently occurring response) is the only measure of central tendency that can be used. Individual frequency percentages can also be determined. Even though nominal scales are not compatible with most statistics, they are still quite valuable. In most surveys, attitudes of individual market segments are categorized with nominally scaled questions.

ORDINAL SCALES   These represent an order sequence, where successive responses on the scale express either a greater or lesser preference with no consideration of distance. If respondents were asked to rank their preference for five different hotels with 1 being the most preferred and 5 the least preferred (a *rank-order scale*), the responses would indicate only the order of their preference (see Figure 3.7). There is no assumption of the distance between each response on the scale. Typical statistics are the mode, median (measurement in the midpoint of responses), and frequency percentages.

INTERVAL SCALES   These possess the attributes of nominal and ordinal scales plus equal differences between response categories. The attributes of order and distance give researchers the ability to apply most desired statistical applications. The most frequently used interval scales are the Likert, semantic differential, constant sum, and purchase intent scales.

One of the most effective and efficient measurement scales for assessing customer satisfaction is the *semantic differential scale* (see Figure 3.7). It measures a person's attitude toward an attribute (a variable) by providing a 3–11 point scale bounded by evaluative terms. The most commonly used scale categories are 5 and 7.

The development process for the semantic differential scale involves the selection of bipolar adjectives that help describe some dimension of the attribute. The responses can be scored on a positive only number line (i.e., 1 through 5), or with a neutral center, such as −2, −1, 0, +1, and +2 (also, −3 to +3, and so on). It is important to vary the sides for positive and negative adjectives (Dickson & MacLachlan, 1990). This increases the accuracy of the data by reducing the possibility of a respondent checking off categories without reading them. A problem with varying the polarity of the responses is the increased difficulty of interpreting combined data. For example, if on a seven-point scale a hotel achieved a 5.9 rating for employee warmth (negative/positive polarity) and a 2.4 rating for courtesy (positive/negative polarity), the courtesy rating would need to be transposed to a 5.6 before overall scores could be analyzed [2.4 is 1.4 points from the lowest rating (1); 1.4 subtracted from the highest rating (7) equals 5.6]. Although the majority of data, which primarily target customers' preferences on critical attributes, can be obtained with the semantic differential scale, in some instances categorical (or nominal) scales (explained later) will be needed. *Profile analysis* is a method in which the semantic differential scale is used to present the research data graphically. Essentially, the

CATEGORICAL/NOMINAL SCALE

"What is your occupation?"

Professional _____ Manager _____ Government _____ Clerical _____ Sales _____

Proprietor _____ Craftsperson _____ Retired _____ Student _____

ORDINAL SCALE

Rate the following attributes according to their importance in your decision to dine at a particular restaurant. (1 = most important, 5 = least important)

Service quality _____ Cleanliness _____ Atmosphere _____ Food Quality _____ Price _____

INTERVAL SCALES

SEMANTIC DIFFERENTIAL SCALE (*The recorded data are the means responses from a survey.)

In my opinion, the employees in the hotel were:

Cold	_____	_____	_____	4.6*	5.9	_____	_____	Warm
Discourteous	1.5	2.4	_____	_____	_____	_____	_____	Courteous
Not helpful	_____	_____	_____	_____	5.8	6.4	_____	Helpful
Slow	1.8	_____	3.3	_____	_____	_____	_____	Fast
Inaccurate	_____	_____	3.9	_____	5.7	_____	_____	Accurate

Profile Analysis (for the questions in the above semantic differential scale)

In my opinion, the employees in the hotel were:

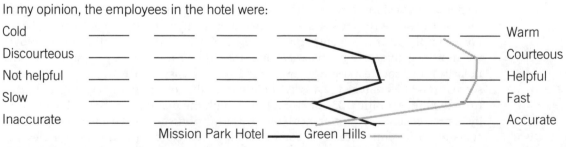

Cold	_____ _____ _____ _____ _____ _____ _____	Warm
Discourteous	_____ _____ _____ _____ _____ _____ _____	Courteous
Not helpful	_____ _____ _____ _____ _____ _____ _____	Helpful
Slow	_____ _____ _____ _____ _____ _____ _____	Fast
Inaccurate	_____ _____ _____ _____ _____ _____ _____	Accurate

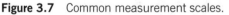
Mission Park Hotel ——— Green Hills -----

Figure 3.7 Common measurement scales.

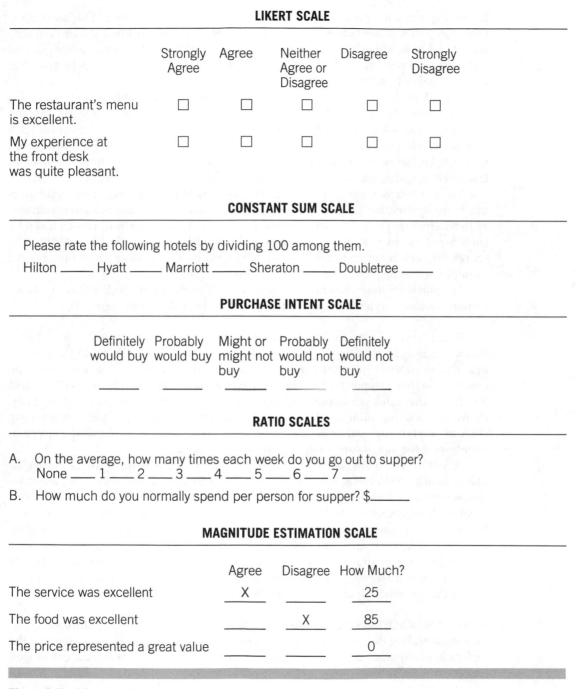

LIKERT SCALE

	Strongly Agree	Agree	Neither Agree or Disagree	Disagree	Strongly Disagree
The restaurant's menu is excellent.	☐	☐	☐	☐	☐
My experience at the front desk was quite pleasant.	☐	☐	☐	☐	☐

CONSTANT SUM SCALE

Please rate the following hotels by dividing 100 among them.

Hilton _____ Hyatt _____ Marriott _____ Sheraton _____ Doubletree _____

PURCHASE INTENT SCALE

Definitely would buy	Probably would buy	Might or might not buy	Probably would not buy	Definitely would not buy
_____	_____	_____	_____	_____

RATIO SCALES

A.   On the average, how many times each week do you go out to supper?
     None ___ 1 ___ 2 ___ 3 ___ 4 ___ 5 ___ 6 ___ 7 ___

B.   How much do you normally spend per person for supper? $_____

MAGNITUDE ESTIMATION SCALE

	Agree	Disagree	How Much?
The service was excellent	X		25
The food was excellent		X	85
The price represented a great value			0

Figure 3.7   (*Continued*)

mean responses for various scores are plotted and then compared. The most common comparisons are between a firm and its primary competitors. Other comparisons could be between businesses of the same firm, different target customer groups, different time periods, and the difference between the business's present standing and its ideal or benchmark position.

The *Likert scale* measures the degree of agreement or disagreement with various statements. It consists of a list of questions or statements to be measured and the evaluative part—the measurement scale. The Likert scale is sometimes called a *summated scale*, because the scores for each individual can be added for a total score that can be compared to that of other respondents. As will be discussed later in interpretation of research information, summated scores are not recommended.

The *constant sum scale* simply asks respondents to indicate their ratings for various items by dividing 100 points among them. Although it is sometimes questionable as to whether this is an ordinal or interval scale, for most research purposes it can be considered as interval. Generally, this scale would be interpreted by adding the scores for each hotel and then dividing the sum by the number of responses. An example of a constant sum scale is presented in Figure 3.7.

The *purchase intent scale* attempts to measure a respondent's inclination to make a certain purchase. Typically, this is a five-point scale as shown in Figure 3.7.

RATIO SCALES   When the responses in the measurement scale consist of consecutive numbers, they can be recorded with a *ratio scale*. These have all the properties of interval scales plus the concept of an absolute zero point. This allows for the assumption that a response of 4 is not only two equal spaces from response 2 but also has twice the value. Examples include sales; market share; the number of menu items, hotels or restaurants, and customers; dollars or percentages spent on anything such as advertising, public relations, or food costs; counts of physical objects or events; and the age of each customer completing the survey.

A hybrid ratio/nominal measurement scale that is increasing in use is the *magnitude estimation scale.* Here, respondents are asked to agree or disagree with a certain characteristic of a sample element. Next, respondents express their level of agreement or disagreement with the answer by allocating up to 100 points to the question. Respondents must be informed that large numbers indicate strong agreement or disagreement, small numbers indicate moderate agreement or disagreement, and zero indicates a neutral position or opinion. While this type of question is highly valid for individual responses, the variation or wide range in individual responses makes the combination of results more difficult to interpret statistically.

SCALE CHARACTERISTICS   There are several areas that must be addressed before most scaling decisions are made. These include the number of categories, the inclusion of a neutral category, the number of favorable and unfavorable categories, and forcing a response.

NUMBER OF CATEGORIES   The key element in this decision is the ability of the respondent to discriminate between the various values. For several reasons, the most commonly used scale category is 5. One reason is that this scale number is relatively simple to interpret. Respondents rate items as "poor," "fair," "average," "good," or "excellent." This means that, if they do not like the object being measured, the question is only whether they think it's very bad or just below average. The opposite would be true if they liked the object. If they think it's neither, they can rate it as neutral. Rating scales of 3 or 4 generally are not thought to have enough categories to allow for effective and worthwhile discrimination. It is impossible for the researcher to determine if a rating of 1 for a three-point scale represents very bad or just below average. A rating of 4 indicates marginal improvement but still retains some of the problems of the three-category rating; also, it does not have a neutral or average response. Additionally, as the number of possible responses goes up, so does the ambiguity and variability of the responses. For example, on a ten-point scale, how does the respondent measure the difference between a response (rating) of 7 or 8? Does an 8 equate with average (80 is an average grade in school) or a 5 or 6 (a score in the middle)? to allow for effective and worthwhile discrimination. It is impossible for the researcher to determine if a rating of 1 for the three-point scale represents very bad or just below average.

NEUTRAL CATEGORY   If the scale is based on an odd number, there is usually a category for a neutral response. To respondents, this generally means that they feel the rating should be average. It could also indicate an inability to make a decision or ignorance about the question or object being measured. Using an even scale removes the neutral category and forces respondents to make a choice of either above or below average. The advantage to management of not using the neutral category is that it lets the business know where it stands, above or below average, and it gives management a tool to use as an motivator for themselves and employees.

NUMBER OF FAVORABLE AND UNFAVORABLE CATEGORIES   The question of whether to use a balanced number of favorable and unfavorable categories or an unbalanced number depends on the likely responses. If customers typically rate various products or services favorably, then perhaps an unbalanced scale with a more favorable response category would yield more actionable results. Instead of the balanced scale of "poor," "fair," "average," "very good," and "excellent," an unbalanced unfavorable scale of "poor," "fair," "good," "very good," and "excellent" would allow for more discrimination. A frequent research problem occurs when people, either out of ignorance or attempts to influence responses, use a four-point scale with three favorable response categories: for example, "fair," "average," "good," and "excellent" or "fair," "good," "very good," and "excellent."

FORCING A RESPONSE   When a scale does not include a response such as "I don't know" or "No opinion" (an unforced response), the researcher is forcing respondents to provide answers on a topic of which they may not have reasonable knowledge. If it is felt that there will be a reasonable number of respondents who cannot answer the question, then an unforced scale should be used. The use of the unforced scale will rarely influence survey results because the response is commonly viewed as if the respondent did not answer the question.

RESEARCH INSTRUMENTS   These include various behavior recording devices previously discussed in observational research and the most commonly used means of recording research information, the questionnaire.

QUESTIONNAIRES   The questionnaire is simply a set of questions asked of an individual, a *respondent,* with the purpose of gathering research data. The following outlines the basic process of developing a questionnaire:

- *Decide the Purpose of the Questionnaire.* What is the company trying to find out? Common objectives are to find out what customers think about present product offerings, prices, and possible future offerings. Along with the purpose-related information, demographic data must be gathered to discover if various customer groups feel differently about a certain issue than other groups.
- *Develop Possible Questions that Will Help Achieve the Stated Purpose.* The questions allow researchers to make reasonably correct inferences about the research objectives. It is best to consider some type of exploratory research before preparing a questionnaire. Since the questionnaire must provide decision-makers with actionable data and information, asking the appropriate questions is imperative. No questionnaire will be perfect. Even the best survey will only give you an approximate picture of what people think. So do not be concerned about the "perfect questionnaire"; it does not exist.

Some of the most important considerations in deciding on specific questions and their order are as follows (Dillon, Madden, & Firtle, 1987):

1. *The questions should be stated in clear, precise, and understandable language.* "Do you feel the impetuosity and verve of our servers are somewhat copious or reticent?" If the question is unclear, the answers will also be unclear.

2. *Avoid double-barreled questions.* This is asking respondents to rate two or more variables in one question. "How do you rate the room service and dining room service at the Hyatt? 1   2   3   4   5"

3. *Adjust for "order bias."* If a respondent is asked to select his/her favorite item from a list, the order of the items in the list will influence the responses. To reduce this problem, alternate the order of the items on questionnaires.

4. *Avoid loaded questions.* Loaded questions influence the respondent to answer in a certain way. For example, "How did you like our new shrimp gumbo?" would be better as "How would you rate our new shrimp gumbo?"

5. *Anything that influences a respondent's answers should be limited.* For example, topics such as abortion, women's rights, or increases in college tuition may cause heightened emotions in respondents, resulting in biased answers to other questions. For this reason, questions on controversial subjects should normally be placed toward the end of the questionnaire. Additionally, when possible, the company for which the survey is being taken should remain anonymous. This helps limit preconceived opinions of the company from influencing answers. An example would be a

mall intercept survey to gather information on the firm's and its competitor's image and level of customer satisfaction. Interviewing people after a good or bad experience may not yield actionable data because of the likelihood that these people do not represent the population from which they were selected. Even so, the derived data could still be used for operational purposes.

6. *Often, marketers are concerned about people's unwillingness to complete multi-page surveys.* Experience has found that, except for "mall intercept interviews," once a person commits to answering the questions, length does not significantly reduce response rates (Luck & Rubin, 1987). To increase the chances of having respondents completing lengthy questionnaires, do not number each question. For example, rather than numbering each question in a 60-question survey, divide the questions into perhaps six groups of ten questions each.

7. *Depending on the information sought, the format of questions can be structured, unstructured, open-ended, or closed-ended.*

(a) *Structured.* A formal list of questions is followed by the interviewer or included in the questionnaire.

(b) *Unstructured.* The interviewer would be given explicit directions for the data sought but would let the respondent's answers guide the process. Because of the wide variations in answers, this format requires an experienced interviewer and is rarely used exclusively. Like open-ended questions that follow, the results may be difficult to interpret statistically.

(c) *Open-ended.* Respondents can answer these questions in any manner they choose. The purpose here is to learn as much as possible about customers' preferences by broadening the allowable responses. However, because of the broad range of answers possible to questions such as "What are some of the reasons you stay at this hotel?" and "What are your five favorite restaurants?" using the data for statistical interpretation is sometimes difficult or time-consuming.

(d) *Closed-ended.* Answers to these questions are limited to those included in the questionnaire. The purpose of this type of question is to locate specific answers that can be statistically tabulated and to make it easier for the respondent to record responses. For example, "Which hotel do you stay at most often? Hotel A _____, Hotel B _____, Hotel C _____" or "How much do you generally spend per day on meals during your stay? Up to $15 _____, $15 to $25 _____, $25 to $35 _____, over $35 _____."

8. *The interview should begin with an introduction and include questions to qualify the individual (sample element) as a participant in the survey.*

(a) *Opening Statement.* Since the respondent has taken personal time out of the day to do something with little perceived value or benefit to him/her, you will need an opening statement to reduce this perception. "We are trying to find out more about people's likes and dislikes about staying at hotels. Could I please ask you a few questions?" (or, "Would you mind answering a few questions to help us serve you better?")

(b) *Qualifying the Respondent.* The first questions should help determine if the respondent is qualified to answer the remaining questions on the survey. If the respondent does not have a reasonable knowledge of the subject being surveyed, or if they are not from the desired target group, it would be best to go to the next respondent. Two common problems in this area are *lack of knowledge*—many people will not admit that they do not know something—and *lack of recall/memory*—the respondent may have eaten at the restaurant or stayed at the hotel but too much time or too many experiences since that time have clouded his/her opinion.

Typical qualifying questions are: "Have you traveled outside the city during the last six months? Yes _____, No _____, Cannot remember _____?" or "Have you stayed overnight at a hotel during the last six months? Yes _____, No, _____, Cannot remember _____?" If the respondent has not traveled or stayed at a hotel, or if it has been more than six months since his/her last visit, that respondent may not be able to provide the proper quality of information necessary for the survey.

9. *The order of the questions should progress from easy-to-answer and nonpersonal to more-difficult-to-answer and personal.*

(a) *Warm-up Questions.* The next group of questions should be warm-up questions that ask for general responses about the survey topic. Their purpose is to stimulate the respondent's memory and to prepare the respondent psychologically for the more specific questions that will follow. It is like stretching before running. These questions should be simple and noncontroversial: for example, "What do you like best about staying in a hotel?" (open-ended) or "What do you like the least about staying in hotels?" Beds _____ Pillows _____ Room temperature _____ Cost _____ Inconvenience of being away from home _____ (closed-ended)

(b) *Specific Questions.* These are the most important questions of the survey: for example, "What is the most frequent reason for you to travel?" "If you travel on business, what is your per-diem for a hotel?" "How long do these trips last?" "How often do you travel?" "Which of the following hotels have you stayed at: Marriott _____, Hyatt _____, Hilton _____?"

(c) *Demographic Questions.* Questions on such subjects as age, education, income, type of work, and value of home will help identify and categorize respondents. Because of their personal nature, demographic questions should generally be asked last. Psychographic information, such as where the respondent shops, political affiliation, recreational activities, and hobbies, could also be included here.

(d) *Conclusion.* Always end the survey with a sincere "Thank you!" (written or oral).

10. *Consider the quality of the questions.* This includes their validity, reliability, pretesting, and revision.

DATA REQUIREMENTS   The primary requirements for assessing the quality of data are as follows:

VALIDITY AND RELIABILITY   The questions should meet the tests of validity—whether or not the questions measure what they are supposed to measure—and reliability—whether or not the responses can be replicated in the future.

RELEVANCE   Whether relevance is measured statistically or by expertise or by common sense, the business must feel comfortable making decisions based on the data and derived information. Since most data are secondary, and possibly may have first been applied toward some other purpose, they should relate to the business's situation and should be applicable to the task at hand.

PROPER QUANTITY   Because both secondary and primary data are relatively easy to gather, there is a tendency to report more than is needed. Years ago, a major problem of research was not having access to enough data. Today, with flourishing periodical and research report businesses, too much data are becoming a frequent problem.

TIMELINESS   Primary data are generally gathered for a specific purpose with associated time constraints. Therefore, the data should be gathered in a timely manner. Available secondary data on past trends may not be actionable.

PROPER COST   A small fortune can be spent gathering information. A major research request from a national research firm could easily cost $50,000 to $200,000 or more. Some firms will have planning staffs of ten or more employees to gather and analyze data. The key is that the money spent should have some relationship to the need. Management must decide subjectively on the importance of the decisions to be made, and on how much should be spent on secondary or primary data to improve the accuracy of those decisions. There are statistical formulas for calculating an approximate value of research, but even these are quite subjective in nature. Many organizations budget between .05% and 1% of sales for research.

MANAGEMENT TIME   Managers need to keep up with the firm's competitive environment. How much time is spent on this will vary, depending on the volatility of the competitive environment, in particular, the company's trade area, its customers, and the economy. Management personnel should set aside between 30 minutes and one hour per day for reviewing the various research sources. The traditional cup of coffee and the *Wall Street Journal* are not a waste of time. It is a relaxing way to engage the mind for the day's work and to see what major competitors are doing or to learn about strategies from other industries.

Contact Methods

The three most commonly used *contact methods* (or methods of gathering information) are personal face-to-face contact with the respondent, sending a questionnaire through the mail, and contacting the respondent by telephone. Although the Internet is currently not a highly effective method of collecting survey information, its use will increase. The key problem now with an *Internet survey* is that its use is concentrated into a small segment of the population that is not generally representative of most hospitality business's target customers. Additionally, this would be a type of convenience or nonprobability sample, since researchers cannot estimate the likelihood of one respondent being selected over another. In spite of these drawbacks, several chains and some independent operators are having a moderate success with the Internet, primarily with opinion polls of company and competitor's products and services.

PERSONAL CONTACT   The face-to-face interview historically took place in the respondent's home. Because of the expense, crime, time constraints, and new technologies, other survey methods have taken its place. The most visible replacement has been the *mall-intercept interview,* where employees of a marketing firm ask shoppers at a mall questions about a product or service. Occasionally, respondents are asked to view a commercial in order to solicit their opinion. One of the least costly means of accumulating primary research, and one of the most frequently used types of survey for the hospitality industry, is the *self-administered* or *in-store survey.* Since it is generally completed immediately after the event to which the questions refer, its accuracy is usually superior to external surveys (surveys taking place after an event are referred to as *ex post facto* surveys). Its limitations are that the number of questions must generally be kept to those fitting on a postcard-sized comment card, and that it is difficult to get a representative sample—often only those who are very happy or very upset with their experience tend to complete the survey. A drawing for free meals or a free stay in the hotel can motivate a more dispersed sample. Another type of personal collection method in wide use in the hospitality industry is the *focus group.* A small group of respondents who have either dined at the restaurant or stayed at the hotel are gathered in a room to discuss their opinions of their experience. The focus interview normally uses open-ended questions and an unstructured style. The interviewer will have a brief written questionnaire but will be given the freedom to guide the respondents to extract the greatest amount of information possible. Because of the unstructured nature of the questioning, the focus group should be recorded by audio or preferably by video equipment. Among the overall advantages of the personal contact method are that questions can be explained and a wider range of question formats is possible.

MAIL   Mail surveys are taken by mailing out a reasonably structured questionnaire to respondents and requesting that the completed questionnaire be sent back. Typical response rates vary with the type of information requested, the targeted sample, and incentives offered to participants, but the average response is about 10%. With attractive incentives, response rates of 50% or more are possible. Since the survey will be self-administered without the aid of an interviewer, questions must be easy to understand. As more syndicated marketing firms create special databases from which to extract custom mailing lists, sampling selection is becoming more accurate. For extensive survey questionnaires, a major advantage of mail surveys is that they are generally less expensive than other contact methods.

Two forms of mail surveys that are increasing in popularity are *mail panels,* where a group of respondents, either for free or minimal pay, agree to complete a reasonable number of surveys, and *diary surveys,* where a record is kept of an individual's visits to a hotel or restaurant (Luck & Rubin, 1987). The response rate for these surveys will obviously be much higher than for standard mail surveys. The business must be careful not to use the same respondent for too long because there will be a tendency for the recording to become tiresome, thereby causing the respondent to simplify answers or write in the same answer each time.

TELEPHONE   Telephone surveys entail phoning respondents to ask them a series of questions. To simplify the process, most telephone interviews are conducted by means of a computer hooked up to a telephone (*computer-assisted telephone interviewing—CATI*). The computer is programmed to randomly select phone numbers to dial. The interviewer must first read specific directions for the interview and then ask the questions at a rapid pace to hold the attention of the respondent. The questions for telephone surveys are, by necessity, simple, since the respondent cannot remember long lists or more than one or two specific details. Because of the verbal contact with the interviewer, the response rate for telephone surveys tends to be high, between 60% and 80% (Dillon, Madden, & Firtle, 1987). Two common problems of telephone surveys are that it is difficult to get respondents to answer questions concerning demographic variables such as income, race, and religion, and the tone of voice of the interviewer will often have an effect on the respondent's answers and willingness to participate in or complete the survey.

Analysis and Interpretation

ANALYSIS OF RESEARCH DATA   Quantitative analysis of the results of the research are generally accomplished with either descriptive or inferential statistics. *Descriptive statistics* focus on an analysis of the distribution of values of a question, essentially summary measures for the data. The primary methods used to describe distribution are as follows:

Location. Mean—average; median—midpoint of the distribution; and mode—the most frequently occurring value.
Spread or Dispersion. Variance—the average of the squared deviations—measures dispersion; standard deviation—the square root of the variance—improves measurement of dispersion by expressing deviations in their original units; range—the difference between the smallest and largest scores in the distribution; and quartile analysis—a comparison between different quarters of the distribution.
Shape. Kurtosis measures the distribution's peakedness or flatness, which shows where scores tend to accumulate.

Each of these measures can be presented in graphic form.

Inferential statistics includes methods that allow researchers to test the significance of the difference between various sample statistics and corresponding population values through hypothesis testing. In hypothesis testing, various assumptions about a population are tested to determine whether they are equal to, greater than, or less than the population from which they were taken. Also included are various types of statistical analyses that attempt to explain the relationship between two or more variables.

The accuracy quality of the analysis can be increased if quantitative support, such as trends in market share, sales, and profit are factored into statistical results. A reasonably detailed analysis of the market by an unbiased third party could also prove helpful.

INTERPRETATION OF RESEARCH DATA   Two simple methods of interpreting survey results are to determine the frequency and mean for each question. While the mean shows the average response, frequencies present the range of responses. The frequency is calculated by totaling the number of responses (173) and then dividing the number of responses for each category by this figure. The mean can be derived by multiplying the scale category (1, 2, 3, 4, and 5) by its respective scores or responses (5, 25, 42, 56, and 45), then dividing the sum of these products by the total number of responses for the question. A perceptual map can be developed using the mean responses for two related product attributes such as value and product quality, room rate and room quality (features and appearance), price and service quality, price/room rate and location, convention facilities and room rate, and service quality and product quality. Knowing the mean allows for comparisons with prior periods and with competitors' scores. For a question about bathroom cleanliness, the data in Figure 3.8 were gathered and analyzed.

Survey scale: 1 = poor, 2 = fair, 3 = average, 4 = good, 5 = excellent

Bathroom cleanliness:	1	2	3	4	5
Total number of responses:	173				
Responses for each category:	5	25	42	56	45

Frequencies—
percentage for each response: (number of responses for category) ÷ (total number of responses)

2.89%	14.45%	24.28%	32.37%	26.01%

Mean or weighted
average calculation: (Survey scale category) × (number of responses for category) ÷ (total number of responses) = (mean response)

5	50	126	224	225

(Total = 630) ÷ (173) = **3.64 (mean)**

Figure 3.8   Frequencies and means.

SUMMING SURVEY RESULTS   While management will find variable information from the analysis of means and frequencies (descriptive statistics) and higher-order statistics (inferential—primarily multiple regression), it is imperative that an overall measure or total score be established for the firm. This composite score is critical, because it is the most effective means of measuring and presenting the firm's overall market position relative to its primary competitors. Performance scores for various categories of questions within the composite score, such as five questions about the guest's experience at the front desk, can be totaled separately to provide functional departments with more specific assessment information.

It would be nice if management could simply add up the firm's means for 20 or so various attributes to be compared with past surveys or with competitors. Unfortunately, this *unweighted rating method* is not valid, since each response has a lesser or greater influence on the firm's actual position (see Figure 3.9). For example, in summing means, the mean for food quality would have the same importance as bathroom cleanliness. If there were 20 variables being analyzed, the sum of the means would be even more difficult to interpret. The *weighted rating method* rectifies this situation by making it possible to rate or weight the different attributes according to their importance as judged by customers. For example, on a scale of 1 to 5 (1 being unimportant, 5 being very important) the customer could be asked to rate the importance of each attribute. The weighted average of the question's value is then multiplied by the question's importance rating. The products are then added together for the firm's performance rating. The average of the importance rating is calculated in the same manner as the mean for the question. The weighted average is the mean of the question times the mean of the importance rating. An advantage of this rating method is its simplicity. One problem is that it may be difficult for management or employees to conceptualize the importance of the answer. This problem can be rectified somewhat with the *ratio rating method,* which develops a ratio for each of the competitor's ratings. In the survey in Figure 3.9, the value totals are summed (31.07 + 29.56 = 60.63) and then divided into 100 (100 ÷ 60.63 = 1.65). This figure is then multiplied by each value total for a percentage ratio (1.65 × 31.07 = 51.27%, 1.65 × 29.56 = 48.77%); the total of 100.4% is due to rounding.

Often, it is desired that the total value for the survey be on the basis of 100 points. If a business is attempting to quantify its position, it might be helpful to know that the business's rating was, for example, 89, compared to a competitor's rating of 94. This can be accomplished by using the *weighted 100-point rating method.* To yield a total possible value of 100, the total of the ratings must be transposed into a number that, when multiplied by the number in the scale, equals 100. If the scale is 5, the total for the rating values must equal 20. Likewise, a scale of 10 would require a rating values total of 10. In the example in Figure 3.9, the ratings are 3 and 5 for a total of 8. To transpose the rating values into numbers that add up to 20, divide 20 by 8. Then multiply this figure (2.5) times the current ratings. The new rating figures then become 7.5 (3 × 2.5) and 12.5 (5 × 2.5). The new ratings are then multiplied by their respective means. The means are then totaled to yield the firm's performance based on a maximum of 100 points.

Unweighted Rating Method (not valid)

	Mean
Bathroom cleanliness:	3.64
Food quality:	4.03

   Total (addition of means): 7.67 Competitor's total: 8.54

Weighted Rating Method

	Mean	Rating	Value
Bathroom cleanliness:	3.64	3	10.92
Food quality:	4.03	5	20.15
		Total performance rating:	31.07
		Competitor's performance value:	29.56

Ratio Rating Method

	Mean	Rating	Value
Bathroom cleanliness:	3.64	3	10.92
Food quality:	4.03	5	20.15
		Performance rating:	31.07
		Competitor's total rating:	29.56

   Percentage comparison: 51.27% to 48.77%

Weighted "100-Point" Rating Method

	Mean	Rating	Value
Bathroom cleanliness:	3.64	7.5	27.30
Food quality:	4.03	12.5	50.38
		Performance rating:	77.68
		Competitor's total value:	74.00

Figure 3.9   Interpreting attribute response totals.

INTERPRETING THE MEAN RESPONSE FOR QUANTITATIVE CATEGORIES   Often, there is a need to calculate or interpret the mean response for various research questions. This method would technically be applied only to interval and ordinal data. The mean response is interpreted using the *midpoint assumption*. This essentially states that individual responses can be assumed to have a mean at the midpoint of the response's range. For example, in a question where the objective is to determine the average household income, the following scale was used:

Under $30,000	$30,000 to 39,999	$40,000 to 49,999	$50,000 or more
1	2	3	4

In this example, the midpoint assumption for response #1 would simply be $30,000 divided by 2, equals $15,000. The midpoint assumption for response #2 is $35,000, or $39,999 minus $30,000 equals $9,999, divided by 2 equals $5,000 (rounded), plus the low range of the response, $30,000, equals $35,000. The midpoint assumption would similarly be calculated for responses #3 and #4.

If the mean response for this question was 2.87, the dollar value of this mean could be calculated by adding the midpoint of the mean response integer (2), plus the fraction (0.87) of the difference between the integer midpoint and that of the next higher response. In the above question, the value of the mean response integer is $35,000 (the midpoint assumption of response #2). The value of the response fraction is $8,700 (the product of the mean response fraction (0.87) and the difference between the midpoint assumptions of responses #2 and #3 ($45,000 − $35,000 = $10,000, $10,000 × 0.87 = $8,700). Using the midpoint assumption, the mean of this question, 2.87, could be interpreted to be $43,700 ($35,000 + $8,700 = $43,700).

REPORTING THE FINDINGS   Whether or not the research up to this point was performed by the firm's research or marketing personnel or by outside researchers, the findings will normally be formally presented to management. If quantitative analysis beyond basic descriptive statistics was applied to the data, it should be explained thoroughly. This is best accomplished by reducing the statistics to basic math, such as percentages, means, and frequency distributions, and presenting key research findings in graphic form (i.e., pie and bar charts, tables, and graphs). If the information or conclusions are not formally presented to management, it will be reviewed at managers' or executive staff meetings as discussed earlier for the marketing information systems process. When this occurs, it is even more critical that the findings be expressed in language that can be understood by those without an in-depth research or statistical background.

QUESTIONS AND PROJECTS

1. Why is research important to strategic marketing planning?
2. Define the term "marketing information system." What are the key tasks necessary to support the system?
3. Draw a diagram to show how you would set up a marketing information system for any hotel or restaurant for which you have worked.
4. Define the following terms:
   (a) Research objective or question
   (b) Data
   (c) Information
   (d) Primary data
   (e) Secondary data
   (f) Cross-sectional surveys
   (g) Longitudinal surveys
5. Define marketing research. List and describe the process used for formal research projects.

6. List and define the three types of research. What is the primary method of collecting data for each of these?
7. List common sources of secondary information.
8. What are the three primary contact methods for a survey? Describe advantages and disadvantages of each.
9. Discuss measurement scales, including the four major types of scale.
10. Discuss the steps in putting together a sampling plan.
11. What are the differences between probability and nonprobability sampling?
12. What is your preference for the number of categories and for neutral categories on survey scales?
13. Define the following types of question formats:
    (a) Structured
    (b) Unstructured
    (c) Open-ended
    (d) Closed-ended
14. Why should you qualify a potential respondent for a survey?
15. What are some questions that can help you assess future wants and demands?
16. What are some independent variables that could be manipulated to see how they influence sales in a hotel? In a restaurant?
17. Explain the problem with the following: "Hi! I'm Howard Yukon with Holiday Inn. Can I ask you a few questions?"
18. Should a respondent be included if it has been one year since his/her last stay at the hotel? Why or why not?
19. Calculate the mean and frequency distribution for the following survey data:

Survey scale: 1 = poor, 2 = fair, 3 = average, 4 = good, 5 = excellent					
Service quality:	1	2	3	4	5
Responses for each category:	43	57	73	96	52

20. One hundred guests at three different hotels were asked to rate the hotel's overall product quality. Their responses follow. Calculate the mean, mode, and median, then interpret the meaning of the responses. What assumptions can you make about the differences in segmentation characteristics for each hotel?

Survey scale: 1 = poor, 2 = fair, 3 = average, 4 = good, 5 = excellent					
Product quality:	1	2	3	4	5
Responses for hotel 1:	3	6	82	5	4
Responses for hotel 2:	21	19	22	18	20
Responses for hotel 3:	38	12	5	8	42

Internal Analysis

Each year we see an increasingly more sophisticated group of competitors and further fragmentation of target markets. This requires firms to be not only more flexible in their actions but also more knowledgeable about the abilities necessary for this more dynamic environment (Day, 1994). The purpose of the internal analysis (also referred to as the *company profile*) is to evaluate how the company is doing, so that its efforts can be directed in the most effective and efficient manner. It consists of an in-depth examination and assessment of the company's performance and competitive position in each of the key functional areas—marketing (sales, marketing planning, and research and development), operations, human resources, administrative or strategic management (overall responsibility for planning and the coordination and efforts of functional departments), finance/accounting, and any other applicable organizational concerns. Each functional department or area, as well as subunits within each, is judged according to various factors discussed in this chapter. The primary determinant is whether the functional component is an asset to the business (a strength) or a liability (a weakness).

The reason that each area of the business must be evaluated is because without a complete picture of the overall operation, the accuracy and soundness of decisions and chosen strategies will be suspect. The marketing department may not have a major influence over the operational or financial aspects of the business, but it must still be cognizant of pertinent performance capabilities. For example, if a strategy called for a sales promotion that would potentially increase business by 20%, could the restaurant or hotel handle it? If advertisements touted the firm's friendly service, does operations deliver? If the restaurant intends to advertise a certain menu item, is there a purchasing system that can obtain supplies at a reasonable cost, in adequate quantity and quality, and in a timely manner? If the strategy for a hotel sales department was to increase personal selling to bring in new market segments, such as a convention of physicians, is the staff effectively trained to serve this more demanding clientele? The goal of the internal analysis is to determine the firm's strengths and weaknesses and, therefore, its abilities in these and other critical performance areas.

Information gathered in the internal analysis will be used in deciding on suitable strategies for the firm. The first focus of the analysis will be to maximize strengths by matching them to the most beneficial opportunities. If the firm has the appropriate strengths to take advantage of an opportunity, it can immediately direct its efforts toward that opportunity. Second, the firm will need to decide what action to take regarding perceived or actual weaknesses. If a viable opportunity must be passed over because of an internal weakness, a decision will need to be made on whether it is possible to correct it, or whether it is worth the time and effort. There is a tendency for firms to focus on taking advantage of opportunities with appropriate strengths, rather than correcting weaknesses. This is an individual decision that must be made with caution. Another common occurrence is that a company will pursue the right opportunity, but because management either ignores or refuses to recognize its weaknesses, the strategy fails (Kotler, 1991).

OBJECTIVITY

One safeguard of an in-depth internal search and review of all critical performance areas is that as hundreds of facts are accumulated, even the most complimentary subjective appraisal of flaws will lead to greater objectivity. Also, patterns of performance, both good and poor, will become evident and hopefully exposed. Even the egotistical manager may have trouble defending the fact that 95% of the customers do not like his grandmother's recipe for cole slaw. The effectiveness of strategic market planning will be minimized to the degree that top management refuses to allow an objective review of the company's performance. Bowles (1991) coined the term *organization shadow* based on Jung's use of the word "shadow" to mean inferior traits that individuals refuse to acknowledge exist within themselves—traits that, unfortunately, influence the individual's or, in this case, the organization's, actions. Among quality-oriented personnel, this inclination often leads to a sinking-ship mentality—get out as soon as possible!

As the name implies, the basis for an objective assessment is a measurable objective. The alternative consists of subjective measurements, which can cause more problems than they solve. Quantifiable objectives become the basis for operational controls by establishing targets for various tasks. There is an old business adage, "What you cannot measure, you cannot manage." Having ambiguous, ill-defined objectives is like trying to hit a moving target. The objectives should, in most cases, be quantified as a dollar amount ($3500), a percentage (20%), a date (June 1, 19XX), a time period (in 6 months, in 2 years), or a certain number of something (150 customers in one hour or a customer satisfaction index [CSI] of 4.3 on a five-point scale).

Manufacturing firms have been quite adept at measuring performance and quality. The definition of quality in the context of business has often been stated as satisfying expectations. The problem with this definition is the ambiguity and variability of each individual's expectations. Crosby (1979, p. 38) defined quality as "conformance to the requirements." Measuring quality in the service industry requires a balance between these two definitions. It is relatively easy to quantify the requirements for a tangible product. When considering the service experience, each individual's needs must be considered. For example, some will enjoy their meal more if they are allowed to linger a while before their check is presented, while others expect the check as soon as they have finished their meal (Martin, 1986).

Service firms are getting better at measuring quality, but there is still much ground to make up. Because of the subjectivity and variability with which the service experience is perceived, the industry will likely never approach the accuracy of manufacturing firms (Albrecht, 1988; Cronin & Taylor, 1992). This lack of statistical support must be made up for by a broad-based and intuitive understanding of the industry and the expectations of each targeted group.

The three key concerns for the internal analysis are *organization and content, standards for measurement,* and *who will prepare the analysis.*

ORGANIZATION AND CONTENT OF THE INTERNAL ANALYSIS

A common approach is to begin the analysis with a historical review of the firm's highpoints related to its past accomplishment of the planning directives. Specifically, did it successfully implement or achieve its mission, objectives, strategies, and tactics? This could also be covered in an executive summary or introduction to the strategic plan.

Functional Organization

The analysis is generally structured along functional areas (see Figure 4.1). Specific areas requiring attention could also be the province of (1) the functional department to which they most relate, (2) every department to which they relate, or (3) the functional area responsible for managing the factor. For example, food cost percentage could be the responsibility of the marketing department that may decide on what to serve and how much to charge, the finance/accounting department, the operations department, or all three functional units. One functional department must have ultimate responsibility for cost control so that the efforts of each applicable department with partial responsibility can be coordinated.

Using the functional approach for the analysis helps to stimulate group participation and interest, because there are a greater number of employees participating in the analysis, and they have a vested interest in the outcome. Key to the functional approach is the understanding that the majority of business problems are solved through cross-functional efforts. Rarely does an issue affect only one functional department. When the internal analysis is performed according to functional areas, the simplest means is to follow the firm's organizational chart. Traditional organizational charts for a restaurant and a hotel are presented in Figures 4.2 and 4.3.

Even though many hospitality businesses normally do not have a research and development department, the business's activities in this area should be analyzed because this is where new menu items and services will come from. If desired, this

MARKETING FUNCTION (Focused on product and market decisions and sales)

- Product and service mix—What to sell.

- Pricing—How much to sell it for.

- Place/location—Where to sell it.

- Promotion—How to let customers know about it and entice them to make a purchase.

In independent restaurants, marketing decisions are generally made by the manager. Some larger independent restaurants may have someone responsible for marketing. In chains, this function is most frequently centered at corporate headquarters. At the corporate level, the person responsible for marketing is usually referred to as the Vice President of Marketing. Marketing people who work with two or more restaurants will have various titles, generally that of Market Manager or Director of Marketing. For most chain restaurants, a national advertising campaign will be supported with local promotions.

In budget hotels that are part of a chain, the marketing function will primarily be at the chain's headquarters or corporate level. Independent budget hotels will perform all marketing tasks in-house. In most other hotels, the responsibility will be divided and shared. The corporate level will decide on marketing strategies that affect the entire chain, such as unit growth and major ad campaigns. The individual hotel will support the national campaigns but also promote their individual property. The title of the person responsible for the entire marketing function is generally the Senior Vice President of Marketing. Below this person at the corporate level may be the Vice President of Public Relations, Vice President of Business Programs, and possibly a Sales Manager for National Accounts. At the unit or business level, the person responsible for the marketing effort is the Director of Sales and Marketing. Below this person will be Sales Managers for different target segments, Sales Secretary, and possibly a Director of Catering.

Operations—producing the product or service. Within operations would be the various functional subunits of the hotel or restaurant: dining room, host/hostess, kitchen, bar, warewashing, rooms, front desk, reservations, housekeeping, purchasing, and maintenance. In hotels, these subunits would have individual supervisors; in restaurants, supervisors would usually be assigned only in larger establishments.

Strategic (or Administrative) Management—someone responsible for planning and the overall coordination and efforts of all functional areas of the business. In a small business, this would be the General Manager or owner. In a larger business, this would be the President.

Human Resource Management (or Personnel Management)—concerning the acquisition and retention of qualified employees for the business. The department is usually responsible for orientation and, in some instances, classroom training programs. In hotels and in some restaurants with more than one location, there will be a Director of Human Resources. Some businesses still refer to this department as the personnel department, and its head as the Director of Personnel. In most single-unit restaurants and budget hotel properties, the General Manager, and perhaps other functional managers, will perform the tasks of the Human Resources Department.

Finance/Accounting—The term *finance* is usually reserved for corporate positions, as it has to do with the acquisition and management of capital (primarily money and other nondeductible assets). *Accounting* refers to the recording of financial information, preparation of financial statements, and monitoring of the business's financial performance. At the unit level, a restaurant generally would not have a person exclusively assigned for accounting work but would have either the manager or secretary record sales figures and prepare deposits, then forward records to the accountant. As the restaurant expands, an accountant or bookkeeper might be hired. In individual hotels, the person responsible for the financial information is generally referred to as the Controller, or, in some instances, the Accountant.

Figure 4.1 Basic functional departments.

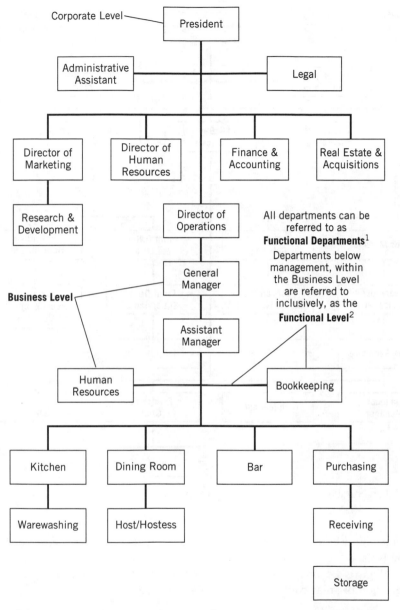

[1]A functional department is any unit of the business responsible for performing a unique group of tasks.

[2]Functional level decisions and actions are relatively short-ranged and focus on carrying out the strategies as written by the business or corporate levels.

Figure 4.2   Typical organization chart for restaurants.

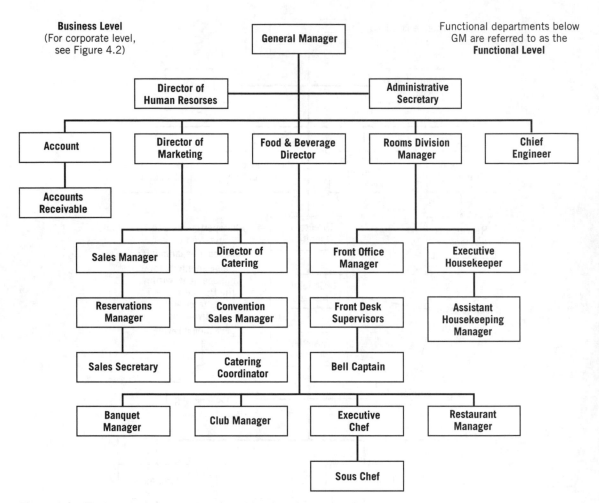

Figure 4.3 Typical organization chart for midscale to luxury hotels.

topic could be considered in operations or in the product section of the marketing analysis.

Figure 4.4 on page 102 shows examples of functional areas for analysis. The selection of areas could be expanded as desired.

INTERNAL AUDIT FORMS   A popular method of analyzing a company is to develop a customized internal audit form to grade or measure key performance areas. The questions that follow are examples; the list could be expanded as necessary with the addition of strategic internal factors included in the next section. The format used could be anything such as questions followed by blank lines, a more objective attempt at categorization, such as the strength and weakness form (see Figure 4.9), or a combination of both.

Marketing

1. Is there a mission statement that communicates the firm's desired direction and corporate philosophies?
2. Have clear marketing objectives and strategies been set?
3. Is there an action plan that details the accomplishment of marketing strategies?
4. Are sales being maximized through effective use of promotional mix variables (merchandising, advertising, public relations, personal selling, and sales promotion)?
5. Do current distribution methods reach profitable market segments (delivery, catering, gift certificates, travel agents, tour operators, and so forth)?
6. Are prices realistic (set according to costs, customer demand, and competitors' prices)?
7. Is there a control system to monitor individual sales representative performance?
8. Are customers satisfied with the services, menu selection, overall product quality, and value?
9. Is research and development into new products and services ongoing?
10. Is there an effective marketing research and information system?
11. Do all employees understand the importance of marketing and customer satisfaction?

Operations

1. Do all levels of management effectively communicate the company's mission and policies to employees?
2. Are the employees performing up to the standards of the company and the expectations of management?
3. Do employees have incentives or are they motivated to achieve customer satisfaction?
4. Are the furniture, fixtures, walls, ceilings, doors, and flooring in good condition?
5. Is equipment functioning properly [from HVAC (heating, venting, and air conditioning) and restaurant equipment, to point-of-sale and property management systems]?
6. Are there any operational practices that are harming the environment?
7. Is the hotel/restaurant clean?

Finance/Accounting

1. Are costs being effectively controlled? Are there any excessive costs that could be reduced?
2. Are corporate and industry benchmarks being achieved?
3. Are cash-handling procedures continuously monitored?
4. Do cash-handling procedures limit the personal risk of employees?
5. Does the firm have adequate reserves for expansion?
6. Can funds for expansion be obtained on reasonable terms?

BY FUNCTIONAL DEPARTMENT

RESTAURANT	HOTEL
Dining Room	Front Desk
Kitchen	Food and Beverage
Personnel	Personnel
Management	Housekeeping
Marketing	Sales and Marketing
Finance/Accounting	Maintenance
Research and Development	Rooms
	Management
	Research and Development

Figure 4.4   Options for the organization of internal analysis.

Strategic Internal Factors

The internal analysis should include all relevant issues that could have a bearing on or impact future decisions and actions. These are primarily the skills and assets (tangible and intangible) necessary for success in any particular industry. The most critical of these issues are known as strategic internal factors, strategic competencies, or critical success factors. The basis for competitive advantage is satisfying the customer at a profit. According to Day and Wensley (1988), the source of this advantage begins with superior skills and resources.

Traditional manufacturing firms will have substantially fewer strategic internal factors than hospitality firms. The key strategic internal factors for manufacturing firms will center on product quality, cost controls, the distribution system, and sales. In hospitality firms, almost every conceivable skill or asset is strategically important because the customer is usually in the facility. Hospitality businesses manufacture their product—a service—either in full view of customers (such as the hotel's front desk or an exhibition kitchen), or while they are waiting in the facility. In fact, the hospitality product—a place to sleep, bathe, and eat and drink—is the most closely scrutinized product sold. No other product or service involves the same level of trust or goes through the same examination process (and then is slept in, bathed in, or placed in the mouth) like the products and services purchased from hospitality businesses (Reich, 1990).

If a genie asked a manager to make three wishes regarding his/her business, he/she could wish for nothing better than profitability and customer and employee satisfaction. While it would be easy to develop a list of 100 factors that should be analyzed, all of these factors eventually would affect one or more of these three key concerns.

PROFITABILITY   Long-term profit is the main determinant of managerial ability and, therefore, is the most important strategic internal factor. Some would argue that customer satisfaction is the most important strategic internal factor. There are problems with this line of thinking: any business can satisfy its customers by selling them a product for a price that is below the firm's break-even cost, and a manager who can satisfy customers may not be able to produce a profit. On the contrary, if the business is showing a long-term profit, it must be satisfying the customer to some degree. Of course, the level of profit will be influenced by the degree of customer satisfaction. Another common argument is that the employee is the greatest asset of the business. This debate can quickly be solved by asking, "Would you rather invest in a firm with marginal employees, but that is showing a substantial profit and a corresponding increase in stock value, or in one with excellent employees, but limited growth and profitability?" Obviously, there would be many other factors to consider, but profit is what keeps businesses in business. When Peter Drucker was asked what management's most important function was, he said, "To stay in business" (Schlentrich, 1993). To stay in business, one must show a profit. In fact, the only way that management can justify its existence is through the achievement of an acceptable level of long-term profit. Sales may be up, operational performance may be excellent, but if profit is down or absent, managerial performance must be suspect. According to Norine Yukon, executive director for Prucare (a division of Prudential Insurance), the reality of business is "the bottom line" is the bottom line. Because of the growing concern for quality-of-life issues, there are many companies that are evaluating managers based on both their financial performance and their operational performance. Managers whose performance is above average in one area, but below average in the other, are being given the opportunity for personal development. Currently, these firms are in the minority; as time passes, this trend will grow.

Each business is financed by some measurable capital outlay, the justification of which is a return or profit to compensate for the particular business's degree of risk. Compensation for degree of risk is normally referred to as the *hurdle rate,* the return necessary before an investment can be considered viable. It is calculated by adding the return from a risk-free investment, such as government bonds, plus a return based on the perception of the risk. For example, if a risk-free investment pays 5% and the business in question has a high perceived risk, then the hurdle rate might be 25% (5% plus 20%). In this instance, if the business did not have a 25% return on its investment (projected for a yet-to-be-opened business, or actual for an existing business), then it would not meet investor expectations, or hurdle rate (Aaker, 1988). Additionally, profit, or the surplus of economic production, pays for societal benefits, such as health care, education, police protection, and museums (Drucker, 1974).

The two key areas of performance that influence profit are *high sales* (marketing and operations) and *low costs* (operations, especially productivity in all areas, and financial and accounting cost controls). This can be understood by visualizing the primary components of an income statement or, as more commonly termed, profit and loss statement

$$(sales/revenue) - (costs/expenses) = profit$$

The higher the sales and lower the costs, the greater the profit. Among the most important means of maximizing sales in the hospitality industry are excellence in relative perceived product/service quality (RPPQ), consistent product/service quality, relative perceived value (RPV), cleanliness, a pleasant interpersonal and physical atmosphere, effective and efficient promotional efforts, and overall image. (Combined, except for cleanliness, these encompass the primary focus of the company's marketing efforts.) The key means of holding down costs and increasing productivity are policies that lead to the effective and efficient performance of tasks, proper training, and enforcement of policies. Obviously, many other performance factors will have an impact on sales and cost control.

CUSTOMER SATISFACTION   After profit, the most important strategic internal factors are customer and employee satisfaction. It is easy to understand why customer satisfaction is important. If customers are not happy with the firm's product or service, they probably will not return. If they do not return, the supply of customers within the trade area soon dwindles to numbers too few to sustain the business. Taco Bell executives have determined that each time a customer comes into the restaurant for the first time, they are potentially worth $11,000 in lifetime sales. Indeed, a Cadillac dealer found that the average customer was worth over $300,000 in lifetime sales (O'Rourke-Hayes, 1993). If employees think about the long-term implications of their actions in terms of $11,000, rather than a $5 sale, the importance of satisfying the customer becomes much easier to understand. Management must learn that in addition to customer service being the "right thing to do," it also produces tangible results through profit and company growth.

RPPQ   The key requirement to satisfying the customer is expressed as relative perceived product quality (RPPQ) (Peters & Townsend, 1986). The business must not only satisfy customers, but it must do a better job of satisfying them than its competitors. (This is discussed further in Chapter 5.) The means to finding out what is necessary to satisfy the customer is embodied in the majority of processes used in preparing the strategic plan. Simply, this is gathering information from the internal analysis about how well the business is currently satisfying the customer; finding out what the customer expects today and in the near future (page 144 in Chapter 5); assessing primary competitors' performance (page 160 in Chapter 5); and then setting new strategies as necessary to meet those expectations.

TECHNICAL AND HUMAN FACTORS   Customer satisfaction consists of more than a smile and efficient service. When customers have finished a transaction with a service business, they are left with little more than an experience. The two key aspects of this experience are the *technical factors*—the food; its efficient delivery; a pleasant, clean room; no excessive waits for check-in or check-out; and a safe environment—and the *human side*—how the experience made the customer feel. No service provider could survive for long without doing a reasonable job with the technical factors. Perhaps one of the most important points of differentiation between service businesses is the ability to leave customers with the feeling that the employees of the business care about them personally—an experience that leaves customers with the sense that their personal needs were met. Customers can go to a restaurant or a hotel and have a very efficient experience, an excellent meal, and a nice room; but when they leave, the overriding thought will often be "How do I feel about the way I was treated?" Obviously, some customers are less concerned with the human side of service than others, but since the business is attempting to please each customer who comes through the door, it must treat each of them as if it is deeply concerned about how the business makes each customer feel. The factors that create this feeling will vary, but each business should consider finding out what it will take (Martin, 1986; Codotte & Turgeon, 1988).

Each functional area of the business should be examined to see how it can change to fulfill customers' personal needs. Or better, a business can ask itself, "What are the memories I want my customers to have after their experience?" One means of locating these customer service attributes is to find other service firms that have them (Bell, 1992). Perhaps for a hotel, it would be a personalized welcome note in the room on the first night of a stay or a thank-you note afterward; or a host or hostess that remembers customers' names and welcomes them with a warm greeting and possibly brings extra bread with a friendly smile. A business that can leave customers with a warm and fuzzy feeling will not only have more business but, as long as the effort to provide the personal attention is sincere, will create an environment that makes work enjoyable.

SPECIAL TREATMENT FOR EVERYONE   One practice that appears to be a problem in many service businesses is the special treatment given regular patrons. Do they deserve special treatment, or do they deserve the same treatment given to every customer? Yes, service personnel know more about the special needs of regular customers or guests, and they should cater to these needs. The problem is that the first-time customers can become irritated and wonder why someone is given the royal treatment, while they are treated like relatives that have outworn their welcome. If employees at each hotel and restaurant would treat every customer like their regular or VIP customers, several things will happen. First, employees at the establishment will have a better image of themselves. After all, their job requires first-class service and they work for a firm with the reputation of providing first-class service. This image will extend to their personal appearance, the way they carry themselves, and their ability to work without close supervision. Second, and equally important, employees will treat each customer according to the standards set by management. Third, as the care that first-time guests receive improves, so will their overall satisfaction, inclination to return, and their motivation to tell friends and associates about their experience. Many firms spend between four and eight percent of sales on promotions. How much of this could go to the bottom line by treating everyone special (Makens, 1988)?

EMPLOYEE SATISFACTION   One of the unfortunate problems in the hospitality industry is that profit and customer satisfaction are viewed as paramount objectives. All other strategic internal factors are seen as playing supporting roles in the business's drive for success. The problem with this philosophy is that the person who caters to the needs of customers and has the greatest impact on profit—the employee—is treated with little more respect than a piece of equipment that needs occasional maintenance. The hospitality industry has developed the image of being a less-than-desirable place to work. Common complaints are low pay, long hours, having to work nights and weekends, fluctuating schedules, poor working conditions, stressful environments, little opportunity for advancement, and limited benefits (Schlentrich, 1993). In spite of this general opinion, a large number of businesses within the industry are making great strides in the treatment of employees.

Historically, employees were viewed as something the business needed, but who could easily be replaced. Today, many firms are waking up to the realization that employees must be viewed as long-term investments as important as the capital necessary to finance and sustain the business. As such, they must be treated in a manner that keeps them interested in satisfying the customer and staying with the company for more than the one-year average tenure.

The Marriott Corporation has the philosophy that first the business must take care of its employees. Satisfied employees will then be more likely to take care of customers. Satisfied customers will return more often, pay more for services, and tell others about their experience. Finally, the satisfied customer will increase profits for the business. Heskett, Sasser, and Schlesinger (1993) developed the *Service Profit Chain* to describe the process required to achieve a profit in service businesses (see Figure 4.5). The process begins with an internal commitment of management to providing superior service. The focus then turns to satisfying employees through benefits, training, and personal growth so they will stay with the company and provide quality service. This leads to customer satisfaction, an increased frequency of purchases, and retention of the customer over the long term. This subsequently leads to profit or, better, to long-term profit. Unfortunately, too many firms forget about employee satisfaction and focus solely on customer satisfaction. As competition for quality employees becomes as fierce as that for customers, these firms will be forced to change.

LOCATING THE DETAILS   To identify customer service gaps or critical areas of the business where performance may be falling short, companies can use some form of gap analysis. Figure 4.6 shows where the main problems occur in meeting the expectations of customers (Zeithaml, Parasuraman, & Berry, 1990; Headley & Choi, 1992). The basic progression from the marketer's point of view is that decision-makers must first develop perceptions of what the customer wants. They then must translate this into strategies, policies, and action plans. Finally, the business must deliver a product and service and external communications that meet the customer's expectations. Customers enter the business with three basic perceptions, garnered from (1) personal needs, (2) past experience (either at the business or with similar, competing products and services), and (3) external communications (either word-of-mouth or

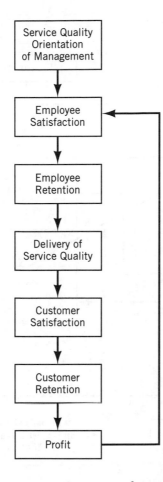

Figure 4.5 The Service Profit Chain. *Source:* Adapted from Heskett, Sasser, & Schlesinger (1993), Achieving breakthrough service, *Harvard Business School Management Programs.*

mass media). From these sources they develop a level of expectations that will either be met or not be met, or that (ideally) will be exceeded.

One challenge that is created when a firm meets or exceeds expectations is that a new expectation is created. This is one of the reasons it is difficult to remain at the top of an industry over the long term. During the experience, the customer will judge product and service quality based on various determinants (those included in Figure 4.6 are samples and will change from customer to customer), and their expectations of those determinants. From these factors will evolve their perception of quality for the firm's products and services. At any point in the model where performance is substandard, this is considered a gap that must be bridged (corrected).

ATTENTION TO DETAIL   The thoroughness and detail with which a firm should analyze its performance are often subject to question. Some strategists feel that a firm should not get bogged down with too many details, whlie others feel that nothing should be overlooked. In the hospitality industry, the latter opinion should probably be adhered to. Even the most minute factor, like placement of bustubs, can lead to a

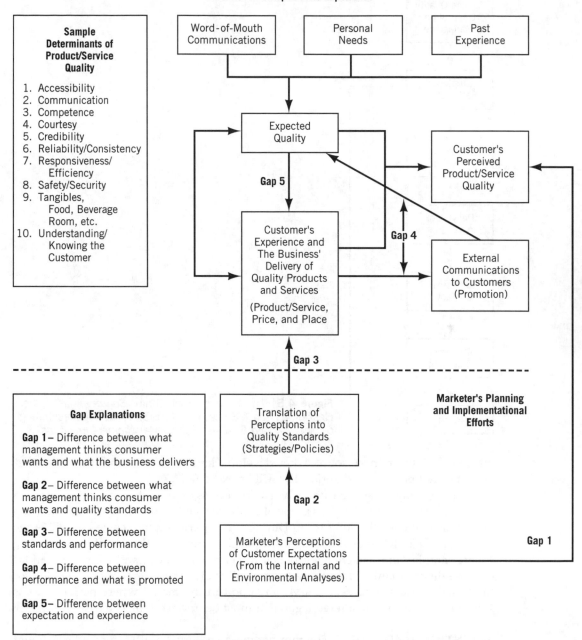

Figure 4.6 Product and service gaps for hospitality organizations. *Source:* Adapted from Parasuraman, Zeithml, & Berry, cited in Headley & Choi (1992), Achieving service quality through gap analysis and a basic statistical approach, *Journal of Services Marketing,* 6(1), pp. 5–14.

decrease in sales. In one restaurant, bustubs were placed in the hallway leading to the dining room—not a welcoming, relaxing beginning to a dining experience. Also, if a major problem occurred because something was overlooked, it is not a pleasant task to tell a superior, "I didn't think it was important." Businesses fail and employees lose their jobs because too many small details were overlooked. In the hospitality business, areas ignored tend to be the areas where problems arise.

Naturally, an inordinate amount of time cannot be spent on hundreds of details, so each factor should be prioritized. For example, decisions on product quality will outweigh those dealing with some barely noticeable scratches on the floor. The primary areas of concern for hospitality firms are profit, customer satisfaction, employee satisfaction, ability to control costs, product and service quality, cleanliness, atmosphere, value, and public image. See Figure 4.7 for examples of strategic internal factors for the hospitality industry. While some of these factors may not generally be considered "strategic" in a long-term sense, they are all "strategic" in their importance to the future of a hospitality business.

STANDARDS FOR MEASUREMENT

The primary measurement will be to determine whether the factor should be classified as a strength or a weakness, or in some other, more detailed grouping. To decide on the particular classification, each area should be analyzed according to some defined criteria. Several options follow:

• *Is performance as good as or better than the competition?*

In what areas does the company do as well as or better than primary competitors, and where does it fall short? Which of these areas is critical to the company's success or that of a competitor? These can be measured by a subjective evaluation of management, or objectively by customers. (Various types of competitor analysis reports and customer surveys can be used to measure the firm's position relative to competitors. See Chapters 3 and 5.)

• *What do the customers think?*

Since the customer expectations and the company's efforts will change over time, an analysis should be made of the company's current performance in light of those changes. Areas relating to overall customer satisfaction, product quality, value, pricing, decor, location, and promotional effectiveness, among others, can be considered. Both *absolute product quality* and *relative perceived product quality* should be measured. Absolute quality is measured in off-premise taste tests (laboratory environment as opposed to field environment, which is in the restaurant or hotel) to eliminate the intervening effect of the customer's impression of other components of the business. Relative perceived product quality would be measured with surveys after the customer's experience. A comprehensive internal analysis should include surveys (formal surveys, comment cards, and focus groups) that provide a reasonably accurate measure of existing customers' opinions of the company's products and

MARKETING

Marketing department's general planning efforts
Product and service offering/mix:

Restaurants—menu mix (types of food offered and number of items of each food category offered—appetizers, entrees, desserts, and so forth); individual product sales; daypart sales; sales by day, week, month, and seasonal fluctuations; the type of service and its compatibility with the restaurant's concept

Hotels—offerings such as the number and types of rooms, meeting facilities, catering services, room service menu, workout facilities, concierge, types of restaurants, menus, meals offered (e.g., breakfast, Sunday brunch), and a breakdown of sales for each revenue-producing area

Atmosphere and furnishings for both restaurants and hotels (meets customer's expectations and state of repair):

Interior—dining room, hotel rooms, lobby, bar, meeting space, restrooms, hallways, elevators (condition and responsiveness), recreational areas

Exterior—building, parking lot, landscaping

Market share or REVPAR* compared with primary competitors
Relative perceived value (RPV), price/value relationship
Pricing strategies—how set; and flexibility—ability to raise or lower prices
Locations—penetration of geographic market, quality, convenience to target customers, accessibility to traffic, parking, traffic count, traffic generators
Effectiveness of promotions—advertising, public relations, sales promotions, personal selling, merchandising
Creativity of promotions
Reservations system
Research and development of new products, services, and other strategies
Customer satisfaction index (CSI) and relative perceived product quality (RPPQ)
Sales maximized by food and beverage servers and front desk employees
Brand loyalty and image

*The hotel industry is currently increasing the usage of the term REVPAR because it is a better indicator of the hotel's financial position than occupancy percentage or average daily rate (ADR). A hotel with an extremely high ADR might sound good to management, but if the occupancy percentage were low, then neither figure would be of much significance. Since REVPAR factors in both ADR and the occupancy percentage, it is a better representative of the hotel's performance and therefore lends itself to comparisons between hotels of the same chain or other hotels within its market segment. The REVPAR is calculated by multiplying the ADR times the occupancy percentage. If a hotel with an ADR of $85 had an occupancy percentage of 60%, its REVPAR would be $51 ($85.00 × 60% = $51.00). Hypothetically, if Econo Lodge had a REVPAR of $45, while Hampton Inns' REVPAR was $55, and both had the same approximate cost of construction per room or debt, it would be easy to surmise that Hampton Inns are performing much better than Econo Lodge. Under the old focus on the ADR or the occupancy rate, actual performance would be slightly more difficult to analyze, especially between properties. They still can serve their purpose as monitors of their specific areas, average dollars brought in for each room sold (ADR), and the percentage of rooms sold each night (occupancy percentage).

Figure 4.7 Strategic internal factors for the hospitality industry. *Source:* Adapted with permission from Pearce & Robinson (1994), *Formulation, Implementation, and Control of Competitive Strategy*. Homewood, IL: Richard D. Irwin, pp. 181–182.

Compatibility of the firm's subjective position with its objective position:
  Objective position (in essence, the image of the business)—the position the product holds in the minds of consumers compared with competing products (e.g., convenient, fast, high status, great food, cheap, fried, dirty, RPPQ, etc.)
  Subjective position—the position for the product as intended by management
Marketing information system—keeping track of and utilizing information from internal records and the environmental analysis
Ability to determine consumer demands

OPERATIONS

General performance of management
Employees' performance according to policies
Effectiveness of controls (scheduling, purchasing, quality, operations)
Equipment—cleanliness, state of repair, and utility—serves its purpose
Functional layout of restaurant or hotel
Cleanliness—internal and external
Sanitation
Safety and security
Economies of scale
Purchasing and inventory systems in use
Specifications written for all recurrent purchases
Employee scheduling
Written policies covering all tasks
Communication and enforcement of policies

HUMAN RESOURCES

General performance of human resources activities
Management skills
Management morale and motivation
Management empowerment, initiative, and entrepreneurship
Incentives, rewards, and benefits for management
Management turnover percentage
Employee skills
Employee morale and motivation
Employee empowerment, initiative, and entrepreneurship
Incentives, rewards, and benefits for employees
Employee turnover percentage
Personnel policies (employee handbook) available
Procedures for trainers
Training manuals for each position
Employee benefits
Leadership ability of manager(s)—ability to sell their vision
Open channels of communication for all levels of the company
Achievement recognized and rewarded

Figure 4.7   (*Continued*)

Opportunities for internal promotions and personal growth
Working conditions conducive to peak performance
Recruitment procedures/available pool of employees and managers
(*Note:* Small independent operations will often combine operations, personnel, and administration into a single area—management.)

FINANCE AND ACCOUNTING

General performance of finance/accounting activities
Profitability—reasons for the company's current ROS (return on sales)
Sales/revenues
Financial strength—applicable financial ratios
Ability and cost of borrowing relative to competition
Effective cost controls
Total cost of sales percentage
Food and beverage cost percentage
Labor cost percentage
Management's knowledge of cost control principles
Overhead compared with industry averages
Effective and efficient accounting system—DSR, monthly statements
Internal cash control
Computerized accounting/management system

STRATEGIC (OR ADMINISTRATIVE) MARKET MANAGEMENT

Overall performance of top management
Organization structure—chart available, technically correct and followed
Record of anticipating trends
Record of achieving objectives
Flexibility to change course when needed
Ability to change course when needed
Makes use of appropriate technologies
Overall success and growth of business
Vision for company
Communicates vision
Corporate culture
Sensitivity to diversity of local community
Systematic procedures for decision-making
Top management's leadership ability
Management and marketing information system—effective and easily accessible
Strategic planning system in place
Strategic plan followed

Figure 4.7   (*Continued*)

services. The survey could also be used to measure future tendencies of customers, such as how they see their diets changing in the next year, or what changes they would like to see in a product or service.

The environmental analysis considers and measures general attributes of the overall market or target customer groups using the four bases of segmentation (see p. 149 in Chapter 5). This is usually measured through surveys taken from a random sample of potential market segments, in addition to existing customer/market segments. This information could be used to calculate how well the firm is positioned to meet broader needs of the market. For example, existing loyal customers may appreciate and like the quality of service that a hotel provides, but the broader target group that contains potential customers with loyalties to competitors may feel that their favorite brand/hotel has better service. This means that while the hotel may rate its service as excellent based on existing loyal customers' ratings, it may be neglecting the fact that there are many more customers in the target market that expect better service. These customers in the broader market with infrequent experiences at this particular business might, in fact, rate the business's service as only average.

• *Current performance in strategic areas is compared with past performance to note prominent trends in operational execution.*

Basically, is performance getting better or worse? Any area that can be quantitatively measured and monitored can be examined, such as customer satisfaction ratings, employee satisfaction ratings, and financial performance. Has the company set appropriate objectives in the past related to the factor being considered? Was the company successful in achieving those objectives? What did the company do effectively or poorly that had an impact on attaining the objectives?

• *Current performance in strategic areas should be compared with short-and long-term forecasted changes in the environment or internal business requirements.*

There are essentially four time frames to be considered:

1. Past performance (past performance can be compared to current performance to note trends)
2. Current performance
3. Projected performance over the next year
4. Projected performance beyond the next year and up to about five years

Will new abilities be required in the next year or perhaps in several years? Does the firm have these abilities or are they developing those that will be necessary to compete in the future? Perhaps a strength in the past will be a weakness in the future, or vice versa.

1. Since downsizing for multi-unit businesses is accelerating, how is the company positioned to compete with these leaner firms?
2. Will employees with new skills be required?
3. Will it be difficult to retain existing key personnel?
4. Will new skills or technologies be required?

5. Will changes in competitors' strategies and tactics require a greater degree of innovation in any functional area?

Strengths and Weaknesses

The main goal of the internal analysis is to perform a detailed analysis of the company to expose its strengths and weaknesses, and, secondarily, its minor strengths (major and minor strengths together are referred to as capabilities), minor weaknesses (both weakness categories can be referred to as limitations), and its neutral performance areas (Kotler, 1991). Strengths will be used later to match up with opportunities in the environment. Weaknesses will be assessed to determine whether action to improve the situation should be taken.

As a general rule, the better or stronger a company's performance, the less likely the need for radical changes in strategy. However, there are instances when even the strongest firms must consider extreme strategic changes: for example, if the environment is changing, as when a competitor is beginning to siphon off business, or when excellent performance creates the opportunity for expansion.

Increasing the Specificity

To improve the accuracy of measurement of internal areas, firms should consider using a broader scale than the traditional strength or weakness rating. Rarely would any survey question be accompanied by a scale of two possible responses. While there are benefits to the classification of something as being either acceptable or not acceptable, such as the simplification of measurement, there are often far more liabilities. Since the firm will be matching its strengths (generally groups of strengths) with opportunities in the environment, it would be helpful to know more about how the strength compares to those of competitors and if there is still room for improvement.

PRIORITIZATION   The first option for increasing the specificity of the measurement would be to group each strength and weakness according to a specified format, such as by functional areas. Each strength and weakness could then be prioritized according to its perceived importance. A further segmentation could be to classify prioritized groups of strengths and weaknesses by categorical labels, such as Categories 1, 2, and 3. Category 1 would include factors that must be addressed immediately, Category 2 factors would subsequently be dealt with as time permits, and Category 3 would be considered a low priority or possibly ignored.

Expanding the traditional strength and weakness scale is another alternative. The key element in this decision is management's ability to discriminate between the various values. For the reasons discussed in Chapter 3, the most commonly used number of categories for surveys is the five-point scale. The primary advantages of this scale are that it is relatively simple to classify and interpret. Management personnel (or other respondents) rate items as "poor," "fair," "average," "good," or "excellent." This means that if management is not satisfied with the firm's performance in an area, the question is only whether one considers the performance to be poor (a major weakness) or fair (a minor weakness). The opposite would apply if management was satisfied with the applicable performance. If management was neither satisfied nor dissatisfied, then the item could be rated as neutral. If there is a desire to increase the discrimination between the variables in each category, the choice would be between increasing the number of categories beyond five and prioritizing the factors in each category. Prioritization is an excellent option because, as previously discussed, this will assist managers in determining how the factor should be considered in strategic decisions. The following five-point scale recommended below can improve the accuracy of the internal analysis and assist management in determining what factors can be used immediately for gaining a competitive advantage and what factors need to be improved upon.

- *Strength (or Major Strength).* A substantive advantage that a company has, relative to competitors and the demands of the current or potential market. Until the past 10 to 15 years, the dominant approach to measuring performance was by means of comparisons with competitors. Porter (1980), for example, stressed that the objective was to find a position in an attractive industry that could be defended. The key skills were to achieve a lower cost than competitors or to differentiate one's product. Competitive advantage was achieved by keeping rivals off balance through random changes in strategies. Another view of the assessment of a firm's strengths and weaknesses is the capabilities approach. This approach focuses on finding a defendable position through the use of distinctive abilities (Day, 1994). The premise is that certain abilities, generally combinations of abilities, are difficult to duplicate and therefore represent an advantage over competitors. These abilities can be categorized as assets or skills. Assets would include both tangible and intangible factors, such as financial condition, equipment and buildings, product or service quality, brand equity, customer loyalty, and quality locations. Skills are intangible and include activities and accumulated knowledge, such as strategic planning, implementation of a strategic plan, departmental planning and implementation, corporate culture, marketing and a market-driven attitude/aptitude, financial, purchasing, legal, and overall quality of employees and management.
- *Minor Strength.* Basically, any area where the company's performance is above average or adequate to keep the company competitive. The factor may not necessitate special attention, but its position may not be adequate to deserve being included as a major strength. For a skill or asset, this would be something either that the company has the ability to accomplish or that does not detract markedly from profitability or competitive position. For example, a decor that is acceptable or food quality that is slightly better than average, but not excellent, will allow a business to keep many of its present loyal customers. The problem is that it may not allow the business to attract competitors' customers or to increase the frequency of visits or average amount spent by regular customers.
- *Neutral.* An area of average ability or position. Even though all functional areas should set goals for improvement, the correction of a neutral factor is lower on the priority list than weaknesses. There is only so much time, money, and energy available for improving performance. If the marketing department's performance

in the area of promotional effectiveness had little effect on the company's success, but was not particularly weak, it could be considered neutral. The key reason for the neutral category is that some areas are simply neither a strength nor a weakness. If the measurement of an internal factor shows that some improvement is needed, then the factor should probably be recognized as a minor weakness. Most scales based on odd numbers (5 in this case) contain a category for a neutral response. To the evaluator this generally means an area of average ability or position. It could also indicate the inability to make a decision or ignorance about the issue being measured. In case of the latter situation, an indication should be made of the reason for the neutral rating.

- *Minor Weakness.* Any area that does not represent a serious weakness but hinders the ability of the firm to perform at the desired level—something that could not be considered as neutral but does not greatly limit the company in its selection of key strategies. For example, limitations in the ability to borrow, name recognition, or the culinary skills of employees in a casual dining restaurant could affect a company's ability to expand locations or add to its menu mix but would not substantially affect its ability to compete.
- *Weakness (or Major Weakness).* Essentially, the opposite of a strength; substantive disadvantage that hinders the firm's strategic efforts at retaining or gaining a desired competitive position. Decisions must be made as to which weaknesses will require corrective action.

DEBATE OVER PERFORMANCE CATEGORY   While it is important to be aware of minor strengths, minor weaknesses, and neutral factors, management must make sure that their consideration as a separate component of the strategic analysis does not develop into an academic debate. If there is doubt about whether a factor should be considered as a minor strength, a neutral, or a minor weakness, then perhaps it will be better to include it in the lower of the categories, to increase its chances of being addressed. The majority of firms simply use the strength and weakness categories, with some listing the factors in order of importance.

CORRECTING WEAKNESSES   There are several options in assessing what should be done about a weakness. If the weakness does not affect overall performance, then the status quo may either be accepted or perhaps tolerated, because the cost to correct it is proportionately too high. Even though a potentially detrimental weakness cannot currently be corrected, it should be addressed as a long-term objective. Basically, put it on the back burner to be focused on again when the timing is better. If the area of weakness represents a skill or asset necessary to pursue a critical opportunity or minimize a major threat that could impact the company's future, then serious consideration must be given to actions necessary to correct it.

As will be seen in Chapter 9, one of the first steps in correcting a weakness is to set an objective that, if accomplished, will improve the company's performance. For example, an objective might be to reduce restaurant service time to 10 minutes (from its current 13 minutes). Subsequently, strategies and policies to achieve the objectives will be formulated and acted upon.

PROBLEM	NORMAL RESPONSIBILITY
1. Poor planning (including strategies, policies and action plans)	All levels of management—unit managers, functional managers, and corporate-level management
2. Poor implementation	Functional and unit managers
3. Lack of objectives for critical areas	Functional and unit managers
4. A control system without provisions for immediate follow-up Strategic controls Operational controls	 Corporate and unit managers Unit and functional managers

Figure 4.8   Problem areas and responsible personnel.

If, for some reason, it is not possible to correct a weakness in an area that is necessary for the pursuit of an opportunity, then the company has two choices. One is to pursue the opportunity realizing that there may be problems. Recently, a major hotel chain expanded with an exceptionally high percentage of borrowed capital. When the economy slowed, the hotel chain was not able to meet its payments and had to renegotiate the debt with its creditors. The other choice is to select another opportunity.

Weaknesses can be traced to problems in four general areas, shown in Figure 4.8.

LOCATING WEAKNESSES   Most weaknesses can be avoided or solved through effective strategic planning, but locating the true weakness is sometimes difficult. Often, when a problem or weakness shows up, the first sign is actually only a *symptom* of the problem. The goal in identifying weaknesses is to identify the primary *cause*.* Once the cause of the weakness is corrected, then the symptoms should disappear. Slow check-out times in a hotel are the symptom of a weakness. If the cause can be found and corrected, then service times should improve. In this case, the cause could be inexperienced employees, improper training, short staffing, inefficient procedures or computer system, no computer system, attitude or motivational problems, front-desk design problems, or weak management or supervision. After management recognizes the symptom of the problem, they must find and solve the root cause of the problem. As was previously discussed, not all weaknesses will require attention.

Focusing on correcting weaknesses can also create surprises for competitors that incorporated other companies' weakness(es) in their own competitor analysis (Perry,

*In case studies, students may not have an extensive knowledge of the inner workings of a company, so to varying degrees, logical assumptions will have to be made about the root cause of a weakness. Then objectives, if required, and strategies to correct the weaknesses can be written.

1991). For example, Hotel A has a reputation for dreadfully poor service—a weakness. Because of this well-known fact, competing Hotel B set the objective of reaching an annual occupancy rate of 70%, from its current 67%. Since this objective served as the primary target of Hotel B, all of its strategies were based on increasing occupancy by 3%. Hotel A rapidly improved its performance in the area of service and successfully promoted the fact through guarantees, media, telemarketing, and sales blitzes. This correction of Hotel A's weakness allowed it to take 5% of the market from Hotel B. Now Hotel B must reconsider its objective of a 70% occupancy rate and redesign its marketing strategies to compete with a stronger opponent. The new strategies for Hotel B would probably include a marginal shift from offensive strategies of attracting new clients to an increased emphasis on defensive or counterstrategies to protect its current client base. Often, when a business corrects a major weakness, competing businesses will not make appropriate changes until their next planning period or when sales have been significantly affected.

SALVAGING PEOPLE   It is important that the categorization of internal factors be accomplished in as objective a manner as possible. Blaming and finger-pointing should be eliminated. In cases of gross incompetence or illegalities, upper management must be notified so the proper actions can be taken. There is not a company or individual without weaknesses. Some flaws may be obvious or glaring, some quite minor; still, the perfect company or individual does not exist. When a weak link is either discovered or exposed during the analysis, the fact should be viewed as objectively as possible. Degrading or embarrassing fellow employees does not solve problems; it only serves to let others know they could be next. Additionally, the problem may be caused by improper policies or procedures, rather than by subpar performance. Employees or management whose performance is categorized as a weakness should, in most cases, be given the chance to improve. This not only salvages the employee for the benefit of both the employee and the business, but it lets the remaining employees know that problems are solved with cooperation, not with termination.

AUDITING PERFORMANCE   Figure 4.9 can be used for recording and ranking the strengths and weaknesses of a hotel or restaurant. Each firm would select the areas to evaluate based on its priorities and past internal analyses. The strategic internal factors can be used as a menu from which to select pertinent items to include in a customized analysis form. Objectivity should be stressed when completing the form. Connecting the ratings vertically (profile analysis) will help management visualize where its strengths and weaknesses are. Period-to-period comparisons created by overlaying transparencies of the connected ratings can graphically show improvements and performance declines (known as a profile analysis). Each factor can also be rated based on its importance to the success of the functional department or the business. In research terminology, the strategic internal factors that will be monitored are the variables. The population would be all employees, suppliers, consultants, customers, and so forth, that could help determine the firm's performance. The sample will consist of those selected from the population to rate the firm's

	PERFORMANCE					IMPORTANCE		
	MAJOR STRENGTH	MINOR STRENGTH	NEUTRAL	MINOR WEAKNESS	MAJOR WEAKNESS	HIGH	MEDIUM	LOW

MARKETING

	MAJOR STRENGTH	MINOR STRENGTH	NEUTRAL	MINOR WEAKNESS	MAJOR WEAKNESS	HIGH	MEDIUM	LOW
1. Company image	___	___	___	___	___	___	___	___
2. Market share	___	___	___	___	___	___	___	___
3. Quality reputation	___	___	___	___	___	___	___	___
4. Service reputation	___	___	___	___	___	___	___	___
5. Value reputation	___	___	___	___	___	___	___	___
6. Promotional effectiveness	___	___	___	___	___	___	___	___
7. Sales staff	___	___	___	___	___	___	___	___

MANAGEMENT

	MAJOR STRENGTH	MINOR STRENGTH	NEUTRAL	MINOR WEAKNESS	MAJOR WEAKNESS	HIGH	MEDIUM	LOW
8. Employee attitude	___	___	___	___	___	___	___	___
9. Speed of service	___	___	___	___	___	___	___	___
10. Accuracy of check-out	___	___	___	___	___	___	___	___
11. Cleanliness of lobby	___	___	___	___	___	___	___	___
12. Cleanliness of rooms	___	___	___	___	___	___	___	___
13. Purchasing skills	___	___	___	___	___	___	___	___
14. Organization skills	___	___	___	___	___	___	___	___
15. Effective scheduling	___	___	___	___	___	___	___	___

FINANCE

	MAJOR STRENGTH	MINOR STRENGTH	NEUTRAL	MINOR WEAKNESS	MAJOR WEAKNESS	HIGH	MEDIUM	LOW
16. Profitability	___	___	___	___	___	___	___	___
17. Cost controls	___	___	___	___	___	___	___	___
18. Communication with management	___	___	___	___	___	___	___	___
19. Financial stability	___	___	___	___	___	___	___	___

ADMINISTRATIVE MANAGEMENT

	MAJOR STRENGTH	MINOR STRENGTH	NEUTRAL	MINOR WEAKNESS	MAJOR WEAKNESS	HIGH	MEDIUM	LOW
20. Capable leadership	___	___	___	___	___	___	___	___
21. Vision for the future	___	___	___	___	___	___	___	___
22. Entrepreneurial orientation	___	___	___	___	___	___	___	___
23. Flexible/responsive	___	___	___	___	___	___	___	___
24. Adequate planning	___	___	___	___	___	___	___	___

Figure 4.9 Strength and weakness analysis. *Source:* Adapted with permission from Kotler (1991), *Marketing Management: Analysis, Planning, Implementation, & Control,* 7th ed. Englewood Cliffs, NJ: Prentice-Hall.

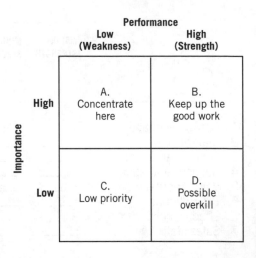

Figure 4.10 Performance/importance matrix. *Source:* Reprinted with permission from Kotler (1991), *Marketing Management: Analysis, Planning, Implementation, & Control,* 7th ed. Upper Saddle River, NJ: Prentice-Hall, p. 51.

performance. Inferences about the firm's actual performance would be made based on information gathered from the sampled groups (McClave & Benson, 1994).

Figure 4.10 details what actions could be taken based on the company's performance in an area and the importance of that area. If a hotel had a check-out time 30% faster than its competitors, and this was valued as important by its target customers, it would be placed in cell B and no new strategy would be considered. At another hotel where personal service is more important than speed, the 30% faster check-out time might be considered a weakness, and therefore ranked low, perhaps placing this concern in cell A. If the catering department developed a reputation for being late to set up for events, and this was considered very important to target customers, it would be placed in cell A. Action would be taken as soon as possible.

When examining a company's performance in each functional area, the level of expenditure devoted to it compared with the national or local average should be examined closely. It is possible that the company is extremely efficient, and therefore does not require a high expenditure, but it could also mean that the company is not maximizing its efforts in that area, or does not consider it to be important. This is particularly true in nonoperational areas: for example, 2% of sales for marketing, when the national average is over 4%; or a one-person financial staff, compared to the average of several finance and accounting personnel. Many companies are proud of their low labor, food, or maintenance costs, while the apparent efficiency may, in fact, be mismanagement that will lead to reduced long-term profit and low customer satisfaction.

WHO WILL PREPARE THE INTERNAL ANALYSIS?

There is no getting around the fact that regardless of who prepares the internal analysis there will be some type of bias involved. Even when an outside consulting firm is hired to prepare the evaluation, the level of subjectivity must be questioned.

The basic options are to use *inside individuals or groups,* use *outside consultants,* and, for applicable areas, have *customers* complete surveys or comments cards (see Chapter 3 for survey information).

The advantage of inside people is that they know the business and where to look for both strengths and weaknesses. The obvious disadvantage is that they will tend to be subjective or biased if a poor ranking affects them, someone they know, or a superior.

The advantages of external consultants are that they tend to be more objective, are usually experts in the field, and have a broad level of experience in recognizing and correcting problems. The objectivity of some consultants must be called into question if they appear to be glossing over or minimizing the seriousness of some problems in hope of gaining further work. Customer surveys should be a constant source of information on company performance. These can range from comment cards to extensive questionnaires. It must be remembered that customers cannot measure every aspect of the business. Questions related to financial performance and strategic market management are generally outside their base of knowledge. (See Chapter 3 for information on customer surveys.)

Preparing an Internal Analysis for New Businesses

Do not go into detail for the internal analysis for a new business. The reasons for this are as follows:

1. There is little to analyze other than perhaps a general introduction of the basic concept, the management team, and finances.
2. An analysis of the environment must first be performed before specific strategies are proclaimed. Stating what will be done before research is performed would not make sense. The specifics of what you intend to do will be addressed later in the functional strategies section (see Chapter 10).

Here, some of the same topics for existing businesses can be discussed, that is, marketing, operations, personnel, and finance, but the information will be based on the general perception of the plans for the business—basically an introduction. For example, the basic concept can be described, using most or all of the following information:

- Possible menu items and service style for a restaurant.
- Possible services for a hotel.
- Pricing structure.
- Location, if a decision has been made. An analysis of the location could be included, such as whether it has adequate visibility, parking, or enough of your projected target customers or targeted segments.
- Location decision parameters, if the decision has not been made. (What are some of the desired features—size, parking, neighboring businesses, and so forth?)
- Interior and exterior design of the building and the general type of atmosphere being considered.

- Key management/personnel, their experience, how they will be compensated, who will be responsible for functional aspects of the business.
- Source of funding.
- General or unique marketing ideas could be discussed.

Again, very little of what is included in the internal analysis for a new business will be set in stone. Basic ideas are presented to help guide research of the environment.

Situational Analysis

The situational analysis is an all-inclusive term used for the examination of the business and the environment in which it operates—the internal and environmental analyses. It is included here only as an optional reference term or title. It is not mandatory that it be included as a specific component of the strategic marketing plan. For example:

Situational Analysis (title only, if desired)
    Internal Analysis . . . (information). . .
    Environmental Analysis . . . (information). . .

THE BRYAN HOUSE AND CITY GRILL INTERNAL ANALYSES

The Bryan House

MARKETING

Products and Services

The Bryan House is an independently owned, three-star, 300-room, upper-midscale hotel (five stars is the maximum; most competitors have four stars). The hotel is managed by Ribak Hotels, a small management firm with eight hotels under contract. There are 275 standard rooms, 20 business suites, 4 two-bedroom suites, and one presidential suite. Half of the rooms are nonsmoking. The hotel has 15,000 square feet of meeting space, which has always been adequate for past functions. There are no secretarial services. The only business services are copy and fax machines. The hotel does not offer newspaper delivery, 24-hour room service, or a fast lunch service. It has been considering adding a concierge. There is a shuttle service between the hotel and the airport, but nothing for the convention center or local attractions. The hotel has a 24-hour security guard service, and entrance is allowed only through the front door and parking garage. All other outside doors are for emergency only and are equipped with panic bars. Guest room locks use a keyed system.

Amenities include name brand soap, shampoo, conditioner, shoe-shine cloth, hair dryer, and a coffee machine for brewed coffee.

The hotel has complete food and beverage services for banquets and meetings. There is one restaurant outlet and a casual dining facility with 150 seats that is open from 6 a.m. to 11 p.m. Menu selection is limited (both banquet and restaurants), and neither includes many healthy alternatives.

The design of the hotel is traditional with a brick exterior; the front doors are carved wood with etched glass; each room has a Chicago double sash window (solid glass in the middle, with windows on each side that open vertically); the lobby has a four-story atrium with several 30-foot tall plants, overstuffed couches, and large oil paintings and mirrors framed in gold-leaf. The hotel was completely renovated in 1992, including new furniture, plumbing fixtures, heating and air conditioning units, and major pieces of restaurant equipment.

Price

Average Room Rates

Individual business travelers (IBTs), 30% of sales, $110
Corporate group business, 25% of sales, $95
Association group business, 15% of sales, $80
Leisure business, 15% of sales, $110
SMERFS (sports, medical, educational, religious, fraternal, social), 15% of sales, $75

The prices for food are quite reasonable, with a range of $6 to $15 for the restaurant, $7 to $12 for banquet lunches, and $10 to $25 for dinner. The problem is that since the quality is low, the relative perceived value is lower than it should be.

Place

The hotel is located one mile from the state's capital, two miles from Gabriel's Row (an exclusive shopping district), and one-half mile from a regional convention center. The city's population is one million. The economic base is made up of a variety of service and manufacturing businesses, governmental agencies, and the headquarters for over 300 associations.

The building is at the intersection of two busy roads. Parking is underground and is accessed from the less busy of the two roads. Ingress and egress to the property are excellent. The downtown area where the hotel is located is undergoing revitalization. Many of the state's prominent businesses have offices in downtown buildings.

Promotion

Merchandising: The hotel has posters showing sophisticated people enjoying themselves at various types of events. Each guest room has a guest services book, but since there are few services available, there is not much to promote. A newsletter has been considered, but not yet implemented.

Advertising: The hotel's advertising efforts are minimal. No radio or television spots are used. Five 4 × 4 ads were run in the state's main monthly magazine. Because several guests mentioned the ads, they judged them to be moderately successful. The hotel is on the SABREvision hotel information and booking system, a worldwide reservation system used by travel agents. No message has been created for promotions (e.g., Hilton—"So nice to come home to," Ramada—"Ramada is in, Holiday is out").

Personal Selling: There are three salespeople on the marketing staff. (Comparable hotels in this market have an average of five salespeople.) One is assigned state group (corporate and associations) business, one handles national group business, and one covers transient business (individual business travelers and the leisure market/tourists).

Public Relations: No charitable donations have been given during the last several years. Likewise, no charitable events have been held or sponsored. The hotel has been involved in recycling for several years. Currently, there are special bins for paper, newspaper, and aluminum cans. Other means of recycling and waste reduction are being considered.

Sales Promotions: Currently, there is only a weekend package that includes a double occupancy room for $79 with a room service breakfast.

OPERATIONS

Overall Customer Satisfaction Index (CSI) 4.0
(Poor=1, Fair=2, Average=3, Good=4, Excellent=5)

Hotel: front desk courtesy—4.4, front desk speed—3.4, housekeeping—4.0, general
   hotel cleanliness—4.3
Meeting and Banquest Services: food—3.2, value—3.6, service—4.3
Restaurant outlets: food—2.7, value—3.3, service—3.6

Check-out transaction times have been between two and three minutes while competitors' times have been between one and two minutes. This is partly because of an older computer system and improper scheduling of help during peak dayparts.

There is no formal operations or cash and financial management manuals.

HUMAN RESOURCES

The human resources department consists of a department head and assistant who perform both secretarial and some administrative tasks. Before applicants are hired, they must be interviewed by someone from the human resources department and by management of the department they will work in. All applicants must pass a drug test and a security audit (police records are checked). Each new employee is given an orientation to help ingrain him/her into the Bryan House way of doing things. The orientation covers general rules, including fire protection and evacuation, scheduling, personal hygiene, and job performance, and emphasizes the importance of teamwork and customer service. Since the overall effectiveness of employees is relatively high, it appears to be working. Training for hourly employees is primarily on-the-job, with minimal reliance on formal procedures. The management firm has been talking about preparing a training manual, but they appear to be a long way from being finished. The currently available personnel manual is outdated.

Management training is done through a limited number of the management firm's in-house seminars and those put on by the American Hotel and Motel Association.

The hotel offers life insurance, health insurance, sick leave, a one-week vacation for the first year and two weeks after five years. There is a 401K pension plan available. The employee locker room is equipped with showers and individual lockers. The employee cafeteria serves a reasonable quality breakfast, lunch, and dinner.

Employee turnover is 90% (average for the local market is 70%). Management turnover is 20% (average for the local market is 35%).

ADMINISTRATIVE MANAGEMENT

The general manager, Mary Douglas, has been doing a good job. Her management/leadership style is charismatic. The majority of employees in most departments willingly help out however they can. The main problems seem to be centered around the marketing department that was brought in by the management firm. Since the Ribak Hotels are relatively new in the market, they still have some management bugs to work out of their system. Greater decentralization of managerial decisions would perhaps be helpful, giving Mary the autonomy she needs to maximize financial and marketing results. All ADA (Americans with Disabilities Act) regulations have been complied with.

FINANCING/ACCOUNTING

Occupancy is currently at 55%. This is 5% below average for the area. The average daily rate (ADR) is $97, $10 above the average hotel in the same market. Average monthly sales during the last year-to-date were $720,225. Business was highest during the mild winter and lowest during the hot summer. Sales for the last three calendar years, beginning with the most recent, were $8,642,700, $8,353,560, and $8,546,400. The income statement for the most recent calendar year reported a loss of 3% of sales. The hotel projected a break-even for the same period.

Food and labor costs for all the food and beverage outlets are 40% and 32%, respectively.

City Grill

The City Grill is a casual, upscale restaurant located a few miles from the Galleria (expensive shopping district) in a mixed business and residential area. Bob Wilson has owned the restaurant for seven years. Although Bob has a degree in Hotel, Restaurant, and Institutional Management, he did not take a marketing strategies course and therefore needs help in guiding the future of his restaurant.

MARKETING

The positioning of our restaurant is well established. Customers commonly think of us just as we view ourselves—a casual, upscale restaurant serving great food.

Product

(A breakdown of product sold, and the internal and external features of the building, its layout, and atmosphere. Sales by daypart (e.g., 5 to 6 p.m., 6 to 7 p.m., and so forth), day, month, or year could be included here, or in the financial section. In this plan, they are included in the financial section.)

Our chefs have developed new menu items that are selling well, allowing us to discontinue those that were not moving. The vast majority of our customers are very happy with our menu mix. Few customers are happy with our rolls.

Menu

Appetizers—all nacho style, either on flat chips or soft flour tortillas @ $5.95 to $7.95
Two steaks—ribeye, 10 oz. @ $10.95 and filet, 7 oz. @ $8.95
Pot roast, 8 oz. @ $9.95
Pollo verde—chicken with green salsa, 6 oz. @ $7.95
Chicken parmesan, marinara sauce and Swiss cheese, 6 oz. @ $8.95
Fried catfish, 8 oz. @ $8.95
Three to five varieties of fresh fish, 8 oz. @ $9.95 to $14.95
Dinner salad, $2.25, and chef salad, basic @ $5.95
Fresh vegetables
Prebaked dinner rolls
Desserts $2.95 to $3.75.

There are 150 seats in the dining room. The decor consists primarily of natural wooden furniture, off-white walls, brown pattern carpeting, and modern art. The atmosphere of the restaurant is still current. Since it is a casual, upscale restaurant with a heavy emphasis on wood and subdued tones, we should not have to worry about remodeling for at least another three to five years. There are some areas that need immediate attention, such as the carpet showing signs of wear, the padded seats on several booths that have tears, and some ceiling tiles that should either be cleaned or replaced.

We feel the primary reason for the increase in sales was the introduction of new menu items that attracted a broader customer base (a new market segment), including families, and those with household incomes at the upper end of our target customer range of between $35,000 and $65,000 per year.

Price

The current pricing policy of costing each new item with a built-in labor factor has reduced past discrepancies in the pricing of prepared versus from-scratch items. For example, an item prepared from scratch has a factor approximating the additional labor required added to its food cost total in calculating its menu price.

(A copy of the menu, comments on present prices—higher or lower than competitors', for example—and a menu analysis could be included.)

Place

(Geographic location, and all related facility factors should be given here.)

The location is relatively good, on a primary road with a traffic count of 35,000 cars per day. We have adequate visibility, and access is fine. Being in the strip center, we lose some visual impact, but this is not a major problem since we have an endcap location. A problem could arise if the center sells pad sites in front of us. Parking is occasionally a problem during lunch. There are several primary competitors close by, which bring plenty of new customers. Since we serve beef, chicken, and fresh fish, we are better able to accommodate our trade area customers' desires than most other restaurants in the neighborhood.

The Galleria, one of the premier shopping districts in the state of Texas, attracts 25,000 shoppers per day to the area. Over 25% of the shoppers are tourists. There is a huge concentration of office buildings occupied by professionals from all fields.

Promotion

(The promotional mix is the use of advertising, sales promotion, public relations, personal selling, and merchandising. See Chapter 6 for an explanation of the components of the promotional mix.)

Promotions have been limited. An ad agency has been producing most of the campaigns. The advertising agency did a good job in designing the new menus, but it was felt that merchandising through point-of-purchase materials could have been increased, lowering the need for costly advertising. Internal promotions, such as sales promotions and merchandising, were almost nonexistent. The radio advertising campaign (focusing on fresh fish) was only moderately successful and probably should not be attempted again unless the rates are exceptional. Dollar for dollar, we feel that we experience greater returns by focusing on in-store promotions. Our primary form of advertising is word-of-mouth because of our high quality and image. Also, our good location lessens the need for advertising.

Marketing Information System

(Internal records, marketing intelligence, and market research should be included here.)

No primary research has been attempted in the last two years. The information about customer's opinions is out of date and not adequate for our needs. In addition to being two years old, it details customer satisfaction of previous customer segments but does not present breakdowns for the newest segments added during the year's menu and market development efforts.

The new file system to accumulate environmental analysis information has helped tremendously in this year's strategic planning.

OPERATIONS

Product and service quality have been good and consistently maintained at high levels. The biggest problem we have is our slow ticket-time from the kitchen. Primary competitors have ticket-times averaging between eight and ten minutes, while our is between twelve and fourteen minutes. Though this has kept us from realizing our potential at lunch, it does not have a great effect on dinner business.

Management controls are better than average, but there is always room for improvement. Menu items are priced out, but food cost does fluctuate for some unknown reason.

The chef is doing a great job but could be more creative. The overall Customer Satisfaction Index (CSI) is 4.4 (Poor=1, Fair=2, Average=3, Good=4, Excellent=5). The food CSI is 4.5, service is 4.3.

PERSONNEL

Management turnover increased from 20% to 40% last year. This was probably caused by the increased hours required of managers. Although this helped our bottom line, it may eventually end up hurting us through increased training and motivational problems.

Employee morale is high and, consequently, turnover at 35% is much lower than industry standards. We feel this is because our reputation for high quality has given our servers higher than average tips and allowed us to schedule a 40-hour work week for any employees desiring it. Cooks are currently making between $1.50 and $2.00 more per hour than at most competitors.

The personnel manual has not been altered for five years and is in need of revision. Since company manuals have been used as legal contracts in many states, our greatest concern is to make sure that we are protected.

Our skill level is good for the items we now serve. This poses a potential problem because we are dependent on five excellent cooks who are receiving regular offers from other restaurants.

Half of the servers have taken the alcohol service course.

ADMINISTRATIVE MANAGEMENT

Because of our obvious success in meeting our sales and profit goals, top management must be commended. Most functional strategies set down in last year's planning meeting were implemented and institutionalized into the restaurant's organizational structure, culture, and leadership style without major glitches. The key will be to continue this trend.

Currently, only half of the servers have taken state-approved alcohol service courses.

FINANCE/ACCOUNTING

(Financial statements could be included here.)

The company had a 10% increase (adjusted for inflation) in sales for the current year. Sales reached $1,000,000 for the first time. Capital City's current 15% return on sales is one of the highest in our area. The return on sales for 19xx and 19yy, respectively, were 10% and 8%. This increase is due not only to improved sales and a strong internal cost control system, but also to recently added management and employee development programs and incentives. Sales on Sundays average $1300, Mondays and Tuesdays $2000, Wednesdays and Thursdays $3000, and Fridays and Saturdays $4500. Lunch business is averaging between $300 on Sunday and $1000 on Friday.

	Sales	Profit
19xx	$909,091	10%
19yy (this past year)	$1,000,000	15%

The debt-to-equity ratio at 65% is much too high. If the economy slows, causing industry sales to drop and interest rates to rise, our entire ROS (return on sales—profit) could disappear quickly. Food cost is 32%; labor cost is 25%.

QUESTIONS AND PROJECTS

1. What is the basic purpose of the internal analysis?
2. Define strengths and weaknesses.
3. List and explain the three primary concerns for completing an internal analysis.

4. What is the most important determinant of success in any business situation?
5. Explain Figure 4.5.
6. Explain Figure 4.6.
7. Analyze a restaurant or hotel using certain selected or applicable strategic internal factors. This could include only the firm's marketing efforts, or any combination of the various functional departments.
8. What are the implications for some of the strategic internal factors? Basically, how would the firm's strengths or weaknesses in the various areas affect its selection of opportunities and its ability to carry out related strategies?
9. When a weakness is located, should it always be corrected? Explain your answer.
10. What are the advantages and disadvantages of having internal personnel completing the analysis? Answer the same question for outside consultants.
11. Eat a hamburger (or chicken sandwich), french fries, and a soft drink at McDonald's, Burger King, and Wendy's, or any group of three similar restaurants. Rate each product and restaurant on a 1 to 5 scale (1 poor, 5 excellent) on the basis of value (record the price paid), quality, service, and cleanliness. Compare your responses and reasons for them with others in your class.
12. What are the factors that influence customer perception of value?
13. Customers want more ethnic foods. What strategic internal factors might be needed by a traditional American cuisine restaurant?
14. Customers are more concerned about their health. What strategic internal factors would help a hotel take advantage of this opportunity?

CHAPTER 5

Environmental Analysis

The environmental analysis is used to locate current and future trends or events that represent potential opportunities or threats to the business. Since there is no way to collect data on and analyze the millions of changes taking place in the environment, each firm must decide which data will have the greatest impact on its success and survival. On the contrary, it is also important that the range of data, and usable information derived from it, be somewhat broad so that potentially important factors are not ignored. To most companies, a 1000-page environmental analysis for a single-unit hotel or restaurant might be overkill, but it may also expose key trends. (It is quite conceivable that an environmental analysis could reach 1000 pages if articles from magazines are included along with the firm's interpretation of critical areas.) Of course, what is important is not how long the environmental analysis is, but the quality of data and information it contains. Ideally, it should accurately represent both current and future critical environmental factors, especially those that will likely impact the firm, its customers, and its competitors. In the environmental analysis, potentially important data are gathered, organized, and stored. In Chapter 6, Strategic Analysis, each factor will be scrutinized more closely for the possible value or harm it could bring.

The environmental analysis is not compiled on an annual basis just before the strategic plan is written. It must be an ongoing process, generally part of the firm's marketing information system and control process.

OPPORTUNITIES AND THREATS

The goal of the environmental analysis is to allow the firm to locate the opportunities that the firm should attempt to take advantage of, and the threats that have the greatest potential to negatively affect the future of the business.

Opportunities

An *opportunity* is an event or trend that represents a chance for the firm to increase its sales, growth, or competitive position—anything that would have a positive effect on the business. If a hotel did not have an exercise facility and there were requests from its guests for such a facility, this would represent an opportunity. Of course, if the hotel did not add the exercise facility, it could also be a threat, particularly if other hotels have taken advantage of the opportunity. If annual sales of pizza were going up 10% per year, while average restaurant sales were going up 3%, this would represent an opportunity for a pizza restaurant to expand, or for a restaurant that is considering serving pizza to add it to the menu.

Often, opportunities may directly be related to or hindered by operational weaknesses, such as the problem of slow delivery of food or waiting in line to check in or out of a hotel. For example, if a restaurant's target customers expected service times of 10 minutes, this would represent an opportunity in the environment. If the business had an average service time of 15 minutes (a weakness), serious operational changes would need to be considered to allow the firm to take advantage of the opportunity. If a substantial number of primary competitors had service times of around 10 minutes, this fact would represent a threat. From a strategic standpoint, the slow service time must be corrected or the business will not be maximizing its potential. From an theoretical standpoint, the 10-minute service time would be an opportunity that, if met by competitors, would be a threat.

Some examples of opportunities are:

- Target customers in trade area want delivery.
- People are taking more frequent but shorter vacations.
- Target customers in trade area want fast service.
- The firm's target segments are seeking good values.
- Target customers are drinking more nonalcoholic specialty drinks.
- Large segment of active 60 to 70 year-olds live in trade area.

Threats

A *threat* in the environment is anything that could cause a decrease in sales, represent an obstacle to success, or conceivably cause the demise of the business. When threats are recognized, the firm will have to decide whether a strategy will be needed to defend against it. Examples of threats are:

- Major competitors with many locations, who are well financed and expanding quickly, have high profit and excellent image/name recognition, and are recognized for their high quality and value orientation; or any competitor with a sustainable competitive advantage
- Recessions or inflation
- Trends away from a restaurant's primary menu item, or away from a firm's segment of the market, such as fine dining

- Governmental regulations, or the potential loss of the government as a customer and
- Lack of quality personnel at reasonable wages

ANALYSIS AND AWARENESS OF ENVIRONMENTAL FACTORS

The basic task of the environmental analysis is to sort through the millions of pieces of available data to retrieve that which should be considered important and included in the firm's information database. In information jargon, this is termed "filtering out the static." In the internal analysis, the three key concerns were *organization and content, the standards for measurement,* and *who will prepare the analysis.* The environmental analysis can be viewed from a similar approach. The organization and content will be based on an analysis of the remote environment, where the firm will have very little control, and the operating environment, where it will have varying degrees of control (see Figure 5.1). Most hospitality businesses will have similar remote environmental factors, while each will generally have more diverse operating environmental factors to consider.

Because of the need to focus more on future occurrences, rather than present performance as in the internal analysis, the standards of measurement for the environmental analysis will be much more subjective. A substantial share of this analysis will be based on opinions of authors of articles, books, and research data, and the interpretation of marketing managers. As for who will prepare the environmental analysis, the options are essentially the same as for the internal analysis: inside individuals or groups; outside sources, including consultants and marketing firms; and, for applicable areas, customer-completed surveys or comment cards. The primary difference is that since the firm's management deals with internal aspects of the business on a daily basis, it will have more experience and, therefore, be able to more accurately assess internal performance than external conditions.

REMOTE ENVIRONMENT	OPERATING ENVIRONMENT
Political regulations and actions	Personnel
Economy	Ecology
Societal trends and shifts	Customers
Technology	Competitors
(Acronym—PEST)	Suppliers and creditors (Acronym—PECCS, pronounced *pecks*)

Figure 5.1   Environmental analysis.

No means of measuring the future can give the firm complete confidence in its estimate of what will happen, but a carefully thought-out system can improve its accuracy. As in baseball, where a batter with a .300 batting average might be paid around $3 million a year while one with a .250 average may earn $400,000, slight improvements in an environmental analysis can yield exponential advantages.

The analysis of environmental factors requires the following:

- A minimization of subjectivity
- The ability to forecast trends
- The realization that the firm will have little control in dealing with most environmental factors

Minimizing Subjectivity

When major mistakes are made in the strategic planning process, the reason is often either a bias in data collection or a subjectively caused misreading of the firm's apparent opportunities or threats. This means erroneously assuming that either something will or will not happen or that customers want a certain benefit or attribute, based on its compatibility with personal opinions. Therefore, it is imperative that information used in the environmental analysis be as factually and objectively based as possible. Subjectivity can be the downfall of an environmental analysis. For example, the wrong market might be targeted—a major mistake—or it might be thought that the current target market desires a fancier decor when, in fact, it wants a simpler decor (Makridakis, 1991).

Forecasting

In the environmental analysis, forecasting concerns the ability to anticipate how consumers and other external factors are likely to change under a given set of circumstances. This broad category for estimating demand can be divided into *quantitative and qualitative forecasting*. Quantitative forecasting consists of using mathematical models such as times series analysis, econometric models, and multivariate analysis. Because of its intricacies, complexity, cost, and the increasing dynamics of environmental changes, quantitative forecasting is used considerably less than qualitative methods. Primarily only larger chains are making extensive use of quantitative forecasting methods; however, their use appears to be declining. This is occurring, even with the current fast pace of technological change and improvements in software, because "people" issues are playing a more significant role in strategy formulation, especially in the hospitality industry. The numbers can present current and past facts, but, in the end, a subjective interpretation must be made of their importance and future direction. The primary quantitative method still used by a majority of hospitality firms is trend extrapolation. This is simply an analysis of past quantitative records for any particular environmental factor (or internal business concern), with an assumption of where the figures will be headed in the future. For example, if inflation for the last three years has been 4% and each recent month's economy has mirrored the previous year's, then, all thing being equal, it could be forecasted that inflation for this year will probably be about 4%. If new information was available that could impact inflation, it might be appropriate to alter the forecast.

Qualitative forecasting is the dominant means used in the hospitality industry. It consists of various means of forecasting based on direct observation or opinions of small groups of people with specific knowledge about a subject. Since factors in the hospitality environment change rapidly, qualitative forecasting through expert opinions, debates, or surveys can quickly construct a picture of possible future events. Methods of qualitative analysis include the following:

- *Brainstorming.* Open sharing of ideas. Brainstorming begins with one person presenting a topic to a group. Then the group members would very briefly express their ideas about future trends for the topic. One member would be assigned the task of recording each member's ideas. The objective is for one person's idea to stimulate the thoughts of others, leading to the accumulation of a large number of implications or options. Quantity is stressed over quality. It is critical in brainstorming sessions that no one person speak for too long—no war stories.
- *Juries of Executive Opinion.* Forecasts from various levels of management, based on a reasonable in-depth analysis of the issue.
- *Delphi Method.* This is generally a series of survey questionnaires designed to obtain a consensus among individual experts in a particular field. Information from the first survey is interpreted and tabulated to derive the average opinion of the group. The group's opinions are then disseminated to the respondents through further surveys until a reasonable consensus is reached. The delphi method (or delphi technique) is designed to allow for independent thought, as opposed to roundtable discussions that may be swayed by formal and informal leaders (McClave & Benson, 1994).
- *Customer Surveys.* Asking relevant people about their knowledge, preference, and attitude about something. This would include nonprobability samples (Descriptive Statistics) only. Probability samples for inferential statistics would be considered as quantitative analysis. (See Chapter 3 for more information on surveys.)
- *Scenario Analysis.* Creating a hypothetical projection about the future, based on one or more events occurring. For example, if the economy improved, how would the hotel position itself to take advantage of the increased demand? Or if air fares increased what might happen to occupancy percentages and room rates?
- *Sales Force or Employee Estimates.* Soliciting opinions from employees with access to key information. Since all categories of employees in the service industry will have valuable knowledge about important issues, level of organizational responsibility should not determine the value of someone's opinion.

Limited Control Over the Environment

Since few companies exert a substantial control over all environmental factors, the objectives here are as follows:

1. *Be aware of it.* If a company knows that a certain environmental factor can affect it, the factor should be monitored. In the vast majority of cases, the primary factors

that must be carefully monitored are the business's customers and its competitors. Most other environmental factors are generally secondary in nature in that they first affect either customers or competitors before impacting one's business.

2. *Be prepared to act as changes occur.* Many strategies are good only as long as the environment is static. Since this is not a luxury most hospitality businesses enjoy, individuals responsible for making key decisions must be prepared for all realistic occurrences. If it is known how a particular factor might affect a business, then a contingency plan can be prepared to allow for a more purposeful and directed reaction. Additional advantages of contingency plans are that they give the company confidence that it is prepared for most situations, reduce response time, and force in-depth analysis of situations.

3. *Be financially and operationally strong.* A company with a 15% bottom line profit is much better prepared to deal with uncertainties than one with a 5% profit. Likewise, a firm with a quality product has a much better chance of withstanding threats than one with a marginal product.

ENTREPRENEURIAL VIEWPOINT   It is often thought that entrepreneurial firms, with their maverick or innovative strategies, will focus less on environmental data than conservative firms. Actually, the opposite is often true. The general tendency is for entrepreneurial firms to track environmental data more closely than conservative firms. The conservative firm is normally well established and may not feel that it is overly susceptible to external trends. Because of the need to be more in touch with what the market wants, entrepreneurial firms tend to track environmental data very closely. This is what allows them to take a proactive stance in the offering of new products and services. Even though this may appear to be indicative of high risk, in many ways it actually reduces risk by increasing the soundness of proactive strategic decisions (Covin, 1991). Though entrepreneurs will always be characterized as doers, not analyzers, they generally will not act before careful consideration of the consequences.

REMOTE ENVIRONMENT

The remote environment (or *macroenvironment*) is concerned with factors that the business generally has very little control over: political (or governmental) regulations and actions, *economic*, *societal*, and *technological* (represented by the acronym PEST). For example, the 1990 war with Iraq had a devastating effect on the hospitality business throughout the world. Since no business could effectively deal directly with the governments to stop the war, the only option was to deal with its consequences—fewer customers. The strategies most often used in this case were to lower prices, develop promotional packages, cut overhead, and wait for the war and its consequences to end.

Political Regulation and Actions

These include an infinite number of legislative actions purchase behavior by political entities that can influence sales or methods of operations. Primary examples of legislation are various types of taxation and legislated methods of collection (such as TEFRA—the Tax Equity and Financial Responsibility Act—tip credit laws, and changes in the meal deductibility), city ordinances and zoning, health codes and inspectors, building codes, minimum wage laws, workers' compensation laws, building and road construction, contraction or expansion of governmental employment and purchasing, the defense budget, wars, the Federal Reserve's setting of interest rates, and the President's Council of Economic Advisors. Since the government can change methods of operation without regard to individual economic considerations or input, it represents a very difficult external factor to monitor. Political or governmental sense and business sense are frequently two entirely different matters. Unfortunately, in the past, many activities of the government have been politically driven; they might be set forth to aid constituents of politicians to increase the likelihood of reelection, or they might be mandates from officials that have little knowledge or concern for the potential detrimental effects of their actions. For example, both federal and most state legislative bodies have not dealt adequately with the problem of an inefficient and ineffective health care system. This has caused workers' compensation insurance and health insurance premiums to rise to unacceptable levels. Also, the federal government has increased the national debt to the point where the interest on the debt absorbs much of the available funds for business loans and drives interest rates up.

In light of the poor past record of the federal government and its inability to competently deal with the nation's problems, it is widely hoped that future administrations will make some positive changes. The American people are becoming impatient and expect a new set of ground rules. With the recent changes in Washington, hopefully things will take a turn for the better. No one knows exactly what mix of stimulative spending, tax incentives, and means of reducing the federal deficit and national debt will work, but everyone agrees that something different must be done (Dodge, 1992).

There are means of influencing governmental actions, but they are generally limited to large, well-financed groups, such as the National Restaurant Association (NRA), the American Hotel and Motel Association (AHMA), and their state and local chapters. Dues-paying members help finance lobbyists and officers that attempt to sway politicians toward voting on legislation that will benefit the industry. Many find the thought of lobbyists distasteful, but until the rules of the game change, NRA and AHMA lobbyists are the industry's key defenders against costly or encumbering legislation.

An often-ignored aspect of political and governmental influence in the hospitality business is the government's actions as a consumer of services. The government can represent a substantial percentage of sales for many hotels. If a restaurant is located near a military base or local, state, or federal office buildings, a large percentage of its business may be government related, especially after payday. Hospitality firms dependent on military bases or defense-related businesses will suffer as the trend to cut military spending and close bases persists.

Economic Conditions

Since the one constant about the economy is that it will always be shifting between peaks and valleys, businesses must be prepared for inevitable decreases and increases in demand for their current product or service at current prices. Common economic concerns are increases or decreases in disposable income (after-tax dollars) or discretionary income (after all bills are paid), customer's propensity to spend, recessions, inflation, high or low interest rates, easy or tough credit, high or low unemployment, escalating oil prices, oil embargoes, multi-national trade agreements, trade barriers, and tariffs.

Historical information for an individual business or industry segment can shed light on the possible effect of economic shifts. Some hospitality businesses may actually benefit from recessions or inflation, while others may suffer. While one business sees inflation as a threat—because people have less to spend on food in restaurants and hotels—another sees it as an opportunity to bring in new customers—because of their reputation for quality food and service, or because of their value orientation. During the economic downturn of the late 1980s, Taco Bell realized that people had less money to spend and were seeking a good value. The company's decision to lower prices and emphasize value-meals led to a phenomenal increase in sales. In economic downturns, declining profits force many businesses to try to hold down expenses by limiting travel or lowering per-diems. This, of course, brings down occupancy rates for many hotels, and sales for restaurants that rely on business travelers. Hotels and motels in the budget segment and value-oriented restaurants may actually see increases in business during the same period.

Businesses must also understand how the various macro- and microeconomic factors affect its sales. Based on current projections for the next decade, the world economy will grow, but at a marginal rate, around 2%. Most Asian countries will show growth in the 7% range, with China at 13% (Alm, 1992). This fact could indicate a potential market for the expansion of businesses that cater to the Asian market, such as luxury motels or tours. In a national downturn, almost all hotels will see declines in business. Between 1988 and 1991, the national economy went from a growth rate of 3.9% to -1.2% (Organization for Economic Cooperation and Development, 1992). This downturn combined with an overcapacity problem and led to decreased occupancies and profit for most segments of the industry. When the local economy is down, hotels will see reductions in business to the degree that those areas of decline affect their customer's clients—the reason they have come to the city. For example, in the city of Houston, Texas, the mid- 1980s saw a major decline in the oil industry, which, in turn, had a devastating effect on the local hotel industry. Fewer reasons to visit the city translated into lower occupancies.

Restaurants that rely on local traffic, which is the majority of them, tend to show only a moderate effect from global or moderate national economic downturns. Other food-service establishments, such as caterers and institutional food-service firms, will usually be affected by economic trends to the extent of their reliance on national or multinational business clients.

A related economic issue that hospitality operators are facing is the globalization of markets and interdependence of national and foreign economies. Twenty years ago it was somewhat rare for American hospitality firms to pursue growth overseas. In the near future, some operations will show a greater sales or profit from foreign-based units than from those in America. As globalization of the industry races ahead, the economic position of America in relation to major industrialized economies, such as the Pacific Rim and Europe, will have a major impact on operations and opportunities. In a debt-laden America of the 21st century, foreign firms will have greater access to our markets. If America can successfully attack the national debt, there will be more money available for expansion-supporting loans. Solving other serious national problems, such as a decaying infrastructure, low capital investment (new equipment used in production), and deficiencies in secondary education, can fortify economic stability through a larger GDP (Gross Domestic Product)—the total value of all goods and services produced in the United States. A broad-based improvement in the GDP will not only brighten the outlook for American firms operating in this country but will increase their ability to expand overseas. The ability to expand globally will force foreign firms to concentrate on defending their turf, lessening their likelihood of entering our markets.

Lester C. Thurow (1992) expresses the view that, consistent with current trends, Europe has the greatest potential to be the leading economy of the 21st century. This is based on advantages such as a well-educated workforce, vast natural resources, strong capital markets, and a strong creative flair. If his prediction is true, major opportunities and threats lie ahead for American firms. He adds that America must shift its resources away from consumption to investment in the future, increase spending on research and development, and improve elementary and secondary schools. Thurow feels that our university system is what allows college graduates to catch up with the rest of the world, but those who do not pursue a college degree may not measure up to world standards.

Societal Trends

Shifts in the broad makeup of our population have always had and will continue to have a profound effect on the way hospitality firms do business. The following are among the most dramatic changes for our industry during the last 20 years:

TWO-INCOME FAMILIES   The percentage of meals eaten away from the home has increased, as mothers who once prepared the traditional evening meal are now in the workforce. Also, if more discretionary income is available, higher quality meals will be purchased, higher quality hotels will be sought, and more vacations will be taken. The higher the percentage of two-income families in a trade area, the greater the opportunities for both restaurants and hotels.

INCREASED PROPENSITY TO TRAVEL   Both domestic and foreign travel will increase as people are exposed to more information about available vacation spots and place more emphasis on quality of life rather than on materialism. Cities or areas where social unrest is well publicized will find it increasingly difficult to attract domestic or foreign travelers. Countries such as Ireland, South Africa, and Egypt have seen their tourism dollars eroded through internal conflicts. As refugees from Eastern bloc countries flood western European nations, protests and attacks by right-wing radical groups are undermining attempts at increasing tourism (Schlentrich, 1993).

INCREASED DEMAND FOR ETHNIC FOODS   The increase in ethnic minorities in America has led to a greater variety of ethnic restaurants and consequently a greater demand for and acceptance of ethnic foods. As people eat out more often, they are becoming bored with traditional American foods.

INCREASED DEMAND FOR QUALITY AND VALUE   The increased focus on "getting your money's worth" and the greater exposure of customers to quality experiences are forcing hospitality firms to improve their offerings. The perception that a hotel or restaurant does not represent a good value must be avoided at all costs.

INCREASE IN THE DESIRE FOR NUTRITIOUS INGREDIENTS AND EXERCISE   One of the most powerful movements in America is the increased awareness of the need for and benefits of a healthy life-style. Customers who one ate burgers and fries on a daily basis are now eating fish and steamed vegetables. Hotel guests who went to the bar after their business meeting are now going to the workout room. People who are eating foods with less salt (sodium), fat, and sugar are making up for the reduction in flavor by the addition of spices; this has fueled a trend toward spicier foods and ethnic cuisines.

There has also been a contradictory move toward the consumption of foods that are considered richer and more flavorful. For example, Marketing Intelligence Service Ltd., a research firm, says that the percentage of new product introductions claiming to have low or no fat or cholesterol has actually declined in recent years. The Yankelovich Monitor survey of consumer trends found that the percentage of people who say they frequently consume salty snacks increased in the mid-1990s from 40% to 45%. This trend has been attributed to various causes, the most popular of which are that people have been getting tired of eating bland foods, and that the recession of the late 1980s and early 1990s has caused a great deal of stress that is being soothed by thick gooey ice cream, burgers with bacon and cheese, and soft chewy cookies. This obviously does not mean that foodservice operators should abandon the health bandwagon; it only shows that each business must know its customers' tastes and consider having foods that satisfy their desire for healthy fare one day and rich foods the next (Bhargava, 1993).

THE AGING OF OUR POPULATION.   Since the baby boomers are having fewer babies than their parents, the average age of Americans is quickly increasing. Few hotels or restaurants can ignore the needs of older customers, or their viability as target segments. The American Association of Retired Persons (AARP) has not only become one of the strongest lobbying organizations in the country, but it is also an extremely productive market for many hospitality firms. One frequent-guest program for seniors found that their average household income was over $70,000 per year. The National Association for Senior Living Industries, based in Annapolis, Maryland, provides a worldwide network of firms that provide services to people 55 and over.

FEWER BABIES AND A REDUCTION IN THE NUMBER OF AVAILABLE EMPLOYEES TO FILL MINIMUM WAGE JOBS   This has forced employers to take various strategies, such as paying higher wages, increasing benefits, accepting less qualified workers, hiring the elderly or homemakers in the neighborhood, purchasing new equipment to reduce the number of employees needed, and work simplification.

WOMEN'S INCREASING ROLE IN THE DIRECT PURCHASE OF HOSPITALITY SERVICES   Women have always greatly influenced purchase decisions, but today they are participating with more financial strength as they take clients to lunch or dinner, travel on business, and decide where their company will go for its meetings or conventions. The increase in women traveling for business was one of the influencing factors that guided the creation and proliferation of the all-suites hotel concept.

THE DESIRE FOR A BETTER QUALITY OF LIFE (QOL)   Increases in both restaurant and hotel sales have been guided by people wanting to experience more of the pleasures of life. QOL issues have also led to changes in hospitality work environments.

- In the 1960s, few kitchens had air conditioning; today, it is rare to find a kitchen without it.
- Traditionally, schedules have been almost completely based on the needs of the restaurant or hotel. This practice, in many cases, has been reversed.
- In the past, professional management was not as critical as it is today. With more professionalism have come demands for better working conditions and pay for managers.
- The average work week for hospitality managers used to be approximately 60 hours. Today, it is edging down toward 50 hours, and five-day work weeks are becoming the norm.

SOCIAL RESPONSIBILITY   As business ethics recover from the "profit at all costs" stigma of the 1980s, social responsibility will become a necessary component of business objectives and strategies. Many firms have virtually eliminated advertising from their budgets to focus on socially responsible public relations efforts.

AIDS   How will the threat or fear of acquiring AIDS affect people's willingness and tendency to visit various types of bars or restaurants and certain countries where the disease is widespread? Countries with a weak medical infrastructure will experience the greatest decline in tourism due to fear of HIV contamination (Schlentrich, 1993).

Technology

In industries heavily dependent on innovation and technology, a discovery by a competitor could make a product virtually obsolete overnight. The hospitality business, on the other hand, has changed relatively little over the decades. Since the industry is heavily dependent on labor as opposed to equipment, technological changes, though beneficial, have not had the impact they have had for manufacturing industries. In the hospitality industry, technological change is normally concerned with changes in accounting and reservations systems, kitchen equipment, guest check processing, safety and security, and energy usage. The most pronounced changes have been in increased efficiency or speed of service and recordkeeping.

Modern equipment allows us to prepare a greater variety of foods faster than traditional methods. Computerized accounting and reservation systems help speed routine duties, help reduce errors, and free management to work more closely with customers rather than staying in the back office. Historically, the hospitality business has been behind most industries on the adoption of technology. Recent years have seen a rapid move toward equipment that will make work easier, safer, more consistent, and less costly.

As with anything new, operators must be aware of potential problems. For example, when a popular point-of-sale (POS) system first entered the market in the early 1980s, there were many problems. Competitors copied the advantages of the new system and eliminated most of the problems. Eventually, the glitches were solved and there are now many reliable systems, but the initial customers were used to test and debug the system. When trying a new technology, the company should consider leasing on a short-term basis, so that if the system does not work as promised, it can be returned without a major loss of capital. It is also beneficial to establish a close working relationship with the supplier, so that the introduction can be managed effectively. If the piece of equipment is strategically important to the operations of the business, it may be necessary to have backup modules or units or to maintain the old manual or electronic system as a backup in case of breakdowns.

Every business must thoroughly analyze its requirements for technology. For some, a lack of technology is part of the concept. Others may be in the opposite situation. Operators should ask themselves the following: (1) "Are there new methods or pieces of equipment that will make operating the business simpler, less expensive, or more productive?" Examples include computers, point-of-sale terminals, convection steamers, and conveyor ovens. (2) "If I do not take advantage of any of these, will my competitors do so?" (3) "Are there current or possible future technologies in related industries, such as less expensive substitutes, frozen dinners, or complete-meal takeout services, that may capture part of my market?"

Be careful of idiot-proofing operational systems. When the challenge is taken out of a task, the company could end up with unskilled employees that cannot adapt to the unique requirements of the hospitality industry. Intelligent employees will rarely perform monotonous tasks for more than brief periods before quitting. This is essentially what happened to the auto industry in the 1970s. They found that some people had been performing the same task for 20 years. Not only was this bad for the employee, but it resulted in more errors and reduced ability to use critical thinking to solve problems. Each major task of a business should be designed with the needs of the employee, customer, and business in mind. If a particular task is redundant, perhaps some mentally challenging components could be added.

OPERATING ENVIRONMENT

The operating environment (or *microenvironment*) is concerned with those areas in the external environment over which management has the most influence; *p*ersonnel, *e*cology, *c*ustomers, *c*ompetitors, and *s*uppliers (represented by the acronym PECCS;

pronounced *pecks*). While the remote environment generally necessitates a forecast, then a wait-and-see position, the operating environment requires forecasting with an active involvement. In gathering information on the operating environment, management must rely heavily on primary research from the particular individuals, groups, or businesses being studied. Obviously, journals, business periodicals, seminars, and electronic databases will provide a great deal of information, but primary research will generally yield the best results.

Personnel

In the operating environment, personnel are discussed from the vantage point of the business's ability to attract suitable employees. (The personnel working *in the business* are discussed in the internal analysis.) The key factors will include the company's reputation as a good or bad place to work, how its work environment compares with that of its competitors, the image of the employees that work for the company, the unemployment rate and wages in the local community, and the skill level of those employees generally available for work.

There will always be a struggle to find qualified employees. As time passes, there may be fewer young people who have traditionally filled hotel and restaurant positions. With these changes have come new trends in hiring retired workers and homemakers from local neighborhoods. There is also a major trend to provide a more stable employment environment by scheduling regular 40-hour work weeks and including benefits, such as retirement, insurance, and vacations. Businesses that fall behind in this trend will find themselves with unqualified, unmotivated employees.

Ecology

As the national and world focus on the environment increases, the action of each restaurant and hotel will carefully be monitored by various public agencies to see how they affect the air, water, land, and all living things. Companies that take the lead in improving their ecological image will gain a potential competitive advantage. To take an assertive or proactive approach (rather than a defensive, after-the-fact approach) to "green marketing," firms must find out how they affect the ecological balance in their markets, what can be done to improve in each of those areas and what various consumer groups and governmental entities consider to be important. Then they must incorporate reasonable changes into corporate strategies (McDaniel & Rylander, 1993). *Ecology* is defined as the study of the relationship between living organisms and their environment. The *environment* means the conditions surrounding the development of an organism (*Webster's New World Dictionary*, Prentice-Hall, 1986).

Among the questions that should be considered are the following:

- What product, packaging, garbage disposal, air quality, and wastewater issues are being discussed in local, state, or national governing bodies?
- Does the company comply with existing or soon-to-be-passed laws?

- Will any new laws affect operating procedures and methods? Many municipalities are requiring companies to limit solid waste or to use recyclable packaging.
- How easily and quickly can the business accommodate changes in these areas?
- What are the sentiments of target customers regarding ecology?

As the world's concern for protection of the environment continues, all firms, especially those that deal directly with the public or have brand name recognition, will need to be certain that they are doing whatever is possible to reduce activities that harm the environment (Hooper & Rocca, 1991). These decisions will influence a destination's ability to attract tourist dollars (Schlentrich, 1993). Some countries are capitalizing on their efforts at restoring or preserving the environment by sponsoring "ecotours" that spotlight those efforts. Ecology is normally addressed first in the mission statement (what it should do); second, in the internal analysis (what it is doing); third, here in the environmental analysis (what is expected, what others are doing or options to pursue); and finally, in the functional strategies and applicable policy or action plan sections (what it will do).

Customer Analysis

The purpose of the customer analysis is to identify the distinguishing characteristics and attributes of market segments (or markets) that have the potential to generate the greatest sales and profits. Markets in this context may be either *consumer markets* that buy products and services for personal consumption or *organizational markets* that buy products and services that are used for the production or sale of other products and services. The term customer is used to refer to both consumer and organizational markets. The vast majority of a restaurant's sales will come from individuals. The opposite is generally true of many midscale to luxury hotels. Corporate and association meeting planners are perhaps the hotel's most important clients. Corporate meeting (travel) planners are responsible for booking hotels for both group business (from small meetings to conventions) and individual business travelers (employees traveling on their own or in groups of less than 10 people). Most associations have at least one large annual meeting and several smaller meetings each year. They generally have offices near a state capitol and/or Washington, DC. Locating the companies and associations that the hotel can best serve is one of the most crucial roles of the Director of Sales and Marketing. Restaurant and hotel marketing managers locate and decide on viable market segments through market targeting.

Each business must develop a substantial base of knowledge and understanding regarding their primary customers: who they are; where they live, work, shop, or spend their time; what their life-styles are like; and how they spend their money. They must be identified as accurately as possible to allow the business to direct its marketing efforts—products, services, pricing, location, and promotion—in an efficient and effective manner. One of the problems that marketers frequently encounter is that current plans are developed with information from several years ago. As time passes, the implications derived from various characteristics for each target segment may change, as well as the identification variables themselves. Some changes will occur frequently, such as trends in music or entertainment: others will be more consistent, as in value orientation—monetary values, family values, and opinions on philosophical issues (McDaniel & Burnett, 1990).

The amount and type of information necessary will depend on a multitude of factors. The specificity will normally increase with the strength of the competition, if customer frequency is decreasing, and if serious strategic changes are being considered. Possibly the greatest need for customer information is for promotions, especially on television. This is because if the business were concerned only with developing suitable products and services for its market it would need to know only what the customer expects of those products and services. But if a commercial was going to be produced, then the firm must also know the range of emotions and sensory considerations required to script the commercial. Additionally, if a multi-media campaign was being planned, the unique characteristics of each type of medium and the target customer's related emotional and sensory factors would need to be addressed.

IDENTIFYING THE TARGET CUSTOMER   This process of identifying the customer's needs, wants, and demands consists of two steps: *segmentation* and *target marketing*. Once these characteristics have been identified, the firm must decide on the ideal image or position for its product in the eyes of its customers, then develop strategies to satisfy that position. The firm's desired *position*, also referred to as subjective position, is decided in the strategic planning section (see Chapter 6). The general and specific actions that support that desired position are formulated in strategic plans, functional strategies, policies, and action plans.

MARKET SEGMENTATION   *Segmentation* is the division of a product's market into groups that have distinct buying habits and will consequently require the use of different strategies. Within all segments will be subsegments that will require additional unique strategies and tactics. For example, a segment such as group business for a hotel will have several subsegments, some of whom want a broad selection of imported beer, while others want vegetarian entrees and a place to run. For most hospitality businesses, there will be from one to four market segments that account for the majority of its sales. There will then be several smaller groups that individually do not provide a good deal of business but collectively may comprise as much as 10% of sales. To avoid marginal returns on research, and since the firm would probably not be developing specific strategies for less profitable markets, normally only the sizable target groups are considered. If substantial growth was expected in a smaller market, and the firm wanted to be ahead of its competition in attracting them, only then would it be viable to research the segment. Typically, markets are divided according to their characteristics as detailed in the four bases of segmentation—geographics, demographics, psychographics, and buyer behavior. (These are explained in the following.)

For most firms, the customer is the focus of the majority of research efforts. Even when looking at competitors, or any other components of the environmental analysis, the key consideration is: "How does this factor affect my target customers?" In past years, marketers were concerned with mass markets—trying to serve broad segments of the population with little concern for specific requirements. Today, the guiding rule in marketing is that *without a specific market to target, there will soon be no market at all.*

There will always be some exceptions to the push for segmenting markets, but when closely analyzed, even these businesses utilize some form of segmentation and market targeting. Segmenting the market allows the company to efficiently utilize its resources and customize its offering for each market's unique requirements. A hotel, for example, might decide to advertise in the *Wall Street Journal* rather than *Time* magazine, because that is the most popular source of information for its particular target market. Another hotel could find the exact opposite to be true. A restaurant learning that 20% of its customers are vegetarian could add several vegetarian entrees and promote this fact in a local periodical with a high vegetarian-segment readership.

This trend towards segmentation is evidenced by the increasing diversification of restaurant and hotel concepts being introduced. In a fast-paced world, markets tend to fragment. What appears to be a safe and secure market today may not be there tomorrow. This has forced marketers to work harder to decide which markets they should try to target, and how they could most effectively and efficiently position their product offerings to satisfy those targeted markets.

Historically, customer markets have passed through three stages: mass marketing, product variety marketing, and target marketing.

MASS MARKETING   The firm does not consider individual differences between customers when designing its marketing strategies. Its principal advantage is that it is the most cost-effective means of reaching the largest possible market. For select new industries with little competition, there may still be some mass markets. For hospitality industries, there are probably no longer any mass markets, at least not on a national scale. The exception is that some small rural communities will act as mass markets by frequenting certain established restaurants. As competition brings greater choices, the market will fragment.

PRODUCT VARIETY MARKETING   The firm offers several different products and services with the purpose of maintaining the loyalty of its present customer base. Since customers eventually become tired of static product offerings, many firms will provide various choices to reduce monotony and give its present customer base less of a reason to seek out competitors. The problem with product variety marketing is that it attempts to temporarily satisfy customers without keying in on their true wants. As competitors target the needs of increasingly fragmented markets, firms that utilize product variety marketing as their primary focus will see their markets erode.

TARGET MARKETING   The firm identifies the distinguishing characteristics of various segments of the overall market, targets one or more of the segments, then designs its marketing strategies to cater to the demands of those targeted markets. The *target market* (or markets) then becomes the identifiable market segments that accounts for the majority of the firm's sales and strategic efforts. There will always be occasional survivors of past eras that continue to satisfy customers without specific targeting strategies, but as time passes their numbers will dwindle.

Many businesses are currently developing databases with the ability to keep track of each customer's individual likes and dislikes This is referred to as *database marketing, individual marketing,* or *customized marketing* (Kotler, 1991). As these firms proliferate, competitors will likely be forced to adopt similar strategies. Currently, many luxury and some upper-midscale hotels are utilizing the customized approach to support their traditional targeting strategies. Software systems are available to allow restaurants to track customers' demands, but their use has been quite limited. How deeply customized marketing will impact the hospitality industry remains to be seen, but as the information superhighway brings technological advancements to the fingertips of the middle-class, one can assume that major changes are around the corner. Ordering meals via television is currently being tested and will likely be commonplace during the next decade.

SEGMENTS TO RESEARCH   The first step in the segmentation process is to decide which of the firm's market segments should be researched, and how they should be classified. Restaurants will usually classify target groups first according to age. For example, customers could be divided by their age—children up to 6, 6 to 12, 12 to 17, 18 to 34, 35 to 50, and over 50. If customers' occupations were the most valuable means of differentiating between market segments, then office workers, professionals, trades (carpenters, plumbers, electricians), and salespeople could be grouped. Fine dining segmentation could be according to household income—up to $29,999, $30,000 to $39,999, $40,000 to $49,999, $50,000 to $59,999, and $60,000 and up. Hotels will normally categorize their segments according to their traditional markets: individual business travelers, group business, and the leisure/tourist markets. Further divisions could be by room nights purchased, by income categories within each of the traditional market segments, by company, by geographic territory, or by type of organization (e.g., associations, nonprofit, religious, education, sports). The information gathered would be recorded for each selected segment.

The next step would be to decide what information should be gathered. The four bases of segmentation are the starting point. Here the marketer decides which are the most important variables (customer characteristics) within each segmentation base. The last step is to gather information for each of those variables. This can be done through the marketer's experience and available secondary information, or through some type of formal research such as observation, survey, and experiments. For hotels and restaurants, the majority of the information should be internally available through the firm's marketing information system. If this is not the case, then a system that will provide the necessary information should be implemented. (See Chapter 3.)

After the information is gathered, it should be subdivided or organized to allow for a closer appraisal or prioritization. A matrix analysis of the most promising customer segments is a common option. If a restaurant was thinking about adding healthy items to its menu, it could use segmentation variables to categorize each group's characteristics (see Figure 5.2 and 5.3). Possible categories might be vegetari-

SEGMENTATION CHARACTERISTIC	VEGETARIAN	NUTRITIONALLY CONSCIOUS	WEIGHT WATCHERS	MODERATE DINERS	INDULGENT DINERS
GEOGRAPHICS					
Distance from home to center of trade area	An average of 6 miles	An average of 4 miles	3 to 4 miles	An average of 3 miles	Up to 2 miles
DEMOGRAPHICS					
Household income	$43,500	$38,350	$34,600	$33,250	$24,800
Education	20% high school 20% some college 60% college	20% high school 30% some college 50% college	30% high school 40% some college 30% college	30% high school 30% some college 40% college	60% high school 30% some college 10% college
Family cycle	Singles, families with one or two children	Singles, families without children	35- to 45-year old singles and married couples	Singles up to 25 and 45 to 55	18 to 45 singles and couples
PSYCHOGRAPHICS					
Political orientation	Liberal to moderate	Liberal to moderate	Moderate to conservative	Moderate to conservative	Broad mix, liberal to conservative
Sports orientation	Active	Moderately active	Some active, some sedentary	Watch sports, occasional participation	Watch sports, some sedentary, some active
BUYER BEHAVIOR					
Percentage of diners	8%	22%	24%	33%	13%
Price sensitivity	Low	Low to moderate	Moderate to high	Moderate	High
Frequency of dining out (evening meal)	Two times per week	Three times per week	Two times per week	Three times per week	Four times per week
Brand loyalty	High	High	Medium	Medium	Low to medium
Product/service quality orientation	High	High	Medium to high	Medium	Low to medium
Principal benefits sought	Flavor, selection, truth in menu	Quality, selection, information	Information, taste, selection	Taste, price, selection	Price, quantity, taste
Menu category concentration	Salads, and creative vegetarian entrees	Vegetables	Chicken and fish	Variety	Red meat

Figure 5.2 Segmentation of casual diners' eating habits for Richland Hills subdivision.

RATING	NUTRITIOUS DINERS	MODERATE DINERS	INDULGENT DINERS
Critical	Low fat choices	Flavorful food	Large quantities of food
Important	Flavorful food	Quantity of food	Low price
Moderately important	Service	Price	Flavorful food
Somewhat important	Price	Service	Service
Unimportant	Atmosphere	Atmosphere	Atmosphere

Figure 5.3   Target segment characteristics: needs, wants, and demands.

ans, nutritionally conscious, weight watchers, moderate diners, and indulgent diners. An alternative to customer segments is to divide the market based on products purchased or cuisines or restaurants frequented. In any market there will be customers that prefer seafood, beef, chicken, or pork; or Mexican, Italian, or Southwestern cuisines: or Matt's El Rancho, Juanita's, or Jalapeno's.

The Four Bases of Segmentation

Traditionally, in the hospitality business, especially for independent operators, customers have been identified primarily by geographic and demographic factors (*geodemographics*). As experience accumulates, we are learning more about the uses of psychographics and buyer behavior. Some type of primary research must be implemented to identify customer segments and their desires. A survey questionnaire is normally the most effective means of accumulating the appropriate information. Research should focus on identifying the following customer characteristics.

GEOGRAPHIC DATA   This concerns where actual and potential customers live or work and trends in population shifts. This is another way of asking: Where is the market? A major consideration is the size of the *trade area*—the geographic area(s) from where the majority of customers come. For example, for most restaurants, more than 70% of the customers live or work within the restaurant's trade area. For a fast-food restaurant this could be as little as a 1-mile radius. Three to five miles is the norm for casual dining concepts, and 20 to 30 miles, and even up to 50 miles, is not unheard of for fine dining or highly differentiated casual dining restaurants. For hotels there will always be certain cities that supply the hotel with a majority of its business. (See The Bryan House example at the end of this chapter.) In states with several large metropolitan cities, the majority of the guests will often come from other cities in the state. The geographic customer base of a hotel in a state with very few metropolitan communities will generally depend on its location in relation to the nation's highway system. Those in between major cities will often attract people on their way to or from the larger city. People who would rather stay in a rural or small city environment will also be potential guests. As globalization becomes more of a reality, the percentage of international guests in U.S. restaurants and hotels is quickly increasing. Primary markets include the Pacific Rim, Europe (especially after unification), and South America. With the implementation of the North American Free Trade Agreement (NAFTA), travel to and from Mexico and Canada has increased.

DEMOGRAPHICS   This is the statistical breakdown of defined populations by various categories, such as the following:

- Age, sex, religion, race, ethnicity, and nationality.
- Size of the demographic group: —3.5 million, 143,000.
- Family size: 1, 2, 3, 4, 5, 6 + .
- Family cycle: single; young married, no children; young married, youngest child under 6 years; young married, youngest child 6 years or over; older, married, with children; older, married, no children under 18; older single; etc.
- Income: measured by "household income," but also per capita (average for each person) income, and income per wage earner. Household income under $15,000, $15K to $20K, $20K to $25K, $30K to $35K, $35K to $40K, $40K to $45K, $45K to $50K, $50K to $60K, $60K and above. According to the U.S. Census Bureau, the current average household income in the United States is approximately $33,000 (U.S. Bureau of the Census, extrapolated based on a moving average, 1990).
- Occupation: professional, technical, managers, officials, proprietors, clerical, sales, craftpeople, farmers, retired, students, homemakers, unemployed.
- Education: grade school or less, some high school, high school, some college, college graduate, postgraduate.

PSYCHOGRAPHICS   This is the study of people's personality characteristics, social classes, and life-styles as exhibited in their attitudes, interests, and opinions (AIO). Basically, what they like to do, how they occupy their time, and what they think of themselves and various issues. These characteristics may not be directly related to their preference for a certain type of product. They are used primarily to help decide what products and services this type of person most likely would purchase, and to provide information for the creation of promotions to which the target customers can relate. For example, marketers must determine whether customers are outgoing, active, and sportsminded, or family-oriented and conservative, then consider these issues in decisions on food and beverages, the personality of its employees, and its advertising. The fact that men who drink beer tend to like sports and women had at one time a considerable impact on beer commercials. This was followed by a period where advertisements took on a tone less demeaning to women. Since the Ritz-Carlton knows that its customers are generally conservative, they train employees to be dignified and formal in their appearance, manners, and language. Marketing firms, such as Simmons Market Research Bureau, Inc., are starting to measure the *affinity* of their readers, listeners, and viewers toward various media. It was found that there is a direct relationship between audience loyalty and advertising effectiveness. The higher the level of affinity, the more likely they are to read, listen to, or watch advertising; believe in the message, and buy the product or service. One media vehicle with a high affinity is MTV. While most television audiences are either ignoring or taking a break during commercials, MTV viewers are inclined to closely watch commercials to learn about the latest trends in fashion and food and their culture. Figures 5.4, 5.5, and 5.6 provide some common forms of analysis of customers' personality, social class, and life-style characteristics.

BUYER BEHAVIOR   There are a number of possible means of segmenting consumers based on their behavior. The most relevant for the hospitality industry concern usage and consumption patterns, brand loyalty, general attitudes, and benefits sought (e.g., price sensitivity and elasticity, quality and value sensitivity, and speed of service). This is possibly the most important category of segmentation, because of its value in identifying actual purchase behavior (Peter & Donnelly, 1991). While psychographics exposes general attitudes and personality characteristics that may lead to a purchase decision, buyer behavior concerns the customer's specific attitudes and actions related to the evaluation and purchase of a particular product or

---

Affectionate, warm, loving, caring people, appreciate a compatible attitude on part of people with whom they come in contact.

Conservative, do not like change, generally a serious attitude toward life, concerned with image and formality.

Dogmatism, an unchangeable attitude, based on the assumption of absolute truth.

Egocentric, concerned with themselves before most anything else, style conscious in most purchases (clothing, restaurants, and hotels), appreciate being the center of attention and catered to.

Extroverts, want to see and be seen, preferably at "in" places; most every sensory factor should be exciting or dramatic in some way.

Impulsive, purchases made based on how they feel at the moment, little thought of needs, concerned with wants and possibly materialism.

Introverts, prefer quiet, sedate atmosphere that offers a degree of privacy.

Liberal, broad-minded, accepting of new and different things, generally easy to please, do not get upset over minor inconveniences, concerned about the environment.

Penny-pinchers, do not spend money without absolute need, make sure they get their money's worth.

Pioneers, tending to be first to try something. (In descending order, the classifications for a person's propensity to purchase a new product or service are innovators, early adopters, early majority, late majority, and laggards.)

Planners, to varying degrees fastidious in preparing for trips and evenings out, make reservations well ahead of average consumer.

Self-assured, confident, do not need social acceptance of actions, buy based on what is best for the situation, analytical more than emotional.

Risk takers, tendency to try something that represents a gamble; for example, a vacation at a new resort could be a $2000 risk.

Figure 5.4 Personality characteristics.

Upper-upper class—less than 1%; inherited wealth; consumption patterns are imitated by others
Lower-upper class—2%; high income through exceptional ability in professions or business; otherwise similar to upper-upper class.
Upper-middle class—12%; neither family status or unusual wealth; concerned with career; civic minded; like entertaining.
Middle class—32%; average pay; white and blue collar; own homes; want children to have worthwhile experiences and go to college
Working class—38%; average pay; blue-collar workers that lead a "working class life-style," whatever their income, school background, or job; sharper sex-role divisions and stereotyping
Upper-lower class—9%; working, not on welfare; living standards just above poverty; unskilled work for poor pay; educationally deficient.
Lower-lower class—7%; on welfare; visibly poverty-stricken; usually out of work

Figure 5.5   Social classes. *Source:* Adapted with permission from Kotler & Armstrong (1990), *Marketing, An Introduction,* 2nd ed. Englewood Cliffs, NJ: Prentice-Hall, p. 149.

ACTIVITIES	INTERESTS	OPINIONS
Work	Family	Self
Hobbies	Home	Social issues
Social events	Job	Politics
Vacation	Community	Business
Entertainment	Recreation	Economics
Club membership	Fashion	Education
Community	Food	Products
Shopping	Media	Future
Watching sports	Achievements	Culture
Participation in sporting activities	Music	Religion
Relaxation	Latest trends	Decor and design

Figure 5.6   Life-style dimensions. *Source:* Adapted with permission from Kotler & Armstrong (1990), *Marketing, An Introduction,* 2nd ed. Englewood Cliffs, NJ: Prentice-Hall.

service. The analysis of customer attitudes and preferences will begin to expose possible changes that should be considered for products and services, and other marketing mix variables. A guiding objective in the description of customers' behavior in each category is the identification of their "hot button"—what it is that motivates them to act. This identification will come from an analysis of the entire profile of the customer (the four bases of segmentation). Buyer behavior is generally analyzed according to the following categories.

FREQUENCY OF USE   This is based on how often customers use a business's product; they are generally categorized as *heavy, medium,* and *light users.* The goal is to identify the characteristics of the groups that purchase a proportionately greater amount of a product or service or visit a business more frequently than other groups. These groups will usually be the business's target customers. If one group proportionally purchases twice as much of a company's products and services as another group, then promotional dollars spent on that group will likely be twice as effective. In many fast-food markets, one-eighth of the population accounts for almost three-quarters of all transactions. These heavy users tend to be 18- to 24-year-old males, often students. Frequency of use segmentation is what has driven the proliferation of frequent-flier, guest, and diner programs (Reid, 1989). If a group of customers are heavy users, then the business should do whatever it reasonably can to attract and keep them. Upscale restaurants will be focusing their efforts on customers that spend $15 to $20 or more per person for lunch, $30 or more for dinner, and dine at restaurants a minimum of five times per week—heavy users. Light users, who will visit an upscale restaurant once or twice per year, will be welcomed but generally will not merit menu changes or a large percentage of the marketing department's budget. Many hotels find that a high percentage of their business comes from companies in certain industries, or from major businesses, such as those in the Fortune 500. In Texas, oil companies will provide some hotels with 20% to 30% of their occupancy. In certain areas of California, electronics firms are a major target segment for hotels.

OCCASIONS FOR USE OR CONSUMPTION PATTERNS   These are the occasions or times that identifiable groups are most likely to patronize a business—breakfast, lunch, dinner, late night, Friday or Saturday only, special occasions, more often during the summer, less often during December, weekdays only, weekends, and so forth. In many Southern states, for example, hotel occupancy rates are highest during their mild winters and lowest during hot and humid summer months. One objective of segmentation for these hotels is to find groups that are willing to bear the heat of the summer in exchange for discounted rates on rooms or, meeting space. Northern cities may find just the opposite to be true. Often, a restaurant will have entirely different target customers for lunch than for dinner. For example, many popular casual dining restaurants cater to 25- to 45-year-old businesspeople for lunch and 21- to 30-year old singles at night. Occasion segmentation may also assist in locating groups of whom the business was previously unaware. A value-oriented restaurant that is near a night club district may find a sizable demand for late-night dining. Even though customers have been going out for dinner in large numbers, many are purchasing their food in restaurants for consumption at home, known as *home meal replacement*. Eighty percent of the fast-food pizza dinner business consists of off-premise dining (drive-thru, carry out, or delivery) Sandelman & Associates, 1994).

The special occasion market, such as birthdays and anniversaries, for upscale restaurants is quickly gaining ground. One of the reasons for this is that as people have been eating out more frequently, they do not want to go to one of their regular places for the celebration. Many hotels are increasing their business for small banquets by capitalizing on the fact that companies have become more focused on providing their employees with quality, out-of-the-norm experiences.

BRAND LOYALTY   The degree of customer loyalty to one's business and that of competitors will greatly affect potential sales volume. If a business is competing in a certain market, it must attempt to measure and compare the loyalty of its customers in the trade area to that of its primary competitors. Loyalty is usually measured based on frequency of visits during a certain time period compared to competitors' experiences. For example, if a survey shows that the average customer dines at the restaurant three times per month and has an average of 12 dining experiences per month, then the *loyalty factor* would be 25 (i.e., $3 \div 12 = 0.25$; $0.25 \times 100 = 25$). This formula can be applied to all restaurants or hotels as in the above example or only to those considered as primary competitors. If customers are extremely loyal to a competitor, then this will seriously impact the business's strategy selection. These customers will require a much more refined strategy or an extremely attractive offer: a simple ad will not suffice. Generally, a combination of tactics such as special meals, discounts, an extra night free, and promotional incentives, such as a Cross pen, umbrellas, T-shirts, and baseball caps, may be necessary to entice them to change brands.

GENERAL ATTITUDES   These consist of the positive and negative attitudes people have about dining, staying in hotels, and traveling. There will always be certain problems that are inherent in traveling or dining. Through research, those problems should be identified and analyzed for importance. Finding solutions to people's problems can be a great source of opportunities. Depending on its effect on business, not acting on consumers' sources of problems can lead to potential loss of business—a threat. For example, significant opportunities and threats were uncovered in the Excedrin Travel Headache Report, a survey of 750 adults (Traveling Can Be a Big Headache, 1992):

Sitting too long in one position	72.9%
Road construction	69.5%
Lack of legroom	47.3%
Fed up with fast food	45.8%
Cutting it too close	45.6%
Need for fresh air	40.2%
Canceled or delayed flight	39.8%
Tired of traveling	38.5%

Are we there yet, Mom and Dad?	36.2%
Too much luggage	36.1%
Stale-and-smoky hotel room	34.1%
I'm lost	33.6%
Brought wrong clothes	32.4%
Desperate for home cooking	31.3%
Who do I tip and how much?	31%
State trooper in the rearview mirror	29.8%
Forgotten toothbrush/necessities	27.6%
Lost luggage	26.4%
Carry-on luggage bin is full	25.6%
Out of money	25.3%
Car problems	21.2%
Out of film/broken camera	15.9%
Motion sickness	15.8%
Eating alone	14.5%
Forgotten wakeup call	10.7%
Out of gas	8.4%
Rental car broke down	7.2%

ATTRIBUTES (OR BENEFITS) SOUGHT   Discovering what attributes customers desire can help lead to a better understanding of how a firm's current marketing mix variables match up to its environment, and what changes should be considered. Attributes can be composed of simple or complex concepts. A customer may mention the desire for larger portions but that same customer may not be willing to volunteer or express the fact that he/she wants to be shown respect or is seeking status more than anything else. Customers of fine dining restaurants may be motivated by the desire for great food, service, or ambiance. They may also be seeking status of one form or another, such as aspiring to belong to a higher social class or just to experience the rewards of their financial success. On a simpler level, customers may be seeking certain product attributes, some of which may currently be offered, while others may be unmet wants. For example, would a restaurant's customers want a grilled fish sandwich or a 5-ounce instead of a 4-ounce chicken breast? Would they be willing to pay 50¢ extra for the extra ounce of chicken? Are they willing to sacrifice some services in exchange for quicker meals? What are their preferences for items such as plastic or stainless steel silverware, a drive-thru window, homemade bread, heart-healthy menu items, fresh or frozen fish, and so on? A hotel might consider a concierge, shuttle service to additional locations, faster service times or better-quality food for room service, upgrading food quality, adding fresh bread, homemade cookies, a workout room, and so forth. The firm that comes closest to offering the benefits customers seek will rule its territory.

If management knows that a large proportion of various target customer groups seek certain attributes in a restaurant or hotel, it should contemplate incorporating them into the business. If a new restaurant surveyed potential target customers in its trade area and found that 60% of them wanted good home-style food at reasonable prices in a comfortable environment, this should be considered in the restaurant's plans. Depending on the percentage of business from foreign countries, perhaps food and beverages, amenities, or various services indigenous to that country could be considered. Many California hotels have been adding Asian newspapers, beer and wine, entrees, kimonos, and teapots to make Pacific Rim guests feel more at home.

PRICE SENSITIVITY AND ELASTICITY   The range of prices that potential segments are willing to pay for a business's product must be considered. What change in sales will result from a certain change in price? For example, in most cases, the lower a person's income, the more sensitive he/she will be to an increase or decrease in price—somewhat elastic. Fast-food customers are sensitive to changes in price and, consequently, are relatively elastic—changes in price will produce relatively proportionate changes in product demand. The midscale to upscale market for both hotels and restaurants is relatively inelastic—changes in price will not produce proportionate changes in sales volume.

Related to price is the need to consider the relative value of one's product offering. This is sometimes termed *relative perceived value* (RPV). *Value* is the perception that you are getting your money's worth. *Quality* is the ability to satisfy a customer's requirements or meet or even exceed the customer's expectations. Customers in the budget market look first for value, placing quality second. Midscale customers tend to balance the two. Upscale markets generally consider quality to be extremely important, much more so than price. In fact, occasionally, an inflated or exorbitant price will be a key attribute (status) and represent a value. "I eat at Windows on the World several times a year." "When I travel I always stay at the Ritz-Carlton." Value, in the traditional quality/price sense—getting a lot for the money—for this group tends to become important primarily for major purchases, such as cars or homes.

SPEED OF SERVICE   This concerns any time in a hospitality business that the customer must wait for a product or service: waiting to be seated, for a server to appear, for food to be delivered, or for the check in a restaurant to be delivered; the time spent checking in or out of a hotel, waiting for room service or for an elevator, and any other occasion where a customer must spend unproductive time. As constraints on personal time increase, the speed of service for all segments of the hospitality business will increase. Twenty years ago, a three- or four-minute wait in a fast-food restaurant was tolerable. Today, anything over one minute seems too long. A few years ago, Church's Fried Chicken had a goal of transacting an order in 22 seconds. Casual dining concepts have realized that speeding up service not only helps to meet the demands of the customer for speed but also increases table turnover, the number of customers that can be served within any given time span. Since competition has forced most people to work longer hours, time has become a more valuable commodity, forcing even upscale restaurants and hotels to begin focusing on shortening service times or at least offering options to guests in a hurry.

In many cases, such as during lunch time at a busy restaurant or Tuesday afternoon check-in for some hotels, customers will be required to wait in line. When this occurs, management must learn as much as possible about the time customers are waiting, and what can be done about it. Essentially, there are two ways of handling it;

1. *Operations management* — speeding up to shorten the actual time. This could be through automation, better design of work flow, faster people, better or additional training, or having the customer or an employee complete some of the work—a food order or registration card, for example—before the customer gets to the front of the line.
2. *Perceptions management* — reducing customers' perception of the amount of time they are waiting (also known as queue psychology) (Katz, Larson, & Larson, 1991).

David Maister developed the following principles that influence customers' satisfaction regarding the amount of time they wait in line (adapted from Katz, Larson, & Larson, *Sloan Management Review,* Winter 1991):

Unoccupied time feels longer than occupied time.
Preprocess waits (buying a ticket) feel longer than in-process waits (waiting for the product or service).
Anxiety makes waits seem longer.
Uncertain waits seem longer than known, finite waits.
Shorter-than-expected waits elicit appreciation.
Unexplained waits seem longer than explained waits.
Unfair waits seem longer than equitable waits.
The more valuable the service, the longer people will wait.
Solo waiting feels longer than group waiting.

Because of these principles, it is common for restaurants to overestimate the amount of time that a customer will have to wait. An expected 20-minute wait that turns out to be 15 minutes seems shorter than an expected 10-minute wait that turns out to be 15 minutes. At Disney World, in Orlando, Florida, customers willingly wait in line for 20 minutes or longer for a three- to five-minute ride because they are kept busy through being exposed to views of the ride, people having fun, and other attractions and activities.*

STAGES OF BUYER BEHAVIOR   Technically, a consumer goes through five stages before making the decision to purchase a particular item (Kotler & Armstrong, 1990).

1. *Problem Recognition.* The person is sufficiently motivated to satisfy a need. A *need* is a state of felt deprivation, something that would be very difficult to do without. Typical needs are for food and water, shelter, clothing, status, sense of belonging, and love. The recognition of a need is strongly influenced by internal or

*In America, the term *queue,* or *queuing,* is used in production engineering (efficiency experts) and marketing. In many other parts of the world, especially England and Europe, the term "queuing" has similar meanings but is also commonly used instead of the term "waiting in line." "I've been queuing for 20 minutes."

personal factors, as opposed to external factors. Needs related to food can be explained by many theories, including the peripheral and central theories. *Peripheral theories* hold that body functions outside the central nervous system, such as contractions of the stomach and a dry mouth, are the motivating factors controlling hunger and thirst. *Central theories* focus on the concept that parts of the brain control a human's motivation for food and drink. Related to central theories are those that stress that specific hungers for certain components of food, such as fat, carbohydrates, protein, minerals, and vitamins, can be triggered by dietary deficiencies (Beck, 1990).

2. *Information Search.* The information search will be influenced by the consumer's wants. A *want* is a need that is influenced by the personal characteristics of the consumer. These include personality, age, occupation, social class, culture, and the opinion of their reference group(s). (*Reference groups* are the people that influence a consumer.) If the want is for an item that is purchased frequently and is relatively inexpensive, such as convenience goods or some shopping goods (defined below), there may not be much need for additional information. If the want is for a shopping product they have little experience with, or for a specialty product, then more information may be necessary. (*Convenience goods* are relatively inexpensive items that are purchased frequently, without much consideration to quality or cost, such as fast food or an economy hotel. *Shopping goods* are those that the average consumer will compare based on differences in its quality or features and price including casual dining restaurants and midscale hotels. *Specialty goods* are those that the customer is willing to make a special effort to attain, for example, fine dining restaurants and luxury hotels.) Generally, the more expensive the purchase relative to the consumer's income or available funds, the more consideration or information the consumer will seek. If the consumer requires additional information, he/she can get it from several possible sources: *personal sources,* such as family, friends, co-workers, acquaintances, and prior purchases or examination; *nonpersonal sources,* such as advertising, reviews, and travel agents.

Of all means of gathering information the strongest influence is from people the consumer trusts, such as family, friends, and personal acquaintances. This is because advertising or most types of promotion communicate messages from people who have a vested interest in the sale of the product or service. When the endorsement is from a person who does not have a vested interest, the level of trust in the opinion is heightened. This is known as a *third-party endorsement,* or *word-of-mouth advertising.* This is why the greater the level of trustworthiness of a commercial spokesperson, the more likely target customers are to feel positive about and be influenced by what is said.

3. *Evaluation of Alternatives.* The search for information has turned up several possible choices; now the consumer must decide between them. There is no set pattern that every consumer will use to evaluate a product before making a purchase decision. Sometimes, it may be on an impulse; other times, the purchase will be made only after considerable study.

The basic process is that the consumer will first compare attributes of the product, such as the technical attributes, those that can be touched, smelled, or tasted, and the human side or experiential attributes that relate to how the product makes the customer feel. *Brand beliefs,* customers' subconscious and conscious beliefs about particular brands, such as Friday's and Steak And Ale, or the Marriott and the Hyatt, will influence brand comparisons and choice.

Consumers will then compare the differences between the product's or service's attributes to decide how important each is, how closely each comes to meeting their needs and wants, and which of the attributes will matter in the final decision. Does a particular product satisfy consumers' desire for a great experience, or is the most important attribute more utilitarian, such as needing an economically priced place to spend the night?

4. *Purchase Decision.* At this point, the consumer is now ready to make a decision and purchase the product or service that has been evaluated. Frequently, there may be *intervening factors,* such as the attitudes of others, risk perception, or unexpected situational factors, that alter or stop the process (Kotler & Armstrong, 1990). If the choice is between two different restaurants, a friend may be the one to make the actual decision on which to visit. In addition to physiological motivations discussed in problem recognition, there are external cues that can stimulate humans to eat or drink. Sometimes, people eat because they are with others who are eating. Other times, people eat because they are bored or are trying to fill a void in their life.

If there is some degree of risk attached to one of the alternatives, then the one that minimizes the consumer's risk will be selected. This is why it is critical for businesses to examine the perceived risks they represent to their target customers and reduce them in some way. Perhaps they can reduce the uncertainty through advertising and public relations, or through improvements in operational performance. *Unexpected situational factors,* such as a friend saying that a particular restaurant is not worth the price or that another is much better, or not getting a raise or losing a job, could influence the consumer to modify, postpone, or avoid the purchase (Peter & Donnelly, 1991).

When comsumer need reaches a level where it must be satisfied, customers will then decide what will satisfy the need (what they want), then make a purchase (what they demand). In marketing terminology, the purchase is referred to as demand. *Demand* occurs when wants are backed by dollars. For example, travelers may need a place to stay and may want to stay at the Four Seasons Hotel, but budgetary constraints require them to demand the Holiday Inn.

5. *Postpurchase Behavior.* This is a combination of the consumer's feelings after the product has been purchased. If the product met or exceeded expectations (satisfied the need and want), the response or purchase will be remembered as a positive experience and will likely be repeated in the future. The consumer's expectations for the product will be influenced by reference groups and claims made by the business. This is why it is dangerous to raise the expectations of potential customers through biased statements. The higher the customer's expectations, the more difficult it will be to meet them. An advertising adage that has much merit is "underpromise and overdeliver."

If the product is repeatedly purchased with positive results, or, even better, if the firm's product exceeded expectations, then a sense of loyalty to the business may develop. This is one of the reasons why businesses that are first on the scene with a product tend to continue to do well, and why high volume tends to perpetuate itself. Customers are creatures of habit, making it difficult for competing firms to alter their feelings of loyalty (Peter & Donnelly, 1991). Postpurchase feelings will also influence the consumer's interpersonal discussions with family, friends, and acquaintances. The level of satisfaction will result in positive or negative work-of-mouth advertising.

Another concept that businesses must be concerned with is that of *cognitive dissonance* (also known as *postpurchase anxiety*). This is the feeling of doubt or second thoughts after a purchase. Cognitive dissonance is especially common after a financially or psychologically important purchase. The product may have exceeded the customer's expectations, but there is the feeling that another alternative may have been a better choice. A vacationer may have had a wonderful time in Cancun but might wonder if Cozumel would have been better. When dissonance occurs, customers may attempt to reduce it by one or more of the following actions (Peter & Donnelly, 1991):

1. By seeking information that supports the intelligence of their decision
2. By perceiving information in a manner that supports their decision
3. By deciding that alternative products were not preferable to the one selected
4. By minimizing the negative aspects of the purchase and focusing on those that are positive
5. By seeking satisfaction through a product substitution, reduction in price, or a refund

RETURN CUSTOMERS   In the skirmish for customers, the central concern for the business is to keep its current regular customers and to attract enough of its competitors' customers or new customers to increase sales and replace regular customers that are lost. Saying that the regular customer is the most valuable asset of any business is somewhat elementary, but this is based on the fundamental concept that customers are the entity that gives the business the nutrients necessary for its life and growth. What is not always made clear is the secondary effects of dealing with regular rather than with new customers. Because the regular customer is familiar with how the business operates, less time is required to explain ordering procedures, or how long something will take, or where something is located. This customer also feels more at home and relaxed, so he/she will be more likely to enjoy the experience. Finally, the regular customer is much less costly to attract than new customers and is great for word-of-mouth advertising.

Competitor Analysis

The key activities of business are no different from those of any sport or game. Individuals or teams of players physically and mentally compete with one another to attain quantitative objectives through qualitative effort. Their success is based on their specific abilities, knowledge of the game, strategies they develop and implement, and the abilities of their opponents. An opponent's weaknesses that can be attacked with a strength may represent viable opportunities, while the opponent's strength may represent threats. In most games, the stronger competitor will generally win, but, as they say in the National Football League, "on any given day, any team can beat another." Since each team will compete with the same rules, and on the same field, a team's success will depend on its planning and implementational abilities relative to its competitors. All characteristics, including the abilities of the players and the effective formulation and implementation of the coach's strategies, must be viewed from the context of advantages they represent over competitors. Talented players that are well-coached will outscore opponents the vast majority of the time. Less-talented players with a minimal number of relative strengths or excellent strategies may not dominate all opponents, but they will win a reasonable share of their games. The three critical research components for the setting of competitive strategies are thorough analysis and understanding of the organization's abilities, customers, and notable competitors. It must be stressed that while the primary focus of strategic marketing planning will always be the customer, much can be learned from an increased emphasis on one's competitors.

THE COMPETITIVE FIELD   Every business operates within an environment consisting of remote factors, such as political regulations, the economy, societal trends, and technology; and operating factors; such as personnel (availability, quality, and cost), ecological trends, customers, competitors, suppliers, and creditors. All means of traversing the competitive field that lead to organizational goals pass through one of the most critical environmental components—the firm's competitors. All research and every analysis, strategy, and action must be considered in light of what competing firms are doing. Tom Peters, of *In Search of Excellence* fame, says that companies should seek the highest possible *relative perceived product quality* (RPPQ) (Peters & Townsend, 1986). What this suggests is that a primary goal of businesses should be to be better than the competition in critical product and service attributes. This sounds logical. After all, how many successful long-term competitors try to be average? They certainly do not try to be average for their segment of the market or when compared with primary competitors.

This further implies that most actions of the firm should be supportive of a high RPPQ. Since many of the important actions of a firm are formulated in the context of competitors' strategies and actions, the firm must have an organized process to analyze its competitors. How can a firm have a high RPPQ without knowing the level of its competitors' RPPQ? A firm may be able to occasionally outscore a competitor with minimal information about them; to do it consistently, the firm must know the level it is trying to surpass. Playing a game without knowing a competitor's score makes it difficult to judge how well one's team is doing.

RPPQ and the Strategic Planning Process

All primary activities of strategic planning—internal (company) analysis, customer analysis, secondary environmental concerns (all environmental factors except customers and competitors), a strategy formulation, and strategy implementation—must past the test of RPPQ or the customer's perception of competitors' products

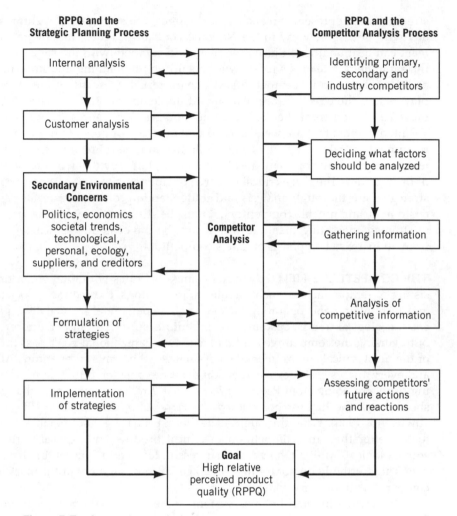

**RPPQ and the
Strategic Planning Process**

**RPPQ and the
Competitor Analysis Process**

Figure 5.7   Competitor analysis.

and services (see Figure 5.7). This means that all key analyses and actions of the firm must be cast in light of the abilities of the firm's competitors. In the following section, each of these five areas will be discussed from the context of RPPQ; later, a competitor analysis process will be offered to help support a firm's existing information or intelligence gathering systems (see right side of Figure 5.7).

RPPQ AND THE INTERNAL ANALYSIS   Not knowing the specific abilities of one's firm is akin to not knowing whether one's football team should be playing recreational, semiprofessional, or professional football. Management must complete an objective analysis of its strategic internal factors before it can decide what strategies it can or cannot implement, and with whom it can compete. The categorization of the firm's abilities, generally recognized as strengths or weaknesses, will, of course, be somewhat subjective, but the key parameter used to guide much of the classification will be RPPQ. How do customers perceive the attribute compared with that of competitors? For areas such as financial flexibility and profitability, which customers cannot directly compare, the firm must make an objective appraisal of its comparative (relative) performance or ability. (These will also be the areas where it may be difficult to assess the abilities of competitors.)

RPPQ AND THE CUSTOMER ANALYSIS   A major goal of any business is the satisfaction of the business's target market and the individual customers within it. Each market has a relatively stable amount of money that will be spent on any given product or service. This means that the degree of success of any business will be measured by the number of dollars attracted from the particular market. Although all factors in the firm's environment will affect its ability to attract dollars from a given market, none will affect it more than the company's competitors and their particular level of RPPQ.

Historically, the hospitality market was a near-ideal world without major competitors. Until the 1950s and 1960s, and, for smaller towns, the 1960s and 1970s, there was a small selection of primarily independent competitors for each market. For example, for restaurants, there were a few steak houses and diners, a number of independent burger stands, and family-style fried chicken restaurants. This limited competition allowed a firm with an average quality product to do quite well. This was because there were few competitors with which to compare a firm's product. RPPQ was based on a limited number of competitors. In many cases, the comparison was not between commercial competitors, but between one's business and the need to get Mom out of the non-air-conditioned kitchen.

The problem is that the world is no longer so wonderful or serene. The more success a company had, the more attractive their market segment became. As aggressive competitors invaded the market, RPPQ entered customers' minds, causing them to remove below average and, in some cases, average quality firms from their mental list of viable options.

Attracting and retaining the target customer are best stated by the definition of the marketing concept: determining the needs and wants of customers, then satisfying those needs better than competitors (Kotler & Armstrong, 1990). Sound familiar? Yes, this is RPPQ. To compete under the marketing concept, the firm must develop an in-depth and detailed analysis of the characteristics of the firm's target customers; know what its abilities are related to those characteristics; develop effective strategies for attracting the target customers; then effectively implement those strategies so well that customers have little desire, other than an occasional change of pace, to visit competitors (see Figure 5.8). The overriding concern in each of these requirements, and in the definition of the marketing concept, is that the business must do a better job of satisfying its customers than competitors. As a company must have detailed information about itself and its target customer, it must also know every detail possible about the businesses with which it competes.

Every restaurant and hotel competes first on its key attributes—those deemed

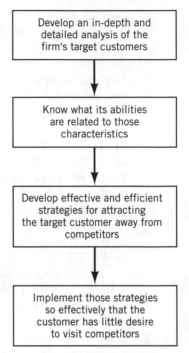

Figure 5.8 Competing under the marketing concept.

most important by the customer. These include abilities and characteristics such as the business's quality of food, quality of service, price–value relationship, atmosphere and furnishing, location, and image. (Key attributes are sometimes divided into the core product—the basic requirement that the business satisfies, such as the satisfaction of hunger and a place to sleep; and the formal or actual product—the tangible and intangible attributes that the customer purchases.) Here is where each business must carefully examine its offering and that of its competitors to be sure that target customers perceive its offering to be the best, one of the best, or at least a viable option. When the situation arises that most of the key attributes are quite similar, then the difference will most often be the quality of service delivered by the business's employees. The reason for this is that it is easier to control repetitive non-customer-contact actions than attitude, personality, and courtesy. Many restaurants have exceptional food; fewer have exceptional service. Likewise, most hotels in each market segment have somewhat similar facilities, so the firm's people and their performance are ultimately the key points of differentiation between competitors. RPPQ for employees? Sure! Service is the main product of the hospitality industry. If customers are satisfied with the service they receive at one hotel, they will be unlikely to spend much time searching for an alternative because of the risk involved in switching brands. This would especially be true if the decision was being made by a corporate meeting planner whose firm was satisfied with the hotel's performance at recent meetings or conventions. Cadotte and Turgeon (1988) conducted an extensive survey, which showed that of the top ten customer attributes that garnered compliments, 50% were service-driven for hotels while 40% were service-driven for restaurants.

After the customer compares key attributes, secondary attributes (sometimes referred to as the business's augmented product) are analyzed. These are generally confined to services that support the formal product. They include such things as acceptance of credit cards, billing services, a travel agency in the hotel, a gift shop, secretarial or business services, fax machines, convenient reservation system, guarantees, concierge, personal attendant during functions, child care, exercise facilities, and incentives such as gifts or frequent-guest programs. Secondary attributes are an extremely rich source of competitive advantage. While most competitors are justifiably focusing on key attributes, a firm can emphasize a secondary attribute as a point of differentiation. This could, in turn, lead to the business being recognized as a leader in customer service.

SECONDARY ENVIRONMENTAL FACTORS For every business, the customer and competitors will garner the majority of concern. The remaining factors of the operating environment and the remote environment that the business must deal with will be similar for most businesses within any industry segment and specific geographic area. However, their effect will be based on specific abilities and characteristics that allow the firm to deal with each factor.

FORMULATION OF STRATEGIES For the hospitality industry, setting competitive strategies, and therefore competing, is somewhat simpler than it is in the manufacturing industry. The reason for this is that it can be assumed with some certainty that present and future customers will need hotels to stay at when they travel, and restaurants to patronize when dining out or ordering for delivery. Luckily for the industry, it is rare for a business to come along with a product so innovative that it renders another's obsolete. It is also relatively uncommon for a competitor to develop a new strategy that could force competing firms to make major changes in current strategies. However, it does occur, as when Taco Bell forced most fast-food competitors to follow its lead of value pricing and nutritious low-fat fast-food. This analysis does not minimize the importance of setting competitive strategies for the hospitality industry; it only illustrates the fact that, while important, competitive strategies rarely have the near immediate life-or-death characteristics they take on in the manufacturing industry.

Hospitality strategies are usually based on the success of past strategies. If a strategy is successful and the premise on which it was based—the abilities of the company and the environment—has not radically changed, then the same or a similar strategy should generally be continued. The vast majority of hospitality strategies are tried-and-true variations of past winners. If a viable strategy was not successful, then the roadblocks to its success must be sought. Perhaps the strategy was not well thought out, or it was not implemented effectively. In any case, if it is felt that the strategy, its objective, or the environmental concern (external environment) are important to the success of the business, then a revised strategy should probably be set (all in the context of RPPQ).

Technically, in marketing, the ideas for potentially desired strategies come first from the customer. Since few organizations have the skills or initiative to analyze customer trends enough to forecast unmet wants or major product gaps, most new strategies evolve from proactive risk-takers. In the average case, an independent operator had a hunch or a customer recommended something. The pursuant strategy was a successful, so others copied it. Competitors are not only a yardstick against which to measure success, but they also supply many of the new ideas that keep a business vital and strong. Management must be careful not to use too many ideas from any one business. This could be construed as a *trade dress* violation. This occurs when one business has several unique characteristics that when combined may become protectable by civil law.

IMPLEMENTATION OF STRATEGIES   The previously mentioned small competitive advantage over manufacturing industries is neutralized by the fact that the execution of service-based strategies, by nature of their heavy dependence on labor, is more difficult to orchestrate. A hospitality firm must make sure that it keeps up with or, ideally, surpasses its competitors in the implementation of a reasonable number of strategic internal factors, or critical facets of the business (a higher RPPQ in important areas). The cliches of being number one or being the best are more than trite philosophies, because the customer *is* searching for the number one or best place to spend his/her money. If when analyzing the differences between the company's and a competitor's offering, at least one or more attributes do not stand out as being as good as or better than the competition, then it can easily be understood why the customer selects a competitor. Generally, the more glaring the difference in strategic internal factors, the more likely a customer will notice and patronize the better of the choices.

Competitor Analysis Process

Hospitality firms must develop reasonably sophisticated competitor analysis processes or systems, not only to keep up with competitors' current strategies but also to project with reasonable accuracy what a competitor might do in the future. Failure to do so could result in substantial losses of sales and profit, if not the demise of the business. An effective intelligence gathering system should be at the base of all key strategy decisions (Porter, 1980). How could a firm decide whether to add a certain product or service without first finding out whether competitors are offering it and customers have embraced it? According to Herring (1991), very few American companies have fully developed competitive intelligence systems, and almost two-thirds have either no system or one that is not organized. Most collect information haphazardly and act on the basis of impressions and intuition, rather than a thorough competitor analysis. On the positive side, there was a commitment by a majority of the firms to increase their efforts. Companies headquartered in foreign countries, on the contrary, tend to have detailed competitive intelligence systems, along with selected strategies of acquiring language skills and increasing global experience.

Since the hospitality industry is nearing saturation in many of its markets, the ability to formulate effective competitive strategies will dictate success. This can come only from an ongoing information gathering system that accumulates competitive intelligence.*

The basic steps in implementing and preparing the analysis consist of the following:

- Deciding who the competitors are
- Deciding which factors are strategic to the competitive situation and analysis
- Gathering competitive information
- Analyzing how competitors' past and present strategies affect relative perceived product quality
- Determining competitors' future strategies and their potential reactions to offensive strategies

The goal of the process is to assist the firm in strategy formulation by uncovering how competitors are currently positioned, and where they might be headed in the future.

IDENTIFYING COMPETITORS   The business's relative perceived product quality (RPPQ) is measured against alternative choices. Each business must determine who its competitors are and to what degree they might affect a customer's perception relative to one's product or services. Most hospitality businesses must be concerned with primary and secondary competitors and the industry in which they compete. Another perspective is gained by viewing customers, suppliers (Porter, 1980), and personnel as additional forces affecting competition.

Primary Competitors   Each business will have one or more customer segments toward which it targets the majority of its marketing efforts. Other businesses in competition for these customers are generally considered to be primary competitors. Basically, these are businesses that compete for the same target customer, with the same or a similar product or service, in the same trade area, for the same occasion. This grouping will provide the business with the most accurate comparison of competitive strategies and performance, without having to contend with the complexity of the industry as a whole (Bogner & Thomas, 1993). They are, therefore, the group with which a business must be most concerned. Chili's, Friday's, and Bennigan's in a certain trade area will usually be primary competitors, as will Hilton, Marriott, and Sheraton hotels.

Not all primary competitors will have identical target customer groups. Some will have several of the same target customer groups but will also have target groups that are quite different. For example, normally, any particular Hilton hotel and Marriott hotel could be considered as primary competitors. Upon closer analysis, because of differences in location, recreational facilities, meeting space, and other features, it can be shown that while these two hypothetical hotels may be primary competitors for a few markets, they may not be primary competitors for one or

---

*The term *competitive intelligence* can be used interchangeably to describe a business's competitors, or general intelligence gathering from the entire environment, both remote and operating.

several substantial markets. One hotel could be located near an airport and cater primarily to transient guests and small meetings, while the hotel with extensive meeting space and recreation facilities will, in most instances, be competing fiercely for group business.

If there is any question of exactly who should be considered as a primary competitor, customers can be asked, "If you did not choose us for your meal/hotel stay, who would you have selected?" What may also be exposed by this line of questioning is the brand loyalty or preference index of one's primary competitors and of key secondary competitors.

Strategic Groups.   A subset within primary competitors is the strategic group. This is a group of firms that pursues similar competitive strategies and have similar strengths and weaknesses (Aaker, 1988). For example, if a hotel is considered to have quality catering and banquet services, its strategic group would be others in its trade area with the same strength. Because of the relative similarity of many hospitality offerings, the strategic group method of competitor segmentation is probably not used as much in the hospitality industry as it is in other industries. Generally, independent restaurants and hotels will simply focus on all primary competitors that are, for the most part, in their trade area. Chain establishments, because of their relatively small group of primary competitors, would likewise focus on all these competitors. A major advantage of the strategic group is that once the competitors are divided into their respective groups their potential actions can be evaluated more efficiently. For example, a hotel in a certain trade area has nine primary competitors. Three are focused on value, three on service, and three have large sales and advertising budgets. Rather than develop nine separate analyses, an option would be to reduce this number to three by analyzing them in their strategic groups.

Secondary Competitors   These are competitors with related (not the same or similar) products or services, viewed as alternatives by the same target customer, for the same or similar occasion—essentially, an alternative to the primary product or service needs filled by one's business. These businesses are normally in different segments of the same industry, such as fast-food and casual dining restaurants being secondary competitors to each other. Competitors in this category may or may not be located in the same trade area. For example, potential guests seeking a short getaway could consider a hotel in or near their city, or one in another location within several hours' drive or flight. A question that can be asked of customers to discover secondary competitors is, "If you were going to spend a little more or less on a meal/hotel stay, where would you go?" (Aaker, 1988). Also, since fast service is becoming more and more important for restaurants, another good question is, "If you had less time to eat, what would your choice have been?"

It is important to include at least some secondary competitors in a competitor analysis to allow an examination of their operations and learn what they do to attract customers. One can never know what opportunities could surface from the analysis of a business that was not considered as a primary competitor. For example, the primary competitors for a fast-food restaurant would be other fast-food operations in the trade area. Secondary competitors could be other types of businesses operating in the trade area that have the possibility of attracting the fast-food customer. These could include casual dining restaurants, convenience stores that sell ready-made sandwiches and other prepared items, and grocery stores with salad bars or delicatessens. By examining secondary competitors, a business can learn about attributes that customers seem to prefer but are not being offered by most primary competitors. Romano's Macaroni Grill, a Brinker International concept, has successfully combined the atmosphere of an Italian deli with that of an upscale Italian restaurant at casual dining prices.

Another reason for a business to consider secondary competitors is that each of the businesses may have the same target customers for different occasions. For example, a Hyatt (upper-midscale hotel) customer on an expense account may turn into a La Quinta (lower-midscale hotel) customer on weekends or vacations. Similarly, a McDonald's customer for lunch may become a Friday's customer for dinner. This means that, on the weekend, La Quinta is a secondary competitor of the Hyatt; for dinner, Friday's is a secondary competitor of McDonald's. Since the customer is already loyal to the business, some means of getting the customer back at other times might be considered.

The importance of the examination of and distinction between primary and secondary competitors is that the business will generally have limited resources available to pursue competitors' customers. Therefore, it should first focus its efforts in areas with the greatest potential return. Subsequent analysis can be directed at lesser rivals.

INDUSTRY COMPETITORS   The business's industry includes all firms selling related products. Here, there will be an overlapping of primary and secondary competitors and those businesses that are rarely considered in a competitor analysis. The *foodservice industry,* for example, includes all businesses that offer prepared food products, (such as fast food), casual dining and fine dining restaurants, catering and banquet services, institutional foodservice firms, and various types of foodservice outlets in grocery or warehouse-type discount stores. A broader definition of the *food industry* would consist of the aforementioned firms, plus all growers, producers, and sellers of food for personal consumption or organizational use. This would include one of the restaurants' major competitors—the grocery store. There is a constant battle between grocers and restaurateurs as to where consumers will spend their food dollar. As of the 1990 census, food purchased in foodservice establishments of all types garnered approximately 42% of the market, while food purchased for preparation and consumption in the home stood at around 58%. As income rises, the percentage of food eaten away from the home also increases. Families with household incomes above $50,000 per year spent 51% of their food dollar away from the home (U.S. Bureau of the Census, 1990). Upward trends in sales for the grocery industry tend to eventually have a detrimental effect on restaurants and vice versa.

Sales for the foodservice industry will surpass $300 billion in the late 1990s. According to Ronald N. Paul, president of Technomic, Inc., growth for chain restaurants will outpace independents (Therrien, 1993). This trend is likely to continue for some time. It is due to their much larger cash reserves, which allow the chains to upgrade existing facilities, expand locations, and acquire or initiate more accurate consumer research. For the independent operator, this means that maintaining existing profit margins will become more difficult. Of the projected increase in sales for the near future the fast-food industry is expected to account for about 45% of the future foodservice sales growth; full-service will garner about 27%, with education, business and industry, health care, retail, lodging, transportation, and recreation dividing the balance, about 28% (Bertagnoli & Chaudhry, 1994).

Coopers & Lybrand (cited in Koss, 1994) reports that hotel industry occupancy will be edging up toward the 70% plateau in the late 1990s. This information is important to all competitors in the hotel industry, but much more for chains and franchisors than for independents and franchisees. These businesses must focus more on their local or primary and secondary competitors.

MARKET SEGMENT COMPETITOR ANALYSIS   As previously discussed, most hotels and foodservice establishments compete with one another for several different target markets. For this reason, it is important to decide, at the minimum, who the business's primary and secondary competitors are for each market in which it competes. This assists the firm in deciding *how* it can best compete, or *whether* it can compete with certain businesses for any given market. For example, by knowing which hotels are in direct competition for group business, the marketing department can determine what specific attributes make the competitor a viable option for customers (see Figure 5.9). If two hotels are competing for group business, their rates,

MARKET SEGMENT	MARKET SEGMENT COMPETITORS
MISSION PARK HOTEL	
Corporate group	1. Green Hills
	2. Sonoma Valley
	3. Town Lake
	4. Great Gorge
	5. Crested Butte
GRAND CAFE	
Couples under 35 years of age	1. Willow Bend Cafe
	2. Red River Bill's
	3. Sarah's on the Lake

Figure 5.9   Market segment competitor analysis.

amount of meeting space, hotel location, the condition of their facility, and quality of service would be important attributes. A hotel's position on these attributes could lead to a variety of possible strategic choices: perhaps improvements in critical areas, rate discounts, or increases in advertising or personal selling. Restaurants could similarly be compared according to attributes such as food quality, value, service, cleanliness, and atmosphere. If the segment competitors are not immediately known, the majority of the information necessary can be derived by completing a competitor analysis. (For competitor analysis options, see Figures 5.10, 5.11, 5.12, and 5.13)

To complete the market segment competitor analysis competing hotels or restaurants are listed according to their relative strength, 1 being the strongest competitor for a given market and 5 being a less capable or weaker opponent. More competitors could be included if necessary. The decision of whether or not to list a competitor and its relative position would be somewhat subjective depending on the accuracy of the competitor analysis and knowledge of the person completing it. In some cases, a competitor may be included based on accurate statistical facts. In most cases, the information will be a group decision of the firm's marketers derived from an interpretation of or survey of customers' opinions. For example, it can reasonably be assumed that when deciding between two hotels, customers on a budget will usually select the one with the lowest rates. To allow for the greatest objectivity, the source of information that guides the decision should be known by all decision-makers.

THE FORCES OF COMPETITION   One tool used to conceptualize and analyze the various competitors within an industry is The Forces Driving Industry Competition, developed by Michael E. Porter of Harvard (1980) (see Figure 5.10). This approach broadens the view of competition by considering more than just traditional competitors in the analysis. The model has been extended to improve its applicability to the hospitality industry. Personnel have been added and industry competitors have been separated into primary and secondary competition. Rivalries among primary and secondary competitors, potential entrants, and substitute products or services (frozen dinners, home delivery) are considered in the conventional sense. Porter adds that a business must also compete with suppliers and customers. For example, while a firm will generally try to purchase supplies at the lowest possible price, suppliers are attempting to charge the highest price the market will pay. This puts the business and supplier in direct competition. Their abilities to reach individual goals will depend on their relative positions of strength. If there are many suppliers with alternative products, then the hotel or restaurant may have a good position from which to bargain. This, of course, would depend on the size of the buyer, whether or not purchasing agents were knowledgeable and experienced in their field, and their degree of organization (needs assessment, product specifications, accurate inventory, and ordering procedures). On the other hand, if there were only a few sources for a particular product, or the business and its purchasing agent lacked knowledge and experience, then the supplier would be powerful.

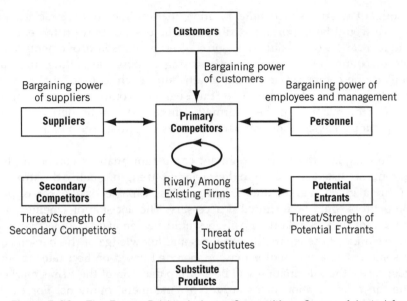

Figure 5.10 The Forces Driving Industry Competition. *Source:* Adapted from Porter (1980). *Competitive Strategy: Techniques for Analyzing Industries and Competitors.* New York: The Free Press.

Hospitality customers must likewise be considered based on their relative strength. Generally, hospitality customers can be considered as powerful competitive forces because there are many other places to which they can take their business. When competing hospitality firms within any particular market segment have similar or undifferentiated offerings, customers tend to be price sensitive and pursue the most convenient options. This weakens the bargaining position of the firm, unless it has penetrated the market with locations or delivery capability. For example, a majority of the fast-food restaurants and budget hotels or motels have undifferentiated products. This fact makes it very difficult for these competing firms to raise their prices beyond those of their primary competitors or to attract new customers without comparatively large ad budgets or incentives. This increases the likelihood of limited profit margins. As the degree of differentiation of a product or service rises (in particular, its level of quality or image), there is a tendency for the customer to focus more on quality than price. This consequently gives the firm greater bargaining power with the customers against whom it is competing.

One implication of this is that, ideally, firms should try to find suppliers and customers who have the least amount of power to influence prices. In our industry this is not always easy, but it can be pursued by creating the greatest degree of differentiation between the firm and its competitors. This is what Fuddruckers, the hamburger chain that grinds its own beef for burger patties and bakes its own buns, and Guest Quarters, the first all-suites hotel, did in their respective market segments. Each developed a concept that was unique, or differentiated from the competition, and reaped the rewards of high comparative sales and occupancies. Resorts in some areas can all but name their price. Profitability will generally be highest when a firm's relative strengths outnumber its customers' or suppliers' strengths.

To Porter's forces of industry competition the author has added the fact that most businesses also compete for personnel. The core concept of marketing states that the business must have attributes that make it attractive to customers, relative to competitors. If service—something performed by one party for another—is the hospitality business's primary offering, then people are the foundation of the hospitality experience. It follows that the business must likewise have attributes that make it a place where people would enjoy working, relative to competitors. A business's ability to attract the highest quality employees available at a reasonable cost is one of the greatest competitive advantages for hospitality businesses. Since the service industry is so labor intensive, the people within a hospitality business could theoretically be considered its main product.

Like differences in target customer groups, there will be differences in factors that make a business suitable for employment. Probably the most important personnel-related attribute is employees and management people who are happy and proud to work for a particular business. Since a large percentage of the industry's employees are young, the business's image will add significantly to its ability to attract personnel. Other factors are the quality of management, working conditions, pay and benefits, job security, opportunities for personal and career advancement, recognition, and participation in decision-making (Reich, 1990). Firms that offer many of the above attributes should be able to attract employees who will help it compete. When this is not the case, the business will end up with a high turnover percentage, marginal employees, and the many other problems that result. Among them are increases in customer complaints, labor cost, food cost, maintenance, breakage, theft, low morale, and supervision time and expense.

DECIDING WHAT FACTORS TO ANALYZE   The competitor analysis should include all reasonably attainable information about primary and secondary competitors and relevant industry information. [Factors concerning customers, suppliers, and personnel as competitors (from the forces driving competition analysis) can be included in their applicable portion of a strategic or marketing plan.] Ideally, the factors considered should be similar to an internal analysis and should contain as many of the strategic internal factors as possible (see Figure 4.7). However, because of limited access to information, it will rarely be as thorough. This section is used only to identify those factors that should be considered for analysis. The competitor's performance will be assessed later in the process. The list should, at the minimum, include the following information:

1. Unique characteristics of the competitor's customers. This would include a breakdown of various target market groups according to standard segmentation variables: geographics, demographics, psychographics, and buyer behavior.
2. Information about the competitor's strategy selection and its degree of success (generally measured as a strength or weakness). This could include areas such as

menu and service mix, price ranges for all products and services, external and internal atmosphere (layout, design, and decor), condition of facility, type of location(s), promotional media used, common promotional targets, characteristics of ads (purpose, tone, appeal), and specific operational strategies or policies (how the company logistically performs key tasks).

3. Factors that could be included separately are attributes known as *unique selling propositions* (USPs). These are characteristics of a business that are out of the ordinary, help the business stand apart from its competitors, and are appreciated or desired by target customers. Unique lighting, colors, decorations, design, in-house bakeries, exhibition kitchen, and larger-than-normal platters for entrees are examples.

GATHERING INFORMATION   Each company should gather and record data about its competitors on a regular basis. The data should be stored and appropriately organized, then incrementally added to as new data are gathered. Usually, as the quantity increases, so does the quality of inferences and implications derived from the data. Also, seemingly unimportant pieces of data, when viewed as a whole, will often uncover opportunities that present the firm with a potential strategic advantage or strategic options. The two key types of data or sources are secondary and primary, which were discussed in Chapter 3.

SURVEYS   Pertinent or problem-specific information may require a survey. A simple survey, such as shown in Figure 5.11, can help determine the standing of a firm's strengths and weaknesses compared to that of its competitors (Kotler, 1991). More formal surveys may necessitate the retaining of a marketing research firm. One means of gathering extremely detailed performance-related information on

Please rate the following businesses for each of the factors in the column on the left. 1 = poor, 2 = fair, 3 = average, 4 = good, and 5 = excellent. Circle your selection.

	TOWN LAKE HOTEL	GREEN HILLS	TOWN LAKE
Convenient location	1 2 3 4 5	1 2 3 4 5	1 2 3 4 5
Friendly employees	1 2 3 4 5	1 2 3 4 5	1 2 3 4 5
Cleanliness of restrooms	1 2 3 4 5	1 2 3 4 5	1 2 3 4 5
Quality of food	1 2 3 4 5	1 2 3 4 5	1 2 3 4 5

(Other applicable key attribute factors would be included.)
Thank you for your time.

Figure 5.11   Key attribute survey.

competitors is to have regular and trusted customers complete a customer survey for one's business and its competitors. For methods of analysis of survey data, see Figure 3.7.

MARKET SHARE REPORTS FOR HOTELS   (Also known as a *Fair Share Report*) Many hotels will exchange reasonable detailed information on sales with primary competitors in their trade area. One of the main reasons for the willingness of hotels to share this information is that it is generally available anyway through the office of the state comptroller (tax collector) (Sharp, 1993). Since everyone has access to the information, the competing hotels decide that it is easier to share than to contact the comptroller each month. In some states there are marketing firms that compile available data. The Texas Hotel Performance Factbook, published by Source Strategies, Inc. of San Antonio, includes the hotel's city and zip code, number of rooms, room revenue, average daily rate, occupancy percentage, and revenue per available room (average revenue per room). The immediate past two years are included with the percentage change for each category (Source Strategies, Inc., 1991).

Knowing whether a hotel is garnering its fair share of the market is helpful in deciding whether it is keeping up with competitors and maximizing revenues. Market share reports for a minimum of three months or more can be used to forecast future performance of market competitors. Market share is figured by first calculating the percentage of rooms that a hotel has for its segment or competing group. For example, if the Mission Park Hotel (see Table 5.1) has 305 rooms and there are a total of 1725 rooms in its group, then it has 17.68% of the available rooms (305 divided by 1725). Each hotel would then volunteer its occupancy percentage and ADR (average daily rate) for the month. If Mission Park had an occupancy percentage of 62.5%, then its market share would be 17.28%, or 0.4% below its 17.68% fair share of the available rooms (5338 divided by 30,892). The *ADR × room nights = rooms revenue* for the period. REVPAR, revenue per available room, could easily be added by multiplying the ADR by the occupancy percentage. With formulas in place in Lotus or Excel, this report will take only a few minutes per hotel to prepare. It is important that the information not be used for the discussion of establishing a market price. That might be considered price-fixing, which may be subject to civil penalties.

Table 5.1   Market Share Report by Occupancy

Hotel	Number of Rooms	Rooms Available for Month	Fair Share	Occupancy (%)	Room Nights	Market Share	Market Variance	Rank	Average Daily Rate	Rooms Revenue
Mission Park	305	8,540	17.68%	62.50%	5,338	17.28%	- 0.40%	4	$62.21	$332,046
Green Hills	422	11,816	24.46%	68.40%	8,082	26.16%	1.70%	1	$64.29	$519,601
Sonoma Valley	340	9,520	19.71%	66.30%	6,312	20.43%	0.72%	2	$68.43	$431,914
Town Lake	310	8,680	17.97%	64.70%	5,616	18.18%	0.21%	3	$61.05	$342,854
Great Gorge	348	9,744	20.17%	56.90%	5,544	17.95%	-2.23%	5	$68.92	$382,116
Total	1,725	48,300	100.00%	63.76%	30,892	100.00%			$64.98	$2,008,531

RESTAURANT SALES   Since sales volume information for restaurants is not generally available through the comptroller's office, most operators attempt to limit the number of people aware of their sales volume. Many of the larger independent operators freely allow sales data to be published in various trade magazines' annual reports on foodservice companies. Industrywide data are available through many state restaurant associations. Through its *Bill of Fare* magazine, the Texas Restaurant Association publishes data on food and beverage sales for each city, including change from the previous year, average sales per outlet, total population, index of consumer spending, index of restaurant sales, percentage of food dollar spent dining out, and change in grocery store sales.

In some states, sales levels of alcoholic beverages are public information. When this is the case, the information can be obtained from the state or through marketing research firms that publish composites of outlet sales.

COMPETITOR ANALYSIS REPORTS   Generally, the most effective means of gathering information about competitors comes from regularly scheduled (at least each three months) investigative visits to the competitor's business. This visit should be analyzed in light of a similar visit or experience at one's own business so that a reasonably objective comparison can be made. The competitor analysis forms in Figures 5.12 through 5.15 can be used to record important information for hotels or restaurants.

Figure 5.12 is a typical competitor analysis that can be used for both hotels and restaurants. It contains a sample of possible comparison factors and a hypothetical evaluation (Reid, 1989) between the Mission Park Hotel and one of its primary competitors, Sonoma Valley. The analysis should be as objective and accurate as possible. A brief summary of Competitor A's various strengths and weaknesses follows. Environmental factors such as major clients, could be added. On an actual form, more space would be provided for each category. The majority of the qualitative information can be obtained through a visit to the competitor's property. Quantitative data can be obtained directly from the owner or others with applicable knowledge, from published sources, or can be estimated. The source of quantitative data could be included to assist decision-makers in judging the data's accuracy and improving the outcome of the analysis. Figures 5.13 and 5.14 are more simplistic competitor analysis forms commonly used for on-site visits of hotels or restaurants. Figure 5.15 is used for hotel rate comparisons. Any of the competitor analysis forms can obviously be expanded to fit one's particular needs. The listing of strategic internal factors from Chapter 4 can be used to develop a more detailed or customized analysis. In addition to these reports, files should be kept for each competitor so that all articles and other information will be available as needed.

ANALYSIS OF COMPETITIVE INFORMATION   After the data have been gathered, they may need to be organized or categorized to be useful in the strategy formulation. A simple review of the information gathered may be adequate for some decisions. An analysis of information gathered from Figures 5.12 through 5.15 would

POSSIBLE AREAS FOR ANALYSIS	MISSION PARK HOTEL	SONOMA VALLEY
Market share or sales	$8,000,000 annually	$12,000,000 annually
Hotel's general market	Midscale, full service	Midscale, full service
Target customer(s)	Corporate, group	Corporate, group
Product/services offered/ capabilities	Secretarial service, workout room, pool, computerized check-in/out	Workout room, pool, computerized check-in/out
Relative perceived product/service quality	4.5 (5-point scale)	3.7
Relative perceived value	4.4	3.8
Room rates	Rack $85 Corporate $70 Group $63	Rack $90 Corporate $78 Group $67
Location(s)—quality and penetration of market	Excellent	Excellent
Facilities—atmosphere, design, layout, and upkeep (number of rooms, number of seats, square feet of meeting space, parking, condition and type of furniture, carpeting, linen, fixtures, and HVAC)	250 rooms 15,000 sq.ft. Meeting space rooms need remodeling, excellent HVAC, excellent audio/visual (AV)	300 rooms 30,000 sq.ft. Meeting space rooms recently remodeled, problem with AC, AV department
Cost advantages	Monthly mortgage $110,000	Monthly mortgage $265,000
Administrative management (GM)	Little focus on planning	Little focus on planning
Operations	Problems with speed at front/desk	Problems with food service
Human resources (morale, motivation, quality)	4.2	3.8
Research and development	Nothing planned	Nothing planned
Financial position and flexibility	Excellent	Moderate
Types of promotion strategies used	Newspaper, heavy sales calls	Travel magazines, moderate sales calls
Success of past promotional strategies	Newspaper—good; sales staff—excellent	Travel magazines—excellent; sales staff—average
Marketing department	Excellent	Good
Competitor's future possible strategies		Lowering rates by $5, will likely target associations

Figure 5.12   Competitor analysis (hotel or restaurant).

Hotel/Motel Name _____

Address _____

Number of Rooms _____ **Number of Floors** _____

Type of Hotel (Business, Airport, Roadside) _____

Primary Target Customer Groups _____

_____

Attribute Analysis:

Food and Beverage (number, types, styles, menus, size, quality)

_____

_____

Guest Rooms (availability, number, size, and condition)

Handicapped _____ Executive Level _____

Nonsmoking _____ Women's Level _____

Suites _____ Features _____

Meeting Facilities (availability, size, and condition)

Audio/Visual Equipment and Services_____

Meeting Space and Group Accommodations_____

Recreation Facilities

Pool ____ Exercise Room ____ Other_____

Amenities

Airport Transportation _____ Newspaper _____ City Shuttle _____ Concierge _____

Toiletries_____Other_____

Rates/Occupancy:

Rack_____Corporate Rates_____Group_____

Other Pertinent Rates_____Occupancy (%)_____

Market Mix Percentages (corporate, group, leisure, crews)_____

_____

Primary Competitors:

_____

_____

General Comments:

_____

_____ Compiled by: _____

Figure 5.13 Competitor analysis form for hotels.

Competitor's Name:_____ **Date of Visit:**_____

Address:_____ **Time:**_____

Distance from Our Location:_____

General Concept of Competitor:_____

Menu Description and Quality (attach copy, if possible):_____

_____

_____

_____

Check Average and Price Range:_____

Alcoholic Beverages Served, Quality and Prices:_____

_____

Service Style and Quality:_____

_____

_____

Atmosphere, Design and Decor:_____

_____**Seating Capacity:**_____

Cleanliness:_____

_____

Unique Selling Propositions (e.g., in-store bakery, exposed kitchen):

_____

_____

_____

Sales Volume During Visit(s), Rate 1 (very slow) to 5 (very busy):

_____

_____

Estimated Daily, Weekly, or Monthly Volume:_____

General Comments:_____

_____

_____

_____

_____ Compiled by: _____

Figure 5.14 Competitor report form for restaurants.

HOTEL (YOUR'S FIRST /# EACH)	EFFECTIVE DATES	RACK ($)	CORPORATE ($) CORPORATE GROUP ($)	ASSOCIATION GROUP ($)	SMERFS ($)	LEISURE ($)	PACKAGE ($) (DESCRIBE)

Figure 5.15   Marketing and sales plan room rate comparison.

provide the company with a reasonably detailed examination of comparative and unique aspects of each competitor. It could easily be seen that one or several competing hotels have more meeting space, or that a restaurant is attracting more customers. In most cases, additional extrapolation is required to help expose the significance of relative strengths and weaknesses and assist in the search for potential and actual opportunities or threats. For example, knowing more about the abilities of the competitor to compete, and the implications of those abilities, and having a graphic display of the information will yield a clearer picture of the firm's competitive situation. Later in the planning process, this information will help the firm weigh the relevance and suitability of future strategic and tactical decisions.

COMPETITOR'S SWOT ANALYSIS   From the completed competitor analysis in Figure 5.12, a company could develop a reasonable detailed listing of a competitor's performance or strengths and weaknesses (Figure 5.16). This analysis would also highlight areas where one's own firm must improve if it is to become a viable competitor. The yardstick for measurement could be based on one or more of the following:

- Management's opinion of the competitor's performance compared to one's own company
- A survey to obtain an objective appraisal of what target customers think of the competitor's performance
- Its current performance compared to its past performance
- Its current performance in any strategic areas compared to forecasted changes in the environment or internal business requirements

STRENGTHS	WEAKNESSES
High sales	No secretarial services
Meeting space	RPPQ and RPV average, but below our rating
Good marketing plan	High mortgage
Rooms recently remodeled	Moderate financial flexibility
	No on-site audio/visual ability

OPPORTUNITIES	THREATS
Tourism within the state is up 15%	Corporate business is down 10%
Customers are requesting healthy menu choices	The economy is not recovering as quickly as had been hoped
Of the five primary competitors, two have weak sales and marketing departments	Larger firms have the ability to purchase equipment to speed check-in and check-out

Figure 5.16   Strength and weakness analysis.

A competitor's strength may be considered a threat if it might be used to gain a competitive advantage. A weakness might represent an opportunity if it is worth pursuing and if the firm's present related performance is superior to competitors. Knowing a competitor's strengths and weaknesses increases the likelihood of success for strategies by allowing the firm to pinpoint areas where it can most effectively and efficiently compete. Three types of strategies are generally associated with competitive actions. An *offensive strategy* can be any action to increase sales or improve a firm's competitive position or, more seriously, a move to take away a portion of a competitor's market. This could be through comparison advertising, heavily targeting the competitor's key accounts, or through discounting. A *counterstrategy* is a direct response to a competitor's offensive or defensive strategy. A *defensive strategy* is any response to environmental factors (including counterstrategies), such as the economy or another firm's offensive strategy. For example, if a competing hotel has a large experienced sales staff and a larger-than-average travel budget, it could be surmised that many of these sales managers will be spending proportionately more time on out-of-town sales calls. The counterstrategy or defensive strategy might include trying to attract the competitor's key accounts through more personalized service, added value attributes, or price; focusing on a market that the competitor has ignored; concentrating efforts on a limited number of origination cities; and upgrading key areas of the hotel's facilities or services a level above the competitor.

If, for example, a primary competitor has a name recognition advantage, some means of overcoming this strength must be sought. If a small independent hamburger restaurant was operating in the same trade area as McDonald's, it would be facing a multitude of threats. This would force the independent restaurant to develop a strategy that would minimize McDonald's impact. For example, if the market was receptive, it could serve its burgers on homemade buns, use fresh-ground meat, use fresh potatoes for fries, serve beer, or have a more sedate atmosphere. To some, this could be considered an attack on McDonald's weaknesses. It would also be locating unmet needs or gaps in the market and positioning its product to meet those needs. A change without an intended and targeted market is not a prudent choice. An independent hotel in a trade area with a national chain would need to protect itself by developing strategies that would drive revenues and allow it to compete— perhaps adding some USPs, such as free homemade cookies and ice-cold milk each night or afternoon, home-style meals with free seconds, or a free (with stated limit) or at-cost fax machine.

When a competitor is weak in an area, such as a hotel that has not been remodeled in several years, offensive strategies such as comparison advertising can be considered. In cases such as this, extreme caution should be used when focusing on a competitor's apparent weakness. If Hotel A attacks Hotel B by going after its key customers, several outcomes are possible. One is that Hotel B will become a weaker player in the market. This could force Hotel B to defend itself with a pricing counterstrategy, which could, in turn, force Hotel A to also drop its prices. Another possibility is that Hotel B could be weakened to such an extent that a major competitor takes it over, remodels, and begins taking business from Hotel A.

MARKET POSITION ANALYSIS   After management has determined which hotels it is competing with in each major market segment, and has gathered information about them, it will need to analyze the specific attributes that make each property desirable. The focus would be on the hotel or restaurant's primary attributes, as they relate to competitors in a particular market. Basically, how do representative guests or customers from one market segment view a company's attributes compared with those of competitors? (see Figure 5.17.) This information is used to help determine the best way to position one business against another. The basic theory is that a business should target another business's weakness with a strength. (Hotel market segments could include corporate transient, corporate meetings, groups, tourists, and so forth; restaurant segments could include office workers, retail sales, professionals, blue-collar workers, young adults, married couples with children in grade school, and so on.) A sample market position analysis is given in Figure 5.17.

POSITIONING MAPS   The positioning map in Figure 5.18 shows that Molly's Diner is competing with Restaurants A and B. (See Chapter 6 for an explanation of positioning maps.) Molly's Diner is equal to its strongest competitor in product quality, but it must correct problems with its value position before it can directly compete with Restaurant A or B. Though Restaurant B has a problem with its quality perception, it is rated reasonably high for value. As long as sales volume for Restaurant B is respectable, this implies that its customers are willing to accept the lower quality because of lower prices. Possible strategies for Molly's Diner would be to add

MARKET: CORPORATE GROUPS

MISSION PARK HOTEL	GREEN HILLS	SONOMA VALLEY
Hotel/Restaurant	Competitor #1	Competitor #2
1. Condition of meeting space	1. Price	1. Location
2. Service quality	2. Amount of meeting space	2. Amenities
3. Size of rooms	3. Location	3. Amount of meeting space
4. Price	4. Amenities	4. Size of rooms
5. Location	5. Service quality	5. Condition of meeting space

Remarks: Green Hills does have lower rates, but their facility has not been remodeled in eight years and is showing signs of wear. Their property is well managed.

Figure 5.17 Market position analysis.

several items that have a high perceived value, improve plate presentation, increase vegetable portions, or lower prices. This, of course, assumes that the restaurant needs to bring up sales volume. Even if this were not the case and sales were fine, being viewed as a poor value could still be a long-term threat that should be dealt with before sales decline or before competitors develop offensive strategies to take advantage of the restaurant's position. (Figure 5.19 explains how the points were plotted.)

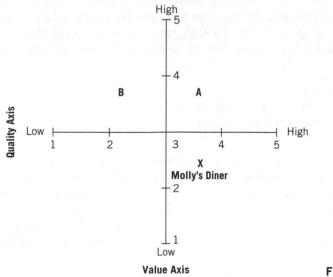

Figure 5.18 Positioning map.

Molly's Diner

Product Quality

	Scale:	1		2		3		4		5		Total Responses
	Responses:	7	+	10	+	46	+	40	+	18	=	121

Calculation of the mean for Product Quality: 7 + 20 + 138 + 160 + 90 = 415 ÷ 121 = 3.43

Weighted Total Responses = 415 ÷ 121 = Mean 3.43

(Product quality responses multiplied by each scale category, add products, divide total by total responses.)

Value

	Responses:	26	+	34	+	47	+	12	+	2	=	121
	Mean:	26	+	68	+	141	+	48	+	10	=	293 ÷ 121 = 2.42

Competitor A

Mean (weighted average) for Product Quality: 3.45

Mean (weighted average) for Value: 3.67

Competitor B

Mean (weighted average) for Product Quality: 2.31

Mean (weighted average) for Value: 3.79

Figure 5.19   Plotting a positioning map.

FORECASTING COMPETITOR'S FUTURE ACTIONS AND REACTIONS   The final step in the competitor analysis process is to attempt to assess the competitor's potential strategies or actions, and their reactions to one's own firm's strategic moves.

FORECASTING COMPETITOR'S FUTURE ACTIONS   After a competing firm's existing strategies have been thoroughly analyzed, an attempt can be made at forecasting its potential actions or strategies. The first step in the forecast is to get inside the mind of the competitor, essentially acting the role of a consultant hired to help with strategic decisions. This is best done by analyzing the competitor's market situation through:

• SWOT analysis
• Market segment competitor analysis
• Market position competitor analysis
• Positioning maps

A primary competitor's opportunities and threats will, for the most part, be quite similar to one's own business. These competitors will generally be targeting the same or similar customer segments and have much the same group of competitors. Remaining environmental factors, such as the economy, societal trends, technology, and suppliers, will vary only marginally. Positioning maps market segment competitor and market position analyses should expose the competitor's strategic position in the market.

A reasonably detailed analysis of a competitor's market position, along with a basic knowledge of its past strategies and the degree of its success, can provide a firm with much the same information that the competitor itself will be utilizing in setting its strategies for the coming year. Additional analytical tools could increase the accuracy of the analysis, but normally, this is unnecessary. One of the problems with an analysis that is too detailed is that the competitor itself will often not progress much beyond the SWOT analysis in its research. Therefore, it will be unaware of information gained from the higher-order analysis, and so will not be using it to assist in formulating strategies. Estimating the level of sophistication of a competitor's research function can help determine the extent of the analysis.

Another reason for the forecast is to uncover weaknesses that the competitor itself fails to recognize or acknowledge. For instance, it would be rare for a marketing department to admit in its marketing plan that one of the firm's major weaknesses is the performance of the marketing department. Therefore, this business would likely continue with present less-than-ideal marketing strategies or possibly formulate new strategies based on false abilities or conjecture, rather than proven skills and bonafide research. Knowing this information, the firm could assume that if, in the past, the competing firm failed to recognize its weaknesses and therefore correct them through applicable strategies, it would probably continue to do so in the future. Since there is the possibility that the competing firm would correct noted weaknesses, a contingency plan might include new potential strategies derived from the competitor's improved analysis and strategies.

FORECASTING COMPETITOR REACTIONS   Being able to calculate the reactions of a competitor to the strategic moves of one's own firm will help forecast the viability and, hence, future success of any selected strategy. It will also help assess the need to have counterstrategies ready, contingent upon a competitor's anticipated response.

In the hospitality industry there tends to be an inverse relationship between the level of product and service quality and the likelihood of a competitor's defensive strategy. Economy-minded consumers are not searching for quality as much as convenience and basic satisfaction of the applicable need—food or a place to stay—at a value-oriented price. To meet this need, fast-food and economy hotel segments focus on the bare essentials, which, in turn, increases the likelihood of minimal product and service differentiation. The consumer's search for the satisfaction of a lower-order need subsequently lessens the tendency to develop a strong loyalty. Because of this, budget market segments must usually develop a rapid response to a competitor's promotional strategies. Otherwise, they face the prospect of losing sales and market share. McDonald's found this to be true when it was slow to react to Taco Bell's value pricing strategy. Reaction to advertisements without incentives will usually be limited to trying to remain visible in the market. If comparison or attack advertising or promotional discounts are used, then a competitor reaction should be expected and planned for.

Generally, midscale to upscale or luxury market segments have mild reactions to competitor's strategies. This is because the target customer is looking for attributes associated with quality, comfort, and status, such as an establishment's food, room size and appointments, attentive service, and overall image. These attributes tend to engender a degree of loyalty and therefore lessen the possibility that a special offer will induce them to switch brands. Price, though a consideration, is secondary to these higher-order needs. Contrary to this traditional view, as the search for value becomes pervasive in all levels of society, all firms will need to consider a primary competitor's possible reaction to a threatening value-oriented strategy. During recent slowdowns in the economy, many fine-dining restaurants formed gourmet dinner clubs that offered various types of discounts, up to 2 for 1. To remain competitive, many luxury hotels have dropped their average daily rates well below their desired level.

COMPETITOR ANALYSIS OVERVIEW   Each time a customer patronizes a business, the image or opinion of the business with which he/she leaves will be based to a great degree on how the business satisfied the customer's expectations compared with competing businesses. This is best described by the term relative perceived product quality (RPPQ). Before a firm can develop a set of viable strategies, it must first be acutely aware of the abilities and actions of its competitors.

For all levels of competition, knowledge of competitors' abilities is important when deciding with whom the business can compete, when to compete, and how to compete. Focusing on a competitor's weaknesses or finding a niche or gap in the market that is not adequately being served is highly preferable to attacking a competitor's strengths. If it is clear that a market has major competitors with strategic advantages that cannot be overcome, then differentiating strategies should be sought or perhaps another market should be considered.

It is said that one should pick his/her fights carefully. Competing for diners and hotel guests is a fight, and a business that enters a market unprepared, unarmed, or ill-equipped, relative to its competitors, may end up a casualty.

Suppliers and Creditors

Suppliers and creditors offer both opportunities and threats to all hospitality businesses. This category includes the companies from which the business purchases its products or services, or its financial creditors. Critical attributes are that the suppliers should be helpful and dependable, that is, provide timely and accurate deliveries; and offer consistent quality at a reasonable price. Offering certain products that competing hotels or restaurants may not be able to get would be an opportunity. Sales representatives should be knowledgeable about specific needs. The relationship must be one of mutual trust and respect. Transactions with suppliers should always be conducted in the most professional manner to assure continued supplies and dependable deliveries. Firms that do not pay their bills on time will find it difficult to develop beneficial relationships.

The business may suffer if prices go up, if quantities and quality fluctuate, or if competitors have access to unique products or better prices or quality. It is important to keep abreast of what suppliers have to offer to be able to take advantage of opportunities to either gain an advantage or, at least, remain competitive.

TYPES OF SUPPLIERS   For hotels and restaurants, there are two major types of suppliers: full-line suppliers and specialty suppliers.

Full-Line Suppliers   These are generally very large companies who can deliver almost any product a restaurant or hotel could need. In the past 20 years, a handful of national or regional companies have been buying smaller supply firms; so as time passes there are fewer full-line suppliers from which to choose. Their primary advantages are that, because of their size and purchasing power, their prices may be lower than smaller competitors and, since they can deliver most of the hotel or restaurant's purchasing needs, less time will be spent on purchasing, fewer deliveries will be made, fewer people will be walking in and out of the back door, and there will be less paperwork with which to deal. Their primary disadvantages are that they offer less personal service and are sometimes not as quality conscious as smaller suppliers.

A relatively new type of full-line supplier is the *custom distribution service*. This is a large regional supplier that will normally charge a set percentage over its cost, based on the distance of a hotel or restaurant from its warehouse and the volume of products purchased. Custom distribution services are most popular among chain restaurants with relatively static menus.

Most businesses purchase dry goods and many other nonspecialty items from a limited number of full-line suppliers, normally about three, based on the suppliers' current prices. If the suppliers know that they are competing with other businesses, they will be more concerned about fair prices and good service; and if one supplier is out of a product, there are two others to buy from, without having to deal with a new supplier. Recently, there has been a trend to purchase the majority of one's products from a single full-line supplier, in exchange for a consistently low price. Care must be taken to make sure the prices remain at the agreed level.

Specialty Suppliers   These suppliers normally carry a single line of products, such as linens, cleaning supplies, bathroom amenities, meats, poultry, seafood, dairy, or produce. Their primary advantage is that, since they specialize in a limited number of items, their ability to deliver a consistently high-quality product is greater than that of a full-line supplier. Their prices are often higher than full-line suppliers but, when high-quality products are required, the additional cost may be justified. These products will often be purchased from one or two very reputable, quality-conscious suppliers. The reason is that if these important items were purchased from several different suppliers, the quality would not be consistent and customers may not be satisfied.

Competitive Prices and Quality   The hotel or restaurant should always be aware of competing suppliers' prices for all recurring purchases. New sources should be considered if there are price increases, if another supplier offers a better quality product at the same price or a similar product at a lower price, or if the quality of the product that the hotel or restaurant currently is receiving begins to drop or become inconsistent. A backup source should be available for all products. Buyers should be aware of *low-ballers* who attempt to attract business with an initial low price, then raise prices after the business has gone through the effort of switching suppliers.

CREDITORS   For most foodservice businesses, the main creditors are suppliers. Based on food cost, cleaning, breakage, and paper supplies, one-third to about one-half of each sales dollar will go to pay for supplies purchased on credit. Businesses considering any type of financing, such as for equipment, leasehold improvements, and buildings and land, must make sure that the debt will not create an undue burden or seriously increase financial risks. Loans with fluctuations in interest rates can cause substantial variations in payments. Also, do potential creditors view the business as being a good risk for future loans?

THE GLOBAL ENVIRONMENT

An additional consideration for the environmental analysis is the degree to which a firm seeks opportunities for growth outside the United States (or its current geopolitical boundaries). Competing in foreign lands will obviously produce dramatic changes in a firm's environment. Each factor in the operating and remote environments becomes a little less familiar, a little less stable. In America and most developed countries, the majority of environmental concerns either change slowly or are not overly disruptive to the business. Once outside the boundaries of the firm's homeland, Murphy's Law and political whim may replace consistently applied regulations. A firm with its headquarters in one country and doing businesses in another is referred to as a *multi-national* company.

Some of the more notable and humorous problems experienced by multi-national businesses were detailed in David A. Ricks, *Blunders in International Business.* Among them were Gerber Foods distributing baby food in a country with a low literacy rate. The jars had pictures of smiling babies on the label, which to the horrified consumer were interpreted as its contents. Coco-Cola's name in Taiwanese meant "bite the wax tadpole." Pepsi's slogan "Come alive with the Pepsi generation" was translated rather poorly into Taiwanese as "bring your relatives back from the dead." KFC's slogan, "Finger lickin' good," in Chinese was translated as "Eat your fingers off." When Coors tried to translate its "Turn it loose" slogan into Spanish, the result was, "Drink Coors and get diarrhea." Braniff Airlines was promoting its new leather seats in a Spanish-speaking country by recommending that travelers "fly naked." U.S. Air promoted its new routes from Hong Kong by presenting its fliers with white carnations. Unfortunately, to many Asians this is a symbol of death and bad luck (Berkowitz, 1994).

Considering Foreign Expansion

The first question that must be asked is: Why should the firm consider foreign expansion? Hopefully, reason will guide the decision, rather than the romanticism of having operations in foreign ports. As in any situation, when egos override reason, problems generally follow. The most logical impetus for foreign expansion is profit. If there is a large unmet demand for certain products or services, then the decision can be considered. Other common reasons for foreign expansion are preemptive strategies and saturation of the domestic market. A very important reason for foreign expansion is simply to be the first to operate in the region. Being first (a *preemptive strategy*) may establish the business as the leader. This will make the expansion decision for competitors more difficult, and, if pursued by other U.S. firms, the new business will have many possible hurdles to overcome. An established operation will generally have the advantaged of brand loyalty, more stable sources of supplies, relationships with local officials and the community, and perhaps some degree of market penetration. If the domestic market is becoming saturated with company-owned units or competing units, and the firm is afraid that volume will decrease as new businesses are opened, then foreign expansion could be an option. In any of the above cases, the business must be sound—marketing abilities, operationally, and financially—before expansion can be considered.

Stages of Multi-national Expansion

There are generally two stages of foreign expansion for hospitality firms; *franchising* and *investment*. The first stage, franchising, consists of licensing the firm's name and systems to operators in other countries. The purchaser of the franchise, known as a franchisee, purchases the franchise rights from the franchisor, the owner of the concept. The franchisee will usually pay a one-time franchise fee and a monthly royalty based on a percentage of sales. The American franchisor will assist the foreign franchisee in setting up the business through consulting, preopening training, and ongoing operational assistance. This is normally the first step in foreign expansion because it has few inherent risks. Since the franchisor does not generally invest in the franchisee's business, there is little or no monetary risk, and the environmental risk is predominantly the responsibility of the franchisee. Other advantages of franchising in foreign lands are that it is an inexpensive means of testing the waters in an unknown territory, and it is a way of speeding market penetration, increasing name recognition, and raising capital for expansion elsewhere. One problem to consider is that if the franchisee is not successful, future attempts of the franchisor to operate in that country or particular part of the world may be hindered.

The second stage in foreign expansion occurs when a firm invests money in the overseas unit. When the firm has a vested interest in the operation, the competitive environment in the foreign land must be analyzed thoroughly to reduce the possibility of unpleasant surprises. The first concern for any business is to determine if there are enough potential target customers in the country. This can be answered with some accuracy through surveys, field testing of the firm's product or service, and an analysis of similar competitors. In many cases, the residents are so enthralled with foreign products, American or otherwise, that they will quickly adapt to the new flavors. Generally, when changes are required, they are usually minor, such as a few additional items on the menu, different spices, and condiments. If the local culture does not consume certain integral ingredients of a firm's signature items, then the country may not be a feasible choice. For example, since McDonald's is not a Kosher restaurant, it took many years to get approval to open in Israel.

Political Stability

Probably the most critical and uncertain environmental factor is the stability of the local government. Foreign governments will vary in their support for outside operators. In many countries, officials will go out of their way to make sure that everything possible is done to make the transition as smooth as possible. These countries appreciate the investment and realize that the majority of revenues will stay in the country in the form of wages, taxes, utilities, advertising, and the purchases of other goods and services. There are still some countries or cities where operators will have to spend countless hours dealing with antiquated bureaucracies and questionable local officials. Hopefully, a detailed analysis will reveal potential problems. In some countries it is a tradition, legal or not, to pay local officials a small stipend. In many instances, this is actually an informal method of taxation. Generally, one of the best solutions to the payoff problem is to let people know up front that there will be no illegal transactions. This stance can be smoothed over by agreeing to pay all legitimate taxes and fees, and showing officials how the firm will be a socially responsible member of the community. Having dinners for local festivals, charitable events, or supporting popular causes will go a long way to help the business assimilate into the local culture.

In various parts of the world, profit is synonymous with exploitation. Often, undeveloped countries or those with a history of colonialism have many suspicions about outsiders opening businesses for the purpose of making a profit. When this is the case, social responsibility may move from being a secondary to a primary goal. A carefully worded mission statement may help allay fears. Again, being a responsible member of the community will help allay most skeptics.

Operational Concerns

The first problem often encountered by growth is how one owner manages two operations. This will usually call for bringing in a trusted individual and setting up policies, systems, and controls to simplify the overseeing of the new location. When the move is not across town, but halfway around the world, all problems are magnified. The decrease in the ability to closely monitor and control the operation and its environment increases the need for a professionally prepared strategic marketing plan. Since many problems cannot be avoided, the best solution is to be prepared. In the strategic marketing plan's control section, a series of contingency plans should be developed to speed reaction time and lessen the effect of radical environmental changes.

A common concern for multi-national firms is the decision of how to divide responsibility for key functional departments. Should financial or marketing activities be centralized or is it prudent to shift their responsibility downward? Can marketing decisions made for a hotel in Atlanta work for a hotel in Tokyo? The general solution is that some broad or long-term marketing strategies may be made in the home office, but the majority of the strategies and action plans must be developed by those who live with the situation on a daily basis and must carry out the plan or policies.

Supplies

One of the more common problems encountered by both hotels and restaurants opening in foreign countries is finding a consistent source of food supplies. The most frequent problems are with perishable items. If the product is grown or raised locally, delivery problems will generally be confined to seasonal fluctuations. Products that must be brought in are at the mercy of the quality of the distribution system of the country or area. Since perishable items, such as produce, must be shipped in at least once a week, there may be periods of limited supply. There are generally fewer problems with the delivery of dry goods. This is because items such as canned goods, paper, and cleaning supplies can be imported in larger quantities with a limited concern for shelflife.

Multi-national Environmental Analysis

The best method of locating opportunities and threats in the foreign environment is to perform a detailed analysis on each of the components of the remote and operating environments. This analysis will be significantly more accurate if it is done in cooperation with a business or hospitality consultant from the country under consideration. It is beneficial to meet with customers, key local officials, and product vendors during this visit.

THE BRYAN HOUSE AND CITY GRILL ENVIRONMENTAL ANALYSIS

The Bryan House

REMOTE ENVIRONMENT

Politics

The current president is attempting to solve many of the country's major problems. This may have a negative impact in the short term but will hopefully produce a more efficient social and physical infrastructure for the future.

Economy

The spending has been improving but appears to be greatly influenced by interest rates. Disposable income is not keeping pace with inflation. Because of cutbacks in business overhead, many of our regular guests are having to limit their travel and reduce the cost of each trip. Since our ADR is about $5 higher than the competition, this is a cause for concern. The increase in foreign travelers is welcomed, since their average daily expenditures in the hotel average $30 higher than U.S. guests.

Societal Trends

Each year has seen an increase in the percentage of the hotel's and city's guests originating from foreign countries, especially the Far East. Even the overall customer base from U.S. cities is becoming more diverse. Every day the public is bombarded by new facts related to nutrition and exercise. Those in upper-income brackets appear to be most concerned, even though they are the same people who order our richest desserts. People are so busy today that time itself will be one of the most important commodities of the future. Security has become a critical issue. The leisure market is traveling more often but taking shorter trips. People are not charging as much on credit cards as they once did.

Technology

There are several types of effective trash compactors and pelletizers that would help reduce waste volume and trash disposal costs. There are many new property management systems that can serve all the hotel's computer needs. Some can come near the goal of the "paperless business." Competition, increased production, and new technologies are bringing down prices. Interchange systems that serve as intermediaries between the hotel and the card-issuing bank can remove the need for manual batching and mailing of credit card vouchers. Customer databases are important now but will become mandatory in the near future.

OPERATING ENVIRONMENT

Personnel

Attracting employees is somewhat difficult for the Bryan House. The main problems are name recognition and, since sales are not at the level of most competitors, the hotel cannot match their wages. Because the hotel is not part of a chain, it has limited chances for advancement. Small cash bonuses are awarded to employees who recommend someone who is hired. The award is made after the new employee's third month of satisfactory work.

Ecology

Customers are demanding that the firms with which they do business take proactive stances in the areas of recycling, waste reduction, and energy management. Failure to do so will put any business at a competitive disadvantage. The state's legislature is discussing bills that would require various levels of mandatory participation. Most chain competitors have begun recycling programs through corporate and unit committees. Each year they are upgrading their recycling efforts. Since ecological strategies are less expensive than many advertising options, they should be pursued as a major part of the firm's public relations effort. One local firm is carving out a niche as a recycler of glass, plastic, and paper. Through increased cleanliness and reliance on nontoxic pesticides, such as boric acid, the hotel should minimize its use of pest control firms.

Customer Analysis

The hotel's key market segments are:

Individual business travelers (IBTs)
Corporate group business
Association group business
Leisure business
SMERFS (sports, medical, educational, religious, fraternal, social)

Individual Business Travelers (IBTs are described as an example.)

Geographics The following are the major feeder cities for all guests of the hotel:

	Total Visits (Average Room Nights per Visit—2.4)	Total Dollars Spent
New York	13,348	$2,002,200
San Francisco	8,992	1,348,800
Dallas–Fort Worth	7,429	1,114,350
Washington, DC	3,932	589,800
Boston	3,657	548,550
New Orleans	2,890	433,500
Chicago	2,185	327,750
Los Angeles	1,946	291,900
San Diego	1,805	270,750
Philadelphia	1,620	243,000
Atlanta	1,468	220,200
Other U.S. cities	5,142	771,300
Tokyo, Japan	881	158,580
Taiwan	437	78,660
Other foreign cities	1,352	243,360
Total annual guests	57,084	
Total dollars spent		$8,642,700

The following are the major feeder cities for individual business travelers:

	Total Visits	Total Dollars Spent
New York	4,004	$ 600,660
San Francisco	2,697	404,640
Dallas–Fort Worth	2,229	334,305
Washington, DC	1,180	176,940
Boston	1,097	164,565
New Orleans	867	130,050
Chicago	656	98,325
Los Angeles	583	87,570
San Diego	542	81,225
Philadelphia	486	72,900
Atlanta	440	66,060
Other U.S. cities	1,543	231,390
Tokyo, Japan	463	83,340
Taiwan	337	60,660
Other foreign cities	541	97,344
Total annual guests	18,762	
Total dollars spent		$2,689,974

Demographics

- The age range for target customers is between 30 and 55.
- The average household income is between $55,000 and $60,000 per year. (The average household income for the U.S. is around $33,000.)
- IBTs are on expense accounts and require business services.
- Ninety percent of the customer base is college educated.
- Those without college degrees are generally either successfully self-employed or have worked hard to establish themselves in their firms.
- Sixty percent have children below 18 years of age.
- Eighty-five percent of those with children feel that experiences shared with the family are important.
- Most consider themselves as upper-middle class.
- Racial breakdown: 70% white, 10% black, 10% Hispanic, 5% Asian, 5% other.

Psychographics

Most IBTs

- Are family oriented
- Are active investors in the stock market and take other financial risks
- Are generally conservative
- Enjoy the challenges of their work
- Take two or more vacations with their families, and one with just their spouse
- Enjoy movies
- Go to religious services ten times per year
- Consider fashion to be important
- Are more concerned about quality than price
- Get most of their national news from television and *USA Today,* and financial news from trade newspapers such as the *Wall Street Journal*
- Feel that the future is bright
- Enjoy participating in and watching sporting events
- Consider cultural events such as the symphony, plays, and opera to be important

Buyer Behavior

- *Benefits Sought.* Quality amenities; concierge; a secure property; workout facility; fast lunch; quality 24-hour room service, or at least from 5 a.m. until 1 a.m.; a quiet room; a clean room that smells fresh; clean bathrooms; firm beds with down pillows; a desk with adequate lighting, fax and modem hookups in each room; a miminum 19-inch television with a movie channel; superior service (both courteous and efficient); 90% of the U.S. guests request nonsmoking rooms, 80% of foreign guests request nonsmoking rooms; hotel locations within 10 minutes of business and 20 minutes of entertainment; no waits in line of longer than three minutes for check-in or check-out; check-in transaction time should be under two minutes; check-out transaction time should be under one minute; availability of a shuttle to the airport (independent shuttle service for a fee is acceptable, if few stops are made and the trip does not take more than 10 minutes longer than a direct trip; good quality food at a reasonable value; restaurant food that has not been sitting under a heat lamp for too long; and meeting space for up to 20 people.

- *Price Sensitivity.* Not overly price sensitive for quality products and services; $90 to $110 is the going rate for most comparable hotels.
- *Frequency of Use.* Most guests stay in the hotel an average of 3.6 times per year.
- *Loyalty.* Sixty-five percent of the guests always stay at The Bryan House when visiting the city.

Competitor Analysis

The primary competitors in the area are the Hilton, Marriott, Sheraton, and Hyatt hotels. All of these hotels have room rates that average $5.00 less than The Bryan House. Each is located within the same market area and has concierges, secretarial services, newspaper delivery to each room, workout facilities, and an outlet for a fast lunch. All primary hotels have been renovated within the last six years, have occupancies of around 65%, and are either breaking even or showing a small profit. Their main strengths are their name recognition, brand loyalty, and reservation systems. The chain affiliation also offers an efficient operations system.

Secondary competitors include Ramada, Holiday Inn, Hampton Inn, Motel 6, and two independent motels. Room rates vary from $40 per night to $65 for Ramada and Holiday Inn. Their locations are not quite as convenient to the convention center and area attractions. Ramada and Holiday Inn are the only secondary competitors with banquet and meeting services. Food and beverage prices are about 30% less than primary competitors.

SAMPLE INDIVIDUAL COMPETITOR ANALYSIS

Hilton Hotel (Hypothetical)
2255 Elm Street
Austin, Texas

Rooms	378; standard—344, suites—30, penthouse suites—4, presidential suite—1.
Year property opened	1982
Last renovation	1993
Owner	Roy Contreras Interests, Inc.
Operator	Simon Rodriquez International Hospitality Management
Mobil rating	4 stars (5 stars is the top rating)
Special floors	Concierge's floor with hospitality suite; a continental breakfast is included
Amenities	Quality personal care products, newspaper delivery by request, coffee maker with coffee in each room
Business services	Complete services, including secretaries, computers, fax machines, copy machines, modem hookup in rooms and in business center, office supplies
Building type	Eight floors with atrium
Smoking floors	One floor for smokers
Distance to convention center	1 mile
Meeting rooms	Total space—12,000 square feet; largest room—7000 sq. ft.
Catering services	Flexible, includes banquets, meetings, and special events; cost per person range—$6.00 to $35.00; average—$16.00.

Restaurants	Casual dining concept with bar, 175 seats, South-western theme, check average for lunch $10.00, for dinner $17.00; fine dining, 85 seats, European ambi-ance, check average for lunch $15.00, for dinner $24.00
Recreational facilities	Workout room, outdoor pool, golf and tennis within 10 minutes
Market segmentation	Individual business travelers, 30%; ADR, $103 Corporate group business, 35%; ADR, $90 Association group business, 10%; ADR, $75 Leisure business, 15%; ADR, $100 SMERFS, 10%; ADR, $70
Average daily rate	$94
Average occupancy	65%
Annual sales	$11,343,548
Key strengths	Part of major chain, concierge, concierge-level floor, swimming pool, 24-hour room service, 750 parking spaces, all customer satisfaction ratings are above 4.4 (5-point basis), video check-out is available, cre-ative and aggressive marketing department, profit-able since opening
Key weaknesses	Long walk from front desk to elevators; audio/visual department improperly equipped

Suppliers

The hotel is on excellent terms with all suppliers. If required, most will make emergency deliveries. Because this is the state's capital, there is an ample number of dependable suppliers for every hotel need. This competition has increased quality and decreased prices. A new firm that offers a complete line of American-made linens should be contacted.

City Grill

REMOTE ENVIRONMENT

Politics

The political environment appears to be stable. We have been in the same location for three years but are considering expansion in the future. Increased liquor taxes will affect margins and perhaps cause a slight decrease in consumption. Our main concern is the possibility of increased local, state, and federal taxes. If this occurs, we are certain that our sales will be reduced.

Economy

The economy is sliding into a recession, but because of the higher oil prices and the heavily oil-dependent economy of Houston, we should be able to hold present sales. If we decide to expand beyond Houston, this could present a problem. Also, if interest rates were to rise, the cost of expansion would increase.

If the economy causes many restaurants to close, those empty locations would offer us the opportunity to expand at a lower initial cost.

Societal

Because of the decrease in the number of teenagers, we are beginning to have problems hiring dishwashers and busers. The increase in two-income families has given us the opportunity to increase our business by offering more home-style meals. The aging population is enlarging the number of elderly customers in our trade area.

The trend toward healthier eating does not appear to be going away. Nutritional awareness is increasing by 15% per year. Seafood consumption is up 5% over last year. Since we have been serving wholesome food, and about 20% of our menu consists of seafood, we are in accord with these trends.

Technology

There are several new pieces of equipment that will allow us to reduce our ticket time and energy consumption. Our electronic registers have been adequate for many years, but a new point-of-sale system should be considered to provide better information with less effort and allow managers to finish closing duties sooner.

OPERATING ENVIRONMENT

Personnel

The current market for employees is stable. Since the restaurant has a high RPPQ (relative perceived product/service quality), good value, and offers employees better than average pay and benefits, we have very little problem attracting employees. If we plan on growing or maintaining our present level of excellence, we may need to do something else to retain highly qualified personnel.

Customer Analysis

We have abstracted the following information from our just-completed questionnaire. Our primary target customer segment is between 25 and 40 years of age, white collar, with an annual household income of $35,000 to $65,000. the residential neighborhood consists of homes in the $150,000 to $400,000 range; apartments start at $500 for an average one-bedroom that would be $400 in most other areas of the city. Segment members participate in sporting activities twice per week; visit the restaurant six times per month; are conscious about the nutritional value of the foods they eat, but still eat some rich foods and desserts; and seek a high RPPQ over value.

Their main alternative choice is Jake's Grill. Jake's menu includes similar items, at a lower cost. (They will be analyzed further in the next section.)

There is a significant number of elderly customers compatible with our target customer segment. Special discounts and meals for the elderly have been used successfully by many restaurants. We should consider them as an option.

Competitors Analysis

Our primary competitors in our trade area are Jake's Grill, Chili's, and Jeffery's. Even though McDonald's does not represent direct competition, we will include them in our competitor group because we must find out why some of our customers will take their families to McDonald's instead of visiting us.

There is no competitor in the trade area currently serving seafood in a casual upscale dining restaurant.

(For the sake of brevity, only Jake's Grill will be analyzed.)

JAKE'S GRILL

- *Marketing.* Food quality was marginal; excellent menu mix—primarily home-style cooking; no fresh fish; average service; prices at or below reference prices for all products (reference prices are the prices customers carry in their minds for any particular item); locations in every major trade area of city; always plenty of parking; decor attempts to duplicate Southern ranch house with lots of wood, knick-knacks on the walls, and blue gingham; advertising is backed by a major budget; consistent, and focuses on food quality.
- *Management.* Managers are obviously concerned about the efficiency of their operation. Rarely do you see customers complain. Service times were below ten minutes during a busy lunch and below eight minutes during dinner. Average RPPQ. Moderate quality food was compensated for by ample servings and free rolls.
- *Finance.* Based on what I have read, their sales are about $100,000 per month, with a month profit (ROS) of 14% or $14,000. Labor cost is 23%; food cost is 34%.
- *Personnel.* Since the company is very well organized with policies for each task and complete training schedules for each position, there is little need for superstars. This gives them an advantage over us because we must generally hire people with experience, rather than training them for an extended length of time.

  The morale of their employees seemed to be a little low at our last visit. They followed orders and did a good job, but their attitude could have been better.

Suppliers

Our suppliers have given us consistent prices and dependable deliveries. We have stayed with our current suppliers for over three years and have developed strong relationships that have aided us. For example, when we occasionally run short of an item most of the suppliers will give us a "hot shot" (when a business runs out of something between receiving dates, some companies will make a special delivery of the item).

One problem is that if we lost our supplier for seafood, it would be difficult to get another at the same prices or quality.

QUESTIONS AND PROJECTS

1. Do entrepreneurial or conservative firms place more of an emphasis on an accurate and relatively complete environmental analysis? Explain your answer.

2. Define the terms *opportunities* and *threats*.
3. Why is the minimization of subjectivity important when analyzing environmental factors?
4. List and explain three or more of the qualitative methods of forecasting.
5. Since no firm can exert complete control over environmental factors, what are its options?
6. List and briefly explain the factors in the remote and operating environments. What are the acronyms for each?
7. What do you feel are the most important societal trends that are currently affecting hotels or restaurants? What do you feel will be the most important societal trends of the next five years?
8. List and discuss three or more ecological factors that can affect a company's image, sales, and profits.
9. List the *four bases of segmentation*, and explain the primary components of each.
10. List and explain the *stages of buyer behavior.*
11. Describe the difference between primary, secondary, and industry competitors.
12. What is the importance of the market segment competitor analysis?
13. Explain Porter's *forces of competition.*
14. Complete a competitor analysis on a selected or assigned hospitality firm.
15. Complete a market position competitor analysis for any selected or assigned group of hospitality businesses.
16. How would you solve the problem of inequitable waiting times in a fast-food restaurant? (In this particular restaurant, there are three cash registers, each with separate customer waiting lines. The problem centers around customers already in one line watching customers in other lines who came in after they did have their orders taken before them.)
17. If you were going to open a casual dining concept, such as a Chili's, Bennigan's, or Friday's restaurant in France, what are some of the factors you would consider? (Answer the same question, but for Japan, Brazil, or any other assigned country.)

Sources of Environmental Data

American Business Information (ABI Inform), 5711 South 86th Circle, Omaha, NE 68127; Tel: (402) 593-4565 (business database).

American Demographics, 127 West State Street, Ithica, NY 14850.

Annual Reports of publicly traded companies, from company or CD ROM.

Associations Yellow Book, Monitor Publishing Company, 104 Fifth Avenue, 2nd Floor, New York, NY 10011

CD-ROM Databases—Business Dateline (regional magazines and newspapers), *Compact Disclosure* (annual reports), *Predicast's F&S Index* (citations to business trade publications and forecasts), *Monthly Catalog of U.S. Government Publications* (index to U.S. Government publications), *National Trade Databank* (Department of Commerce publications and information, including market research reports for foreign countries), *Thomas Register* (listing of manufacturers in United States and Canada and food industry file), and local and national newspapers.

Bernan Press, 4611-F Assembly Drive, Lanham, MD 20706-4391 (statistical abstracts from governmental sources).

Brand Advantage, 3004 Blenview Road, Wilmette, IL 60091; Tel: 1-800-323-4588. (Consumer purchase information for target market subsets, including gender, age, household income, employment, geographic region, and county).

Bureau of Labor Statistics, Division of Labor Force Statistics, Room 4675, 2 Massachusetts Avenue, NE, Washington, DC 20212; Tel: (202) 606-6378.

BusinessWeek Magazine.

CACI—1100 North Blebe Road, Arlington, VA 22201; Tel: 1-800-292-2240 (full-service research firm, *Sourcebook of Demographics for ZIP Codes*, ACORN Market Segmentation System).

Census Bureau's Data User Services Division; Tel: (301) 763- 4040. Also, Superintendent of Documents, P.O. Box 371954, Pittsburgh, PA 15250-7954; Tel: (202) 512-2250 (*Census Catalog and Guide: 1993*).

Chambers of Commerce, local, state, and national.

CIS Index (Congressional Information Index).

Claritas—NPDP, P.O. Box 610, Ithaca, NY 14851-0610; Tel: 1-800-234-5973 (full-service research firm, demographic data, PRIZM® Lifestyle segmentation, boundary files for mapping, consumer expenditure estimates, business information, healthcare data, etc).

Cornell Hotel and Restaurant Administration Quarterly, Elsevier Science Publishing, Madison Square Station, P.O. Box 882, New York, NY 10160-0206.

Encyclopedia of Associations, Gale Research Colk Gook Tower, Detroit, MI 48226.

Equifax—National Decision Systems, 5375 Mira Sorrento Place, Suite 400, San Diego, CA 92121 (full-service marketing research, including Restaurant-Facts).

Geographic Data Technology, 13 Dartmouth College Highway, P.O. Box 377, Lyme, NH 03768-0377; Tel: 1-(800)-331-7881 (desktop mapping for target marketing).

Harvard Business Review, P.O. Box 52623, Boulder, CO 80322-2623.

Hospitality Research Journal, the professional journal of the Council on Hotel, Restaurant and Institutional Education (CHRIE), 1200 17th Street, NW, Washington, DC 20036-3097; Tel: (202) 331-5990.

Hotel Business Magazine, 1393 Veterans Highway, Suite 214 North, Hauppauge, NY 11788; Tel: (516) 979-7878.

Journal of the Academy of Marketing Science, JAI Press, Inc., 55 Old Post Road–No. 2, Greenwich, CT 06836-1678.

Journal of Culinary Practice, Haworth Press, Inc., 10 Alice Street, Binghamton, NY 13904-1580.

Journal of Hospitality & Leisure Marketing, Haworth Press, Inc., 10 Alice Street, Binghamton, NY 13904-1580.

Journal of Nutrition in Recipe & Menu Development, Haworth Press, Inc., 10 Alice Street, Binghamton, NY 13904- 1580.

Journal of Services Marketing, 108 Loma Media Road, Santa Barbara, CA 93103.

Journal of Travel & Tourism Marketing, Haworth Press, Inc., 10 Alice Street, Binghamton, NY 13904-1580.

Lifestyle Change Communication, Inc., 5885 Glenridge Drive, Suite 150, Atlanta, GA 30328; Tel: (404) 252-4295 (specializes in psychographic data).

Maritz Marketing Research Inc., 1297 North Highway Drive, Fenton, MO 63099; Tel: 1-800-446-1690 (full-service custom research).

National Association for Senior Living Industries, 184 Duke of Gloucester Street, Annapolis, MD 21401-2523; Tel: (410) 263-0991 (national surveys of senior adults).

Nation's Restaurant News, 425 Park Avenue, New York, NY 10022.

Marshall Cohen Associates, 1971 Palmer Avenue, Larchmont, NY 10538; Tel: (914) 833-3400 (media consulting).

Psychology & Marketing (journal), John Wiley & Sons, Inc., 605 Third Avenue, New York, NY 10158.

Restaurant Briefing, published for American Express Establishment Service by Walter Mathews Associates, Inc., 799 Broadway, New York, NY 10003; Tel: 1-800-342-2788.

Restaurant Business (magazine), 633 Third Avenue, New York, NY 10017.

Restaurant & Hospitality (magazine), 1100 Superior Avenue, Cleveland, OH 44197-8104.

Restaurants & Institutions (magazine), Cahners Plaza, 1350 East Touhy Avenue, Des Plaines, IL 60017-5080.

Roper CollegeTrack, 205 East 42nd Street, New York, NY 10022; Tel: (212) 599-0700.

Sandelman & Associates, Inc., 2942 East Shamrock Avenue, Brea, CA 92621; Tel: (714) 993-7116; also, 9191 Garland Road, Suite 638, Dallas, TX 75218; Tel: (214) 319-0794 (in-depth surveys of foodservice consumers).

Simmons Market Research Bureau, 420 Lexington Avenue, New York, NY 10170; Tel: (212) 916-8900 (The Kids Study, Affinity, Custon Studies, Custom Media, The Hispanic Study, The Study of Media & Markets for the Foodservice Industry, and others).

Statistical Abstracts of the United States (local libraries).

Strub Media Group, Inc. P.O. Box 1274, New York, NY 10113-0920; Tel: (212) 242-1900 (gay and lesbian lists).

Superintendent of Documents, P.O. Box 371954, Pittsburgh, PA 15250-7954; Tel: (202) 512-

2250 ($21, a book of over 3000 sources of governmental assistance for Census Bureau information).

The Numbers News, 127 West State Street, Ithaca, NY 14850; Tel: 1-800-828-1133.

Urban Decisions Systems, 2040 Armcost Avenue, Los Angeles, CA 90025; Tel: (800) 633-9568 (demographic information on United States and Mexico).

U.S. Bureau of the Census, Tel: (301) 763-4100.

U.S. Bureau of Economic Analysis, Tel: (202) 523-0777.

U.S. Bureau of Labor Statistics, Tel: (202) 606-7828.

U.S. Department of Agriculture, Family Economics Research Group, Tel: (202) 720-7507.

U.S. Government Printing Office, Washington, DC 20402; Tel: (202) 783-3238 (various sources of government information).

U.S. News & World Report.

U.S. Postal Service, Tel: (202) 268-2000.

Value Line (financial data, libraries).

Wall Street Journal.

World Travel & Tourism Council Research Report, WTTC, P.O. Box 6237, New York, NY 10128-0300.

CHAPTER 6

Strategic Analysis

Strategic analysis consists of (1) determining what factors in the firm's situational analysis are important, (2) deciding which of those factors may have the greatest impact on the firm's future, and (3) analyzing these important factors to determine possible corporate, business, or functional level strategies. The primary purpose of strategic analysis is to give planners a platform from which to review the significance of their firm's market situation and to think about options in dealing with it. Strategic analysis consists of the SWOT analysis (SWOT is the acronym for strengths, weaknesses, opportunities, and threats) and the strategic analysis questioning sequence.

SWOT ANALYSIS

The SWOT analysis is the detailed search and listing of factors from the situational analysis that might or will impact the business's strategy. Strategic marketing is based on the SWOT analysis. The process by which SWOT factors are derived is to carefully review the internal analysis for strengths and weaknesses, and the environmental analysis for opportunities and threats, and to then record, in the appropriate category, every factor that has a reasonable possibility of affecting the short- and long-term future of the firm. Any thoughts that come to mind or occur after the situational analysis has been prepared can also be added. Although prioritization is normally saved for the strategic analysis questioning sequence later in this chapter, various factors can be listed or grouped according to perceived importance. If desired, subcategories may be established within each SWOT component, such as by functional departments or key operating areas—sales, profits, customer satisfaction, and so on.

The list should be as comprehensive as possible so that all factors that may have an impact on the selection of a strategy can be studied (see Figure 6.1). Care must be taken not to record an inordinate number of SWOT variables, but it is better to err on the long side.

STRENGTHS	WEAKNESSES
Experienced management team	Low profit/poor cost control
Good location	Last advertising campaign ineffective
Customers highly satisfied with product and service	Potential customers in trade area confused about what you sell
Fast kitchen times	Sales slow December and January
Corporate business up 10%	Individual business clients down 15%
Superior kitchen equipment	Poor image/reputation
Low unit cost	High food or labor costs
Ready access to capital	
Good marketing information system	

OPPORTUNITIES	THREATS
Recession coming (for low-end concepts)	Recession coming (for midpriced concepts)
No direct competitors in trade area	Major competitor is advertising heavily
Weak competition	Major competitor will open in trade area within three months
Customers want variety	
Company with 300 employees opening soon	Planned road construction may limit access
Target customers in trade area need fast service	Demographic profile of customers does not fit menu
Consumption of spices up	
Consumer-research-identified target customers want delivery	Strong, quality competitors doing poorly (possible reduced demand for the product or service)
New business in trade area	Trade area business slow on Sunday and Monday nights
Large population of elderly in trade area	

Figure 6.1 Typical SWOT analysis variables.

From a marketing standpoint, the primary purpose of the SWOT analysis is to serve as a framework to guide the selection of key opportunities in the environment. These opportunities will subsequently be matched up with appropriate strengths of the business. The secondary purpose is to identify and analyze potential or actual threats that could hurt the business, and weaknesses in key areas that may need to be upgraded to allow the business to compete more successfully. Collectively, weaknesses and threats are often referred to as "problems." On paper, most weaknesses can be corrected; but in the real world, a business may have to live with some imperfections or less than exemplary skills or assets.

The selection of opportunities to pursue, threats to defend against, and weaknesses to correct is not a simple matter. The company's abilities and trends in the marketplace, particularly customer demands and competitors' strategies, are always changing. The purpose of the SWOT analysis is to offer a menu from which one can objectively view the possible alternatives, not to make the selection automatic. As previously stated (Chapter 1) a business's decisions are as good as the facts with which they are made. A properly prepared SWOT analysis simply presents a focused summary of the business's database of available information so that better decisions can be made. The most important information gleaned from the SWOT analysis will usually revolve around details of the internal, customer, and competitor analyses.

STRATEGIC ANALYSIS QUESTIONING SEQUENCE

Developing strategies is not a great challenge. Most firms prepare annual marketing plans that contain reasonably well-thought-out strategies that will keep the firm at or near its present competitive position. But the challenge and the ultimate responsibility of market managers are not to keep firms in their current position. To survive in a dynamic environment, businesses must grow in strength by finding strategies that allow it to stand out from competitors (Schaffer, 1986). Finding the right strategy does not guarantee success. But neglecting the search for viable strategies for more than brief periods of time will all but assure failure (Thomas & Pruett, 1993).

The Need for Models

Once management has decided that it is worth its effort to search for viable alternative strategies and attempt to settle on probable strategic directions for the firm, a major question surfaces. "How do I distinguish between what is important and what is not?" Before this question is answered it is important to understand four issues. First, no human on earth can know everything about a situation as complicated as a firm's competitive environment (Molloy & Schwenk, 1995). Even if he/she did, too many things can change, making the initial prediction at least partially obsolete (Tsoukas, 1994). The objective is not to know everything, but to know and understand what is important and relevant to the issues being addressed. Second, a million dollar research program can help explain and predict certain phenomena. However, no amount of research will ever be complete enough to encompass all potential issues. Third, corporate culture and politics will often have a greater influence on decisions than the facts on which the decisions are based (Feltenstein, 1992; Rodrigues & Hickson, 1995). And fourth, managers with different mental models (images and assumptions about how the world/business works) will describe the same situation differently (Senge, 1992; Valentin, 1992). The answer to the question posed at the beginning of this paragraph is that management must use models to simplify the decision-making process. Humans have limited intellectual capacities in relation to the complexity of the problems they face (March and Simon, 1958, cited in Molloy et al., 1995). Therefore effective decisions require models that encompass the main concerns of the issue without involving every detail. In other words, since it will not be possible to know everything about an issue or to quantify all factors related to the issue, much of the strategy selection process will be subjective. Models reduce subjectivity by forcing a sequential and relatively thorough analysis of the issue.

The Crucible of Strategic Decisions

In the planning process, management develops extensive lists of SWOT factors. These various situational factors are then analyzed to decide which are important enough to act on, which should be monitored and considered for the future, and which should be given tertiary status. While most firms view the strategic analysis process as important, few give it the attention it deserves. Since selected strategies are the foundation for the success or failure of the company, strategic analysis is the crucible of the decision-making process.

Strategic Decision-making

Whether explicit or implicit, all firms have some type of plan for the future. The quality of these plans is often correlated with the quality of information and processes or models used to develop them. If management has historically developed successful strategies, then these efforts should probably be continued, regardless of their foundation in managerial science and theory. When management has had difficulty in producing effective strategies, or strategic options are not forthcoming, a formal means of analysis—a model—should be considered.

Too often when the word strategy is used an aura of permanence is assumed. Thirty or forty years ago this may have been true. Today, change comes quickly. What appeared logical a few months ago may appear half-baked today. Strategy is the first step or starting point of business decision-making. It is initially conceived as a business strategy that will be supported by functional strategies and tactics (policies and action plans). As various factors inside the firm and in its environment change, management must assess its totality of actions in light of the new information. This assessment normally works its way backward through the decision-making process. "Are our tactics appropriate for the current situation?" "Will changing them correct any perceived problems?" If not, the viability of strategic decisions must be reassessed. Strategy can be viewed as a synthesis of constantly evolving and vacillating facts. The cognitive challenge to management is not to keep the firm on course but to make sure it is on the right course.

The Theoretical Foundation for All Decisions

Regardless of the decision style employed, all decisions involve the concepts of strategic issues diagnosis and vigilant information processing.

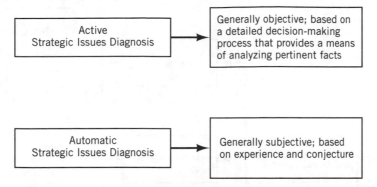

Figure 6.2 Decision-making alternatives.

STRATEGIC ISSUES DIAGNOSIS (SID)   This analytical concept refers to the degree of effort utilized when diagnosing or examining an issue. Strategic issues diagnosis is divided into two categories, active (reflective) and automatic (unreflective) SID (see Figure 6.2). Active SID is a systematic means of reviewing information for decision-making, especially for critical issues. Because of the issues' importance, management must utilize a process or model to assure that critical information is on hand and that alternative solutions are thoroughly examined (Dutton, 1993). Active SID is also known as *procedural rationality*. Rationality is this instance is defined as the extent to which information is collected for a decision and the degree of reliance on analysis of the information to make a decision (Dean & Sharfman, 1993).

The alternative to the active SID (or procedural rationality) decision-making processes is termed automatic SID. This occurs when the decision-maker's experience with the issue induces an automatic diagnosis—intuition. There are both problems and advantages with automatic SID. The primary problems are that one's experience may produce outdated means of addressing the issue, and that new, perhaps more suitable, means are ignored or are given only cursory attention. Another problem with automatic SID occurs during the annual planning process or during crises. In these circumstances decisions are being made that will impact the long-term future of the business; they should therefore be given reasonable consideration before strategies are selected. There are advantages to automatic SID, but caution must be used. The primary advantage is that it preserves executives' valuable time and capacity for attention to a variety of decisions by letting them utilize their experience and judgment (Dutton, 1993).

VIGILANT INFORMATION PROCESSING (VIP)   Herb Simon developed a model of decision-making similar to the active/automatic SID typology (Jago, 1994). He said that decisions (planning decisions, in this case) are made under low, medium, or high stress (see Figure 6.3). Decisions made under low stress tend to result in either doing nothing, utilizing the existing strategy, or acting without searching for more viable alternatives. Though the vast majority of hotels and restaurants do not operate in low-stress environments, they tend to make marketing decisions as if they were.

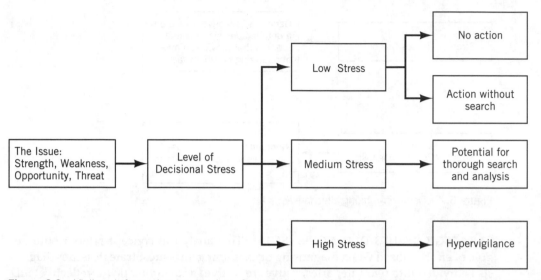

Figure 6.3   Vigilant information processing. *Source:* Adapted from Jago (1994), "Simon's vigilant information process." Speech at the University of Houston College of Business.

This is evidenced by the fact that too many of these firms simply dust off last year's marketing plan and reuse it. Moderate-stress decisions have the best chance for a thorough search and appraisal or vigilant information processing. This is the optimal level of stress for decision-making. Marketers know that the decision is very important, but since they are in control of the situation, they can summon all their abilities to make the necessary decision(s). The steps for vigilant information processing include (1) setting an objective that, if met, will satisfy specific and overall organizational goals; (2) searching for strategies and tactics that will achieve the objective; and then, (3) when a strategy (or tactic) is found that would likely achieve the objective, the search is stopped and the strategy is incorporated into the organization's plan. One of Simon's theories was that a business can rarely optimize its strategy search. Optimizing meant that marketers would search for all possible alternative strategies or tactics. Marketers must instead suboptimize, or find the best alternative after a reasonable search. The two primary threats to VIP are procrastination (putting off the decision) or buck-passing (letting someone else make the decision). Decisions made under high stress are generally not effective because the decision-maker cannot function at his/her optimal capacity (Jago, 1994).

Strategic Analysis Questions

The key tasks of the marketing information system were earlier described as deciding which data are necessary, then gathering, storing, and analyzing the data for decision-making purposes. Decisions on necessary data gathering and storing of data are relatively simple tasks. As long as an organized process is in place, most activities prior to analysis (formal research being the main exception) can be accomplished by personnel with limited research experience. Basically, management must make sure that a sufficient database has been compiled that will help decision-makers see the big picture. Effective analysis, and the subsequent diagnosis and decisions that follow, will require a much higher level of cognitive skills. Sitting around a table with a few environmental reports and internal records will not likely produce the most favorable results. A problem with the all-too-common cursory analysis is that five people will come up with five different solutions to the same situation. Unfortunately, since their opinions may be subjective and based on conjecture rather than analysis, each solution will be defended personally, producing dissension rather than consensus. The most skillful debater and those with political power will be heard above those with worthy and substantive concepts, perspectives, and strategic options.

While most firms view the analysis and diagnosis process as important, few give it the attention it deserves. Since it leads to decisions on future objectives and strategies, and therefore the potential success or failure of the company, the analysis of SWOT factors is actually the crucible of decision-makers and the planning process. This is the primary area where inferential skills (defined in Chapter 1) come into play. To improve the likelihood of consensus and to reduce the inherent risk involved in business decisions, some type of organized review or process of analysis should be considered.

The primary purpose of analysis at this point in the planning process is not to finalize the firm's strategies: it is to make sure that decision-makers have a detailed knowledge and understanding of the firm's competitive position and available strategic choices and to develop a consensus on the general direction in which many of its most important strategies should be headed. This analysis aids in the setting of long-term and annual objectives; corporate, business, and functional strategies; and related policies and action plans. For example, a preliminary assessment of a firm's opportunities for growth and related optional strategies will lead to a more realistic setting of objectives and better strategy selection. It also provides a platform for brainstorming of "alternative" strategies that may not have been considered in a formal discussion and forces the company to review its existing strategies for soundness in light of new environmental data and the changing abilities of the firm.

Strategic analysis of SWOT factors [a form of active strategic issues diagnosis (SID)] entails asking a series of ten questions to elicit and guide management's opinion of the relevance and value of a particular factor or group of factors and the firm's potential strategic direction (see Figure 6.4). Though the process might at first appear somewhat laborious, it can actually be accomplished very quickly. The choice is basically between an organized process that guides the business in thoroughly analyzing key factors, and random subjective opinions that lead to strategies with minimal factual support.

The number of SWOT factors that should be strategically analyzed depends on their perceived importance to the success of the business. In the actual planning process, only the most significant SWOT factors or groups of factors will be formally analyzed. Since many firms will group related SWOT factors, such as those concerned with increasing banquet business, the process may need to be reviewed only

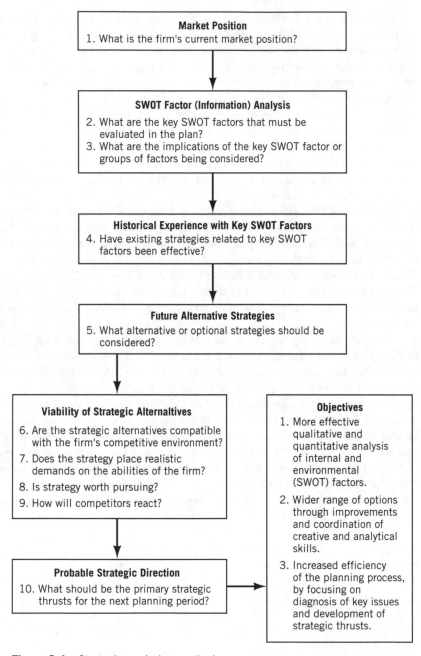

Figure 6.4   Strategic analysis questioning sequence.

a few times. It can be completed via written reports or oral review. As the questioning process is ingrained in the subconscious thought processes of management and marketing decision-makers, most SWOT factors can quickly be reviewed for their implications, importance, and possible solutions or strategies. Some factors can be processed in a few minutes. Others will take several days or longer if critical information is required for a thorough analysis. Occasionally, an item is weeded out after one or two of the questions, if it is felt that further discussion for that SWOT factor is not necessary.

The first three questions set the stage for the remaining questions by establishing a base for analysis—how well positioned the firm is in the market, the key SWOT factors that should play a role in future strategy decisions, and the implications of those SWOT factors. Questions 4 and 5 consider past strategies that were related to the SWOT factors, and potential future strategies that might be considered. Questions 6 and 9 address the viability of the potential future strategies. Question 10 sets the stage for the rest of the marketing plan by establishing probable strategic thrusts or directions for the firm.

MARKET POSITION

1. *What is the firm's current market position?*

Before a firm can attempt to capitalize on opportunities from its particular competitive situation, it must first have a reasonable idea of how it is viewed by its current target customers (its objective position). The categories include the following: position #1, a leader in the market; position #2, somewhat ahead of the market; position #3, meeting current market demand (or meeting expectations); position #4, slightly behind market demand; position #5, seriously behind market demand. With its current position in mind, the marketers can then decide on the degree of strategy change appropriate for its particular competitive position. (See the discussion on positioning on pages 296–299 for guidance in determining the firm's position.)

SWOT FACTOR ANALYSIS

2. *What are the key SWOT factors that must be evaluated in the plan?*

The business must now select those factors from the SWOT analysis that have the greatest possibility for impacting the firm in a positive or negative manner. Since the SWOT analysis is a summary of the situation analysis, this question is essentially asking, "What information do we have that is important enough to require action?" For example, in a firm's SWOT analysis, there could be 100 or more potential opportunities listed. It would not be economically or logistically feasible to try to take advantage of each, so only those with the greatest potential to further the firm's competitive position will be selected. Since the primary objective of the marketing department is to increase sales, opportunities with the potential to increase sales are generally considered first. Subsequently, the firm should address threats that must be defended against, weaknesses that must be corrected, and whether strengths are being fully maximized. Problems noted in the position analysis (question #1) will provide insight into which factors should be considered as important to the business's future.

For some companies there will be many factors that must be studied, each of nearly equal importance. For others there will be one central issue, or perhaps a few fundamental problems.

GROUPING OF FACTORS   When possible, related issues should be grouped together into a smaller number of major issues. This combining of factors allows the firm to effectively broaden the number of issues that will become part of its analysis and possibly its strategy. For example, weaknesses in the areas of per person revenue, front-desk courtesy, cleanliness, and food waste might be attributed to the larger problem of a lack of or ineffective training, no training manuals, weak management, and so on. The fact that people want more security in hotels and are taking shorter trips, that the Americans with Disabilities Act mandates accommodations for most disabilities; that there are more older people traveling; that older people are quite value-conscious and want health-oriented meals and enjoy continental breakfasts, could be combined to go after the senior citizen market.

JUDGING THE IMPORTANCE OF SWOT FACTORS   Some means such as prioritization, impact/immediacy analysis, or confidence assessment should be utilized to assess the importance of the various factors in the firm's situational analysis.

PRIORITIZATION   If SWOT factors, or groups of related SWOT factors, are prioritized by degree of importance, it will allow management to focus its efforts in areas that will produce the best results. Prioritization could be indicated by listing and numbering according to degree of importance, or by assigning levels of importance such as A = high priority, B = secondary or medium priority, and C = low priority. An entirely new marketing department for a competing hotel made up of experienced veterans might be labeled "A," a new director of sales or the creation of an in-state sales manager's position for this competing hotel might be given a "B" rating, and the hiring of a new sales manager might be labeled "C" or possibly ignored if the skill level of the new sales manager was approximately the same as the former sales manager. Figure 6.5 can be used to help prioritize SWOT factors.

	Opportunity	Threat
Strength	Pursue if worthwhile	Depending on the severity of the threat, use available abilities to defend against it
Weakness	Correct, and if worthwhile, pursue or select another opportunity	Depending on the severity of the threat, correct any weaknesses necessary to defend against the threat

Figure 6.5 General strategic option matrix.

IMPACT AND IMMEDIACY   A means of determining the importance of a threat or opportunity as well as a strength or a weakness is to assess its potential:

- *impact*—how great an effect it could have
- *immediacy*—the likelihood of it occurring, how soon it might take place, and if it did occur, how long the firm would have to prepare a strategy or tactic for it

If the determination is that it would have very little impact and no potential effect for several years, then it may not be necessary to include it in the analysis. If, on the other hand, the determination was positive, then it should probably be included in the analysis. In essence, this helps marketers and management differentiate between burnt toast and tragedy. Two factors may be serious, but one may have the potential for great harm, while another is simply a nuisance. For example, if a budget hotel had an excellent location in an area with several hotel sites, the company would have to consider the immediacy of a competitor constructing a hotel on the site and the impact it would have. If the determination of immediacy could be expressed as "potentially within a year," and its impact could be significant, then an applicable strategy would be implemented, or at least a contingency plan would be written and available if needed.

The matrix in Figure 6.6 graphically displays the relationship between the impact and immediacy of any particular environmental concern. Each quadrant is identified with a category number based on its importance to the business. A Category 1 factor would require a quick response, where Category 4 would not. The recommended actions for each level are included in the pertinent cell. Larger firms or those with many options may want to expand the matrix from four to nine cells, with low, medium, and high designations (McDonald & Leppard, 1992).

CONFIDENCE   The revelance of data or information can be assigned to categories based on the level of confidence attached to its probability of occurring. The categories

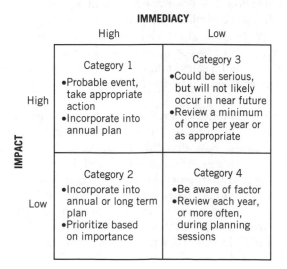

Figure 6.6 Impact/immediacy matrix.

could be identified by various titles. Most commonly used are *high, medium,* and *low confidence data.* This labeling could assist and alert marketers so that when a factor is discussed, decision-makers within the firm would understand how likely the event is to happen or how much weight the firm gives to its occurring. For example, the likelihood of increased demands for nutritious foods could be considered as high-confidence information, while the measurement of the availability of Alaskan salmon and the assessment of its market price might be low-confidence information.

3. *What are the implications of the key SWOT factor or groups of factors being considered?*

Of the key SWOT factors listed, the firm must determine their relevance for further analysis. This question is central to the analysis and extrapolation of information from the selected key SWOT factors. It is essentially asking the question, "How does or could this factor (or group of factors) affect the firm, its customers, or competitors?" One of the abilities required to develop potential implications of a SWOT factor is a manager's inferential skill—the ability to identify relevant issues and recognize the degree of their importance. Essentially, this means being able to analyze information and form valid assumptions that will assist in decision-making. For example, a high level of guest satisfaction (a strength) may imply that there is an opportunity for sales growth through both existing units and expansion. Lower sales than desired (a weakness) could have many implications: for example, the firm's product or service mix is not what customers want; the firm has been promoting an inferior product or service; the firm has not promoted its offering effectively (assuming a quality product or service); or the firm is not in a position to expand at the present time. If customers want more seafood (an opportunity), this would imply that additional seafood items should be considered, possibly an image change or repositioning is needed, and area competitors' seafood offerings should carefully be examined along with competitors that may also be considering adding seafood. If there is a possible price or value war (a threat), the implication could be that value should be a primary concern in the pricing and production of all menu items; that to remain competitive, costs should be minimized to the greatest extent possible; and that some or all menu items should be positioned as good or great values.

Another way of expediting the implications process is to ask questions that begin with, "What about . . . ?" For example, in the analysis of a major nearby competitor, a marketer might ask "What about the competing hotels' poorly decorated rooms, their larger auditorium, their smaller sales staff, or their new reservation system? The answers to this complex question would be the implications.

INTUITION   Knowing something without conscious reasoning (Guralnik, 1986) plays a part in the analysis of implications. The part of the mind used for this level of thought is the subconscious. Basically, this is where all previously acquired knowledge—the sum of a person's experiences—is stored. Developing implications requires a deep thought process that generally accelerates based on the degree of experience and ability of an individual to bring that experience to bear on the analysis. Where brainstorming, also an excellent method of eliciting ideas, brings an active, vocal participation from group members, intuition is best utilized in a quiet, relaxed atmosphere (better individually than in a group) allowing people to bring up their deepest thoughts. Frequently, the most in-depth understanding of a situation comes within about 30 minutes after lying down, when an individual is almost asleep, or the following day, by remembering dreams. The reason why relaxation, meditation, or sleep increases mental ability is because the mind is most effective when the brainwave cycles are at lower levels. There is much validity to the adage, "I'll sleep on it." Intuition can also be used to help develop optional strategies or the solutions to other problems or situations.

HISTORICAL EXPERIENCE WITH KEY SWOT FACTORS

4. *Have existing strategies related to key SWOT factors been effective?*

In other words, has the firm had any experience with strategies based on the SWOT factor being analyzed? Essentially, every existing strategy the firm now has was directly or indirectly based on a particular past SWOT factor.

If a particular strategy has been successful, and its related SWOT factors have not changed, the company should consider keeping it as long as it is compatible with the new environment. If related environmental factors have changed, then the strategy will need to be reassessed and perhaps discontinued, markedly changed, or at least modified.

In cases where the strategy has not been successful, it should either be dropped or reconsidered based on the new SWOT analysis. If the cause of the problem is with execution and not a misreading of the competitive market, it must be addressed as a weakness. In this instance, a determination should be made as to whether the weakness is possible to correct or its cost in resources, including time, are worth the effort.

For example, a hypothetical restaurant is analyzing the SWOT factor of customers wanting a place to eat after 2 a.m. when the bars close down. In the past, the firm had tried to take advantage of the opportunity, but it was not successful. The firm would have to consider whether there have been changes in its strengths and weaknesses that might allow it to be more successful this time. Additionally, are there any changes in the impact or immediacy of the opportunities? Is there a larger market for late-night food service now than in the past, or is the market more willing to frequent a restaurant offering late-night service? Perhaps there are more restaurants or clubs in the vicinity that are helping to increase the size of the market and their inclination to visit the area.

Overall, everything the company now does should be put on trial for its life (Drucker, 1974). The only sacred cow for a business should be its morals and philosophy of doing business. Strategies, like consumer behavior, must be flexible. Unfortunately, there is a tendency for firms to continue existing strategies whether they were successful or not (Mintzberg, 1972). Executives who have decided to pursue a certain course that has not been successful will often not want to change positions because it is tantamount to admitting failure. Naturally, this unwillingness to change will almost invariably lead to the executive's replacement. The primary reasons for this are that:

- Millions of dollars may have been lost and stockholders want a change.
- A new executive with appropriate skills may be needed to help select and implement new strategies.
- The executive is unable or unwilling to change.

Hospitality trade magazines frequently detail stories about changes in the executive suite. Because of stockholder distrust and increased publicity regarding high pay for poor performance, it is expected that these changes will not only continue but are likely to surge.

FUTURE ALTERNATIVE STRATEGIES

5. *What alternative or optional strategies should be considered?*

The alternative strategies will be developed from a screening of the SWOT analysis for potentially profitable opportunities, strengths that should be maximized, weaknesses that must be corrected, and threats that should be avoided or defended against. For example, if a new market segment has been identified that could increase sales—an opportunity—then alternative strategies to take advantage of it would be developed. Alternative strategies must be based, as much as possible, on an objective appraisal of the firm's situational analysis (what customers want, not what management thinks they want). Marketing planners' experience or personal feelings about the environmental concern or optional strategies often lead to an automatic diagnosis (Dutton, 1993). In some cases, this may be the most effective and efficient means to the strategy decision. After all, most decisions (strategies and tactics) are the result of personal experience and the success of past decisions. To determine their viability, the alternative strategies (also referred to as strategic options) would then be subjected to strategic issue diagnosis, through the remaining strategic analysis questions.

If a firm has certain exceptional strengths, especially sustainable competitive advantages, with which to take advantage of the SWOT factor, it can develop strategies to extract the greatest value from the strength. For example, if a hotel's strength was having a location near every major airport in the United States, then alternative strategies based on this could be developed. The firm would take advantage of the opportunity of potential business from airline customers and employees based on the strength of its locations. The marketing department could develop a promotional strategy around that fact, such as offering a special rate to all major firms that fly into those airports, offering a special rate to airline crews and placing signs in the airport stressing the convenient location. When a firm's strengths are not considered formidable, the goal might be to direct the company's efforts at developing strategies designed to fill a niche in the market not currently being addressed. An independent restaurant operator could focus on personal service, high-quality menu offerings, specials, serving regional favorites, and other strategies that might differentiate it from chain operators (Thompson & Strickland, 1992).

Similarly, when a firm considers weaknesses it must develop alternative strategies to correct them. When a skill that is needed to take advantage of an attractive opportunity does not exist—a weakness—management must decide whether it is worth the effort to make appropriate changes—implement a strategy to correct it.

Defending against threats (defensive strategies) poses a more difficult problem. If the actions of a competitor, societal trends, changes in traveling habits, or trends in any other area of the environment indicate a possible or probable threat, management must decide if it is necessary to prepare a strategy to defend against the threat.

Often, other actions of the firm are normally already helping to defend against the threat. For example, if a threat is posed by a primary competitor's high RPPQ (relative perceived product/service quality), or if such a competitor is planning on moving into an existing firm's trade area, the existing firm would probably already have a strategy in place to upgrade its products and services. Under normal circumstances, this practice should be a never-ending strategy. Additional defenses, such as price, quantity, or plate appearance adjustments, might also be considered. The key question here would be, "What do I need to do (what strategy or tactic is needed) to successfully defend the firm against the perceived threat?"

Not acting on some SWOT factors is unavoidable. The company can only do so much. But an increasingly common characteristic of business strategies is the inaction on imminent and serious threats. Unfortunately, too many firms, especially smaller businesses, view themselves as being unable to mount a defense against a larger competitor. In almost all cases of fair competition, there are strategies by which even the smallest competitor can protect itself and even thrive in the midst of large competitors. In fact, smaller and leaner competitors often have major strengths that can be exploited, such as the ability to adapt quicker to changing market conditions, more personalized service, and lower overhead. A decision must be made as to which factors should be acted on immediately, spread out over the short- or long-term future, or put off indefinitely. Someone must lead the firm and take responsibility for deciding which path to take.

LOCATING OPTIONAL STRATEGIES   The search for strategies is analytical, creative, incremental (Pearce-Robinson, 1991), and political.

ANALYTICAL   Historically, marketing has been perceived as a discipline where creative thought was the predominant requirement. This attitude does not do justice to the study. Creativity is important, but it makes up only a small portion of the marketer's requisite skills. The primary reason people perceive marketing as a creative activity is because most firms lack a formal plan to guide the decision process (Reich, 1991). It is true that marketing does require some creativity, but the critical academic requirement for hospitality marketing is actually analytical. The marketer first does research to establish various facts about the firm and its environment. Marketing creativity flows directly from the quality and quantity of that research. From this information, marketing managers decide what products or services the customer will purchase, other marketing mix variables such as pricing and atmosphere, and, finally, how to communicate these to potential consumers.

CREATIVE   Everyone is creative to a degree: but the difference between average creativity and superior creativity is the difference between an occasional jogger and an Olympic athlete. The first step to creativity in a business organization is to have an environment conducive to creativity. The following are some of the characteristics of a "creative organization" (Hayes, 1994):

Receptive to new ideas, sensitive to different possible approaches, withholding judgment or criticism

Attitude of the organization as a whole
Attitude of each individual's supervisor
Recognition
Time for creative thought, away from normal responsibilities
Freedom of choice to do what is reasonably necessary to pursue one's ideas
The physical environment of the workplace
The amount of interaction between workers

For marketing, the process of developing a new product or service includes *idea generation* (seeking a reasonable quantity of new ideas that appear to solve the issue at hand), *idea screening* (deciding which ideas have the most potential), and *concept development* (creating and testing the ideas). Creative idea generation begins by getting into the minds of customers. What do they want? How do they think? What are their behaviors relative to the firm's products and services? When the average firm attempts to use creative thinking it will normally use *convergent thinking*—focusing on the one best solution. One of the keys to maximizing the creative process is the use of *divergent thinking*—not setting parameters on ideas and attempting to gather the largest quantity of options rather than the best quality options. Qualitative concerns would be addressed later if an option was considered for adoption. Some basic forms of creative thinking are the following:

- *Attribute Listing.* Simply list the various attributes for which the customer is looking—ideally, those that delve into the psychology and motivational characteristics of potential customers.
- *Forced Relationships.* Select any stimulus word, list the characteristics of that word, and then determine which of those words have any possible relationship or application to the firm's strategies or procedures. For example, the stimulus word is "canned tomatoes." Its characteristics and uses are: red, watery, salty, acid, bright, mushy, crushed, seeds, silver (the can), metal, paper, Italian, spaghetti sauce, tomato soup, and so forth. These characteristics would then be viewed as to how they could be applied to any desired strategy or procedure. This could range from another food item to the decor of a restaurant. Perhaps the plate appearance should be brighter and more colorful, or there should be an Italian entree on the menu. The same goes for the decor—maybe some silver on the walls to add richness.
- *Fantasy Technique.* This method is utilized by an individual in private. The person sits in a comfortable chair in a quiet room. (Several major corporations have designated "quiet rooms" where employees can go to think or meditate about solutions to problems. These rooms are pitch dark, except for small directional lights near the floor.) The task is to visualize oneself as a customer going through the hotel or restaurant, while sensing all the smells, sounds, decor/atmosphere, furniture/fixtures, and people one would encounter. Immediately afterward, all thoughts, feelings, and ideas are recorded. The insights are used to develop possible improvements, modifications, and innovations.
- *Heuristic Ideation Technique (HIT).* (Heuristic refers to a self-guided method of developing solutions to a problem.) This is the utilization of a matrix to establish possible

SALADS	INGREDIENTS		
	RED BELL PEPPERS	ARTICHOKE HEARTS	MUSHROOMS
Chef Salad	Yes	Maybe	Yes
Tuna Salad	Yes	No	No
Chicken Fajita	Yes	No	No
Salmon Chef	Yes	Yes	Yes
Dinner Salad	No	No	No

Figure 6.7   Heuristic ideation technique.

relationships. On the vertical side of the matrix could be the entrees that will be served in the restaurant. On the horizontal side could be the various styles of serving pieces that are available (see Figure 6.7). Then, each block or grid in the matrix would be considered for its possibilities. The selection of plates, entrees, and the analysis could be more extensive. (The selection of ingredients, salads, and the analysis could be more extensive.) The HIT grid is commonly used to develop new menu items. The available meats, poultry, and seafood items would be placed on one side of the matrix, and the possible accompaniments on the other. For example, a chicken breast could be paired with mushrooms, green onion, garlic, basil, wine, tomatoes, and mozzarella cheese. The objective in this case is not only promotion of creativity but also cross-utilization of existing products.

• *Collective Notebook Method.* This is simply a small notebook that is carried at all times. When a thought comes up, write it down. It is especially useful if placed by the bed, because as the mind relaxes (brainwave cycles are lowered), its capacity for creativity increases. Analyze the material for possible application.

Conventional wisdom should be discarded when developing potential strategies. Often, unconventional strategies or tactics that initially sound far-fetched bring up other ideas with potential for implementation. A television commercial showing pizza with cheese that stretches throughout the house is definitely not mainstream, but it worked. The target customer desired humor. These "illogical" strategies may also offer a window to the future needs of the customer—the potential to reach position 1. Since strategies are developed for the short and long term, the longer the lead time the stranger the potential strategy will sound. Figure 6.8 shows what can be done with a few facts from a customer analysis.

Operational and financial creativity are concerned primarily with effectiveness and efficiency. How can we do something better, faster, or at a lower cost? It is important not to have preconceptions of how things should be done.

If a hotel were trying to develop a TV commercial, it would ideally have hundreds of pieces of information in its customer analysis. Assume the following information must be utilized for the production of a commercial for a hotel: (1) guests like fresh flowers and nutritious foods; (2) feel they are not getting the respect they deserve from hotel employees in general; (3) are homesick while traveling; and (4) do not feel they can fully relax in a hotel room.

With just four facts, and a little creativity, the draft for a storyboard for a commercial could be developed. The desired message for this commercial is that the hotel's employees do everything possible for their guests. A bit of humor is used to help differentiate the ad from competitors' ads and to attract and hold the viewer's attention.

Music: Have the song "Respect" by Aretha Franklin playing in the background. Ms. Franklin would make a cameo appearance, as a guest.

Scene One:

The tired guest walks into a lobby full of flowers. She takes a breath of the fragrant air and breathes a sign of relief. Immediately afterward, she is asked to sit down in a chair that has poles attached to the sides in the style of those used by ancient royalty. The chair is lifted by the general manager, the marketing director, the chef, and the concierge. As she is taken to the front desk, the clerk recognizes her by name and asks if she would like a hometown newspaper in the morning and reminds her that she has accumulated enough frequent-guest points for an upgrade to a suite. She replies that the suite would be great.

Scene Two:

The guest is now relaxing in her room in an overstuffed chair. Her feet are on an ottoman resting on a satin pillow. She is talking on the phone to her family, while sipping a fresh fruit smoothie. She tells her husband that she finally found a hotel where the service is first class and the people really care about and respect their guests.

(The respect issue could be a point of differentiation by making it a #1 priority with employees. It could be supported with internal marketing efforts such as contests and external pressure on employees such as creating some type of slogan used in the media that communicates the expectation that guests will receive respectful and courteous service.)

Figure 6.8   Combining analysis and creativity to develop a commercial.

INCREMENTAL   The search is incremental because the selection process begins by analyzing past strategies, policies, and marketing action plans to decide what has been successful and what has not. Actions that have been successful are kept, those that are not are discontinued or modified, and new strategies are "incrementally" added to existing strategies, policies, or action plans. For example, if a functional strategy to control costs has been successful in reducing costs by the amount set in the annual objectives, then the strategy and its corresponding policies should be kept. If a promotion targeted at corporate clients of a hotel has been marginally successful, it will be analyzed according to its merits and either modified or discontinued. If a new strategy is called for, perhaps a sales promotion of giving an umbrella with the company's logo to corporate guests who stay over for one weekend night, it will be incrementally added to existing strategies. This is essentially saying that the vast majority of strategies, with some modifications, will remain the same. Marketing strategies, because of their dependence on the environment, are the functional area most subject to change. The majority of other functional areas will normally focus on improvements in execution.

CORPORATE POLITICS   A common occurrence in strategy selection is that executives enter into the process with preconceived strategic agendas and are simply searching for compatible opportunities that support their biased views. This attitude negates the purpose of the planning process. Each participant must be open enough to realize that as new information comes to light, new strategies may be required. Plans must be based on valid information, not just opinion or one's position on the organization chart (Aram & Cowen, 1990).

One common characteristic of corporate politics is that the lower one is in the corporate hierarchy, the more factual support must be presented when expressing views or opinions on possible strategies. This is a legitimate requirement in that those who are new to the business world will have fewer experiences to draw from when analyzing SWOT factors. "Great ideas" from young managers without proper research and support will seldom attract more than passing attention. But ideas that have been analyzed thoroughly and appear to show promise must be heard.

VIABILITY OF STRATEGIC ALTERNATIVES   The remainder of the strategic analysis questions focus on the advantages, disadvantages, and viability of the strategic options and, finally, the most preferred options.

6. *Are the strategic alternatives compatible with the firm's competitive environment?*

The perceived opportunity (or other SWOT factor) must be based on factual data and a realistic appraisal of the situation, not on management's subjective speculation. If a strategy calls for improved quality at a higher price, customers must want higher quality and be willing to pay for it. An occasional problem for independent fast-food restaurant operators is that they generally offer a higher quality product and charge more than chain fast-food operations. If this is what the customer demands, there is no problem, but if the restaurant's target customers resist higher prices for similar menu items, then it will need to find a way of reducing the price or increasing the perceived value of the meal. If a hotel company decides to build smaller, but luxurious, hotel rooms that will be offered at a midscale price, it must be sure there are enough customers who have a need for a less expensive, luxury hotel room. A problem with this strategy could be that the majority of guests desiring higher quality or luxury hotel rooms work for companies that pay for the room. Therefore, they may not be motivated by the opportunity to save money. On the other hand, if there is a limited supply of the smaller rooms—less competition—then even if the demand is low, a niche (small protected market) might be available. If the firm had an experienced marketing staff—a strength—it might be possible through personal selling to contact companies with travel needs that would like to reduce their travel expenditures.

TIMING   A key factor related to environmental compatibility is timing. Is the timing right for any certain course of action that may be selected? As mentioned in Chapter 1, one of the goals of strategic market management is to be proactive—seeing an opportunity or threat before others and taking advantage of it. Though generally a benefit of strategic planning, it can also cause severe problems. If a company acts too soon, thinking it will be a leader in an untapped market, the result may not be pleasant. Everyone knows what happened to many of the pioneers crossing the plains.

For many strategies there may be a window of opportunity. A strategy executed during this time might be successful; afterward, the risk goes up. A popular sandwich chain was purchased from its creators in the early 1980s. People inquiring about purchasing franchises were told that none were going to be sold until the company was reorganized. At this time their part of the country was experiencing rapid growth with expansion in almost all business segments. Unfortunately, the reorganization took several years and by the time the company was ready to sell franchises again, this region of the country was in recession, and few buyers were available. An additional problem was that while the firm was stagnant, another sandwich chain penetrated the local markets, making expansion even more difficult.

Also in the 1980s, D'Lites, a small chain of health-oriented fast-food hamburger restaurants, opened. Because of the great initial curiosity on the part of consumers, many restaurants were opened within a short period of time. Once the novelty wore off and the company was not able to cover its debt, stores quickly began closing. Several imitators of this company also closed. They were trying to pioneer a concept before its time. Although customers were requesting healthier foods, only a small number were willing to change their present eating habits.

A related issue that will be garnering much strategic thought is the subject of smoking. At some point in the future it is likely that smoking will be banned from all public access buildings. Until this law is passed, there will be a great many people trying to minimize their exposure to smoke. Many hotels and most restaurants have rooms or areas that are designated as nonsmoking. This has made these establishments more attractive to those who do not wish to be exposed to smoke. If a hotel or restaurant prohibits smoking altogether before a law is passed requiring it, are there enough nonsmokers to replace current smokers? Also, will smokers continue to frequent these establishments in spite of their self-imposed prohibition? Before a hospitality company adopts the strategy of prohibiting smoking, it must make sure that the timing is right.

7. *Does the strategy place realistic demands on the abilities of the firm?*

This requires an objective appraisal of the firm's strengths and weaknesses. A key opportunity can rarely be taken advantage of without a compatible strength with which it can be paired. For example, if consumer research indicates the need to upgrade the quality of food or service, or if a more demanding customer is added to the target customer base, then correspondingly greater skills in cooking, service, purchasing, and quality control will be necessary. If a hotel company sees an opportunity to expand and desires to do so, financial resources, profit stability, operational systems, and adequate key personnel will be among the requisite skills. If customers are seeking value, and the firm has a low profit margin, it may not be in a position to effectively take advantage of the opportunity without major operational changes. If a skill that is needed to take advantage of an attractive opportunity does not exist—a weakness—then management must decide whether it is worth the effort to make appropriate changes.

An important skill related to the implementation of any strategy is the firm's current ability to effectively and consistently execute policies and action plans. If most activities of the business are already carried out according to standardized policies, then implementation and control of new policies or strategies will normally be simplified.

8. *Is the strategy worth pursuing?*

First and most important are the answers to the following questions: What are the financial or other competitive advantages, such as cost reductions (productivity), sales increases, improvement in image/public relations, quality and employee relations benefits, that will accrue from the strategy? (Porter, 1980). What are the potential benefits of a $20,000 ad campaign for a midsized restaurant chain? Based on historical information and knowledge of the market, what might be the increase in sales during the campaign? Is the quality of the campaign such that it will have a residual effect either on sales or on the firm's image? Is the campaign a necessary evil to defend against a strong competitor? Would another strategy, such as targeting existing customers through internal merchandising, be more lucrative, easier to implement, and less of a risk? Can the costs involved in the campaign be reduced through co-promotions with vendors or other restaurants or hotels, limiting ad agency input, or sponsoring a charitable event?

Are the risks involved acceptable, and what might be the likely results from pursuing a certain strategy? Obviously, the hope is that something positive will result, but this is often based on some degree of optimism—blind or factually based. Generally, there is a double-barreled decision to be made. If 100 rooms are added, what could happen? On the other hand, if the 100 rooms are not added, what might happen to business? Customers may go elsewhere. There will always be risks involved in pursuing an opportunity, but there may often be greater risks involved in ignoring it.

9. *How will competitors react?*

A business must consider whether a competing firm will react to any specific strategic choice. If so, how soon, will it happen, what might that reaction be, what amount of effort will be brought to bear on it, and how could it affect the firm and its new strategies? Some industry segments react quickly to competitive moves, while others react slowly, if at all (Porter, 1980). The majority of competitive reactions in the hospitality business are instigated by a competing firm's promotion of new products and services or reductions in price for popular offerings. In the convenience or economy segment of the market—fast-food and budget or limited-service hotels and motels—most counterstrategies are related to changes in a competitor's price or other means of promoting prices, such as value meals. The reason for this is that since there is often a lack of differentiation between these competitors—the products and services are so similar that brand loyalty is low—the customer will quickly change buying habits according to who has the best deal. As we learned from Porter's forces of competition that, in some instances, the customers have more power than the business, so they can dictate terms (Porter, 1980). When one fast-food restaurant lowers its price, primary and even secondary competitors are generally quick to follow. The alternative is a loss of market share or sales. There are, of course, instances where a fast-food restaurant's promotion of new menu items brings a reaction, but so far in the 1990s value promotions appear to garner the quickest response.

Pricing counterstrategies for midscale and luxury markets are much less obvious and are rarely used in promotional campaigns. Each firm will keep up with competitors' room prices and menu prices and utilize this information when making seasonal or scheduled price changes. Competitors' reactions in the midscale to upscale markets generally involve either a response to the addition of menu items or services, an increased emphasis on general advertising, or a focus on expansion.

Any type of promotional campaign that could affect a primary competitor's sales should take into account possible responses. The degree of potential effect, between minimal and severe, will generally match the competitor's reaction. Any such campaign should generally be accompanied by a contingency plan focused on defending against possible counterstrategies, especially attack or comparison advertisements. In many cases, this response would be a continued focus on the original campaign. For example, a hotel promoting its friendly service to the point of positioning itself as the "friendly hotel" would probably want to continue the promotion. As the competitor tries some type of diversion for the customer, through comparison ads or otherwise, the continued focus on friendly service during the battle would reinforce the attribute in the customer's mind. Of course, there is always the possibility that a competitor might develop an extremely effective comparison ad campaign that belittles the firm's "friendly service" ads. If this occurs, it is up to the marketing department to outgun the competitor with a direct response, begin working on another positive ad campaign, or lay low for a time to avoid an expensive promotional battle.

A common strategy by most large hospitality firms is that of expanding locations in order to be number one in a market. The possible counterstrategies are to select other markets or, if the market in question is strategic, to follow a competing firm's expansion strategy in an attempt to limit its ability to achieve the competitive advantage of being number one in a market (through sales, image, or obtaining the most prominent locations).

PROBABLE STRATEGIC DIRECTION

10. *What should be the primary strategic thrusts for the next planning period?*

After pertinent SWOT factors or groups of SWOT factors have been analyzed and potentially viable strategic alternatives have been selected, probable strategic thrusts and the general direction that new strategies will take are decided on. The purpose of this, as with the rest of the strategic analysis process, is to increase the likelihood of an objective diagnosis of key issues and a platform from which to discuss remaining components of the strategic plan. It is not imperative at this point that selected strategic thrusts be set in stone. Through the questioning process many advantages and disadvantages will have been considered, but more will come forth as the planning process continues.

Strategic thrusts can be a single strategic alternative, such as "Promote more weekend packages"; or a combination of strategies that focus on increasing promotions, such as "Increase the promotional budget." This might include strategy alternatives, such as the above promotion of more weekend packages, increasing the use of radio, adding in-flight and meeting planner magazines to the promotional mix, doubling spending on the secretary's club, and so forth. Other examples of strategic thrusts are focusing on new products, improving product or service quality, increasing the value perception, opening new locations, and remodeling hotel lobbies and restaurant dining rooms.

The strategic analysis questioning process provides planners with a methodical means of determining key situational variables and potential strategies. This planning step not only saves time, as objectives and various functional strategies are set, but also improves the effectiveness of the overall planning effort. No planning process or model will ever detail specifically what must be done to assure success, but attempts must be made at clarifying these complicated decisions and improving results. In the end, management must simply gather the best possible information, analyze it in an organized logical manner, and then make a decision. The ten-step strategic analysis facilitates this process.

THE BRYAN HOUSE AND CITY GRILL SWOT ANALYSES

The Bryan House

FACTORS

Strengths

Airport shuttle
24-hour security guard, limited access to hotel
Quality room amenities, including coffee maker with coffee
complete renovation in 1992
Atrium in lobby
Luxurious appointments in lobby
Located at busy intersection, with easy ingress and egress
Near state capitol, shopping district, and regional convention center
Many corporate and association headquarters are located downtown
Downtown is undergoing revitalization
Advertisement in state travel magazine was moderately successful
Recycling bins have been set up for paper, newspaper, and aluminum cans
All new employees have passed a drug test
Comprehensive orientation program has been successful
Excellent benefits for employees
Management turnover is 15% below average for area

Neutral Factors

15,000 square feet of meeting space
One restaurant, a casual dining concept
Some in-house merchandising
Reasonable-quality lunch and dinner for employees

Weaknesses

Independently owned
300 rooms (smaller than most competitors)
No secretarial services
No newspaper delivery to rooms
No fast lunch
No concierge
No workout facility
Keyed-lock system
No healthy alternatives in any of the F&B outlets
Guest services book with few services available
Understaffed sales department by at least one person, possibly two poor performance
    by marketing department
The hotel has not been involved in any charitable events
The $79 weekend package with in-room breakfast is $10 to $15 higher than competitors
Front desk speed—3.4
Banquet food—3.2; restaurant food—2.7
Restaurant service—3.6
Check-out times are 2 to 3 minutes, about 1 minute over competitors' average
There is very little formal training, except on-the-job training
Employees are not paid quite as well as those of competitors
Employee turnover is 20% higher than the average for area competitors
Occupancy is 5% below the average for area competitors
The ADR is $5 above competitors
The hotel lost 3% on sales during the past year
F&B prime costs: food costs 40%, labor costs 32%

Opportunities

Recycling is important to guests and, if promoted, can help minimize promotional
    expenditures
A local company will pick up most recyclable items
New York City, San Francisco, and the Dallas–Fort Worth areas are bringing us almost
    half of our sales
IBT Characteristics (again, for the sale of brevity, only the IBT factors are listed):
    Average household income for guests is nearly double that of the U.S. average
    IBTs require business services
    60% of IBT customers have children below 18 years of age
    85% are family oriented
    Are active stock investors
    Generally conservative
    Take two or more vacations each year, one with just their spouses
    Enjoy movies

Moderately religious
Concerned about fashion
Concerned about the quality and value of everything they purchase
Concerned about nutrition, exercise, and quality-of-life issues
Watch news on television
Read *USA Today* and the *Wall Street Journal*
Enjoy participating in and watching sports
IBTs want the following that our hotel currently does not offer:
Concierge
Business services
In-room movies
90% of guests are requesting non smoking rooms
Freshly prepared, quality food from the restaurant
Most hotel guests are loyal to The Bryan House
Because of the new political climate, the average American may have more disposable
    income in the future
Foreign guests spend about $30 per day more than U.S. guests
The number of foreign guests is increasing
People

Threats

Easier for competitors to attract employees
Less of a change for advancement for employees than at competing hotels
Most competitors are recycling
There are several quality secondary competitors with rates of up to half of our ADR
Secondary competitors that have banquet and restaurant facilities charge about 30%
    less than we charge
Most primary competitors have:
Brand name recognition through chain affiliation
Approximately 25% more rooms
Average ADRs $5 below our ADR
Concierge's desk; half have concierge's floors
Workout facilities, including weights, bikes, and pool
Business services, including secretaries, computers, and fax machines
Up-to-date property management systems
Interchange systems that electronically approve and bill card-issuing bank

City Grill

FACTORS

Strengths

10% increase in sales
ROS continues to rise (15%)
New menu items very popular
High RPPQ and RPV

Effective cost control system
Atmosphere well suited to concept
Flexible menu offerings
Employee turnover low
Average employee skill level high
Effective implementation of functional strategies

Weaknesses

Debt-to-equity ratio 65%
Marketing department used money instead of creativity
Some minor remodeling needed
Customer survey information not adequate
Ticket-time over 12 minutes, most competitors under 10 minutes
Management turnover too high

Opportunities

Two-income families increasing
Elderly customers in neighborhood
Nutritionally conscious customers
Takeout and delivery business increasing steadily
Most restaurant menus look the same
Our target customer appears to be the baby boomer
Frequency of customer return higher than average restaurant
Can generally attract employees easier than competition
No major competitor is serving fresh fish
Moral of Jake's Grill employees appears low
Good prices and quality from suppliers
Low interest rates
Good supply of seafood of which competitors are unaware

Threats

National economy is weak
Several major competitors in trade area
Over-reliance on one seafood supplier
Our marketing budget is lower than most of our competitors
Fewer people looking for low-paying jobs such as busser and dishwasher
Liquor taxes were raised

THE BRYAN HOUSE AND CITY GRILL STRATEGIC ANALYSES QUESTIONING SEQUENCE

The Bryan House

1. What is the firm's current market position in relation to customer demand? We are between Positions 3 and 4 (Position 1 = far exceeding customer demand, a leader in the industry or market; 2 = ahead of basic customer demand; 3= meeting customer demand; 4= not meeting customer demand in critical areas). The people end of service has been good, but we need to focus more on the technical side of execution and offer more services.

2. *What are the key SWOT factors that must be considered in the plan?* (Each key SWOT factor is referred to hereafter by its letter designation—A, B, C, and D.)

A. Limited business services
B. Poor-quality food
C. Lack of name brand recognition
D. Slow check-out at front desk

3. *What are the implications of the SWOT factor or group of factors?*

A. Business guests frequently have to go outside the hotel to have their business needs taken care of. Regular guests know about the lack of business services, but several have been asking us why we don't add them. We have probably lost sales because of this, so at some point, we must either add them or continue to see sales decline.

B. The low food quality will drive away banquet business and limit the sales for our restaurant. Employees and management are getting tired of food complaints. Because of this, morale is slipping and it is becoming more difficult to hire employees.

C. Our reservation system has been providing us with about 20% of our sales, but because of the lack of name brand recognition, we are not getting our share of new business.

D. Hotel guests are getting tired of standing in line and sometimes become impatient with front desk employees. Like the food problem, this is hurting morale.

4. *Have existing strategies related to the key SWOT factor been effective?* No, there have not been any major attempts at solving any of these problems. To a degree, most can be corrected with effective strategies and implementational efforts.

5. *What alternative or optional strategies should be considered?*

A. One of the small meeting rooms could be converted to a business center. To maximize the use of secretaries' time, they could also be given hotel assignments.

B. The chef should hold meetings with existing employees to get their ideas of how some of the current problems could be solved. Either a new chef should be hired or an outside consultant should be brought in. The layout and equipment in the kitchen must be analyzed for efficiency and effectiveness. New recipes must be written and adhered to. Servers must be trained and given the appropriate help to deliver the food when it is ready.

C. Since there is no way of having our name in the public eye as much as our primary competitors, we should focus most of our efforts on exceeding current customers' expectations, limited advertising in the most efficient travel-related magazines, some direct mail, and a first-class personal selling program that includes telemarketing. A new brochure that describes the hotel's features is needed. A video featuring the hotel's attributes would be helpful. Since the hotel is already tied into the SABREvision system, it could also add the JAGUAR hotel directory service, which gives each of the SABREvision accounts access to video displays of the hotel features, surrounding attractions, and a map of the area. The travel agent can make copies of pictures and maps for clients.

D. The hotel needs to purchase a property management system. An analysis of the hotel's needs and available systems should begin as soon as possible. Until the system is in place, the front desk manager should have meetings with employees to discuss the reason for getting the system, what features the employees would like to have, and how check-out time could be reduced until the new equipment is in place.

6. *Are the strategic alternatives compatible with the firm's competitive environment?*

A, B, & D. Customers want a reasonable level of business services; fresher, better tasting food; and faster check-out times.
C. Name recognition must be improved.

7. *Does the strategy place realistic demands on the abilities of the firm?* All potential strategies are within the abilities of the hotel. The marketing and F&B strategies may require help. Hopefully, the management company will assist us; but if not, someone else must be brought in. APMS (property management system) must be purchased that fills our needs without inordinately adding to our expenses.

8. *Is the strategy worth pursing?* Since we are losing money, changes must be made as quickly as possible. Each strategy must be viewed from the stand-point of potential financial return and improvements in the hotel's image. A budget should be established, so that costs are known prior to implementation, and so that functional departments will have budgets to maintain.

9. *How will competitors react?* For the following reasons, minimal competitor reaction is expected:

- Since our hotel is not part of a chain, minimal increases in promotional efforts will hardly be recognized by competitors.
- Potential increases in sales will be small in comparison to the hotel's market.
- Most competitors have already implemented our proposed strategies.

The Hilton, our closest competitor, may step up personal selling efforts.
10. *What should be the primary strategic thrusts for the next planning cycle?*

A. Add business services as soon as possible. Implement a survey to determine the quantity and type of services necessary.
B. First try to internally correct the problem with poor-quality food. If this does not work, then do whatever is necessary to solve the problem.
C. Decide on what steps are required to increase our image. Set detailed objectives to measure results.
D. Find a PMS that is functional and affordable. Make sure it is tied to an electronic credit-card-processing system.

City Grill

See Appendix B: Strategy Selection Process, Example #1, in Chapter 7

QUESTIONS AND PROJECTS

1. What is the purpose of the SWOT analysis?
2. Describe the process by which it is developed and optional formats for its presentation.
3. How do you determine the importance of SWOT factors?
4. Why do people use models to solve problems?
5. Describe what is meant by strategic issues diagnosis and vigilant information processing.
6. Related to the strategic analysis, what does the term "implications" mean?
7. Select a potential factor for any business, then given examples of how the business's experience with that factor in the past will influence its action in the future.
8. Discuss the analytical, creative, incremental, and political aspects of selecting strategy options.
9. What is the difference between convergent and divergent thinking?
10. When developing optional strategies, why is it generally important for younger management personnel to have more supportive evidence for their strategic options than older personnel?
11. Select one weakness, opportunity, or threat for a firm, then prepare a strategic analysis for it (the strategic analysis questioning sequence).

Malcolm Baldrige National Quality Award*

As part of the national quality improvement campaign, industry and government have joined together in supporting an Award for business excellence—the Malcolm Baldrige National Quality Award. Created by public law, the Award is the highest national recognition for business excellence that a U.S. company can receive.

The Award promotes:

• Understanding of the requirements for performance excellence and competitiveness improvement; and
• Sharing of information on successful performance strategies and the benefits derived from using these strategies.

The Baldrige Award is presented each year at a presidential ceremony.

CATEGORIES

Awards can be made to qualifying companies in each of the following categories:

• Manufacturing
• Service
• Small business

Award recipients may publicize and advertise receipt of the Award, provided they agree to share information about their successful quality strategies with other U.S. organizations.

*Reprinted with permission of the U.S. Department of Commerce; National Institute of Standards and Technology, Gathersburg, MD, 1996.

CRITERIA

The Award Criteria provide organizations with an integrated, results-oriented framework for implementing and assessing processes for managing all operations. These Criteria are also the basis for making awards and providing feedback to applicants. The following are the Criteria's seven examination Categories:

- *Leadership* The company's leadership system, values, expectations, and public responsibilities.
- *Information and Analysis* The effectiveness of information collection and analysis to support customer-driven performance excellence and marketplace success.
- *Strategic Planning* The effectiveness of strategic and business planning and deployment of plans, with a strong focus on customer and operational performance requirements.
- *Human Resource Development and Management* The success of efforts to realize the full potential of the work force to create a high-performance organization.
- *Process Management* The effectiveness of systems and processes for assuring the quality of products and services.
- *Business Results* The company's performance and improvement in key business areas—product and service quality, productivity and operational effectiveness, supply quality, and financial performance indicators that are linked to these areas.
- *Customer Focus and Satisfaction* The effectiveness of systems to determine customer requirements and satisfaction and the demonstrated success in meeting customer's expectations.

Malcolm Baldrige National Quality Award
National Institute of Standards and Technology
Administration Building, Room A537
Gaithersburg, MD 20899–0001

Telephone: (301) 975–2036
Telefax: (301) 948–3716
E-mail: oqp«nist.gov

The Baldrige Award Program's World Wide Web
home page address (or URL) is
http://www.nist.gov/quality–program/.

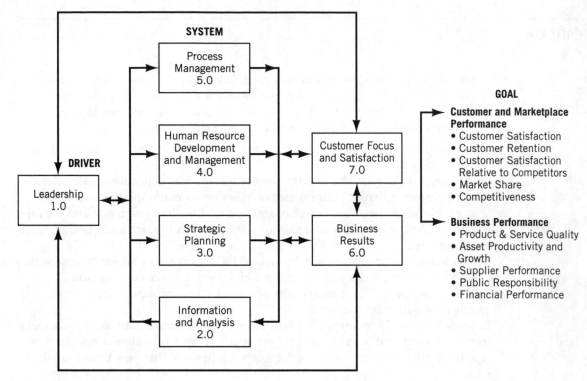

Malcolm Baldrige National Quality Award (1996). Reprinted with permission of U.S. Department Commerce; National Institute of Standards and Technology, Gaithersburg, Maryland 20899.

Strategic Decisions

STRATEGIC MARKETING

Strategic marketing is the set of basic actions the company will follow to achieve its long-term objectives and to serve the long-term demands of the market. The *primary goals of strategic marketing* for a single business (business-level strategies) are (1) to maximize the firm's position (image in the minds of customers relative to competitors) within its chosen markets by establishing a clear distinction between its offering and that of competitors; (2) to determine what factors are necessary for the firm to attain its strongest position; (3) to allow the firm to specialize in an area where it can either be the best of its competitive segment or one of the best (domination is the ultimate goal); (4) to provide marketing managers (and other functional managers) with a target on which their efforts can be focused; and (5) to continuously learn from experience and seek ways of improving the firm's position. Strategic marketing for a multi-business firm would include the majority of decisions made at the corporate level (see Corporate Level Strategies, Chapter 1) and Portfolio Analysis (this chapter).

The *primary focus of strategic marketing* is on *grand strategies* (both corporate- and business-level strategies) the decisions concerning the products and services that will be offered, the market or markets for which the firm will compete, and the timing of any new product/service introductions or market additions (both customer segment and geographic markets). These strategies are critical because they are what the business will be known for—what it sells and to whom it sells it. There are normally very few major changes in a firm's grand strategies, but there may well be many minor ones. For example, a midscale hotel will rarely upgrade to the luxury market, but it may add new customer or market segments, find new means of promoting to existing customers, renovate the hotel, or add new products or services. Sometimes marketers will begin to consider how the *marketing mix variables* (product, price, place, and promotion) will be used to support the grand strategy. However, this task is normally determined later in the planning process.

Concurrently with the setting of grand strategies, the firm should examine the extend to which *generic strategies*, *product life cycles*, *portfolio analysis* (for multi-business corporations), and factors related to its *industry position* should be incorporated into the grand strategies.

Prior to the setting of grand strategies, the firm must have created a *SWOT analysis* or summary of the firm's situational factors. Then, through the *strategic analysis*, it will determine the most critical factors that could influence the firm's future and develop optional strategies to address these factors (Chapter 6). Based on the grand strategies and other strategic considerations, the firm would decide on its desired *position* in the market (Chapter 8).

Time Frame (Horizon)

There is no explicit time frame for strategic marketing plans. They are essentially the plans for the long-term future of the business. The time frame for the plan and its implementation will vary by need and importance. Some areas of the strategic plan will be focused on the immediate future; others will be planned for several years in the future. If it is decided in the strategic plan that menu changes reflecting lower fat entrees are needed now, then objectives, marketing strategies (or any other functional area), and action plans will begin detailing their immediate implementation. If management feels that the change will not be necessary for three years, then it will be noted in the strategic plan, and applicable long-term objectives will be set with little further attention until managerial actions are necessary to prepare for implementation. If changes in the environment occurred that would affect the long-term strategy, then the time frame or the strategy could be altered or simply not implemented. Some companies, especially those that anticipate vast expansion, may have several time frames, such as for the next five, ten, and fifteen years in the future. One of Japan's largest electronics firms, Matsushita, has strategic plans for the next 250 years!

Specificity

The strategic plans are often general, such as to add new services to remain competitive and to satisfy existing target customers. The method of achieving the above long-term strategy would best be included in the functional strategies section. For example, begin offering room service until 12 midnight, and add a workout room with professional equipment. The details of their implementation would be included later in the marketing action plan.

GRAND STRATEGIES

There are two primary categories of grand strategies: intensive and extensive (normally referred to as diversification). These are sometimes known as growth strategies, because they focus on growth within the firm's current products and markets or growth in related or unrelated businesses. As any of these possible strategic actions are incorporated into the firm's strategic marketing plan, marketing managers will need to decide which of the specific *marketing mix variables* (product, price, place, and promotion) will be used to accomplish them. If, for example, it was decided that a new market (intensive growth) will be added, then perhaps new or modified *products or services* at an acceptable *price* must be adopted, the product must be in the right *place* (distribution channel or location), and the changes must then be *promoted* (communicated) to the new market segment. The marketing mix variables in this context are referred to as *strategies* because they help guide the strategic direction of the firm. Here, they are used in the general sense, by stating that a certain strategy, a pricing strategy, for example, will be used to help achieve the grand strategies. The specifics of how they will be used are known as *marketing action plans* or, in generic planning terms, *tactics*, which describe exactly how they will be carried out in the next planning period. This explanation must be made because in various marketing textbooks the marketing mix variables are described as either strategies or tactics, or as both strategies and tactics. Each of these uses is correct based on the author's interpretation. What is critical is not what they are called, but how they are used to increase the effectiveness of the firm's planning efforts.

Intensive Strategies

Intensive strategies are concerned with improving the performance of existing businesses. They focus on various internal means of retaining and expanding the firms' market share or sales. Most activities will relate to increasing the frequency of present customers, increasing their average amount spent, or attracting new customers (either competitors customers or those from a different market segment).

1. Concentration or penetration—focusing on the current market with the current product
2. Product and service development—focusing on the new products and services targeted at existing markets
3. Market development—focusing on new markets (customer segment or geographic markets with existing products (see Figure 7.1)

CONCENTRATION OR PENETRATION   *For existing products and services in existing markets, this basically means selling more of present products or services (or slightly modified versions) to the existing customer base, or simply doing a better job of what is currently being done.* The key advantage of concentration is that the company is doing what it does best—dealing with known competencies. It knows its product and market, and knows what works and what does not. One disadvantage of concentration is that a company can become lulled into inactivity or complacency by not focusing on changes in the environment. If a company becomes overconfident in its present product or service mix, it may lose touch with shifts in demand and suffer dearly for it later. For example, for many years McDonald's concentrated on a limited product line, and average-to-high prices relative to competitors. As consumers' tastes

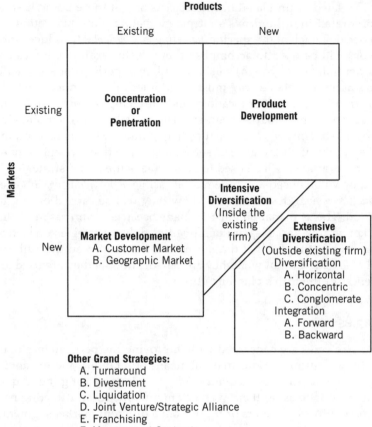

Products

	Existing	New
Existing	**Concentration or Penetration**	**Product Development**
New	**Market Development** A. Customer Market B. Geographic Market	**Intensive Diversification** (Inside the existing firm) / **Extensive Diversification** (Outside existing firm) Diversification A. Horizontal B. Concentric C. Conglomerate Integration A. Forward B. Backward

Markets

Other Grand Strategies:
A. Turnaround
B. Divestment
C. Liquidation
D. Joint Venture/Strategic Alliance
E. Franchising
F. Management Contracts
G. Acquisitions and Mergers

Figure 7.1 Grand strategy matrix (also product/market matrix and growth strategies). *Source:* Adapted from Ansoff (1957), Strategies for diversification. *Harvard Business Review*, 35(5), 113–124.

changed and pocketbooks were squeezed, McDonald's sat by, watching as competitors adapted. They changed only after Taco Bell's value-focused menu garnered a substantial increase in sales and market share. For many years Holiday Inn controlled the middle market in the hotel industry. In the 1970s that market began breaking up into smaller segments. Holiday Inn did not respond to these changes and saw competitors like La Quinta and Days Inn take a major share of its market.

Being on automatic pilot or doing what was done in the past is acceptable for brief periods of time. But changing times require changes in the fundamental offerings of firms, and this necessitates the consideration of improvements in current products and services, or the development of new products and services, or the addition of new markets. If new locations were opened in the same city, in trade areas with similar target customers, the strategy could still be considered penetration—trying to sell more to existing customers. The firm is trying to penetrate its market. If new locations were opened in new cities, the strategy would generally be considered *market development*. When locations in the same city are opened in trade areas with significantly different target customers, it would be best to refer to it as market development. The purpose for this is to increase management's focus on matching existing product with the new market.

When very serious problems exist or there is an opportunity to sell the business at a profit the strategies of turnaround, divestment, or liquidation should be considered.

- *Turnaround.* When a major effort is required to correct the downward direction of sales, profits, or operational performance a form of concentration strategy referred to as a *turnaround* should be implemented. In this situation, everything must be viewed as suspect, but in most such circumstances there will be pockets of good mixed in with the major problems. In one turnaround situation, two weeks of management training and the simple elimination of wasted advertising expenditures resulted in a 10% turnaround in profit. If a turnaround is neither successful nor feasible, then perhaps the entire business or parts of it should be sold.
- *Divestment.* Sell the business as an ongoing concern. In all but the rarest circumstances, it is best for a business to be sold while it is operating rather than when it is closed. If sales volume for a restaurant is terrible, then it may be best to close to minimize losses. Because of the extraordinary issues in maintaining a closed hotel, such as cost of security, vandalism, and mildew, it is uncommon for a hotel to close.*
- *Liquidation.* Sell the business in parts. This could be a large hotel or restaurant company selling off one or more of its properties. It most often refers to the selling off of components of a business, such as the hotel or restaurant building company or selling furniture, fixtures, and equipment.

CONCENTRATION STRATEGIES AND TOTAL QUALITY MANAGEMENT (TQM)

> Quality makes it possible for the customer to have a love affair with your product. (Unknown)

Buzzwords come and go, but perhaps one of the most beneficial concepts in modern business history is *total quality management (TQM)*. It is defined as "a structured process for establishing long-range goals, at the highest levels of organization, and defining the means to be used to reach those goals" (Juran, 1992, p. 300). This structured process refers to quality planning, quality control, and quality improvement. Quality in relation to business has been defined in different ways but can generally be expressed as satisfying the customer's expectations, or simply keeping the customer happy. Inherent in this definition is consistency, a term not lost on long-term high achievers in the hospitality industry.

The drive for quality has been so intense in recent years that customers are

---

*Mildew is a major headache for many owners and managers, especially in humid climates. A hotel that is closed for even a few weeks may need its interior repainted and carpets, upholstery, and wallpaper replaced.

beginning to expect quality in everything they buy. Companies not joining in are watching their customer bases quickly erode. Spender (1993, p. 11) tells us that "excellence, vision, commitment, teamwork, and service have recaptured the attention of top management." The implicit ramifications of a quality product or service are increased frequency of use or habitual purchases and exponential increases in word-of-mouth advertising. Except for variable costs, much of the increased business volume goes directly to the bottom line. Another benefit of TQM has been increased productivity. The service sector has not enjoyed the productivity returns realized by the manufacturing industries, primarily because of its high labor intensity.

Much of what has been written on TQM has focused on the manufacturing sectors. This has occurred for two reasons: (1) the decline in America's manufacturing dominance and (2) the increased ease of measuring and controlling the production of a product as opposed to a service. The 1970s brought the realization that products manufactured in America were no longer the standard against which the world's products were measured. The decline first became apparent in the automotive industry, then was closely followed by almost every conceivable product. The service sector was somewhat insulated by the fact that it was more difficult to penetrate the hotel and restaurant markets than manufacturing or product markets. Panicking companies scouring the world for the answer to decreased market share found it in an increased respect for quality. What was astonishing is that the key proponents and theorists of quality, W. Edwards Deming and J.M. Juran, had been trumpeting its importance since the 1920s, but their pleas had fallen on deaf ears. The problem in America was that there was plenty of business to go around, so few companies were concerned enough to listen and learn. Both Deming and Juran found their most enthusiastic audiences in Japan. As "Made in Japan" changed from being a symbol of cheap workmanship to one of excellence, and American market shares dwindled, American firms were forced to listen.

The reasons American firms have fallen behind much of the world in the area of quality are numerous, but a businessman from Japan had the following observation. He said that in the Asian culture, sensitivity to other people guides their proclivity for quality. Americans tend to focus on what is good for themselves, thereby neglecting details and quality. It appears that American companies respond to quality only when red ink replaces black ink.

As gains developed from TQM and processes became standardized, service sector firms began attampting to adopt its principles. They soon found that measurement of service quality was much more difficult than product quality. While products are quite tangible and can be measured by defects per hundred thousand or million, service is an intangible whose performance is based on customer and management perception. Additionally, this perception varied among each customer and manager, based on geographic, demographic, psychographic, and behavioral characteristics. Some measurements were possible, such as check-out time or the average time necessary for the kitchen to process a food order, but this did not present a complete picture of how the company was doing. To improve the transferability of TQM from manufacturing to service sectors, hotel and foodservice companies had to find alternative means of measuring quality. This fact has led to an increased use of customer surveys to find answers to questions on such things as what customers thought of the level of quality of their services, differences between the customer's expectations and perceptions, how often they returned, and how often they bought from competitors. Survey information was then incorporated into all segments of the business. Proactive companies began taking a daily measure of customer satisfaction and taking immediate action to correct problems before they become endemic to the business.

Initial attempts at service quality improvement were to make sure that employees offered an obligatory "May I help you" (which was sometimes pronounced, Melpew), or "Hi, I'm Susan, I'll be your waitress." Customers quickly saw through this lip service. More was needed to make sure the customer left with a positive feeling about the company and would be likely to return. Management realized that it was not they but their employees who were responsible for assuring customer satisfaction. In fact, for most service companies, the lower an employee is on the organizational chart, the greater his/her impact on quality. With this acknowledgment came an increased focus on empowering employees to do whatever is necessary to make sure that the customer is satisfied.

TOTAL QUALITY MANAGEMENT PROGRAM   The steps for developing and implementing a TQM program for the hospitality industry are essentially the same as those of strategic marketing.

1. *Find out what product and service attributes are judged to be important by the customers.* Also, find out what factors are considered important to employees, stockholders, and other stakeholders. Rank each attribute or factor based on how important each is to the success of the business. (See Research and Customer Analysis.)

2. *Determine how the company is presently performing in each area.* (See Internal Analysis.) A common recommendation of TQM practitioners is to locate the company's biggest problems and begin by focusing all efforts there first. A version of this approach is to locate and begin solving the most serious problems in each functional area of the business. The easiest place to begin for line workers is to start with the big picture. Have them create a flowchart detailing their movement when performing their jobs. This helps give them a simple place to start their analysis. Next, have them review the procedures required to perform each major task.

One of the keys to identifying performance deviations is that management must have some means of statistically measuring the performance of key tasks, especially those that affect customers or are considered critical to their satisfaction. Without measurement, control is relegated to the inconsistency of qualitative and subjective opinions. This is a not a totally negative circumstance, but is less accurate. (See Objectives and Controls.) Measurement for line workers is often easier than for management personnel. To measure management efficiency, begin by deciding what a particular manager's most important responsibility is. Then calculate how much of his/her time is spent on that task and other less important tasks. If too much time is spent on tasks that do not improve quality—for example, paperwork or excessive meetings—then those impediments to better performance should be removed.

3. *Set objectives that will lead to incremental improvement in areas where present perfor-*

mance is not at an acceptable level. Objectives should be as detailed as possible and follow the categories of social responsibility, profitability, productivity, employee development, employee relations, competitive position, and technology. (See Objectives.) One method of deciding on how high to set objectives, and in exactly which areas to set them, is to use the performance of excellent companies as a *benchmark* (known as benchmarking). The company should be careful not to set objectives too high or to focus on too many areas at once. Luckily it is much easier for hospitality firms, to make quantum leaps in quality than it is for manufacturing firms. The manufacturing firm may require months of retooling and redesigning of products, while hospitality firms can with much less effort change a few policies, retrain, and motivate employees to meet the new standards.

4. *Decide what strategies will most effectively lead to the achievement of objectives.* (See Strategic Planning, Functional Strategies, and the Marketing Action Plan.) It is critical for management to not only include line employees and middle management in the process, but to give them the responsibility and authority to make reasonable changes in operating procedures. Once employees are effectively trained and rewarded, and supervisors are coaching employees to keep their performance in line with objectives, then the company should be on its way to major improvements in quality.

There are various terms used for attracting employee input in the decision-making process: quality circles, task teams, and self-managing work teams. Each offers a successively greater degree of employee control over the work environment. *Quality circles* are groups of employees doing similar or related work who meet regularly to identify and analyze means of improving their input into the overall quality of the firm's product or service. Their popularity has been losing ground because employees are not given much guidance as to the problems that need to be addressed and their input is not always considered by management when deciding on necessary change. *Task teams* are similar to quality circles, except they are given relatively explicit directions as to what they should focus on. *Self-managing work teams* are given the responsibility of total control over their portion of operations (line) or support (staff) process. They have control over all tasks for which they are responsible, including the setting of schedules and division of assignments. Obviously, the "total control" freedom is monitored and measured by the achievement of stated objectives (Ross, 1993).

5. *Institutionalizing the new strategies.* (See Institutionalization.) A number of companies have looked upon TQM as a series of operational steps that lead to excellence, but it generally involves an overhaul of the organization's corporate culture, structure, style of leadership, and reward systems. From the president down to the lowest paid employee, everyone must buy into the company's quest for quality. Few people readily accept change. TQM must be sold to employees just as the company sells its product to customers. Each target group of employees must be analyzed to determine the best method of introducing necessary changes. Of course, if employees were to help develop the new strategies and policies, cooperation would be much more likely. Additionally, some type of system should be in place to reward workers for improvement.

6. *Postimplementation efforts.* Monitor performance for deviation from objectives. (See Controls.) Ideally, all employees should have their efforts measured daily. Keeping the employees aware of how they are doing in critical performance areas lets them know what the company considers to be important. When corrections are necessary, update policies and action plans. (This would be performed in the applicable section of the strategic marketing plan.)

The key to successful quality control in the hospitality industry is to build the philosophy of quality into the operational system and corporate culture of the business. This is accomplished through management's enthusiasm and support for the program's policies and its recognition of employees when objectives are reached. Most employees want to do a good job and are proud of their efforts; they simply need to be shown what constitutes a quality performance and to be recognized for it. The company's efforts, both good and bad, should be regularly discussed at employee meetings, during evaluations, and during everyday supervision. Ideally, TQM should be viewed as a worthy challenge to employees. The goal is to increase the entrepreneurial spirit of employees by showing them that reaching objectives is good for both them and the company.

PITFALLS OF TQM   Too often executives voice their concern for the importance of quality, but their personal actions or managerial style do not provide the foundation for a quality-directed effort. A TQM program requires much more than saying quality is important, then waiting for employees to make quality happen. It entails a detailed set of plans and actions that must be integrated into every part of the organization. Before a firm initiates a total quality management program, it should be aware of the pitfalls that may be encountered both before and during implementation. In his article, "Why Customer Focus Strategies Often Fail," Richard C. Whiteley (1991) presented nine common areas where problems occurred. To avoid implementation problems, organizations should address these before beginning a TQM or strategic marketing program.

1. *False Starts.* Total quality management (or strategic marketing) takes time. Often, executives will get people overly excited about the new changes, then, because of the length of the process, will not get back with them for months. In the meantime, employees' initial enthusiasm drops, and they become cynical about the effort.
2. *Disconnection from Customer Issues.* An excellent quality product or service may be worthless if it is not what the customer wants. Close customer contact and feedback are required for total quality, because the firm must determine how it is currently doing, plus be aware of new demands.
3. *"Do" Versus "Develop."* W. Edwards Deming's framework for managing and implementing total quality focuses on four phases: (a) a plan for improvement is created; (b) the plan is put into effect; (c) during implementation, checkpoints are monitored and adjustments made; and (d) when all the fine-tuning is completed, the final phase is to freeze the process and continuously improve it. In Japan, the emphasis is on phases (a) and (c), because they are aggressive in determining

whether or not their plan is on course. In the United States, too many companies have a bias for action and end up focusing on production quantity more than quality. This often results in work that must be redone because it was not done right the first time.

4. *"We're Doing Okay."* Frequently, businesses feel that if profits are good, then quality is good. The Malcolm Baldrige National Quality Award has a requirement that quality be integrated into all activities and be an overriding concern for all decisions (See Chapter 6, Appendix A, for information on the Malcolm Baldrige Award). Donald E. Petersen, former chairman of Ford Motor Company, said, "The principle by which we live and die is that, once we do something well, we have to figure out how to do it even better." David Kearns, chairman of Xerox Corporation, echoed this idea when he started, "As we get better, so does our competition. We are in a race for which there is no finish line."

5. *The Quick-Fix Syndrome.* Normally, quality problems cannot be corrected quickly. Since the development of a new process that allows for continuous improvement may take several weeks or months, results may not be immediately apparent.

6. *Mandate and Move on.* Executives frequently implement a quality program, then neglect it to focus on other things. Total quality management requires that managers assume an active, hands-on role.

7. *No Space on the Agenda.* Executives must master the skills necessary to implement a quality program. U.S. executives spend an average of 40% of their time on routine matters and 60% solving problems. Winners of Japan's Deming Prize for quality spend 20% of their time on routine work, 20% on problems, and 60% on actions that lead to continuous quality improvement.

8. *Look Who's Running the Show.* Since it is generally necessary to put someone in charge of the business's quality effort, someone whose past work exemplifies quality should be selected.

9. *No Guts at Crunch Time.* When the pressure is on to reach financial objectives, the quality effort must not be put on the back burner.

THE THREE COSTS OF QUALITY   As successful strategies necessitate proactive planning, so does quality control. The causes of quality control problems should be found and their solutions built into routine activities. At the root of quality control issues are the related costs of quality. According to Labovitz and Chang (1987), costs can be divided into three areas:

1. *Prevention Costs — Good Costs.* Costs of quality are "good" if they relate to preventing mistakes that affect product costs and customer complaints. It is always preferable to prevent a problem before it occurs than to correct it afterward. Examples of prevention costs are effective hiring policies; quality-conscious personnel; training and supervision that focus on supporting quality-oriented standards; and tying compensation, evaluations, and promotions to quality performance. These costs represent a long-term investment, rather than a short-term temporary fix, in solving problems of substandard quality.

2. *Inspection and Correction Costs — Bad Costs.* Obviously, inspection and correction in

the hospitality business will always be a primary component of a supervisor's job. A dilemma arises because even though it is good to find and correct the problem, this is only a short-term solution and, unfortunately, it must be repeated over and over. The objective here is to minimize the amount of time spent on locating and solving problems, especially those that occur frequently. This allows a greater focus on the customer and other more productive endeavors. If a hotel's general manager is having trouble with food cost, high labor costs, and a less-than-friendly front-desk staff, these are symptoms of a greater problem—the failure to allocate time and money for prevention costs.

3. *Customer Complaints—Ugly Costs.* If prevention or inspection and correction do not stop substandard performance, customer complaints are the result. It is important that the business apologize for its mistakes, but it would be much better off if it avoided them instead. Since word-of-mouth advertising is the most important means of communicating a product offering to customers, negative word-of-mouth must be avoided at all costs.

Labovitz and Chang (1989) also developed the "1–10–100 Rule" to compare the three costs of quality. Basically, every $1 spent in prevention costs (good) will save the company $10 in inspection and correction costs (bad) and $100 in customer complaint costs (ugly). Obviously, this is an approximation, but it does emphasize the relative importance of each cost of quality.

PRODUCT AND SERVICE DEVELOPMENT   *This category includes the development of new or modified products or services for existing customers.* There will always be a need to consider what new products and services will be demanded in the future. Most companies will concentrate primarily on their existing product offering, then have a constant ongoing search for potential new products (termed research and development or R & D). Most often, product or service additions are modifications of existing offerings. If competition is fierce or the product or service has reached the end of its life cycle, then an entirely new or innovative product or service may be needed.

Technically, this definition uses the broad interpretation of "existing customer," such as customers of fast-food restaurants or guests of a luxury hotel. However, in the hospitality business, the categorization of product development as new products and services for existing customers is not always used in this manner. This is because when a business adds a new product or service, it may also add customers from other market segments as well. For example, if a restaurant adds fresh vegetables, a salad bar, or a new category to a menu, such as seafood, existing customers may appreciate the change and return more often, but a parallel result (and purpose) is that is will likely bring in new customer segments. How many will depend on the degree of divergence from the existing offering and individual variances within existing customer segments. If a fast-food restaurant adds mushrooms and avocado to a burger, existing customers may purchase it or come back more frequently for it, but it may also attract a new customer segment in search of a better tasting, higher quality, or more regionally acceptable burger. If the same restaurant adds a grilled chicken breast sandwich and a selection of salads, then a new segment will almost certainly be added. If a hotel adds a workout room, it will have the objective of increasing the loyalty of existing customers, but it may also bring in customers, however small the number, from other market segments. A hotel adding computerized check-in and check-out and business services would generally be focusing on product and service development in the technical sense. It would simply be allowing the hotel to better meet the demands of the current target market. But if this hotel were in the midscale market, such as a Holiday Inn, it may also have an eye on adding customers from the bottom end of the upper midscale market—customer's that stay at Hiltons and Marriotts but who may temporally or permanently be on a tight budget.

When a fine dining restaurant or luxury hotel adds almost any product or service to its products or service mix, this could be considered product development in the strictest sense, because these firms generally have only one target market and are not usually concerned about attracting other segments.

When the goal of new products or services is specifically to bring in new market segments, some planners will use the term diversification or, more properly, intensive diversification (i.e., a new product and a new market). In most cases, if a firm wanted to add new products, it would be appropriate to use the terms product development and diversification interchangeably (e.g., "diversify our product offering"). Perhaps a better definition of product development would be researching and developing new products and services with the primary purpose of increasing brand loyalty of existing customers, the secondary purpose being the attraction of new market segments. In any case, the terminology used is secondary to application. It does not matter what it is called, as long as it is effectively executed.

MARKET DEVELOPMENT   *This includes selling existing products to new customer segments — market segment development — or to customers in a new location — geographic market development.* The need for *market segment development* will vary greatly depending on the dynamics of the business's customer base. Most businesses will have the same primary target customers each year but will find permanent or temporary opportunities in secondary target customer groups. A business could add primary customer segments, such as catering, meeting, or banquet services, or try to attract senior citizens, college students, those who are willing to pay more for their meals or rooms, or guests who will stay for a week or longer. Subsegments of the business's target segments could be added with minor modifications of existing strategies, such as products, services, prices, atmosphere, or promotion. Improving a hotels' workout facility, adding heart-healthy items to the menu, and promoting these changes may attract health-oriented customers within the hotel's present individual business traveler market segment. Decisions related to adding new customer segments are based on information from customer segmentation research and market-targeting decisions.

MARKET TARGETING   The primary purpose of segmentation (accomplished in the customer analysis section of the environmental analysis) is to learn enough about the various segments of the market to be able to determine which will have the potential to become viable target markets. Effective targeting is the result of an adequate base of information concerning the personal characteristics of the target customers. This will allow the business not only to select the appropriate markets but also to more effectively position its products and services for that market. Most firms will have one or more primary target markets, possibly some subsegments within primary markets, and secondary target markets. Because of limited returns, secondary markets do not generally attract a great deal of the marketing department's attention or time.

Far too many firms assume that what their customers wanted last year is what they will want this year. Often this is true; but when changes do occur, the firm that realizes it first and takes the appropriate action has the opportunity to reap substantial benefits.

Selecting Target Markets   A decision must be made on whether or not to target one market, a new markets, or several markets (Cravens, 1991). *Single-market targeting* allows the firm to focus on just one market, and therefore to maximize valuable resources and its opportunities. The problem with focusing on a single market is that changes in the market will have a proportionately greater effect on a business that adopts this approach than on firms that rely on several market segments. There is also a tendency for firms to drift into complacency and become aware of changes in demand only when it is too late. Firms using the single-segment targeting strategy should do so only with the knowledge that they are the best (or one of the best) alternative for their targeted group. An additional reason for deciding on a single segment is the location of a niche that can be protected, or that is likely to be ignored by others. This strategy has been particularly effective with upscale restaurants and luxury hotels. In the future, because of broad societal and demographic shifts and increased competition for each market, single-market targeting will most likely increase in importance.

Selective targeting, or targeting a limited number of markets, expands the business's opportunities and limits its dependence on a single market. It gives the firm the option and flexibility of going after multiple segments to fill rooms and restaurant seats during off-peak times. Selective targeting essentially allows the firm to maximize its market penetration while remaining focused on only a few specific segments.

Extensive targeting, or *full marketing coverage,* is attempting to gain a large market share by targeting the majority of the potential users of one's products or services (Kotler, 1991). This mass-market targeting strategy can be approached from two perspectives:

1. *Differentiated Market Targeting.* The Marriott hotel chain could not satisfy all customers with its upper-midscale hotels. It was also reaching a saturation point in many geographic markets. The strategy it selected was differentiated market targeting— developing different concepts for each market segment within a product or service category. Most of the major hotel chains are pursuing this strategy because it allows them to maximize their brand's image, sales, and synergy in many functional areas, such as reservations, advertising, and operations.
2. *Undifferentiated Market Targeting.* The focus of firms utilizing undifferentiated mar-

keting is to offer one product or service to all market segments. The objective of this targeting strategy is to reduce costs by focusing on larger markets. The problem is that larger markets often attract well-financed, established firms that are relentlessly attempting to hang onto market share. Since few businesses can satisfy broad segments of a product's market, it is generally best to either reduce one's scope with the use of selective targeting, or to expand one's offerings with the use of differentiated market targeting.

Requirements for Target Markets   Since not all segments will have the same potential, some means of analyzing each segment must be used to decide which of them to enter. The target customer segments identified for a restaurant or hotel can be evaluated according to the following criteria:

- *Measurable.* Each segment chosen must be measurable by components of the four bases of segmentation, such as number of people in the segment, zip code, income, age, life-style activities, frequency of use, and price sensitivity. Companies that do not measure their markets tend to focus on either mass markets or ill-defined target markets.
- *Substantial.* The segment must be large enough to be worthwhile pursuing. The focus for most businesses will be their largest potential markets. Occasionally, as subsegment of a market (members of the target market with unique demands such as the disabled or those on special diets) or a secondary market may be substantial enough to pursue, as long as the business realizes that it probably cannot expect sizable returns. If the smaller market has been ignored, then this could be considered a niche that could be exploited. Secondary markets include college students, senior citizens, salespeople with small firms, or construction workers who travel for their companies.
- *Profitability.* Since profit is the driving force behind business, marketing managers must be confident that selected target markets both want and will purchase their product at a satisfactory price. Profitability will normally be estimated based on actions of existing target customers or through researching the experience of other firms.
- *Product Differentiation.* The segments selected should allow for maximum differentiation between a company and its competitors. *Differentiation* can be defined as brand awareness and loyalty based on attributes such as product or service quality, atmosphere, cleanliness, past advertising, image, locations, and value. This term usually refers to positive differences that customers feel are important in the selection of one business over another. If management does not feel that it can compete head-on with its primary competitors with a similar product and price, then it must continue its search for a market that will value its offering. If the market does not see a noticeable difference between two products, then brand recognition and loyalty will be a primary influence on the purchasing decision.

For example, it would probably be unwise for an independently owned casual hamburger restaurant to open up in the same trade areas as a Chili's restaurant, unless it has something that differentiates its offering from Chili's—perhaps an in-store bakery exhibition kitchen, more seafood than Chili's, or a very popular signature dish.

Management should also try to find *market gaps* or *niches* in the market—needs that are not currently being met. In the ideal situation, the gap or niche represents an area of the market that can to some degree be protected or that will be ignored by primary competitors. These gaps could be in any areas that represent the potential for increases in sales or business expansion, such as location, atmosphere, price, concept (e.g., fast-food restaurant or economy hotel), menu items, and services (Aaker, 1988). For example, the only sandwich shop in a trade area with a high percentage of office workers finds out that pizza is the only lunch item available for delivery. If customers are receptive to ordering sandwiches for delivery, then a potentially profitable, measurable, and accessible gap in the market has been located.

- *Accessible.* Either the target customer must be accessible to the business, through being in the business's trade area, or, if the business must rely on promotional activities, promotional options must be available at a reasonable cost. Targeting decisions for restaurants revolve around customers in their trade area—the area immediately around the location where approximately 60% to 70% of its customers either live or work.

  Obviously, the trade area for a hotel will be much larger, and therefore require a much more sophisticated promotional effort. Hotels at the budget end of the market will rely on travelers that are driving through their trade area. As their sophistication and promotional budget grow, they may become part of reservation systems such as SABRE, or the travel agents' Red Book, which will help promote the hotel to callers requesting hotel rooms. Most chain hotels will try to attract guests from the United States or internationally using their own reservation system. Each city will generally find that a disproportionately large percentage of its guests travel from only a few cities, states, or countries. For most hotels in Texas, other Texas cities supply the majority of guests. For a growing number of hotel chains, Mexico is an increasingly large target market. Many hotels in San Francisco will focus a substantially larger percentage of their promotional budget on the Far East than will hotels in most other U.S. cities.

- *Stable.* Decision-makers must be confident that the market will be around for a long enough period of time to allow for a reasonable return on the business's investment. If the investment is low, as when a restaurant adds a menu item that may be a fad, there is no major problem. If the investment concerns remodeling, expansion, or major strategies affecting the firm's products and service, pricing structure image or promotional campaign, marketers must be confident that the market will be there for the foreseeable future.

GEOGRAPHIC MARKET DEVELOPMENT   This concerns opening new locations of the same business in other areas—generally other cities. The new geographic markets would normally be located and identified in the customer analysis, and occasionally in the competitor analysis. Care must be taken not to expand too quickly out of one's area of strength. For restaurants, it is generally better to focus on penetrating a single geographic area first (existing customers in one's existing market) and then to expand to nearby areas. There are several reasons for this. First, as the succeeding locations are opened, they will be within arm's reach, so as problems arise, management can handle them quickly. Second, selecting a location in a city where owners and managers have lived for several years is much easier than finding a location in another city after a two-day visit.

Since the future of the business may depend on the success of new geographic locations, it is best to prepare a detailed site analysis and to have someone from the company live on the site for about a week to see it under all possible conditions. As expansion takes place in the business's present market, customers will recognize the name and, based on its good reputation, be much more likely to patronize the restaurant than one they have never heard of. For this same reason, once the decision has been made to expand out of one's current market, it is generally best to expand into the nearest suitable markets.

The question of expanding to new geographic markets for a hotel will largely depend on whether it gets the majority of its business from walk-ins or reservations. A new, quality-oriented roadside motel can open up in almost any new geographic area with satisfactory results, as long as it is located near similar successful motels. Chain hotels with excellent name recognition and reservation systems can open a hotel in almost any location that is in need of more or newer rooms. Small chains or independents with limited name recognition should generally penetrate their current markets first, then focus expansion on nearby markets. Since expansion normally is derived from takeovers of other properties, there may be more emphasis placed on the "deal" than on the location. Recently, when a relatively new five-unit hotel chain took over and reflagged a top brand hotel, the occupancy dropped 25%. It took one year for the hotel to increase volume to 10% below its predecessor. To a large degree, success will depend on how well management was able to limit overhead in the deal and on the aggressive work of their marketing department.

GRAND STRATEGY SELECTION MATRIX   Figure 7.2 is a matrix format that can be used to graphically display grand strategy options or to inspire brainstorming. Simplistically, the marketing department's main objective is to increase sales, and there are three primary ways to do this. The purpose of the matrix is to develop options for each grand strategy that will help achieve that objective.

Diversification

This involves developing a new product for a new market. Diversification concerns adding businesses that will increase the firm's competitive advantage. This could be through lowering costs, increasing quality, increasing market penetration, improving efficiency, raising sales, or increasing profits. Diversification generally refers to opening a new business outside the current business. When used in this context, it is more properly termed *extensive diversification.* Categories include horizontal, concentric, and conglomerate diversification. Technically, it is either getting into a new

STRATEGY	CONCENTRATION PENETRATION	PRODUCT DEVELOPMENT	MARKET DEVELOPMENT
Raise check average	Improve quality Increase training Increase promotion Raise prices Product bundle pricing Suggestive selling	Improve presentation Higher priced items Add new options such as a wider selection of drinks or desserts	Add new market segment with higher discretionary income
Get customers to come back more often	More interaction with customers Lower prices Sales promotions and merchandising Better service	New items Survey customers to find needs and wants Better quality Emphasize differentiation	Add market segment that has a higher usage frequency
Attract new customers	Promotional mix options Increase word-of-mouth advertising Open new locations in existing markets	Expand product offering Promote new products	Attract new market segment Advertise in different media vehicles Open locations in new geographic markets

Figure 7.2   Grand strategy selection matrix.

business that is similar to the existing business, into one within the same industry but in a different segment, or into a new type of business altogether. Colloquially, the term can also be used to connote adding a new product to an existing business (theoretically termed *intensive diversification*). Each firm may have different meanings for diversification. The primary point is that everyone involved should understand the context in which the term is being used, so that functional strategies can be written that support the intended grand strategy.

One major study of 33 firms' efforts in diversification found that it was not usually an effective strategy (Porter, 1991). The measure of success of the diversification strategy was whether the acquired firm was retained or divested. In this particular study, the overall divestment rate was well over 50% of all acquisitions. It was also found that it was the lawyers, investment bankers, and original sellers that profited from the acquisition and consequent divestment of the subsidiaries.

COMMON PROBLEMS WITH DIVERSIFICATION

1. Competition occurs at the business unit not at the corporate level. Therefore, corporate officers must either have experience with the acquired firm or be willing to relinquish responsibility to others.
2. Diversification can add cost and constraints to the acquired business units. For example, in most cases the acquired business will have to pay its share of its new corporate parent's overhead. There may also be corporate philosophies and cultures that differ from that of the new subsidiary.
3. Shareholders can diversify their own portfolios. Unless the acquired business adds value to the bottom line of the parent corporation in an amount that is greater than the two individual businesses, the shareholders would be better off purchasing the stock themselves. What happens in these acquisitions is that the parent company has maximized its growth in its base industry or has a significant amount of retained earnings and thinks that it can add value to its company with the acquisition. Too often its motivation is not what will happen to the acquired firm's bottom line, but how it can increase the growth of the corporate parent.

CONDITIONS FOR ACQUISITION   Porter (1991) described the conditions by which true shareholder value could be created. (These would also apply to integrative growth, page 253.)

1. *Attractiveness Test.* The broad structure of the industry of the acquisition must represent opportunities for the potential subsidiary. Often, there will be businesses that for one reason or another are not achieving their potential. If the parent firm has certain competencies that can help the potential acquisition maximize its competitive position, then a purchase could be considered.
2. *Cost-of-Entry Test.* The purchase price must allow for a reasonable return on investment (ROI). If the parent firm is not confident that future profits will amortize the investment, the purchase should not be considered.
3. *Better-Off Test.* The new business unit must bring the parent firm a competitive advantage or vice versa. (Because of the close functional ties with the parent firm, this would be particularly important for integrative growth.)

HORIZONTAL DIVERSIFICATION   This category includes opening another business that competes for the same customer, or purchasing a primary competitor; essentially getting into a business in the same level of the marketing channel. Examples include a midscale hotel purchasing another midscale hotel, or a fast-food restaurant chain acquiring a competing fast-food chain.

CONCENTRIC DIVERSIFICATION   This involves the acquisition of a business that is related to the hospitality business or that would use similar skills. This could be through direct similarities or through common operating characteristics; for example, a restaurant buying a specialty grocery store. Horizontal diversification and vertical integration could be included in this category.

CONGLOMERATE DIVERSIFICATION   This category includes the purchase of unrelated businesses. This strategy rarely works because of the lack of synergy of skills. For example, someone who operates restaurants should probably stay away from the printing business.

VERTICAL INTEGRATION   This consists of opening or purchasing a supplier to one's business—*backward vertical integration*—or purchasing an organization that is a customer to one's business—*forward vertical integration* (the act of integration is a type of diversification since it involves the acquisition of a new business or at the minimum, a combining of two or more components of the marketing channel.) Although it does not happen very often, there are many ways of utilizing backward vertical integration, such as when a restaurant or hotel gets into the bakery, linen, or produce business or an equipment supply or service company. Several restaurants have had problems obtaining quality produce or seafood, so they bypassed their wholesaler and began buying directly from farmers and fishermen. Eventually, some began selling to other restaurants. Forward vertical integration in the hospitality business is not as common. Some examples would be a hotel purchasing a travel agency or reservation system that supplies it with customers and a franchise headquarters purchasing its franchisees.

Other Grand Strategies

Often, firms that want to pursue diversification or integration strategies do not have adequate funds or expertise. Common options include joint venture, strategic alliance, franchising, management contracts, and acquisitions and mergers. *Joint venture* is the combining of resources with another company for mutual benefit. A *strategic alliance* occurs when a smaller company, generally with expertise, time, and little money, joins with a larger company with money or available credit, and a broad business background, including the opportunity to achieve a competitive advantage, such as an expanded reservation system (Tse & West, 1992). *Franchising* is the licensing of others to operate a business using the firm's operating system and brand name. *Management contracts* include a variety of agreements between those that have the expertise and reputation for successfully operating a particular type of business and those that own the business. Management contracts have become quite common in the lodging and institutional segments of the foodservice industry. Though not widespread in restaurants, their use will likely increase in proportion to competitive intensity. *Acquisitions* are basically the outright purchase of another business that may continue to operate under its own name. *Mergers* occur when two or more firms are combined to create one firm.

GENERIC STRATEGIES

Generic strategies were designed to help guide the overall strategic selection process. The most popular generic strategy is that of Michael Porter (1980). He proposed that the generic strategy typology* of *overall low-cost leadership, differentiation,* and *focus* could be applied to any industry and that his accompanying theories would result in higher than average returns [*stuck in the middle* (between low-cost and differentiation), a fourth option, was not viewed as viable]. He added that each firm should select one generic strategy to focus on and that the suitability of each would vary based on the industry's stage in its product life cycle. To this mix, other authors have added *preemptive* and *synergy.*

There is no doubt that these generic strategies have made a major impact on the science of business. And no one can argue with the fact that each if effectively pursued in the appropriate environment can lead to improvements in a firm's competitive standing. But in the context of strategy-setting, "What additions did they make to the strategists' tool box?" and "Can strategists rely on a relatively static generic strategy for deciding their business's future?" For example, all businesses know that they must keep costs as low as possible to remain competitive and that there must be some relative uniqueness about their product or service offering that attracts an adequate number of customers. Also, it is rarely possible for marketers to select either a low cost or differentiation strategy. Both must be pursued. The real foundation for Porter's generic strategies are actually based in marketing and financial theory—to yield the highest profit, adopt strategies that keep sales at the highest possible level and costs at the lowest possible level (see Figure 7.3). The question of the appropriate strategy is more complicated than deciding on one generic strategy to pursue. The people who should actually receive the credit for these generic strategies are Smith (1956), for proposing the concept of differentiation, and Drucker (1954), for introducing the marketing concept.

Most generic strategy typologies were created during a time when America was still the preeminent manufacturing power in the world. Today, with the rapid transformation toward service- and knowledge-based core competencies, the achievement of competitive advantage is no longer a simple matter of deciding in which of three or so strategic directions a firm should be headed. The purpose here is not to suggest that these generic strategy typologies be placed on the strategic planning history shelf, but simply to describe an alternative means of viewing their application in the strategy formulation process.

Strategic planning is as much as artform as a science. Multi-dimensional decisions are made that attempt to achieve a harmonious balance between the firm and its environment. As such, individuals with the broadest palette or widest array of beneficial theories and strategic options have the greatest potential to create successful strategies. The process is simply too diverse and even cryptic to be relegated to a "matching the round block to the round hole" procedure. Generic strategies focus on parts of the strategic puzzle but do not offer a complete picture or package that can be utilized to determine he firm's most viable position in the market and, therefore, the business- and functional-level strategies it should pursue. Their essential value is

---

*A typology is the categorization of any group of related elements such that all elements fit into one of the typology's categories. For example, a typology for business organizations is *for-profit* and *not-for-profit.*

Overall Cost Leadership
Often based on the experience curve and economies of scale, this strategy requires aggressive pursuit of cost reductions wherever possible.

Problem
Opportunities for economies of scale in the hospitality industry as compared to manufacturing sectors are limited. While very few service firms can become low-cost leaders, every firm in a competitive and fragmented market must attempt to keep costs at the lowest reasonable level.

Differentiation
Being perceived as having something unique. Includes brand image, technology, past advertising, product, or service quality, and loyal customers.

Problem
This is simply a rewording of the *marketing concept,* the foundation for beginning the search for strategy options. It is the equivalent of saying that the firm should consider the area of marketing when determining its strategic direction. Additionally, firms must balance the need for differentiation with that of stability.

Focus
Focusing on a relatively narrow segment of the market (customer or geographic segment), or a limited product line.

Problem
In 1980, many industries were in the transition to target marketing. Today, this strategy is not a choice, but perhaps the only choice. It is best expressed by the concepts of *segmentation, target marketing, and positioning.*

Stuck in the Middle
A firm that does not develop its strategy in at least one of the three other generic categories. This firm will rarely be profitable. May lose cost-sensitive business to low-cost leaders and high-margin business to firms focusing on differentiation.

Problem
While there are many firms that could be labeled as stuck in the middle with problems, there are also many firms that have found this strategy to be reasonably successful and profitable. These are primarily small independents and non-franchised chains that realize they cannot compete in areas such as product quality, low price, or innovation, so they limit their promotional and R & D expenses and are content with average sales and returns

Figure 7.3   Problems with Porter's generic strategy typology.

that of reminding firms that the marketing concept (differentiation) and costs control are the central tasks of management.

Generic strategies are not normally included as a separate component of the strategic plan but are emphasized in each area to which they apply. For example, if the *low-cost* strategy was being used, concentration or product development strategies could include lowering the average cost of entrees with a high food cost. To allow for more price flexibility or profit, management or marketing strategies might focus on finding ways to decrease operating expenses and overhead. Financial accounting strategies could include regular meetings with the purchasing department to identify opportunities for reducing costs.

Of the following generic strategies, differentiation and low cost are generally considered the most important.

Differentiation

Differentiation can be defined as product identification and brand loyalty based on such unique features as superior product or service quality, fast service, good location, recognizable name and associated image factors, a protected source of supply, and past advertising. Essentially, this is any unique selling proposition (USP) that customers view as different from competitors and desirable, and that offers an advantage over competitors. The ideal differentiation strategy yields an SCA (sustainable competitive advantage) or at least a competitive advantage. The more difficult the advantage is to understand or replicate, the greater its benefit and the longer it can be used as a competitive weapon (Grant, 1991).

Differentiation is a valuable strategy because it allows the firm to effectively position itself against competitors while at the same time gaining customer loyalty. Customer loyalty may then allow the firm to decrease its advertising expenditures and, in many circumstances, increase its prices (Porter, 1980).

The strategy of offering an excellent-quality product will usually help a firm survive. The problem with this line of thinking is that there are many firms doing just that. But positive points of differentiation will help the firm become a solid competitor. Matching a competitor is often relatively easy: observe its strategies and actions, then imitate them. Replicating critical points of differentiation may be considerably more difficult. If the point of differentiation consists of excellent locations, large sums of money and time will be required. On the contrary, an exhibition kitchen would be somewhat easier. Imagination and research into customer wants and demand will help locate the most effective differentiation strategies.

McDonald's has several major points of differentiation with its many convenient locations, recognizable sign, billions of dollars in past image-building advertising, and its reputation for consistency. The Hyatt is known for quality services and large atriums. Subway Sandwich Shops are known for their fresh-baked bread and many locations. Houston's Restaurants are known for offering an upscale atmosphere with professional service and excellent food at casual dining prices. Because of each of these firms' size and financial strength, their points of differentiation are also sustainable competitive advantages.

One of the problems involved in the setting of grand strategies for the hospitality industry is that few strategies have the ability to develop into sustainable competitive advantages. Since there are relatively few firms with well-protected advantages, a business must realize that even though it should not stop looking for a major competitive advantage or points of differentiation, it will need to focus more on satisfying the customer with a quality product or service.

Kotler and Stonich (1991) propose that there are four stages of competitive marketing: making goods less costly; designing products to be different; making better products; and making and delivering goods and services faster than competitors (called *turbo marketing*). All four stages focus to a great degree on product differentiation—less costly, better, different, faster. (The making of less costly products in this instance is construed to be a form of product differentiation.) To increase its competitive position, a firm must recognize and satisfy a market's demand for products and services in less time, that is, before competitors. A firm must also be able to reduce the time necessary for the delivery of those products or services. As the importance of the target market's time becomes more apparent, all classes of hotels and restaurants are doing whatever they can to speed and simplify the delivery of food, beverages, and various services. For a lawyer or sales representative, waiting up to an hour for a table at an upscale restaurant represents lost billable hours or less time with clients. Each business must analyze its target customer or peripheral markets to identify their wants for present and potential products and services. Kotler and Stonich theorize that as traditional sources of competitive advantage, low cost, and differentiation have been exploited, time compression or *turbo marketing* should be added to the next generation's list of generic strategies.

Low Cost

Low cost means simply having an advantage in terms of any product costs and operating expense factors. Examples are economies of scale from a large market share or relatively large purchases, inexpensive land or building, efficient operations, and cost minimization in such areas as advertising, sales, research and development, labor and supplies. A low-cost generic strategy can have a multitude of benefits, such as helping to ride out a recession, being able to compete more aggressively through pricing strategies, absorbing increases in costs of goods, offering a lower price to customers, reducing the attractiveness of a new competitor entering the market, and overall financial flexibility. In essence, low-cost leadership provides the firm with the ability to be a more nimble competitor by increasing its financial options.

The typical low-cost leader has a large market share. This allows for larger purchases relative to competitors, which leads to economies of scale. Since this option is not available to every competitor, most firms must seek alternative means to gain cost advantages. Possibly the most important time to consider costs is when the business's concept is being planned. At this time, decisions such as sites, building, equipment, product and service, and labor requirements are made that will have a major impact on costs for the life of the concept. If a restaurant concept were centered around a limited rather than an extensive menu, it might be possible to save money on the building (less space), equipment (fewer menu items), food costs (purchasing larger quantities of a smaller number of items), and labor costs (fewer cooks are generally required for smaller, simpler menus).

A major sandwich shop chain was established on a low-cost strategy. At one time it was one of the fastest-growing small chains in the country. New owners decided that the decors should be upgraded—at a considerable expense. Sales did not improve, so 20% of the previously successful shops closed their doors because they could not absorb the higher overhead. In various recessions businesses can sign 20- to 30-year leases or purchase buildings that are frequently 20% less than prior market rates. Some firms have as their expansion strategy the takeover of businesses with these low-cost, long-term leases.

A low-cost strategy is imperative in the hospitality industry. This is because customers have a reasonable base of knowledge that allows them to compare each product or service with another. For example, it would be difficult for a casual restaurant to charge $14.95 for a chicken entree for which primary competitors are charging $9.95. Customers know what chicken costs at the grocery and at other restaurants, so they will likely refuse to order it. Because of consumers' product knowledge and their ability to compare a product with other similar products, hospitality industry competitors must focus on having the lowest possible cost in their segment, which will allow them to offer a good value and show a reasonable profit. In many other industries, when a company comes out with a new product or service that has previously not been available, the average customer may have nothing with which to compare its value. For example, a new computer component may cost little to produce but can be marked up several times more than related products. (This is called *market-skimming pricing*—setting a price well above traditional mark-ups, the highest price that consumers are willing to pay.) As competitors introduce alternatives, then price comparisons and customer knowledge will help force the price down.

Focus

The focus strategy means concentrating on one primary product, a single or narrow market segment, or a limited geographic area. The core concept of the focus strategy is that the firm concentrates on a narrower strategic target and therefore is able to operate more effectively and efficiently than competitors with broader goals. Generally, when a focus strategy is successful, the result is either low-cost leadership or high differentiation (Porter, 1980). For example, most upscale restaurants focus primarily on a single menu category, such as steaks or Italian or French cuisine, and a limited market segment, generally upper-middle- to upper-class. Market focus could include a geographic focus, as when a restaurant or hotel goes into locations that others do not want, or where there is not as much competition. The purpose of this and most focus strategies is to locate a protected niche that can be exploited and defended.

Preemptive

When a company is the first to bring its product or service to market or is first to introduce a unique strategy, it may achieve an advantage (also referred to as *first-mover advantage*) over future entrants or adopters. Domino's made the first major effort at offering pizza delivery. Fuddrucker's was first with a made-from-scratch hamburger. Taco Cabana was first with a quality fast-food Mexican restaurant. During the late 1980s, Taco Bell was the first major chain to focus on value. McDonald's was first with clean, inexpensive fast-food hamburgers. La Quinta was first with upgraded budget-priced hotel rooms for business travelers. The founders or leaders of each of these firms had highly developed inferential skills. The fact that they were first to offer their products helped position their companies as first in customers' minds when they needed their particular product or service. This fact, in many cases, fueled explosive growth that resulted in much higher than average P/E ratios (price of a share of stock divided by earnings per share). When the average P/E ratio was around 15, several companies were over 50, some over 100. To put this perspective, the average privately owned restaurant is worth in the neighborhood of four to six times earnings, irrespective of assets. A growing chain of restaurants, also irrespective of assets, might be worth around 10 to 20 times assets. A fast-growing restaurant chain that is publicly traded and is utilizing a preemptive strategy could be worth between 50 and 100 times earnings. Hotel figures are less dramatic since expansion is generally less dramatic and the value of their real estate plays a much greater role in the assessment of their value.

One of the considerations when using a preemptive strategy is the number, size, and duration of the barriers that hinder competitors from duplicating one's own efforts. High-tech firms, because of patents and other proprietary technologies, have the greatest barrier-building assets. Some manufacturing firms may gain control of raw materials or establish economies of scale in purchases, production, distribution, and so on. Service companies, because of their heavy reliance on labor and limited reliance on protected technologies, have fewer barriers available with which to defend their strategies. Since service industries find it difficult to protect a first-mover advantage, establishing a pattern of preemptive moves will help maintain the advantages of the strategy (Patterson, 1993). This is what Jack-in-the-Box did reasonably successfully with its "Always something new" campaign. Taco Bell is continuing it value focus with frequent introductions of new value-oriented menu items.

To reduce the obvious risk of being first with a concept, many companies will take an idea that is successful in one part of the country or world and bring it to their area.

Synergy

When firms are considering any type of expansion, one of the key skills that must be available is that of synergy. Synergy, in the context of strategy, is already having some of the skills necessary for the new business. For example, if a business expands outside its current geographic markets, having good real estate people, trainers, and a corporate culture supportive of expansion would be synergistic generic strategies.

PRODUCT LIFE CYCLE

The product life cycle (PLC) is an analysis of the actual or potential sales of a product or business segment through the various stages of its marketable life. It is also a means of mapping the strategic direction of the hotel or foodservice industry as a whole, by industry segments and concepts (referred to as the *business life cycle*), or by the brand itself. The setting of effective strategies for the long term requires some knowledge of the general direction of similar businesses and the potential strategies that competitors will use. Although there cannot be a set rule as to what strategy a

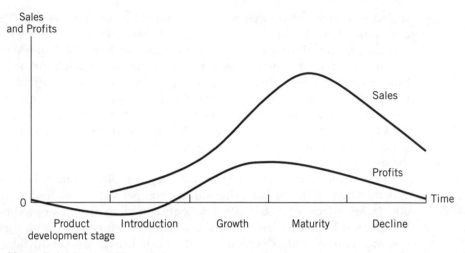

Figure 7.4   Product life cycle.

business should pursue, various circumstances within each state of the PLC tend to support a narrow range of options. The analysis can be used to ascertain the most reasonable strategic options for a business and can help to determine the potential strategies of competitors (See Figure 7.4).

INTRODUCTION   The introductory phase for hospitality businesses is applicable only for new individual brands or for new concepts. The industry as a whole must be considered to be in the maturity stage because of its longevity. Hospitality concepts considered as being in the introductory stage will generally be new types of business within market segments, such as gourmet delivery or a mini-room luxury-class hotel. Occasionally, it will include a new segment, as when La Quinta Inns opened its first economy business-class hotel. For an individual business or brand, introduction is the highest-risk stage because the business is new and untested. It is also generally going up against competitors with loyal customers, a solid base of experience, and greater cash reserves. Profits will usually be limited by high opening costs and normal inefficiencies caused by a lack of experience. Frequently, restaurants will open with limited cash and show an excellent profit from the start. In fact, many new restaurant concepts will have their best months during the introduction stage. This is caused by customers in the trade area anticipating the opening, then flocking to try the new establishment. Once this *curiosity factor* wears off, the restaurant will need to rely on its quality to keep sales up.

Since few customers may have heard of the business before, there will likely be a need for extensive use of promotional strategies. However, the ingenuity of the operator and other factors can limit the need for promotion of a new business. The most common and frequently inherent problem with preopening and opening pro-motional campaigns is that a new business will generally have very little available cash for an effective campaign. This will force most businesses to rely heavily on product, pricing, and place (location and atmosphere) as their primary opening marketing strategies. The need for promotion may be reduced with some type of pricing strategy, such as *market penetration pricing*—opening with a price lower than the competition with the purpose of attracting customers from competitors— or personal selling in the neighborhood. If the hotel or foodservice business has a good location (place strategy), much of the need for special promotions may be negated.

If the business is being opened as an extension of a well-known brand or, for hotels, if there is an effective reservation system in place at its introduction, such as for the Marriott's Residence Inns, then increased promotion may be limited to preopening selling. Afterward, the business could conceivably be on a firm footing from its opening day. If a product is unique in a way that creates an exceptional amount of word-of-mouth advertising, then promotion will not be as necessary.

GROWTH   If the business, concept, or segment survives the introduction stage, then there is normally a period of accelerated growth in sales. At this stage the product has been accepted by target customers as a suitable alternative to previous choices. This is generally the most profitable stage for any product category (see section on Categories for the Product Life Cycle, later in this chapter). When the business is new, mistakes are made that often limit profits and sales. Experience will generally produce the most efficient employee schedules and the most effective product/service mix and promotional mix. Suppliers are more numerous and also in their own growth stage, so prices for food, beverage, and operating costs may be lower. Since profits are up, and it is evident that concept or segment will be growing for some time to come, competing firms will enter the market. Schlotzsky's Sandwich shops, based in Austin, Texas, was one of the original sandwich shops to bake bread fresh each day in the restaurants. As the brand entered the growth stage, numerous competitors began employing similar concepts. If the leader can retain its position during this stage, surviving attacks from new entries and smaller followers, then, unless major mistakes are made, it will most likely retain its position. If a business can dominate a market through a penetration strategy, high entry costs, or a reputation for excellence, then competitors may think twice before entering. Houston's Restaurants of Atlanta, Georgia, have established a foothold in the casual upscale restaurant market, and though some competitors have surfaced, few are competing with them head on.

MATURITY   Since the primary problems faced by most restaurants and hotels are saturated markets, declining profits, and price competition, as a group they can be said to be in the maturity phase of the product life cycle. At this stage sales are either increasing slightly or have leveled off. Sales increases will be limited to natural market expansion, much as the growth of the population in the region or country, or when new occasions for use are developed. Individual brands, concepts, and segments may be at this or any stage in the PLC, but this is the current stage for the entire hotel and foodservice industries. At maturity there are often too many competitors chasing the same customer. Each segment will see its share of closings as stronger concepts take business away from weaker competitors. Promotional strategies will be stressed, but quality and value will be the lasting competitive advantages. Product differentiation will also come into play as people grow tired of the same offering and as societal trends and other environmental factors change. Entry or expansion for smaller competitors will come through the establishment of niches in the market. These will be either through a protected or as yet unexploited location, or through developing a differentiated product. Tejas Cafes based in Conroe, Texas, have grown by opening restaurants in cities generally thought too small for major casual-dining competitors.

The restaurant industry appears to move in a relatively consistent pattern from early to late maturity, then back to early maturity. As too many restaurants are opened, weaker businesses, for one reason or another, will not be able to compete and begin to close down. This is termed a *shakeout* and can happen for the entire industry or for a segment, concept, or brand. The mid-1980s saw many concepts either go out of business or close many of their locations.

DECLINE   Both the foodservice and hotel industries have experienced periods of decline. Foodservice establishments have quickly rebounded after dips in sales. However, hotels have not fared as well as the foodservice industry in recent years. Because of financial problems caused by overbuilding and overcapacity, the hotel industry during the late 1980s and early 1990s entered a period of decline. In the early and mid-1980s, money for expansion was easy to come by, so a large number of chains, franchisors, and independent operators were building at slightly inflated costs. When the economy dipped, many operators in the overbuilt and heavily mortgaged industry were not able to survive, or they decided to keep the hotel as a real estate investment rather than for its value as a business. Even though the average hotel had been losing money for several years, each year it was losing less, and as of 1993, just over half of the industry was showing a profit. Things are expected to improve into the next century. Like the restaurant industry, segments within the hotel industry are enjoying varying degrees of success. While the upscale and upper-midscale segments have been struggling, the midscale to lower-midscale and economy segments have been holding their own and in some areas showing moderate growth. The all-suites segment has fared the best but because of its higher rates is more vulnerable to a value-conscious consumer. During the late 1980s and early 1990s, the government-owned Resolution Trust Corporation (RTC) through hotel foreclosures became one of the largest hotel operators in the country.

When restaurants experience major declines in revenues and negative bottom lines, closing the doors is a viable option. This is because there is little value to be gained, under the circumstances, from keeping a restaurant open. It will probably continue to lose money and could eventually lose much more than its salvage value. On the other hand, a hotel losing $15,000 per month, while not the best of circumstances, would pose a different problem than a restaurant with losses. Since the hotel could have an asset value of several million dollars, owners are motivated to hold onto the property until a regular profit returns, or until a buyer is found. It is also more expensive to close a hotel than to keep it operating at minimal capacity. Once closed, carpeting, furniture, and paint tend to mildew, HVAC systems (heating, venting, and air conditioning) break down, 24-hour security is required, the property must be fenced in, vandalism becomes a problem, and so forth.

Some operators in the foodservice or hotel industries feel that because of the unique needs they serve—food and a place to sleep while traveling—they will probably never reach the end of the product life cycle. This is true to an extent. The hospitality industry as a whole will survive, but only those brands, concepts, or segments that modify their offerings to keep pace with consumer trends will be among the survivors. As competitors develop newer, more effective, and more efficient means of satisfying the customer, less viable concepts will die off.

Categories for the Product Life Cycle

The PLC can be used to explain a product's potential for any relevant product category grouping, such as its industry, concepts, and primary product offering. Each product grouping analysis will yield a unique picture of a business's potential opportunities and threats. Since each category of the PLC encompasses many conceivable factors that may affect a business, there is no set position in any one PLC that would unquestionably indicate what strategy a business should pursue. Product categories for the product life cycle follow.

INDUSTRY   The broadest category is the industry. This product life cycle would show how the sales for all hotels or all foodservice establishments are progressing. The degree of effect on a particular business or brand will depend on many factors. If the industry PLC is growing at moderate pace, the company can generally assume that the economy and the majority of environmental factors are conducive to growth.

INDUSTRY SEGMENT   The industry segment would represent sales for a segment within the industry. There are several possible methods of segmenting the hotel and foodservice industries. The foodservice industry is commonly divided into fast-food, casual-dining, fine-dining, and institutional foodservice. Hotels segments could include economy, midscale (or limited-service midscale and full-service midscale), upper midscale and luxury.

CONCEPTS   This would include types of businesses within each industry segment. Within the fast-food segment there are hamburgers, Mexican food, fried chicken, pizza, and Chinese food, among others. In the midscale hotel segment, typical classifications are downtown, airport, business, shopping, roadside/highway, suites, inns, and resort.

BRAND   This includes each different hotel or foodservice company, for example, Hilton hotels, Taco Bell restaurants, and ARAMARK Corporation for institutional foodservice.

PRODUCT OR SERVICE OFFERING   Each year unique products or services appear in restaurants and hotels. Many of these quickly perish as fads, while some will survive for varying lengths of time. Trends are new products or services, or variations of existing products and services, that have been accepted by various customer segments and widely adopted by business. Paul Prudhomme's blackened style of cooking first appeared to be headed toward extinction—a fad. Few conceived that customers would want their fish, steak, or chicken essentially burnt. As the converts grew, the blackened style of cooking became a major trend. Other new products, such as butter sauces or California compilation sauces like blueberry vinaigrette for meats, can be considered as fads and have quickly faded. The ability to discover what new products or services customers will want is not easy. For some it is akin to using a crystal ball. Companies with well-developed marketing information systems, especially a thorough customer analysis, will have clues as to the next product or service customers will desire. Generally, the safest approach, and one used by most operators, is to allow someone else to take the risk of introducing (pioneering) a new product (or service). If the product appears to be catching on, then being one of the first to offer it may be better than risking the fate of the pioneer. This strategy must, of course, be weighed against the sacrifice of not being the first to market a highly demanded product.

Occasionally, there will be products that are obvious fads but, because of their current popularity, should be considered for the business. If customers currently want five different flavors of cheesecake, it may not be in the interest of the business to argue with them.

LOCATION   Each of the above categories can also be considered by their location. This could refer to country, region, state, county, city, or part of a city. For example, at the same time hotels may be suffering in one region, business could be booming in another.

PORTFOLIO ANALYSIS

In portfolio analysis, a corporate-level strategy decision, individual businesses are viewed on the basis of such key performance factors or indicators as profit, market share, the competitive nature of industry, and the strengths and weaknesses of the business. Perhaps the most popular form of portfolio analysis has been the *Boston Consulting Group (BCG) growth/share matrix* (see Figure 7.5). The primary purpose and contribution of the BCG matrix analysis is two-fold:

1. To provide a systematic means of integrating several businesses into a comprehensive corporate strategy. The analysis adds a measure of objectivity to the strategic selection process by quantifying a business's position.
2. To assign a purpose for each business unit. Under the BCG matrix each business is given a designation as one of the following:
   (a) *Star.* Businesses with a high market share in a high-growth industry will normally be generating reasonable profits but, because of the necessity of financial investment for growth, may not be producing a positive cash flow.

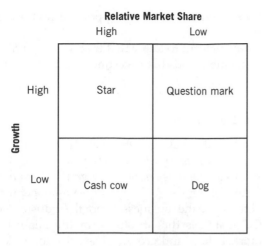

Figure 7.5 BCG growth/share matrix. Source: Adapted with permission from Pearce & Robinson (1991), *Formulation, Implementation, and Control of Competitive Strategy.* Homewood, Illinois, p. 263.

The business strategy will generally be for growth fueled by externally acquired capital.

(b) *Question Marks.* businesses with a low relative market share in a high-growth industry will usually be in a growth phase, but with a weak financial position. This will normally necessitate investments from other corporate business units. The business strategy for most question marks is usually for growth with funds being supplied from cash cows (see below). If the business does not live up to expectations or if industry growth slows, then the question mark may become a dog (see below).

(c) *Cash Cows.* A business in a low-growth industry but with a high market share will often produce substantial profits and cash flow to be used for business units in other categories. The most frequent business strategy for a cash cow is to be milked for investment in stars or question marks. If there is little optimism for a stable future for the business, then the corporation might decide to pursue a harvest strategy of limiting maintenance investments.

(d) *Dogs.* Businesses with a low market share in a low-growth industry will vary between significant cash users to moderate cash generators. The business strategy for a dog is most often to divest, but occasionally to hold for possible strategic repositioning as a question mark or cash cow.

Though the BCG matrix was at one time at the forefront of corporate strategic planning theory, it is now studied primarily from a historical perspective and as a means of establishing a better understanding for more advanced methods of portfolio analysis. Among the key problems of the BCG matrix is that it focuses only on growth and market share. Obviously, these two indicators are important, but much more is needed. For example, a restaurant could have a low market share with minimal industry growth but be producing an excellent profit. It also ignores many internal and environmental influences that will impact the business's future. For example, in a declining market, businesses will be closing down and be put up for sale, reducing supply and increasing the likelihood for improved demand for remaining competitors. This would also increase expansion opportunities through the acquisition of marginal performers.

Finally, few business managers want to know that their business has been designated as a "dog" by top management and that divestment (sale of the business) is a real possibility.

Business Strength/Industry Attractiveness Matrix

To solve some of the problems of the BCG growth/share matrix, a more thorough matrix analysis, the *business strength/industry attractiveness matrix,* was developed (see Figure 7.6). (It is also referred to as the *nine-cell planning grid* and is credited to both General Electric Corporation and McKinsey & Company—a management consulting firm.) The primary improvement of the business strength/industry attractiveness (BS/IA) matrix over the BCG matrix is that it allows for the analysis of multiple variables rather than only market share and growth. The selection of key indicators of success of any business can be included so that a more realistic, if still somewhat subjective, view of the business unit can be made. A list of the key factors can be derived from the strategic internal factors listed in Chapter 4. Also, with the expansion from the BCG's four cells to BS/IA's nine cells, a more precise measurement and visual distinction can be made.

The matrix is flexible in that it can be used to assess the performance of a single

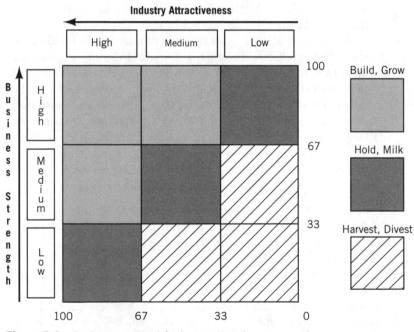

Figure 7.6 Business strength/industry attractiveness matrix.

TABLE 7.1 Business Strength/Industry Attractiveness Values

Business Strength	Weight (Importance to firm; must add up to 10)	Rating (Performance; 1 = poor, 10 = excellent)	Value (Weight x Rating)
Profit	3	8	24
Product/service quality	3	8	24
Management skills	2	7	14
Locations	1	6	6
Atmosphere	1	5	5
Total value for business strength			73

Industry Attractiveness	Weight	Rating (Present trend; 1 = not attractive, 10 = very attractive	Value
Growth	2.5	5	12.5
Profit margins	3.5	7	24.5
Competitive intensity	3	5	15
Remote environment	1	7	7
Total value for industry attractiveness			59

company or a group of companies under the same corporate umbrella, or as a tool to analyze the comparative strength of competitors.

Each of the key variables used must be given a weight, rating, and value (see Table 7.1). The process follows.

- The weight will be based on its importance to the company, relative to other selected variables. The total points must equal 10. If desired, decimals, such as 1.4, may be used. The weights can be based on their importance as determined by management or, when possible, by customer surveys. For example, financial performance would be weighted by management, whereas the weighting of operational performance factors could be determined by asking customers to complete a short survey that ranks the importance of selected factors.
- A rating (or grade) will be given for each business strength variable, designating the company's level of performance. For example, a strength would receive a high score, a weakness would receive a lower score. The ratings would be calculated on a ten-point basis as recommended for the category weight.
- The rating for each variable is then multiplied by its weight to obtain the variable's value.
- The values are individually summed for total value for business strength for that particular business.
- For industry attractiveness, influencing variables will be given a weight based on their importance to the business, and a rating based on favorable or unfavorable conditions in the environment relative to the variable. Primarily, does it indicate an opportunity or threat, now or in the future?

- The total value for industry attractiveness is calculated in the same manner as for business strength.
- The two scores for each business unit are then used to position the business on the matrix.
- As with the BCG matrix, the position on the matrix will indicate whether the overall business strategy for the individual firm should be to grow (invest in the business to expand it), hold (keep operating the business without liquidation of assets, invest only enough capital to remain competitive), harvest (keep operating the business but do not invest beyond that necessary to stay in business), or divest (sell the business).

Neither the BCG matrix nor the BS/IA matrix will provide all the answers to corporate-level business strategy decisions. Each business and its competitors must be analyzed in depth to make the most accurate strategic choice possible. The matrix analysis at least adds some consistency to the process. An additional use for matrix analysis is to construct a competitor's portfolio matrix to forecast what potential strategies might be selected (Porter, 1980). It can also be utilized as a more sophisticate form of a competitor's perceptual map. Rather than factor in two primary variables, any desired number could now be included.

STRATEGIES FOR DIFFERENT INDUSTRY POSITIONS

There are hundreds of thousands of hospitality firms, each with varying amounts of resources and abilities and different objectives. Each business will decide, based on its position in the industry, what strategies are possible and logical for it to pursue. While there is no set strategy that every business of a particular type, size, or financial strength should follow, there are historical parameters of engagement that can be utilized to increase the possibility of success. Much of what is practiced in marketing strategies comes from military terminology. Flanking attacks, guerrilla attacks, counter-offensives, encirclement attacks, and many other strategies are not unique to marketing, but originated and were perfected in the ultimate struggle—war—where lives and countries were at stake.

Various marketing and strategic business writers have different terms for a business's position in its industry. The categorization selected for this book is that of the market leaders, market challengers, and market nichers (Powers, 1990; Kotler, 1991). Each market position will dictate different strategies.

The Leader

Each segment within the hotel and foodservice industries will have a leader. For the hospitality industry, the primary measure of leadership is overall sales, plus unit sales for restaurants and REVPAR for hotels (average daily rate times occupancy percentage). Sometimes this is a clear and well-recognized leader, such as McDonald's in the fast-food sector. For some segments, the lead position may not be as easily recognized as in the case of upper-midscale hotels, with the Hilton, Marriott, and Hyatt. Unlike in many industries, where certain leaders capture enough of the market to deter most competitors, costs of entry are exorbitant, and economies of scale rule, leaders in the hospitality business must compete head-on with rivals on a near-even footing. The greater a firm's reliance on people rather than equipment, the fewer advantages there are for the leader of that industry. There is no room in the lightbulb industry for 10,000 competitors to attack General Electric, but there are well over 600,000 foodservice establishments vying for the customer's food dollar.

Leaders in the hospitality industry will benefit from name recognition and financial resources that allow for larger ad budgets and faster expansion, but each leader's primary focus will be on competing with rivals in its trade area. It is often more important for hotels to face competition within each market rather than on a national basis. National campaigns will always be important in gaining customers for their initial visit, but individual business units of the chain will have the responsibility of keeping them. A Marriott across the street from a Crowne Plaza (Holiday Inn) enjoys a name recognition benefit, but not much else. Each hotel will have to compete based on its relative individual merits rather that fact that one is an industry leader and one is a challenger. Even McDonald's, the Goliath of the fast-food industry, must address each trade area challenger as a potentially worthy opponent.

For leaders to remain on top, they must focus on protecting their strengths, essentially the continuation of what got them to their present position. They must also incorporate strategies that will make it more difficult for challengers to gain momentum. This could be through increasing market penetration, product additions, or diversifying into related businesses (concentric diversification). A common problem for market leaders is that they focus so much on their strengths that they miss major shifts in their competitive environment. A more and more frequent strategy of market leaders is that of a commitment to core strategies, plus the adoption of successful strategies of market challengers and nichers. Holiday Inn has imitated several of its largest challengers by adding five different classes of hotels to its portfolio (Holiday Inn Express, SunSpree Resorts, and Select; and Crowne Plaza Resorts and Hotels).

Also, unlike in most industries, a leadership role or high market share does not equate with profit or growth. McDonald's is the leader in fast food and it does show a good profit, but that profit is from running an efficient operation. Burger King, Hardee's, and the Marriott, at various times, found that being a major player carries few benefits. The lesson learned is that the results of strategic actions are essentially proportionate to the size of the company. A small company selecting the wrong strategy may lose $20,000, perhaps a major percentage of their cash reserves. When a major firm errs, the figures are now potentially in the hundreds of millions of dollars.

Challengers and Market Nichers

Quite often, most firms within an industry segment will utilize very similar strategies, regardless of their position. When this happens, the results are generally that the business with the largest market share will win. The leader has more experience, money, penetration, recognition, and customer loyalty, so it can easily defeat an opponent that plays by their rules. Imitating the leader may allow a business to survive, but in today's competitive environment trying to survive may lead to demise. For long-term success, every business must gain some type of an advantage. If a challenger or nicher is to increase its share of the market, it must change the rules of the game with the goal of neutralizing or temporarily paralyzing the leader or significant competitor. Large corporations have set ways of doing things, and after all, they are the leaders, so it has worked for them. They also generally have rigid organizational structures that make a rapid response difficult. While the leader is stunned, or sitting back thinking that things will soon be back to normal, the challenger can make significant gains (Robert, 1991).

There are various types of attacks for the challenger or nicher. One is a flanking attack to circumvent the strengths of the leader. Pizza Hut and Pizza Inn thought little of Dominos' strategy of delivery until their market shares were severely eroded. La Quinta Inns developed a strategy based on the theory that business and pleasure travelers would accept fewer services in return for lower rates. Choice Hotels International, composed of Sleep, Comfort, Quality, Clarion, Econolodge, and Roadway, among others, decided to set up an advanced reservation system, then assemble a menu of hotels so they could offer each caller a hotel room within their price range.

The safest strategy for the nicher is to find a geographic niche that leaders or challengers are not likely to pursue. For a restaurant, this could provide years of relative protection from major competition. While hotels can still find geographic niches, because of the much larger investment and broader customer base, they must be certain that the location is worth the risk.

THE BRYAN HOUSE AND CITY GRILL GRAND STRATEGIES
The Bryan House

Concentration

The hotel is doing average to above average in most areas. Service and attitude have been acceptable. The performance of the kitchen and marketing department should be given considerable attention and support. All levels of management must aggressively focus on improvements that will help the hotel achieve its objectives.

Some means must be found to increase the length of stay of guests, especially on weekends. A new weekend package should be developed. Special event banquets for groups, such as a Brazilian Carnival, could help increase catering sales.

Product Development

The hotel will need to add business services and a concierge in order to become more competitive. Other services should be considered as our customers request them.

Market Development

No new markets will be added at this time. The main concern is maximizing existing market segments.

City Grill

Concentration

We will continue to serve high-quality, high-value foods and beverages with first-rate service. We must strive to hold product costs at the lowest level possible by supporting an effective purchasing policy.

Our primary market will continue to be existing target customers, those 25 to 40 years of age with annual household incomes between $35,000 and $65,000. Growth will come from increasing the frequency of visits of present customers, attracting competitors' customers (especially from Jake's Grill), and attracting other customers in our trade area who have not yet eaten at our restaurant.

Product Development

We will continue to add nutritionally oriented menu items, but we must make sure we do not appear to be a health-food restaurant. We will increase the percentage of seafood items on the menu to 30%.

Table d'hôte dinners and specials should be considered.

We will add freshly baked rolls to our menu.

New menu items and services must be justified by increases in sales, contribution to profit, possibly attracting a new market segment, and hopefully not cannibalizing sales of other menu items or services. All products and services must support the image of a high-quality casual dining restaurant.

For food and beverages, consider cost, compatibility with existing menu items, preparation and line cooking and assembly requirements, cross-utilization of ingredients, and kitchen time.

We plan on adding fried chicken. We already have the sauce, the chicken breasts, breading mix, and deep-fat fryers.

Market Development

We will begin promoting discounts for senior citizens.

We will promote takeout business to compete with fast-food restaurants. After we have established that takeout service can be done successfully, we will consider delivery.

If the sales and profit for the first quarter of 1991 continue at their present pace, we will begin looking for a second location in the city.

QUESTIONS AND PROJECTS

1. Draw and describe each quadrant of the grand strategy selection matrix.
2. Prepare a grand strategy selection matrix for a selected or assigned hospitality firm.
3. Explain the term "total quality management."
4. List and explain the three costs of quality.
5. Explain the "1–10–100 rule."
6. What two categories are included in market development?
7. What is the difference between intensive and extensive diversification? What are the four main types of extensive diversification?
8. What are generic strategies? List and explain the purpose of the five different generic strategies.
9. What is the product life cycle?
10. Why might it be important to consider different product categories for the product life cycle? Apply the PLC to any hospitality firm's primary product and service offering. What hospitality firm's primary product and service offering. What stage is it at now and what might happen to it in the future?
11. What is the purpose of portfolio analysis?
12. Prepare a business strength/industry attractiveness grid for any single firm by creating your own values table as in Figure 7.1
13. Use the business strength/industry attractiveness grid to analyze any corporation with two or more businesses. You can estimate the plot points. Be prepared to discuss your decisions.
14. Discuss strategies for different industry positions as they relate to some of your local hotels and restaurants.

Scenario Analysis

Scenario analysis is an optional form of strategic analysis and consists of matching a selected strategy (or strategies) with a company's strengths and weaknesses and environmental opportunities and threats. The goal is forecasting the possible outcomes if a certain strategy is selected to pursue a certain opportunity (correct a weakness or protect the business from a threat). The result would be a contingency plan outlining the most prudent action for the firm to take.

The first scenario to be developed would be the one most likely to occur. Other scenarios could be developed as appropriate. The scenarios could be developed for pessimistic, realistic, and optimistic possibilities.

City Grill

SCENARIO ANALYSIS

Scenario #1

What would be the possible outcome if we added several seafood items to our menu and became known primarily for fresh seafood?

Additionally, what if we make this change, and then seafood prices double?

Possible Outcomes for Scenario #1

Seafood is becoming so popular that this can only help our sales and image. We will always have a minimum of two chicken and two beef entrees for customers wanting something other than seafood.

If our prices increased, so would those of most other restaurants. Our major problem would not be other seafood competitors, but customers changing their dining habits away from seafood.

If we stopped serving seafood, we could lose customers who have come to expect it from us.

We could still serve seafood, but charge the extra price. If we did this, it could change our image from being a moderate-priced restaurant to a more expensive one.

We could develop recipes that called for less seafood, such as gumbo, seafood thermidor, and shrimp creole.

We could look for direct sources to reduce middleman markups.

Scenario #2

We open a new restaurant in Houston, sales are lower than expected, and the restaurant is losing $10,000 per month.

Possible Outcomes for Scenario #2

1. Since we are now making $12,500 per month in our first location, this would give us a net income of $2500.
2. A worse-case outcome would be if we had to close the restaurant and absorb a debt of $150,000 or payments of $7500 per month for 30 months.
3. Strategies could be developed to fix the problem.

Strategy Selection Process

The following examples are designed to show the progression of decisions from the recognition of the opportunity, weakness, or threat, through to the setting of policies and marketing action plan. (This appendix will include parts of the strategic model that have not yet been covered. An understanding of the entire process is not mandatory at this time. If something is not understood, do not be concerned; if there are questions, read ahead and preview the appropriate section.

Example 1

SWOT ANALYSIS (WEAKNESS, OPPORTUNITY, OR THREAT)

Customers want a 10-minute service time.
　　The first example could be viewed as a weakness, an opportunity, a threat, or all three.

- The weakness for the restaurant is a slower service time.
- It is definitely an opportunity because present customers desire faster service time.
- This is also a threat if competitors have a 10-minute service time.

STRATEGIC ANALYSIS QUESTIONING SEQUENCE

　　1. *What is the firm's current market position in relation to customer demand?* We are currently between Positions 2 and 3; slightly ahead of current demand. Since our service time is slower than competitors', this is a potential sign that we are slipping further behind market demand.
　　2. *What are the key SWOT factors that must be considered in the plan?* Here would be listed applicable key SWOT factors, including the focus of this example.
　　3. *What are the implications of the SWOT factor or group of SWOT factors?* Of the key SWOT factors listed, the firm would select those that will require further analysis.
　　The planner must consider how the weakness, opportunity, or threat could affect business. For example:

- Competitors can deliver food faster, which speeds lunch turnover for their restaurant and takes up less of the customers' time.
- Food will not sit in competitors' pass-through windows as long, so it will appear fresher.
- Our restaurant will develop the image of having slow service.

- Morale could be affected, from customers asking servers when their food will be out.
- Investors will be upset and try to exert more control over decision-making if the problem is not resolved.

4. *Have existing strategies related to the key SWOT factor been effective?* No. Current service times average 14 minutes, with 10 minutes being desired by customers, and 10-minute times being offered by competitors.

Reason—Poor design is the primary cause, but training methods, operational policies, and an extensive menu may also influence the slower times.

5. *What alternative or optional strategies should be considered?* We do not have the money to remodel at this time, but something should be done. Our options or alternative strategies* are:

- Find an inexpensive way to make needed changes. (Management: Administrative and Operations, Finance)
- Borrow the money to remodel now, and pay it back over several years. (Finance)
- Modify the menu to get rid of the items that take more than 10 minutes. (Marketing, Management: Operations)
- Rearrange the kitchen equipment to reduce the number of steps necessary to prepare orders. (Management: Operations)
- Purchase new equipment that will reduce kitchen times. (Management: Operations, Finance)
- Pre-prepare some items to reduce the number of steps and time needed when the item is ordered. (Management: Operations, Marketing)
- Increase training, and have meetings with the goal of finding ways to reduce average ticket times. (Management: Personnel)
- Write a new kitchen policies manual. (Management: Operations and Personnel)
- Give rewards to staff for meeting goals of lower ticket times. (Management: Personnel)

Each of the above strategy options would be viewed from the perspective of the remainder of the eight strategic guidelines questions:

6. *Are the strategic alternatives compatible with the firm's competitive environment?* Customers want 10-minute ticket times.

7. *Does the strategy place realistic demands on the abilities of the firm?* We have the potential; if we are going to remain competitive, we have no choice.

8. *Is the strategy is worth pursuing?* Yes, if the appropriate action is taken.

9. *How will competitors react?* Some competitors could view this as a threat, but minimal reaction is expected. If we began taking business from competitors within our trade area, perhaps they would increase promotions of some type. For this reason, after we reach our goal, we will have a small promotional campaign featuring a new entree.

10. *What should be the primary strategic thrusts for the next planning cycle?*

Speed up Ticket Times (the Strategic Thrust)

- Find an inexpensive way to make needed changes.
- Modify the menu to get rid of the items that take more than 10 minutes.

*All options, if selected, will require action—a strategy—by one or more functional areas of the business. The normal responsible area is in parentheses.

- Rearrange the kitchen equipment to reduce the number of steps necessary to prepare orders.
- Increase training, and have meetings with the goal of finding ways to reduce average ticket times.
- Write a new kitchen policies manual.
- Give rewards to staff for meeting goals of lower ticket times.

GRAND STRATEGY

(These will be general actions to achieve long-term objectives.)

Product Development: Modify the menu to eliminate items that have kitchen times longer than 10 minutes, and make sure that the number of orders received at each kitchen station is balanced.

Long-term Objectives
(These are the results expected over the long-term.*)

Technology: Remodel the kitchen in 2 years, set up a fund exclusively for this. (Finance) Reduce kitchen time to 9 minutes. (Operations) (This problem is placed in the technology area because even though it is a rudimentary form of technology, it has to do with the speed of delivery.)

Employee Development: Organize training sessions for each area impacting the kitchen timing problem, primarily in the kitchen, but also for servers. (Management: Operations and Personnel)

Employee Relations: Improve employee morale by 30%. (Management: Operations and Personnel) (This would often not be measured for a small company; instead, simply *improve employee morale.* The measurement could be in reduced turnover. Larger companies will have employees complete a questionnaire to measure changes in morale. This would be a longitudinal survey, since it would measure morale before and after implementation.)

Annual Objectives

(These are the objectives for the first year of the plan and are supportive of the long-term objectives.)

Technology: Purchase a convection oven by 5/3/19X to reduce times on baked items. Reduce kitchen time to 10 minutes. (It may be difficult to reduce the kitchen time to the desired level within the first year. The long-term objectives are expressed in terms of what you expect over a period of more than one year. The annual objectives are what the business is

---

*Each long-term objective is set for the entire company, but its responsibility should be assigned to a specific functional department or individual.

expected to achieve this year, so they will normally be less ambitious. There could perhaps be intermediate objectives, such as lowering the kitchen time to 12 minutes within the first six months. The accomplishment of the objective would depend on the specific problem and the means by which it could be solved. If the problem could be solved by rearranging the kitchen front line and buying one piece of equipment, then three to six months would be logical. If the entire menu would need to be changed along with many pieces of equipment, then more time would be necessary.) (Management: Operations, Finance)

Employee Development: Beginning on 3/20/19xx have training sessions for kitchen employees every two weeks, focusing on the timing problem. The sessions will continue until the goal of 10 minutes is reached. (Management: Personnel)

Employee Relations: The level of employee morale should be increased by 50% during strategy implementation of kitchen time reduction. (Management: Personnel and Operations) (This would be accomplished through incentives—making a game out of the objective; and preshift meetings to pump up the staff—letting them know the importance of the objective to the employees and the company. Trying to keep employees at an extremely high level of enthusiasm for extended periods of time can lead to burnout.)

Functional Strategies

(These are actions taken to achieve the annual objectives and the grand strategy.)

Management

- Rearrange some pieces of equipment.
- Organize work so that orders can be started as quickly as possible.
- Implement a reward/bonus system for meeting designated company goals, specifically, the reduction of kitchen times.
- The kitchen manager will be responsible for all aspects of the training sessions, including scheduling of employees, content, record of performance, and follow-up performance toward objectives.

Finance: Set up a fund to save $20,000 to remodel the kitchen and purchase new equipment.

Marketing

   Product

- Discontinue serving baked-to-order lasagna, 16-ounce New York Strip.
- Reduce the number of sauteed items from seven to five by discontinuing our two veal dishes.
- Add two salads—Southwest Chicken and the Fresh Catch Chef. This will reduce the overload on grilled items and help balance the work being done in the pantry with other stations. (The reasoning or justification for each change should be included. To make the necessary decisions in this example, you could complete a menu analysis report, sometimes called *menu engineering,* to see which items are producing the most revenue and profit. To this analysis report you would add the time necessary to prepare each item or

any logistics problems encountered. A breakdown of the items being prepared at each station should be included.)

Price. Cost out each new menu item. (Recipe Cost and Procedure Worksheet.)

Promotion. Have our current ad agency design and produce a poster showing our new salads. The poster will be displayed in our lobby and in the dining room. Small versions will be used for table tents.

Management Policies

- All orders must be started within one minute of being received in the kitchen. (Kitchen manager is responsible.)
- Kitchen times will be monitored on a continual basis with the aid of a kitchen timer that stamps a time-in and time-out on each guest check. (Kitchen manager)

Financial Policies

The accounting department will be responsible for setting aside money for remodeling and new equipment. Three thousand dollars per month should be appropriated.

Management Action Plan

- Rearrange kitchen equipment by 1/15/xx.
- Training sessions will begin on 2/5/xx. These will be conducted by the kitchen manager.
- Bonus requirements:
    - For the month of September when 80% of the orders go out in less than 12 minutes, the kitchen staff on that shift will get $20-per-person bonuses.
    - For the month of October when 90% of the orders go out in less than 11 minutes, the kitchen staff on that shift will get $40-per-person bonuses.
    - For the month of November when 100% of the orders go out in less than 10 minutes, the kitchen staff on that shift will get $60-per-person bonuses.
- The kitchen manager will be responsible for issuing bonuses for meeting objectives.

Marketing Action Plan (Matrix Format)

Activity	Person Responsible	Date Completed and Initials
Product		
Delete lasagna, NY Strip and veal on 8/22/xx	Mary Wilson	8/22/xx
Have new menus printed by 8/18/xx	Bob Johnson	8/15/xx
Add Southwest Chicken Salad and Fresh Catch Chef Salad by 8/22/xx	Mary Wilson	8/22/xx
Price (All prices must be ready by 8/16/xx)		
Southwest Chicken Salad $4.95	Mary Wilson	8/15/xx
Fresh Catch Chef Salad $5.95	Mary Wilson	8/15/xx
Promotion		
Posters and table tents completed by 8/18/xx	Bob Johnson	8/15/xx
Placed on walls and tables by 8/24/xx	Bob Johnson	8/22/xx

Example 2

The following is a simplified example of a restaurant that believes there is an opportunity to attract a new market segment—college students.

SWOT ANALYSIS (OPPORTUNITY)

College campus within trade area, two miles from restaurant, 33,000 students, most have jobs and cars, 50% live within 10 miles of campus.
Internal Analysis—College students amount to only 15% of total customer counts.

STRATEGIC ANALYSIS QUESTIONING SEQUENCE

1. *What is the firm's current position in the market?* We are currently in Position 4. The firm has not done much to take advantage of its environment. Its product offering is out of date and new businesses have opened up that are siphoning off current customers. Something must be done to reposition the company.

2. *What are the key SWOT factors that must be considered in the plan?* Here would be listed applicable key SWOT factors, including the focus of this example.

3. *What are the implications of the SWOT factor or group of factors?* (How could the existence or selection of this strategic choice affect the business?)

- This is a definite opportunity to increase sales.
- There are some opportunities to increase night business.
- Students prefer less expensive menu items, and beer.
- It could help take business away from some competitors.
- Students like delivery during midterms and finals.

4. *Has the existing strategy related to the key SWOT factor been effective?* No specific attempt has been made to attract college students.

5. *What alternative or optional strategies should be considered?**

- Develop a menu that targets students in addition to our present customer base. (Marketing)
- Focus on foods that can be prepared quickly, are filling, and that can be sold for under $3.00. (Marketing, Management: Operations)
- Provide delivery to dorms and apartments in the trade area. (Marketing, Management: Operations and Personnel, Finance)
- Add recreational activities to the restaurant, such as darts or pool tables. (Marketing, Management: Operations, and Finance)
- The decor could be updated to appeal to younger customers. (Marketing, Finance)
- The musical selection could be changed. (Marketing)

Each of the above strategy options would be viewed from the perspective of the remaining questions: 6. *Is the strategy compatible with the firm's competitive environment?*

*All options, if selected, will require action—a strategy—by one or more functional areas of the business.

7. Will the firm be able to execute the strategy? 8. *Is the strategy worth pursuing?* 9. *What are the possible competitor reactions?* 10. *What should be the primary strategic thrusts for the next planning cycle?* Do whatever is reasonable to increase sales form college students. (In this case, all of the strategic alternatives should probably be adopted.)

- Develop a menu that targets students in addition to our present customer base.
- Focus on foods that can be prepared quickly, are filling, and that can be sold for under $3.00.
- Provide delivery to dorms and apartments in the trade area.
- Add recreational activities to the restaurant, such as darts or pool tables.
- The decor could be updated to appeal to younger customers.
- The musical selection could be changed.

Grand Strategy

Concentration: Increase the frequency of visits of college students from the University of Houston campus. (Marketing)

New Product Development: Add new products to increase percentage of college students. (Marketing, Management: Operations, Personnel)

Long-Term Objectives

Profitability: Increase profit from 8% to 12% (based on the cumulative total of all new strategies geared toward increasing profit—including the new market segment). (General Manager, all functional departments)

Competitive Position: Increase sales by 15% (based on the cumulative total of all new strategies geared toward increasing sales). (General Manager, Marketing, Finance, all other functional departments)
  Increase number of customers under 25 years of age by 30%. (Marketing, Management: Operations)

Annual Objective

Profitability: Increase profit by 2%. (Management: Operation, Marketing, Finance)

Competitive Position: Increase sales by 10%. (Marketing, Management, Finance)
  Increase number of college students to 30%. (Marketing, Management: Operations)

Functional Strategies

Management: Develop system to offer pizza by the slice.

Finance: Set aside $1000 for heated holding cabinet.

Marketing

Product. Add pizza-by-the-slice.
Price. Offer meals under $3.00.
Place. Update decor to attract college students.
Promotion. Advertise in the *Daily Cougar* (campus newspaper) and offer a discount.

Management Policies

- The basic cheese pizza will be used for all by-the-slice orders.
- Toppings will be added as requested by the customer.
- Amounts will be as follows:
  Cheese—6 ounces for any pizza
  Pepperoni—12 slices of pepperoni
  Sausage—1/2 cup
  Onion—1 Tablespoon
- Maximum holding time will be 20 minutes.
- A par stock of ten unbaked plain pizzas will be refrigerated and ready for the oven. Between 11:30 a.m. and 12:30 p.m., a par stock of six baked cheese pizzas will be stored in the heated holding cabinet.

Financial Policies

By 6/15/19xx, the financial manager will set aside $1000 for purchase of heated holding cabinet.

Marketing Action Plan

Product. Add new menu item by 8/16/19xx.
Price. Cheese pizza with drink will be $2.45. The price for additional toppings will be 10 cents for vegetables and 25 cents for meat items.
Place. Paint dining room, add neon signs, bring in a CD juke box, all by 8/16/xx.
Promotion. Advertise in the *Daily Cougar* newspaper each Monday and Friday.
Offer: Introductory price of $1.95 for pizza and drink.

Example 3

The following is an example of a hotel that has a problem with courtesy and speed of service at the front desk.

SWOT ANALYSIS (WEAKNESS)

- *Guest check-in and check-out times of 4 minutes.*
- *Employees are not smiling as much as they should and are not conversing with new guests to make them feel welcome.*

STRATEGIC ANALYSIS QUESTIONING SEQUENCE

1. *What is the firm's current position in the market?* We are currently between Positions 1 and 2. Luckily since we are a luxury hotel, customers have been interpreting our slower service and lack of smiling as "formal service." If we are to retain our position, we must change quickly. Segment competitors are focusing on customer service and lower check-in and check-out times. As customers discover the difference, our position will begin to decline and we will experience lower sales and ADRs.

2. *What are the key SWOT factors that must be considered in the plan?* Here would be listed applicable key SWOT factors, including the focus of this example.

3. *What are the implications of the SWOT factor or group of factors?*

- Hotel guests are getting tired of standing in line.
- The lack of courtesy on the part of some employees is not good for the image of the hotel.
- If this continues, it will be easy for competitors to take our business.
- Employees and management are getting tired of complaints. Morale is slipping.
- It may become harder to hire employees.

4. *Have existing strategies related to the key SWOT factor been effective?* Competitors have times of between 2 and 3 minutes with the same computer system that we use. Part of the reason for the excessive time is having the keys too far from each work center (defined below). Something must be done immediately about the lack of courtesy. After research, we feel that the problem is rooted in lack of proper initial training, with no ongoing training, few benefits, and no breaks.

(The *work center* is the immediate area where each employee works. For example, there may be four or more work centers in the front desk area of a hotel. *Work stations* are combinations of work centers where one or more employees perform a functional task, such as the entire front desk of a hotel, the serving line of the kitchen, server pickup area, and warewashing area.)

5. *What alternative or optional strategies should be considered?*

- Schedule more employees during busy periods.
- Maximize efficiency of present equipment.
- Change layout of front desk area.
- Purchase a more advanced computerized guest registration system.
- Schedule regular breaks around peak periods.
- Establish reward system for reductions in check-in and check-out times.
- Purchase computerized entry system for guest rooms.

Each of the above strategy options would be viewed from the perspective of the remaining questions. 6. *Is the strategy compatible with the firm's competitive environment.* 7. *Will the firm be able to execute the strategy?* 8. *Is the strategy worth pursing?* 9. *What are the possible competitor reactions?*

10. *What should be the primary strategic thrusts for the next planning cycle?* Increase efficiency at the front desk.

- Schedule more employees during busy periods.
- Maximize efficiency of present equipment.
- Change layout of front desk area.

- Schedule regular breaks around peak periods.
- Establish reward system for reductions in check-in and check-out times.

Grand Strategy

In this example, no change is required in the grand strategy.

Long-Term Objectives

Technology: Reduce time for check-in and check-out transactions to 1 minute. (Management: Operations) (In Example 1, the problem with the production speed was due to technology—equipment and design. In this example, the problem is due partially to design and partially to employee-related problems.)

Employee Development: Implement a training system focused on customer service that all hotel employees must go through. (Management: Personnel)

Employee Relations: Improve employee morale by 50%. (Management: Operations, Personnel)

Competitive Position: Achieve a customer satisfaction index (CSI) for front desk service of 4.8.

Annual Objectives

Technology

- Move key storage area closer to the desk clerks' work centers.
- Reduce average transaction time to 2 minutes.

Employee Development

- Beginning on 10/15/19xx, have training sessions for all front desk personnel twice a month. Focus on the timing and courtesy problem. The bimonthly sessions will continue until the goal of 2 minutes is reached. Afterward, sessions will be monthly.
- Have customer service training for all employees during our monthly employee meetings.

Employee Relations

- Improve employee moral by 30%, by rewarding employees who reach the time reduction objectives.
- Breaks will be scheduled around peak periods.
- All employees will be cross-trained in at least one other position (to reduce monotony).

Competitive Position: Achieve a customer satisfaction index (CSI) for front desk service of 4.5.

Functional Strategies

Management

- Rearrange front desk area. Have a meeting with front desk personnel to discuss the problem. Mutually agree on a new design and procedures that will help reduce check-in and check-out times.
- Have training sessions to introduce new procedures.
- Morale must be improved through praise of improvements.
- Move the keys closer to the work centers.

Finance: The financial manager should appropriate $3000 for rearranging the front desk area.

Management Policies

- The front desk manager will be responsible for the training sessions.
- Transaction times for all new guests must be under 3 minutes during the first six months. (Front desk manager)
- Times will be monitored and measured four times daily by the front desk manager and the general manager. All management personnel should praise improvements.
- When the average check-in and check-out times are under 3 minutes for each peak period during an entire month, all front desk employees will receive a jacket with the hotel's logo.

Financial Policies

The head of the finance department will be responsible for appropriating $3000 for the redesign of the front desk area, and necessary funds for the incentives.

POSITIONING

Once the firms's target market or markets have been selected, management must decide how it wants the individual customers within its target markets to view its product offering relative to competing offers. This process, termed *positioning,* can be defined as creating a positive and unique image of the company in the minds of customers, relative to competitors (Boyd & Walker, 1990; Kotler, 1991). A firm's position can be discussed from two perspectives—the firm's strategized position and the opinion of the target customer—respectively termed *subjective position* and *objective position.* Most successful companies will have their subjective and objective positions in relative agreement. For example, if the subjective position (or management's view) is that one's hotel is a first-rate midscale hotel with clean rooms, excellent menu, quality food, and friendly personnel, the objective position should reflect this. If not, there may be a problem. If management thinks that its menu offering is just what the customer wants but, in reality, it is not, sales volume will suffer and future opportunities may be missed.

Sometimes the problem of nonalignment of subjective and objective positions is not serious. For example, if management does not think that the implications that its hotel is near a city recreation center are important, yet guests consider this to be a primary benefit, then there is no major problem but simply a missed opportunity. It is possible that a certain number of potential target customers will select the hotel if they know about the nearby recreation facilities. Management, in this case, is not maximizing its potential within its market. If this is what guests value, then this attribute should be included in positioning decisions and promotional efforts.

REPOSITIONING

When major changes in the firm's current position are required for the firm to remain competitive, it will attempt to *reposition* itself in the market. Firms that let their market position slide, whether through neglect or poor strategic decisions, are gambling with their business's future. Keeping a firm at its present position is far simpler than being forced into a repositioning situation (Hurley, 1990). Making incremental improvements to the firm's position on an annual basis carries only minimal risks and consistent levels of effort and expenses. Repositioning places the entire future of the firm in jeopardy. While generally not as risky and expensive as opening a new business, changing the perception of an existing business's target market has led many a chain down a long, perilous road. Hundreds of millions of dollars, and even billions of dollars, have been lost because of weak repositioning decisions.

POSITION AS A FACTOR OF PRODUCT, PROMOTIONAL, AND PUBLIC IMAGES

In the hospitality industry, the majority of a business's objective position is based on its *product offering*. This occurs because the public's perception of the industry's products is based on either first-hand experience or the experience of a friend or acquaintance. The market penetration of the vast majority of restaurant and hotel concepts is nearly 100% of American consumers. At some point in time, the vast majority of major hotel and restaurant chain's potential market has patronized the concept. In contrast, the objective position of many manufacturing firms is based more on promotional efforts. Most consumers buy a refrigerator only once every 10 to 15 years. The promotional and public images are important because of their influence on potential customers. They are also a means of increasing the loyalty of existing customers.

The *promotional image* concerns the overall message that has been communicated through personal and nonpersonal channels (mass media). As with the customers' perception of the firm's product mix, there may be a vast difference between what customers think of the firm's promotional efforts and what management thinks. Oftentimes firms with excellent or satisfactory sales assume that no changes are necessary in their promotional efforts and the image or message they project. In some cases, this will be true. Yet, a problem arises when the firm's internal efforts are at standards that keep existing customers returning on a regular basis but external promotional efforts are lacking. Subpar promotions may not be adequate to replace regular customers who are siphoned off by competitors, move from the trade area, or no longer travel to the trade area. This should be viewed as a positional weakness that must be evaluated and corrected (Deighton, Henderson, & Neslin, 1994). External communications should set the firm apart from competitors; offer benefits that target market demands, including those that are most critical to the purchase decision; communicate a mental image of what the business stands for; and deliver on what the message promises (Lewis, 1990).

The firm's *public image* (also referred to as corporate image) should be considered not only among its target customers but also in the local communities in which it operates, and in the broader public. This image is derived from individuals' exposure to any information about the firm. Sources include publicity from charitable and other community-oriented efforts, its reputation as a good place to work, the reputation of its management, word-of-mouth advertising, and the business's external appearance (Schmitt, Simonson, & Marcus, 1995). The importance of public image increases when buying power is concentrated and represents a major risk to the decision-maker. For example, a corporate travel planner will be making a career-defining decision each time a hotel is selected for a national convention.

POSITIONING'S PURPOSE

Positioning serves the firm in four critical areas: (1) it exposes the relationship between customer satisfaction and the firm's and competitors' performance; (2) it helps to identify new market opportunities (Lovelock, 1991); (3) it matches the firm's product offering, price, and location with that desired by the firm's target market; and (4) it communicates to the target market through personal and nonpersonal communication channels that the firm's product offering (benefits offered) is unique and preferable to competitors' offerings (DiMingo, 1988). The basic goal is to achieve *top-of-mind awareness* (TOMA), also referred to as being first on the customer's *product ladder.* This is the conscious or subconscious list that businesses review each time a purchase is considered. A business's place on its customers' product ladder is based on (1) its strategists' selection of a positioning strategy, (2) the functional strategies chosen to articulate the positioning strategy, (3) the success with which the functional strategies are implemented and communicated, and (4) the degree to which competitors' positioning and supportive functional strategies have met the demands of the target customers.

THE POSITIONING PROCESS

When developing corporate- and business-level strategies, marketers decide on the broad actions that should be taken in setting marketing strategies. These would include long-term strategies, such as adding new target markets (customer or geographic markets), significant changes in product and service offerings, and efforts to increase the penetration of existing markets with existing products. Since the positioning process is where the business will narrow its focus and decide on more specific parameters, the corporate- and business-level strategies establish the target for positioning decisions—the customers to target and the basic product that will be offered. To position a product or service in the market, the firm must (1) determine the customers' preferred combination of attributes, (2) locate the firm's current position, (3) analyze its current position and determine its desired position, (4) decide on the appropriate level of strategic aggression (degree of change necessary to achieve the firm's desired position), and (5) select a positioning or repositioning strategy. (See Figure 8.1.)

1. *Determine the target customers' preferred combination of attributes.* To develop a positioning strategy, marketers must have first systematically identified their target customer(s) and their demands from the segmentation and market targeting process

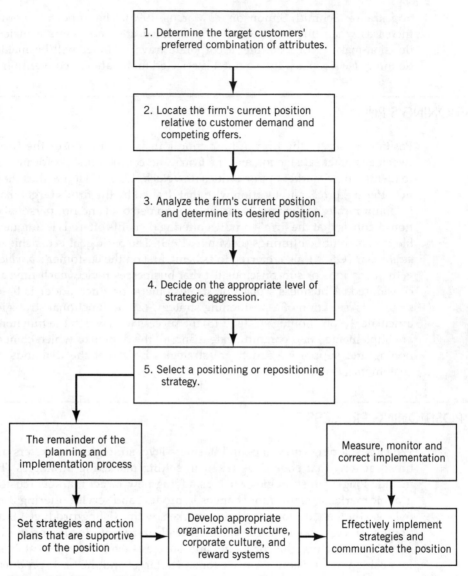

Figure 8.1 The positioning process.

(Cronin & Taylor, 1992). The *segmentation process* is essentially an analysis of the broad customer market to locate differences in buying patterns and personal characteristics between various groups (Swinyard & Struman, 1986). This is a commonly neglected area for potential sales increases for most hotels and some restaurants. To varying degrees, most hospitality marketers analyze their existing customer bases for unique characteristics, but very few take enough time to analyze the broader markets for untapped sources of customers. The reasons for this vary, but most common are the financial and career risks of focusing on new target groups and the fact that it is easier to repeat what has been done in the past. A frequently used basis for segmentation includes four factors: geographics—where the potential customers live, work, or travel; demographics—a statistical breakdown of the characteristics of applicable customer groups (age, income, education, etc); psychographics—centered on personality, social class, activities, interests, and opinions (characteristics not specifically related to purchasing the firm's product); and buyer behavior patterns—including user status, frequency of use, price sensitivity, attributes sought, and brand loyalty (characteristics that are specifically related to purchasing the firm's product). *Market targeting* is deciding which of those groups or segments the business can most effectively and efficiently attract.

Locating Small Gaps in Customer Information

If the customer characteristics already identified are those that are commonly known and utilized in competitors' positioning strategies, then other factors must be sought that will allow the firm to stand out from competitors. Before the Medallion Hotel Corporation opened their first property under the Medallion name (formerly a Marriott in Houston, Texas), they surveyed their target markets to see what needs and wants were being satisfied and which were not. Among the many things learned was that, after a long day of work, business people wanted to walk into a more relaxing lobby, not a monument to the hotel's designer. This resulted in a lobby that looks more like a contemporary upscale home, rather than a sensory overload of color and design. They also learned that customers were becoming desensitized to years of frequent guest programs and that they were also tired of waiting for benefits. The Medallion Hotels quite successfully took advantage of this situation by providing guests with gift certificates from Eddie Bauer clothing stores after a specified amount was spent at the hotel (about what would be spent for three nights at the hotel). While there was an initial drop in revenue after the name change, in less than one year occupancies were more than 10% higher than when the property was under the Marriott flag.

MAGNIFYING SMALL GAPS   There are few physical differences between many of the Hilton and Marriott Hotels. They offer many of the same services and generally are in close proximity to one another. In fact, some hotels, through changes in franchise contracts, may have been Hiltons or Marriotts that switched from one brand to the other. If their offerings are similar, management will have four key choices in their positioning decisions (Levitt, 1980). They could (1) find out what services would be valued by the market that are not currently being offered (Getty & Thompson, 1994), (2) attempt to magnify irrelevant attributes (e.g., promoting Viennese desserts when target customers know nothing about Viennese desserts) (Carpenter, Glazer, & Nakamoto, 1994), (3) improve strategy implementation to a level that is obviously above that of primary competitors (Snow & Hrebriniak, 1980; Day & Wensley, 1988), or (4) focus on differentiating their properties through promotions (Porter, 1980). Promotions could attempt to magnify any minor differences between the two hotels, especially those related to various customer-demanded attributes. For example, Hilton Hotels positioned themselves away from "America's business address" and toward "So nice to come home to." The purpose was to capitalize on Hilton's reputation as the standard for the upper midscale market, while at the same time creating a more relaxing image than *a place for business*. The winner in the positioning battle between similar concepts will likely be the hotel that first, locates the most meaningful tangible or intangible attributes, and then packages and promotes them to the satisfaction of its target customers.

In some instances, there may be noticeable differences in product and service strategies between primary competitors, such as between the Bennigan's and Friday's Restaurants. When this occurs, management must find out what differences are most valued by its largest target customer groups, then attempt to highlight those differences in its positioning strategies and communicate them through promotional strategies. Again, the creation of the appropriate image will play a major role in determining which restaurant is positioned most effectively.

Future Desired Attributes

As a firm tries to find that unique position in its market, it must obviously study its customers' preferences and competitors' offerings. But a critical component is the determination of what customers will desire in the near and long-term future. While this is not a simple task, it can often be determined by asking customers questions, such as "What do you not like about the current products and services we offer?" or "How would you change our products and services to better make them meet your needs?" (Questions similar to these could also be asked about primary or secondary competitor's offerings.) "What are your favorite three restaurants/hotels?" and "Do any of these businesses come close to your ideal restaurant/hotel?" "Why?" and "Why not?" Finding out what customers like about current products is valuable, but, in today's fast-changing market, this may not yield enough of a differentiation to locate a unique and defendable position.

2. *Locate the firm's current position relative to customer demand and competing offers.* One of the most important tasks necessary for determining a positioning or repositioning strategy is to locate where the firm currently stands relative to customer demand and competing offers (Dodson, 1991; Kara, Kaynak, & Kucukemiroglu, 1995). Concurrently, it must find out why the firm occupies its current position. Porter (1980, 1991) says that the position is based on "lower cost than rivals, or the ability to differentiate and command a premium price that exceeds the extra cost of doing so." While this is true, it is an overly simplistic view of strategy. Knowing that one should keep costs low and offer something different is the foundation of business—the basis for financial decisions and the marketing concept. The basis for a firm's position requires a detailed analysis of its competitive marketplace (this topic is discussed later in this section).

In the previous step, management found out what target markets think is important and other characteristics that will help the firm improve its competitive position.

Now management will attempt to measure the degree to which its performance has satisfied the demands of its target customers. Performance in this context will be expressed as the firm's position in its market. This position, while being a unique place in the minds of target customers, is like an individual's personality, made up of many elements. While the details of the position are critical to its measurement, the primary purpose here is not an in-depth analysis of the many variables that form the basis for the firm's position, but simply to locate the firm's overall position relative to competitors. The details will be reviewed and analyzed in Step 5 of the positioning process, deciding on a positioning or repositioning strategy.

Locating the Firm's and Competitors' Positions

To determine a firm's or a competitor's position, management can either subjectively decide how the business is positioned or objectively query its customers to discover how they view the firm. The objective position will be preferable in the vast majority of instances. If adequate information is not available or if time is short, then the subjective position may have to suffice. Since the customers of any one firm will also patronize other similar businesses, it is not difficult to accumulate adequate and relevant information about primary competitors (Haywood, 1986).

DETERMINING THE FIRM'S SUBJECTIVE POSITION   The subjective position can be based simply on management's opinion or determined by reviewing historical records, such as strategic or marketing plans. Subjective accuracy can be increased with quantitative support or with an analysis of the market by an unbiased third party with extensive industry experience. If these additional steps are not taken or are minimized, then whoever makes the assessment must attempt to be as objective as possible. For a subjective assessment of the firm's position management should analyze:

- Changes in sales, profit, or growth patterns from year to year
- Changes in competitor's sales, profit, or growth patterns from year to year
- Whether or not competitors have ceased offering products or services that are similar to one's firm's products and services
- If competitors with similar target customers are outperforming the company with an updated or innovative concept or new products and services
- If traffic counts for the location are decreasing or potential customers are passing through on their way to other businesses.
- Whether the decor or general atmosphere of the interior or exterior appear dated
- If customers have been commenting or complaining about anything

DETERMINING THE FIRM'S OBJECTIVE POSITION   The objective position can be determined informally by interviews or formally by surveys. Much can be learned by asking a reasonable number of customers about their perception of the business—for example, what they think of when the business's name is mentioned (Callan, 1994). As respondents air their opinions more specific data could be gathered from

Figure 8.2   Factors influencing the objective position.

follow-up questions. Focus groups are one of the most beneficial methods of gathering this type of qualitative or exploratory data. Many successful firms hold focus group interviews on a weekly or monthly basis to keep in touch with target customers' sentiments. Quantitative or statistical analysis, usually obtained through various types of survey instruments, may be necessary if locations are geographically dispersed, if there are several target customer groups, and if competition is intense and sophisticated. Because of the diverse variables to be addressed for each hospitality firm, questionnaires will normally need to be customized for each market segment (Cronin & Taylor, 1992; Getty, Barclay, & Ryans, 1994). Figure 8.2 includes a generic list of some of the most important topics. Common categories for attributes for hotels include: image, location, price/value, competence (quality of core product), access, security, additional services, guest rooms, food, and leisure facilities (Callan, 1995).

Restaurant questionnaires could include categories such as location, price/value, food quality, selection (taste, variety, and nutrition), cleanliness/sanitation, service quality, consistency, and brand image (Reich, 1990). Specific recommendations on questions to be included are beyond the scope of this chapter, but generic questionnaires such as SERVQUAL (Parasuraman, Zeithaml, & Berry, 1988; Lee & Hing, 1995), LODGQUAL (Getty & Thompson, 1994), and SERVPERF (Cronin & Taylor, 1992) can act as a starting point. Other sources of survey questions are offered by the following authors: Fitzsimmons & Maurer (1991), Martin (1986a), and Martin (1986b).

Before a survey questionnaire is approved for the study, individual questions must be analyzed and pretested to determine their validity of value to the research project. Key is each question's benefit toward the objectives of the research. The business's choice of the type and number of questions to ask and scaling (response) formats should be based on management's knowledge of research and statistical theory. There is no need in asking 40 questions if the results cannot be effectively tabulated and interpreted. If there is no one inside the firm with these skills, then questions should be held to a minimum or the hiring of an outside marketing consultant should be considered. The critical point is that effective consumer research can vastly improve the business's knowledge of its target customers, its performance in meeting their needs, and therefore its ability to identify the most viable present and future opportunities (Tse, 1988; Price, Arnould, & Tierney, 1995).

ALTERNATIVE DECISION-MAKERS   While it is important to monitor individual customers' image of the firm, it is also essential for hotel management to monitor the opinions of decision-makers who may never stay at the hotel. Meeting planners, travel planners, corporate secretaries, sales managers at various tourist bureaus, travel agents, and government officials will have vastly different objectives and desired attributes than individual customers. Rather than being primarily concerned with product, service quality, and price, monetary incentives and the decision-maker's personal reputation may surface as key attributes.

USER STATUS   In a survey with the purpose of finding out the objective position, it is best to ask groups with various levels of product usage and frequency. This allows management to expose potential problems with its image or positioning (Barich & Kotler, 1991). For example, nonusers of the business's product or service may have a poor image of the business based on something that happened years ago. Low-frequency users may have somewhat different images of the business than high-frequency users. This information can be used to understand how these various interpretations influence the firm's overall market position.

3. *Analyze the firm's current position and determine its desired position.* The market position and market position/profit models assist firms by providing graphic means of displaying position information. A firm must also determine its desired position, because this will tell all within the firm where it wants to be and how resources should be allocated. Step 4 requires management to decide how aggressive they must be for the firm to achieve its desired position.

Market Position Model (Linear Positioning)

The market position model (see Figure 8.3) is designed to help with the explanation and quantification of a firm's position and with most major decisions related to the selection of a future or desired position. The main advantage of the market position model over positioning maps is that it represents the firm's overall position, as opposed to its position on selected attributes. The purpose here is not to discriminate between variables (attributes), but to position the firm based on how customers perceive it on a global basis. For example, if customers say they like competitor A more than competitor B, competitor A will occupy a better position than competitor B. Competitor B will be faced with the decision of the importance of attempting to change its current position. In addition to graphically showing the firm's position in the market, it also reveals the interaction between the environment and the competitive set of businesses in that environment (the business's industry).

LINEAR COMPETITIVE COMPARISON   This linear form of quantification allows for a comparison with competitors and is a means of showing how well the market (or environment) has received the firm's product offering. For example, knowing that a firm's fiercest competitor is one position ahead gives management rich information to help with strategic and tactical decisions. Management would analyze the reasons for the disparity in positions, then decide to remain in its current position or to narrow the gap through strategies similar to the competitor or by differentiation. It is important to stress that strategies would not be selected solely on the basis of relative

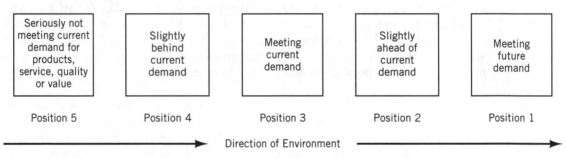

Seriously not meeting current demand for products, service, quality or value	Slightly behind current demand	Meeting current demand	Slightly ahead of current demand	Meeting future demand
Position 5	Position 4	Position 3	Position 2	Position 1

Direction of Environment

Historical progression over time

Position 5
A firm that does not react to changes in the environment for an extended period of time.

Position 4
Sometime after Position 3 with little or no change, and only a weak attempt at meeting customer demand.

Position 2, then 3
A. This is where most new firms begin.
B. If a firm begins at Position 1, it will likely become a Position 2 or 3 firm after the market selects another firm as a Position 1 choice.
C. If this firm does not keep up with customer demands, it will become a Position 4 or 5 firm.

Position 1
A. A proactive firm, generally during its introduction.
B. It is rare for a Position 1 firm to remain there.

Figure 8.3   Market position model.

positions. The firm's level of profit and additional specific research information (the survey used to pinpoint the position) would serve as the primary justification for these decisions. Management experience and intuition would also be considered.

ENVIRONMENTAL CHANGE   Another major purpose for the market position model is that it shows what happens to a company's position over various periods of time, based on its selected strategies. Since the environment is constantly changing, a company that continues to offer the same products and services, with the same level of quality and value, can only lose its current position in the market. There will always be exceptions, but as a general rule, customers' demands do not remain static. Some positions may be defendable for a decade or more. At some point though, customers' preferences change and competitors begin catering to those new demands.

The positions are categorized as follows:

POSITION 1   Firms in this position are highly proactive or innovative firms that have found a major gap in the market—an unmet need, sometimes referred to as meeting future demand—that is, finding out what the customer will want in the future, then offering it now. Position 1 firms will essentially create demand rather than following the pack by meeting current demand. Position 1 generally includes only 2% to 5% of the businesses for any segment. Since this is a high-risk, high-return position, it may be tenuous, based on the strategies chosen, implementation, and sustainability.

On a national basis, few firms have been able to remain at Position 1. Some could argue that McDonald's is a Position 1 firm, but based on national surveys, they are rarely rated number 1 in any category but convenience (McDowell, 1995). Their success is based on two strategies: heavy promotions and having products ready when customers place their order. While the latter strategy speeds up service, it reduces the quality of many of their products. Most competitors cook to order, which requires more time and thereby reduces the number of customers that can be served. McDonald's is certainly the leader in sales, brand awareness, and number of locations, but Position 1 requires more than big numbers. It requires a high degree of relative product quality and a proactive strategic stance, in addition to customer satisfaction. McDonald's, now a Position 2 firm, was a Position 1 firm up until the early 1980s. Its position has since been heavily challenged and eclipsed by several quick service firms (primarily Wendy's and Burger King) focusing on the key attributes of food quality, variety, service, and value. A more comprehensive view of McDonald's position is offered by the position profit matrix that follows this description of linear positioning. Here, McDonald's would be a 2, 1 firm, that is, Position 2 and a profit level of 1.

Regionally, there are a number of firms that, through highly proactive strategies, sustainable competitive advantages, and superior implementation, have remained in Position 1. The Pappas family restaurants in Texas (several different concepts, primarily casual dining, Mexican, and seafood) currently have a solid hold on Position 1 in their respective market segments. Several highly proactive and well-financed hospitality firms may begin here; few will stay.

In the short-term, proactive firms do not necessarily have to remain proactive if they hope to continue their success, but they do need to be poised for change before the position is lost (Miller, 1994). For instance, a Position 1 firm could take a passive strategic stance for several years, but at some point it would need to renew its proactive image to hold on to its Position 1 standing. The Outback Steakhouse chain has been in Position 1 in the casual dining market for several years. It will continue to hold this spot until either a competitor provides customers with a more attractive alternative or customers simply tire of the concept. Domino's Pizza, a former Position 1 and now between a Position 2 and 3 firm, rested on its laurels for several years and saw its market share drop significantly. Through renewed efforts, they are regaining some of their lost share, but they will most likely never attain their former position. This is because, once Position 1 is lost, whether to competitors or simply vacated through inactivity, it is difficult to convince the market that a firm is again the leader in meeting future demand (a leader in customer-valued innovation). There is no simple means of finding out what it will take to reach Position 1, but theoretically what must be done is to find a gap between what is being offered and what customers want and then supply it. The gap that Domino's filled to attain Position 1 was delivery. The Outback Steakhouse is filling the gap of a reasonably priced, quality steak restaurant with a comfortable trendy atmosphere. Hampton Inns is filling the gap of modern, quality, budget hotel rooms. Since there will always be challengers scanning the environment to forecast what will be demanded in the future, these companies and others in their position will need to stay continually ahead of current demand.

Because of the greater degree of difficulty to change or upgrade concepts for the hotel industry, it is likewise more difficult for them to remain at Position 1. The vast majority of leaders in the hotel industry are at Position 2—moderately innovative firms that excel at implementing the basics on a consistent basis (McKee, Varadarajan, & Pride, 1989).

Position 2   These firms are ahead of basic consumer demand, but not leaders in innovation. Some Position 2 firms may never utilize innovation. Instead, they will simply react to successful strategies of competitors (often segment leaders), then focus on near flawless implementation to distinguish themselves. This position can be achieved in two ways. As difficult as it is for a firm to reach Position 1, it is probably more difficult to remain there. Since few firms can continue hitting home runs, as time passes Position 1 firms will usually slip to Position 2. Risk-averse management and comfort with success are the two primary factors that cause this decline. To remain at Position 1, marketers must at some point develop new strategies: possibly not as innovative as those that brought them to Position 1 but exciting enough to gain the market's attention. Occasionally, a Position 3 or 4 firm through radical or persistent changes and wide market acceptance will move forward to Position 2. This move will require extensive changes in all functional areas of the firm and promotions that saturate the firm's target market. Because of the difficulty of remaining at Position 1, the primary and realistic goal of most marketers is to keep their firm at Position 2.

POSITION 3   These firms are meeting current demand for products and services with average quality and value. They may have begun here or slipped to this position by not keeping up with environmental changes. In some circumstances, this position may, in fact, be quite advantageous. If customers are conservative and the business has an established reputation, then meeting the current demand could be just what the customers expect. However, there normally comes a time when even the "We've been going there for years!" establishment needs to make some changes. Position 3 occupants are in a comfort zone that can reap the benefits of stability. The chief problem, like that of Positions 1 and 2, is waiting too long to upgrade its offering and subsequently seeing its position decline. The Position 3 firm can best hold its position by waiting for trends to solidify before attempting to adopt them.

POSITION 4   A somewhat outdated concept. This firm has not kept up with what customers are demanding or what competitors are offering. Frequently, firms that have centered their concept around a single product end up here because of their product, rather than market focus. Rarely does a business start out in Position 4 or 5. Those that do will generally not last for more than their working capital allows. The most common Position 4 firm is one that has been around for a long enough period of time to allow it to build up cash reserves and a small but relatively loyal customer base. As management becomes complacent, the firm gradually lets its market standing slip to this position. A firm in Position 4 that updates it product offering or decor will rarely move beyond Position 3 without several major innovations. This is because there is a substantial brand image that must be overcome. To move beyond Position 3, the firm needs to implement highly innovative strategies and saturate its target market to make customers aware of the changes. Normally, this is unlikely because of the financial risk of attempting to rejuvenate an outdated concept and the difficulty of changing the image of a lackluster firm. Taco Bell prior to John Martin was a Position 4 firm. It appeared that the concept was on the decline. Currently, it is one of the most innovative and ground-breaking concepts in the hospitality industry. In a period of a few years, sales increased by about 60%. They are now certainly in Position 1.

Position 5   A seriously outdated concept. A major turnaround strategy is necessary that will likely encompass all functional areas of the business. Position 5 firms have either recently reached this position or have adequate reserves or other competitive advantages that allow them to linger with a poor image. Few firms have the reserves to linger at Position 5. Over 90% of these firms are losing money. Rarely will any strategy allow a Position 5 firm to move immediately to Position 3 or higher without a major concept and perhaps name change. Because of the expense involved and the probability that existing shareholders will not accept the risk, Position 5 firms are most often sold to firms in Position 3 or above for renovation and rebranding.

Market Position/Profit Model

Figure 8.4 is a market position model that adds the concept of profit to the analysis. The reason for this addition is that a firm may be in one position but may be

Direction of Environment/Market

← Market Position →

Position Ranking (Relative to primary competitors)	5 Far behind customer demand (outdated)	4 Slightly behind current customer demand	3 Meeting current demand	2 Ahead of current demand	1 Meeting future demand	Profit Position ↓	Profit Level Ranking (Relative to primary competitors)
1= Recognized as a leader in the industry, highly proactive, exceeding customer demand, top 5% of firms in market segment.	5,1	4,1	3,1	2,1	1,1	1 High	1= Upper 90% to 100% of industry range.
2= Somewhat proactive, ahead of basic customer demand, upper 80% to 95% of firms.	5,2	4,2	3,2	2,2	1,2	2 Above Average	2= Upper 70% to 90% of industry range. 3= Middle 30% to 70% of industry range.
3= Generally reacts to strategic moves of other firms, meeting basic customer demands and expectations, middle 30% to 80% of firms.	5,3	4,3	3,3	2,3	1,3	3 Average	4= Lower 10% to 30% of industry range.
4= Not quite meeting customer demands or expectations, lower 10% to 30% of firms.	5,4	4,4	3,4	2,4	1,4	4 Below Average	5= Bottom 10% of industry range.
5= Far behind current customer demand, marketing strategies are very outdated and execution is not meeting customer expectations, lower 10% of firms.	5,5	4,5	3,5	2,5	1,5	5 Low	

General Directions

1. As objectively as possible, rank a reasonable number of primary competitors.
2. Record the reasons for your positioning of the competitors.
3. Rank your firm.
4. Record the reasons for your firm's ranking.
5. Does your ranking need improvement? If so, what possible strategies might be considered?

Figure 8.4   Market position/profit matrix.

producing the profit of firms in other positions. For example, a Position 3 firm that is producing the profit of a Position 1 or 2 (Position 3,2 or 3,1 in Figure 8.4) firm may decide that it is best to continue with existing strategies rather than risk change. Conversely, a Position 3 firm with the profit of a Position 4 or 5 firm (Position 3,4 or 3,5) may decide that its market position is okay but that either costs must be reined in or sales must be increased. If cost reduction is not the most effective remedy, then strategies targeted at increasing sales and probably its position should be considered.

There have been instances in which firms were extremely proactive but, for one reason or another, were not realizing the benefits of their position. The most frequent reasons for this have been financial problems, such as a massive debt, a large corporate overhead, or ineffective financial or accounting control systems. There may also be management or marketing problems, such as maintenance or repair problems with capital assets, inefficient operations, an entrenched bureaucracy, many poor locations, or possibly the market that has enthusiastically accepted the product or service is too small to allow for a reasonable profit.

The Limitation of Positioning Maps

Most managers are familiar with positioning maps. Their purpose is to graphically display a business's position or performance on various attributes, generally relative to competing firms. The problem with positioning maps is that they display the firm's relative performance based on two broadly defined (image and quality) or narrowly defined (quality of room and price) variables. Since a firm's position could be made up of 40 or more individual attributes, positioning maps can only provide minimal assistance in determining the firm's overall position. Yes, some variables can be combined, but the information is still too fragmented for assisting management in pinpointing the firm's position. The main disadvantage is that it cannot provide the composite score required to measure accurately the firm's position or to pinpoint where the firm stands in comparison to its chief rivals. Information from surveys is far more suitable for this purpose.

Certainly, if desired, positioning maps can play a supportive role in this task, but they are more valuable and useful in determining a firm's future position, rather than determining its current overall position. Therefore, various examples of positioning maps will be described that help to determine the firm's positioning or repositioning strategy.

4. *Decide on the appropriate level of strategic aggression.* Once management has located the firm's current position, it will then be faced with the task of deciding on the appropriate level of strategic aggression (level of change) necessary to move toward its desired position. Since, at some point, the majority of existing strategies will need to be changed, management should not be too pensive when hanging on to old habits (Mayersohn, 1994). Firms that lack at least a moderate degree of uniqueness when compared to competitors will invariably be positioned behind them. The choices are Level 1, proactive; Level 2, reactive; Level 3, passive; Level 4, adaptive; and Level 5, discordant (not a viable selection, generally one that is acquired rather than chosen) (see Figure 8.5).

PROACTIVE   Being *proactive* can be defined as accessing future opportunities and threats, deciding which could provide avenues or hindrances to growth and profit, and then acting on the assessment before competitors. A proactive stance can come

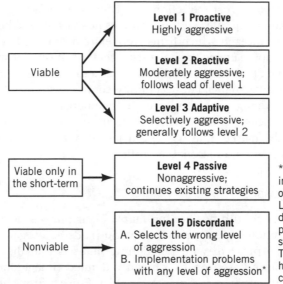

Figure 8.5 Levels of strategic aggression.

from the development of an entirely new or innovative strategy (Drucker, 1985; Ross, 1985), capitalizing on an existing trend by incorporating more of its elements into the business than competitors (Quinn, 1985), seeking incremental innovation through improvements in existing practices (Brown, 1991; Stalk, Evans, & Shulman, 1992), or reviving a strategy from the past. Normally, being proactive is associated with the future. The key yardstick of proactiveness is actually being first. By the time Hyatt Hotels implemented their strategy of offering rooms with a wide array of business services, all of these services had been available for many years. They were simply the first to promote them as a package.

In the ideal case, early innovators will accrue advantages of increased sales, profit, and improvements in image that can lead to sustainable competitive advantages (Makridakis, 1991). McDonald's, the first national fast-food franchise; Taco Bell, the first major fast-food Mexican food franchise; Domino's, the first major pizza delivery franchise; Holiday Inn, the first major midpriced hotel chain; and Motel 6, the first major budget hotel chain—all attest to the fact that being first with something desired, but not currently offered, can be quite beneficial.

Important to the selection of proactive strategies is the firm's ability to carry out the strategies (Feltenstein, 1986; Covin, 1991). The need for an accurate assessment of the firm's ability increases with the degree of risk involved. Also critical to the proactiveness decision are the cross-functional cooperation of the firm's different functional departments and the timing and aggressiveness of the new product announcement. Empirical research by Olson, Walker, and Ruekert (1995) show's that highly innovative strategies are best implemented by cross-functional teams, where less innovative strategies, such as product improvements, are more effectively directed by the individual functional department closest to the product's production. New product announcements (NPA) obviously serve the purpose of informing customers, with the ultimate objective being to increase sales. However, they also let competitors know about the introduction. There are two options to decreasing or reducing competitor reaction. One is to keep the introduction secret until the new product is available for purchase. If this is a new location, secrecy may be a problem. If it is a major menu introduction, then this strategy may be a reasonable option. The second option for NPAs is to limit the aggressiveness with which the announcement is made. An announcement that proposes a major change in product offerings or one that is heavily focused on comparisons will often bring a quicker and stronger response from primary competitors (Green, Barclay, & Ryans, 1995; Robertson, Eliashberg, & Tymon, 1995).

A key to earning the designation of being a proactive firm is the speed with which a new product is brought to market. Time lapses can dilute potential impact, allowing competitors either to catch up or to beat the firm to market. A study by Arthur D. Little (cited in Topfer, 1995) shows that increases in research and development costs associated with speeding up product introduction results in only minimal reductions in revenue as compared to delays in introduction.

One of the reasons that entrepreneurial firms frequently outperform conservative firms is because of an increased propensity toward risk. They are usually smaller, less bureaucratic, and in need of strategies that help differentiate themselves from larger competitors. This allows the entrepreneurial firm to assume a more proactive stance when it comes to taking advantage of potential opportunities. Conservative firms, on the other hand, tend to be risk-averse, noninnovative, and reactive (Covin, 1991).

REACTIVE   Probably the largest number of hospitality organizations choose to adopt a *reactive* posture. These are firms that react to, or pursue, proactive firms' viable strategies. The primary benefits of being reactive are that strategic mistakes are generally minimized and there is an above-average degree of stability in functional areas. For example, earnings for reactors are generally stable, as are management tenure, operational performance, and customer loyalty. The problem is that, because the firm is just a little late in recognizing a trend, the firm's full potential is not realized. The quicker a business can identify and begin posturing toward an opportunity-producing trend, the greater its lead time, the stronger its applicable skills, and therefore the greater its competitive advantage over rivals. Also, being known as a firm that utilizes "copy-cat strategies," rather than "innovative strategies," does little for a business's image. Progressive, conservative firms tend to take the reactive position of quickly following innovators—after it has been established that the new product or service is viable and profitable.

PASSIVE   *Passive* firms simply do what they have been doing. There are two basic types of passive firms. Position 1 or 2 firms, and firms in Positions 3 through 5. After a firm moves up to Position 1 or 2, it must generally take a respite of about one year to allow customers to get used to the new offering and for the firm to maximize its new image. There would be little point in making aggressive changes after achieving this position.

Most firms that choose the passive level of aggression do so with little or no focus on changes in their competitive environment. Instead, efficiencies through standardized, high-volume products and services, and cost minimization in all functional areas are the focus of strategic efforts. Proactiveness and even reactiveness are discouraged, because this would be counterproductive to the firm's abilities and philosophies. Passive firms may follow the lead of reactive firms, but only after the success of the strategic change is unquestionably evident and sales have shown a significant downward trend (Miller, 1986). Occasionally, there will be a market for passive firms. When, for example, the elderly constitute a firm's primary market, the business can often successfully pursue passivity, because this is what its market expects.

ADAPTIVE   These firms choose to be flexible to allow them to adapt to their relatively stable environment. Sometimes this level of aggression is chosen by Position 1 or 2 firms when management wants to continue with its current highly or reasonably successful strategies but remain open to appropriate changes if the right opportunity presents itself. This works because the firm has acquired the image of Position 1 or 2 and can rest on its current reputation until it is ready to pursue a more aggressive strategy or market demand for its current product/service mix begins to weaken. This does not mean that the firm ignores the environment; it simply chooses to be opportunistic about its strategic moves. In some cases, rather than make major strategy decisions during their annual planning meetings, adaptive firms will make minor strategy decisions throughout the year. Firms in Position 3 or 4 may select this strategy because they are satisfied that their current position is probably as high as their concept, management, or finances can take them.

The adaptive level of strategic aggression differs from the reactive level because the firm is not aggressively following proactive firms' actions. Instead, it is searching for the most suitable strategy for its specific circumstance. This new strategy could be proactive or reactive, but it could also have the purpose of simply keeping the firm in its present desired position. The adaptive level differs from the passive level in that the firm is actively monitoring its market in pursuit of potential strategies; it has simply not found an appropriate choice.

DISCORDANT   The discordant firm will usually be in Position 4 or 5, has had problems with past strategic decisions, and is unsure about how to deal with its current position, particularly deciding where its best opportunities lie. This strategy is not usually selected but rather acquired through poor performance. The causes vary but include disagreements between management personnel, doing too many things at once, misperceptions about the environment, preconceived (personal) strategic agendas, and analysis paralysis (fear of action). Discordant firms are generally in need of a turnaround but unfortunately may not realize it until it is too late.

PAST, PRESENT, AND FUTURE CHANGES IN AGGRESSION AND POSITION   A further application of the strategic aggression analysis is the study of how a firm's present position can influence management's future strategic aggression choices, and subsequently how these decisions have influenced the firm's position. Firms that have

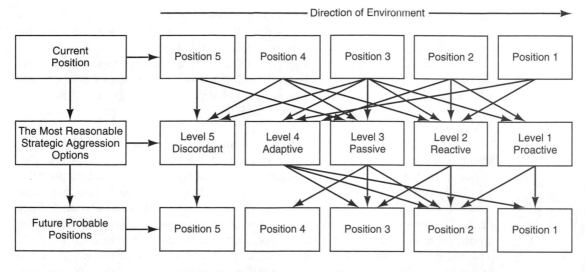

Arrows denote most probable paths and possible results.

Figure 8.6   Position/strategic aggression sequence.

been complacent or have attempted to minimize risk in their strategic choices and have subsequently not achieved their desired positions may want to consider more aggressive strategic options.

In Figure 8.6 it can be seen that each firm has certain realistic options available to it based on its current position. These strategic aggression choices will result in some type of modification to the firm's position. An important domain assumption for this model is that it will be possible to change a firm's position based on its tenure at its current position. For example, a firm in one position generally cannot select a higher than normal level of aggression and expect to reach the position most often associated with that level of aggression. If a firm in Position 3 selects a Level 1 or proactive level strategic aggression, it will not likely result in vaulting it to Position 1. The reason is that this Position 3 firm has normally been there for some time and therefore has acquired the image of this position. Thus it will be difficult to convince the target market that the firm has gone from being an average option to being one of the best options. Assuming that the proactive strategy was implemented effectively, the most likely result would be to raise the firm to Position 2.

An additional application of this concept is to assist in forecasting competitors' strategic actions.

5. *Select a positioning or repositioning strategy.* Up to this point, management has gathered information on

- Its target customers' desired attributes
- The firm's and its competitors' performance and current positions
- The desired future position for the firm and forecasted positions of competitors
- The appropriate level of strategic aggression

Now management must begin the process of deciding which attributes should be focused on to achieve this desired position. For planning purposes, the positioning or repositioning strategy is expressed in a positioning statement.

Since there will be almost always an effort to incrementally improve the firm's position, a decision must be made on the relevance of current market research and information. If research efforts have not provided possible options, then marketers must reanalyze existing data to determine if something was overlooked or if new research data are required.

Before positioning decisions are made, management must thoroughly understand its internal abilities and review environmental factors to learn about the unique needs of the targeted markets—the goal being to satisfy customers in a manner that lets the business stand out from the multitude of competing firms. When there is no cost-effective way to compete head-on with a larger competitor, a position focused on this competitor's weakest points should be considered. Another alternative would be to develop creative ways of serving customers that would likely not be adopted by these larger competitors (Stalk et al., 1992). Some of the key considerations for deciding on a position in the market are service quality (courtesy, personality, relationships, personal attention, and speed), product quality, customization, quantity, variety, consistency, convenience, value, technology, delivery speed and efficiency, and image.

POSITIONING AND IMPLEMENTATION   Positioning is accomplished by a multitude of decisions, primarily those relating to the products and services the firm sells, the markets to which it sells, and its selection of marketing mix variables. However, the true measure of the firm's position is not determined exclusively by strategy selection, but also by how well customers perceive the firm to have delivered on their positioning decisions. For this reason, implementation of strategies is as important as the strategies themselves.

Positioning Maps

Positioning maps (also referred to as *multidimensional modeling*) help the firm analyze its performance based on selected attributes. Their purpose is to show how the market perceives a certain set of brands (firms) or products. Each firm competes based on how the market views its products as being close substitutes for other products. The positioning map graphs the spatial relationship between the products or brands based on specified attributes. The closer the distance between two products or firms, the closer is the market's perceived relationship. In addition to helping determine the firm's most suitable position, they can also be used to track actual market changes and potential market changes, such as when a new product or strategy is being proposed (Dillon, Madden, & Firtle, 1987). Generally, data for the positioning maps will come from survey information. When survey data are not available, then management's best judgment is a common alternative.

Most positioning maps are based on a four-quadrant matrix that is made up of two axes and multiple coordinates or scores. The axes specify the dimensions on which the firms or products will be judged. The coordinates represent the position of each brand (product) on the axes. When descriptive statistics are used, the coordinates (plot points) are the mean responses for each attribute (variable) (see Figures 5.18 and 5.19 for detailed examples). Frequently, graphed attributes include price and product quality; room rate and room quality, features, or appearance; price and service quality; price/room rate and location; convention/meeting facilities and room rate; convention/meeting facilities and location; convenience and quality; convenience and price; or service quality and food quality. If more variables are desired, then several positioning maps can be created, possibly one with room rate and room quality, and others with room rate and amenities, or location and amount of meeting space. When necessary, it is acceptable to use a form of factor analysis to combine related variables into one category. A restaurant could combine portion size, flavor, taste, and plate appearance into one variable—food quality. A hotel could similarly combine courtesy of front desk staff with that of their restaurants, banquets, housekeeping, concierge, and bellmen into one variable—service. These attributes can be combined by adding their means, then dividing by the number of variables that were factored together.

AWARENESS   Two positioning maps that are helpful in highlighting a firm's marketing image are brand awareness/brand loyalty and image/attribute importance (Barich & Kotler, 1991). In Figure 8.7, brand awareness and brand loyalty are plotted for four different hotels. Hotel A's customers view it favorably, but it has not maximized its awareness. Hotel B is currently in the ideal position and should consider growth strategies that allow it to capitalize on its position. Few of Hotel C's target customers are aware that it exists, and those that are do not consider it as a first

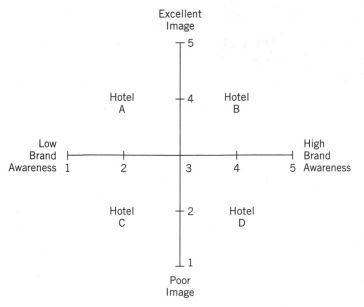

Figure 8.7 Positioning map—awareness/image. *Source:* Adapted from Barich & Kotler (1991), A framework for marketing image management. *Sloan Management Review*, Winter, 94–104.

option. Before this hotel can attempt to solve its awareness problem, it must first find out what it is doing wrong internally. The advantage of hotels over restaurants in this quadrant is that, although potential hotel guests are dispersed throughout large geographic areas, a restaurant's market is in a narrowly defined trade area. The hotel in this position could correct some of its problems, then focus on attracting new guests. A restaurant, because of the increased likelihood of exposure to its target customer base, would generally not be in this quadrant. If it were located here, like the hotel, it would first have to correct problems before attempting to attract new customers. Hotel D is in the worst position by far. Its customers are not happy with its performance, and the majority of its target market is aware of this fact. Here, the firm will not only need to improve its internal standards but also will need to focus heavily on promotions targeted at reversing its negative image. A restaurant in this quadrant may have alienated too large a percentage of its potential market to allow it to make a few changes that attempt to attract the same individuals again.

Figure 8.8, an image/attribute importance position map, shows how company A compares on several key attributes with its closest rival, company B. Company A's different positions would first be analyzed based on why it is where it is, and then based on its comparison to company B. Positioning strategies would subsequently be developed that improve the firm's current position relative to competitors. It is always best to work with prioritized attributes so that management can focus on those most critical to success. It should also be remembered that, since positioning primarily concerns the firm's overall image, all relevant attributes must be considered.

POSITION DECISION MATRIX   This is a type of analysis that allows for comparisons between two firms on multiple factors. It also provides a format for marketers to

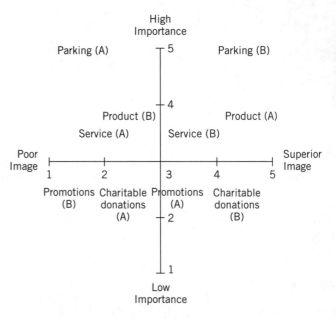

Figure 8.8 Positioning map—image/attribute importance. *Source:* Adapted from Barich & Kotler (1991), A framework for marketing image management. *Sloan Management Review*, Winter, 94–104.

ATTRIBUTE	COMPANY STANDING 1–5	COMPETITOR STANDING (1–5)	IMPORTANCE OF IMPROVING STANDING (H–M–L)[a]	ABILITY TO IMPROVE (H–M–L)	COMPETITOR'S ABILITY TO IMPROVE (H–M–L)	RECOMMENDED ACTION
Product quality	4.3	4.2	M	H	M	Hold
Service quality	3.4	3.2	H	H	M	Improve efficiency
Friendly service	4.3	3.5	H	H	M	Focus
Operations	3.5	3.6	H	H	M	Improve consistency
Atmosphere	4.4	3.5	M	L	L	Secondary focus
Cleanliness	4.6	3.7	M	H	M	Secondary focus
Points of differentiation	3.9	3.6	M	M	M	Focus

(e.g., unique features such as fresh bread, exhibition kitchen, workout facility, tennis courts, golf, well-known chef)

[a] H = high, M = medium, L = low.

Figure 8.9 Position decision matrix. *Source:* Adapted with permission from Kotler (1991), *Marketing management: Analysis, Planning, Implementation, & Control.* Englewood Cliffs, NJ: Prentice- Hall, p. 305.

determine how each factor could be incorporated into positioning decisions. In the example in Figure 8.9, the product and service quality of the two firms are about even. Improvement could be made in service quality, but the firm is not satisfied enough with its performance in this area to emphasize it in its positioning decision. The company's standing on friendly service is considerably higher than its primary competitor. Since this is highly valued by customers, and the competitor's ability to improve is rated as medium (its performance has historically been average), friendly service may be an attribute to focus on in the positioning decision.

Similarly, in this matrix, the company scored higher than its competitor in atmosphere, cleanliness, and points of differentiation categories. While each of these categories is important to customers, all categories do not have equal appeal for purposes of positioning. For most restaurants, the average customer will prefer good food and service over atmosphere. So, while atmosphere is important, it may not be a critical issue in the positioning decision. Cleanliness, again, is an important issue for customers, but this is expected as a minimum standard of operating a restaurant. If this were a major concern to the target customer, then it could tactfully be included in advertising by showing a bright, spotless restaurant. Some firms owe a portion of their success to having facilities that are much cleaner than their competitors. A riskier approach in this situation would be some type of comparison between the company's clean restaurant and a hypothetical restaurant that happens to be quite dirty. The fact that the restaurant serves fresh bread, large portions, and has an exhibition kitchen would likely help the restaurant's image and should therefore be included in the positioning decision.

RESTAURANT POSITIONING   Positioning decisions will be somewhat simpler for restaurants than for hotels. Restaurants will generally focus on one (fine dining) and perhaps two or three target groups (fast-food) with a relatively homogeneous product—its menu, service, pricing, and atmosphere. They will, of course, offer products that will be desired by a small number of members of other target groups, but there are generally very few changes that must be made to accommodate these secondary target groups. Perhaps a special menu for children, lower prices for senior citizens, or one or two entrees for smaller targeted groups. A positioning statement is written as a guide for the setting of marketing strategies. It must answer the question of how the business wants to be viewed by customers relative to competitors. The following is a sample positioning statement for a restaurant:

> We serve a variety of fresh seafood,
> including shrimp, crab, lobster, and a minimum of
> ten varieties of fish. Preparation methods include
> broiled, baked, grilled, blackened, steamed, and fried.
> Salad, baked potato, a choice from three vegetables,
> and fresh bread will be offered with each meal.
> Cooks must be trained in the intricacies of seafood preparation.
> We have a full-service bar with a premium well.
> Service is casual, but very professional. Prices are
> moderate and will be slightly above our competition to
> allow for higher quality products. As much as possible,
> fish will be purchased from day boats. Promotion will
> be held to a minimum, focusing on employee contests
> and public relations.
> We want to be thought of as *seafood experts.*

HOTEL POSITIONING STATEMENTS   Hotels will need one general positioning statement and possibly several individual positioning statements if the hotel caters to two or more market segments. An average hotel could have four or more target segments, such as business transient (individual business traveler), leisure (tourist), group, and catering. A sample overall positioning statement follows along with statements for various targeted segments:

> We are a quality hotel that offers competitively
> priced rooms and food, a broad array of meeting
> and banquet services, a casual restaurant that
> serves three meals, and a variety of recreational
> facilities. Our lobby will emphasize relaxation
> with comfortable couches arranged for informal

meetings, beverage service, and an abundance of
live plants. All employees will be trained to deliver
"friendly service" that cannot be equaled in our market.

- *Individual Business Travelers.* "A full service hotel that is conveniently located in the Williamsburg area, with immediate access to Interstate Highway 45, near suburban and downtown business districts, and provides travelers an extraordinary level of business-class services at a highly competitive rate."
- *Tourists.* "A full-service hotel with a variety of activities, including jogging trails, hiking, and indoor/outdoor swimming pool, tennis, and shopping in one of the largest malls in the Southwest. Major league sports, first-class museums, a lively theater district, an exceptional variety of live music, and exceptional restaurants help assure a fun getaway at an affordable price."
- *Groups.* "We are a full-service hotel offering everything necessary for a successful group function, from modern facilities, exceptional personalized service, on-property recreation facilities, and a location accessible to local airports, shopping, and highways. The hotel is located in a dynamic city with activities for all ages, from sports activities and world class shopping, to some of the country's best educational entertainment venues and museums. The individual guest's satisfaction with our hotel is a commitment of all employees."
- *Catering and Banquets.* "We provide catered events that exceed guests' expectations in quality of service, food and beverage, and atmosphere, at a price that represents a great value. An extensive catering menu will be available to serve the needs of guests in the middle to upper-middle income range. The hotel will be capable of a variety of functions from the traditional to special events and theme parties."

POSITIONING SLOGANS   Often a slogan, a brief and memorable summary of the firm's desired position, can be written. Its purpose is to help communicate the business's positioning strategy and help to influence and support its overall image. The first step would be to decide what it is that customers want most that the business can supply better than competitors, or at least be convinced of this. The previous restaurant positioning statement offers an obvious possibility—"seafood experts." A hotel could adopt a portion of its positioning statement for its positioning slogan: The Bryan House, "A first-class value in a business-class hotel." The slogan would then be used on signage, on stationery, and in advertising and other promotions.

Strategies Supportive of the Position

Once the positioning decision has been made, management will then be faced with the task of deciding how it will utilize various functional strategies and tactics (tactics include action plans and policies) to support the position. Since most of the attributes that management has decided to focus on are expressed in the positioning statement, the essential task is to prepare strategies and tactics that guide their implementation. Previously gathered information from the market position analysis, positioning maps, and the positioning decision matrix should be reassessed as these decisions are made.

Positioning and the Mission

The firm's positioning decisions, like the mission statement, help establish the foundation for objectives and strategy decisions developed in the marketing plan. The mission statement could be viewed as the firm's attempt to position itself for the long-term future, perhaps the next five or more years, while the firm's positioning decisions are targeted at meeting the demands of its market for the next year or possibly two years. Consequently, the portion of the mission statement that covers product and market characteristics is somewhat general to allow for flexibility in strategic direction and quick responses to new opportunities. The positioning of the firm will state more explicitly where the firm should be now or in the short-term future, specifying in greater detail what products or services will be offered for each target group. For example, a mission statement for a restaurant could include a description of the product: "A casual seafood restaurant specializing in high-quality fresh seafood." The positioning statement would usually, but not necessarily, be more explicit, including those features that the target market considers important, such as the quality of the seafood, and how it will be procured, stored, inventoried, and prepared.

THE BRYAN HOUSE AND CITY GRILL POSITIONING STATEMENTS

Utilize the examples at the end of the chapter.

QUESTIONS AND PROJECTS

1. Define positioning and repositioning.
2. Describe positioning as a factor of product, promotional, and public images.
3. What are the four main purposes of positioning?
4. Describe any business's place on a hypothetical customers's product ladder based on (a) its functional strategies, (b) the success of the functional strategies, and (c) the degree to which competitor's positioning and supportive functional strategies have met the demands of the target customers.
5. Explain the two major options for measuring a firm's position.
6. Explain the five steps in the positioning process. Describe the market position model and the concept of strategic aggression in detail.
7. Use the position strategic aggression model to suggest what any hospitality firm should do for its next planning period. Based on the chosen level of aggression what might be the change in the firm's position?
8. Create a position decision matrix for any two firms.
9. What is the difference between the mission statement and a positioning statement?
10. Prepare a positioning statement for any hospitality business for which you have worked. Give your reasons for the specifics of the statement.

OBJECTIVES

Every business will need to set objectives to guide and challenge its managers and employees. Objectives help clarify the direction in which each task will lead by quantitatively and, in some cases, qualitatively describing desired outcomes. They are also the basis for operational controls in that they establish targets for various tasks. Effectively communicated objectives can become self-fulfilling prophecies that consciously and subconsciously guide management and employees towards their accomplishment. Companies that attempt to manage without clearly defined objectives will find themselves in the same predicament as a traveler without a destination—lost. Some will argue that strategies must be set before objectives, and vice versa. Since nothing is final until the entire plan is complete, it matters little which is set first. If strategies are considered first, then the initial objectives might be more realistic. This is one of the advantages of answering the strategic analysis questions. To the contrary, strategies are normally created to achieve objectives, so if objectives are set first there may be a greater motivation to locate strategies that achieve their lofty goals. Basically, strategies and objectives are developed based on a series of compromises. Each are subject to adjustments, depending on what is realistic and achievable. The firm should set both long-term and annual objectives.

CHARACTERISTICS

Objectives should be measurable; motivating; flexible; compatible with the company's mission, culture, abilities, and environment; and understandable.

MEASURABLE   The objectives must provide specific, measurable targets that will ideally lead to the achievement of the organization's goals. There is an old business adage, "What you cannot measure, you cannot manage." Having ambiguous, ill-defined objectives is like trying to hit a moving target. The objectives should, in most cases, be quantified as:

- Dollar amount ($3500)
- Percentage (20%)
- Date (June 1, 19xx)
- Time period (in six months, in two years)
- A certain number of something (150 customers in one hour)

All objectives should have a completion date (Feltenstein, 1992), for example, achieve a 32% food cost by January 1, 19xx. Generally, interim completion dates could be included with the objective or in the controls section of the plan. If the objective itself is not quantifiable, such as a training program, then an explicit description of what is expected and a targeted completion date are critical. This helps clarify tasks and allows for the measurement of results. Where it is not possible to measure the objective other than by observation, some means of quantification, such as a customer survey, customer comment cards (customer satisfaction index, CSI), or employee satisfaction index (ESI), should be considered. When the objective is difficult to measure and management is close to the situation, such as in employee morale, an accepted practice (alternative to survey) is for management to monitor the level of performance and record impressions in the manager's log book (Bungay & Gould, 1991); for instance, "Everyone worked well together tonight. Attitudes have improved since our last meeting." There will be some instances where long-term objectives will not require dates. This occurs when a corresponding annual objective will detail the accomplishment of the long-term objective in the first year or when the long-term objective concerns something that would likely become a policy in the future. For example, "Have all servers complete 'alcohol awareness' programs."

MOTIVATING   Most employees are sensitive to the level of their personal performance. They like to know where the company is going, what is expected of them, where they stand, and what they can do to improve. Objectives set the foundation for measuring company performance. Since it is the individuals and groups who work for the company who are personally responsible for the achievement of the objectives, each should be realistic and motivating. All employees must accept the objectives as achievable and worth the personal effort necessary to accomplish them. If employees do not see objectives as personally rewarding, they will probably not be achieved. "What gets rewarded gets done" generally holds true.

It is important to consider the degree of difficulty employees of the firm will have in achieving the objectives. If objectives are set too high, employees may view them as impossible and not work to achieve them. A possible advantage of setting some objectives too high is that employees will be motivated to muster every ounce of creativity and effort to achieve them. A staggered approach to setting objectives, such as weekly sales of $20,000, $22,500, and $25,000, with appropriate rewards for the achievement of each, provides a buffer against setting too high an objective. When objectives are set too low and easily reached, employees may relax after their achievement and not seek to maximize their effort.

One of the quickest ways of lowering morale is by changing an incentive program to make it more difficult for employees to achieve company and, therefore, personal objectives. Years ago, one of the primary causes of the downfall of the Sambo's restaurant chain was that the bonus system, "Fraction of the Action," was changed, cutting managers' salaries nearly in half.

If objectives, like any part of the strategic or functional plans, are to be met, it is best to prepare them with the assistance of those who will be trying to achieve them. To effectively accomplish this, participating employees must understand the ingredients for success of the firm and how their efforts will help. For example, if front desk personnel are asked how many guests they can check out in one hour, they might volunteer additional input to actually increase the number that would have been set by management (Bungay & Gould 1991).

FLEXIBILITY   Objectives should not be set in stone. Adjustments may be required as the environment changes, as the firm's abilities change, or as it is found that they were set either too high or too low. Since the future is somewhat unpredictable, the longer the period projected for, the greater the need to adapt.

COMPATIBLE   The objectives should help set the course for the company's future. They should be compatible with the company's mission, environment, abilities, and culture of its management and employees. If employees or management are not comfortable with new objectives that they consider to be personally degrading or that change their image of the business, then they will probably not succeed. An objective of lowering food cost through reducing the quality of certain ingredients is usually not popular with cooks or servers who take pride in what they serve, and who must listen to complaints from customers.

UNDERSTANDABLE   First, the objectives should be thoroughly reviewed to make sure that they say exactly what the writer intends. Second, whoever reads and is responsible for achieving the objective must have the same perception of what is meant as the person who wrote the objective. The objective of a 33% monthly food cost is suitable: if applicable employees understand how their individual tasks play a part in the achievement of the objective (e. g., cut steaks within 1/4 ounce of specified weight); if they are kept updated on their progress; and if it is understood whether employee or complimentary meals are included.

MANAGEMENT BY OBJECTIVES

The joint preparation of objectives is often referred to as *management by objectives* (MBO). Through MBO, functional-level managers participate in setting their own objectives and strategies (or policies and marketing action plans) in cooperation with their subordinates; therefore these managers know precisely how they will be evaluated, the date by which specific objectives should be achieved, and how the work should be performed. MBO programs frequently improve functional-level managers' morale by:

- Increasing their understanding of their position in the company.
- Increasing their understanding of objectives and strategies.
- Increasing their support of the new strategies, through pride of authorship.
- Opening lines of communication with supervisors.

The old management adage, "Employees will allow you to succeed to the degree they want you to," may not be 100% correct—management can change attitudes or employees—but having employees working with the firm rather than against it will certainly prove beneficial. It also helps managers of firms to develop realistic objectives and strategies. Who knows better whether something is achievable than the person who deals with it on a daily basis? The process works as follows (Boone & Kurtz, 1987):

- The supervisor, normally a general manager, and a functional-level manager discuss successes and failures in reaching past objectives and strategies.
- Based on this information and the firm's long-term objectives and grand strategies, new annual objectives and functional-level strategies are jointly established and agreed upon. (The functional-level managers can participate in the preparation of long-term objectives and grand strategies.)
- Intermediate checkpoints are set to measure progress toward objectives and strategies. This could be decided when the objectives are first set or during the control phase. For example, for an annual objective of 32% food cost (reduction from the present 38%), the dates for meeting the objective could be set as follows: by March 31, 19XX—36%; by June 30, 19XX—34%; by December 31, 19XX—32%
- The functional-level manager meets regularly with the supervisor to discuss progress toward objectives and the effectiveness of the strategies and their implementation.
- At the end of the year or other prescribed period, the functional-level manager and supervisor meet to evaluate the results of the subordinate's efforts.

If a more detailed plan is desired, each functional-level manager may prepare individual objectives for each employee. For example, a cook could be given the objective of preparing 300 meals during dinner with no ticket times over 12 minutes.

LONG-TERM OBJECTIVES

Long-term (or strategic) objectives can be defined as the results expected over a specific period of time. Although there is no standard period of time, it is generally three to five years (Pearce & Robinson, 1991). The general business meaning for long-term is anything over one year. The long-term objectives are based on an appraisal of factors from the SWOT analysis, strategic analysis questions, grand strategies, and the firms's desired position. In the mission statement, management sets broad goals that should be focused on as the strategic marketing plan is written. The first quantification of the mission statement will generally be the firm's long-term objectives.

Accuracy

The question of the accuracy of five-year projections frequently surfaces and is worth discussion. No one knows with certainty what events will influence the firm over the next six months, much less five years. The answer can be found in the alternative to long-term objectives—not setting them and being forced to face the future without a long-term course. With no long-term objectives, strategies will not be focused, and, therefore, the firm will not have a sense of direction or purpose. A company without sales, profitability, or growth objectives for the long-term future is unlikely to succeed.

Process for Setting Long-Term Objectives

The following is an example of the theoretical process for setting long-term objectives:

OPPORTUNITY   Two-income families in the trade area:

- Are eating out more often
- Have an average of $10,000 more in household income than single-income families
- Are increasing by 5% per year

STRATEGIC THRUSTS   (From the strategic analysis questions, both long and short term options)

- Offer a special dinner-for-two at a set price,
- Have family-style meals where additional servings of everything are free; or perhaps only one additional entree,
- Have frequent-diner promotion. For example, if a customer eats at the restaurant seven times during a specified period of time, the eighth meal is free,
- Offer more nutritious meals to attract families.

LONG-TERM OBJECTIVES

COMPETITIVE POSITION

- Increase customer counts of two-income families by 30%, by January 20xx (any number of years in the future).
- Increase the number of different vegetables being served by 60% by January 20xx.
- Have a minimum of 30% of the entrees noted as "heart-healthy" by January 20xx.
- The institution of a frequent-diner program would be saved for inclusion with annual objectives.

EMPLOYEE DEVELOPMENT

- Train employees to serve families in a professional, personal manner. The training should focus on the special needs of families. (Since this would begin within the next year, an annual objective with a greater specificity of measurement would be written.)

Reducing Strategic Myopia

Long-term objectives help assure continuity of the business by reducing *strategic myopia,* the inability to see the future. Without long-term objectives, the result is usually short-term thinking (shortsightedness), which lessens the chances of stable growth. One of the major problems in American business today is the short-term view of profit. Executives are often employed at the whim of stockholders and stockholders' primary concern is the value of their stock. The executive's efforts in increasing the stock's value is the first measure by which he/she is evaluated. Managers of individual units will likewise be paid or retained based on their profit for the month, quarter, or year, promoting short-term views of the company's future. The ideal situation is to have a purposeful division of profits between growth, updating and maintaining facilities, employee benefits, dividends, and research and development of new or better products and services. This approach would generally lead to a more competitive firm and increased stock prices over the long-term. In America, the primary concern of business owners is profit. In Japan, the focus is on market share, quality, and innovation—profit and higher stock prices follow, if theses objectives are achieved. Japan and other Asian firms are willing to accept smaller returns in the short-term with the expectation that returns will increase in the long-term. Since this places fewer constraints on management and operations, it has been termed "freedom in patience" (Gemmell, 1991).

Without planning for the future by building a solid base, the chances of long-term success are limited. The apparent cause of this dilemma is that short-term rewards have led to short-term goals and, consequently, the short-term goals have led to profit-taking and greed, and ignoring what is best for the business. There has been an attitude, symptomatic of the 80s, of "I'll be gone in a year or two, so I'll get mine while I can." For example, if a manager's bonus is based strictly on annual profit or current stock price, there will be a tendency to neglect ways of improving the company's competitive position or long-term profit outlook. Building maintenance, employee benefits, and product research could be neglected in favor of a higher profit that drives up the firm's stock price. Another problem is the institution of anti-takeover devices, which insulate management. These include strategies such as golden parachute contracts for executives that guarantee exorbitant settlements if the applicable executive is terminated, or the imprudent use of cash to reduce attractiveness to potential suitors. Therefore, one of the primary purposes of long- term objectives is to reduce the strategic myopia of both management and shareholders.

Objective Ambiguity

There will be instances when a certain objective will not seem to fit into one of the categories. If it is analyzed carefully, it can generally be accommodated in one of the seven listed. If not, a new heading can be created.

One alternative is that the objective may be utilized as a strategy. For example:

1. Using promotions to increase sales would normally be a strategy, not an objective. Although if past performance indicated that promotions in general, or certain

types of promotions, were helpful, then related objectives, such as "We will spend 3% of sales on promotions" or "We will mail out 25%-off coupons to each trade area twice a year," might be appropriate.

2. Using a daily food cost report would likewise normally be a strategy or policy, not an objective. If desired, a statement such as *Management will complete a food cost report on a daily basis* could be an objective, but it would be much better suited as a policy. The objective related to this policy might be *Lower food cost to 32%.*

3. Concentrating on new menu items could be a long-term or annual objective, or grand or functional strategies:
   - *Annual Objective*
   Competitive position (objective category)
   - *Long-Term Objective*
   Competitive position
   Add four new entrees each year. Delete the four least productive entrees.
   Add four new entrees this year (annual).

   It could also be included in the strategy sections:
   - *Grand Strategy*
   Product Development (category)
   Add new menu items to keep up with customer demand.
   - *Functional Strategies*
   Marketing (category)
   Add chicken with green chile sauce.

4. Trying to attract more of a certain demographic market segment would be recorded in the Competitive Position objective section. The method used to accomplish it would be a strategy. Its potential or hopeful impact on sales and profitability would be factored into the long-term objectives section.

Categories for Objectives

Long-term and annual objectives are set in the following seven areas (Pearce & Robinson, 1991) (see Figure 9.1): social responsibility, profitability, productivity, employee development, employee relations, competitive position, and technology. (The

---

Social Responsibility—image through being a responsible member of society
Profitability—return on sales percentage or net profit
Productivity—ratio of input to output for various cost categories
Employee Development—improving the inventory of employee skills
Employee Relations—improving morale and motivation
Competitive Position—marketing-related factors that lead to increased sales
Technology—innovations that improve quality or speed

Figure 9.1 Categories for objectives. *Source:* Adapted from Pearce & Robinson (1991), *Formulation, Implementation, and Control of a competitive strategy,* 4th ed. Homewood, IL; Irwin.

acronym for long-term objectives is SPPEECT, pronounced *spect.)* Marketing department personnel will not have direct control over all of these objective categories. However, they should be involved in their creation because to varying degrees each of the objectives will have an impact on the firm's marketing efforts and its competitive position. The classification system used is not as important as the fact that the long-term objectives should be set in areas that help the firm achieve a long-term advantage over competitors. Another means of categorizing objectives is by dividing them between those that are financially related, and those that are strategic or important for the business to achieve a competitive advantage. The primary advantage of multiple categories is that it forces planners to address specific areas important to the firm's future.

Following are explanations, with examples, of the seven areas for objectives.

Social Responsibility

Social responsibility is managing the company's image and being viewed as a contributing part of the community. Businesses that take a responsible attitude toward helping others generally find many benefits.

- Increased morale of employees and management
- A more stable community
- Being recognized by the community as an organization run by professionals who care about something besides making a dollar

In the past, social responsibility was viewed by many as a waste of money and not something in which business should be involved. Today, social responsibility and long-term profit are generally inseparable.

EXAMPLES

Contact a charity, such as the Battered Women's Shelter, to discuss supporting it as an ongoing project, to include fundraisers and employee volunteers.

Help the Salvation Army during Thanksgiving and Christmas.

Cater a meal for residents of a local nursing home.

Begin a recycling program. Within the next three years, a program for recycling every possible item should be totally integrated into operations.

Join and serve on the board of at least two civic organizations, such as the Chamber of Commerce, or the local symphony or a museum.

Profitability

This is primarily the return on sales (ROS) of the business or other desired measures, such as return on investment (ROI), return on equity (ROE), and return on assets managed (ROAM). This objective category could also include liquidity ratios, such as the current ratio (current assets divided by current liabilities), and leverage ratios, such as the debt-to-equity ratio and the debt ratio (total debt divided by total assets).

The return on sales is calculated by dividing the operating income—the profit before interest and taxes—by sales.

$$\frac{\text{Operating income}}{\text{Sales}} \frac{\$15,000}{\$110,000} = \text{ROS of } 13.64\%$$

Using net income—the profit after interest and taxes—produces the firm's true profit picture but is not as useful for comparisons among industry rivals. This is because the differences in amount of debt and tax reporting methods affect net income, and thereafter comparisons of operating efficiency.

Other commonly used profitability ratios are:

$$\text{Return on assets managed, (\%)} = \frac{\text{Net income}}{\text{Total assets}}$$

and

$$\text{Return on equity, (\%)} = \frac{\text{Net income}}{\text{Owner's or stockholder's equity}}$$

Leverage ratios are calculated in a similar manner:

$$\frac{\text{Debt}}{\text{Equity}} \frac{\$224,000}{\$560,000} = 0.40 \text{ (or 40\%)}$$

This means there is $40 of debt for every $100 of equity. Assets minus liabilities equals equity.

EXAMPLES

Reach a return on sales of 15%.
Keep debt-to-equity ratio below 40%.

Productivity

Productivity is the ratio of input to output. For food cost, this is the food cost percentage—food cost divided by food sales. (Alcoholic beverage cost is calculated in the same manner.)

$$\frac{\text{Food cost}}{\text{Food sales}} \frac{\$26,000}{\$80,000} = 0.325 \text{ (or 32.5\%)}$$

$$\frac{\text{Beverage cost}}{\text{Beverage sales}} \frac{\$2,500}{\$12,000} = 0.208 \text{ (or 20.8\%)}$$

For labor cost, labor dollars are divided by total sales. If desired, labor cost can be calculated for specific areas such as the kitchen or front desk.

$$\frac{\text{Labor dollars}}{\text{Total sales}} \frac{\$18,500}{\$92,000} = 0.201 \text{ (or 20.1\%)}$$

Other ratios of productivity could be laundry expense, paper, rent, and utilities, and are calculated in the same manner. Since most statements of income (profit and loss statements—P&L) include applicable percentages, many companies include their entire statement of income as their productivity objectives.

SETTING PRODUCTIVITY OBJECTIVES   If the firm's current food cost is 38%, the long-term objective might be 33%—if management could support that figure through hypothetical menu changes and increased efficiencies of production. Care should be taken in attempting to lower any productivity percentage. If the cost is lowered without increases in efficiency or productivity, customer dissatisfaction could result. For example, a restaurant lowering food cost by reducing portions or quality might incur problems. As an alternative, it could obtain lower prices through effective purchasing or by adding new menu items that have a high perceived value and a low food cost.

PROBLEMS WITH PRODUCTIVITY IN THE HOSPITALITY INDUSTRY   One of the greatest productivity-related problems in the hospitality industry is its labor intensity. Productivity gains driven by reductions in costs relative to output are much more difficult to achieve than in manufacturing industries (Senn, 1990; Ozol, 1991). This occurs because productivity increases in capital-intensive industries are made by technological improvements in machines, as opposed to the human capital focus in labor-intensive industries. According to the U.S. Department of Labor, improvements in productivity for manufacturing industries between 1980 and the first quarter of 1991 were 37%, while productivity gains for service industries were less than 1% (Pomice, 1991). Productivity gains in the service industry in the 20 years after World War II were somewhat higher (Mansfield, 1980). This is generally due to the lack of competition in the hospitality industry prior to World War II, which allowed management to profit in spite of inherent inefficiencies. Since World War II, the progressively increasing number of competitors and their greater degree of sophistication have forced firms to be more productive. Consequently, incremental increases in profit due to increased productivity have likewise been more difficult to attain, especially in labor-intensive industries (Reich, 1993).

This is one of the greatest dangers of our national economy becoming increasingly service based. Capital-intensive industries (manufacturing-based economies) can make improvements with the addition of new equipment, a new plant, or new technology. A machine can be purchased that, holding other inputs constant, could potentially double output. One server can still wait on only a limited number of customers per meal period. Though industry wide improvements may be hard to come by, individual businesses can generally find areas in which productivity can be increased. Improvements in the service sector are most often made through:

- Increased manual dexterity (through training or selective hiring)
- Reduction of distances between tasks
- Work simplification

- Reduction of inefficiencies of production
- cost controls

Increasing the productivity of hospitality firms is usually first achieve through various methods of cost control. Accounting of financial departments establish the lowest reasonable level for expenses, set reasonable long-term and annual objectives, and then establish financial strategies for achieving them. Part of the process of setting the objectives can be a discussion of the necessary strategies, if this was not already reviewed during strategic analysis meetings. The second most popular method of reducing costs is through changing methods of producing a product, or eliminating certain labor-intensive items or services. Conventional wisdom must be challenged if the outcome is to achieve its fullest potential. If this course is chosen (unproven strategies), objectives will be set based on management's best estimate of the results. Strategies will be developed and later specifically designed to achieve the desired results. For peak effectiveness of productivity, both cost control and changes in production methods must used (Vajta, 1991).

The shift to fast food, takeout and delivery, and budget hotels has been fueled not only by societal shifts but by business's dual drive to increase productivity while reducing fixed overhead. There has also been a drive to reduce the labor required of casual and fine dining concepts and midscale and luxury hotels. This can be seen in the increased use of point-of-sales and back-of-the-house computer systems, hand held terminals, convection steamers, conveyor and microwave ovens, equipment with self-cleaning options, and automated laundry equipment. The key problem is that it is substantially more difficult for service industries to find technologies to increase productivity than it is for manufacturing industries. Though there will always be an occasional technology that will increase productivity in the hospitality industry, the industry is at the mercy of customers who want personal service, and competitors who offer it. The fact that productivity gains will always be more difficult in the hospitality industry must be realistically accepted but should not keep firms from seeking incremental improvements.

EXAMPLES

Reach a 32% food cost by 20xx.

Reduce labor cost to 20% by 20xx.

Increase revenues per sales manager (hotel) by 20% (could also be placed in competitive position).

Reduce linen cost to 2.3% of sales by 20xx.

Reduce utility costs to 3.6% by 20xx.

Decrease overall operating costs by 7% by 20xx.

Employee Development

If there are problems with the firm's image, or the firm has operational weaknesses, or new products or service will be added, or management simply seeks to improve its competitive position, there will generally be a need for the improvement of existing training efforts, or the addition of new specific training programs. All companies, regardless of situation, must have some type of ongoing training to make sure that employees and management are functioning at their potential and effectively supporting the firm's objectives and operating standards. Additionally, development efforts must assure that employees and management are trained not only for current needs but also for the future. Will the profile of the ideal employee or manager change in the next few years? In the fast-changing environment of the hospitality industry, this scenario is highly possible. Management must find ways of identifying the skills that will be necessary for current and future needs, assess the competency level of current personnel, and then decide what actions are required to bridge perceived gaps (Mirabile, 1991)

Traditionally, hospitality businesses and many managers have not allotted enough time to training or development of skills necessary for proper performance. Training efforts have been thought of as time consuming, costly, another task to take care of in a manager's already busy schedule, and not a revenue-producing activity (Reich, 1990). As more is learned about the benefits of training, a greater number of companies are instituting extensive programs for all positions from dishwashing to manager. Improved morale, increased opportunities for employees, fewer customer complaints, and less hectic atmosphere are common outcomes of training programs.

There is also a major trend to push decisions to the lowest reasonable organizational level of the firm. The recent buzzword for this trend is *empowerment,* but for many years it has been known as decentralized decision-making. This strategy will require greater cognitive skills of all the firm's personnel. This is especially true of the hospitality business, where the inappropriate handling of a situation can lead to dire results. A single dissatisfied meeting planner can decimate a hotel's business.

Often the strategies of the marketing department are not effectively carried out by the operations department because of poorly trained employees. For example, the marketing department has designed product strategies around having a quality product of service. If operations does not execute the strategy as designed, this could force a change in marketing strategies. Rather than having a focus on offering a quality product and service and promoting that fact to customers, it may need to consider discounting. Effective employee development objectives and corresponding strategies can help remedy this situation.

EXAMPLES

Prepare/write a comprehensive operations manual; revise manual each six months.
  (If this objective was to be completed this year, then the annual objective would
  be the same, with perhaps more specifics such as completion dates and possibly
  priorities for the various sections.)
Have all employees who serve alcoholic beverages, or who have contact with customers who consume them, take alcohol awareness courses.
Have all employees that handle food take certified sanitation courses.
Always have at least one employee on duty who is certified in CPR.

Have a crisis management plan ready for emergencies such as fire, robberies, fighting, unruly customers, and restroom or sewer backups.

Employee Relations

This basically concerns the morale of employees—generally expressed in the employee and management turnover percentage. The costs of high turnover are extensive, the most important being low customer satisfaction. Employees with little tenure may not have the knowledge and abilities of those who have been with the company for a substantial period of time. Questions to consider are:

- Do employees feel good about working for the company?
- Can the company offer employees the opportunity for a better future, a stable environment, good working conditions, decent wages and benefits, and quality supervision?

In strategic planning, the firm can lay the groundwork for success, but employees may not be motivated to support it if they do not feel that they are given opportunities to provide input into decisions that affect their jobs and performance, recognition of their importance, and the chance for a better future.

EXAMPLES

Find a group health insurance program for employees with a tenure of six months or more. Implement partial coverage within the year.

Consider increasing coverage after the first year.

Reduce employee turnover to 70% by 20xx.

Reduce management turnover to 25% by 20xx.

Institute employee vacations policy. (A specific date could be included, or it could be understood that it will be acted on in the annual objectives.)

Increase the amount of time for management vacations.

Maternity leave for both women and men should be considered in the future.

An employee profit-sharing plan should be implemented at some point in the future.

Recognize employees for volunteering their time for any charitable cause or for giving blood.

Encourage open and active channels of communication between all levels of staff and management.

Competitive Position

Most objectives in competitive position are marketing related and serve to support market share or sales objectives. They also include objectives such as those relating to innovation or image that lead to an improved strategic posture, especially as compared with chief competitors. The primary considerations for competitive position for most firms are relative market share, average unit sale, and total sales. If the current market share were 4%, a long-term objective could be a 6% share of the national or local market. (Market share is a business's percentage share of the total dollars spent for that product or industry. This could be the hotel industry or a segment such as economy hotels. It could also be for the national, regional, state, or city market, or for the immediate trade area.) For most hospitality businesses, total corporate sales, unit sales, and a comparison of various sales figures with those of other primary competitors could be used. The second most common objective for competitive position is customer satisfaction.

EXAMPLES

Open six new units during the next three years.

Achieve $900,000 in sales for 20xx, and $950,000 for 20xx.

Increase average daily customer count to 400.

Achieve a 4.2 overall CSI (customer satisfaction index) or 3.8 CSI for food, 4.2 CSI for service, 4.5 for rooms, 4.3 CSI for front desk efficiency by 20xx.

Increase sales on Sunday and Monday nights by 30% by 20xx.

Increase overall occupancy by 10% by 20xx.

Increase corporate business segment by 15% by 20xx.

Increase percentage of families by 25% by 20xx.

Add workout room to hotel. (As discussed in measurement, if the long-term objective will be accomplished within the year, a date for the long-term objective is not necessary.)

Increase average room rate to $97.00 in 20xx and to $105.00 in 20xx (second and third years of the plan).

Increase senior citizen segment by 25% by 20xx.

Increase delivery business by 15% by 20xx.

Have at least four major promotional events each year geared to increasing customer loyalty and improving the image of the hotel (or restaurant).

Technology

Technology has influenced some hospitality businesses more than others. Some restaurants use a wood-burning grill, others use an Impinger oven (a heated-air conveyor oven), or a combination microwave-convection oven. Some hotels use an electronic cash register, others use an integrated property management system. Some hotels are adding digitally controlled water systems that maintain a desired water temperature for the bath or shower. Video check-out is becoming increasingly common. Technology in the hospitality business is basically anything mechanical or electronic that improves the effectiveness or efficiency of the business—primarily in the areas of speed, productivity, quality, convenience, and accuracy. If desired, it can include operational technology such as changes in layout based on a detailed job analysis.

Since our industry has relied on manual labor for most of its history, it has been somewhat hesitant in adopting new technologies. An additional factor, as shown in the above discussion on productivity, is that productivity gains in labor-intensive industries are more difficult and take longer to realize than in capital-intensive industries.

The increasingly competitive nature of the hospitality business is forcing many firms to consider the latest technological advances. The president of Hyatt Hotels estimated that by the year 2005 customers will be able to access a hotel's computerized room inventory to make their own reservations (DeLa Cruz, 1994). This is already occurring to a limited extent on the Internet. Because of consumer surveys that expressed the desire for business travelers to be more productive, Hyatt has developed "Business Plan" rooms with computer and modem hookups, facsimile machines, and a copier on each Business Plan Floor. Most major hotel chains are rushing to add similar business services. In the future, as the need for lines of communication with the traveler's home office and the pressure to be more productive continue, customer demand for technology in the hotel room will increase rapidly. It is not currently known which segments of the hotel industry will need to add extensive in-room business services, but it will certainly push its way down to the lower midscale level in the not too distant future (referred to as *amenity creep*).

As security increases as an issue in both hotels and restaurants, the need to assess what is reasonable care will continue to be critical. While the industry cannot guarantee the safety of a guest, each business must attempt to stay current with the de facto standards of similar businesses for its trade area, if it expects to limit its liability. This essentially includes two steps: first, finding out what the typical trade area breaches of security have been; and second, based on what similar businesses are doing, estimating what changes in operational procedures or technological applications are necessary to assure that the business is in relative compliance with both "reasonable care" and "de facto standards" for that particular trade area. Because of the "deep pockets" philosophy (individuals suing people or businesses with the greatest ability to pay), many businesses will continue to be sued whenever a problem occurs. While there will never be a guarantee against being sued, suits can more easily be prevented and defended against by utilizing the above recommendations (Reich, 1994b).

PURCHASING EQUIPMENT   The goal in purchasing equipment is to choose equipment that will most economically meet the needs of the restaurant. In the long run, the least expensive piece of equipment is rarely the most economical. Equipment decisions should include the following factors (Reich, 1990).

PERFORMANCE   The equipment that is chosen should perform as efficiently and effectively as alternative pieces of equipment. It should produce a quality result and be durable enough to withstand heavy use. Utility consumption is a primary consideration.

REPUTATION   Contact other businesses that are using the equipment. Find out whether they are pleased with the equipment and whether they have experienced any specific problems with it.

SERVICEABILITY   Find out whether there is an authorized local repair service. If so, ask the service representative whether parts are available from them exclusively or from other distributors. Also inquire about the cost of labor and parts for common or potential problems.

EASE OF USE   Determine whether most employees can be trained to properly use the equipment in a reasonable amount of time.

CLEANING AND MAINTENANCE   Calculate how long routine cleaning and maintenance take and how often they must be done. Decide whether an inventory must be kept of maintenance supplies (such as lubricants, cleansers, heating elements, ink cartridges, ribbons, and attachments of various types).

PRICE   Consider how the price of each piece of equipment fits into the business's budget. A certain piece of equipment may be the best performer, but the business may not be able to afford it.

EFFECTIVE UTILIZATION   There will be some pieces of equipment that the business absolutely must have. But for equipment that is not critical, the cost must be justified according to how it will be used and the potential demand for its benefits. For example, in the near future, computer and modem hookups will be expected in upper-midscale and luxury hotel rooms. But are they needed now?

EXAMPLES

Reduce service time from 14 minutes to 10 minutes.
Continually reevaluate present kitchen equipment (also dining room, front desk, accounting, or housekeeping) and update where needed to speed service and improve product and service quality.
Consider all possible and affordable means of making the hotel (or restaurant) more secure.

ANNUAL OBJECTIVES

Annual, or short-term, objectives are the specific statements of what an organization is expected to achieve within the next year. These should flow directly from the long-term objectives. They are the first step in attempting to assure that the business achieves its long-term objectives. Annual objectives convert long-term thinking into day-to-day operations (Bungay & Goold, 1991).

The title is somewhat misleading, because with minor modifications the annual objectives are also for the immediate future. For example, if the annual objective is to reach an occupancy of 75%, and the current occupancy is at 67%, interim objectives might be set at a 2% increase per quarter. An annual objective to correct a problem might have a target date three months in the future. As soon as the annual objectives are set, the company will begin setting functional strategies, policies, and action plans directed toward their accomplishment. The majority of the remaining sections of the strategic marketing plan will be based on and guided by the annual objectives.

Relationship to Long-Term Objectives

The annual objectives must relate logically to the long-term objectives and be supportive of the grand strategies. For example, if the grand strategy is for market development, and the long-term objective is to open six new units, the annual objective might be to open two units.

If the present food cost is 38% and the long-term objective is 32%, the annual objective would be between the two figures, based on what the restaurant thought was achievable during the first year of the plan. If the cause of the high food cost is mismanagement, then, through proper procedures and controls, the percentage could perhaps be brought down quickly to the 32% to 33% range. If mismanagement is not the main problem, then 35% or 36% might be more realistic. The primary reason for this less-ambitious decrease is that too quick a reduction in food cost may be noticed by customers through increases in price, reductions in portions or quality, or radical changes to the menu mix. In a situation where there is no mismanagement, attempting to lower the food cost from 38% to 34% means that there will be 10.5% less food on the plate (38% − 34% = 4%; 4% ÷ 38% = 10.5%). Obviously, if the business was approaching bankruptcy, quick changes would be necessary, but the customer's perception of the changes must still be considered. Interim objectives might also be set, such as bringing the food cost down 1% each quarter.

If a hotel with an average daily rate (ADR) of $75 and a revenue per available room (REVPAR) of $54 ($75 times a hypothetical 72% occupancy—75 × 0.72 = 54) had long-term objectives of a $90 ADR and REVPAR of $66.60 (90 × 0.74 = 66.60), the annual objective for each would normally be in between the two.

There is no set rule stating that food and labor costs, or any productivity-related objective, for that matter, must always go down. For example, if one of the primary strategies of a restaurant or hotel was to offer an exceptional value, a possible objective might be to raise the food cost from 33% to 35% over the long-term, or this year. The need to improve service could potentially lead to an increase in labor cost. When this decision is made, management must either do so on the theory that sales will increase or that other costs can be reduced.

Supporting Objectives

The annual objectives may need to have supporting objectives to improve implementation. If a long-term objective indicated the general need for a security system or that a particular type of system should be added (e.g., long-term objective: *a security system must be added as soon as possible*), the annual objective could specify what will be added, with appropriate installation target dates.

Supporting objectives might include the following:

- Reduce the number of incidents of crime from twelve per year to three.
- Increase the hotel's score on the security section of the guest survey from 3.5 to 4.5 by October 20xx.
- Increase lighting so that there is complete visibility around the hotel at night. Complete this by January 20xx.
- Immediately increase the number of patrols in the parking lot from one each hour to one every 30 minutes (also a tactic, but acceptable here).

Objectives supportive of lowering the food cost might be as follows:

- Implement a new computerized purchasing system by 5/1/20xx.
- Train all kitchen employees in the fundamentals of receiving by 3/15/20xx.
- Immediately begin comparing prices among suppliers for all regular purchases on a monthly basis.
- Increase sales of the restaurant's special chef salads (a low food cost item) by 20% by March 20xx.

If the business desired to open two new units during the coming year, supporting objectives could include the following:

- Put aside $20,000 per month for expansion.
- Hire people with skills in site location and construction.
- Train two additional general managers.
- Develop a marketing plan for the new locations.

Another consideration, which can be seen in the above example, is that some objectives will take priority over others. Before property can be purchased, suitable financing will have to be obtained. A common sequence is that before service time can be significantly reduced, either the menu must be modified or kitchen production procedures (also known as *kitchen logistics*) must be changed.

There will be cases when the long-term objective and the annual objective will be identical. For example, if the long-term objective was to increase annual profit (or sales, customer counts, unit growth, etc.) by 10% per year, the annual objective would be to increase annual profit by 10%. If the long-term objective was to have all employees trained according to the company training manual, the annual objective could be the same. In the last example, the objective would be replaced by a policy before the next plan was written. Time frames could be added for specificity.

The following annual objectives are derived from the examples in the long-term objective section. The current year is assumed. Compare the long-term with annual objectives to develop a better understanding of the relationship and sequence.

Social Responsibility

EXAMPLES

All edible scraps will be saved for local hog farmers beginning March 1 of this year.

As much as possible, all glass, plastic, and paper will be recycled beginning February 15 of this year.

The Battered Women's Shelter will be supported through a charity dinner by mid-summer. Each employee will be asked to volunteer eight hours of service during the year.

Have at least five employees help the Salvation Army serve Thanksgiving and Christmas dinners.

Cater a meal for residents of the Golden Manor Nursing Home once a year. Check with their director for a suitable date.

Join and serve on the boards of the Downtown Chamber of Commerce and the Museum of Fine Arts.

Profitability

EXAMPLES

Show a return on sales of 10%. (A new hotel may have a goal of breaking even during its first year. A restaurant should show a positive ROS.)

Keep debt-to-equity ratio below 0.45 (i.e., 45%—$45 of debt for each $100 of equity; assets minus liabilities equals equity).

Productivity

EXAMPLES

Achieve a 34% food cost by May of this year.

Reduce labor cost to 22% by May of this year.

Reduce linen cost to 2.5% of sales by March of this year.

Through conservation, reduce utility costs to 3.8% of sales by July of this year.

Decrease overall operating costs by 4% by July of this year.

Employee Development

EXAMPLES

All supervisory employees will become certified in CPR within the first three months of the plan's implementation.

All kitchen employees will be cross-trained in each position by March of this year.

Each manager will attend a seminar during the year that will increase his/her value to the company. The manager attending the seminar will present a summary of the key topics at a managers' meeting.

Complete the rough draft for an operations manual. Field-test each section before making it policy.

Write training manuals for each position by June of this year.

Write trainers' manuals for each position by June of this year.

Have all employees who serve alcoholic beverages, or who deal with customers who consume them, take alcohol awareness courses by March of this year.

Have all employees that handle food take a certified sanitation course by March of this year.

Have a crisis management plan ready for emergencies such as fire, robberies, fighting, unruly customers, and restroom or sewer backups.

Have groups of managers and employees go to seminars on emergency-related topics and report back on what they learned.

Hire four new managers and new employees as needed to replace those transferred to the new units.

Hire consultants to help in site location, financing, and construction of the new units.

Employee Relations

EXAMPLES

Employee turnover will be reduced to 150%.

Employees will be given one-week vacation after each year of employment. This will include part-time employees.

Management turnover will be reduced to 40%.

Management vacations will be increased this year. (A later policy might read: *Managers will be given vacations of two weeks during the first two years, then three weeks for the next five years, and four weeks thereafter.*)

Management work weeks must limited to five days and no more than 55 hours.

By August of this year all employees with tenure of six months or more will be enrolled in a group health insurance program. Coverage will be offered at cost during the waiting period.

Paid maternity leave of two weeks will be offered to both women and men.

An employee profit-sharing plan consisting of dividing up 20% of the net profits proportionate to pay will be implemented by June of the year.

Employees volunteering time for any charitable cause or for giving blood will be rewarded with free dinners: target date, February of this year.

Open and active channels of communication between all levels of staff and management will be encouraged. This will be measured by the achievement of an ESI (employee satisfaction index) of 4 or higher (5-point scale)

Management must meet with each employee at least once a month for a few minutes to see how each is doing personally and to review his/her job performance.

Competitive Position

EXAMPLES

Open two new units this year.

Achieve $850,000 in sales for the coming year.

Increase average daily customer count to 360 by June and to 375 by December of this year.

Achieve a 4.0 overall CSI (customer satisfaction index) or 3.6 CSI for food, 4.0 CSI for service, 4.3 CSI for rooms, and 4.1 CSI for front desk efficiency by July of this year.

Increase sales on Sunday and Monday nights by 20% by December of this year

Increase overall occupancy by 6% by December of this year.

Increase corporate business segment by 10% by December of this year.

Add workout room to hotel by February of this year.

Increase average room rate to $72.00 by December of this year.

Increase senior citizen segment by 15% by August of this year.

Increase delivery business by 10% by December of this year.

Have at least four major promotional events each year geared to increasing customer loyalty and improving the image of the hotel (or restaurant). (These would be detailed in the marketing strategies and marketing action plan sections.)

Technology

EXAMPLES

Reduce service time from 14 minutes to 12 minutes by May of this year.

Add a convection steamer to improve the quality of vegetables by March of this year.

Add a computerized door entry system (keycard system) by August of this year.

Add a video surveillance system by March of this year.

THE BRYAN HOUSE AND CITY GRILL OBJECTIVES
The Bryan House

Unless otherwise stated, all long-term objectives are for three years; annual objectives are for the first full year of the plan.

Social Responsibility

Long-Term Objectives

Select a local branch of a national or international charitable or civic organization that our target customers support and can identify with. A minimum of one major event that receives city wide publicity must be held. All financial assistance and time given must be compensated for with increased exposure and an improved image.

Annual Objectives

Join the local branch of the American Cancer Society by February 1 of this year.

Have at least two employees of the hotel go to all meetings and play an active part on one or more committees.

Have one major ACS event at the hotel each year.

Hold a minimum of six charitable (at-cost) events at the hotel each year.

Profitability

Long-Term Objectives

ROS of 3% in three years, 5% in five years.

Annual Objectives

Reduce 3% annual loss to break-even by year's end, and to below 1.5% within the first six months of the plan.

Productivity

Long-Term Objectives

Lower food cost to 35%.
Lower labor cost in food outlets to 27%.
Reduce check-out time to a 30-second average.
Increase annual production per sales manager in marketing department from an average of $800,000 to $1,200,000.

Annual Objectives

Lower food cost to 37%.
Lower labor cost in food outlets to 29%.
Reduce check-out time to a one-minute average.
Increase annual production per sales manager in marketing department from an average of $800,000 to $1,000,000.

Employee Development

Long-Term Objectives

Develop a comprehensive training system with manuals, schedules, test, and training sessions.
Hold monthly meetings to review departmental performance and to discuss methods of improvement.
Send each manager to a minimum of one educational program per year.
Build to a staff of five sales managers.

Annual Objectives

Develop training manuals covering the fundamentals of each position one month or more before the restaurant opens.
Hold bimonthly training meetings to review departmental performance and to discuss methods of improvement. Solicit ideas for improvement from employees.
Send each manager to a minimum of one American Hotel and Motel educational program seminar per year.
Add one experienced sales manager within six months.

Employee Relations

Long-Term Objectives

Have complete health insurance for all employees (pending federal regulations).
Have an employee stock ownership program in place within two years.
Turnover ratio—employees 50%, management 20%.
ESI (employee satisfaction index)—4.8 (on a 5-point scale).

Annual Objectives

Have a new HMO by October of this year (pending federal regulations).
Turnover ratio—employees 70%, management 20%.
Have employee stock ownership plan researched and ready to implement within six months.
ESI—4.4.

Competitive Position

Long-Term Objectives

Restaurant average daily customer count for breakfast—150 (150 seats).
Average daily customer count for lunch—200
Average daily customer count for dinner—150
Check average for lunch (including beverage)—$14.00 ($11.00 food, $3.00 beverage).
Average restaurant sales per hotel guest, per day—$15.00
Check average for dinner (including beverage)—$18.00 ($14.00 food, $4.00 beverage).
Sales for breakfast—$900 per-day average, $6300 per-week average (150 customers × $6.00)
Sales for lunch—$2800 per-day average, $19,600 per-week average (200 customers × $14.00)
Sales for dinner—$2700 per-day average, $18,900 per-week average (150 customers × $18.00)
Weekly sales for restaurant—$44,800
Gift shop sales—$500 per day.
Market segment percentage and ADR objectives:
  Individual business travelers (IBTs), 35% of sales, $130.
  Corporate group business, 30% of sales, $115.
  Association group business, 10% of sales, $100.
  Leisure business, 15% of sales, $130.
  SMERFS (sports, medical, educational, religious, fraternal, social), 10% of sales, $90
ADR—$118.
Occupancy—65%.
Total room nights—71,175.
REVPAR—$77.
Total sales of $11 million per year
Overall CSI—4.8 (customer satisfaction index/5-point scale).
Overall service— 4.8.
Value for room rate—4.8.

Banquet/catering food—4.5.
Banquet/catering service—4.7.
Room service:
   Food—4.7.
   Service and attitude—4.8.
Restaurant food:
   Breakfast—4.5.
   Lunch—4.5.
   Dinner—4.5.
Restaurant service:
   Breakfast—4.7.
   Lunch—4.7.
   Dinner—4.7
Check-in speed—4.8.
Check-out speed—4.8.
Service and attitude:
   Front desk—4.8.
   Reservations—4.8.
   Concierge—4.8.
   Telephone operators—4.8.
   Housekeeping—4.8.
   Maintenance—4.8.
   Gift shop—4.8.
Intent to return—4.8.
Would recommend hotel to friends—4.8.

Annual Objectives

Restaurant average daily customer count for breakfast—150 (150 seats).
Average daily customer count for lunch—200
Average daily customer count for dinner—150
Check average for breakfast—$6.00
Check average for lunch (including beverage)—$14.00 ($11.00 food, $3.00 beverage)
Check average for dinner (including beverage)—$18.00 ($14.00 food, $4.00 beverage)
Average restaurant sales per hotel guest, per day—$15.00
Sales for breakfast—$600 per-day average, $4200 per-week average (120 customers × $5.00)
Sales for lunch—$15,400 per-day average, $10,780 per-week average (140 customers × $11.00)
Sales for dinner—$1800 per-day average, $12,600 per-week average (120 customers × $15.00)
Weekly sales for restaurant—$27,580
Gift shop sales—$500 per day.
Market segment percentage and ADR objectives:
   Individual business travelers (IBTs), 32% of sales, $110.
   Corporate group business, 30% of sales, $95.
   Association group business, 13% of sales, $80.
   Leisure business, 15% of sales, $110.
   SMERFS (sports, medical, educational, religious, fraternal, social), 10% of sales, $80

ADR—$103.
occupancy—60%.
Total room nights—65,700.
REVPAR—$77.
Total sales of $9.6 million for the year
Maintain room nights with Clara's Cosmetics at 850
Increase room nights with Nancy Giles Textiles from 345 to 450
Overall CSI—4.6 (customer satisfaction index/5-point scale)
Overall service—4.7.
Value for room rate—4.7.
Banquet/catering food—4.4.
Banquet/catering service—4.6.
Room service:
    Food—4.6.
    Service and attitude—4.7.
Restaurant food:
    Breakfast—4.4.
    Lunch—4.4.
    Dinner—4.4.
Restaurant service:
    Breakfast—4.6.
    Lunch—4.6.
    Dinner—4.6.
Check-in speed—4.7.
Check-out speed—4.7.
Service and attitude:
    Front desk—4.7.
    Reservations—4.7.
    Concierge—4.7.
    Telephone operators—4.7.
    Housekeeping—4.7.
    Maintenance—4.6.
    Gift shop—4.8.
Intent to return—4.7.
Would recommend hotel to friends—4.7.
Increase advertising budget by 20%.
Add a concierge by March 1 of this year.
Add a workout facility by June 1 of this year.
Convert a meeting room into a business center by April 1 of this year.
Sign up for the SABREvision JAGUAR hotel directory service by January 15 of this year.

Technology

Long-Term Objectives

Keep up-to-date with the available technology related to both the hotel and F&B outlets.
Do not let competitors take major technological leaps ahead of us.

Annual Objectives

By March 1 of this year, purchase a property management system with an interchange system that electronically approves and processes credit car payment.

City Grill

LONG-TERM OBJECTIVES

Social Responsibility

Hold one major charitable fundraiser each year.
Participate with other businesses in charitable events at least three times per year (to keep name in public eye and uphold image).

Profitability

Reach an ROS of 18%.

Productivity

Keep prime factor (the combination of food and labor cost) at or below 57% (25% for labor cost and 32% for food cost).
Lower operating expenses by 2%.

Employee Development

Send each manager to at least one restaurant seminar per year. (Have that manager report back to the management staff on what was learned.)
Institute training program for every position in the restaurant.

Employee Relations

Reduce management turnover to 20% per year.
Reduce employee turnover to 30% per year.

Competitive Position

Increase sales by 10% over each prior year (10% compounded annually).
Increase sales on Sunday, Monday, and Tuesday nights by 30%.
Increase sale of seafood by 25%.
Improve overall customer satisfaction index to 4.6.

Technology

Attempt to reduce our average ticket-time from 12 minutes to 10 minutes.
If a new location is opened, a back-of-the-house computerized register system should be purchased.

ANNUAL OBJECTIVES

Social Responsibility

Hold fundraiser for the local women's shelter by September 15 of this year.

Serve dinners for three charity events where the name of the restaurant will be mentioned in return for the donation. (Ideally, these should be spread evenly over the year.)

Profitability

(An entire projected income statement could be included here.)

Reach an ROS of 17%.

Productivity

Keep prime factor at or below 57% (25% labor cost and 32% food and beverage cost).

Lower utility expense to 4.5% of sales (from 5.5%).

Lower linen expense from 2.3% to 1.8% of sales (from 6¢ to 5¢ per person).

Lower repair and maintenance expenses from $500 to $350 per month average.

Employee Development

Send each manager to one seminar per year.

Institute a training program for every position by June 1 of this year.

Employee Relations

Reduce management turnover to 25%.

Reduce hours worked per week to a maximum of 50.

Increase annual vacation time to two weeks.

Reduce employee turnover to 35%.

Increase benefits by 10%; add health insurance and employee vacations.

Competitive Position

CSI 3.2 (customer satisfaction index).

Increase sales by 10% over the prior year.

Increase sales on Sunday, Monday, and Tuesday nights by 20%.

Increase sale of seafood by 15%.

Technology

Reduce ticket-time to 11 minutes per order by July 1 of this year.

If a new location is opened, install a back-of-the-house computer system.

QUESTIONS AND PROJECTS

1. List and discuss some of the ideal characteristics or qualities of objectives.
2. Discuss the accuracy of long-term objectives.
3. What do you feel are the main advantages of having long- term objectives? Why?
4. Which of the following are best suited as objectives or as strategies? Explain your answer.
   (a.) Increase promotions.
   (b.) Add a workout facility by June 15 of this year.
5. What is the relationship between an opportunity and an objective?
6. List and define the seven categories for setting objectives. What is the collective acronym for objectives?
7. Prepare both long-term and annual objectives for each of the seven categories for any company for which you have worked.
8. Discuss how various firms in your community have improved their image through socially responsible activities.
9. Approximately how much less value, in terms of percentage, is on a plate as the result of a restaurant dropping its food cost from 36% to 31%? What would be the possible negative outcomes if this occurred? Is there any way to do this while minimizing negative outcomes and perhaps turning it into a positive situation?
10. Review an income statement for a restaurant or hotel to determine possible productivity objectives for the future.
11. What are supporting objectives?
12. Discuss the impact on marketing of a high employee or management turnover rate.
13. Set long-term objectives (LTOs) and annual objectives (AOs) for each of the seven objective categories for the following company (include supportive objectives—those that increase the likelihood of achieving LTOs and AOs). (Assume today's environment.)

Objectives Exercise

The following is a brief summary of the internal analysis of a hypothetical upper-midscale hotel in a combination business and shopping district.

Category	Date: Prior Year	Date: Last 12 Months	Next 12 Months
Sale	$13M	$12M	_____
Profit (loss)	($400K)	($500K)	_____
Occupancy rate	65%	61%	_____
ADR	$82	$85	_____
Labor cost	20%	15%	_____
Food cost	40%	42%	_____

Employee turnover	150%	170%	_____
Management turnover	25%	25%	_____

CSI (customer satisfaction index 1 = poor, 5 = excellent)

Overall	2.8	2.6	_____
Courtesy	2.0	1.8	_____
Efficiency	2.5	2.3	_____
Food	3.5	3.5	_____
Cleanliness	2.5	2.7	_____
Crime incidents	15	20	_____

Sales mix (% of total room sales)

Business	35%	35%	_____
Group	25%	35%	_____
Leisure	40%	30%	_____
Share of local market is 13%			_____

The hotel's fair share (percentage of rooms for local competitors) of the local market is 15%.

The colors in the hotel's lobby are dark brown and red.

Two of the five primary competitors in the market have remodeled in the past year.

Computer system at front desk is ten years old.

The hotel recycles 60% of its paper, plastic, aluminum, and glass.

The only charitable activity was giving a total of $1000 to a few local organizations.

Insurance benefits for employees begin after one year of work.

No training program last more than two days. There is no follow-up.

Examples of the Objective-Setting Process

Unless otherwise stated, all long-term objectives are for three years in the future. All annual objectives should be accomplished by the end of the year.

SOCIAL RESPONSIBILITY

Being a responsible member of the community.
Giving money or time to charities and civic organizations.
Recycling or reducing business's impact on environment.

Internal Analysis

Currently giving about 2% of profits to charities, and not recycling anything.

Long-Term Objectives

Select one charitable organization to provide with 5% of profits.
Recycle all items that can be taken to a suitable recycling center.

Annual Objectives

Give 5% of profits to the Adopt-a-School program.
Recycle all glass, paper, cans, and edible scraps.

PROFITABILITY

Generally, the return on sales (ROS), which is profit divided by sales:
    Realistic for hotel—5% ROS.
    Realistic for restaurant—10% to 15% ROS depending on the concept.

Internal Analysis

8% ROS.

Long-Term Objective

15% ROS.

Annual Objective

10% ROS.

PRODUCTIVITY

The ratio of input to output is as follows:

$$\frac{(\$20{,}000 \text{ labor input})}{(\$80{,}000 \text{ sales output})} = \frac{\$20{,}000}{\$80{,}000} = 25\% \text{ labor cost}$$

The entire P&L could be used for productivity objectives.

Internal Analysis

Food cost—36%.
Labor cost—31%.
Laundry and linen—0.9%
Kitchen time for Friday night—25 minutes.

Long-Term Objectives

Food cost—32%.
Labor cost—25%.
Laundry and linen—0.6%.
Kitchen time for Friday night—18 minutes.

Annual Objectives

Food cost—34%.
Labor cost—29%.
Laundry and linen—0.8%.
Kitchen time for Friday night—22 minutes.

EMPLOYEE DEVELOPMENT

Training.
Personal/professional development.
Hiring quality employees.

Internal Analysis

No training manuals.
No continuing education for managers.

Long-Term Objectives

Develop a comprehensive training system with manuals, schedules, test, and training sessions.
Send each manager to a minimum of one seminar per year.
Hire construction superintendent when four restaurants per year are being built.

Annual Objectives

Develop training manuals covering the fundamentals of each position.
Send each manager to a minimum of one seminar per year.
   Send general manager to a productivity-related seminar.
   Send first manager to a human resources management seminar.
Nothing necessary during the next year.

EMPLOYEE RELATIONS

Keep morale high.
Morale is measured by turnover ratio: average number of months divided by 12

$$12 \div 12 \text{ months} = 100\% \text{ turnover}$$
$$12 \div 9 \text{ months} = 133\% \text{ turnover}$$
$$12 \div 20 \text{ months} = 60\% \text{ turnover}$$

Internal Analysis

No health insurance for employees.
Turnover ratio—employees 120%, management 50%.
Kitchen equipment breaks down frequently.

Long-Term Objectives

Have complete health insurance for all employees.

Turnover ratio—employees 60%, management 25%.
Kitchen equipment—(see technology objectives).

Annual Objectives

Have $500 deductible policy by October of this year.
Turnover ratio—employees 100%, management 40%.

COMPETITIVE POSITION

Primarily marketing-related objectives.
Sales—day part: lunch or dinner; day week; month; year.
Market share—national, state, local (fair share).
Customer counts—usually day part.
Occupancy (%) and ADR.
REVPAR—ADR times occupancy.
CSI—customer satisfaction Index.
ESI—employee satisfaction index.
Opening new locations.

Internal Analysis

3.7 CSI.
Annual occupancy—58%.
Average occupancy on Sunday—34%.
One restaurant in hotel.
Environmental analysis.
Customers requesting 24-hour breakfast.

Long-Term Objectives

4.5 CSI.
Annual occupancy—70%.
Average annual occupancy on Sunday—50%.

Annual Objectives

4.0 CSI.
Annual occupancy—63%.
Average annual occupancy on Sundays—38%.
Test 24-hour breakfast by June 12, of this year; use existing kitchen facilities, lobby as the dining room.

TECHNOLOGY

Speed and efficiency.
Reducing service time.
Check-in or check-out time.
Upgrade equipment
Security—technology or competitive postiton.

Internal Analysis

Kitchen equipment needs replacing.
Kitchen time is 25 minutes.
Food cost is 36%.
Labor cost is 31%.

Long-Term Objectives

Replace all kitchen equipment as needed to improve productivity.
Lower kitchen time to 18 minutes.

Annual Objectives

Replace broiler by May 15, of this year.
Replace any equipment that will help kitchen reach annual objective of 22 minutes.

CHAPTER 10

Marketing Mix Variables

All marketing decisions to accomplish the firm's grand strategies and annual objectives can be expressed in terms of the *marketing mix variables* of product, price, place, and promotion. The details of how they will be used are described in marketing strategies and tactics. *Marketing strategies* are plans of action to show how the marketing mix variables will be used to achieve annual objectives and grand strategies. *Marketing action plans,* or in generic planning terms, *tactics,* would include the specifics of how the marketing mix variables would be used to implement the strategies. Action plans would supply answers to questions such as: *What* will be done? *Where* will it be done? *When* and *how* will it be promoted? *Who* will be responsible for implementation? and *How much* will be budgeted?

STRATEGIES VERSUS TACTICS

There are always questions in marketing as to how many of the details of the marketing mix variables should be in the marketing strategies and how much in the marketing action plan (tactics). This decision is left up to the marketer. Most would say that, technically, the strategy would be the decision to use a certain marketing mix variable and the action plan or tactics would be all the details of its use. Others will include the majority of the details of its use in the strategies section, then use the action plan primarily for the specifics of its implementation such as when, where, responsibility, and budget. The decision of which method to use is up to each marketing manager. Results are more important than theoretical decisions. To simplify the explanation of marketing mix variables, this text will use the method chosen by most authors, that is, to discuss options for using the marketing mix variables whether for strategies or action plans. Then, in a section on action plans and policies focus is on implementational details. The only issue is that desired actions must be included in the action plan (or policies); otherwise, they may not be implemented (general rule #2 for strategic market management, Chapter 1).

The following shows the hierarchy of steps used to create strategies and action plans:

- *Grand Strategy*
  Market development—Add families with children under 12 years of age to the target market mix.
- *Annual Objective*
  Competitive position—Increase occupancy of families with children under 12 years of age from 5% to 10%.
- *Positioning Strategy*—Be viewed as a fun place to stay for short vacations or weekends.
- *Marketing Strategies*
  Products and services—Weekend package, including breakfast, adult-supervised activities for children, coupon book for entertainment and sporting attractions, and the use of free games and videos.
  Price—Couple with one child $89, $5 extra for additional children.
  Place—All Mission Valley Hotels located in the continental United States.
  Promotion—Develop a promotional campaign, directed at the targeted market, that supports the positioning strategy; a promotional budget of $35,000 will be allocated.
- Marketing Action Plan
  (The marketing action plan could again follow the format of the marketing mix variables with the applicable specifics of what, where, when, who's responsible, and how much. An alternative would be to use what, where, and so forth as titles, then include pertinent information for each category.)

Product   *What:* The weekend package for families with young children will include breakfast buffet on Saturday and Sunday mornings from 7:00 a.m. to 9:30 a.m. [scrambled eggs, pancakes, five flavors of muffins, selection of five different cereals, toast, orange juice, Colombian and French vanilla coffees (regular and decaffeinated for each), real butter and low-fat margarine, maple-flavored syrup]; one employee trained in child-care will be available for every ten children and will have both indoor and outdoor activities and games to keep them busy from 9:00 a.m. to 5:00 p.m.; as weather permits, there will be a children's cookout and pool party; board games and videos for all ages will be available at the front desk for free use (limited to two games or videos at a time); the marketing department will assemble a coupon book with discounts to museums, IMAX theaters, amusement parks, department and specialty stores, and tours.
When: April through August of 19xx.
Who is responsible: Ryan L. Abrams, Vice President of Sales and Marketing.

Price   Couple with one child $89 per night, $10 extra per night for each additional child.

Place   *Where:* At all Mission Park Hotels in the continental Unites States.

Promotion   *What:* Use the headline of "Live like Royalty with the Mission Park
                 Weekend Getaway." Copy: "Leave your cares at home and take the
                 whole family away for a fun-filled, exciting weekend. The Mission
                 Park Weekend Getaway gives you everything you need for a care-
                 free mini-vacation at a great price. While adults take in the city at
                 specially discounted prices, the kids take in the fun with profession-
                 ally supervised games and activities. Let us give you the Royal
                 Treatment at the Mission Park Hotel of your choice. Cost? Only $89
                 for two adults and one child, $10 extra for each additional child.

                 Who is responsible: Myra Ribak, Vice President of Promotions.

                 Where: The travel section of the Sunday newspapers in each of our
                 primary feeder cities.

                 When: March 19xx through July 19xx.

                 Budget: $35,000.

Cross-Functional Implementation

Marketing strategies are one part of the firm's overall functional strategies. Strategies must also be developed for the operations, human resources, finance, and other applicable departmental or functional units of the business. (These are addressed in Appendix A at the end of the chapter.)

Sustainable Competitive Advantage (SCA)

Most firms should attempt to have at least one or more strategies that can be classified as sustainable competitive advantages. (See Sustainable Competitive Advantages in Chapter 1.) Many of today's fast-food restaurants like to claim value as their SCA. For this to be an SCA only one or perhaps a limited number of chains could assume this to be true. In a recent survey, Rally's drive-through hamburgers had the SCA for value; Wendy's for food quality, menu variety, atmosphere, and cleanliness; Sonic Drive-ins for service; and McDonald's for convenience (McDowell, 1995).

PHILOSOPHIES OF STRATEGY PREPARATION

There are two contrasting philosophies of strategy preparation; *top–down* and *bottom–up*. Top–down strategies are developed by upper management, occasionally with assistance from those below. Bottom–up strategies, while still orchestrated by various levels of management, are developed with considerable input from all staff personnel unit managers, first-line supervisors, and line employees. There is no set rule of strategy preparation related to the type or size of the firm, but the trend is currently to solicit input from everyone in the organization. This is especially true of the hospitality industry, where the dishwasher may know more about the business than many other employees. For example, the dishwasher will often see when employees are stealing or disregarding certain company policies, and know what foods customers are eating or leaving on their plates. Executives often will not understand the magnitude of effort necessary to carry out the plan or are not able to specify in sufficient detail the specific strategies required to carry them out. Also, with limited knowledge of the details, appropriate objectives and rewards are unlikely (Judson, 1991).

In general, it will be difficult to develop effective strategies without input from the personnel who will implement them. Strategies developed by top management and delivered to those who will carry them out will never be supported to the degree of those created by workers responsible for executing them. The key is to have workers buy into, or *own*, the objectives and strategies (Brooker, 1991).

MARKET DRIVEN VERSUS PRODUCT DRIVEN

The actual and potential customers for any given product or service are the primary consideration in strategy selection. This is because all strategies must be driven by the firm's applicable market and environment rather than exclusively by internal product forces. To achieve any degree of success, a firm must be market driven, rather than product driven. Additionally, without considering the importance of a firm's market, supporting policies of operations and finance would be misguided. There are several distinctions between market-driven and product-driven firms that merit discussion.

Market Driven

Research focus

Environmental (PEST and PECCS) and the company's abilities to extract the maximum advantage from it.

Product focus

Based on customers' wants. "But the aim of marketing is to make selling superfluous. The aim of marketing is to know and understand the customer so well that the product or service sells itself" (Drucker, 1974, p. 64).

Product Driven

Research focus

Company.

Product focus

Based on making an excellent product. "If you build a better mousetrap, the world will only beat a path to your door if they need a better mousetrap." Likewise, there may not be an adequate demand for the best hamburger in town at $9.95. Product-driven firms generally stay with the same product offering too long.

Unfortunately, too many companies are product driven. One cause is the ego of the top manager or owner of the business. "I know what the customers want!" is often the equivalent of "famous last words" in the hospitality business. The primary rationale for being product driven is a general lack of business knowledge and information. Few firms gather an adequate amount of research. Many know very little about carrying out a research plan or analyzing information from a situational analysis. Others feel that they either do not have the time or that it would be too expensive.

Many independent restaurateurs are product focused because they became successful with a certain product—often by accident—and are hesitant to change course. In 1963, Darrell Royal, the famous football coach from the University of Texas, when asked if his team would use the pass in the Cotton Bowl replied, "We'll dance with who brung us," meaning that the team would stay with a running game rather than passing. His team won the national championship that year. Soon afterward, as most football fans know, most teams had to switch to the passing game. In fact, today, there are virtually no major college or professional football teams that base their offense on the running game. In business, as valuable and rewarding as existing product or service mixes may be, at some point changes must be made to keep up with changes in the competitive environment.

DEVELOPMENT PROCESS

The general manager of the business will normally have the administrative responsibility for the preparation and implementation of functional strategies. In small multi-unit companies and large chains, the director of operations, or other functional department manager (director, vice president, senior vice president, or other titles), may have the ultimate responsibility for preparation of the functional strategies. The process should begin with a meeting between the general manager and individual managers, department heads, or supervisors from each functional department. Here the general manager will explain the long-term objectives and grand strategies as they apply to each functional department. (Ideally, each of these managers and functional department supervisors should also have input into the setting of the long-term objectives and grand strategies.) Participants should review present strategies to see which are compatible with new objectives and which are not. The amount of required new strategies will vary based on the dynamics of the environment and the desire for change on the part of various levels of management. In many instances, there will be relatively few changes. The decision to keep any number of the same strategies or to institute new ones is important because this is the basic direction of the firm for the next year. Part of this analytical process may have been completed earlier in the strategic analysis section. Each department head or strategy committee will then be responsible for submitting what they feel are the most effective annual objectives and strategies for reaching the long-term objectives and satisfying any parameters set in the grand strategies. These suggestions are then submitted to the general manager for review and approval (or to whomever is responsible for the planning process). The various people responsible for carrying out the final plan should come to an agreement with management on the objectives and strategies that are adopted.

In many cases, strategies will be created and implemented during the year based on operational controls. For example, as various managers and employees see that objectives are not being met or that strategies, for one reason or another, are not effective, they are changed or modified. Hopefully, they have the autonomy to make the change.

It is not necessary that all employees be involved in the actual strategic planning meetings, but input, within reason, should be solicited from all workers who will carry out the functional strategies. For example, in a hotel, the general manager would be responsible for the compatibility of the functional departments and would assist the supervisors in the preparation of their specific functional strategies. Through a series of meetings, the opinions of employees would be solicited to attempt to achieve a consensus on the most beneficial strategies. The general manager will occasionally be required to have the functional strategies approved by an immediate supervisor, usually a regional manager, director of operations, or other middle- or upper-management executive.

Functional Departments

The simplest means of determining the number of functional areas is to divide the responsibility for developing strategies according to the major departments in an organization. Like the internal analysis, it matters little whether a department is considered on its own or in a category with other departments, as long as the same information or strategies are addressed. When the firm's management style follows a well-defined organization chart with detailed policies and structured lines of authority, such as that followed by most hotels, then each department—sales and marketing, food and beverage, accounting, and rooms—could be classified as a separate functional area (see Chapter 4). An alternative would be to group these departments into sales and marketing, accounting, and operations. The most efficient method of functional assignment is to use the same division used for the internal analysis. This will allow for consistency in the planning process and make it easier for personnel to understand what effect they have on the operating results of the company.

Minimal Changes

Often, management and financial strategies and their supporting policies will change very little each year. Since most firms infrequently make major changes to their style of operations, a few new strategies may be incrementally added to those the company already has. Most operations strategies and policies are already in place in the organization's operations and personnel manuals. If the firm has a problem with food quality, it may already have a policy calling for all cooks to use recipes, so in this situation management must simply enforce the policy. Financial and accounting parameters set by the company, such as various cash control procedures, the desired debt-to-equity ratio, working capital position, and profit and cost goals, will generally not vary much from year to year. These are located in a financial policy manual, sometimes referred to as the *Cash and Financial Management Policy Manual*. The primary change in this area will be the financing of the current year's projects or dealing with shifts in interest rates.

While grand strategies related to marketing may or may not indicate the need for drastic changes, functional marketing strategies will almost always represent the greatest area of change. This is because there are more factors to consider—PEST and PECCS, grand strategies, and the 4 P's—and these factors are subject to greater fluctuations than those for opeations or financial strategies. Restaurants, because of the need to keep menus current, will generally have more changes than will hotels. Both hotels and restaurants should seriously consider regular promotional strategy changes to keep current with target customers, to avoid monotony, and to stay ahead of competitors' opposing efforts.

Pretesting Strategies

Strategies can be tested in any of three ways:

1. Conceptually or intuitively, based on the personal experience and judgment of those setting the strategies.
2. Theoretically, based on published research on the topic (public domain research).
3. Empirically, by trying them out on employees, customers, or those toward whom the strategy is directed. Many large firms conduct lab tests (experimental research) to determine the acceptability of new recipes. (A lab test is an experiment that takes place in an artificial environment.) Smaller firms conduct field tests (in natural surroundings of the restaurant or hotel). Testing a new menu item as a special is a form of field test. It is relatively simple for a hotel to design a field test to determine the feasibility of new or modified products and services.

CAUSES OF INEFFECTIVE STRATEGIES

Each firm must make sure it is maximizing its strategy selection by reducing roadblocks. Among the common causes of unsuccessful strategies are the following:

1. *Limited Cross-Functional Cooperation.* This happens for various reasons, such as turf wars and interdepartmental rivalries, lack of an effective organizational structure, a counterproductive corporate culture, or ineffective leadership. Functional departments often neglect to coordinate their strategies with other departments within the firm.

2. *Overambitious Management.* Taking on too many tasks may result in a draining of financial, physical, and mental resources.

3. *Product Driven, Rather than Market Driven.* Strategies that focus on producing a product that has satisfied the market in the past may not be the product that will satisfy it in the future. Ideally, the firm must take a proactive stance and focus on a

balance between today's market and potential forecasted markets. Strategies should not be viewed as reverent icons that cannot be altered. Change is the way businesses grow.

4. *Subjective, Rather than Objective, Appraisal of the Environment or the Abilities of the Business.* Imposing one's judgment over factual evidence to the contrary may produce ineffective strategies. Setting strategies is simple. Setting effective strategies requires an open mind willing to seek out and listen to the ideas of others.

5. *Too many strategic plans ignore threats.* Generally, the main impetus of strategies are to advantage of opportunities. In the excitement of adding more units, updating products and decor, and developing new promotional campaigns, management should not overlook the fact that defensive strategies may be necessary to defend against threats. A major benefits of many defensive strategies is that while they are making the firm a more viable competitor, they also improve the bottom line and operational efficiency.

6. *Not Seeking Consensus Among Those Who Will Carry Out the Strategies.* As taught in the most basic management courses, participative management helps to enlist the willing cooperation of workers. It also tends to bring to the surface a greater variety of possible alternatives, while providing management with a reality check of seemingly logical strategies. In many cases, the management will approve strategies that even the dishwasher knows will fail. The problem, of course, is that no one bothered to ask the dishwasher.

7. *Forgetting that the ultimate objective is to win the war,, not every battle.* Management must focus on strategies that serve the purpose of improving the firm's competitive position over the long-term. Strategies, action plans, and policies should be orchestrated to be compatible with long-term objectives.

8. *Rubberstamping of Strategies.* Since selected strategies will lead to changes in present actions, they should carefully be reviewed before being accepted for implementation. At first glance, many decisions seem appropriate and sound, but upon closer scrutiny, they begin to appear illogical.

9. *Not Setting Effective Policies and Action Plans.* The strategies for each functional department must later be translated into specific policies and action plans; otherwise, no formal plan for their implementation will be available.

MARKETING STRATEGIES

The marketing strategies will focus on marketing mix variables to specify a game plan for the business. The key concerns will be how the firm can increase or improve its sales, profits, competitive position, and image. As has been previously emphasized, customer demands and competitors' strategies are constantly changing. Where operations and financial strategies focus on effectiveness, efficiency, and consistency, marketing strategies focus on measured change or adaptation. Present marketing strategies should not be discarded for no reason; but without some modifications, concepts become tired and customers move on to more contemporary competitors. Some competitors have adopted the adage that "a moving target is harder to hit."

They are constantly introducing new menu items or are offering new services or promotions for guests. While this strategy can be very successful, the downside is that, once started, it must generally be continued because it is expected. The middle-of-the-road tack would be to focus on making moderate changes each planning period to keep things fresh for the customer, without creating a logistical nightmare for marketers and unit-level managers.

As discussed in Chapter 6, Strategic Analysis Questions (see questions 2, 3, and 5), it is important to use one's creativity when developing all strategies, especially marketing strategies. A popular term is "thinking outside the box." This means that companies should consider unconventional ideas. Thinking *inside* the box refers to limiting one's strategies or options to those that are already in use, or those that are either commonplace or already being utilized by competitors. Different ideas, even those that sound crazy at first, may become the catalyst for an effective, exciting new strategy. Differentiation and the marketing concept must be guiding tenets when deciding on marketing strategies. If the offering is not unique in some way or satisfies the customer better than competitors' offerings, there may be little reason for the customer to visit.

The marketing strategies, or marketing mix variables—product, price, place, and promotion—are the methods the firm will use to achieve its marketing-related objectives and grand strategies. The marketing action plan and, to a lesser extent, policies will present a detailed explanation of how (the means by which) the firm will carry out the strategies.

PRODUCTS AND SERVICES

These include new products or services to be offered, as well as changes to be made in existing products and services, packaging, and design of the physical facilities, such as exterior appearance and internal atmosphere and the firm's brand (its name and logo). Businesses will frequently become complacent about the quality of the products they are offering and will occasionally not know or care if those offered are desired by actual and potential customers in the trade area. In the grand strategies section, discussions concerned possible changes in the firm's offering; here, and in the action plan and policies sections, discussions will center on the specific changes to implement.

An important consideration in the search for new products and services is the fact that customers are usually much more concerned with a quality and safe experience than with innovative new services or differentiation. In a major survey of business travelers, McCleary and Weaver (1992) found that the attributes desired most were clean rooms, a comfortable mattress and pillow, good-quality bath and wash towels, and good lighting for reading and working. Friendly service, various security and safety issues, and nonsmoking rooms made up the next most important attributes. An interesting discovery from the survey was that women and married men encountered the most serious problems with the above issues, while top management guests had fewer complaints than middle managers. Too often, firms attempt to be leaders in innovation or differentiation when what the customer wants is professional execution of the basics. Innovation as a strategy does have its place in the hospitality industry, but it should focus on means of improving what the customer came to the hotel or restaurant for in the first place: professional service, quality food, and a clean, comfortable room. The addition of new value-added features or services should normally play a secondary strategic role. This study is supported by West and Olson (1990), who found that differentiation without adequate emphasis on internal abilities and market demand yielded a below-average return on sales (ROS).

Food and Beverage Product and Service Decisions

The key concerns for restaurants will center around menu development, analysis of current offerings, packaging or presentation, brand decisions, design and decor, music, and layout. Decisions for hotels (with foodservice) will include those for restaurants, plus decisions on rooms, meeting space, and services to be offered.

MENU DEVELOPMENT   Probably the most important decision a restaurant operator can make concerns the type of foods and beverages that will be offered. Almost everything else in the restaurant in one way or another is affected by the menu. Additionally, the image of the restaurant will generally center around what type of food is served (a seafood restaurant, Indian restaurant, Chinese restaurant, and so forth).

CONCEPT COMPATIBILITY   The first consideration when selecting the menu is the restaurant's concept. The menu for an Italian restaurant should generally focus on dishes that target customers will associate with Italian food. Next, the operator must consider which individual menu items to offer.

DESIRES OF THE TARGET CUSTOMERS   As in most aspects of marketing, the primary focus of menu selection will be the target customer. The primary concerns of the customer are derived from the customer analysis in the environmental analysis section. Simplistically, the first desires of customers are that the food taste good and that it be reasonably familiar. Having too many items that the target customer has never tried or seen on a menu may be risky.

QUALITY   The food should represent quality to the target customer, that is, meet or exceed the customer's expectations. An individual who normally eats in a gourmet hamburger restaurant will not likely consider a fast-food burger to represent quality. This is something that must be defined by the target customer group. In the case of fast food, quality may be characterized by its convenience and low price, rather than its ingredients, taste, or appearance. (Price is addressed in the next section, Pricing Strategies.)

SELECTION   The number of items on a menu is generally unimportant. There are successful restaurants with four or five entrees and those with over 200. Consistent quality, value, compatibility with the concept, and logistical requirements are more important than the mere number of items. There is a tendency for many restaurant operators to have an extensive menu so that there will be something on the menu for everyone. When this occurs, order preparation time and equipment costs increase, food costs escalate, spoilage increases, quality generally suffers, labor costs go up, and the morale of kitchen personnel goes down, along with the restaurant's image.

SIGNATURE ITEMS   One of the most effective means of menu development is to begin with a signature item. This is an entree that is somewhat unique to the trade area and its customers. Either the actual food item could be new, or the manner in which it is prepared or served could be novel. Among the key considerations of the signature item is that it should generally have a reasonably low food cost, be relatively simple to prepare, have a shorter kitchen time than most other entrees, be exciting in some way, and elicit positive word-of-mouth advertising. Deviations from the above factors are acceptable if additional costs are balanced by improvements in competitive position or profit.

EXPERTISE OF THOSE PREPARING THE FOOD   A common error is to try to offer a menu that is beyond the skills of kitchen personnel. If the restaurant operator and target customer want certain menu items that require an above-average level of culinary skill, cooks or chefs should be hired with the ability to deliver the items. Many hotels have menu items that can only be prepared by skilled chefs. Unfortunately, many of these chefs normally work day shifts only, leaving lesser skilled cooks to work the night shift when these more challenging items will be ordered. In addition to the basic skills in preparation, the cooks should be able to serve the food within an acceptable period of time.

COMPETITORS' MENUS   Whether or not to offer foods similar to that of primary competitors is an individual decision. There is no set rule. Some restaurants have menus that are almost identical to primary competitors, while others have only a few or no similar items. If the restaurant is attempting to establish a unique image, duplicating a competitor's menu is probably not a good idea.

CROSS-UTILIZATION   This is the use of a limited number of ingredients to prepare several different menu items. Chinese restaurants may use less than 30 basic ingredients to prepare over 100 different entrees. Cross-utilization makes ordering easier, decreases the amount of storage space needed, reduces preparation and service time, reduces waste, and improves freshness by increasing the turnover of perishable inventory. Care must be taken not to overemphasize cross-utilization and end up with a boring menu.

NUTRITION   How much of a focus a restaurant should place on nutrition depends on the target customer. Few restaurants, even those specializing in red meat, can ignore the fact that more and more people are concerned about what they eat. Twenty years ago the average American consumed red meat at least once a day and, in many cases, three times a day. Today, chicken consumption in most markets has surpassed that of red meat.

An interesting observation is that many people who have been trying to eat things that are good for them are now becoming tired of foods lacking in flavor. This has led to a slight reversal of the chicken and fish trend, back toward beef and snack foods. Another outcome of the lack of flavor of many healthful foods is that there has been a large increase in the amount of spices being consumed. This can be verified by the expansion of concepts that offer well-seasoned foods, such as Mexican, Chinese, and other ethnic cuisines, and the fact that Mexican salsa has surpassed catsup as the number one condiment.

Generally, the best approach is to offer a variety of foods that can be enjoyed by people of all nutritional inclinations.

OFF-THE-MENU ITEMS OR SPECIALS   To increase the variety of foods offered, and to reduce the monotony of offering the same selection day after day, specials can be offered either daily or weekly, depending on the concept, competitors' strategies, and the expectations and wants of the target customer. The specials can be promoted with clip-ons attached to the permanent menu, written on a blackboard, or announced by the server. The blackboard menu with a reminder from the server is preferable, as long as it is compatible with the restaurant's concept, because it denotes freshness and quality. Advantages of specials are that they allow the restaurant to:

- Test an item before committing it to the menu.
- Give the cooks an opportunity to be creative and showcase their skills.
- Help the restaurant move overstocked items.
- They are also generally considered exciting by customers.

Among the common problems with specials are:

- The blackboard may not be visible to customers.
- Servers may forget to mention the specials.
- Most of what was prepared is left over at the end of the day.
- The kitchen runs out of the special while orders are still coming in.
- Preparation of the special requires either special skills or equipment that are not available.

TYPES OF MENUS   The average restaurant will require one menu. Others may decide to have additional menus for wine or desserts, or separate menus for breakfast, lunch, or dinner. Fast-food restaurants will most often use wall-mounted menu boards, instead of individual menus. It is generally a good idea to have a copy of the restaurant's menu printed on a small flyer that customers can take with them. Hotels and resorts will generally have a different menu for each meal, plus an extensive menu album for banquet sales. It is important for the hotel to destroy all old menus when new menus are introduced. This lessens the chances of surprises for both front and back-of-the-house personnel.

MENU DESIGN AND LAYOUT   The menu should be arranged so that a customer can easily order without having to search for items or categories. Most menus begin with appetizers in the upper-left corner, then continue with one or more entree sections, then end with desserts and possibly specialty drinks. The letters or font should be easy to read with available light, especially if the elderly are frequent customers. For most restaurants, menu items should be accompanied by appetizing descriptions to entice customers and to differentiate the restaurant's offering from that of competitors. To increase the sales of any particular menu item, place it as the first or second position in its category. Some experts add that the last position on a list is also advantageous.

There are several different software programs available for use that make it relatively simple for anyone to design and print his/her own menus. The programs include different typefaces (fonts), layouts, and graphics to allow for complete customization. Menu Designer, a software package from a firm based in Mountain View, California, has gained wide acceptance for its ease of use and reasonable cost.

SOURCES OF MENU IDEAS   Among the possible ways of coming up with menu ideas are visiting other restaurants, talking with other restaurant operators and the staff of the restaurants, reading cookbooks and consumer and industry magazines, taking vacations or business trips to other cities or countries, asking friends, joining restaurant associations (national, state, and local) and employees.

MENU ANALYSIS   One of the most difficult tasks related to the menu is deciding between those items that should be kept and those that should be discontinued. The majority of restaurants make this decision either qualitatively or perhaps simply according to the item's sales volume. Kasavana and Smith (1982) developed a somewhat more effective and quantitative method of ascertaining the value or worthiness of an item to remain on a menu. They coined the term *menu engineering* (see Table 10.1). The analysis will reveal which items have the lowest food cost, highest sales,

TABLE 10.1   Menu Analysis

Menu Item	Number Sold	Menu Mix (%)	Food Cost (%)	Menu Price	Menu Item Food Cost	Total Item Sales	Total Item Food Cost	Item Contribution Margin	Total Contribution Margin	Contribution Margin Rating	Menu Mix Rating	Menu Item Classification	Labor Intensity (1–10)
Chicken Fajitas	450	29.76%	32%	$8.95	$2.86	$4,028	$1,289	$6.09	$2,739	L	H	Plowhorse	8
Ribeye Steak	306	20.24%	38%	$12.95	$4.92	$3,963	$1,506	$8.03	$2,457	H	H	Star	2
Filet	85	5.62%	42%	$11.95	$5.02	$1,016	$427	$6.93	$589	L	L	Dog	2
Pork Chops	67	4.43%	36%	$8.95	$3.22	$600	$216	$5.73	$384	L	L	Dog	3
Snapper Vera Cruz	336	22.22%	35%	$13.50	$4.73	$4,536	$1,588	$8.78	$2,948	H	H	Star	6
Lobster	43	2.84%	48%	$16.50	$7.92	$710	$341	$8.58	$369	H	L	Puzzle	4
Veal	38	2.51%	39%	$13.50	$5.27	$513	$200	$8.24	$313	H	L	Puzzle	9
Chef Salad	187	12.37%	32%	$6.95	$2.22	$1,300	$416	$4.73	$884	L	H	Plowhorse	3
Column Totals	1512	100.00%				$16,664	$5,981		$10,683				

Average Menu Mix: 100 ÷ 8 = 12.50%; 12.50% × 0.7 = 8.75%.
Average Contribution Margin: $10,683 ÷ 1512 = $7.07.
Food Cost Percentage: $5981 ÷ $16,664 = 35.89%.

highest contributing margin, and lowest labor requirements. If an item was a poor performer in any of these categories, the options would be to raise its price (to lower its food cost), reduce the portion size, improve its presentation, give it a more prominent position on the menu, discontinue serving the item, and so on. Although no form of menu analysis can detail the exact composition of a menu, the exercise does show how individual items affect the profitability of the restaurant and is certainly much more objective than using product sales or personal preference. The most critical menu category for the analysis is the entrees. Other categories, such as appetizers, salads, or desserts, can be included if desired. Table 10.1 contains a menu analysis from a hypothetical restaurant.

The procedure to complete a menu analysis follows:

1. List the menu items for one particular menu category.
2. Record the number sold of the menu item for the period covered by the analysis.
3. Record the *food cost percentage* of the menu item.
4. Record the menu price of the item.
5. *Menu item food cost* is item price multiplied by the food cost percentage. For example, a 34% food cost percentage (0.34), times a menu price of $8.95, equals a menu item food cost of $3.04.
6. Record the *total item sales* for the period the analysis covers.
7. *Total item food cost* is the total item sales multiplied by the food cost percentage. For example, total item sales of $3689.25, times a 34% food cost percentage (0.34), equals a total item food cost of $1254.35.
9. *Total contributing margin* is obtained by subtracting the total item food cost from the total item sales: $4028 − $1289 = $2739. This figure also represents the gross profit of the item.
8. *Item contributing margin* is the menu price minus the menu item food cost. For example, a menu price of $8.95, minus a menu item food cost of $2.86, equals an item contributing margin of $6.09.
10. For the *contribution margin rating,* divide the total contribution margin by the number of meals, then categorize menu items with contribution margins above the average figure as high (H) and those below it as low (L). For example, a total contribution margin of $10,683, divided by 1512 meals sold, equals an average contribution margin of $7.07.
11. For the *menu mix rating,* divide 100 by the number of menu items to obtain the average percentage for each menu item. To allow for the fact that sales for a reasonably popular menu item are slightly below the average, a multiplier of 0.7 is used to lower this average (100 divided by 8 menu items = 12.5% times 0.7 = 8.75%). If the menu item's menu mix percentage is above 8.75%, it is labeled as high (H), if below that percentage, it is labeled as low (L).
12. The *menu item classification* is a means of grouping items so that further analyses can be made. Items noted as high in contribution margin and menu mix are referred to as *stars,* those with high contribution margins and a low menu mix are *puzzles,* those with low contribution margins and a high menu mix are *plowhorses,* and those with both low contribution margins and low menu mixes are *dogs.*

TABLE 10.2   Menu Analysis Ranking—Strategies, Action Plans, and Policies

Menu Item	Number Sold	Food Cost (%)	Total Item Sales	Total Contribution Margin	Labor Intensity	Menu Analysis Totals	Menu Analysis Ranking
Chicken Fajitas	1	1	2	2	5	11	2
Ribeye Steak	3	4	3	3	1	14	3
Filet	5	6	5	5	1	22	5
Pork Chops	6	3	7	6	2	24	6
Snapper Vera Cruz	2	2	1	1	4	10	1
Lobster	7	7	6	7	3	30	7
Veal	8	5	8	8	6	35	8
Chef Salad	4	1	4	4	2	15	4

13. *Labor intensity scale* is calculated by ranking each menu item based on its labor intensity. This would include both preparation and assembly for service, and any special requirements that make the item more or less complicated to deal with relative to other items. Menu items are ranked from 1 to 10, with 1 having minimal labor requirements and 10 being very labor intensive.

MENU ANALYSIS RANKINGS   The five most critical categories from the menu analysis are ranked according to their relative position and value to the restaurant (see Table 10.2). The ranking begins with a 1 for the highest or best item in each menu analysis category. This could be the highest sales or contribution margin, or the lowest food cost. For the menu analysis totals column, add up the rankings for each menu item. The menu analysis ranking is calculated by assigning an order to the menu analysis totals according to the item with the lowest score.

A menu analysis should be completed just before a menu is changed, once again about one or two months after it has been in effect, about each six months thereafter, and before considering a major menu change. The menu analysis rankings must not be taken as the final ruling on menu decisions. This quantitative presentation should be balanced with a subjective opinion, especially if the analysis indicates that an item should be discontinued. For example, dropping a low-ranking item that is popular with a few regular customers may not be a wise decision. The entire menu analysis can easily be accomplished on any spreadsheet program.

BRAND DECISIONS   All businesses and many of their products and services must have a brand—a name or symbol—for purposes of identification and differentiation. The part of the name that can be spoken is termed the *brand name*. Any symbols or logos, such as the golden arches, is termed a *brand mark*. The federal government provides legal protection of the brand name and brand mark through the issuance of a *trademark* (Kotler & Armstrong, 1990). If a firm uses a name without seeking trademark protection, it is possible that the name could become "generic" and available for use by the general public. For example, *aspirin* at one time was the name of a business's product.

Before the brand name is selected, careful consideration must be given to the business, the product or service and its uses and target market, and competing firms. While it is not likely that a business will fail because of the wrong brand name, an effective brand name can improve its outlook. In the long-run, the customer's perception of that brand name is more important than the name itself. A study in England reported that one of the key valuations of a firm is the potential the brand name has for future earnings growth, for example, through geographic expansion (brand extension strategies). It was found that only 7% of consumers disregard a brand name (Thomas, 1993).

A frequent mistake made by many small restaurants is to avoid using product identifiers such as restaurants, grill, or bar in their name. "Joe's" may have great food, but if the majority of passing traffic does not know what "Joe's" is, Joe has a problem. While many marketers have various rules of thumb for naming a business or its products and services, each rule has been repeatedly broken with great success. For example, the belief that names should be short and easy to spell and pronounce has been ignored by Fuddrucker's Hamburgers and Schlotzsky's Sandwich Shops. Probably the best reason for a short brand name is that one of the major determinants of the cost of signage is the number of letters. If there is a possibility of becoming a multinational firm, the name should not have a derogatory meaning in targeted countries. For example, Chevrolet tried to sell the Chevy Nova in Latin American countries. *Nova* in Spanish means "will not go/run." In Spain, Budweiser was promoted as the "queen of beers," and Bud Lite was "filling and less delicious," (Berkowitz, 1994).

With the ever-increasing frequency of brand changes for existing hotels, marketers must set specific strategies to deal with all ramifications of that change. Does the new name have a better, similar, or less stellar image than the former name? What about the image of the specific hotel whose name will change? To assure guests that only improvements are foreseen, it is best to contact all regular guests through a mailed announcement and high-occupancy accounts through phone calls or personal visits. On some occasions, such as when a Hilton is rebranded as a Ramada Inn, the change will be to a lower level of service. If it is assumed that it may be difficult to hold on to many of the existing guests, then the marketer's task, though not as challenging as opening a new hotel, will require an exceptional effort.

PACKAGING   Many years ago brown paper bags, menu tissue, and aluminum containers sufficed for the majority of packaging needs for restaurants. As competition forced differentiation and new packaging materials became available, white paper bags with colorful logos and Styrofoam became the norm. Today, with society's focus on ecology, the trend is to return to the brown paper bag and aluminum containers. The key requirements for packaging are that it retain the product's temperature, protect the product from being crushed and the customer from being burned, facilitate takeout and delivery, and, as necessary, identify the product or business. Companies that can factor recycling into this equation will likely improve their image.

PRESENTATION   What type of plates and silverware should be used will depend on the type of restaurant, the style of service, and the desired atmosphere. While fast-food restaurants must present the food in an appetizing manner, they are limited by the amount they can spend on dinnerware. Casual restaurants must focus primarily on durability, appearance, and cost. Fine dining establishments will focus first on appearance, then on durability and cost. The general rule is that white sets off the color of food best. Other colors can be used for uniqueness. The wider the rim (the slanted area on the perimeter of the plate), the more substantial the food appears. Also, the closer the border (the painted stripe around the rim) is to the flat portion of the plate, the greater the perceived quantity of the food.

SERVICE STYLE FOR RESTAURANTS   The decision of whether to use one style of service or another is fairly simple. Fast-food restaurants will focus on varying types of self-service where the customer orders at the "customer counter," then either receives the order immediately or returns when his/her name or number is called. A variation of the self-service style is for restaurant personnel to deliver the food to the customer, rather than requiring the customer to return to the counter. Casual and fine dining restaurants will almost exclusively use table service (technically, American service), where the customers' orders are taken at their table by a server, who then also delivers the orders. Many restaurants have adopted the food-runner system, where any server can deliver the table's order when it is ready. This increases the efficiency of the servers and helps assure that the food is promptly delivered. French service, another type of table service, focuses on partial preparation of the food in the dining room and requires an additional number of personnel, such as a maitre d', captains, front waiters, back waiters, and bussers; its use is limited almost exclusively to fine dining establishments. Russian service consists of bringing the food to the dining room on an attractively arranged platter that is presented to the host and guests. Servers will then plate each customer's meal.

Hotel Product and Service Decisions

Product and service decisions for hotels are relatively simplistic when compared to those for restaurants. The major product and service decisions for a hotel are made during its planning stages, when developers decide in which market to compete. This target market decision will dictate the basic design of the building and the layout and size of rooms, type and number of food-service facilities and restaurants, meeting space, ancillary services such as workout rooms and business services, and public areas. It will also indicate the level of service provided by personnel in each department. For example, in the economy market, personnel at the front desk have one primary responsibility, to check guests in and out. In the midscale and luxury markets, front desk personnel, and concierges if available, will receive messages, help arrange itineraries, help solve problems with meeting rooms, make reservations at restaurants, recommend local entertainment venues, and, to varying degrees, act as the host of each guest during his/her stay. Subsequent decisions would be whether to offer such services as a concierge or late-night room service, a newspaper, quality toiletries, in-room service bar, or a continental breakfast. Perhaps the fastest-growing service is the use of various forms of technology that either expedite the logistics of the guest's stay or increase his/her productivity. Examples include video check-out, computerized keycard entry systems, in-room computers or computer and modem hookups, fax machines, and copy machines for business floors. Hilton's BusinesSavers includes such amenities as free local phone calls, outgoing faxes, movies, and health-club use for $10 to $20 more than the corporate rate. Hyatt's Business Plan includes an in-room fax machine, free telephone calling-card and 800-number access, continental breakfast, and a phone on the desk and on the bedside table for $15 above the regular corporate rate (Stone, 1994).

Various weekend, vacation, honeymoon, and business packages are marketed by combining available hotel services. Each hotel will have different opportunities for unique packages. For example, in Los Angeles, California, several downtown hotels have developed "trial packages" for the abundance of visiting attorneys. The package includes a special rate for the several-week average stay, plus an in-room fax and a computer (Seal, 1991). If these packages are for the short-term and would later be discontinued, they would generally be referred to as sales promotions (see the Promotion section in this chapter).

Design and Decor for Hotels and Restaurants

The average customer is concerned with courteous, efficient service and good food or comfortably appointed rooms, at a good value. This can be accomplished in a hotel or restaurant with a simple design and decor as well as in one that is very expensively designed. For most businesses, money is the single most important and least expendable asset, so it is necessary to closely watch what is spent on design and decor. To get the most mileage out of each dollar spent, imagination and ingenuity should be used to create a design that is compatible with the customer's demands and showcases the business's products and services. Consider the following when designing and decorating the hotel or restaurant.

RENOVATING AN EXISTING LOCATION   The key to renovation is to attempt to use existing features and limit extensive remodeling. It is not necessary to do something unusual with every surface, unless required by the concept or desired atmosphere. It is generally more economical and esthetically pleasing to concentrate on one or two areas or surfaces that could be developed into a focal point, then finishing the remainder of the room in an tasteful, subdued manner. Track lighting can be used to emphasize the chosen focal point. Focal point could be a grouping of large or unique plants, a wall with various types of unusual art or artifacts, a mural, an unusual ceiling, an antique bar, or an exposed kitchen.

DESIGNING A NEW LOCATION   A new hotel or restaurant can be designed with a philosophy similar to that of designing an existing facility. The difference is that there is more flexibility in creating the focal points. For hotels, the lobby offers the greatest challenge and benefit. Guests in the upper-midscale to luxury hotel market segments expect an eye-catching ambiance that differentiates the hotel from less expensive alternatives. There are a few properties with quite modest lobbies that were originally designed for the upper-midscale market, but because of higher guest expectations they have had to lower their rates nearer the level of midscale competitors. Essentially, the lobby must match the concept. Hyatt Hotels have proved the importance of the lobby, through their use of atriums. Historically, lobbies were viewed as nonproductive space that should be minimized (Hilton, 1957). They are now the focal point of many hotels.

Many people will strongly equate the size of the building, referred to as *building mass* or *curb appeal,* with its overall image. For example, a restaurant in an in-line position in a strip shopping center will not have as much visible building mass as one located on the end of the strip center. A hotel can increase its visible building mass by having its longest side facing the primary street from which people enter.

FURNITURE   Since customers in restaurants spend the majority of their time in a chair or booth, this piece of furniture should be of the top affordable quality and comfort. Couches, chairs, and tables in a hotel's lobby are equally important for a different reason. Lobby furniture and decor items, to a degree, set the tone for the hotel's image. Furniture in hotel rooms should be compatible with the hotel's image, be viewed as tasteful by targeted guests, and be functional, sturdy, and ideally one grade above that of the competition's. If a hotel can provide leather when its competitors have cloth, all else being equal, it will have a higher level of guest satisfaction.

AVOIDING OVERLY EXPENSIVE DESIGNS   Unless the property's concept is centered around a particular theme or is attempting to target a well-defined customer base, care must be taken to minimize expenditures. Too often, money is spent on hotels and restaurants so that the designer can showcase his/her talent at the willing or sometimes unknowing expense of the owner. Sometimes the owner will want to spend a large sum of money to create a certain unique feeling or ambience. This is actually good for the industry, because there is always a need for someone to stretch the limits of creativity to see what the customer will accept. These successful and unsuccessful attempts set the yardstick for acceptable designs.

AVOIDING GIMMICKS   One problem encountered more in restaurants than hotels is that overdone, gimmicky theme designs and decors can detract from the customer's experience. Some customers may initially be impressed with the decor, but, in the majority of cases, this is not what will bring them back. Most hotel guests prefer tasteful, conservative decor, while most restaurant customers prefer comfortable but interesting surroundings.

DESIGNING WITH FLEXIBILITY   In the past, design and decor had to have a direct relationship to the business's concept. "American customers have now become more sophisticated—we no longer need to eat Italian food off a table with a red-and-white checkered tablecloth lit by a candle in a Chianti bottle" (Reich, 1990 p.

13). Design and decor must become more versatile and flexible to accommodate passing trends for food, design, decor, color, furniture, fixtures, and so forth. This approach can also limit expenses when renovation is required.

EMPHASIZING ACTIVITIES OVER DESIGN   Today's restaurant customers desire brighter, more casual, open dining rooms that allow them to see and be seen, to interact with others, and to be part of something fun and exciting. Rather than making design or decor the main emphasis, many operators today make the activities taking place in the restaurant the attraction. For this reason, exposed kitchens and bakeries have become popular and quite effective for their entertainment value. Customers enjoy seeing the mechanics of an operating restaurant, especially appropriately attired cooks preparing their food. It gives them something to look at and something to talk about, increases their trust in the food's preparation, and relieves the monotony of staring at the same pictures on the wall, time after time.

DESIGNING WITH COLOR   Because of the ability of color to act as a mood changer, knowledgeable use of it is one of the most effective and inexpensive design tools. Blue, green, white, gray, and black tend to sedate and fatigue customers and employees. Yellow, brown, beige, red, gold, pink, and peach increase energy and promote activity. Decors that focus on bright and varied colors can make areas conducive to frivolity and excitement. Dark colors tend to moderate personalities and create a feeling of privacy and intimacy. To reduce fatigue among kitchen employees, try light beige walls instead of white.

Music and Public-Address Systems

Music is a major aspect of the atmosphere for most hotels and restaurants. A quality music system, proper musical selection, and appropriate volume can have a positive effect on the success of the business. Mistakes in these areas can be a major contributing factor in customer dissatisfaction.

The system, music selection, and volume should be geared to the hotel or restaurant's target customer, but be pleasing to the majority of customers. It is common to ask customers about their general experience, or how their room or food was; occasionally, someone should question customers about the music. It is important to consider the tastes of not only target customers but also secondary markets. Rarely will one type of music be the first choice for all customers, so a compromise must be sought.

One theory of musical taste is that people most enjoy the music they listened to when they were teenagers. For example, someone in their 60s would prefer music from between 40 and 50 years ago (the big band era), a customer in their 40s will prefer light rock 'n' roll (the Beatles and James Taylor), and those in their 20s and 30s will appreciate more contemporary music (U2 and Metalica). Basically, each generation's rock 'n' roll becomes easy listening music for the following generation. This means that musical choice in the future will likely be toward more aggressive types of music such as that of U2.

Since music influences the psychological and physiological well-being of customers, the selection and volume should have a positive effect on their state of mind and digestive system. Music for the mind and digestive system should be melodic, without loud bass (low-pitch) or treble (high-pitch) sounds, with no dramatic changes in volume or harsh beats, and should be as pleasant for the average customer who may not notice the music as for the customer who consciously listens. Music can also be used to help cover up less desirable sounds of ventahoods, bussers, kitchen activities, and dishroom noise. For bars located in restaurants, the music system should have separate volume controls to allow proper balance between the bar and the dining areas.

If there is a public-address system for paging customers, it should be tied into the music system so that it cuts off the music while a customer is being paged. To remove this interruption, many restaurants are now using pagers to notify customers.

Because of their ease of placement and unobtrusiveness, ceiling-mounted speakers are generally used for most hospitality businesses. These speakers should be omnidirectional, meaning that they will disperse the sound in all directions, rather than just straight down. For proper sound coverage, ceiling-mounted speakers should be spaced at intervals of about twice the ceiling height, with a maximum distance between each of about 25 feet. For example, if the ceiling height is 10 feet, the speakers should be approximately 20 feet apart.

The sound absorption qualities of all surfaces in the hotel or restaurant will influence the power of the amplifier, the type and quantity of speakers, tonal qualities, and the volume of the music. Softer surfaces, such as carpet and unfinished wood, absorb sound. Hard surfaces, such as metal, plastic laminates, and vinyl, reflect sound.

There are three major categories of music for hotels and restaurants:

- *Background Music.* This is instrumental music (no lyrics), only slightly louder than the ambient sound in the room. The "ambient sound" is the average, constant sound in the room, including people talking, moving, and working; and air-conditioning and heating systems. Background music is generally used in hotel lobbies, public areas, and meeting rooms, and for upscale or formal dining rooms.
- *Foreground Music.* This is music with or without lyrics and loud enough to be easily heard over the ambient sound of the room without interrupting conversation. This could be easy-listening music at a higher volume, or mellow rock 'n' roll. Foreground music is used in most fast-food and casual dining restaurants.
- *Recreational Music.* Loud enough to dominate the atmosphere of a room, recreational music is generally reserved for bars and discothèques. Generally, the higher the percentage of alcohol sales in a restaurant, the greater the customer's tolerance and desire for louder music.

Hotel and Restaurant Layout

Layout is the logical placement of all major activities in a way that allows employees and customers to work and transact their business at maximum efficiency. The layout for an economy hotel will be extremely simplistic, geared toward functional needs and minimization of space. Midscale and luxury properties will also focus on functional needs but will generally not want to create the image that space was sacrificed to reduce costs. The type of food and beverages to be served and the service style are the most important elements to be considered in the layout and equipment needs of a restaurant. The best layout usually results from the cooperative efforts of the architect or designer, the general manager of the hotel or restaurant, the chef or kitchen manager, the head server, the owner, and consultant, if one is retained.

Hotel and restaurant layouts should be based on the development of the work centers and work stations.

WORK CENTERS   This is the smallest grouping of closely related tasks that are normally performed by one person. The primary goal of a work center is to reduce the time and number of steps an employee or customer must take to complete recurring activities. A work center would include the concierge's desk, a front desk employee's station, a broiler cook's station, a salad bar, bar station (for alcohol), a wait station, and a desk in a guest room.

Requirements for a work center include the following:

- A work center where an employee works while standing should be approximately 4 linear feet. As the distance goes beyond 4 feet, speed decreases while fatigue increases. For example, keys or entry cards should be not more than two or three steps away from a front desk employee's normal work area.
- When more than 4 feet of space is necessary, parallel work lines or a U-shaped work center should be considered. Both configurations greatly limit the amount of steps necessary to complete tasks.
- When feasible, everything needed to complete a normal task in a work center should be within arm's reach.
- Grouping related items such as condiments and paper supplies reduces the time it takes to locate them.
- Dry and refrigerated storage and the dish and pot washing area should be no more than 20 feet (ideally 10 feet) away from any point in the preparation area.
- The bartender's work center, or station, should have all needed supplies and equipment so that the bartender does not have to leave the station except for unusual drink requests.
- Any other areas should be viewed with economy of motion in mind.

WORK SECTIONS   These are a group of related work centers where one type of activity occurs, such as the front desk, laundry room, preparation area or the cooking line in the kitchen, warewashing, the server's food pickup area, the bartender's work area, customer greeting and waiting areas, and dining room seating.

LAYOUT   The layout consists of the work sections being joined together to promote the greatest degree of work and employee efficiency. The following are among some of the more common requirements:

- The work should proceed in sequence, with as little backtracking or wasted movement as possible.
- The employees, customers, baggage, food, beverages, meeting tables and chairs, and so forth should move the shortest possible distance.
- Customer service time should be the shortest time attainable, compatible with the concept.
- Floor space should be used efficiently.

At the preliminary design stage, exact dimensions are unimportant. The primary purpose of this information is so that hotel or restaurant developers can work effectively with architects or designers to lay out the hotel or restaurant according to known facts rather than averages or estimates. Far too many hotels and restaurants are laid out and designed improperly by "professionals" (architects and designers) because of the hotelier's or restaurateur's trust or lack of knowledge. Also, with this additional knowledge and information, developers can locate problems before they become permanent mistakes that can:

- Cost dearly in money and time to correct
- Negatively influence the operation of the hotel or restaurant because of inefficient work flow, slow service, high labor cost, low morale, and high employee turnover
- Reduce the number of potential customers and thereby sales because the production areas were poorly laid out

Typical Considerations for Product Strategies

1. Are new products geared to the elderly market or any particular market necessary?
2. Are improvements in product quality necessary? (Obviously, decisions here will influence management strategies.)
3. Where does the company stand as far as its relative perceived product/service quality (RPPQ) and relative perceived value (RPV), and what changes should be considered to reach the desired RPPQ or RPV ratings?
4. Which products or services have the greatest gross margin?
5. What USPs (unique selling propositions) will be offered, such as fresh-baked bread or desserts, large platters for entrees, extensive wine list or drink menu, signature appetizers or entrees, complete workout facility, free movies, or an in-room stocked bar?
6. Does the name of the company, and its products and services, create the type of image that is sought? What graphic form should the name or logo take? (Chajet, 1991).
7. What USPs related to decor, such as an exhibition kitchen, bakery, or fish tank, might be incorporated in the design of the hotel or restaurant?
8. Should the layout be changed to improve efficiency?
9. What type of music should be played, background (soft, without words), foreground (heard over the ambient sound of the room, with or without words), or recreational (dominates room)? Should it be varied, depending on the meal or day of the week? Is live music a consideration?

10. What colors should be used in the lobby, guest rooms, dining room, bar, and kitchen?
11. Should plants be used as a focal point, or as a complement to the design? What type of plants will be used? How large and how many?
12. What aromas will customers be smelling while they are in the building or around it? Which aromas will have the greatest impact on customers' inclination to make a purchase and ability to relax? Most restaurants will have a distinctive smell. The operator must decide if it is a positive one. Should the hotel, through disinfectants and deodorizers or perhaps a bakery, also have a distinctive smell? The scientific term for the utilization of aromas is *olfactory-evoked recall*. This refers to the relationship between the aroma/smell, one's experience with it, and its physiological effect on individuals. For example, lavender tends to be relaxing, while jasmine can be stimulating.

PRICE

For the pricing strategies section of the strategic marketing plan, there is generally a discussion of the pricing strategies that will be used, with the actual prices included later in the marketing action plan. If desired, a listing of the prices for each product or service and the reason for them (the appropriate pricing strategy) could be included in the strategies section, with only the prices in the action plan. It is acceptable for presentation purposes to combine prices with the product sections of the marketing plan (e.g., title: Products and Prices). For example, the menu could be included with its prices or hotel rooms and suites with their applicable rate schedules.

It is important that the business's prices reflect its overall and specific marketing objectives and be set according to an organized process rather than simply by personal opinions. No amount of personal experience is a substitute for careful analysis of all pricing considerations. Mistakes in pricing, such as charging too much, too little, or not knowing if the current price is suitable for the firm's market, can develop into serious problems that are difficult to overcome.

The frequency with which prices must be changed will vary considerably. Restaurant prices for most menu items will normally be relatively stable. Each six months or so, management will review the cost of each item sold, its current price, and various other internal and environmental concerns, then determine whether the price should be increased, left as is, or, in rare instances, lowered. When the price of an item with a high food cost fluctuates, a decision must be made whether to include the item on the menu at "market price," on a clip-on addition to the menu, on a blackboard, or simply announced by the server as a special.

One of the advantages, and often problems, of the hotel business is that prices are quite flexible. A room with a rack rate (the highest rate charged) of $100 could have a range of prices, beginning at a crew rate (airline crews) of around $35, with most between $55 and $80. (The main reasons for the lower crew rate are that the rates are contracted on a very large quantity basis, the rooms would go empty, it's good public relations, and the hotel will still show a small profit.) Most prices for a hotel room would be negotiated between the buyer and seller. The hotel sales manager understands this going into negotiations, and if he/she has forgotten, the potential customer will certainly make the manager aware of it. Even front desk personnel and reservationists are learning more about negotiations. (Yield management, a method of balancing price with demand, will be discussed in this section.)

Pricing Objectives

Each firm must attempt to charge a price that will help it achieve its long-term objectives—the most important of which is long-term profit (McCarthy & Perreault, 1993). Marketers must also consider how price will influence the business's overall image, its ability to afford a certain type of facility, and its capacity to expand. In the short term, more specific pricing objectives dealing with profit, survival, market share, sales maximization, quality, and must be considered.

PROFIT MAXIMIZATION   This is selling at a price that will yield the greatest profit. In the past, this was generally the price point beyond which people would begin selecting alternative sources: in other words, a price that will yield the greatest profit, but not so high that customers would go elsewhere. Because of today's value-oriented public, the chosen price is often not the highest acceptable price, but the one that maximizes profits. A gross profit of 75% matters little if sales and net profits are low. There are instances when this strategy will work, such as when competition is weak, but an overcharging strategy may unfortunately sacrifice long-term objectives for short-term profits. Competition will eventually enter the market, resulting in drastic reductions in sales and the business's image. A business would be much better off with a lower gross profit, but hopefully higher sales and net profit. Several restaurant chains have recently adopted the approach of increasing their food cost percentage (resulting in a lower gross profit) because of its positive impact on sales and net profit. In this case, customers realize that they get more for their money, so they return more often and tell their friends.

SURVIVAL PRICING   This is lowering the business's price in a last ditch effort to stay in business or remain competitive. This occurs much more frequently in hotels than restaurants. If a restaurant's food and service quality are inferior at $6.95, then they are still inferior at $3.95. If this restaurant was losing $5000 per month, it would likely be closed down (especially if operated by an independent without substantial financial resources) or preferably sold. If problems could be solved, such as through a turnaround strategy, then the business might be saved. Large chains would have more flexibility if faced with this situation. For example, the promotional value of operating the restaurant may be greater than the monthly losses incurred (e.g., if the monthly losses were $5000 and the cost of having two billboards in the city was over $5000, then the loses might be justified). The restaurant could also be used as a training site or place to test new products. Various types of temporary reductions or sales promotions are a possibility, but this option is generally viable only for the fast-food market. (Sales promotions are discussed in the Promotions section of this chapter.)

Hotel survival pricing is actually quite common, especially during periods of oversupply, such as in the late 1980s and early 1990s. Unlike a restaurant that is losing money, if a hotel is losing $10,000 per month, it will likely stay open to minimize losses. The reasons for this are twofold. Since the hotel owner has a major investment in real estate, he/she will not give up a several million dollar asset in the face of a relatively small monthly loss. Another factor is that it is usually more expensive to close down a hotel rather than to operate it at low occupancy. Also, if the hotel were still operating, it would be much easier to sell than if it were closed.

MARKET SHARE   This is the business's percentage share of dollars spent on a particular product in a particular geographic or customer market. This objective is more important to large companies than smaller ones. McDonald's keeps track of its market share of the fast-food dollar. If it is holding steady, then its management knows that, as the market grows, its sales and perhaps number of units will also grow. Businesses with few locations are more concerned with their individual sales objectives, rather than market share. Hotels chains know about their share of the national, regional, state, and local markets. Individual hotels in a certain trade area, whether affiliated with a chain or not, will often exchange information that is used to produce a market share report. This is sometimes referred to as a *fair share report*, because it calculates the percentage share of the market for each hotel weighted by its number of rooms (see Chapter 5). The objective will be to select a pricing structure/ strategy that will provide the business with its highest potential market share.

SALES MAXIMIZATION   Most businesses have the objective of achieving the highest possible level of sales. Sometimes this is by charging a higher than average price, other times by charging a lower than average price. If a business is maximizing its capacity (seating or occupancy), then the primary means for it to increase sales is by increasing prices (it could also increase the capacity of the business or expand to new locations). If the business is not a market leader and has weak to average demand, then prices may need to be lowered to realize the highest possible sales. Since the decision to raise or lower prices will impact costs and customers' perception of the business, it should not be made without thorough consideration of all ramifications.

QUALITY FOCUS   Generally, the higher the company's product quality, especially its *relative perceived product quality* (RPPQ), the more it can charge its customers. Among many affluent customers, a purchase that represents anything other than the highest or one of the highest quality alternatives available is not an option. If these people make up a considerable percentage of a business's target customers, then keeping its quality and price above that associated with average products and services is critical. Each business must determine the importance of quality to its customers, then make sure that not only the product or service meet the demand, but that the price charged is compatible with the desired quality perception. To many, a low price, regardless of the product's quality, represents low quality.

VALUE FOCUS   Value is best explained by the equation

Price + (Quality and Quantity) = Value

The correlation between quantity and quality will depend on the business's target customer. Some groups will demand both; others need only one to meet their demands. Each business must decide how important value pricing is to their overall objectives. The most effective method of analyzing value is by comparing a business's value to that of its primary competitors, referred to as *relative perceived value* (RPV). While all businesses must be concerned about their value perception, those in the middle and economy sectors will need to factor value into their pricing decisions more than those in the upscale market. The value pricing trend in the hospitality industry has been on the increase since the late 1980s and it appears that this can only continue.

Pricing Approaches

There are three major approaches to setting prices: cost-based, customer-based, and competitor-based. Every business's situation will call for a unique combination of the pricing approaches. Restaurants tend to focus primarily on costs and what competitors are charging. Hotels focus more on what customers are willing to pay and competitors' prices.

COST-BASED PRICING   This can be either cost-plus pricing or break-even pricing. Cost-plus pricing involves a standard markup based on the total cost of the product or service. The objective is to maximize the gross profit on each sale (revenue − cost of goods sold = gross profit). The most common pricing method used by food-service operations is to base the selling price on the desired food cost. For example, if the cost of the menu item is $3.50 and the desired food cost is 32%, the approximate menu price would be $10.94 (calculated by dividing the cost, $3.50, by the desired food cost percentage of 0.32). The actual menu price would likely be $10.95.

Some restaurants mark up food and beverages by multiplying them by a *pricing factor*. The pricing factor is calculated by dividing 100 by the desired food cost: for example, 100 ÷ 35 (35% is the desired food cost percentage) = 2.86 (rounded off); 2.86 × $3.50 = $10.01. Alcoholic beverages will have different pricing factors, generally between 2 and 5, based on their category, such as domestic beer, well liquor, house wine, and so forth. The tendency is to mark up bottles of wine by a lower pricing factor, often between 2 and 2.5. Among the reasons for the lower pricing factor for bottled wine are that since wine makes a meal more enjoyable increasing the likelihood of a wine purchase increases satisfaction; a higher pricing factor would price the wine out of the range of many customers' budgets; and if a customer buys the same wine for the home, he/she may not like seeing it for three to four times as much in the restaurant.

Another variation of cost-based pricing is to use a certain percentage markup, such as a 200% markup, which would equate with a pricing factor of 3. An entree that costs $3.00 with a 200% markup would sell for $9.00 (200% of $3.00 is $6.00; so $3.00 + $6.00 = $9.00.)

Though it does not happen very often, when a business sets its prices below its costs with the idea of driving a competitor out of business, it is termed *predatory pricing,* which is illegal. Since there are often more factors influencing the setting of a price for restaurants and hotels than for manufacturing or product-oriented retail businesses, attempts at predatory pricing are not common in the hospitality industry.

BREAK-EVEN PRICING   This is calculating the point at which the company would break even, then adjusting the price to yield a profit. Break-even pricing is most often used for estimating the most appropriate per person average for a yet-to-be opened restaurant.

The following is a break-even analysis for a restaurant

Per person average (PPA) = $7
Fixed costs = $30,000 (costs that do not change or change very little as sales volume changes; e.g., rent, insurance, accounting, and prorated utilities)
Variable costs = 60% (costs that change in direct proportion or approximately in direct proportion to sales; e.g., a food cost of 35% and a labor cost of 25%)

$$BE = \frac{\text{Fixed costs}}{(1 - \text{Variable costs})}$$

$$BE = \frac{\$30,000}{(1 - 0.60)} = \frac{\$30,000}{0.40} = \$75,000$$

The break-even figure of $75,000 divided by a PPA of $7 equals 10,714, which is the average number of customers per month needed to break even. If the restaurant wanted to use break-even pricing, it would attempt to raise prices above the break-even point or find ways of increasing the number of customers. If, in this example, the PPA was raised by $1.00 to $8.00, the increase could potentially bring in an additional $10,714 for the month ($1.00 times 10,714 customers). Since the restaurant has a 60% variable cost, the additional profit would be approximately 40% of the $10,714 increase in sales or $4286 (rounded off).

Another way of using this formula is to calculate the sales needed to generate a specific level of profit or sales necessary to cover the cost of a promotional campaign. If the restaurant (or hotel) wanted an $8000 profit, it would simply add the desired profit to the fixed cost. If the business wanted to calculate the increase in sales necessary to cover a certain promotional campaign, it would similarly add the dollar cost of the campaign to the fixed cost. If marketing expenditures were increased by a certain percentage, such as 2%, it would add the 2% to the variable costs:

$$\frac{\$38,000}{0.40} = \$95,000 \quad \text{the sales needed to show an \$8000 profit}$$

Divided by a $7 check average, the new break-even price with profit factored in equals 13,571 customers per month necessary to provide the restaurant with an $8000 profit. Carrying this a step further: 13,571 customers per month ÷ 30 = 452 customers per day needed to show an $8000 profit. If the restaurant's maximum capacity is 400 customers per day, it would have several options:

1. Raise the check average (an $8 check average divided into $95,000 equals 396 customers per day).
2. Lower variable costs (the largest percentage of these are food and labor costs).
3. Lower fixed costs (very difficult).
4. Expand the dining room.

The following is a break-even analysis for a hotel.

Hotels use break-even pricing for calculating both the break- even point for sales and the average daily rate (ADR) required to break even. These figures are then used as reference points for sales and pricing objectives.

Assume an occupancy rate of 70%, in a 250-room hotel with fixed costs of $350,000 and variable costs of 20%:

$$BE = \frac{\$350,000}{(1 - 0.20)} = \frac{\$350,000}{0.80} = \$437,500$$

Calculating the ADR necessary to break even:

1. Determine the average room nights per month, or for any particular month, week, day, or other time period:

   0.70 (70%) × 250 rooms × 30 days = 5250 room nights per month
2. Divide the BE by the room night figure:

   $$\frac{\$437,500}{5250} = \$83.33 \quad \text{ADR to break even}$$

CUSTOMER-BASED PRICING   This is basing the price on the customer's perception of what the product or service is worth. If the product or service is similar to that offered by competitors, then the customer's *reference price*, the price a customer is accustomed to paying, should be considered. Every lodging or foodservice organization should find out through surveys and personal conversations what the customer thinks of the prices the business charges. Since the price that a customer will pay is based on perceived values derived from the product, it behooves the business to do whatever it can to increase the perceived value by means that do not add to the cost of the product or service. For example, developing an image of superior service will enable one hotel to charge more than another. Often, the difference in cost for excellent service will be insignificant, perhaps a combination of better training, reward systems, and quality supervision. In some cases, the cost will be less because more employees want to work for the hotel and thus turnover is reduced.

There is also the question of whether it is easier to establish a high perceived value for a product than for a service. Since it is generally easier to have a consistent product than a consistent service, establishing a high perceived value for a service will likely be more difficult. At the same time, since the service is intangible, it creates unique opportunities for a company to set the quality of its services apart from that of its competitors.

THE ECONOMICS OF HOSPITALITY PRICING   All pricing is essentially based on negotiations between sellers and buyers (supply and demand). In hotels, this is accomplished when a sales manager discusses price with a corporate travel planner and when reservationists or front desk personnel attempt to extract the highest reasonable rate from individual travelers. Because the majority of hotel rooms are sold through a reservation system, negotiations take place directly with individuals, or the representatives of individuals or groups. In restaurants, negotiations are more subtle. Rather than negotiate with individual customers, restaurants negotiate with their customers in the marketplace by establishing a certain position or image supportive of a certain price. If the restaurant sets menu prices lower than what could be obtained, then the customer has gotten the better deal. If the restaurant can still make a satisfactory profit at the low price (because of increases in customer counts), then each party is happy. If the restaurant attempts to charge too much for its food or beverage, then the customer will refuse further negotiations until the price is reasonable.

In setting prices, marketers must be aware of the *price elasticity* of their targeted customers—how sensitive customers are to changes in price. In economic terms, hospitality pricing has traditionally been *relatively inelastic*. This means that, as the price goes up or down within a moderate range, the level of *demand* (total sales) will change very little. Like everything in marketing, things change, and the economics of the hospitality customer is no exception. Currently, because of intense competition, many sellers are offering discounted prices and specially priced packages of different sorts. As customers are getting used to looking for the best deal, demand is becoming more *elastic,* meaning that, as the price changes, total sales or demand will also change. Of course, other issues such as quality, consistency, and atmosphere will affect the degree of the target customers' elasticity. Businesses, whether budget or upscale, with a reputation for quality will be able to limit the degree of price elasticity. A business viewed as an option only because of its low price will find its demand to be highly elastic.

VALUE PERCEPTION   Another means of exposing key elements in the customer's purchase decision is to determine how the customer perceives the value of the product or service (Kotler, 1991). This theory says that customers will first calculate nonmonetary values of the product, such as the product itself, service, convenience, atmosphere, and image. (These comprise the total value customers are receiving.) They then calculate the price they are willing to pay for these values. This includes the monetary price, time, effort, energy costs consumed during the purchase or experience (e.g., the time and effort necessary to get the family ready and drive to the restaurant and the cost of the gas), and the psychic cost (level of comfort and risk). Based on the target customers' value assessment, the business then sets a price for the product or service.

COMPETITOR-BASED PRICING   Setting a company's price based on what competitors are charging is referred to as *competitor-based* or *going rate pricing*. Because of the tendency for a hotel's customers to compare prices, and the fact that a hotel room costs the customer considerably more than a meal in a restaurant, hotels are generally forced to use competitor-based pricing to a greater extent than restaurants. The primary problem with competitor-based pricing is that there may be a substantial difference in cost of sales and expenses between one competitor and another. The justification for it is that customers know what competitors are charging for similar accommodations and, therefore, will be wary of hotels charging a higher relative price.

THE IDEAL PRICING APPROACH   It is best to consider each of the three pricing approaches and the business's particular situation in determining prices. For example, if competition is intense, then competitor-based pricing will generally be the primary approach. This situation will likely drive the price down to the point that customer-based pricing will not be a major factor in the decision. However, a problem could develop if a low price became associated with low quality. Cost-based pricing would need to be a consideration since the business must show a profit.

Pricing Strategies

Pricing strategies are the easiest of the strategies to change and, therefore, the most abused. Quite frequently, hotels will lower their room rates rather than focus on other means of maintaining a stable price. Erratic changes should be avoided because price is generally one of the most sensitive issues for the customer. Having a customer say or think "I wonder why the price has gone up? I'll take my business elsewhere!" is not a desired outcome. General pricing strategies follow.

RAISING OR LOWERING PRICES   There are several basic rules that can be followed in changing prices. They do not apply in all circumstances because every situation has different variables that must be considered.

1. Try not to raise prices by more than about 10%. Raising a price from $9.00 to $9.90 is quite noticeable to a person who orders the item on a regular basis. An increase to $9.45 would not stand out as much. If increases in costs forced the 10% increase, then the adjustment could be made easier to implement if the item's plate presentation, accompaniments, and perhaps name were modified. Because the customer is accustomed to hotels raising and lowering their prices based on the time of year and occupancy levels, the 10% rule does not always hold true. Even so, a hotel should consider the option of adjusting prices upward gradually. If, for some reason, the occupancy level during a brief period of time increased from 60% to 90%, then there would be a justification for raising the price by more than 10%, depending on the actions of competitors.
2. When price increases are unavoidable, spread the increase over several items rather than increasing only one or a few items. Raising the price of several items on a menu by 10¢ to 15¢ will be less noticeable than raising the price on one or two items by 70¢ or 80¢.
3. Every price point will have a different meaning to each target customer group, depending on such factors as income level, frequency of purchases, and whether their company is paying for the meal or room.

The price for most hotels can be upgraded psychologically by using *even-dollar pricing*. A price of $74.00, to many customers, sounds better than $73.60 or $74.50. Certain groups connote even-dollar pricing with quality. For example, antiques are generally priced in even-dollar increments. An exception to this rule is when a price is being raised above a *price break-point*—the highest amount the customer is willing to pay. For restaurants, the price break-point is generally the next dollar level. A $7.95 dinner will often sell better than an $8.25 dinner. The break-point for hotels will vary depending on the target customer and existing pricing structure. The average hotel will have a break-point of the next $10 increment, for example, within the $60 range up to about $70. An exception to this would be that as prices approached $100 or higher, there will be less resistance to the $10 break-point. Of course, as previously mentioned, this will depend on the target customer's perception and budget.

For restaurants, it is generally better to end prices with the numbers 5, 9, or 0. This is what people are used to, so being a pioneer could present risks. A price of $8.47 for a meal does not register in the customer's mind as easily as a price of $8.45 or $8.50. An exception would be cafeterias, where items are often priced based on their exact food cost. For example, if the cost of a portion of squash is 18¢, and the desired food cost is 32%, the price charged would be 58¢ (57.6 rounded off).

REACTIONS TO CHANGES IN A COMPETITOR'S PRICE   Generally, in the hospitality business, a company should react to a competitor's price changes if it thinks it is going to lose sales or if it does begin to lose sales. Prices should not be lowered if it is not necessary. Figure 10.1 shows possible options in view of a competitor's price decrease.

Typically, when a restaurant lowers its prices, the reaction will depend on the competitiveness of the market and the level of service. Fast-food or quick-service restaurants tend to follow price changes of their primary competitors; casual dining

---

The Green Valley Hotel has a corporate rate of $90. The Town Lake Hotel nearby (very similar facilities and location) lowers its corporate rate from $90 to $80. Possible options and considerations for Green Valley follow:

1. Wait to see what happens to reservations.
2. Find out why Town Lake lowered its price (lower occupancy, losing money, or wants to increase its market share and then return price to previous level).
3. Is it a temporary reduction?
4. Do Town Lake customers care about the $10?
5. Do Green Valley customers care about the $10?
6. Are present occupancy and future reservations satisfactory to maintain sales?
7. Has this happened before? If so, how did it affect sales?

Figure 10.1   Reactions to price reductions.

and fine dining restaurants generally disregard changes, unless they begin to affect sales. Basically, the total package for casual and fine dining establishments is more important than price.

YIELD MANAGEMENT   To give the hotel a means of adapting for varying demand, many hotels use what is termed *yield management.* This is essentially making adjustments in the hotel's rate based on either present occupancy, in the case of guests for any certain day, or forecasted occupancy (reservations). Historically, the majority of hotels have charged more during peak season and less during slack times, but yield management is the utilization of current supply and demand pricing strategies, in addition to a seasonal price change.

The purpose of yield management is to allow a business to achieve a fair market-adjusted price for its products or services. Though yield management is most often associated with the hotel industry, its theories are used by most businesses because of the practice of adjusting prices to reflect the level of demand for their products or services. There are several different applications of yield management. For hotel guests who do not have a reservation, the room rate will vary depending on the hotel's projected occupancy for the night. For example, if the hotel's projected occupancy was 50%, its corporate rate might be $65. The next day, if the occupancy was projected at 65%, then the same rate category might jump to $70 or $75 depending on competitors' rates for a similar room. Some guests have called this unfair because in either instance there will be rooms unoccupied at the end of the night, but this has proved to be one of the fairest means of adjusting the hotel's price. After all, this is based on the theory of supply and demand. As more buyers are demanding a room, the available supply goes down, forcing prices up. The alternative would be a flat rate regardless of demand. Though the flat rate appears to be a viable strategy for lodging's economy sectors, it is not widespread in midscale and luxury markets.

Generally, a software package such as a property management system would determine the hotel's yield management rates. Manually, a hotel would first forecast its occupancy for the requested dates (see Figure 10.2). Assume that the expected occupancy for the Mission Valley Hotel 100 days out (days out refers to the days before a specified date) is 78% and its corporate rate is $95. Then, based on historical reservation patterns for various categories, the hotel's management would create a model detailing a normal range for reservations for certain periods of time, such as each 10 or 20 days, that precede the specified date. For example, 100 days out, for this particular time of the year, the hotel's yield management model shows reservations at 20% to 25%. At 80 days out the reservations are normally at 25% to 35%, and at 20 days out the reservations are normally at 50% to 60%. If actual reservations were within the reasonable range of the yield management model, then rates would be set at the normal corporate rate of $95. If reservations were below the range, then rates would be lowered to attract more business. If reservations were higher than the model's range, then rates could be increased. In some cases, hotels will turn down business because it is felt that it could sell the rooms at a higher rate closer to the specified date (Relihan, 1989). If a sales manager brought in a piece of group business for 100 rooms (30% of the hotel's rooms) at 60% of the corporate rate, using yield

DAYS OUT	HISTORICAL RESERVATION RANGE (%)	ACTUAL RESERVATIONS (%)	RECOMMENDED RATE
100	20% to 25%	24%	$95
80	25% to 35%	28%	$92
60	35% to 40%	32%	$90
40	40% to 50%	47%	$95
20	50% to 60%	65%	$98
10	60% to 70%	75%	$105
Within 10 days	75% to 80%	83%	$105

Figure 10.2   Mission Valley Hotel: yield management model.

management, the Director of Marketing might decide to turn it down because, according to the model, a majority of these rooms would normally be sold at a date nearer the specified date at the full corporate rate. At 60% of the corporate rate, the gross revenue for the 100 rooms would be $5700 ($0.60 \times \$95 = \$57 \times 100 = \$5700$). At the full corporate rate, only 60 of the rooms would have to be sold to yield the same gross revenue ($\$5700 \div \$95 = 60$ rooms). The decision would not be based solely on the yield management model. Factors such as the group's potential to bring in future business or its use of the hotel's banquet facilities would influence the decision. Obviously, this is a nice problem to have, but this type of decision is becoming more frequent with the increased usage of yield management.

PRODUCT BUNDLE PRICING   This is packing several products or services together to make them more attractive to potential purchasers.

HOTEL EXAMPLES

Modified American Plan—two meals, usually breakfast and supper
Full American Plan—three meals
European Plan—no meals
Weekend, vacation, honeymoon, or other special packages

RESTAURANT EXAMPLES

A la carte—individual prices
Prix fixe—one price with some choices; usually a several course meal with a limited choice for each course
Table d'hôte—one price, set menu; generally several courses
Special dinners for two for a set price

Price

	High	Medium	Low
High	**1. Premium strategy.** People willing to pay for the best. Relatively small market with few competitors.	**2. High value strategy.** For most firms this is one of the strongest positions. Customers get their money's worth, visit regularly, and tell their friends.	**3. Superb-value strategy.** Unless this firm is showing a reasonable profit based on high volume, it should probably consider raising its price.
Medium	**4. Overcharging strategy.** People paying more for the image than for quality. Often a business that, through negligence, slipped from a high-quality strategy.	**5. Medium-value strategy.** A fair price. Is not differentiating itself based on price. If competition is not aggressive, this strategy may work.	**6. Good-value strategy.** The firm hopes that by offering a reasonable quality product at a low price, increased sales will make up for higher costs.
Low	**7. Rip-off strategy** Near total purchase is for image rather than product. Longevity may be limited to speed of bad word-of-mouth advertising.	**8. False economy strategy.** The firm thinks that the customer cannot differentiate between low and medium quality and will therefore pay more than the product is worth.	**9. Economy strategy.** There will always be people who do not care about quality or do not have the available money to afford a better product.

Product Quality (vertical axis label)

Figure 10.3   Price/quality strategies. *Source:* Adapted with permission from Kotler & Armstrong (1990). *Marketing, An Introduction,* 2nd ed. Upper Saddle River, NJ: Prentice-Hall, p. 306.

QUALITY-PRICE OPTIONS   Figure 10.3 is a matrix showing several of the choices a company has in formulating its desired relationship between quality and price. Marketers should first locate competitors' positions on the matrix. They can then attempt to find a position that has the potential to yield a competitive advantage that is compatible with the firm's overall strategies. The matrix could be applied to all the business's products and services or only to specific products or categories.

MARKET-SKIMMING PRICING   This is charging the highest price possible to skim maximum revenue from segments willing to pay the higher price. This generally does not happen much in the hospitality industry, although it is not unheard of. Some fine dining restaurants will charge more simply because there are few competitors with which to compare their product or service. In the lodging industry, upscale resorts and spas can often use market-skimming pricing until competitors enter the market and compete on price. An old saying in business, "Charge what the market will bear," applies to this and other similar pricing situations.

MARKET-PENETRATION PRICING   This is charging a low relative price to penetrate the market quickly and attract a large number of buyers. Although it does occur, penetration pricing is difficult to pursue in the hospitality industry because most businesses have similar costs. To use market-penetration pricing, the business must be able to do at least one of the following:

1. Find a cost advantage (food, labor, operating expenses, overhead) not immediately available to competitors.
2. Reduce portions or quality.
3. Hope that increased volume will make up for decreased margins.
4. Be willing to accept lower profits. Sometimes there is no other choice: for example, to remain competitive, most hotels must lower their rates during the off-season.

TYPICAL CONSIDERATIONS FOR PRICING

1. What is the desired food cost percentage, alcoholic beverage, labor, or any other major applicable cost categories that must be factored into the price?
2. Are costs controlled at the lowest effective level (purchasing, finance, accounting, operations, and marketing)?
3. Should prices be adjusted upward or downward, based on costs, customer perception, or competitor's price structure?
4. Does the hotel or restaurant take surveys to find out what customers think of its prices (pricing strategies)?
5. Can the company economically afford seasonal discounts or can other, more creative options be sought? (Temporary discounts are considered sales promotions and are included in the Promotion section.)
6. How can individual prices be adjusted to yield the greatest profit?
7. How sensitive are customers to changes in price (elastic—very sensitive; or inelastic—not very sensitive)?

PLACE

This includes all factors relating to the distribution of the product to the customer. Place refers to where the business is in the distribution or marketing channel. In the hospitality industry, hotels and restaurants are considered to be retailers (see Figure 10.4). The primary consideration for a retailer in regard to the marketing channel is its location, so this becomes the main issue to be addressed.

In addition to its normal distribution channels, hospitality businesses will need to determine if there are alternative means of delivering the product/service to the customer or making it available to them. Most firms tend to stay with their primary or traditional marketing channels, such as individual business travelers, group, and

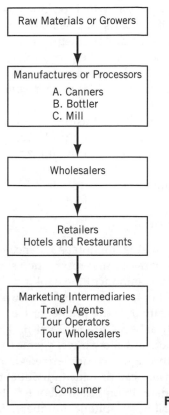

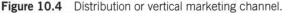

Figure 10.4   Distribution or vertical marketing channel.

leisure. Since this is where most of the competitors are, a less desirable channel may offer less resistance (Kotler, 1991). These niches may represent great opportunities for growth for innovative sales managers. Some hotels near hospitals sell between 20% and 30% of their rooms to insurance companies for out-of-town patients and their families. There is still a high percentage of the small business market that does not know of the benefits of having meetings away from their office. Many service organizations, colleges, and universities have not had sales managers call on them to offer special rates (McCann, 1995). Targeting major travel agencies is an option that has been used by many of the larger hotel chains, but not as much by smaller chains or independents. International, national, and regional travel clubs offer another potential source of business. To improve the effectiveness of both marketing and operational aspects of the catering function, many hotels that were previously without a catering sales manager have added one.

In some areas, customers are able to order food for delivery through the Internet. Some hotels are offering discounted rooms through the Internet. Many casual dining and even fine dining concepts have implemented delivery strategies. Competitors at all levels of the restaurant business are adding catering (in-house and on-site) to their marketing channels.

The *vertical marketing system* refers to the way in which portions of the channels of distribution are related. For example, if all parts of the marketing system are owned by one company, it is called a *corporate* vertical marketing system. If there are signed agreements to supply products or services or help coordinate efforts, it is called a *contractual* vertical marketing system. If a dominant member of the marketing channel controls activities through its size and power, it is an *administered* vertical marketing system.

Place strategies may not be critical for an existing business if no changes in the marketing channel are contemplated. If the location was a problem, it should have been noted in the internal analysis section; then the firm should consider a strategy to reduce its detrimental effect on sales. (A promotional message, such as "A great hotel is hard to find," along with a map might be used to minimize the situation.)

Marketing Intermediaries

One area of concern for the marketing channel is the hotel's reliance on marketing intermediaries, such as travel agents, tour operators, and reservation services. For an agreed fee based on a certain percentage of the amount of the booking, the marketing intermediary, generally a travel agency, will book an individual or group at participating hotels. The booking can be made manually over the phone, or it could be placed through electronic booking services, such as Apollo and SABRE. These systems provide a variety of travel-related information and allow travel agents to book flights, hotel rooms, and ground transportation through a computerized database. Travel agents equipped with the appropriate software can provide individual travelers and corporate meeting planners with up-to-date information about hotels for their chosen destination, such as room availability, telephone numbers, fax numbers, recreation facilities, and rates. With the addition of the JAGUAR electronic hotel directory (for SABREvision), the agent can access maps and pictures of the hotel that can be described or faxed to the client. The *Official Hotel Guide* (Secaucus, NJ), the *Hotel & Travel Index* (Secaucus, NJ), and *The Red Book*, the official American Hotel & Motel Association Lodging Directory (Walnut Creek, CA) for the business traveler, provide printed listings of hotels.

Importance of a Good Location

The original description by E. M. Statler of the three most important factors to consider when opening a hotel, "location, location, and location" (Powers, 1990, p. 154), can apply equally to almost any retail business. Obviously, there are other factors and strategies to take into consideration, but without a good or excellent location the business's chances of success are greatly reduced. No single decision will have a greater impact on the business's investment and success than its choice of a location. Its primary importance concerns the number of potential customers that can be attracted. Other significant factors include the available labor pool; a multitude of zoning requirements that could place limits on hours of operation, the serving of alcoholic beverages, or even whether a hotel or restaurant can be opened or built on the property; local health codes; construction costs; available parking; and various operating costs, such as monthly rent, taxes, insurance, maintenance, utility costs, and trash disposal. Every city has a restaurant or two in terrible locations that are doing an exceptional amount of business. These restaurants should be viewed as exceptions, and any attempt to duplicate their location strategy should be approached with caution.

The term *location* is used to describe the piece of land on which the building is located (its address). A location survey will include all variables that make the location suitable or unsuitable for a particular use. *Site* refers to the place on that piece of land where the building will be or already is located. Sometimes a particular location will be excellent, but the site has various problems, such as lack of visibility, parking, or access; or being too small, narrow, or too large.

Though location research is becoming much more scientific, it is still a soft or social science impacted by human nature. Current geographic, demographic, psychographic, and behavioral attributes can be reasonably quantified, but constantly changing consumer trends, competition, economic conditions, and other environmental factors are difficult to discern with accuracy. Frequently, the statistics for a particular location will appear to be ideal, when operating results prove disappointing. Unfortunately, there is no known method of assuring the success of a location decision. For the independent firm or small chain, the most suitable option is to complete a detailed location report to help gather necessary research. (See the discussion on location considerations below.) Large chains have the strategic advantage for location decisions of vast statistical data that enable them to compare the characteristics of a proposed location with similar, existing locations. This allows them to determine with greater accuracy the potential of the proposed location. Another major advantage of the large chains, or even well-recognized smaller chains, is that with their increased name recognition, larger advertising budgets, and increased promotional expertise, the impact of selecting a less-than-ideal location is reduced.

In the end, the decision on a location, like that of most strategies, is based on research, inferential skills, experience, the advice of others, and a gut feeling.

Location Considerations

The following factors should be included in any analysis of a location. It should be recognized that not every location will be perfect in every category. Alternatively, a limited number of excellent location variables should not be equated with probable success. Since there are many factors to consider and a great many differences between individual locations, a careful analysis should be made to determine which factors will impact success and which could lead to failure (Reich, 1990).

TRADE AREA   Perhaps the most important concept related to place is *trade area*. This is the area from where the majority of a business's customers will come. This percentage in generally thought to be around 65 percent. Fast-food restaurants will generally have trade areas of approximately 1 to 1½ miles. The reasons for this relatively small trade area are that, since there are usually many competing fast-food restaurants, the customer does not have to travel far to find something to eat, and that because one of the primary attributes of the fast-food restaurant is convenience, the customer will not drive far. Casual dining concepts will normally have trade areas of approximately 3 to 5 miles or the distance their target customers are willing to travel. This again will depend on the number and quality of its competitors. Fine dining restaurants may have trade areas of up to 20 miles or more, again, depending on the distance the customer is willing to travel. Hotels will sometimes consider trade area from the standpoint of multiple trade areas. In other words, the majority of their customers will tend to come from several cities, termed *feeder* or *origination cities*, while some will also come from the local residential and business communities. The reason for the importance of knowing the expanse of one's trade area is that this allows the restaurant or hotel to focus its marketing efforts—all 4 *P*'s—in an area that has the potential to produce the greatest results. When considering many of the location characteristics below, the business's trade area should be a guiding concern.

VISIBILITY   Potential customers should be able to find the hotel or restaurant without searching for it. Since a meal at a restaurant is more of an impulse purchase than a night in a hotel, visibility for a restaurant is generally more critical than for hotels. In the ideal situation, hotel and restaurant sites should be visible for about 300 to 400 feet in the right lane (the adjacent lane) and 400 to 500 feet in the left lane. This allows customers time to see the business and turn in before they pass it.

Since the majority of purchase decisions for hotels come from advance reservations, the primary requirement for a hotel is that it have a location that makes it reasonably accessible to the destinations of its target customers. For example, if most target customers are from the corporate segment, then the hotel should be located near the business district where these customers will be working. Excellent visibility may not be critical in this instance. However, all things being equal, the most visible location will receive the most business. The trade-off, of course, is that the better location, because of higher land costs, will have a higher overhead and be at a competitive disadvantage on price flexibility.

Restaurants located in *strip centers* (several businesses under one roof, normally in a straight line or L-shaped) should be clearly visible to traffic. At the very least, a sign on a pylon (signpost) should be available to help direct customers. Because of its increased exposure, the *endcap* (the end of a strip center), rather than *in-line locations* (in between other locations), is most often the best location. Of the two endcap locations, the one with the most potential is normally the right endcap (facing the building), because it will be much more visible to customers driving in the adjacent or right lane. Another reason the endcap is better than in-line locations is that the endcap will generally have about twice the amount of building exposure, and therefore building mass, of in-line locations. For example, two 50-foot by 50-foot locations will have the same square footage, but if one is an endcap, it will have a total of 100 feet of visibility to potential customers. In-line locations should be viewed with caution because the restaurant will tend to blend in, reducing its visibility. This type of location can prove successful for a smaller restaurant, such as a sandwich, yogurt, or pizza shop, and for bakeries, if the store face is visible to traffic on the major street and the landlord allows signage that can be seen from the road.

ACCESSIBILITY   Both restaurant and hotel locations should be easily accessible, with efficient *ingress* (entrance) and *egress* (exit). A close examination of the location should be made to note medians, traffic lights, stop signs, three lanes or less for each direction, and center turn lanes that could positively affect accessibility. Congested intersections, poor road maintenance, one-way streets, and speed limits over 40 miles per hour often have a negative effect on accessibility. It is critical to visit applicable city, county, and state planning departments to see whether any future road construction will affect access to the location or that of competitors.

PARKING   The location should have ample parking spaces for its intended use. For restaurants, most cities require one parking space for every 100 square feet of floor space of the entire restaurant (some cities use 75 square feet to determine parking space requirements). Many restaurants will require more parking spaces, especially during peak hours. For example, a 5000-square-foot restaurant would have a legal requirement of 50 spaces. If this restaurant has a seating capacity of 200 (a dining room of slightly over 3000 square feet, divided by the fire code requirement of 15 square feet per person, equals 200), it would have a minimum peak potential requirement of 50 or more parking spaces just for customers (200 seats where the average table is for four people; $200 \div 4 = 50$). An additional 20 or so spaces may be necessary for employees. A more logical requirement is to have enough spaces for an average number of employees who drive to work and an additional space for each three seats in the dining area.

When considering locations where parking spaces will be shared with other tenants, examine the prospective locations during expected peak hours to see how many vacant parking spaces there are. Conflicts often arise when businesses such as restaurants dominate the parking lot. To many shopping center tenants, a packed parking lot represents additional potential customers. If parking adjacent to the restaurant is limited, valet parking or private, for-pay parking might be considered. Generally, customers view this as acceptable if the restaurant is either a fine dining establishment or one that is worth the extra few dollars for parking.

In most cities hotels are required to have one parking space for each of the first 250 rooms, the equivalent of 0.75 or 3/4 of a space for each room between 251 and 500, and 1/2 space for all rooms above 500. This is a general requirement and will not suffice for all properties. Economy hotels would have enough spaces based on this requirement, because most have less than 250 rooms, very few employees, and many of the employees travel to work by bus. Midscale or luxury properties with up to one employee per room and banquet facilities for three or more times room capacity should consider the need for spaces well beyond the minimum requirements. If parking is limited, nearby lots might be rented, or there may be room for on-street parking, or a more distant parking lot with bus transportation could be considered.

TRAFFIC COUNT   Technically, the traffic count for a location is considered to be the number of vehicles that travel all roads adjacent to the hotel or restaurant site during a 24-hour period. This could be only the street in front of the business or if side streets carry potential customers, both the frontage road and side streets. Because of vast differences in types of businesses and driving habits of target customers, developing a minimum number of cars per day necessary for success is difficult. Businesses with the experience of several locations may have an approximate number that are deemed necessary. Since most hotels derive the majority of their business from reservations, traffic counts, while important, generally are not as critical for hotels as for restaurants. Luxury and resort hotels competing in the upscale market may have locations in exclusive areas with traffic counts low enough to scare off most concepts. Roadside hotels and motels will, of course, depend greatly on street traffic. Some airport properties and those in shopping areas will depend on a substantial traffic count. Downtown, business park, and amusement park locations will rely on being in the immediate area of their target customers' needs more than on traffic counts. For example, being within one-third of a mile from a convention center will have a greater influence on occupancy than the traffic count.

For restaurants, the traffic count requirement will depend on the size of the restaurant, its requirement for patrons, quantity and type of competitors, accessibility (ingress and egress), the image of the restaurant, whether it is a destination or a convenience restaurant, the percentage of the traffic that is seeking a place to eat, and so on. Even though it is difficult to say exactly what the traffic count should be, it is important to know this figure as a means of comparison with other locations, and as a component of the total location decision.

Most local governments have a traffic count for all major roads in their area. Since this count is normally for a 24-hour period, it is necessary to personally take a traffic count during what are expected to be peak business hours for the restaurant.

One common problem is that decision-makers equate a high traffic count with the area being a good location. Some locations with an extremely high traffic count have proved to be horrible locations. Sometimes accessibility is the problem; other times the location may be good only for destination restaurants where customers are willing to make a special effort to visit. Fast-food establishments that rely on convenience may suffer in the same location. In downtown or mall locations that rely on foot traffic, count the number of people walking by and try to calculate whether enough of them are potential customers.

Since no traffic count number will by itself equate with success, knowing the traffic count number and the various factors affecting it will improve the decision-maker's judgment and allow for comparisons with other locations. As with accessibility, check to see whether any road construction is planned that would cause a significant change in the traffic count.

TRAFFIC GENERATORS   Every business will have sources of potential customer traffic that supply it with a large percentage of its customers. For most hotels this will be certain cities and businesses or nonprofit organizations. They may also rely on local office buildings, shopping centers, and amusement parks. Traffic generators for restaurants will include residential areas, shopping centers, office buildings, industrial parks, schools, hospitals, and organizations of various types located within the restaurant's trade area.

In developing strategies for securing a location or finding sources of new business, traffic generators will be a key focus. An important consideration is whether the loss of any of these traffic generators would negatively affect potential or existing business. Additionally, there may be new traffic generators that could positively affect business.

AREA STABILITY   How will the specific location or area change over the coming years? Each trade area will generally progress through various cycles. Knowing the characteristics of those cycles (similar to the product life cycle) may help predict what the area will be like in the future. There will be areas that either will not progress through each stage or will remain in the same stage for a generation or more. For this reason, the stages will not apply to all locations. Determining the present and potential stages of area stability is not an exact science but can generally be done by those who either have lived in the area for many years or have extensive experience in business or real estate development. The stages include initial development, growth, maturity, decline, and revitalization. The characteristics of each are examined in the following.

INITIAL DEVELOPMENT

- There are few open businesses, and, depending on customer traffic, traffic from the local trade area may be minimal for some time. Because of limited demand, the cost of land or rent may be low.
- The operator must be able to cover operating expenses for an unforeseeable period of time.
- For restaurants, sometimes a landlord will agree to a rental abatement of between several months to a year to compensate for the risk. When taking over an existing hotel in such a location, attempts should be made to reduce the price, based on limited sales potential. This can normally be accomplished if the property has previously been foreclosed upon.
- Some trade areas will never get beyond the initial development stage; consequently, adequate sales volumes may never be reached.

GROWTH

- Customer traffic and sales volume are increasing. Empty retail space begins to fill up, while available tracts of land are becoming more scarce.
- Rents and land costs are rising because of an increased demand.
- If the economy is peaking at the same time, rents or land costs may be temporarily high, then decrease as the economy drops.
- Locked-in rents or exorbitant land costs can negate the majority of future profits. Renegotiation of the lease may be necessary.

MATURITY

- The area is still generally profitable, but sales growth will normally be difficult because there are too many businesses competing for the same customer.

- An advantage for the maturity stage is that since there is little room for expansion, the competitive base is known and, except for changes in concept or name, somewhat stable.
- If many of the neighboring concepts are outdated, this may be a good time to remodel or reposition the concept.
- A frequent problem with mature locations is that as nearby areas begin to develop, existing customers may prefer the newer competitors.

DECLINE

- This stage is characterized by an increasing number of empty retail locations, buildings in need of repair, few new businesses, and limited or pass-through traffic.
- Business may still be adequate for some firms, but customer counts are dropping because of growth in other areas, the lack of maintenance on the part of landlords and restaurant owners, and, at some point, a loss of public interest in the concept or area.
- Occasionally, existing hotels and restaurants will begin remodeling or reconcepting. Closed or foreclosed businesses may reopen under new owners.
- Lower rents or building costs may be the major way to justify a location in this area.

REVITALIZATION

- For various reasons, older areas may attract commercial interest. Investors may feel that by virtue of its atmosphere or personality customers can be attracted to the area. Older buildings may lend themselves to unusual concepts.
- Rents and land costs may be low or developers may purchase the property at a price that allows them to renovate and lease at a profit. Revitalization is normally associated with downtown areas.

RECOGNIZED DINING OR LODGING AREA (CLUSTERING)   Generally, a variety of reputable hotels or restaurants in the trade area will increase the likelihood of success. Except when the area is saturated with restaurants or hotels, the more existing target customers around the proposed location, the better. This, of course, produces an increase in competition and the need to excel, but that is exactly what attracts greater numbers of customers and strengthens the long-term position of the firm. Additionally, it is sometimes easier and less expensive to have supplies delivered if the supplier is already in a particular area.

Recent studies have shown that, for many of the same reasons, clustering is critical for a variety of companies. The vast majority of industries have traditionally been located in a narrow geographic area. For example, Solingen, Germany, is home to around 300 cutlery manufacturers; Omaha, Nebraska, has more hotel reservation systems than any other city in the United States; and the manufacturers of the fastest cars in the world, Lamborghini, Bugatti, and Ferrari, are all located in the town of Modena, Italy (Morgan, 1992).

CHARACTERISTICS OF THE TARGET MARKET   This is covered in the environmental analysis, but an in-depth knowledge of the target customers, especially those living or working in the trade area (local and out-of-town), will greatly assist the location decision. If a business knows what its likely target customers desire, it can better estimate the potential for the location.

BUILDING AND LAND COSTS, EXISTING FEATURES, AND PROJECTED CONSTRUCTION COST   The basic options for restaurants are the following:

1. Purchase an existing restaurant that may or may not require remodeling.
2. Lease a building that must be remodeled.
3. Lease land, then construct a building.
4. Buy the land, then build.
5. Buy the land with an existing building.

The basic options for hotels are the following:

1. Purchase the land, then build the hotel.
2. Take over an existing hotel property (nowadays this is a more frequent option).

For restaurants, the rental factor has historically been approximately 6% of estimated sales. If a restaurant projects sales of $1 million per year, a 6% rental factor would equal $60,000 divided by 12 months, for a monthly rent of $5000 per month. Serious and cautious consideration should be given if a landlord is asking the equivalent of more than 6% of sales for rent. Occasionally, a higher rental factor can be justified because it is an excellent location, and there would hopefully be less of a need to advertise. For example, rather than spending 6% for rent and 5% for advertising (11%), the business might spend 8% for rent and 3% for advertising (also 11%). Another justification for a higher rental factor is if the landlord will include additional funds in the tenant's finish-out allowance (money provided by the landlord to complete a shell—an empty location, or to remodel an existing location) or in the landlord's finish-out (the features the landlord provides in constructing the building). This could include various components of the building such as walls, doors, glass, restrooms, and utilities.

If the location exists, a determination must be made as to whether it is the right size (number of square feet), the right layout and ceiling height, and has the necessary utilities available. Locations with storefronts narrower than 20 feet are difficult for designers to work with and require long walks for service personnel. For rectangular locations, the short side should generally equal at least 40% of the long side. For example, a location with a 40-foot storefront should be no longer than 100 feet (or vice versa). If the previous tenant was a restaurant, the building should be inspected for any usable equipment that was left as part of the building, especially ventahoods, HVAC systems, grease traps, walk-in coolers and freezers, and a water heater. Additional equipment beyond these items is obviously beneficial, but these are the ones that are frequently left behind. Is any of the equipment in operable or repairable condition?

If the desired location is an empty shell, a preliminary estimate of the construction costs should be made. An architect or restaurant designer, for a minimal fee, can draw a rough plan or layout with an exterior elevation (outside appearance). With this drawing of the concept, an experienced restaurant contractor can give a cost estimate within 5% to 10%. If the landlord offers a tenant's finish-out allowance of $30 per square foot and the construction estimate is for $80 per square foot, the estimated construction cost would be $50 per square foot. If the landlord's finish-out includes such features as a concrete slab or exterior walls, inform the contractor.

EMPLOYMENT   What are the problems associated with hiring people in the trade area? Every area has unique characteristics that should be thoroughly researched before a commitment is made. Such factors as the prevailing wages paid to various types of employees; their knowledge, experience, and dependability; and distance from the proposed site will affect the efficiency of operations of the business. Some areas will require hotels and restaurants to pay several dollars above normal wages. In some areas, such as upscale suburban communities or downtown sites, attracting qualified help may be difficult.

MAKING THE FINAL DECISION   Hundreds of hours and many dollars can be spent on the process of deciding on a location. The decision comes down to someone or a group of people agreeing that the location will be suitable for the business and compatible with its image (or desired image for new businesses). The location must inspire confidence and be right for the concept. Ideally, the area should offer a reasonable quality of life for management and employees. Unfortunately, the level of crime should also be factored into the decision. A gut feeling, though important, must be coupled with factual data, justifiable reasons, and a thorough analysis. Many companies will complete location analysis reports covering the topics discussed in this section. If desired, the location can be quantified or graded, such as a location with all the firm's desired characteristics would be an "A" location. Anything less would be an "A−", "B+", and so on.

Typical Considerations for Place Strategies

1. What geographic areas are compatible with the business's concept?
2. Should new types of locations or distribution channels, such as pizza restaurants opening up in convenience stores or smaller hotels in niche markets, be sought out?
3. What parameters should guide the decision of whether a particular location is appropriate?
4. What stage in its life cycle is the location?

PROMOTION

Promotion refers to decisions on how the business will communicate its offering to its customers. In the strategic marketing plan, this is the creation of the promotional campaign. The focus will be on the effective and efficient use of the promotional mix variables of merchandising, advertising, personal selling, public relations, and sales

Merchandising	Primarily in-house promotion of products and services
Advertising	Nonpersonal promotion through a mass medium, by an identified sponsor
Personal selling	Promotion of products and services through personal communications channels
Public relations	Promotion of the company's image, rather than its products and services
Sales promotion	Short-term incentives to increase sales, customer counts, and customer loyalty

Figure 10.5 Promotional mix variables.

promotion (these are briefly defined in Figure 10.5 and discussed in more detail later in the chapter). None of the promotional mix variables (MAPPS) are mutually exclusive. They can be used in any combination. For example, if the business as part of its public relations effort is a major sponsor of a charitable event or cause, it may want to advertise its participation or merchandise it in the business's facility. Sales promotions are generally communicated through advertising and merchandising. Advertising often has the additional purpose of improving public relations (the business's image). Individuals involved in personal selling will always have an effect on public relations.

Promotion is the area of marketing where creativity is most valued and where huge mistakes are frequently made. Have you ever seen a commercial and thought, "How could they think this would get anyone to purchase their product?" There are several possible answers to this question. First, you are not a member of the target audience. The commercial is oriented toward attracting people from another target customer segment, who will hopefully be swayed by what the company is attempting to communicate. Second, it may have been placed in the wrong medium or at the wrong time. A Holiday Inn commercial run during a polo match or equestrian competition would probably not produce its desired results. Third, it could be a lousy commercial. For varying reasons, it simply does not entice or create interest in the minds of the firm's target market. Common reasons for this are inadequate research (not knowing what will attract customers' attention, hold their interest, arouse desire, or get them to act) and poor judgment in the creation of the message or in the production of the commercial.

As shown above, the creative process is more than trying to whimsically offer a set of options. *Creativity* in relation to promotion "deals with the ability to generate fresh, unique, and appropriate ideas that can be used as solutions to communications problems" (Belch & Belch, 1990). The effectiveness of creativity can be increased by the following process:

1. *Preparation.* Gathering information about the issues important to the business's product. This would include the situational analysis and other factors applicable to the potential message or method of communicating it.
2. *Incubation.* After consciously reviewing the information, it is best to let the subconscious take over. This happens automatically if the outcome is important.

3. *Illumination.* Coming up with the solution or the creative means of communicating a message.
4. *Verification.* Editing and refining the solution until it is acceptable to decision-makers (Belch & Belch, 1990).

Promotional Misconception

A common misconception in marketing is that low sales can be rectified almost exclusively by promotion. This occurs because hotel or restaurant managers fail to recognize and identify the root cause of the problem and therefore tend to simplify its solution. Few want to admit that they personally may not be operating their business as it should be, and that perhaps room rates or food prices are relatively high, or food or service quality standards are too low. Of course, the catastrophe here is that customers attracted to these establishments by promotions will usually be from the business's trade area. Once these customers are lost through bad experiences, the hotel or restaurant's customer base will be diluted, greatly reducing any future chances of success. At this point, the marketing department is reduced to the chore of buying new customers, until, finally, there are none left (Reich, 1990). This situation is exponentially worse for restaurants because of their significantly smaller trade areas. Once they lose the target customers in their trade area, there are few left to attract. Hotels, on the other hand, have the advantage of a larger trade area and, consequently, a larger group of target customer who have not had a bad experience.

Promotion is a tool that when wisely used can complement the business's execution of the other marketing mix variables—product, price, and place. If these are not satisfactory, then promotion will only make things worse by exposing more customers to a bad experience. Hospitality firms must make sure that their standards or performances are at a level that will satisfy their target customers enough to make them want to return. The message is: execute the first 3 P's effectively, then promote.

Hotel Promotion

Hotels, because of their unique dispersal of target customers, will need to rely more heavily on promotion than most restaurants. Often, the decision-makers for a hotel stay are individuals such as meeting planners, corporate travel planners, and travel agents who make travel plans for entire firms or associations. These people must be sought out personally by the hotel's sales staff through personal selling. Individual business travelers (IBTs) live almost exclusively in cities outside that of the hotel. This necessitates various types of sales promotions and advertising, not only to attract them to a specific hotel, but to keep the brand name and image of the hotel in the minds of these customers.

Restaurant Promotion

Restaurants are generally in a much different position than hotels. Fast-food restaurants, because of their many locations and relatively undifferentiated products, must continually advertise to keep their brands on the minds of target customers and to convince them that their offering is best. Some spend upward of 10% of sales on promotions. For the majority of casual and fine dining concepts, the primary (or ideal) promotional vehicle is their target customers, or word-of-mouth advertising. Since one of the reasons customers select these restaurants rather than fast food is for a higher level of quality and service, this should be not only the primary focus of the business but also the primary method of promotion. If intense competition requires advertising or sales promotions, then they must be considered, but the objective is to keep present customers returning and bringing their friends and not to have to continually buy new customers. Promotions for these restaurants would preferably be focused on public relations or simply keeping the brand name in the public eye.

Internal Marketing

While the major focus of promotion is the target customer, it must also be realized that businesses must have a similar promotional strategy for employees. This is generally referred to as *internal marketing*—actions to improve employees' attitude and performance. Since the hospitality industry's core product or benefit is a service, its true product is the people who will create and deliver that service—employees. Promotion for employees is usually accomplished through incentives, opportunities for personal growth and advancement, quality management, a good work environment (both for social interaction and physical surroundings), and focusing on the personality of employees (such as Bennigan's Blues Busters). The essential tasks are to attract good employees, train them, motivate them, and retain them. The internal marketing plan would be the responsibility of the human resource department. But because of the impact people have on hospitality firms' marketing (and financial) efforts, cross-functional preparation of the internal marketing plan is imperative.

Advertising Agencies

In view of the complexity of making promotional decisions, the vast majority of firms utilize advertising agencies to take care of anything from production of the commercial or advertisement, to complete responsibility for the promotional campaign. An increasing trend is the creation of *house agencies* to better control promotional efforts, reduce agency charges (commissions, hourly fees, and sometimes fixed charges), and take advantage of typical 15% media commissions (except for outdoor advertising). The primary functional units in an advertising agency and their responsibilities follow.

ACCOUNT EXECUTIVE   The account executive acts as a liaison between the client (advertiser) and the agency, gathering information from the client that will be used by agency staff. Results of the agency's efforts are presented at various stages of production to assure that the client's objectives are being met.

CREATIVE SERVICES   People in this department will be responsible for the creation and production of advertisements and commercials. It is made up of *graphic* *artists* who will create illustrations supportive of the message and design or lay out the advertisement. For television, the graphic artists will assist with the creation of *storyboards,* a series of pictures or photos accompanied by verbal messages and instructions for sound effects, music, and camera techniques. *Copywriters* will create the written information, referred to as *headlines and copy* (body text), that supports the client's objectives. Successful copy should be interesting, concise, believable, simple, and persuasive. *Production personnel* will be responsible for the production of the print ad or commercial. Technology is rapidly simplifying the production process. Most print ads are now produced in-house on computers. Some agencies are using video software and digital cameras to produce their own commercials. The majority of agencies use outside production firms for both radio and television commercials.

MARKETING SERVICES   This will consist of media and research departments. Based on coverages and audiences attracted, the *media* department will develop a media plan that includes the communication channels, specific vehicles (e.g., magazines or programs), and schedules that are most effective at reaching the targeted audience. To make these decisions, media personnel must understand the characteristics of each medium (communication channel), the target customer's media habits, and the number of times the target audience should be exposed to the advertisement. Most advertisements are tested on representatives of the target market before being placed in media. The *research* department gathers information about target customers, various media, spokesperson (generally referred to as "talent") credibility, and the effectiveness of various types of messages and production techniques. Some of this information should be available in the customer analysis portion of the strategic marketing plan. For example, psychographic and buyer behavior information will help determine what type of message will persuade the targeted audience and their media habits. Because of the unique characteristics of certain messages and media, additional information must be gathered, generally from research firms, such as the A. C. Nielsen Company and Arbitron.

AGENCY ALTERNATIVES   For firms that need promotional help, but for various reasons do not want or need a full-service ad agency, there are smaller companies and consultants who perform only specific promotional tasks. *Market research specialists* will compile primary and secondary research to help determine attributes of the target market. *Creative boutiques* can prepare anything from the copy draft to the final commercial. *Media buying services* can help select suitable time (media time) buys. Some media buying services will purchase time in bulk from stations, then resell portions of it to advertisers.

Competitor Analyses

An analysis of each major competitors' strengths, weaknesses, market position, and promotional efforts should be prepared before promotional decisions are made (see Figure 10.6). Ideally, this information is available from the competitor analysis in the

Market _____   **Date** _____

Competitor _____   **Primary/Secondary**
                                             (circle one)

Address _____   **Phone #** _____

_____

Competitor's Strengths:

_____
_____

Competitor's Weaknesses:

_____
_____

Competitor's Promotional Strategies:

Television
Stations used: _____
Message: _____
Approximate reach, frequency, and budget: _____

Radio
Stations used: _____
Message: _____
Approximate reach, frequency, and budget: _____

Electronic media
Vehicles used: _____
Message: _____
Approximate reach, frequency, and budget: _____

Newspapers
Newspapers used: _____
Message: _____
Approximate reach, frequency, and budget: _____

Magazines
Magazines used: _____
Message: _____
Approximate reach, frequency, and budget: _____

Direct mail
Description: _____
Message: _____
Approximate reach, frequency, and budget: _____

Display advertising
Locations used: _____
Message: _____
Approximate reach, frequency, and budget: _____

Figure 10.6   Promotional strategies of competitor.

environmental analysis. This information will help the business determine the advantages it has over its competitors and what promotional strategies are necessary to help it highlight those advantages. The objective will be to develop a promotional message and perhaps promotional offers that will help the business stand out from its competitors. The competitor categories for a restaurant could be primary and secondary competitors. A hotel's competitor analysis could include primary and secondary competitor categories for each of the major markets for which it competes (i.e., group, individual business travelers, leisure travelers, etc.).

Fundamental Tasks of Promotion

For each of the promotional mix variables, a target market must be selected, objectives must be set, a budget must be set, a message must be created, media channels must be selected, and there must be some method or standard to measure outcomes. Figured 10.7 presents a graphic model of these tasks. While the first consideration must always be the target customer and promotional objectives, decisions regarding the budget, message, and media may be made in any order that suits the marketer. If the budget is limited, if a certain communication channel is by far the best for a certain target market, or if a campaign was centered around a specified message, then any of these fundamental tasks could be the guiding factor in the promotional decision. Figure 10.8 displays the relationship of the promotional process with the rest of the marketing plan. This section of the chapter will review many of the techniques and tools at the disposal of marketers that help increase the likelihood of an effective promotional effort.

TARGET MARKET   The target market is the customer segment that makes up a sizable percentage of the business's customer base. Most businesses will have several target markets, while some will have only one. From both the internal and environmental analyses, marketers must accumulate an adequate amount of information about the characteristics of their target markets to help make the various decisions necessary to reach them and to achieve the business's desired overall and promotional objectives.

Quite frequently, fortunes are spent on promotions that are creative and attract much attention but do not achieve any of the firm's promotional objectives. Before any promotion can be considered, marketers must first have an extensive understanding of their target market. Each target market will have relatively homogeneous

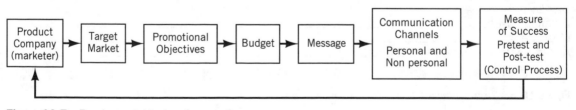

Figure 10.7 Fundamental tasks of promotion.

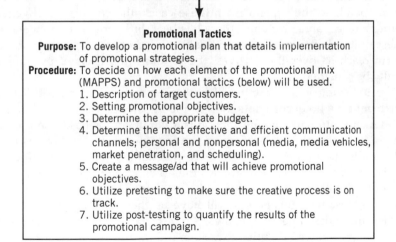

Situational Analysis
Purpose: To determine and understand marketing issues through the development of a SWOT Analysis.
Procedure: An analysis is made of all factors that impact the company and its competitors, including:
1. Size and share of market.
2. Sales history, costs and profits.
3. Current position in market.
4. The nature of that position such as expected changes.
5. Promotional mix strategies.
6. Opportunities to increase sales.
7. Threats that could cause sales to decline.

Marketing Objectives and Strategies
Purpose: To plan activities that will improve the firm's competitive position (take advantage of opportunities and defend against threats).
Procedure: Determine appropriate objectives and effective strategies:
1. Set marketing objectives.
2. Position the company for the future, including identifying the best target markets.
3. Develop products and services.
4. Set prices.
5. Modify current place or distribution strategies as necessary.
6. Decide on elements of the promotion to focus on.

Promotional Tactics
Purpose: To develop a promotional plan that details implementation of promotional strategies.
Procedure: To decide on how each element of the promotional mix (MAPPS) and promotional tactics (below) will be used.
1. Description of target customers.
2. Setting promotional objectives.
3. Determine the appropriate budget.
4. Determine the most effective and efficient communication channels; personal and nonpersonal (media, media vehicles, market penetration, and scheduling).
5. Create a message/ad that will achieve promotional objectives.
6. Utilize pretesting to make sure the creative process is on track.
7. Utilize post-testing to quantify the results of the promotional campaign.

Figure 10.8   Relationship of promotional process and marketing plan.

opinions of products and services, price sensitivity, life-style characteristics, and other segmentation variables. This means that once marketers create the message and decide on communication channels, the general theme of the message should suffice for most members of a particular target market. If there are several different target markets, then several options are available. The simplest communication strategy would be one message and communication channel for all target markets. Next in simplicity would be to keep the same message but utilize different communication channels to reach each specific market. Occasionally, a different message must be created that will be delivered by the same communication channel, or perhaps different channels for each of the business's target markets.

The key consideration for the target market in promotions is that marketers be acutely aware of what it will take to get the customers to think or act as desired. As discussed in the customer analysis section in Chapter 5, factors that motivate people to action can vary considerably. Marketers must find out not only who their target customers are but what it will take to get them to listen and positively act on the firm's promotional message.

PROMOTIONAL OBJECTIVES   Promotions are most effective when there is a specific objective in mind. The characteristics of objectives were discussed in Chapter 7. The primary objectives for the marketing department are normally to increase customer traffic and sales and improve the business's image. If a company has an annual objective of a 10% increase in sales, advertising objectives would likely be developed that were supportive of the sales objective. Supportive advertising objectives could relate to the AIDA hierarchy of promotional goals (attention, interest, desire, and action—explained later in the section on the promotional message).

Frequently, firms spend the majority of their advertising budget without any specific objectives or targets. The thinking is that they have a certain percentage of sales to spend, so they spend it. In these cases, the company has generally been showing a reasonable profit and there has been little pressure to increase the effectiveness of its advertising. To lessen the likelihood of wasting ad dollars and to help the firm reach its overall objectives, the fundamental tasks of promotions should carefully be considered.

The following is an example of how objectives might be set. The marketing department for a hotel considers that people in San Francisco show excellent potential as target customers. Its information is accurate and is based on the fact that for hotels in its segment, 15% of the occupancy comes from San Francisco. Before the hotel can direct its promotional efforts to potential guests, it must find out what it will take to get target customers to visit the hotel. If the target customers have never heard of the hotel, the first objective will be to make them aware of the hotel and its attributes. Most new businesses will have as their first promotional objective to inform or make the target market aware that they exist and extoll their features.

If a survey showed that there was a brand awareness of 5% for the hotel in the San Francisco market, an objective might be to increase the awareness of the hotel in the San Francisco market to 20%. Even though awareness will always be a concern for firms, the ultimate and most beneficial measure is an increase in business from the San Francisco market. If the current sales from the San Francisco market are $200,000 per year, an objective could be to increase them to $600,000.

Frequently, objectives will be set based on the hotel's share of a market. If in this example the hotel's share of the San Francisco market is currently at 3% (of the sales from San Francisco for the hotel's city), the objective could be to increase it to 7%. A related objective for this promotion could be to increase the number of return guests from San Francisco from 50% to 70% (the percentage of customers from San Francisco who return more than once).

PROMOTIONAL BUDGET   There are two major areas: to be concerned with in setting a promotional budget media costs and the overall promotional budget.

The majority of marketing expenses are related to promotional mix variables and marketing-related labor costs. Product, price, and place expenses will generally be limited to research and development and planning time. Even though improvements in decor could theoretically be classified as a marketing cost (the "product" variable of the 4 P's), the standard procedure is to include minor improvements in repairs and maintenance; remodeling of leased space as leasehold improvements; and remodeling of an owned building and the addition of new furniture, fixtures, and equipment as capital expenses.

Many hotels will be able to limit their spending on most areas of the promotional mix (merchandising, advertising, personal selling, public relations, and sales promotions), but the vast majority must utilize some form of personal selling to remain competitive. Personal selling costs, such as salaries and traveling expenses of sales managers, will not normally be classified as promotional expenses but will be grouped as marketing expenses. Since labor costs should always be at a level directly proportional to sales, one of the best ways of holding down marketing department labor costs is to establish sales goals for each sales manager, then monitor and coach performance.

Independent restaurants will focus on their neighborhood or trade area so promotional costs should be limited. Most independent restaurants focus on quality to get customers to return, rather than repeated promotions. Since the trade area for chain restaurants or hotels could include the entire city, state, or country, and differentiation may be limited, costs will be much higher. Focusing on quality experiences and membership programs, such as frequent-guest or dining programs, can help limit promotional expenses.

In addition to traditional external promotional efforts targeted at actual and potential customers, there has been a recent shift to the importance of internal marketing. There are many restaurants that focus entirely on internal marketing, limiting promotions to occasional public relations activities. Figure 10.9 details marketing costs and controls for internal and external promotional strategies.

MEDIA COSTS   Most communications channels can be effective with enough exposure: the key is efficiency or cost relative to other choices. The cost of communications channels is generally measured in two ways. The *absolute cost* is how much the advertiser will pay to the media company for placement of the ad. The absolute cost that can be afforded should carefully be decided, not only by marketers but also by financial managers. What may seem reasonable to the marketing department may seem outrageous to the general manager and managers in other departments. To assess the *relative cost*—the efficiency of the media when compared to the absolute cost—the cost per thousand (CPM) customers or potential contacts is calculated ("M"

Internal Marketing

Cost: Dollars–nonmandated
benefits
Tasks–training, morale
and motivational factors
Effect–long-term
Control: High degree
of control

Management

External Marketing

Cost: Dollars–X % of sales
Tasks–4 P's
Effect–long-term,
promotion is mainly
short-term
Control: High degree, except
for bad publicity

Employees

Actual and Potential
Customers

Interactive Marketing

Cost: Dollars–extra
supervision
Tasks–supervision
of product, price/value,
place and internal
promotion
Effect–long-term
Control: High degree of control

Actual
Customers

Interactive Marketing

Cost: Dollars–None
Tasks–uniqueness,
Quality, and consistency
Effect–long-term
Control: Limited to internal
actions that result in
customer satisfaction

Figure 10.9   Marketing—cost and control.

is the Roman numeral for 1000). While there are other formulas for measuring cost (see below), the advantage of using the CPM method is that different media can be quantitatively compared to one another. Obviously, when comparing the different media, allowances must be made for variations in qualitative effectiveness. While television will often have a greater impact than radio, some radio programs may have a greater impact than many alternative television programs. Many radio talk shows are extremely popular with certain audiences. If the targeted audience closely parallels a business's target market, the program may be more effective and efficient than television. The following are examples of CPM calculations:

- One magazine charges $9000 for a quarter-page ad, while another charges $20,000 for the same size ad. If the target audience or circulation for the $20,000 ad is more than double that of the $9000 ad, then the CPM will be lower for the more expensive ad. For example, an 800,000 circulation for the $9000 time ad equals a CPM of $11.25 ($9000 × 1000 ÷ 800,000 = $11.25), while a 2,000,000 circulation for the $20,000 ad would equal a CPM of $10.00 ($20,000 × 1000 ÷ 2,000,000 = $10,00). The fact that not all readers would necessarily be from the hotel or restaurant's target market may require an additional quantitative estimate of efficiency. For example, if the effective readership or those who are members of the business's target market consisted of 600,000 for the smaller magazine and 900,000 for the larger magazine, their respective effective CPMs would be $15.00 and $22.22. This would reverse the decision on cost effectiveness. The cost of television or radio commercials and newspaper advertisements can be calculated using the same method.

- The CPM for mailings will vary from a low of about $50 ($0.05 $\times$ 1,000 = $50) to $500 and up. The $50 CPM would usually be for what is termed *marriage mail,* where the firm's coupon or flyer is sent with a number of other advertisers by a specialty advertising firm. A relatively inexpensive brochure with a total cost of printing and mailing of $0.50 will have a CPM of $500 ($0.50 $\times$ 1000 = $500). With this increased cost should come increased effectiveness; otherwise, a less expensive medium or form of direct mail must be considered.

There are two other common methods for calculating the cost of a medium. The *milline rate,* used to measure the relative cost of newspaper ads, is the cost per line of space per million of circulation. It is calculated by multiplying the agate line rate (per column line rate) times 1,000,000, then dividing the product by the newspaper's circulation. (For example, $5.85 $\times$ 1,000,000, $\div$ 350,000 = $16.71.)

Occasionally, for television the *cost per rating point (CPRP)* is used. This is calculated by dividing the cost of the commercial by the program rating—the percentage of homes in a survey sample tuned in to a program. For example, the $5000 cost for a 30-second local spot divided by a rating of 35 (35% of the viewers) equals a CPRP of $142.86 (Dunn & Barban, 1978). Assuming that the number of target customers reached was 250,000, the CPM for this spot would be $20 ($5000 $\times$ 1000 $\div$ 250,000).

Through *co-promotions* several hotels in one or several cities or compatible businesses such as airlines and car rental agencies can share the ad or commercial's expense, thereby increasing exposure and/or reducing its absolute cost. Many restaurants and hotels utilize *cooperative advertising* to reduce promotional expenses. Credit card companies and some food and beverage suppliers will pay for a portion of a business's promotional expenses in exchange for mention of their name or use of their logo in the advertisement.

Since most hotels and restaurants are not operating at 100% occupancy or capacity at all times, this excess capacity can be used to *barter* with media companies in exchange for ad space or commercial time. While there are barter firms or third parties that will broker the trade, these should be considered only after careful consideration of monetary costs and obligations. Negotiating the barter agreement is relatively simple. Rather than paying for advertising with dollars, the hotel or restaurant pays with trade credits of rooms and food and beverage. The normal exchange rate will be $1 of services for each $3 of ad space or air time. The reason for this ratio is that the hotel or restaurant has a higher variable cost for each dollar of sales than do media companies. As in any negotiation, it is best to see how desperate the media company is to trade its excess capacity.

PROMOTIONAL BUDGET   The budget required for promotional efforts will be based on many factors, but primarily on sales of the business, geographic disperson of locations and customers, size of the target market, loyalty of customers, brand recognition, strength of the competition, size and ability of the sales staff (hotel sales managers and restaurant servers or counter people), clutter from competitors and others in the same medium, the absolute cost of the medium, cost of the necessary reach and frequency, and production costs. Management's thoughts on the potential of the campaign and what it can afford will also influence the decision. The primary methods of setting a promotional budget include the following:

- *The Affordable Method.* Decide what the company can afford. For many businesses that are short of cash for either opening or operating, this may be the only choice. In many instances, it can actually be the most effective budgeting method. The marketing manager of an existing business could simple focus more on internal marketing in an attempt to minimize the need for advertising. If a new independent restaurant is opening and its trade area is densely populated, many of its potential customers will drive by on a regular basis. This will lead to a greater inclination for word-of-mouth advertising. It will also increase opportunities to visit local businesses that are part of the target market. An additional consideration is that most mass media, other than direct mail, may have too much wasted coverage to be efficient.
- *Objective and Task.* This is essentially just following the basic procedures in the marketing plan: analyze the situation, then set objectives, strategies, and tactics. The objective would be what the marketing department is determined to accomplish. The tasks would include the selection of the media that would most effectively and efficiently communicate the business's message to its target audience. The budget is then set based on the tasks required to meet desired objectives.
- *Percentage of Sales.* A standard percentage is normally between 2% and 4% of sales for hotels and approximately 4% of sales for restaurants. Each figure can vary dramatically depending on the business's market segment and competitive position. A resort hotel, because of its location, will usually need to spend more than hotels in business districts. Some fast-food restaurants will spend over 6% for local promotions and another 2% to 3% for national campaigns. A problem with the percentage of sales method of setting a budget is that it assumes that sales are the cause of promotional expenditures, rather than the other way around. For example, if sales are high, then promotional expenditures are high at a time when they may not be necessary. If sales are low, promotional budgets are also low, but at a time when they should possibly be increased.
- *Competitive Parity.* This means spending about as much as the business's primary competitors. The degree to which this budgeting method should be followed will depend primarily on the loyalty of a business's customers. A few restaurants spend almost nothing on promotions except for public relations and merchandising. Some hotels spend little or nothing on advertising, focusing mainly on personal selling and public relations. These are the exception, rather than the rule. Most hotels and restaurants will need to spend varying amounts on promotions because they need to attract new customers to replace those who are lost to competitors or who no longer live or work in the area.

Even though each is important, ideally, final decisions will be based primarily on the objective and task method. The percentage of sales will usually set the upper limit. Competitive parity will be factored in to objective decisions, by answering questions such as, "Are we as visible in the market and media as our competitors?" and "To what degree does competitive parity on promotional budgets dictate success

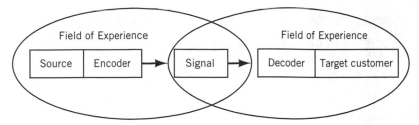

Figure 10.10 Communicating a message. *Source:* Adapted from Dunn & Barban (1978). *Advertising: Its Role in Modern Marketing*, 4th ed. Chicago: Dryden Press, p. 46.

in our market?" The affordable method is the least attractive choice, especially if promotions beyond the business's budget are needed. The budget should be prepared with cooperation of applicable personnel from finance, operations, purchasing, human resources, and administrative management.

MESSAGE   The message generally refers to the *overall message* that the business is attempting to communicate. It can also refer to a *headline* (attention-getting / grabbing word or words), *slogan* (a single word or a few vivid words that describe something important about the product that advertisers want the target audiences to remember), *copy* (written or verbal text), or *illustration* (pictures or graphics). The message can also refer to an individual advertisement or commercial or to an entire *campaign* (a series of coordinated promotional efforts designed to communicate a specific message). The purpose of the message is to provide target audiences with something to consider or think about before their next purchase of products or services sold by the advertiser. They help set the mental agenda for the customer's product ladder—the alternatives that will be considered before a purchase is made. Essentially, the customer first travels mentally, then physically. A desired objective of a message is that it should be of sufficient quality to raise the advertised firm one or more rungs on the customer's product ladder. Few messages will tell customers what to think: that is, the vast majority of people will not act without some degree of rational decision-making process—in this case, an existing need or want for the product and the consideration of alternatives. Sometimes it is not so much the message but the frequency with which the business can afford to communicate it (Sutherland, 1993).

Figure 10.10 traces the essential process for communicating a message. First, the firm must create or *encode* a message that will promote a favorable and desired reaction from the target customer. For the message to reach the target customer, an effective communication channel or *signal* must be sought. Finally, the target customer will hear the message and interpret or *decode* not only its meaning but also its impact based on a lifetime of experiences.

The creation of the ad and its message are generally influenced by the following questions.

What is the objective of the promotion? Not all messages are designed to sell a product; in fact, most are simply to provide information about the product or service.

OBJECTIVES OF COMMUNICATION

1. Get   *Attention*
2. Hold   *Interest*
3. Arouse   *Desire*
4. Obtain   *Action*

Figure 10.11   AIDA response hierarchy model.

For example, if a customer has not yet visited a certain hotel or restaurant, an advertisement will be but one factor in a series that may be necessary to induce a purchase. There are many different response hierarchy models that present the various objectives of promotional communication. The theory is that the firm must decide at what level in the selected hierarchy various potential and actual customers are, then attempt to move them along to the next level. The ultimate objective is to persuade potential customers to make a purchase and existing customers to return on a regular basis (Powers, 1990). One of the most popular hierarchies is the *AIDA model* (see Figure 10.11). This acronym stands for attention, interest, desire, and action. If a firm is new or promoting a specialty product, then its initial goals may be to attract attention and interest in their firm or its products and services. Later ads in a series would have the objective of arousing desire and obtaining action. Since the AIDA response hierarchy is often used to set objectives of promotional communications, it can be also be used to measure the success of a particular advertisement. For example, if the objective included any of the first three steps in the hierarchy, success could be measured with a questionnaire. If the objective was action, then success could be measured by sales or inquiries.

What is the creative strategy? Normally, the first task is to decide on the *creative strategy* (or *copy theme*), the message that will be conveyed to target customers. A creative strategy must be developed that determines which of the product's attributes or benefits to promote. This could be value, convenience, quality, status, luxury, and so forth. Because people tend to think more about what is important than what is not, it is critical that the message being promoted is important to customers. In marketing terms, this is referred to as *salience.* Through research, marketers must determine which tangible and intangible attributes are considered important or salient, and how target customers prioritize them. If the message then focuses on what is important to customers, they will begin to associate that issue with the brand. Before any creative work begins, the attribute or key benefit must be determined.

A restaurant promoting its expensive or stylish decor will find few people who value decor over a quality dining experience. Between the late 1980s and early 1990s,

Taco Bell could have chosen to focus on speed, convenient locations, or nutritional quality, but the company realized that their target customers' primary concern was value, so that was used as their copy theme. Value was considered both salient and a "big idea" to their target customers. In the mid-1990s, as their customers' concerns changed to nutrition, so did the company's promotions and product offerings.

In addition to being important to the customer, the message should ideally contain something referred to as *the big idea*. People rarely watch television or listen to the radio for the commercials. Readership of newspapers and magazines for the ads will vary with the specific publication and the target audience. For the message to be effective in the clutter of advertisements, it must have something that jolts the consumer out of indifference and gets him/her to pay attention and take action. For the message to stand out, it must be outstanding (Dunn & Barban, 1978).

The degree of success of the message will be tied to the credibility of the firm to deliver on the promise and the consistency with which the firm has delivered on the issue in the past. Any advertisement can only be as good as the product it promotes. Also, if past messages were not successfully delivered for past promotions, then audiences will be skeptical. With a large enough budget, potential customers can be led to believe anything within reason, but, once their experience does not meet their expectations, then the customer may be lost forever. In other words, if the company's strengths are also desired attributes of its target customers, then this is what should generally be promoted. Focusing on customer-valued strengths allows a business to promote and establish meaningful differences between itself and competitors, increasing its customer loyalty and brand equity (the intangible value of the company name and image). Any firm that cannot match up a strength with important attributes (opportunities) must consider what it can do to remedy the situation.

What reward will be offered? Closely tied to the creative strategy is the reward or benefit that customers will derive from a purchase. Generally, a person does not buy or consider buying something unless there is a tangible or intangible, immediate or future, benefit. Without the reward, the consumer may not have a reason either to switch from a current brand or to continue purchasing a specific brand.

What creative tactics will be used? After the message or creative strategy is set, *creative tactics* must be developed to communicate the message. This would include coming up with an attention-grabbing headline, the copy (also body text or body copy) that should support the headline, an illustration (picture or graphics), and visualization or artwork for a proposed television commercial (see Figure 10.12). Occasionally, the most effective method of attracting attention to an ad or commercial is the headline (written or spoken), but generally, it is the illustration that first draws people in. Few words can compete with a picture of an experience that target customers find desirable. A creative illustration enables customers to imagine themselves in the scene. It is also as close as a mass medium can get to the real product. For these reasons, a common procedure is to prepare the illustration or storyboard first, then to prepare supportive headline and copy.

How many of the attributes or benefits should be promoted? Customers tend to become confused if an ad makes too many claims, or if the features promoted are changed

VERBAL SYMBOLS	NONVERBAL SYMBOLS
Headlines	Illustrations (pictures)
Copy	Layout/design (where everything goes)
Slogans	Typography (fonts)
Brand names	White space (to attract attention and differentiate ad from others in the communications medium)
Lyrics	Color
	Motion
	Expression
	Voice
	Music
	Sound effects

TV

All of the above

RADIO

Copy
Voice
Music
Sound effects

PRINT AND DISPLAY

Headline
Copy
Illustrations
Color
Layout/design
White space

Figure 10.12 Components of mass media. *Source:* Adapted from Dunn & Barban (1978). *Advertising: Its Role in Modern Marketing*, 4th ed. Chicago: Dryden Press.

too frequently. The best ads promote a single tangible or intangible benefit. This benefit could be supported by several features, but the focus would still be singular.

What type of appeal or attempt to sway the target market would be most effective? A *moral appeal* asks the audience to consider what the right thing to do is. Taking care of one's family through recreation, relaxation, quality time, education, and good nutrition are common moral appeals used by hospitality firms. A *rational appeal* relates to the audience's reasoned values or better judgment. If the company's products and services do a good job of meeting the expectations of the target market at a reasonable price, then some aspect of the promotional message could center around this fact. If a business charges more than most primary competitors, then it must give customers information that will help them rationalize a purchase decision. An *emotional appeal* stirs up positive sentiments about the firm's product, service, or core values. These sentiments can be based on subconscious motivations, such as when comedy, sexuality, self-esteem, or vanity are used to highlight, or in some cases exaggerate, tangible or intangible attributes. Sometimes businesses will focus not on promoting their business but on the image of the people that patronize their business. Marketers know that few consumers will go to a restaurant or stay in a hotel where they either do not have something in common with other customers or would not like to associate with these other customers. This association could be physical or psychological. There are many restaurants that become tremendous successes simply because some opinion leader, such as the mayor or a local sports hero, dines there on a regular basis. An emotional appeal is sometimes used to create negative feelings about competitors. This appeal could be targeted directly at a certain competitor or competitors in general.

In deciding what type of appeal to use, the marketer must consider what the primary motivating factor is for the target customer. Some hospitality consumers will focus on purchasing what they need based solely on the need; others will focus on purchasing what they need based on what they want, and still others will simply purchase what they want, without consideration of need. Each level of motivation will require a different promotional appeal. To clarify, everyone needs to eat and, when traveling, everyone needs to find a place to sleep. If the only concern for customers was meeting their needs, then quality or features (perhaps other than sanitation) would not be much of an issue. Anything within reason that meets their needs would suffice. For these customers, a rational appeal would likely be the most successful, usually one related to price. While there are a good many consumers in this "needs only" category, the majority of consumers will base their purchases on both what they need *and* want. Wants concern the purchase of something that is not only physically necessary but also psychologically satisfying. It is not necessary that travelers stay at the Hilton, but if this is the level of service and quality required to make them feel comfortable, then the cost is justified. Since these customers must be satisfied on two levels, a combination of appeals would generally be most effective. A rational appeal would be used, supported with either an emotional or moral appeal. Then, in the last category, there are those who can make purchases based primarily on what they want. For these customers, the primary appeal will be emotional, with some level of support from rational or moral appeals. The support from secondary appeals would be to bolster customers' egos so that they do not feel that they are engaging in conspicuous consumption. It is not likely that a traveler would suffer undue harm while foregoing a luxury hotel in favor of an upper-midscale property, so to help support the decision, the hotel must support the emotional appeal of status with some rational (or possibly moral) basis for the decision, such as service that improves the guest's productivity (Bly, 1993).

Will left-brain, right-brain, or whole-brain advertising be required? The left side of the brain is the location where analytical processes take place; the right side is where creative thinking occurs. The degree to which one or the other is required depends on whether emotional or rational thinking is required to induce a purchase. An ad for an upscale business hotel that appeals exclusively to the left brain may alter the consumer's image of the company or its products or services, but it will not likely result in a purchase. If right-brain advertising or information were included, such as status or royal treatment, the ad's effectiveness would likely improve. Products with limited differentiation will need to use right-brain advertising (creative) or convince the left brain (analytical) through price incentives (Rapp & Collins, 1987).

What tone would be most effective? Is *humor* appropriate, or should the ads have a *serious* demeanor? Generally, the greater the level of service provided, the less likely humor will be work. Where Garfield may have been effective for Embassy Suites, it would probably not be appropriate for the Ritz-Carlton. The Garfield promotional campaign, using a humorous tone and an emotional appeal, was quite successful at targeting and increasing Embassy Suites' family leisure business. However, its problem was that it was not rated highly by business guests: perhaps too much of a right-brain, emotional appeal, rather than left-brain, rational appeal. The hotel's next campaign is using a more serious tone and rational appeal targeted at business travelers. The new campaign is centered around the slogan, "Twice as Nice," referring to their two-room suites.

Which should be used—believability or exaggeration? The importance of believability will depend on the context of the ad. If the company's claims are exaggerated and it can obviously not deliver on what is the equivalent of a promise, then consumers will not only ignore the ad but likely develop a poor image of the company. If the ad exaggerates benefits or features in a humorous way to make a point, then believability and credibility should not be an issue. In the latter case, image, awareness, or interest, rather than immediate sales (action), would be the objective.

What presentation technique should be used? The *slice-of-life* technique presents the firm's product or service as the solution to a problem. Someone, perhaps a celebrity spokesperson, could talk about their experiences with the product, a *testimonial*. To create a novel approach to communication, *animation* such as cartoons or claymation can be used. The *fantasy* technique presents the product in an unusual or exaggerated setting. The purpose is twofold—to attract the target audience's attention and to get customers to visualize themselves in the situation. *Dramatization* involves telling an exciting or suspenseful story involving the product. The basic process of dramatization includes setting the stage for the story, identifying the problem, intensifying the problem or conflict, and then solving the problem with the advertiser's product (Belch & Belch, 1990).

Does the message clearly and simply position the product? There are only 15 to 30 seconds for the average commercial and a limited amount of time during which a consumer will focus on a print ad. If the ad is to make an impact, the message must quickly communicate what the product is, who it is for, and why it should be purchased (Belch & Belch, 1990). Promotional mix variables should always be supportive of the business's desired position in the market.

Who will deliver the message? Is it worth the cost of hiring a recognized *spokesperson?* When a celebrity is hired, he/she should have some knowledge or expertise about the product or service being sold. The spokesperson should also be likeable and trustworthy (Kotler & Armstrong, 1990). Ideally, the message would be good enough to stand on its own without a costly celebrity. Major problems can occur when a company ties itself closely to a celebrity who falls out of favor with the target market.

What will be the effect of the message? If the company is taking the time and effort to create an advertisement, it should make sure that it has the potential to be effective. There is an old saying in the advertising business, "Half of my advertising dollars are wasted, but I don't know which half!" The concerns and personal preferences of executives are important, but the true test of an ad should be the effect it has on members of the firm's target market. An ad may be cute and make management feel good, but the customer must be the primary consideration. In most cases, ads should be pretested on members of the business's target market (this is discussed in more detail in measures of success).

Should color be used? Studies have shown that the use of color increases audience interest and response by between 50% and 80% (Dunn & Barban, 1978). The problem is that the increase is often not as much as the increased cost in terms of readers per dollar. For example, if the cost for color was twice as high and yielded an increased response rate of 50%, then the business would likely be better off using a black and white ad and perhaps increasing the number of placements. Another option would be to increase the amount of white space in the ad. In television, color is almost mandatory. In other media, its use should be analyzed in light of the incremental increase in audience interest and recall.

COMMUNICATIONS CHANNELS   Marketers can select among various types of *personal and nonpersonal communications channels.* Personal channels include strategies such as personal selling and public relations by employees and management and focus on increasing the level of word-of-mouth advertising of its customers. For *nonpersonal communications channels,* or mass media, there are five primary choices: *broadcast* (television, radio), *electronic* (computers and fax machines), *print* (newspapers, magazines, and newsletters), *direct mail,* and *display* (billboards, signs/posters). How and where a business promotes its offer will be based primarily on its target market and the relative cost and efficiency of the medium.

Corporate headquarters for chain hotels and restaurants will focus much of their promotional efforts on broadcast media. Individual hotels will divide their promotional efforts among personal selling, print, and broadcast media. Hotels and restaurants that are part of a franchise must normally spend a minimal percentage of their sales for advertising and sales promotions. Individual restaurants will use mass media to the extent they have penetrated their respective markets. The current trend for restaurants is to limit advertising, focusing more on internal aspects of marketing, such as good food and reasonable prices—the objective being to increase word-of-mouth advertising. The following discussions on various types of media will apply to advertising, sales promotions, and some public relations and merchandising efforts.

BROADCAST MEDIA   The 21st century will see rapid changes in broadcast media. As consumers become accustomed to technological advances and the conveniences they bring, the role of broadcast media in the marketing of goods and services will significantly expand. Currently, the varying types of direct response advertising, such as the Home Shopping Network and QVC (purchasing products as they are advertised on television and/or radio) are beginning to modify traditional distribution channels. Because of these advances, the use of broadcast media will likely outpace most other forms of media, with the possible exception of electronic media. Much of the growth in broadcast media will come from an increasing variety of cable channels with smaller, highly targeted audiences. This will lead to more effective and efficient use of television advertising, allowing for more local advertising, rather than the current preponderance of national network advertising. Governmental support for public broadcasting will also likely be cut, increasing pressures to allow for paid advertising. If this occurs, and is accomplished in a manner acceptable to viewers, it will become one of the most effective and efficient means of reaching heavy-user, highly attentive, upscale audiences.

There are two primary types of broadcast media, *radio* and *television*. The first radio advertising occurred in Pittsburgh, Pennsylvania, in 1919 on a station where the Hamilton Music Store received endorsements from program hosts in return for loaning records to the station. The first national television commercials were placed by the Texaco Oil Company in 1948 on the Texaco Star Theater that starred comedian Milton Berle.

There are likewise two different forms of operation for radio and television stations: *commercial stations and networks* are supported by advertising and *public broadcasting* is supported by donations and grants. Major donors of public broadcasting receive recognition through *courtesy announcements* during programs they sponsor.

Broadcast Campaigns.   Campaigns can be based on program affiliation or announcements. *Program or sponsorship campaigns* call for the sponsorship of selected programs whose target audiences match characteristics of the firm's target market. Traditionally, the firm would pay for advertising time and for the production of the program. Because of the high expenses associated with many television programs, program campaigns for television audiences are becoming less common. Program campaigns on radio can be very effective when the firm's target market thinks highly of the sponsored program. *Announcement or participation campaigns* are spread over different programs so that the advertiser's budget achieves a broader reach at a lower expense. This category contains the vast majority of broadcast advertising.

Ad Placement.   Broadcast ad placement is divided into three categories based on the desired geographic coverage and the ad's source. *Network advertising* is broadcast simultaneously over two or more network stations (i.e., stations in different cities). This is normally purchased on a national basis by major firms. *National or regional spot advertisements* are placed normally by hotel or restaurant chains (national or regional chains) in selected cities on specific programs where the target audience is closely aligned with the firm's target customers. *Local advertising* is the term applied when local firms advertise in the city in which they operate (Zeigler & Howard,

1991). Advertisements on cable channels can be purchased on a national, regional, or local basis. Superstations, such as WOR in New York, WGN in Chicago, and WTBS in Atlanta, offer national exposure at much lower rates than network stations.

Broadcasting Dayparts.   Commercial time is normally sold based on its daypart and the particular program that will be shown during that daypart. Rates are based on the size of the program's audience as measured by research firms, such as the A. C. Nielsen Company or Arbitron. A. C. Nielsen Company prepares the Nielsen Station Index (NSI) that measures over 200 U.S. markets, known as *designated market area* (*DMAs*). Arbitron similarly measures over 200 U.S. markets, referred to as *areas of dominant influence* (*ADIs*). Each of these areas consists of nonoverlapping counties that view the local major market station over 50% of the time. The reports include audience estimates by daypart, time period, and program. If a hotel was attempting to target housewives, then soap operas aired during daytime television would likely be effective. If a restaurant wanted to target adult males between the ages of 21 and 45, Saturday and Sunday afternoon sports programs or Monday night football may be good choices.

Common Television Dayparts

(Central time zone will be one hour earlier)

Early morning	Sign on to 10 a.m.
Daytime	10 a.m. to 4:30 p.m.
Early fringe	4:30 p.m. to 8:00 p.m.
Prime time	8:00 p.m. to 11:00 p.m.
Late news	11:00 p.m. to 11:30 p.m.
Late fringe	11:30 p.m. to 1:00 a.m.

Common Radio Dayparts

Morning drive time	6 a.m. to 10 a.m.
Daytime	10 a.m. to 3 p.m.
Afternoon/evening drive time	3 p.m. to 7 p.m.
Nighttime	7 p.m. to 12 a.m.
All night	12 a.m. to 6 a.m.

Advantages of Broadcast Media

- *Immediacy.* Radio and television commercials, once produced, can be aired flexibly at desired times on selected media with little advance notice. (Network television will have a longer closing period/lead time.)
- *Media Penetration.* Over 99% of the American public own either radios or televisions.
- *Level of Exposure.* Radio and television advertisers have the flexibility to select *low-intensity, maintenance,* or *saturation campaigns.*

- *Popularity.* Next to work and sleep, radio and television usage is the third most popular activity of the average American.
- *Targetability.* Cable and radio programs allow advertisers to efficiently reach audiences who closely match the characteristics of the business's target market. With the variety of radio programs and the number of cable programs growing almost daily, targeting one's market will become less complicated.
- *Use of Sound.* The sound of the human voice increases the likelihood of the message's effectiveness and spokesperson's persuasiveness. Music and sound effects can help communicate the message and its appeal. A successful jingle—music generally with lyrics (words) written exclusively for a commercial—will have people either humming the tune or recalling the tune long after the last time they heard the commercial. "Two all-beef patties, special sauce, . . ." certainly worked well for McDonald's.
- *Integration of Message with Medium.* When a commercial is run on radio or television, the audience will *generally* hear or see it. Additionally, the message to be communicated is the choice of the broadcaster or advertiser, not the consumer. In other forms of media, the consumer has greater flexibility to decide whether or not to be exposed to a message. Zapping is of course decreasing the viability of this advantage.

Advantages Unique to Television

- *Personal Message.* A spokesperson on television is the electronic equivalent of person-to-person selling. Spokespersons in the more successful commercials give audiences the feeling that they are being personally told about the product or service.
- *Visual Component.* The elements of motion, if used effectively, have the power to create a greater interest in the firm's message than sight or sound by themselves. Television can take audiences on a moving tour of a facility or bring products or services to life.
- *Mass communication.* Even though network television is losing some of its dominance to cable channels, it is still the medium that comes closest to garnering a mass audience.
- *Cost.* Cable channels have brought the cost of television advertising to within the budget of most businesses. In some markets, 15-second cable spots are around $10.

Advantages Unique to Radio

- *Stimulates Imagination.* Effectively used, radio has the ability to customize a message by communicating general concepts, then letting audiences complete the picture. A commercial during evening drive time with words like "sizzling," backed up with applicable sound effects and other verbal descriptions, can induce hungry listeners to salivate.
- *Cost.* Radio is the least expensive method of reaching a national market. Costs on some network programs (ABC, CBS, Westwood, and United Stations) will start at about $5000, with a CPM in the $3 to $4 range. Typical 30- and 60-second commercials in local markets will range from around $10 to over $1000 (see Figure 10.13). Production costs are also reasonable for radio. Someone simply reads a script, then

DAY	DAYPART	RATE
Monday–Friday	6 a.m.–10 a.m.	$ 165
Monday–Friday	10 a.m.–3 a.m.	165
Monday–Friday	3 p.m.–8 p.m.	140
Monday–Friday	8 p.m.–midnight	80
Saturday	8 a.m.–8 p.m.	85
Saturday	8 p.m.–midnight	85
Sunday	8 a.m.–noon	120
Sunday	12 noon–midnight	60
Monday–Sunday	midnight–5:30 a.m.	20

All rates are for 60-second commercial ads. Package and long-term scheduling will reduce commercial rates.

Figure 10.13 Station KLTE rate sheet.

music and possibly sound effects are added. If celebrity talent (spokesperson) is used, then costs can quickly escalate. Radio production costs will often be included at no cost if enough time on the station is purchased.

- *Fidelity.* The quality of sound on most FM stations will often surpass that of television.
- *Targetability.* The majority of stations have well-defined target audiences (see Figure 10.14). Options include rock 'n' roll, classical, country western, tejano, reggae, talk radio, and so on.
- *Flexibility.* Since airing a radio commercial requires little more than playing a taped or digital recording, most radio stations have very short closing periods.

Disadvantages of Broadcast Media

- *No Permanence.* Radio and television lack the permanence of print media. Once the message is aired, it is gone.
- *Zapping.* With the proliferation of remote controls and numerous quality radio stations, a high percentage of viewers are "zapping" commercials in favor of seeing or listening to what is on other stations. Also, the commercial breaks on television are often a time for people to take care of personal needs, such as getting something to eat or drink and restroom breaks. This is one of the reasons that for a commercial to be effective, it must be as interesting to watch as the media vehicle to which it is tied. Rarely will someone call the family in to watch a commercial, but this standard should be considered. Krystal's Hamburgers scored big with body-

Ownership	Harry Abrams Broadcasting, Inc.
Dial position	102.5 FM
Power	150,000 watts at 1650 feet above average terrain
Hours	24 hours daily
Format	Soft adult contemporary
	KLTE is a music-intensive, adult contemporary station programming "lite" rock hits from 1970 to the present. KLTE creates an environment that is always soft and familiar: music with a tempo, but without an edge.
Target audience	Upscale women 25–44
News	News briefs twice hourly 6 a.m.–9 a.m., Monday–Friday
Network	CBS-FM
Inventory	9 units (60-second ads) per hour at :10, :30, and :50.
Features	(1) K-LITE Festival—contemporary jazz and blues Friday and Saturday nights 8 p.m.–midnight
Target audience	Upscale women and men 25–44
	(2) K-LITE JAZZ—soft jazz Sunday mornings 8 a.m.–12 noon
Target audience	Upscale women and men 35–44

Figure 10.14 Station KLTE profile.

less Bob, a spokesperson without a torso. Each commercial has a message that was communicated through a short comic skit. Grey Poupon's commercial with the flatulating plastic container and the English gentleman's response of "pardon me!" was also quite successful at keeping its audience tuned in and focused.

- *Low Attention Level.* Radio audiences rarely actively listen to commercials. If the commercial is on a talk radio program, the listener is much less likely to mentally tune-out the commercial.
- *High Absolute Cost of Television.* Because of the cost of equipment, personnel involved, and increased intricacy, television commercials are considerably more expensive than those for radio. Television production costs vary from a few thousand dollars for local efforts to over a million dollars for commercials using expensive production effects and celebrity talent. Most are in the low $100,000 range.

  Though television ads are quite expensive in absolute terms, when the CPM or relative cost per 1000 exposures is calculated, it can often be quite reasonable. Thirty-second ads on national television networks (NBC, ABC, CBS, and Fox) will vary in cost from below $40,000 to around $1,000,000 (Superbowl), based on the time and program on which it is aired.

- *Long Closing Times for Television.* Commitments for network time must be made well in advance of the actual airing of commercials. If there is a major change in strategy, the flexibility of opting out of time commitments may be limited.

- *Clutter.* Some radio and television stations will run up to 15 minutes of commercials per hour. Because of this, a commercial that is not exceptional will not be able to "break through the clutter" and therefore will not be heard.
- *Wasted Coverage.* Because of the wide coverage of most broadcast media vehicles, there is generally a large amount of excess exposure.
- *Fragmented Audiences.* Once an advertiser gets beyond network television, very few television or radio programs can deliver much more than 5% to 10% of the market. This requires buys on several stations. If radio were selected as the major medium for a national or regional campaign, time would have to be purchased on potentially hundreds of radio stations as opposed to up to four network television stations.
- *Distrust of Broadcast Media.* Because of many questions about the ethics of advertisements, especially commercials targeted toward children and senior citizens, there is a sizable number of people who have a low opinion of television and radio commercials.

ELECTRONIC MEDIA   Various forms of electronic media such as computers and fax machines are quickly increasing in importance to marketers. Currently, the *Internet* is not an overly effective means of advertising, but it is quickly gaining ground. New promotional concepts are being introduced on the Internet on nearly a weekly basis. However, before the Internet can become a force in promotion, customers' affinity for the traditional media of television, radio, magazines, and newspapers will have to diminish. This will likely happen, but the evolution will take some time. Those in the forefront with creative use of the Internet can speed up this evolution and, concurrently, improve their image with upscale customers and be recognized as leaders in the movement. Most major cities have consulting services for firms that want to establish their own *home page*—a point of access on the Internet where information about a business can be displayed. MenuNet of Chicago, Illinois, has started a nationwide restaurant directory on Internet called *Dining Oasis*. Restaurants will be able to promote themselves under such subject headings as geographic location, cuisine, atmosphere, and price.

Faxes (facsimile machines) that transmit printed material over telephone lines have become quite popular for many advertisers. It has also become somewhat of a nuisance for many businesses that must pay for receiving supplies (paper, ink, and equipment) and receive an abundance of extraneous faxes along with important business correspondence. Unless customers request specific information over a fax line, it is generally best not to utilize this channel of communication. Several restaurants that tried it have gone back to direct mail and other media because of complaints.

PRINT MEDIA   While electronic media consume a large piece of the hospitality communications pie, print media are still an effective means of reaching many target audiences. Because people read newspapers and magazines by choice, they are considered *high involvement media.* Television audiences are generally passively waiting for the program to resume. Radio listeners will likely be paying closer attention to driving, work, or some other activity during a commercial.

Newspapers.   Currently, newspaper readership is on the decline, while magazine readership is increasing. Nationally, just over 60% of American households take a newspaper and many of the regular readers are senior citizens (Belch & Belch, 1990). There are still large targetable segments of the population who will read the paper for specific purposes, such as for the travel, food, coupon, sports, or business sections. For this reason, it should not be ruled out as a potentially viable medium. Just over one-fourth of all advertising dollars are spent in newspapers, with the majority of this amount being for retail businesses. Newspaper advertising for hospitality businesses is normally limited to hotel promotions placed in travel sections and coupon inserts for fast-food restaurants.

The majority of newspapers are daily city newspapers. Small towns will generally have weekly editions. National newspapers, such as *USA Today* and the *Wall Street Journal,* and special audience newspapers, such as *Hotel and Motel Management* and *Nation's Restaurant News,* account for most of the remaining categories.

Newspapers charge by the agate line or by the column inch. An *agate line* is $\frac{1}{14}$ inch deep by one column wide. For the majority of newspapers one column is $2\frac{1}{16}$ inches wide. A *column inch* would be 1 inch deep (high) by one column wide. These measurements are known as *standard advertising units* (SAUs).

The two primary types of ads in newspapers are display and classified. *Display ads* will be the traditional form, consisting of a headline, illustration, and copy, and will vary in size from one or two column inches to a full page. If the advertiser wants the ad to be in a specific location in the newspaper, then there will be an extra charge, referred to as the *preferred position* rate. If the ad can be placed anywhere in the paper, it is referred to as *run of paper.* As long as the request is reasonable, many newspapers will not charge preferred position rates. *Classified ads* are primarily copy only and are normally inserted in the classified section with ads of a similar nature. If a display ad is placed in the classified section, it is called a classified display ad.

If the target market is very large or widespread, as for chain restaurants and hotels, then newspapers and magazines (also television and radio) may be effective. Independent restaurants will generally find that city newspapers reach too many customers outside their target market to be cost effective. Consider the following: a restaurant chain has three locations in a city; the average number of customers per month, per restaurant, is 5000 (30 days times 500 customers per day equals 15,000 customers per month divided by the average number of visits per customers of 3, equals an average of 5000 customers per restaurant); and the newspaper readership for the city is 300,000. Theoretically, the small restaurant chain has 15,000 customers, so there would be a potential wasted coverage of 285,000 or 95% (285,000 ÷ 300,000 = 95%). Expressed in other terms, 95% of what was paid for in this media vehicle would not be read by present customers. If the objective was to attract new customers or to improve the restaurant's image, the expenditure would still be questionable.

If an independent hotel's primary market was not in its home city, then for reasons similar to the restaurant example above, the city newspaper may not be effective at reaching target guests.

Advantages of Newspapers

- *Widespread Readership.* Between 50% and 70% of the households in most cities receive a daily newspaper.
- *Targetability.* Both national and many city newspapers will have special editions for certain regions or neighborhoods.
- *Short Lead Time.* Closing time for ads are sometimes only 24 hours before the paper is printed.

Disadvantages of Newspapers

- *Poor Reproduction Quality.* Both print and pictures are not as clear as magazines. The ink smears.
- *Wasted Coverage.* (Previously explained.)
- *Short Life.* Most people throw away newspapers the day after they are received. For this reason, an ideal newspaper ad should be one that the consumer is likely to cut out of the paper.
- *Clutter.* The average newspaper consists of about 65% advertising, leaving 35% for editorial content. This is a higher percentage of advertising than any other major medium.

Magazines.   Magazine readership is increasing for several reasons. Currently, people are more concerned with information than they were in the past. Careers can hinge on knowledge that often can only be found in various types of magazines. There is also a greater variety of magazines than in the past, the majority of which are targeted at narrow markets. This allows for more effective targeting at costs well below those of magazines with large circulations and multiple target markets. If a hotel wanted to target women between the ages of 21 and 35 with household incomes over $40,000, who make family travel decisions, there are magazines whose subscribers would closely parallel these demographic and buyer behavior requirements. Most national magazines have regional editions targeted at specific geographic areas. *Newsweek,* for example, divides the United States into 11 geographic regions. This allows advertisers to more efficiently target their selected markets, reducing wasted coverage.

Magazine circulation is quoted in two ways. *Primary circulation* is the total number of magazines that were sold to the original purchaser. The original purchase may have been through a subscription or at a newsstand (retail) of some type. *Total audience* includes primary circulation and *passalong readers*—the estimate for the average number of people other than the original purchaser who read the magazine.

There are three broad classifications of magazines: consumer, farm, and business magazines. For advertising purposes, consumer and business magazines are of most interest to the hospitality industry. Various farm publications, such as *Progressive*

Farmer and *Hog Farm Management,* are sources of research information for chains that make large-scale commodity purchases. Within the consumer classification there are numerous publications that appeal to consumers from virtually every target market segment. The most effective magazines for hotels and restaurants deal with life-style issues, essentially concerning how to live the "good life." These magazines cover topics such as travel, leisure pursuits, sports, the environment, camping, and cooking. Business magazines are normally either targeted toward the general business market (*BusinessWeek, Fortune, Inc., Forbes*) or to specific businesses (*Hotels, Restaurant Business*).

Because of the clutter in most forms of mass media, it is critical that the promotional effort stand out. The first step in this process is to examine competing ads in the same medium to determine what will be noticed. To help magazine ads stand out, advertisers use a variety of graphic techniques, such as white space, where the majority or at least a large portion on a page is blank; colorful or heavy borders; bold colors; bleed pages, where the color goes beyond the normal boundary; gatefolds, a triple page spread where the third page folds out; special inserts that tend to fall out in the reader's lap; half a page on two successive pages; classical art; caricatures; women and men in sensual poses; and three-dimensional pop-ups.

Advantages of Magazines

- *Excellent Reproduction.* Most magazines use a high-quality paper stock that allows for both high-quality print and picture reproduction. This makes magazines visually appealing, which leads readers to spend more time reading them.
- *Creativity.* The various options discussed above can be used.
- *Permanence.* Most people save their magazines and look through them several times.
- *Production Costs.* Usually, it is cheaper to produce a print ad than a television or radio commercial.
- *Targetability.* Nearly every specific customer group will have a magazine targeted toward them.
- *Prestige.* There are some magazines that can improve the status of a business. An independent hotel advertising in *Forbes* could improve its image, while at the same time increasing its customer base of business travelers. The ad could also be used in other promotion efforts, such as brochures and framed pictures mounted in the hotel.
- *High Receptivity and Involvement.* People buy magazines because they feel they are relevant to their lives. This relevance increases the reader's interest in advertisements. Some magazines are read nearly as much for the advertisements as for editorial content.
- *Split Runs.* Some magazines will allow for split runs, which are two different ads run in alternative copies of the same issue. This allows businesses to test the effectiveness of each ad through recall surveys or coupon redemption rates.
- *Timing.* There are quarterly, monthly, weekly, and daily magazines. The longer the time between issues, generally the longer the subscriber will keep the magazine.

Disadvantages of Magazines

- *Long Lead Time.* Magazines, because of their increased production time, will have lead times considerably longer than newspapers. For some, the closing date is 90 days before publication.
- *Cost.* Many national magazines have rates in the $100,000 range for a full page. Full-page ads in special-interest magazines can be purchased for considerably less, beginning below $5000.
- *Clutter.* The advertising content of the average magazine is 50%.
- *Limited Coverage.* Because there are few magazines that have a truly national audience, advertisers will need to buy space in several magazines to achieve effective coverage.
- *Inaccuracy in Circulation Numbers.* The actual quantity of some magazines in circulation may be difficult to determine. Different media research firms will have estimates of circulation for the same magazine that will vary by as much as 5% to 10%.

DIRECT MAIL   For many years most people has been receiving *junk mail*—advertisements sent to a mass market or a market that has not been qualified in some manner. Mass market in this case does not always mean promoting to everyone without regard for targeted characteristics, but targeting with the assumption that most people in a geographic area or on a purchased mailing list have the same or similar characteristics. As marketers began refining in-house mailing lists or databases to key in on their heavy users, they found that they were able to significantly increase the response rate (also known as redemption rates) for their mailings. Typical response rates for mass mailings are usually in the 2% to 6% range. This would depend on the size or value of an offer and the markets' demand for the product. As marketers began targeting their mailings, response rates increased as much as tenfold. Hilton Hotels Corp., for example, found that by mailing incentives to members of their Senior HHonors (produced "H" honors, the first "H" is for Hilton), their frequent travel program for seniors, response rates climbed to as high as 50%. Direct mail for many businesses, especially those with narrow target audiences, has become the most effective communication channel.

The result of direct (or database) marketing is that marketers are not only increasing the efficiency of their promotional efforts but bettering their competitive position. If one firm's database is substantially more sophisticated than a competitor's, then so is the firm's ability to communicate and attract actual or potential customers. Along with the ability to target customers, and thereby reducing the quantity of mail sent to noncustomers, the business can send specialized messages that pertain to smaller target markets, increasing the likelihood of response. For example, customers with small children and married couples without children may each require unique offers to induce action. A single message targeted at both groups will rarely be as effective at garnering customer loyalty as a customized message.

Another thing to consider is that as the concept of *home meal replacement* increases, major segments of customers for future casual dining concepts may never visit the restaurant, but may instead order over the phone or their computer. Many pizza restaurants have found that their most efficient means of reaching a customer is through a mailing targeted to a mass market within their trade area. Since pizza has been challenging the wide acceptance of the hamburger, this strategy has proved successful: so successful, in fact, that many pizza concepts are scrapping the idea of inside seating. Operators of casual and upscale restaurants are in a much different position than their fast-food counterparts. First, their product offerings are not as widely accepted as fast food. Everybody, or nearly everybody, eats a pizza at least occasionally, but the market for authentic South American food, for example, will be substantially smaller. Second, the trade areas for casual and upscale concepts are considerably larger than for fast-food concepts. Where a pizza restaurant will target trade areas within a 3-mile radius, casual dining concepts will focus on customers within approximately 5 miles, and upscale establishments up to 10 miles or more. As the size of the trade area increases, the number of households within that trade area increases exponentially. For example, the size of an average fast-food trade area is approximately 28 square miles [$\pi r^2 = 3.14 \times (3 \times 3) = 3.14 \times 9 = 28.26$]. As the trade area increases to 5 miles, this figures jumps to 78.5 square miles. Upscale establishments may find themselves with a trade area of over 300 square miles. Mass mailings to these increasingly larger trade areas would not be efficient. If there were an average of 2500 households (both apartments and homes) per square mile (extrapolated from Pop-facts: Full Data Report, EQUIFAX NATIONAL DECISION SYSTEMS, 1994), the number of households for the three product levels would potentially be 70,000, 196,250, and 785,000, respectively. The fast-food concept could target a 10,000-household zip code for sequential mailings. As the number of households grows to nearly 200,000, the expense increases and, ultimately, so does the increase in mail sent to nonusers. To be successful in direct mail marketing for casual and upscale restaurants, marketers will need to increase their ability to target specific members of each trade area who have the same characteristicss as their heavy users.

Advantages of Direct Mail

- *Targetability.* The target for fast-food restaurants could be everyone within a certain zip code or neighborhood or, for casual and fine dining concepts, only selected individuals within the neighborhood or city. The majority of hotels have databases of customers' names and addresses, and more restaurants are beginning to see the merit of keeping in touch with customers through the mail.
- *Continued Contact.* For hotel properties such as resorts, where a year or two may pass between visits, direct mail helps the hotel stay in touch with the clients and communicate special packages and news about the property.

Disadvantages of Direct Mail

- *Poor Image.* Unless what is sent can be considered as valuable to the target customer, it will be considered as junk mail.
- *Clutter.* There is so much junk mail that many customers mentally label something that is not a bill or a personal letter or package as junk mail.
- *Cost.* The CPM for direct mail is the highest of all mass media. The only form of promotion that is higher is outside personal selling.

DISPLAY MEDIA   Billboards and signs will normally play a secondary role to broadcast and print media. Historically, billboards were thought of primarily as directional signs. As marketers began using them in more creative ways, their usage and effectiveness increased. Today, billboards are still sometimes used as directional signs, but they are also used to increase the awareness of a business and its products and services, increase the loyalty of existing customers, attract new customers, and improve the image of the business with the local community. If a quality billboard is on a road or highway with a traffic count of 40,000 cars per day, the billboard may receive as many as 200,000 exposures per month (assuming an average exposure of 0.5 per vehicle and that the average car passes the billboard 10 times per month: $0.5 \times 40,000 = 20,000$; $20,000 \times 10 = 200,000$). If it were estimated that 25% of the people traveling on this particular highway are members of the business's target market, then the effective exposures would be 50,000 per month. Though the CPM for billboards is normally not calculated, it may prove beneficial in comparing its cost to other forms of media. If the cost of the billboard was $3000 per month, the CPM would be $60.00 ($3000 \times 1000 \div 50,000 = \$60.00$).

Billboards are either individually painted or constructed of several panels that are glued in place. They are rented by either paying a certain amount per month for a specific billboard or buying *showings* or *gross rating points.* The latter methods are both similar, gross rating points being the newer of the two. Here, the advertiser is buying the equivalent exposure of a certain percentage of the mobile population on a daily basis. Ten gross rating points means that 10% of the mobile population will see the advertiser's billboards on a daily basis. This could be one billboard or more depending on the traffic at each billboard location.

Because people are generally driving by the billboard at 55 miles per hour or so, it is difficult to include long narratives. Those that attempt to use too many words on a billboard will only serve to frustrate customers, because they will not be able to finish reading what the ad has to communicate. Usually an effective headline along with an eye-appealing illustration will garner the most attention and recall. Three-dimensional billboards, such as those with manikins, have been gaining popularity for their ability to catch the eye of fast-moving motorists.

In some cities, signs can be placed on busstop benches at a very economical rate. Other cities will allow signs to be placed on the sides of buses. The benches have a much greater readership because when people are sitting at a traffic light, waiting for it to change, they will look around and perhaps notice the sign. Many fewer people will see signs on buses. This is because they focus either on the back of the bus or on the entire bus as a nuisance that is slowing traffic. Signs on taxi cabs can be good for restaurants or night clubs that cater to tourists. Since most travelers in a taxi already have a hotel reservation, the sign would likely not attract many new customers. If a large percentage of the firms that advertise on these signs in a particular city are not morally acceptable to a business's target customer, then because of guilt by association, this form of advertisement may not be a wise choice.

Advantages of Display Media

- *Reach.* Billboards placed in high-traffic areas may be seen by between 20,000 and 100,000 people per day. These numbers are only meaningful if a high percentage of these drivers and passengers are part of the business's target market.
- *Frequency.* The percentage varies with the area, but a high percentage of traffic consists of people who are driving to and from work. This means the monthly frequency for many of these people will be over 20.
- *Around-the-Clock Exposure.* The majority of billboards are illuminated, allowing for 24-hour exposure.
- *Awareness.* Because of the high average reach or market penetration, an effective billboard can quickly increase brand awareness.
- *Geographic Flexibility.* Contracts for panel type billboards can be moved on a regular basis, allowing for a broader reach.
- *Creative Flexibility.* Billboards that are unique in some way will attract more attention than those that appear generic. Unusual shapes beyond a rectangle and three-dimensional illustrations will improve the billboard or sign's effectiveness.
- *Cost.* In some areas the absolute cost may be high, but when the CPM is calculated, the relative cost will generally be reasonable.

Disadvantages of Display Media

- *Brief Message.* Because of limited space, drivers being as far as 100 to 200 feet away, and the speed and amount of traffic, the written message must be brief.
- *Wasted Coverage.* Varying percentages of those exposed will not be from a business's target market.
- *Brief Shelf-Life.* After a target customer has driven by the same billboard for several weeks, it will lose its effectiveness.
- *Measurement Problems.* There is less relevant research and information for display media than for most other advertising media. This means that reach and frequency are difficult to determine accurately.
- *Long Lead Time.* Many of the best locations for billboards are contracted out for one-year periods. This may leave only secondary locations or require a long wait for the better locations.

MEDIA VEHICLES   After deciding which media to use, a careful search must be made to assure that the ad will in fact reach the desired target market. The media vehicle is the specific location of the ad within the selected medium. If television was the medium choice, then the media vehicle might be the evening news. For newspapers, the vehicle would be the specific location within the paper, such as the sports section, that would likely deliver the desired audience (males between 21 and 55 years of age). Most media companies have research reports prepared by reputable independent firms that detail probable audiences for each media vehicle. For example, it would be safe to say that the viewers of Monday night football would probably be a viable or representative market for pizza and beer. Since soap operas predominantly attract homemakers, family-oriented restaurants or hotels with weekend getaway packages might find them to be an effective vehicle. When selecting the media vehicle, it is also important to consider the mood of the target audience during their exposure. Each vehicle will create a mood that influences the reader's reception to advertisements. An individual reading *BusinessWeek* would likely be less receptive to visiting a quality restaurant than if reading *Gourmet*.

In most cases, the safest route is to bring in an advertising agency to assist in everything from the creation of the ad to the selection of media, placement, and scheduling or timing of the ads. Traditionally, if a minimal amount of work is required and a reasonable amount of print space or air time is purchased, there would be no cost since the advertising firm would be paid an approximate 15% rebate from the media source chosen. If research, creative, or production work of the firm is required, then appropriate individual fees would be charged.

MARKET PENETRATION   Before any media placement decisions are made, marketers must determine the degree of exposure necessary for the advertisement to achieve its stated objectives. Market penetration decisions revolve around determining the necessary *reach*, the percentage of the market that will be exposed to the message during the campaign, and *frequency*, how many times the average member of the targeted audience should be exposed to the message. The first decision made when developing a promotional strategy is deciding at whom the promotion will be targeted. It naturally follows that for the promotion to have its desired impact, it must be heard or seen not only by the chosen market but by a large enough number to either increase sales or increase the likelihood that those exposed to the ad will become customers in the future. Decisions regarding reach revolve around the breadth of exposure necessary for the message to achieve its objectives. There is generally an inverse relationship between the necessary reach and the awareness of the business or the product or service being promoted. New businesses or products will generally require a greater reach than those that are firmly established. Within the reach decision, marketers must be aware of the *geographic coverage* of the media. A commercial on television may be effective at reaching a large percentage of target customers, but if the geographic coverage is greater than the geographic target market of the business, then there will be *wasted coverage*.

Once marketers are comfortable that the targeted customer will be reached, a decision must be made on the frequency with which the message must be heard before the desired objective will be achieved. No ad seen or heard once will induce large numbers of people to run out in a trance to purchase a product (Sutherland, 1993). Advertising and other types of promotion work in small increments. Depending on, among other factors, the creativity of the ad, the size of any offer, the loyalty of the listener, and the quantity and quality of competitors' advertising, any ad will need to be heard a certain minimum number of times before its desired effect will be achieved. Unfortunately, there is no exact formula for this decision; it is generally based on the experience of the media buyer and an objective appraisal of the message and its potential impact. Common sense tells us that as long as the ad is effective to begin with, the more the targeted audience hears or sees it, the greater its effect. Some ad people say a minimum of three times and a maximum of ten times should suffice. Often, excellent commercials will not achieve their objective, simply because the frequency was not adequate.

A common question in frequency decisions is the actual number of people who are exposed to an ad. If an audience for a particular program averages 50,000, and the marketing department has decided on a frequency of 7, could these figures be accepted as appropriate? The question can be answered by several research studies that show that about 82% of viewers actually watch each commercial (Belch & Belch, 1990). This means that if the desired frequency is 7, then, to allow for nonviewers, it must be increased. Dividing 7 by the 82% that view commercials would yield a necessary frequency of 8.5 ($7 \div 0.82 = 8.5$). Though this formula does take some of the guesswork out of frequency decisions, the question of frequency levels can best be determined by what has worked in the past.

Another issue in the frequency question is the consideration of average frequency. For example, if a 50% reach was chosen and it was thought that, through various media vehicles, 25% of the target market would be exposed to a message eight times and the other 25% would be exposed four times, then the average frequency would be six, or the average of the two figures. The average of six in this instance would be satisfactory only if the desired minimum frequency was four or less. If the minimum frequency was six, then even though the frequency objective (based on the average) was met, only half of the targeted audience would be effectively exposed. In spite of this potential for deception, the average frequency is commonly used in calculations. Marketers must make sure that the minimum number of exposures is achieved for the desired percentage of the targeted market.

The terms reach and frequency can be applied to the overall campaign with several different advertising media or to a single medium. Since there will never be a medium that can guarantee delivery of an exact reach or frequency to advertisers, a third term, *gross rating points (GRPs)*, is used to express the approximate market penetration or weight of the ad or campaign. For example, the potential market for a particular hotel chain is considered to be ten million people. It was determined that a reach of 50 and a frequency of eight would be adequate. A 50% reach of ten million people is five million. For the frequency decision it was determined that, for the average target customer to be exposed a minimum of eight times, a frequency of ten must be purchased (80% of commercials are seen by viewers; $8 \div 0.8 = 10$). The GRPs would then be 500 [50 (reach) × 10 (frequency) = 500 GRPs]. Most advertising is purchased based on GRPs. This is a relative term, since the GRPs, in this instance, could mean that 50% of the target audience will be exposed 10 times, or that 20% of the target audience could be exposed 25 times.

SCHEDULING OR TIMING   Timing of promotion will relate to the specific target of the promotion. For hotels, personal selling will go on throughout the year. Some potential and existing clients will be called on when travel planners make their annual decisions. Contracts for conventions are generally signed several years in advance. Advertising and sales promotions for hotels will be scheduled during the busy season for each target segment and the period before the season or bookings for the season begin. This period before can range from more than a month for the leisure travelers, to a week or two for business travelers, and from a few days to one week for weekend packages. For most restaurant markets, promotions are spread throughout the year. Promotional spending can be reduced for periods when the restaurant is at or near capacity. For periods when sales are lower than desired, promotional efforts can be increased. Many businesses have the promotional philosophy of keeping their name in the public eye continuously throughout the entire year. Every restaurant and hotel will need to analyze its situation and decide on when each or any of the promotional mix variables will be used.

Scheduling for media will vary depending on the objective of the promotion, the quality of the ad or commercial, and the firm's budget. The primary purpose of scheduling patterns is to make the desired impact within the fewest dollars. A promotional event may require a build-up to the event's date. Keeping the company's name in the public eye may require continuous exposure.

The primary forms of scheduling are the following (see Figure 10.15):

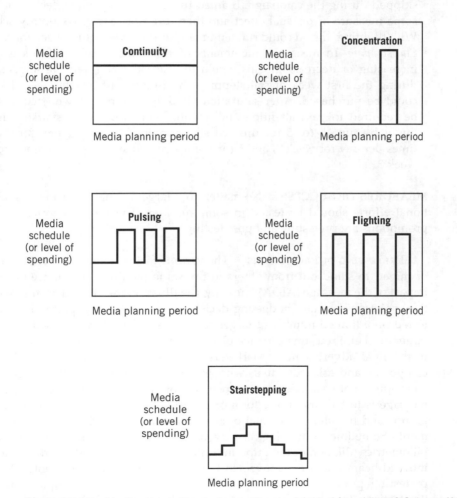

Figure 10.15   Media scheduling strategies. *Source:* Adapted from Hiam & Schewe (1992). *The Portable MBA in Marketing*, New York: Wiley.

- *Continuity.* This is relatively even scheduling over the period covered by the campaign. Using continuity, an ad could be run ten times per day for three weeks.
- *Concentration.* This is focusing all ads for a campaign during a brief period of time. This could be for a grand opening, special event, or other circumstances that called for a media blitz with a minimal budget.
- *Pulsing.* This consists of continuously running the ads, but increasing or decreasing the number run for varying periods of time: perhaps alternating 15 ads one week with 5 ads the next. This creates the illusion of a larger number of ads because many members of the target market will think they are hearing a consistent number of ads during the low week but are really just missing more than they did the previous week.
- *Flighting.* This consists of scheduling ads so that various periods of time are skipped during the campaign. If an ad turns out to be quite effective, it will have some measure of residual effect and therefore not require continuity scheduling. With flighting, the ad could run ten times per day every other week for five weeks.
- *Stairstepping.* In measured increments of time, the number of ads is gradually increasing or decreasing. This would increase the ad's relative impact, because during the first week of stairstepping the highest affordable level of saturation could be purchased. After saturation (or domination), a lower frequency would be required to gain attention and action. With downward stairstepping an ad might be run 15 (or 5 for upward stairstepping) times per day for week 1, 10 times per day for week 2, and 5 (or 15 for upward stairstepping) times per day for week 3.

MEASURES OF SUCCESS   No matter how large or small a business is, all promotional efforts should be tested in some manner. The two categories of testing of promotions are pretesting and post-testing.

PRETESTING OF PROMOTIONS   The various factors to be pretested are the ability of the ad to stand out from others in the same medium, the choice of media, the impact of the message (AIDA), the copy, the illustrations, the music, the credibility of the spokesperson, and budgeting decisions. In most cases, promotions should be tested on a limited number of target customers before they are used on the overall target market. Pretesting can take place at any level of creation from idea generation to the final advertisement. Marketers will commonly visit an area where people congregate and ask individuals who appear to be members of the targeted market their opinion of an ad. Before an expensive commercial is produced for television, its message is tested first in the form of a storyboard. Testing is also done with focus groups and by having potential or actual customers individually rate an advertisement. Sometimes physiological measures, such as galvanic skin response, pupillometrics (dilation of the pupil indicates arousal or interest), and eyetracking (an infrared beam tracks eye movement) are used to test advertisements. One form of pretesting print ads is to give targeted customers several sample headlines and illustrations, then have them select the pair they feel would be most effective. Direct mail ads can be tested by the *postcard test*. This consists of sending different potential ads with identical free offers to a sample of target customers. The ad's quality is measured by the individual response rates. A more expensive method of pretesting print ads is to obtain advanced copies of a publication, replace an existing ad with the ad to be tested, give the publication to target customers, and then, after they have read the magazine, test the effectiveness of the ad through a recall survey.

The advantages of asking people about their opinions or attitudes toward a potential ad are that it is generally inexpensive, takes little time, and provides potentially valuable input from target customers. Some of the disadvantages are that opinions may not equate with action (many people say they will do one thing, then do another); that one ad might be rated as the best, but it is simply the best of several bad ads; and, since advertising is generally based on a cumulative effect, that one exposure may not be enough to truly determine effectiveness.

Post-testing of Promotions   The success of any promotional effort will be measured by the degree to which it achieved its related objectives. Common measures are improvements in awareness and image and increases in reservations, customer counts, sales, and profit. Post-testing includes all methods of determining the effectiveness of a single advertisement or an entire campaign. The most popular of these are readership, unaided recall, attitude change, sales increases, and inquiry tests (Dunn & Barban, 1978).

Readership (or Aided Recall).   Respondents, who are either subscribers or have been given a copy of a magazine or newspaper, are asked questions to determine how effective the ad was. The interviewer turns to an ad and then asks if the respondent remembered seeing the ad (*noted*), if they remembered the brand advertised and read at least some part of it (*associated*), and whether or not they read at least half of the ad's copy (*read most*). The percentage of respondents for each category is recorded for analysis. Though various cost formulas can be developed for each level of recognition or a combination of the three, it is most commonly completed for the *read most* category. For example, if 27% of the respondents read most of the ad, the circulation of the publication was 800,000, and the cost of the ad was $13,000, the CPM or cost per 1000 people in the "read most" category would be $60.19 (0.27 × 800,000 = 216,000; $13,000 × 1000 ÷ 216,000 = $60.19). The calculation is the same as that for the CPM, except that the circulation figure would be multiplied by the percentage of respondents who read most of the ad (or noted it or can associate the ad with the company).

Unaided Recall.   In this test, only minimal assistance is given to respondents. Like the readership test, the interviewer must determine if the respondent has read the publication. But, since this test is more challenging, the respondent is normally tested in some manner to prove that he/she has in fact read the publication. This is generally accomplished with a question about an article in the publication. Qualified respondents are then given a deck of cards with the names of companies with reasonably large advertisements in the publication and are told to take out the cards for each company they can remember seeing. The respondent is then asked to recall what the ad looked like, what basic message the advertiser was trying to communicate, any particular sales points, and if the ad made the respondent want to either learn more about the product or purchase the product. The three key dimensions of the ad's impression are reported as *proved name recognition* (the percentage of respondents who recalled seeing the ad and could describe something about it), *idea penetration* (remembered the message), and *conviction* (wants to know more about the product advertised or is interested in purchasing it).

Attitude Change.   These tests attempt to measure the effectiveness of promotions based on changes in respondents' opinion of the company or its products. These opinions generally concern image, loyalty to the company compared to competitors, and product- and service-related attributes. The questions for the survey could be unstructured or structured. Various types of questionnaire scales can be used, such as the semantic differential, Likert, constant sum, and purchase intent scales described in Chapter 3. For many scales, different adjectives are presented; then respondents are asked to rate how well the adjectives describe the advertisement. Typical adjectives are exciting, stupid, original, ingenious, important to me, ridiculous, humorous, meaningful to me, boring, and eye-catching (Belch & Belch, 1990).

Sales Increases.   Measurement of sales increases are generally tested in two ways, *comparison with past sales* and *field experiments*. Immediate sales increases directly tied to the promotion are difficult to calculate with any accuracy. Essentially, sales during the promotion are compared with sales either during the period immediately before the promotion or for the same period during the past year. A method of calculating a weighted average is to take the percentage increase or decrease in sales for the period prior to the promotion compared to the same period for the prior year (last year $35,000 per week, this year $37,500 per week equals an increase of 7%: $37,500 - 35,000 = 2500; 2500 \div 35,000 = 0.07$). To get this year's "projected sales", multiply 1.07 times the same period one year prior; $34,000 \times 1.07 = \$36,380$. If actual sales during the promotional period were higher than this figure, then, all things being equal, the promotion had a positive effect on sales. (Past company promotions and those of competitors should be analyzed to determine their potential effect on the calculations.) If sales were not higher, then, unless the ad created horrible image problems for the company, it could be assumed that the ad had either no effect or that intervening factors caused the decline in projected sales.

While actual sales increases are generally the key focus, *residual sales increases* should also be considered. For example, in a hypothetical firm with a total variable cost percentage of 60%, a $10,000 ad campaign increases sales by $17,000. Since the 60% variable cost or $10,200 of the increase in sales must be subtracted from the $17,000 increase, there is a net increase in current profit of $6800. This, of course, is not enough to cover the cost of the ad campaign. But given the likelihood that there will be some degree of residual effect or an increase in sales over a longer period, future profit will hopefully cover the cost of the campaign.

In field experiments, there would be a control group, for whom all current strategies remain the same, and an experimental or test group, who are exposed to a new promotion. The differences in behavior are then determined. This experiment could be implemented by sending a brochure to certain customers and not to others or by placing an advertisement in one regional edition of a magazine (or a commercial in one city) and not another.

Inquiry Tests. These tests are generally used in two different situations—to test the effectiveness of different ads in the same medium and to test the effectiveness of the same ad in different media. As was discussed in advantages of magazines, a split-run could be used to find out which of two different ads was most effective.

PROMOTIONAL MIX

The promotional mix is concerned with various means of communicating with actual and potential customers. The promotional mix variables of merchandising, advertising, personal selling, public relations, and sales promotion (the acronym for which is MAPPS) will be utilized in varying degrees, depending on particular needs. Some firms place an emphasis in only one or two areas; others focus on each variable. Restaurants use advertising and sales promotion heavily, while hotels generally concentrate on personal selling and advertising.

The degree of a firm's emphasis on promotion will depend greatly on the amount of competition it has and the competitors' focus on the various promotional variables. If competitors for hotels limit their promotion to occasional ads in travel magazines and personal selling, then this may be all that is needed to keep the business's name in the public eye and compete. If competitors take an aggressive stance, attempting to saturate the market using several promotional media (e.g., travel magazines, newspapers, and direct mail), then a similarly oriented counterstrategy may be required to remain competitive. In some markets, established firms can limit their amount of promotion because their product is well known, it does not frequently change, and a substantial client base exists. If the business is innovative or new in a market, then a greater focus on promotional mix variables may be needed (Covin, 1991).

Merchandising

Merchandising refers to in-house promotion of products and services, which is usually accomplished with table-tents, posters, dessert displays, tableside preparation of entrees and desserts, display cases, brochures, gift shops, stationery, and guest services books. Restaurants with exposed kitchens or bakeries are merchandising their food and preparation. To minimize the perception that some seafood is not as fresh as it should be, Red Lobster restaurants publishes several brochures, two of which are called "The Standard for Seafood Excellence" and the "Red Lobster Fact Book." An often overlooked area for merchandising for hotels is the front desk. Since almost everyone staying at the hotel will visit the front desk at least once a day, brochures, posters, signs, and displays could be used to promote the hotel's services. Clothing with a logo is rapidly gaining ground, not only as a means of promoting a business but also as a source of revenue. Some restaurants rely on T-shirts, golf shirts, caps, and other souvenirs for up to 25% or more of sales.

Advertising

Advertising is the paid, generally nonpersonal, promotion through a mass medium by an identified sponsor. While there are a few hospitality firms that do not need to advertise, the vast majority must have an organized advertising strategy for each marketing planning period. Advertising strategies and tactics should follow the fundamental tasks of promotion (presented earlier in this chapter).

In the ideal situation, advertising should focus primarily on what is termed *image advertising*—establishing a memorable brand identity. Since most hospitality products and services are physically similar, reason will play less of a part in the customer's decision. Some marketers, under pressure to increase short-term sales, will resort to sales promotions (price cuts or giveaways). The problem with sales promotions is that they reinforce behaviors in target customers that lead to a best deal mentality rather than brand loyalty. As long as the company delivers on what it promises in ads, successful image advertising builds sales over the long term, allowing the business to reduce its dependency on discounting. While image may not be everything, it is the next best thing.

Studies have shown that most people would rather feel that they made the decision to purchase, rather than being sold a product (Belch & Belch, 1990). Providing details about a product to help consumers make this decision is accomplished through *informative advertising*. The degree of success of informative advertising is usually closely tied to the education of the buyer and the importance of the purchase. Convenience products will require very little informative advertising. Consumers already have the majority of information necessary to make a purchase and the purchase is not deemed important enough to carefully gather details about the various alternatives. Consumers of shopping and specialty products, on the other hand, will be seeking information on quality and price to help them make a better purchase decision. When consumers are considering the purchase of a specialty product, a considerable amount of information will usually be required before a decision is made.

If a top-of-mind survey shows that a reasonable percentage of the target market knows about one's hotel or restaurant but visits a competitor's establishment, then the business must persuade the competitor's customers to change their habits. This is called *persuasive advertising* and generally focuses on quality, unique features, or pricing. This will mostly be used for firms selling convenience products but also for those firms whose products require minimal awareness or differentiation or possibly having some image problems.

Sometimes the marketing department might feel that it is worth directly comparing the benefits of its business with those of another. This is termed *comparison advertising.* The ultimate goal of comparison advertising is to reposition the competitor's product in the customer's mind. The most famous comparison advertising in the hospitality industry was used by Burger King in the mid-1980s when they compared their broiled burger patties to McDonald's fried burgers. This became known as the "Burger Wars" because many millions of ad dollars were spent by both sides in the court of public opinion. Eventually, the confrontation ended up in court but was not pursued to final judgment. Rather than using broadcast media to communicate the comparison, a portion of a brochure could use a matrix format to highlight differences.

Mild comparison ads that may not mention any competitors by name can be quite successful if used indirectly and creatively. For example, "Other steakhouses usually serve a lower grade of beef" or "No other hotel gives you more for your money." This is because a competitor's response to a direct comparison or attack can almost be assured and immediate, while indirect comparisons will not be viewed with as much concern. Depending on the ferocity of the proposed tactic, contingency plans should be prepared for any possible retaliation. Attacks that draw swift responses can end up like most lawsuits—except in this case, it's not lawyers but the marketers and ad agencies who win.

Occasionally, there will be a need for a more serious form of advertising, termed *attack advertising.* This can be used in several different circumstances but is generally used either in an offensive manner when a firm feels that it is in trouble, or in a defensive manner against a competitor's offensive attack. Attack advertising should be considered only as a last choice. Its message should be communicated in a serious tone, conveying to customers that the business is attempting to communicate the truth. Humorous attack ads making light of a competitor's product or service can be successful, but the humor in the message should be the primary focal point in the ad. It is also important that the ad be communicated in such a way that the customer would not view it as distasteful or immoral.

If customers know about the hotel or restaurant and they patronize it occasionally, then perhaps they just need to be reminded of it. This is called *reminder advertising* and is critical for many hotels and restaurants. In the normal course of time, people develop new habits and forget about other possible alternatives. A simple reminder may work, or it may need to be accompanied by an incentive or sales promotion (described later). If the percentage of return customers is decreasing, then the problem may require a more serious solution than a reminder. Perhaps remodeling, changes in menus or services, or repositioning are in order.

Public Relations

Public relations is promotion of the brand's image rather than its products or services. The objective is to alter the perception of the business in the minds of target customers and the general public. The starting point of positive public relations is the activities where the business is located or where its target customers live or work. There are many kinds of activities that lead to good public relations:

- Energetic participation in causes or charities by donating money, food and beverages, facilities, or personal time
- Informing people of the nutritional content of food items
- Expanding operations and creating new jobs
- Doing new or unusual things (new entrees or desserts, serving a different cuisine on certain nights, bringing in a well-known chef for a special meal, or some type of unique entertainment)
- Recycling, waste reduction, and other efforts to minimize the business's impact on the environment

The most valuable element of public relations is that the proportionate cost, compared with advertising, is minimal. For example, if a manager or employees are members of local civic organizations, or if employees volunteer time for charitable events, there will be little or no cost, but the goodwill created may be immeasurable.

When public relations is announced over mass communications channels, it is called *publicity*—exposure for the company, either for free or well below established rates. Getting a newspaper or TV station to publicize an event or achievement is not a simple task. The keys to acceptance are that the event is unique or unusual and that it is of interest to the target audience of the chosen medium. The press release, or written report of the event, should be formatted as follows: date in the upper left-hand corner, name and telephone number of the contact person in the upper right-hand corner, a catchy descriptive title in the top center of the page, followed by the text. Since the press release is generally coming from people with a vested interest in the business, it is important not to use too many self-venerating words such as "great" or "the best" (Reich, 1990). Unless this opinion is a statement from a third party, publishers and editors will rarely continue reading.

Another form of publicity is attainment of a rating from the Mobil (up to 5 stars) or AAA (up to 5 diamonds) travel services. Field inspectors, committees, and local consultants determine the rating based on cleanliness, maintenance, quality of furnishings, services provided, and degree of luxury. In Europe, the *Michelin Guide* honors restaurants with up to 3 "rosettes." In all of France there are 19 restaurants with 3 rosettes, and 11 throughout the rest of Europe (Marcom, 1990).

Personal Selling

This is promotion of products and services through personal communications channels. In almost all instances, personal selling is more effective than other types of promotion. This is because most purchase decisions are based to varying extents on information and persuasion, and there is not enough time or space in an advertisement to attempt to supply all answers to target customer' potential questions. A good salesperson can, within reason, estimate what a buyer's motivations are, then attempt to satisfy them during the course of a sales presentation. The main problem with personal selling is that it is not as effective at reaching large numbers of decision-makers as are mass media.

Restaurants use personal selling through counterworkers and servers, but rarely through outside sales calls. This is a significant lost opportunity for many restaurants. Since the average restaurant will draw between 60% and 70% of its customers from its trade area, visits to local businesses and organizations may be one of the most effective means of promotion for the business. Too often, a restaurant will take the easy way out by letting their advertising agent spend money on mass media. What this does is focus the majority of the restaurant's promotional budget on people who will never be customers. One-to-one contact with customers who are within the restaurant's trade area would generally prove more profitable than advertising.

The majority of a hotel's promotional and overall marketing efforts will be in personal selling. The fact that there are too many hotel rooms in many markets has forced each property to compete fiercely for customers. No hotel can be expected to keep every present customer, so as they lose existing customers, new ones must be found to take their place. If the sales staff is not aggressively scouring their markets for customers, declining sales will result. The primary steps in attracting business are (1) prospect for clients, (2) qualify the prospects, (3) develop a strategy to attract them, and finally, (4) schedule a meeting to formally present the benefits of the hotel (Hart & Troy, 1986).

PROSPECTING   Finding new potential clients is called prospecting. Sources of prospects include the following:

PAST CLIENTS   Check files for accounts that have not had functions for the past year. This could be an opportunity to see why they have not been back. If there were problems in the past, have answers ready for any potential objections that might be raised.

REFERRALS FROM PRESENT CLIENTS   Ask current accounts, especially regulars, if they are aware of others in their company, or meeting planners with other companies, who may have a need for rooms or meeting services. If a client refers a new account, send him/her a gift such as a complimentary weekend.

LOCAL ORGANIZATIONS AND COMPANIES   Check the *Yellow Pages*, headquarters of trade associations and nonprofit organizations, and local chambers of commerce. A local firm could be a branch of a national company. Even the most frugal companies often have at least one or two meetings each year away from the office. If not, possibly they could be convinced of the benefits of a change of scenery.

FRONT DESK PERSONNEL   Individual guests have the potential to bring group business to the property. Front desk employees can be trained to notice what company someone works for, then offer the hotel's services for their meeting needs (e.g., "Does your company ever have any meetings in this area?"). Generally, people in business do not mind being asked this because they are in business themselves and realize that the way a company gets business is to ask for it. Also, for many people it is an ego boost to have someone consider them important enough to ask them about their company's needs.

EMPLOYEE REFERRALS   Frequently, the hotel's employees are overlooked because they are often not members of the hotel's target market. Employees may be members of organizations or clubs (bowling, darts, baseball cards, antiques, and so forth) that have meetings, events, and conventions. They could also have a personal need for weddings or reunions or have friends who will require a hotel's services.

THE PROPERTY'S COMPETITORS   One of the best sources of leads are clients of the property's competitors. The primary advantage of trying to attract competitors' clients is that they are essentially prequalified. The marketing staff can surmise that clients use a particular type or size of hotel, the services they require, and that they have a need for rooms or meeting space in the hotel's area. The following should be considered when venturing on to a competitor's property:

- *Who are the hotel's primary, and perhaps secondary, competitors?* The primary competitors are those that offer the same or very similar services to the same target market. Secondary competitors will be hotels in different market segments that cater to some of the same target markets. For example, it may be possible to convince a group that for $15 more a day they could have a substantial upgrade in facilities and/or services.
- *Who are the top accounts for each competitor, and what are some of their needs?* Competitors' daily events boards will supply a plentiful list of prospects. Some qualifying can be done on the premises. For example, the number of guests for the client might possibly be approximated by examining the meeting room setup. Various local tourist and visitors bureaus will keep information on the groups in town during any particular week, their number, and the hotels at which they are staying. By checking the board twice weekly, an approximation can be made of the length of a group's stay. The board may list meals and banquets to be served, yielding additional sources of revenues. A reasonable estimate can generally be made of the client's room rate or charges for other services.

QUALIFYING PROSPECTS   Qualifying prospects refers to determining the likelihood that a potential client will be a viable customer. The following information is needed to qualify a prospect:

- *What is the client's need for rooms and meeting space?* For individuals, such details include total room nights per year and rate they are used to paying; for groups, one should know how many rooms, length of stay, time of year, meeting space requirements, and food and beverage requirements.
- *What type of hotel or location does the prospect normally use?* All companies have preferences for hotels located either near airports, in downtown areas, near shopping or business districts, or in resort areas. If the company normally stays at downtown locations, convincing it to stay at an airport hotel may be difficult.
- *Does the prospect need special services or features?* Some companies will have needs that not all properties can satisfy (e.g., a 24-hour restaurant, tennis courts, workout facility, teleconferencing abilities, ice carvings, a kosher kitchen, or valet parking.)

- *Does the company or organization pay its bills on time?* Before committing to work with a company, check with the credit bureau. It may have a good overall reputation but may not have paid all its bills in the past. Margins in the hotel business are too low to suffer the consequences of a company that does not pay its bills. When it comes time to pay the bill, some businesses will complain about things with the hope of having the amount lowered.

PERSONAL SELLING STRATEGY DEVELOPMENT   Restaurants service the needs of individual customers or consumers (individuals who buy for personal consumption) but focus their strategic marketing efforts on identifiable groups to which the consumer belongs. Since hotels offer a much broader range of services than restaurants, they will also have to deal with a broader range of customer requirements. Because of this, each time a new customer is sought, the hotel must make sure that it can service that customer's needs. For hotels, the market will be divided up between corporate individual, corporate group, associations, government, tourist, and possible other miscellaneous markets. The above potential target groups will form the target for the personal selling strategy formulation. Their characteristics are gathered at two primary stages: first, during the strategic planning process in the environmental analysis, and second, from the routine search for new customers (discussed earlier in the sections on prospecting and qualifying prospects). After the characteristics have been identified, and management is satisfied that the hotel has the ability to service the prospective client's needs, the marketing department can begin to develop its strategy for attracting that client.

The key question in developing a personal selling strategy is, "What will it take to get your competitor's major accounts to use your facilities?" A prospect will leave an existing facility for many possible reasons. The most frequent fall under the heading of problems—basically, that the hotel did not meet the overall expectations of the meeting planner, guests, or both. Perhaps the service was less than sterling, the food was not good, the attitude of the hotel's employees was not up to par, or promises were made that were not honored. If there were few or no problems, then other enticements will be needed to influence a meeting planner to change hotels. These could include additional services, lower prices, pampered attention, such gratis services or functions as an opening party, increased quality of service, reputation of food, or a more suitable location. Perhaps the meeting planner was basically satisfied with the competing hotel's services but has the feeling that the grass may be greener on the other side. Since the meeting planner's livelihood may well depend on the success of a meeting, the hotel that can offer quality services at reasonable rates and develop a reputation for consistency will attract more than its fair share of clients (Piner, 1993).

In addition to work-related motivations, such as seeking the best quality and a reasonable price, it must be recognized that meeting planners will also have personal agendas. These could include the desire for power, control, recognition, popularity, respect, and personal attention or perks during the meeting. An assessment of these additional motivators and attempts to satisfy them may help sway borderline clients (Bliss, 1994).

TYPES OF PERSONAL SELLING FOR HOTELS   There are five different types of personal selling for hotels: cold calls, appointment calls, public relations calls, inside sales calls, and presentation sales calls (Hart & Troy, 1986). Each of these in various situations could apply to all hospitality businesses.

Cold Calls or Prospect Calls.   These can be in person, such as a sales blitz, or over the phone (telemarketing). Cold calls are used primarily to gather information about prospective clients, and to let them know you are interested in their business. They are rarely used as an opportunity to make a sale. Of course, if someone is interested in doing business, there is nothing wrong with telling them about the property and perhaps trying to make a sale, but this rarely happens. The secondary purpose of cold calling is to arrange an appointment call.

Appointment Calls.   Their general purposes are to meet a prospective client, to establish a business relationship, and to get information that will further help qualify a prospect. During the conversation, the sales manager should make a point of getting as much specific information as possible, such as the dates and types of events the company will be planning. Any attempt to close a sale would depend on the prospect's interest and be made at the discretion of the sales manager.

Public Relations or Service Calls.   These are visits to companies that are generally already clients. The purposes are to get to know clients personally, to keep up with their needs, and to maintain positive relationships. The call may open up opportunities, such as an event coming up that the company has just begun to plan. The goal is to have the meeting planner think about having the company event with "Anita," rather than with any specific hotel. A professional relationship will make it more difficult for the client to switch to another property. Also, when something comes up, they will often call the last sales representative to whom they talked.

Inside Sales Calls.   These are generally made to potential guests and banquet customers inquiring about the property. If a prospective client is interested in using the hotel for an upcoming event, first find out his/her needs. Then, if the requirements are within the capabilities of the hotel, and the prospect appears amenable, show how the hotel can accommodate his/her event. Many weddings and social and nonprofit organization's events are booked from walk-ins.

The majority of hotel rooms will be sold by reservations systems. Even though the rate will normally be set, through *bottom–up selling,* this guest could be offered an upgrade to a business suite. Walk-in prospects without reservations offer a little more flexibility in pricing strategies. Most common today is the previously discussed yield management method, where the price is based on occupancy percentage. The prospect could also be given the option of two or more different rooms, termed *rate-category alternatives:* for example, a standard room at one price, or a business suite or room with a view for slightly more. Another tactical option, termed *top–down selling,* is offering a higher rate, then reducing it, if there is resistance. *Suggestive selling—* influencing a guest's purchase through recommendations of foods, beverages, or services that will make the meal or hotel stay more enjoyable—is a term generally used in the foodservice industry, but it would also be applicable to front desk personnel or any other area of the hotel where a recommendation could be made. In any case, the goal is to maximize the potential revenue from each prospect or guest.

If the hotel is part of a chain or franchise, guests could be asked if they need a reservation in another city. This is called *cross-selling* and is especially effective for people who are obviously traveling by car or are on a multi-city trip. Also, employees in each department could recommend the services of either their own department, at another time, or the other services in the hotel. For example, the evening host in the restaurant could tell a guest about the great breakfast buffet, or a front desk employee could inform the guest about the workout room with qualified instructor.

It should also be acknowledged that every employee who has contact with guests is part of the sales staff. The most obvious are the employees behind the front desk or in the hotel's restaurants; but this also includes housekeepers, maintenance personnel, bellmen, and various employees in office support, such as those in the accounting or marketing departments. The foundation for improving inside sales with nonsales staff employees is high morale and a warm attitude toward all people in the hotel. Each employee should have a friendly smile for guests, offer a pleasant verbal greeting when within about 5 feet of guests, or, if the opportunity offers itself, be willing to assist in any manner. All employees should know all the features and services of the hotel, hours of operation, and any current special promotions. Inviting all employees to experience the various features of the hotel, such as eating in the restaurant or staying in the hotel for a night, will help educate them on the features, improve morale, and increase their enthusiasm for describing services. Employees should also know about various tourist attractions, shopping malls, and business districts in the city and how to direct guests to them.

Presentation Sales Call.   These are formal presentations, generally with the objective of making a sale. They are made after the sales representative has enough information to show exactly how the hotel can meet the needs of the prospective client. The presentation is almost always ended with a sales close—asking for a commitment.

PRESENTATIONS   The following information on presentations can be used for any type of public speech, whether for selling or to inform. The standard by which to measure a presentation is the same as for a business—it should be better than competitors'. There are several critical areas and concerns for any presentation (Reich, 1992).

FEAR OF PUBLIC SPEAKING   It is rare for people to progress in any field without the ability to communicate in front of groups. The first key to effective communication is practice. Some people feel natural in front of audiences; most do not. Another factor that makes speaking before groups much easier is enthusiasm. There is an old saying credited to Dale Carnegie, "Act enthusiastic and you'll be enthusiastic." Since people can only feel one emotion at a time, this helps reduce nervous tension.

Toastmasters International is a nonprofit organization designed to help people of all levels of ability hone their skills. There are Toastmasters clubs in or nearby almost every city in the United States, plus many clubs outside the country (about 7500 in all).

BODY MOVEMENT   The mind has a short attention span. Motion is a way of relieving mental boredom. If the speaker stands behind a lectern for the entire presentation, prospects are forced to look at one spot for up to one hour. But as the speaker moves from behind the lectern toward the audience, several things happen: listeners' eyes will follow, they will become more interested in the message, and both the speaker and listeners will feel more comfortable. In everyday conversation, people rarely stand statuelike behind something. Body movement increases confidence by allowing the speaker to focus on natural communication rather than excessively relying on notes.

GESTURES   Facial expression and movement of the body and arms are the means by which people physically punctuate their message. Practice a presentation in front of someone and ask him/her to note the number of different gestures used. Be conscious of these, then learn new gestures by watching other speakers or by asking those with effective skills and, if available, professional speakers.

VOCAL VARIETY   Sales representatives should be aware of how many different notes (levels of pitch) they use when speaking. Record a practice sales presentation, then listen to it. Are there frequent changes in pitch, or are most of the notes within a limited range? When a speaker's vocal range is limited, listeners may find it difficult to listen for more than a few minutes. Increasing the number of different notes used during a presentation is one of the quickest means of improving speaking skills and the audience's receptiveness to a message.

In addition to increasing the range of notes, other options are to raise or lower the volume, to speed up or slow down (changing pace), and to use silent pauses to increase vocal variety.

VERBAL PAUSES   Perhaps one of the most disturbing speech habits is the *verbal pause*—sounds or words, such as *uh* and *um*, joining each sentence with *and, you know,* and others. Ask someone to count the number of verbal pauses during a practice presentation. The quickest way to avoid them is simply to *pause* instead of filling the gap with "uh."

EYE CONTACT   In public speaking, there is a term called "eye darting," which means to focus on one person in an area for about three seconds, then to move to another area. This way, each person in the group feels that he/she is being given some attention. If a speaker rarely or never looks at a certain section of an audience, there will be a natural tendency for that section to tune out. If the audience is small, eye contact will depend on the personality characteristics of the potential clients. Some like eye contact for long periods of time; others feel uncomfortable if eye contact is established for more than a few seconds. The presenter must acclimate to his/her audience.

DIRECTED QUESTIONS   The quickest way to make sure that prospective clients listen to the presentation is to ask a question to introduce a topic or after an important point is made. Questions make people think and keep the mind active. They are also the primary means of finding out exactly what features a client may want. Many people will say very little unless asked, and information is the sales representative's best weapon.

HUMOR   Most busy people appreciate a certain amount of humor. It helps them switch gears from an otherwise pressure-filled regimen. They may not have time for jokes, but a light-hearted presentation will usually be better received than one that is dry and filled with mountains of facts. People tend to absorb information more effectively and view that information in a more positive light (less cynical) when they are happy, intellectually stimulated, and relaxed. This occurs because the brain wave cycle rate decreases, allowing for greater concentration and utilization of a greater percentage of the brain's ability.

VISUAL AIDS   People learn in three ways: *auditory* (hearing), *visual* (seeing), and *kinesthetic* (doing). If potential clients hear and see what is being said, they will remember it longer and understand it better than if they just hear it. Typical examples of visual aids are pictures, charts, graphs, short films, overheads, testimonial letters, and newspaper clippings. The hotel's position will be strengthened if visual aids can be combined with a tour of the facility—kinesthetics.

ORGANIZATION OF THE PRESENTATION   The effectiveness of a presentation is increased through proper organization. This includes an opening, a body, and a conclusion. Using this speech outline helps to tell the hotel's (or restaurant's) story in a manner that can easily be followed and understood.

OPENING   In a speech, the opening statement will set the mood for the balance of the presentation. The most logical opening for sales presentations is a statement about the property that makes the listener think about its advantages. Such statements as "Today I'm going to show you why I think we have the best facility and services available for the price in the city!" or "No hotel in town will work harder to assure the success of your meeting!" are possible means of gaining the audience's attention. The opening should also include a short summary of the presentation: "I'm going to review how the Holiday Inn can accommodate your needs and make your upcoming conference a success."

BODY   The body of the presentation will include information about the hotel that is directed at influencing the decision-maker. Through qualifying the prospect, the sales representative should know what is most important to him/her. The key concerns generally are price, that the meeting or conference run smoothly, and that each attendee leaves satisfied about the hotel's selection and performance. During the presentation, it is beneficial to ask questions of the prospective clients. This helps to learn more about their specific needs, as well as keeping their interest and attention. It also presents opportunities to confirm that the property can meet the client's needs.

Often, prospects will raise *objections*—questions about the hotels' features, rates, abilities, and reputation. This application of the term objection is not applied in its traditional use. It could represent a major or minor problem or simply an attempt at seeking more information to assist in decision-making. These questions could be expressed verbally or nonverbally, so it is important to pay attention to prospects' body language as well as to what they say. For example, a raised eyebrow or change of facial expression will often mean that something has either not been understood or is being internally questioned.

Sometimes these questions will be to seek more information; other times they will be serious questions about past problems with the hotel or about its reputation. All sales representatives must be ready to field objections. Past problems can be researched by reviewing the client's files. Hopefully, each of these problems were solved. In any event, have an answer ready if a question about past incidents is raised. Do not become defensive or try to discount a prospect's opinion. This will quickly put an end to the hotel's chances of gaining his/her business. If the objection raised is based on erroneous information, it is proper to tactfully rectify the misunderstanding. Try to address objections as they are raised. If an objection cannot be handled to the satisfaction of the prospect, it is unlikely that a sale will be made. The following are examples of common objections:

Objection: "I heard your food was not very good."
Reply: "Our new chef is from Tony's. Here's a recent review about our restaurant. Can you join me for dinner tonight?"
Objection: "Your rooms are $15 higher than the Green Mountain Inn."
Reply #1: "For your group we will have 24-hour citywide transportation, a 24-hour coffee shop and delicatessen, and one of the best workout facilities in the city with a professional instructor; for extra security we have a computerized entry system instead of keys and quieter, larger rooms."
Reply #2 (if emphasis of features does not work): "What will it take for our hotel to get your business?"

The specific features and levels of service of competing properties will come into play in Reply #2. Perhaps, because of limited budgets on the part of the potential clients or competition with a hotel offering fewer services and therefore lower rates, the piece of business is going to be very difficult to attract. If the potential client responds with a reduced price, it can be accepted, or negotiated between the original $15 more per room and the offer, or the sales manager can ask for time to discuss it with the marketing director. This may be a good time to further discuss which specific events, features, and services are important, and which could be deleted or changed. It is rare that an offer is immediately rejected without an attempt at negotiation.

If the prospect appears (either verbally or through body language, known as a *buying signal*) to be satisfied with the new numbers and has enough information with which to make a decision, a close may be in order. Never give up an opportunity to close a sale during the body of a presentation. If the prospect is ready to sign, then let him/her sign.

CLOSING   This is a brief summation of the benefits of the hotel that were included in the body of the presentation to find out about the readiness of the prospect to commit. The amount of information included in the summarization will depend on various factors. If there were many details or if the decision is a major one for the potential client, then each of the key details should be included. If most details are obvious or the decision is less critical, then the summary should be brief. There are two primary types of closing statements.

Test Closes.   This will be an important question that should indicate how the prospect feels about the hotel or its services. Its purpose is to handle any remaining objections and to solidify the hotel's benefits in the mind of the prospect. It is also a tactful way of leading up to asking for the business without the sales representative having to appear overly aggressive. For example, ask "Do we have the services your company needs?," or "How do you like our meeting facilities?," or "How do you like our rooms?" If there is a negative answer to a test close, this is an objection that must be dealt with. If there is a positive answer to the test close, a major close may be appropriate.

Major Close.   This is asking for the sale. "Can I book the 150 rooms for your convention?" "If we can revise our prices to fit within your budget, then we're set?" After attempting a major close, be quiet. Let the prospect think things over. If a decision cannot be made at that time, then the sales representative should ask when the prospect might have an answer.

AFTER THE CLOSE   If a sale was not made, thank the prospect for the opportunity to meet with him/her and send a brief thank you note: something like "It was a pleasure meeting you last Thursday. You have a lot to be proud of at (*their business*). If I can ever be of assistance in the future, please call." Do not mourn a missed sale for too long. No one has a perfect record and sales is a game of percentages: the more phone calls made, the more personal visits made, the more sales. Rather than being depressed, think about what can be done to improve the chances of closing the next presentation.

If a sale was made, then also send a thank-you letter. More importantly, the sales representative must make sure that everything possible is done to assure the client's satisfaction in every aspect of the relationship. This will generally include several phone calls before the convention to see how the planning is coming; letters to verify meeting times, rooms, and food requirements; personal attention during the function, such as short meetings to make sure that everything is progressing as planned and to keep up with changes; and a meeting the last day to thank the client for the business. A small gift as a token of the hotel's appreciation will help cap off a positive experience and hopefully lead to repeat business and positive word-of-mouth advertising.

Sales Promotions

These are short-term incentives to increase sales, customer counts, and customer loyalty. (The primary exception to the "short-term qualifier" are frequent-flyer programs and many frequent-guest and frequent-diner programs.) Sales promotions include coupons, discounts, contests, samples, premiums (caps, T-shirts, glasses or cups), and product bundling promotions—the combination of several of the hotel or restaurant's products and services. These could include promotions such as a special dinner for two with a good bottle of wine, a summer weekend getaway, a violinist or opera singer for various occasions, or a murder mystery show where the audience takes part (Andreoli, 1992).

If desired, the marketing strategies section could include several separate action plans for specific sales promotions: for example, product plans for a coupon discount, a six-course dinner for two, a weekend package, and a charity event that would occur throughout the year. If the specifics of the promotions were going to be planned for a later date, this could be discussed in the strategies, with a statement that the marketing action plan would be prepared later.

Some important elements of the promotion to consider are the size of the offer or incentive, its cost, its duration, and its long-term impact.

SIZE   The size of the incentive should be large enough to attract the desired target market and achieve the stated objective, without causing the company to lose money. A 10% or even a 20% discount, unless creatively employed, will generally not be large enough to bring in restaurant customers. This is because there are so many buy-one-get-one-free coupons available that anything less will not be acceptable to many customer segments. A 10% to 20% discount will likely be adequate and profitable for a hotel if it is in return for additional night stays.

A temporary discount at an obvious loss may be justified if it increased customer counts and introduced new customers to the firm's products and services. However, it should only be used for a very limited time, such as when a restaurant first opens its doors and desires to fill the seats as quickly as possible. If the restaurant offers turn-back-the-clock prices for the first week, then their purpose may be well served. Of course, the restaurant must have a strategy for dealing with large crowds. A limited menu during this time could speed up service.

Some target markets are attracted by sales promotions (discounts), while others are not. On the whole, the most susceptible market for incentives is the fast-food and economy hotel customer. Markets above midscale for both hotels and restaurants have a marginal attraction to special offers or discounts, but there are always exceptions, as in weekend packages for midscale and luxury hotels. One of the reasons that markets beyond the economy segment are not highly influenced by offers is that they tend to value quality over price. Value to them is based on the experience and the pleasure it brings rather than saving a few dollars. When overhead is high and margins are tight, it is generally best to focus on quality and creativity, rather than on discounts.

Since most hotel customers either have advanced reservations or are on expense accounts, a temporary discount may not increase business at all. A premium, such as a free umbrella, or a patronage reward, such as a frequent-guest program, may be more effective with these groups. The weekend discount by itself has been around for so long and is so widely available that it has lost much of its effectiveness as a promotional tool. Combining the weekend discount with other incentives into a weekend package has proved extremely successful. The originator of modern weekend package promotions, Hilton Hotel's Bounce Back Weekend, accounted for a phenomenal increase in sales.

COST   The cost of the offer will vary with the incentive selected. It would probably not be wise for a fast-food restaurant to give away a $5.00 premium with each purchase, so some amount must be selected that the business can justify. A common practice is to sell an item with either the firm's logo or other advertising attached, such as a current movie, at slightly more than its cost; this way the expense is minimized.

Since most promotions involve discounts of some type, the business must calculate the true cost. The following scenario is used to describe a process for calculating the cost of discounting in foodservice operations:

• A restaurant with a 32% food cost offers a two-for-one special.
• Twenty-five percent of its sales for the promotional period came from the offer.
• These customers spend an additional 50% for drinks or appetizers.

Figure 10.16 shows that if the promotion was successful and either 15% or 25% of the sales during the promotional period were discounted, then the 32% food cost would have risen to 35.2% (at 15% of sales) or 37.3% (at 25% of sales). This would not be an unreasonable cost if the promotion was for a brief period of time and the customers attracted were potentially loyal target customers. If the period of time is too long, then the redemption percentage would probably increase. At a 50% redemption rate, the restaurant's food cost would rise to 42.7%, or an increase of over 10% of sales. This would in turn likely force management to either raise prices in an attempt to lower the food cost percentage, decrease quality or portions, find other methods of reducing overhead, or use a combination of these options. When the option selected is either raising the price or lowering the quality or portions, the restaurant will no longer be recognized as a reasonable value. If the discounting was continuous, then the redemption rate would continue escalating to the point where customers would not frequent the restaurant without a coupon and menu prices would have to be raised to an unacceptable level.

DURATION   The incentives should last long enough to allow target patrons the time to take advantage of it. Since not everyone goes out to eat every week and since patrons may not have the opportunity to dine at a specific restaurant over the very short term, perhaps a month should be the minimum time. If the incentive lasts for

First meal—$10.00
Second meal—Free ($10.00 meal)
Ancillary products—$5.00 (Items other than the main meal)
Total check—$15.00
Food cost of above meal at full price—$8.00, or a 32% food cost percentage ($8.00 ÷ $25.00)

Food cost of above $15.00 meal, with the special offer—$8.00 or a 53.3% food cost percentage ($8.00 ÷ $15.00)

Food cost for entire restaurant if 25% of sales are from the promotion and the balance at full price—
Food cost = 37.3% [0.25 (0.533) + 0.75 (0.32)]

Food cost for entire restaurant if 15% of sales are from the promotion and the balance at full price—
Food cost = 35% [0.15 (0.533) + 0.85 (0.32)]

Factoring in labor cost of 30% or $7.50 for the $25.00 meal ($15.00 full price, $10.00 free)—Food cost $8.00 plus labor cost of $7.50 equals a prime cost of $15.50 for the meal (prime cost = food + labor cost)

Prime cost percentage of $15.00 meal, with special offer—103.3% ($15.50 ÷ $15.00)

Prime cost percentage of full price meal—62% ($15.50 ÷ $25.00)

Prime cost for entire restaurant if 25% of sales are from the promotion and the balance at full price—
Prime factor = 72.3% [0.25 (0.1033) + 0.75 (0.62)]

Prime cost for entire restaurant if 15% of sales are from the promotion and the balance at full price—
Prime factor = 68.2% [0.15 (0.1033) + 0.85 (0.62)]

Figure 10.16   Calculating the cost of discounting.

much longer, it may lose some of its impact. Since many restaurants utilize second-party coupon books, such as Gold C, there may not be much flexibility on the duration.

When a hotel promotes a package of some type, it must make it available for a reasonable amount of time to allow for the fact that potential customers may not be traveling for several months. Of course, if the purpose of the incentive is to increase business during a specific period, such as during January, then a shorter term may be reasonable. When this is the case, it is best to have the offer on the market well before its redemption period.

LONG-TERM IMPACT OF SALES PROMOTION   Figure 10.17 demonstrates the potential positive and negative impact of sales promotions on sales. Sales promotions, primarily discounts, can be a boost to both short-term and long-term sales growth, if their use is limited. An occasional special of some type, such as dinner for two or even an extra night's stay for half-price, is generally appreciated by regular customers and may bring in new customers for a trial purchase. Most successful businesses find that long-term growth is enhanced by focusing on the quality and

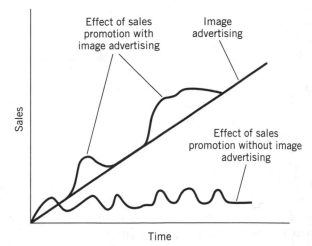

Figure 10.17 Impact of sales promotions on sales.

value of their products and services, and on image or informative advertising rather than discounting. Many companies use discounts (especially coupons) so frequently that customers tend not to make a purchase when no sales promotion is in effect. When this happens, they are only succeeding at convincing the customer to temporarily switch to their product. When the offer stops, most coupon-customers are lost. These companies will also find that saturating the market with discounts diminishes the ability of the firm to build sales over the long term.

Historically, this is what happened to the pizza industry. Beginning in the late 1960s, operators were having problems competing with the much cheaper and more popular hamburger restaurants. Going out for dinner had not reached its present popularity, so there were fewer customers. Rather than focus on value by lowering prices across the board or improving quality, businesses flooded the market with coupons—primarily buy one, get the next smaller size free. For years, this strategy permeated and nearly strangled the fast-food pizza concept. The strategy has become so embedded in the American culture, that Little Caesar's and several other pizza restaurants have centered their key promotional strategy around a two-for-one sales promotion. Though this strategy did not get entirely away from discounting, it did lessen the need for further discounts. One way to succeed with couponing is not to use it as a discount, but as a mini-advertisement. The price may or may not be less than the company's regular price, but since many people are hooked on coupons and specials, they use it regardless of the price. For example a dinner for two, a bottle of wine at a reduced price with a meal (the wine could be purchased in quantity to reduce its unit cost), or an extra night's stay for a reduced price.

Typical Considerations for Promotional Strategies

1. Which products or services should be promoted?
2. Where should each menu item be positioned/placed on the menu or menu board?

3. How important is the overall design of the menu to the customer's perception of quality and value?
4. Should food be displayed in any manner?
5. Will incentives be offered to promote customer/guest satisfaction or to increase sales?
6. Is there a promotional message or slogan needed?
7. Which of the promotional mix options—merchandising, advertising, personal selling, public relations, sales promotion—will be used? Basically, what are the most effective methods of reaching the firm's target customers?
8. What type of media will be used—print, broadcast, display?
9. What percentage of the budget will be spent in each selected medium and on selected target customers?
10. What percentage of the budget will be spent on mass media—broadcast, print, and display—and how much on personal communications—point-of-purchase promotions, merchandising, and personal selling?

ACTION PLANS

Where policies are relatively permanent activities designed to carry out strategies, action plans are temporary activities for the same purpose. Though they can be used for any functional area of the business, by far the most common is the marketing action plan. The reason for this is that, while most activities of other departments such as operations and finance change very little from year to year, marketing activities are composed of temporary events such as promotional or public relations campaigns that may last only a few months. When operations or financial policies do change, the policy is generally updated, rather than issued as a temporary policy or action plan. In spite of this, there will still be the need for occasional operations or financial action plans. For example, if the food cost has been well above budget, a series of intense actions could be taken to carefully monitor receiving, storage, preparation, line assembly, service, and cash control to locate the problem. After the problem was found and brought to resolution, the action plan would be either discontinued or incorporated into new policies.

Marketing Action Plan

The marketing action plan (tactics) details how the marketing strategies will be carried out. It can be organized according to the 4 P's or simply by what will be done, when it should be accomplished, who will be responsible for it, and how much it will cost. It should also include any other planning or implementational parameters or guidelines necessary to increase the chances for success.

What will be done? What new menu items or services will be added? Should the decor be remodeled or repainted? Which prices will change? What are the projected

HOTEL/LOCATION	EFFECTIVE DATES	RACK ($)	CORPORATE ($)	CORPORATE GROUP ($)	ASSOCIATION GROUP ($)	SMERFS ($)	LEISURE ($)	PACKAGE ($) (DESCRIBE)
Competitors								
1								
2								
3								
4								
5								
6								
7								

Figure 10.18 Marketing and sales plan: room rate comparison.

total sales, covers (customer counts for a restaurant), occupancy percentage, and ADR for the coming year? (See Figures 10.18 to 10.21.) The hotel's room rates should be compared with those of primary competitors. This would normally be accomplished in the competitor analysis and be included in the marketing action plan as a reference and justification for new pricing strategies or tactics (see Figure 5.15). What are the tactics for communicating with the business's target customers? All actions should be tied to the firm's overall objectives and specific marketing objectives. The marketing mix variables would be reviewed for options. Figure 10.22 is an example of a marketing action plan form used by many hotels. Other formats include outlines and matrices. Both are used in the hotel and restaurant examples at the end of the chapter.

What communication channels will be used? Marketers must decide between the appropriate mix of personal (direct contact between customers and personnel) and nonpersonal (mass media) channels. This and other issues may have been addressed in the market strategies portion of the strategic marketing plan.

Should national reservation systems, newspapers, magazines, radio stations, TV stations, or billboards be considered? Is merchandising, such as table-tents or food displays, an option? For hotels, the sales department will consume the majority of the marketing budget. Is a spokesperson appropriate?

| MARKET SEGMENT | LAST YEAR'S ACTUAL | | THIS YEAR'S ACTUAL/FORECAST | | NEXT YEAR'S BUDGET | | REVENUE |
	OCCUPIED ROOMS	ARR	OCCUPIED ROOMS	ARR	OCCUPIED ROOMS	ARR	
Individual Business Traveler							
Group							
Leisure							
Packages							
Complimentary							
TOTAL							

Marketing and Sales Plan
Hotel:
Year:
Occupied Rooms and Average Room Rate (ARR) by Market Segment

Figure 10.19 Occupancy and room rates by market segment.

Where will it be done? Once the decision has been made about which types of media will be used, management must decide which specific media vehicles to use. If newspapers were chosen, which newspaper should be used, which edition (citywide or neighborhood), and what section of the paper would be the most effective? (*We will run a 4-column-inch ad in* Texas Monthly *each month for the entire year. The ad placement will be on the last page of the food section.*) If television was used, the station and specific program would need to be selected.

When will it be done? The marketing efforts may be limited and only for the immediate future, or they may be extensive and spread throughout the entire year. Scheduling is critical. Often, a timeline will be used to visually display the timing of each activity. This is a calendar detailing the sequence of events that will need to take

Marketing and Sales Plan

Hotel:	Year:							
	Occupied Rooms and Average Daily Rate (ADR) by Period							
	LAST YEAR'S ACTUAL			THIS YEAR'S ACTUAL/ FORECAST			NEXT YEAR'S BUDGET			
PERIOD	OCCUPIED ROOMS	ADR		OCCUPIED ROOMS	ADR		OCCUPIED ROOMS	ADR		REVENUE
————	————	————		————	————		————	————		————
————	————	————		————	————		————	————		————
————	————	————		————	————		————	————		————
————	————	————		————	————		————	————		————
————	————	————		————	————		————	————		————
————	————	————		————	————		————	————		————
————	————	————		————	————		————	————		————
————	————	————		————	————		————	————		————
————	————	————		————	————		————	————		————
————	————	————		————	————		————	————		————
————	————	————		————	————		————	————		————
————	————	————		————	————		————	————		————
————	————	————		————	————		————	————		————
————	————	————		————	————		————	————		————
————	————	————		————	————		————	————		————
————	————	————		————	————		————	————		————
————	————	————		————	————		————	————		————
TOTALS	————	————		————	————		————	————		————

Figure 10.20 Form for tracking occupancy and room rates.

Marketing and Sales Plan
Food and Beverage Sales

Business _____

Year _____   Meal: Lunch ____ Dinner ____ Other ____

_____

OPERATING PERIOD:	COVERS			PER PERSON AVERAGE (PPA)			SALES		
	FORECAST	ACTUAL	VARIANCE	FORECAST	ACTUAL	VARIANCE	FORECAST	ACTUAL	VARIANCE
Total Year:									

Comments: _____

_____

_____

Figure 10.21   Form for tracking food and beverage sales.

Marketing and Sales Plan

Business:

Year: _____

Action Plan _____

Department: _____

Market Segment:

Objectives: Strategies:	Action Steps:	Date:	Position/Person Responsible:

Figure 10.22 Marketing action plan.

place before, during, and after the promotional campaign. Figure 10.23 is a sample of a timeline for a short ad campaign to promote a new banquet room for a hotel. Figures 10.24 and 10.25 are the forms used to prepare the marketing and related functional schedules for the current marketing plan.

Who is responsible? As in any business activity, if someone is not specifically assigned the responsibility for results, the outcome will be in question. Will an outside agency be brought in? How much responsibility will the agency be given? Will employees and management participate in the campaign and will they be ready for additional business? Is there someone in-house who is capable of managing a

SUNDAY	MONDAY	TUESDAY	WEDNESDAY	THURSDAY	FRIDAY	SATURDAY
	1 Call media contacts	2 Press release	3	4 Morning talk show	5	6
7	8 10 Ads Radio All KMOL	9 10 Ads	10 15 Ads	11 15 Ads	12 15 Ads Symphony benefit	13 5 Ads Cancer benefit

Figure 10.23   Timeline for ad campaign.

campaign? (*John Doe will be responsible for all advertising placement, Mary Smith for point-of-purchase materials, and Ed Williams for coordination of advertising with operations.*)

What will the budget be? Include the cost of salaries and each action taken (see Figures 10.26 to 10.29). Before preparing this year's budget, last year's expenditures should be compared with the results of each related strategy or tactic to see if it is worth repeating and if the expense category should be reduced, unchanged, or increased. Figure 10.30 is used for planning events and costs for various outlets in a hotel, such as a bar, restaurant, banquet services, and special events.

Will a reward system be needed to motivate employees? The success of any plan will be influenced by the degree of motivation of those who will carry it out. If employees and management are rewarded through regular evaluations and corresponding pay increases, rewards for specific marketing efforts may not be necessary. Generally, the closer management links a reward with the employee's actions, the higher the morale of the employee and the more responsive the employee will be to the next promotion.

1. All employees will receive a bonus of 10% of the increase of sales during the promotional period.
2. If the hotel reaches a 72% occupancy (or a REVPAR of $75) for an entire month, each employee will receive a $100 bonus.

POLICIES

Policies are relatively permanent activities undertaken to support strategic decisions. Here in the strategic plan, policies (and action plans) are the specific means by which the business will implement its functional strategies. The primary purposes of poli-

Business:

Marketing and Sales Plan
Year:

Promotional/Operational Timeline
Department:

Personal Selling/

MEDIA ACTIVITIES/ OPERATIONS/ OTHER	JANUARY	FEBRUARY	MARCH	APRIL	MAY	JUNE	JULY	AUGUST	SEPTEMBER	OCTOBER	NOVEMBER	DECEMBER

Figure 10.24 Cross-functional timeline.

Functional Strategies

Business:		Marketing and Sales Plan Year:				
Location:		Monthly Timeline—Month:				
Event/Task:						
Date/Day:						

Figure 10.25 Marketing timeline.

cies are to assign responsibility and authority, and to standardize the execution of repetitive tasks to allow the business to function at its most efficient and effective level. This, in turn, allows management time to focus on strategic issues, such as increasing sales or improving customer satisfaction and operations, rather than on dealing with recurring problems or tasks. For the most part, marketing, operations, human resources, and financial employees will perform their tasks based on the written policies in their respective policy manuals. The policies for most functional areas are generally contained in an all-inclusive operations manual or, if deemed necessary or appropriate, in specific policy manuals, such as for cash and financial management, marketing, and human resources, or in employee and management handbooks.

Marketing, operations, human resources, and financial policies included in the strategic plan will be either additions or changes to existing policies. As in functional strategies, if appropriate policies are already in place, they will not be changed. The

Business:	Marketing and Sales Plan Year:	
Marketing Department: Salaries and Wages		
EMPLOYEE	(No individual pay rates are recorded) **TITLE**	**EXISTING/NEW POSITION**

	Current Year Budget	Previous Year's Total	% Increase (Decrease)
Salary Total			
Benefit Total			
Total S&Bs			

Remarks: _____

_____

_____

_____

Figure 10.26   Salaries and wages.

Business:	Marketing and Sales Plan Year:			
	Sales: Travel and Entertainment Budget			

DESTINATION	EMPLOYEE	PURPOSE	DATES	BUDGET
This Year's Budget	Last Year's Actual or Forecast	$ and % Increase (Decrease)	Total Travel & Entertainment Budget	

Figure 10.27 Travel and entertainment expenditures.

purpose of the policies section of the strategic plan is to decide whether new policies or modifications of existing policies are necessary for the implementation of functional strategies.

Occasionally, there will be modifications, such as temporary or emergency policies, that evolve after the strategic plan has been written. For example, if operational policies state that the host/hostess normally works until closing, but there is not enough business to justify it, a temporary action plan may be required. Usually, this would simply be recorded in the manager's logbook. It may be decided that between 9 p.m. and closing the late servers will act as hosts (known as "watching the front

Business: _____   Marketing and Sales Plan
Year: _____

Sales: Dues and Subscriptions

EMPLOYEE	MEMBERSHIP	COST
	Total Dues and Subscriptions	

THIS YEAR'S BUDGET	LAST YEAR'S BUDGET/FORECAST	$ AND % INCREASE (DECREASE)

Figure 10.28 Dues and subscriptions.

| Business: | Marketing and Sales Plan Year: |
| | Marketing Expenses Summary |

CATEGORIES AND SUBCATEGORIES: TOTALS FOR APPLICABLE COLUMNS	CURRENT YEAR BUDGET	CURRENT YEAR ACTUAL	$ AND % VARIANCE	LAST YEAR ACTUAL	$ AND % VARIANCE

Figure 10.29 Marketing expenses summary.

Business:	Marketing and Sales Plan

Year: _____

Outlet Timeline and Cost

DATE	EVENT	PROMOTIONAL SUPPORT AND COST:				EVENT TOTAL
					TOTAL	

Figure 10.30 Outlet timeline.

door"). In attempting to deal with an increased number of walks (customers leaving without paying), management's desired action may be issued first as an action plan, then, if deemed necessary, included as a policy.

The degree and frequency of change for operational, human resources, and financial policies are normally limited because the company's overall strategies in those areas will not radically change. For this reason there will be relatively little need for action plans in these functional areas.

Writing a Policy

To write a policy, simply ask the following questions:

- What are the functional strategies that must be achieved? For example, *lower food cost through improved efficiencies in purchasing.*
- What are the specific procedures necessary to achieve the strategy? *Dry goods prices will be compared among three suppliers and purchased at the lowest quoted price.* (If the company is buying all of its dry goods from a full-line supplier, then the lowest total price would be appropriate.) *Seafood will be purchased according to the company's quality standards (policies). Seafood as a category must not move above a 36% food cost or be sold for more than $14.95 for an 8-ounce portion.*
- Are there any specific performance standards? *The price of each item purchased should be the lowest reasonable price possible, while at the same time complying with the hotel's specifications. Overall food cost should be kept at or below 33% per month.*
- Who will be responsible for it? *The purchasing agent, under the direction of the food and beverage director.*
- When or how often will it be done? *Dry goods, each Monday and Thursday; seafood, daily as necessary.*
- Will the policies achieve related strategies and objectives? *The objective is to lower food cost by 4%, while maintaining the present level of quality. This will be possible if combined with deleting two high-cost menu items and adding three pasta dishes.*

MARKETING POLICIES

The marketing policies are the parameters within which the marketing department will operate and the guidelines for the selection of marketing mix variables (the 4 P's). This could include site location requirements, relatively permanent food cost objectives (necessary when pricing menu or drink items and selecting items to promote), budgetary limits for the marketing department, the desired image or position (manipulated by the marketing mix variables), and the company's general philosophy toward its marketing efforts, such as focusing on new product development, product quality or consistency, or promotion to drive sales. Strategic or general management will work with the marketing department to set marketing policies.

Many of the routine duties of marketing department personnel will remain the same and be included as policies, such as "Each sales manager will maintain an updated file on all accounts in his/her territory." The specific tactics or actions to obtain business—number of phone calls or accounts to be called on for a certain week—will generally be in the action plan. Similarly, a football team has policies for the way each player should block, tackle, throw, and catch the football; but an action plan detailing where, when, and to whom they will direct their efforts must be developed based on competitive conditions.

Since most independent restaurants do not have marketing departments, the need for marketing policies may be minimal.

THE BRYAN HOUSE AND CITY GRILL STRATEGIES, POLICIES, AND ACTION PLANS

The Bryan House

FUNCTIONAL STRATEGIES

Marketing

Products and Services: Add business center, concierge, and workout facility. Increase hours for room service to start at 5 a.m. and end at 1 a.m.

Prices: Prices for the next year will remain the same to bring the hotel in line with the competition.

Place: No new strategies.

Promotion

Merchandising: Table-tents should be added to each room to promote the restaurant and workout facility.

Advertising: The hotel should have a different ad in each month's state travel magazine and should add the JAGUAR feature of SABRE.

Personal Selling

Hotel

Keep in close contact with present accounts.
Create a system for increasing referrals.
Upsell reservations and walk-ins.
Prospect for new business.
Develop new package for weekend business.
Maintain room nights with Clara's Cosmetics at 850.
Increase room nights with Nancy Giles Textiles from 345 to 450.

Restaurant

Set individual objectives for servers.

Public Relations

Join the American Cancer Society.
Hold six charitable events (at cost) at the hotel.
Send press releases regularly to let target customers and the community know about our charitable efforts.

Sales Promotion: Rates should be flexible (open rates) during the summer to attract association business.

Management

Front Desk: Add property management system by March 1, 19xx.

Housekeeping: Minimize use of supervisors by empowering housekeepers to take care of their assigned rooms. Spot checks will be made as necessary.

Food and Beverage: Have meetings with employees to determine how food costs can be lowered and quality improved. Labor cost for food service employees must be cut to 30% within six months and 28% by year's end.

Purchasing: Update specifications for each product purchased. Review supplier list for opportunities to improve quality and lower costs.

Human Resource Management: Begin work on operations and training manuals immediately. Have meetings with each department to gather recommendations from each employee and manager.

Administrative Management: The general manager will be responsible for monitoring implementation of the plan.

Finance/Accounting

Keep departmental managers and purchasing agent aware of performance toward financial objectives.

POLICIES

Marketing

Advertising: The advertising budget will increase to 2.5% of sales.

Services: Increase hours for room service to start at 5 a.m. and end at 1 a.m.

Management

Front Desk: The maximum time for check-out is 1 minute (with PMS).

Housekeeping: Housekeepers will be held accountable for their assigned rooms. This will include informing the executive housekeeper of the need for maintenance.

Food and Beverage: Training meetings will be held every two weeks until food quality increases. After objectives are reached, the meetings will be held each month.
All steaks and fish entrees will be cut in-house.

Steaks and fish must be cut within ½ ounce of specified weight.
Set up a schedule based on past sales that will achieve labor cost objectives.

Purchasing: Three suppliers must be allowed to bid on recurring purchases on a monthly basis.

Administrative Management: Each department head and his/her assistant will be reimbursed for one American Hotel and Motel seminar each year.

Finance/Accounting

Review costs and financial objectives with departmental managers and purchasing department once per week.

ACTION PLANS

Marketing

Products and Services: The meeting room nearest the front desk will be remodeled as a business center. The head of the maintenance department will be responsible for contracting necessary work. All designs, furniture, fixtures, and equipment must be approved at an executive committee meeting. Costs and budgets will be approved through the accounting department. Remodeling should be complete by March 1, 19xx.

A desk will be moved to the northwest corner of the lobby for the concierge. Maintenance will be responsible for having this done by February 25, 19xx.

A second floor meeting room will be converted to a workout facility. The head of the maintenance department will be responsible for contracting necessary work. Mirrors, improved lighting, and exercise equipment will be the primary additions. All designs, furniture, fixtures, and equipment must be approved at an executive committee meeting. Costs and budgets will be approved through the accounting department. Remodeling should be complete by March 1, 19xx.

Prices: Prices for the next year will remain the same to bring the hotel in line with the competition.

Place: No new strategies.

Promotion

Merchandising

Strategy: Table-tents should be added to each room to promote the restaurant and workout facility.

Action Plan: The head of sales and marketing will be responsible for working with our ad agency to create the message, design, and layout of the table-tents. Production will be handled through the hotel's current printer. These should be ready to be placed in rooms by June 1, 19xx.

Advertising

Strategy: The hotel should have a different ad in each month's state upscale magazine and should add the JAGUAR feature of SABRE.

Action Plans: The head of sales and marketing will work with our ad agency to have a different picture of the hotel in each issue of *Gallery.* Budgeting must be approved by the head of the accounting department. The head of sales and marketing will sign the hotel up with JAGUAR by January 15, 19xx.

Personal Selling: Hotel

Strategy: Keep in close contact with present accounts.

Action Plans:

Make an average of 40 calls per week to existing accounts.

Call each current account a minimum of once each three months to keep relationships strong. Follow up with sales calls as necessary. Keep accounts in a tickler file (a dated file) to make sure that each account is called.

Sales managers will travel to visit key accounts in our major origination cities. While there, prospect for new business.

Have secretaries' luncheon (RSVP) each six months.

Offer FAM trips to meeting planners with potential for business.

Strategy: Maintain room nights with Clara's Cosmetics at 850.

Action Plans:

Continue to offer discount on meeting rooms for training.

Invite Clara's salespeople to General Manager's reception at least once during their one-week stay.

Strategy: Increase room nights with Nancy Giles Textiles from 345 to 450.

Action Plan: Offer a reasonable discount for 100% of their business.

Strategy: Create a system for increasing referrals.

Action Plans: Offer free weekend stay with successful business referral. Record referrals in database so that clients can be rewarded as their referral books business.

Strategy: Upsell reservations and walk-ins.

Action Plan: Reservations manager will train staff to upsell to suites, increase length of stays, and book future nights.

Strategy: Prospect for new business.

Action Plans:

Attend major trade shows related to current market segments.

Actively network at Chamber of Commerce meetings.

Make an average of 50 cold-calls per week.

Increase road trips by 20%.

Organize telemarketing blitzes to attract new accounts.

Public Relations: Join the American Cancer Society by February 1, 19xx.

Sales Promotions

Strategy: Develop new package for weekend business.

Action Plans: Lower weekend package to $69 from $79. Include free workout, breakfast, airport shuttle, and chocolate-chip cookies each night.

Management

Front Desk: Purchase PMS by March 1, 19xx.

Housekeeping: Supervisors will gradually allow housekeepers to make more decisions for themselves.

Food and Beverage: Set sales objectives for each server in the restaurant. The combination of these objectives should equal the daily/weekly objectives for the restaurant.

Purchasing: No action plan for purchasing.

Human Resource Management: Attempt to sign with the new HMO by June 1, 19xx. Fine-tune employee stock ownership plan. Have it ready to implement by June 1, 19xx.

Administrative Management: Discuss objectives at executive committee meetings each week. Meet privately with each department head and assistant each week for a closer analysis of progress.

Talk with employees regularly to see what they think about the new plan and how it is impacting their performance and the performance of their department.

Finance/Accounting

Work closely with general manager to monitor financial performance of each department.

City Grill

FUNCTIONAL STRATEGIES

Marketing

Products/Services

Perform a menu analysis every six months (June 15th and December 15th) to determine which menu items are selling best and providing the highest contributing margin. (Chef Johnson)

Add one vegetarian item to the menu. If it proves popular, consider adding one more. Two should probably be the maximum number of vegetarian entrees.

Add new seafood item every few months. Drop those that are the least popular.

Add bakery for rolls.

Price: No item should take our overall food and beverage cost above 32%. We should keep our prices no more than 5% above those of primary competitors serving similar products. (If for some reason we cannot do this, we must be able to justify the higher price by a higher relative perceived value for the menu item.)

Place (Location, Facility): Begin search for second location if sales and profit hold steady through the first quarter of 1991.

Promotion (Merchandising, Advertising, Personal Selling, Public Relations, Sales Promotion): Our strategy will include a focus on word-of-mouth advertising through our high RPPQ, a good public image through community involvement in charitable events, a takeout promotional effort, and a discount for senior citizens.

Financing/Accounting

We must have approximately $250,000 if we plan on opening a second restaurant. This would be financed partially from cash flow and a loan, not yet arranged, of $150,000. We should begin negotiating a $150,000 loan for a possible second location.

$100,000 should be set aside in a contingency fund for a new location.

Set aside $6000 for an oven and ventahood for baking rolls and desserts.

The accounting department will oversee all monetary transactions and purchases in the restaurant.

Management

Administrative: Write a new strategic plan each year. Management must prepare an employee policy handbook.

Operations: Labor cost will be calculated on a daily basis.

A policy and procedure manual is needed before we add a bakery.

Food cost must be monitored daily with a food variance report.

The production line procedures must be changed to help lower ticket times to a 10-minute average per order.

A bakery consultant will be hired to write a policy and procedure manual for the bakery.

A new operations manual must be written to include new policies and to update existing policies.

Personnel: Medical insurance coverage should be available for all employees.

Training programs will be undertaken to increase the knowledge and performance of each employee.

Management hours are set at no more than 55 per week.

Management seminars will be scheduled through the National Restaurant Association for each manager.

POLICIES

Management

Operations: The manager (or purchasing agent) will be responsible for obtaining competitive bids at the end of each month for all food and beverages and for operating supplies. A minimum of two suppliers will be asked to bid on operating supplies, and three suppliers for food and beverage products. The exceptions to this are produce, meat, and seafood. Since the quality and consistency of these products have been excellent, we will compare prices on these items each three months.

On a daily basis, the chef will calculate a usage variance for our seafood items. For example, if our beginning inventory was 15, we received 20, and sold 30, we should have 5 left. If we have 4 left, we are short by one order.

Every six months (December 15th and June 15th), the manager and chef will calculate our ideal usage for operating supplies. For example, to examine our linen costs we will calculate the exact amount of linen we should be using, then figure our ideal cost.

The general manager (or accounting department) will complete a daily profit and loss statement for three months to access its value.

The chef will review kitchen procedures and timing for the preparation of every item on the menu every three months. Items with ticket times above 11 minutes must be brought down below 11 or removed from the menu.

The kitchen expediter and manager on duty will be responsible for monitoring ticket times for every guest check with a ticket timer.

Hire bakery consultant June 1, 19xx to write bakery manual.

Personnel: Beginning January 1, 19xx, we will include all employees in our medical insurance program after they have been with us for six months.

Beginning February 15, 19xx, each employee will be allowed to participate in our in-house management seminars put on by each manager.

By June 1, 19xx, each employee will be cross-trained in at least one other position.

By February 1, 19xx, management paperwork will be reduced to allow managers to work no more than 10 hours per day.

The human resources department will update position guidelines (job descriptions) by June 1, 19xx.

Each employee will receive an annual bonus based on the restaurant meeting key financial and customer satisfaction objectives.

Each manager will attend at least one National Restaurant Association seminar per year. He/she will report what was learned at the following manager's meeting or all-employee meeting.

Finance/Accounting

The corporate accountant will be responsible for implementation of the following new policies:

The interest rate on any loans must not be more than 1% over the current prime rate.

Before January 15th, open an account for a contingency fund for a new location. Set aside approximately $10,000 per month.

All orders for supplies will be processed through the accounting department so that costs can be compared to bids.

On a daily basis, the accounting department will review the DSR (Daily Sales Report) for accuracy.

Immediately upon receiving the bank's copy of the deposit receipt, the bookkeeper will compare it with the restaurant's copy.

On a monthly basis, the manager on duty will check food servers' guest checks for accuracy. During the month every server must have his/her guest checks audited at least once.

Marketing

The bookkeeper will be responsible for compiling all customer surveys on a quarterly basis for the CSI report.

The annual marketing plan will be updated each six months.

Hold marketing expenditures for 19xx to 3% of sales but concentrate on the objective and task method of setting the marketing budget.

All promotions should be somewhat conservative in nature.

Compile all customer surveys on a quarterly basis for the CSI report. (Jane Wilson)

All locations will be judged by our location guidelines, including good visibility, adequate number of target customers, parking for 60 cars, good ingress and egress, adequate traffic counts and traffic generators, recognized dining area, stable area, and limited crime statistics.

ACTION PLANS

Marketing

Products/Services: One vegetarian item will be added to the menu by February 1, 19xx—vegetarian lasagne. A Recipe, Cost and Procedure Sheet must be included for each new entree. Chef Johnson will be responsible for all menu additions.

The first seafood item will be added to the menu by February 1, 19xx—salmon, grilled or baked. The second seafood item will be added to the menu by April 1, 19xx—pescado verde.

Price: Menu Pricing Worksheets would be attached for new items. (Chef Johnson)

Place/Location: Begin location search if sales and profit hold steady through the first quarter of 19xx. (Bob Wilson—owner)

Promotion (Merchandising, Advertising, Personal Selling, Public Relations, Sales Promotion): Takeout promotion to begin April 1, 19xx. We will use point-of-purchase materials exclusively to announce the service. Our advertising agency will design and produce them. The budget is $400. Kay Wilson (manager) will be the contact person and will be responsible for coordinating the promotion.

Sales promotion of senior citizen discount is set to begin February 1, 19xx. The discount will be 15%. A 1/8th-page ad placed in the June 19xx, *Houston AARP Newsletter* will announce the promotion. The cost will be $250. Our advertising agency will be responsible. (Kay Wilson—manager)

Public relations efforts of fundraiser and charity events will be supervised by Kay Wilson (manager). The fundraiser for the Women's Shelter is planned for March 1, 19xx. This will be a wine-tasting dinner featuring two vineyard owners. The total budget is $800.

Matrix Format for Marketing Action Plan

Activity	Budget	Person Responsible	Target Date	Date + Initials When Completed	
Marketing Management					
Perform menu analysis		Chef Johnson	6/5/xx	_____	_____
			12/5/xx	_____	_____
Product					
Vegetarian entree (lasagne)		Chef Johnson	2/1/xx	_____	_____
Seafood entree (salmon)		Chef Johnson	2/1/xx	_____	_____
Seafood entree (pescado verde)		Chef Johnson	4/1/xx	_____	_____
Price					
Menu pricing worksheets prepared for each new entree		Chef Johnson	2/1/xx	_____	_____
			4/1/xx	_____	_____
Place					
Begin location search if sales continue to increase		Bob Wilson	4/1/xx	_____	_____
Promotion					
Takeout promotion positioned toward upscale market and as an alternative to pizza	$400	Kay Wilson Ad agency	4/1/xx	_____	_____
Senior citizen discount 15%—1/8th-page ad in *Houston AARP Newsletter*	$250	Kay Wilson Ad agency	2/1/xx	_____	_____
Charity Fundraiser for Women's Shelter (the event will be a wine-tasting dinner featuring two vineyard owners)	$800	Kay Wilson	3/5/xx	_____	_____

QUESTIONS AND PROJECTS

1. Are strategies generally set only during the strategic planning session, or are they set throughout the year? Explain.
2. Discuss some of the primary causes of ineffective strategies.
3. Which functional strategy changes the most? Why?
4. Discuss the three ways that strategies can be tested before they are adopted.
5. Which businesses need to change their product and service mix more frequently, restaurants or hotels? Why?
6. Talk to managers at several casual dining and upscale restaurants to find out what their pricing strategies and policies are for wine. Do they use a pricing factor or cost percentage? Do these pricing approaches vary by wine category?
7. (a) What is the average daily rate (ADR) necessary to break even for the following hotel: fixed costs, $365,000; variable costs, 22%; 350 rooms; 70% occupancy; 28 days in the accounting cycle?
   (b) If advertising costs were increased by 2%, how would this affect the ADR?
   (c) If monthly sales for the hotel were $500,000, and the variable costs remained the same, what would the hotel's profit be?

(d) If the building's mortgage of $250,000 was reduced through refinancing to $240,000, what would the new ADR-to-break-even figure be?

(e) By how much would this mortgage decrease, increase the hotel's profit?

8. Contrast cost-based, competitor-based, and customer-based pricing methods.

9. Create a new type of product-bundle pricing for a hotel. Do the same for a restaurant.

10. You are the director of sales and marketing for a Marriott hotel. A Hilton hotel is directly across the street and has nearly the same features and the same corporate rate of $95. If the Hilton reduces its corporate rate to $90, what would you do? If the following month they reduced their rate again to $85, would this change your strategies or tactics?

11. Describe the situations where you would use market-skimming and market-penetration pricing in the hospitality industry.

12. Discuss yield management for economy, midscale, and luxury hotels.

13. Analyze a location for a hotel by the various location factors. Do the same for a restaurant.

14. Locate areas in your community that are in each of the five categories of area stability.

15. Discuss Figure 10.9 from the perspective of promotional budgeting.

16. Discuss the success of a $14,000, three-month advertising campaign that increased sales by $9000 per month, in a restaurant with a 62% variable cost. Consider a residual increase in sales of $3000 per month after the campaign.

17. List and define each of the components of the promotional mix.

18. A certain city accounts for a sizable percentage of the hotel business in your city, but only 10% of the potential guests from this city have heard of your hotel, and only 2% of this potential market frequents your hotel. What are some possible advertising and personal selling objectives?

19. What are some methods of prospecting for potential guests for a hotel?

20. When you locate a prospect, how can you determine whether he/she is a good source of potential business?

21. In a sales presentation, what is the difference between a test close and a major close?

22. Discuss the possible long-term effects of the continuous use of sales promotions, particularly discounts, without image advertising (promote benefits, rather than offer incentives). What restaurants or hotels can you think of that:

(a) Always use sales promotions?

(b) Use an effective mix of sales promotions and image advertising?

(c) Never use sales promotions?

23. Describe the difference between policies and action plans.

24. Create a timeline for any hypothetical campaign. Support each of your tactics/actions.

APPENDIX A

Management Strategies, Financial Strategies, and Policies

OPERATIONS AND HUMAN RESOURCES STRATEGIES AND POLICIES

These strategies will provide the game plan for achieving the firm's annual objectives and grand strategies for strategic (administrative) management, operations (kitchen, purchasing, dining room, front desk, housekeeping, and so forth), and human resources. As previously mentioned, many of these areas of concern already have effective strategies, so this will include only changes or additions. The strategy will include the basic requirements for achieving the company's desired objectives and grand strategies. Policies will detail the specific actions needed for their achievement—what will be done, how it will be accomplished, when it will be done, and who will be responsible. This is the same progression and relationship as that between marketing strategies and the marketing action plan—what will be done, followed by the specifics of how it will be done.

FINANCIAL STRATEGIES AND POLICIES

The financial manager, or any person responsible for financial decisions, is first and foremost responsible for maximization of the owner's interest in the firm. This is accomplished through overseeing the acquisition of funds for the business and deciding how the funds will be used and controlled. The guiding principle of financial strategies is that each decision will carry a certain degree of risk based on the option selected and the option declined. Is the safe road compatible with company philosophy or is aggressive growth desired? The willingness to accept financial risks will depend to a great extent on whether the firm takes a conservative or an entrepreneurial stance toward strategies in general. Conservative firms tend to rely less on outside financing, while entrepreneurial firms generally must have outside financing to fund growth and innovation (Covin, 1991).

Extreme caution should be used when developing financial strategies, because they will be felt throughout the organization. Setting financial strategies will generally

473

require a reasonable base of knowledge related to principles of financial management. The two paragraphs here and other references in the book will not provide this knowledge. Most larger firms will have one or more financial specialists. Common titles are vice president of finance, controller, and, occasionally, treasurer. If someone in the firm is not competent in financial matters, and company size does not merit a full-time professional financial manager, then outside help should be sought. Frequently, banks will take an interest in customers and provide financial assistance. Another option is to bring in an outside consultant. Whatever course is taken, the company's top manager must listen to the advice and then take responsibility for the final decision.

Appropriate financial strategies will first require an in-depth understanding of the firm's objectives. The most obvious objectives are profit and growth, but the majority of all other objectives will impact financial strategies as well. Should the company purchase new equipment requested by the front desk manager, or finance a major advertising campaign proposed by the sales and marketing department? Should profits be used for dividends or for profit sharing and community causes, or should as much as possible be retained for future needs? If objectives specify that employees with certain skills should be hired, such as a chef, a financial decision may be necessary when reviewing compensation packages and the added value to the business of hiring a chef who commands $70,000, as opposed to a $35,000 chef. Also, will there be a secondary impact in hiring the $70,000 chef, perhaps unit management or other kitchen employees requesting more money?

Even when a company has a financial specialist, other departments within the company will participate in finance-related decisions. The sales and marketing department of a hotel will estimate sales. The maintenance supervisor will play a major role in deciding when a new air conditioning system is needed, and how much should be spent. This information will be used to prepare forecasts of future cash flow and to make other critical decisions about how the company's money should be used to finance growth or strengthen its present condition.

The basic principles that guide the selection of financial strategies are the same for both large and small firms. Figure 10.31 presents typical finance-related functions.

1. *Financing and Investments.* Supervising the firm's cash and other liquid holdings, raising additional funds when needed, and investing funds in such projects as repair and maintenance, new equipment expansion, and marketing efforts
2. *Accounting and Control.* Maintaining financial records; controlling financial activities; identifying deviations from objectives; and managing payroll, tax matters, inventories, fixed assets, and computer operations
3. *Forecasting and Long-Term Planning.* Forecasting costs, technological changes, capital market conditions, funds needed for investment, returns on proposed investment projects, and demand for the firm's product
4. *Pricing.* Determining the impact of pricing strategies on profitability
5. *Other Functions.* Credit and collections, insurance, and incentive planning, such as pensions, benefits, and bonuses

Figure 10.31 Typical finance-related functions. *Source:* Adapted from Schall & Haley (1986), *Introduction to Financial Management*, 4th ed. New York: McGraw-Hill.

CHAPTER 11

Institutionalization and Controls

Functional strategies state in general terms what will be done to accomplish the organization's objectives and grand strategies (long-term strategies or the strategic portion of the plan). The policies and action plans detail the specifics for achieving the strategies. Before the policies and action plans can be effectively implemented, management must consider certain characteristics of the firm that will act as either *impediments* or *facilitators* to the strategies' success. These characteristics include organizational structure, leadership, corporate culture, and rewards. Decisions must be made as to the most appropriate means of institutionalizing or ingraining the strategy into the daily routines of the business and its members.

IMPLEMENTATION VERSUS INSTITUTIONALIZATION

The terms *implementation* and *institutionalization* are often confused. Implementation refers to the action of carrying out the policies and action plans. Policies and action plans are what will be implemented. Institutionalization is using a systematic and scientific process (social science) to expedite implementation. The greatest operational policies or marketing plans in the world will do no good if the firm lacks the ability to execute them, if employees are resisting implementation, or if prescribed organizational changes are simply gathering dust in the manager's office. Once policies and action plans are set, they must be meticulously carried out through effective training and management support, and by enlisting enthusiastic, willing employee participation. The key factors for consideration when institutionalizing strategies are the organizational structure of the business, leadership, corporate culture, and a rewards and motivational system (Pearce & Robinson, 1991).

ORGANIZATIONAL STRUCTURE

Simply put, organizational structure is the division of tasks for the most effective (qualitative—best results) and efficient (quantitative—least costly) accomplishment of goals. It should be prepared based on the firm's requirements for strategy implementation and control (Pearce & Robinson, 1991). Strategies and tactics are the firm's response to how it will reap maximum advantage from the competitive environment. The organizational structure details how work will be arranged to implement those strategies and tactics. It is a visual representation of the types of activities and decisions that take place in the firm, where decisions are made, how they are communicated, and the relationship between departments. Each box on the organizational chart details what department, or unit within the department, is responsible for certain activities and tasks. It may also include the name of the person or persons responsible for associated tasks.

While the formal organizational chart attempts to portray how the organization functions, there are other influences that affect its relevance. Out of necessity, convenience, or the desire for social interaction, people will often interact in ways different from the organization's formal structure. Occasionally, people well below the top levels of the chart will make critical decisions based on their experience, reputation, leadership, or social skills. The extent to which this is appropriate depends on the organizational dynamics of the particular firm, the personalities and egos of key personnel, and how deviations from the formal structure are viewed. With the tendency toward increased employee empowerment, the information age versus the industrial age, and decentralized decision-making, the traditional responsibility and authority component of the formal structure is evolving into a less authoritarian presentation of how things get done (Houghton, 1992). At this point, it is difficult to say what new forms of organization will appear in the future, but they will probably be flatter, will rely less on functional departments and more on cross-functional teams, and will be more flexible and customer oriented rather than production oriented (Norris, 1992).

Types of Structure

In the hospitality business there are four common types of structures: *simple*—manager and employees; *functional*—manager, employees, and functional specialists (e.g., marketing, finance, human resources); *divisional*—two or more functional structures for the same business or corporation (an East and West Coast division or divisions based on different businesses); and *matrix*—a combination of the functional and divisional structures (used more in restaurants than hotels). Other structures that will become more common in the future are the *horizontal* structure—in which functional departments are retained but there is a minimal hierarchy and the majority of work is accomplished by cross-functional teams grouped according to customer-related needs (e.g., marketing, food and beverage, and accounting develop a new weekend package)—and *circular* structure—in which each department works closely with other departments and there is virtually no hierarchy (see Figure 11.1). A historical progres-

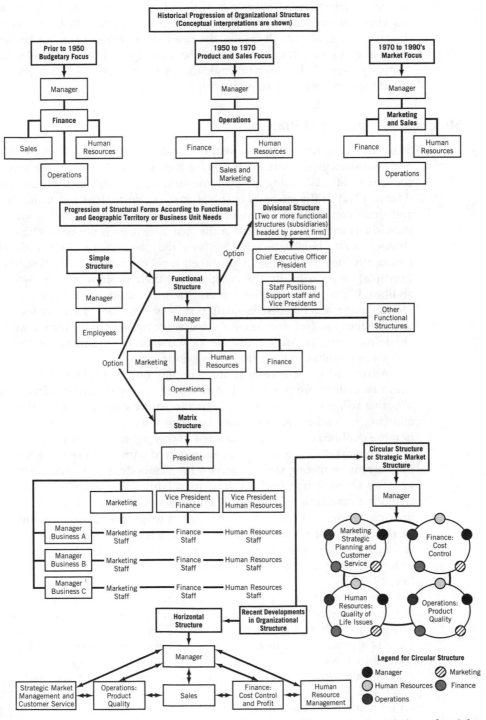

Figure 11.1   Common forms of organizational structure. (There are many variations of each form.)

sion of organizational structures is included to show how the focus of organizations has changed over the years. The normal progression is to begin with the simple structure; then, as growth creates the need for a greater focus on key areas such as marketing or accounting, there would be a change to the functional structure. If the company expanded, either through different concepts or geographically, it might adopt the divisional or matrix structure.

Structural Alignment and Strategy

Structure is important because, without an appropriate structure, the potential of an excellent strategy is limited. Various functional departments of the firm will need to coordinate efforts during preparation and implementation of the strategic plan (Hahn, 1991). If the current organizational structure does not facilitate cooperation and open communications, gaps in planning or implementation will exist. When individuals within the structure or the structure itself is not compatible with the new strategy, a *structural impediment initiative* may be required to remove the obstacle. Frequently, people are promoted to their level of incompetency (known as the Peter Principle) or occasionally the company or their position has grown beyond their abilities. When either situation occurs, there is a tendency for the incompetent individuals to surround themselves with people with similar or greater levels of incompetence so they can feel more secure. Also, since these people may not know what they are doing or may not have a firm mental grasp on the situation, they tend to try to do as little as possible, to keep from being noticed.

A common occurrence in strategy implementation is that after the new strategy is in place, there are problems because the existing structure is inadequate. Generally, this will force a change to a structure more congruent with the new strategy, allowing for successful execution. For example, if a strategy specified new menu items, a qualified chef might be needed. If competition was threatening, an increased focus on marketing would be needed, required a professional marketer, expansion of the current marketing staff, or advice from outside consultants such as advertising agencies or marketing firms. A strategy calling for geographic market development without a structural or functional emphasis on location selection, layout, design, finance, hiring, and training could result in major problems. Of course, it must also be remembered that structural reorganization is not the solution, if the firm's organizational structure is not the problem. Sometimes there is only a need for adjustments in how existing departments cooperate or in the personnel involved (Heyer & Van Lee, 1991).

Generally, the larger an organization, the greater its bureaucracy, and frequently, the more resistant it is to change. The greater the division of responsibilities, the greater the likelihood that departments will have a limited, biased, and self-serving view of the actions required to solve problems and implement strategies. This is sometimes referred to as *organizational arteriosclerosis*. These firms may view environmental shifts (the competitive environment) as fads that will pass in time; new entrants to the industry are noted only as a passing curiosity. Rather than focusing on innovation, actions by key competitors are monitored to see if new products or services are successful. And finally, the most prominent indicator of organizational arteriosclerosis is believing that it is only a question of time before existing policies will bring back the success of the past.

MANAGEMENT

In the hospitality business, or any business, the abilities of the firm's top management personnel in selecting the appropriate strategies and directing the firm toward their accomplishment will dictate success or failure. Consequently, when there is a major problem caused by poor planning, unrealistic strategies, or ineffective communication or implementation of the strategy, it is normally the firm's top manager who is at fault. Since these managers are often tied to the strategies they helped create, when strategies are unsuccessful, it is frequently best either to bring in a new manager who has experience with the new strategy, or to allow greater participation of other management personnel. This could include functional specialists or those with broader project experience.

Among the key skills of a hospitality manager are the ability to assure customer satisfaction, maintain profit, control costs, uphold standards, delegate, communicate, train, maintain a suitable degree of morale, and motivate. This broad base of necessary skills requires that hospitality managers have a combination of education and training exceeding that of many other fields.

The most important skills related to strategic marketing are the ability to:

- Objectively assess the firm's present market position.
- Inferentially identify relevent issues and recognize the degree of their importance (Boone & Kurtz, 1987). This allows for the maximum extraction of benefits from the environment.
- Decide what changes are necessary to take advantage of the environment.
- Communicate and enforce policies through subordinates.

Management Versus Leadership

There have been many attempts, from scientific to mystical, at delineating the difference between leadership and management. Warren Bennis stated that leaders do the right things (in the broad strategic sense) while managers do things right (in the short-term, bottom-line sense) (Norris, 1992). This statement is accurate, in that it represents the essential roles of the leader and manager, but a further explanation is required.

People have five basic sources of power related to interpersonal relationships: legitimate, reward, coercive, expert, and charismatic power (Gibson, Ivancevich, & Donnelly, 1991).

- *Legitimate power* refers to a person's ability to influence others because of his/her position. Someone higher in an organizational structure will likely have legitimate power over others. This has little to do with a personal ability to direct the efforts of subordinates: it is simply because that person occupies a different position than the subordinates. Legitimate power can also refer to how the reputation of one's firm influences the actions of employees.

- *Reward power* concerns the ability to provide followers with something of value in return for achieving desired objectives. The valued reward could be tangible, generally a bonus or raise, or it could be intangible, such as a larger office, recognition, or a new assignment or title.
- *Coercive power* is having the ability to punish followers for not acting in a desired manner. Followers will act out of fear of the negative results of subpar performance. A problem with punishment, and the fear it creates, is that if it is not fairly applied, it may increase anxiety and aggressive tendencies on the part of subordinates. This might be exhibited through low morale and dislike of supervisors or the company in general. Additionally, punishment is supposed to persuade employees to act in accordance with company policies. As employees see peers being punished, they learn to imitate this behavior, thus creating a negative environment that is the opposite of the original purpose of the punishment.

The above three types of power are referred to as *power of position*. It can reasonably be assumed that the average manager will have them available as situations require their use. They are given to people and can therefore be taken away or modified, as through rewriting of policies. The last two types of power are personal. Expert power is earned through performance or experience. Others perceive the manager to be an expert or as someone having above-average competence in a certain area. A manager may or may not have expert power. People generally either have or do not have charismatic power. This trait is generally found only in leaders.

- *Expert power* occurs when a person has particular personal, technical, or administrative abilities that are valued by the organization. Expert power can be held by almost anyone in the organization and increases with the difficulty of replacing them. The only dishwasher who can handle a shift alone has expert power.
- *Charismatic power* is exhibited by people who can influence others through their personalities and behavioral characteristics. The influence is derived from others wanting to either be with this charismatic person or be like him/her. Obviously, this can have both positive and negative effects on the organization, depending on the motives of the person with charisma.

Technical and Interpersonal Skills

Figure 11.2 explains leadership in terms of a two-dimensional construct—technical and interpersonal (Javidan, 1991). The technical dimension refers to the manager's functional and administrative expertise and the ability to control costs and quality. The interpersonal dimension represents how the executive impacts other people in and outside the organization.

Quadrant 1. The *powerless manager* has very little influence in the organization and is not effective in most undertakings.

		Technical	
		High	Low
Interpersonal	High	4. Superior Leader	2. Political Gamesperson
	Low	3. Technician	1. Powerless Manager

Figure 11.2   Leadership. *Source:* Adapted from Javidan (1991), Leading a high-commitment, high-performance organization. *Long Range Planning,* 24(2), 28–36.

Quadrant 2. A *political gamesperson* is someone who has a limited knowledge about how the business should be run but has a charismatic personality and is able to garner personal influence in the organization.

Quadrant 3. The *technician* is a high performer who makes sure the business is operated at a profit but who is not viewed as a leader by subordinates.

Quadrant 4. The *superior leader* elicits the best efforts from employees by showing them that everyone benefits when the company does well. This person is looked up to by subordinates as a role model, someone for whom they will do whatever is needed.

ORGANIZATIONAL CULTURE

Organizational or corporate culture is the unifying belief system that can be identified in any company. It is based on a variety of factors generally stemming from historical philosophies of management, organizational goals, the firm's focus on standards, its successes and failures, and organizational and community norms. The culture of the firm tends to guide employee behaviors through implicit codes of conduct and expected behaviors (Burack, 1991). If it does not consider the attitude and reactions of employees toward change then all planning efforts may be for naught.

Before employees are requested to change the way they have been performing their routine tasks, or to modify their beliefs, a careful assessment of the business's corporate culture should be made and factored into the development of new strategies. After all, one of the main characteristics of corporate culture is its stabilizing nature, or resistance to change, which helps individuals and the firm stay on an even course. For the most part, corporate culture is a positive factor in business. The existence of a corporate culture makes it possible for management to identify characteristics that permeate the work ethic of employees in order to improve implementation of strategies.

Acknowledgment of the power of corporate culture should be incorporated into the plan, with its own strategy. Unfortunately, it is usually only an afterthought: "Tell the employees to do it, and they'll do it" is a common attitude. Perhaps the plan must be marketed to employees in a manner similar to how it will be marketed to the consumer (Piercy & Morgan, 1991). Find out what their needs are, then satisfy them.

Often, most aspects of culture will be easy to identify; at other times, idiosyncrasies will only surface during stressful situations. The corporate culture is critical because it determines what is important to the employees: "Do your best" or "Just take it easy"; "Be proud of what you serve" or "Just get it out"; "Teamwork" or "You're on your own." When strategies are changed, the firm may also have to change cultures—or employees—because if the strategies are not supported by all persons involved, achievement will be hindered (Aram & Cowen, 1991).

Because of the high turnover in hospitality businesses, we generally do not have the problem with corporate cultures that long-established businesses like many manufacturing firms do. Since the employees have not had habits reinforced through time (relative to manufacturing), it is easier to get them to change. Of course, there are hospitality businesses that have a low turnover, but these businesses generally do not have problems with corporate culture because the low turnover is generally indicative of good management and a positive culture.

A strong leader can change the corporate culture of a hospitality business in a very brief time by holding an all-employee meeting, announcing the new rules, and then supporting the new rules with a period of training and coaching. There will be exceptions, but employees will usually want to keep their jobs more than their culturally based/biased habits. They realize that a few changes in their work habits are a much simpler challenge to deal with than looking for a new job. Anyone, employees or management, who does not firmly believe in the goals of the company must not be allowed to linger. Malcontents, even if minutely justified, can destroy morale and thwart the effective implementation of new policies and programs. A serious talk should be had; then whatever actions are deemed necessary should be taken to resolve misgivings about the changes or other philosophical differences. For these reasons, management's leadership skills are one of the most critical elements in the hospitality business for institutionalizing and implementing strategies.

REWARDS AND MOTIVATION

Quality leadership and a positive corporate culture by themselves will go a long way to infusing a sense of loyalty in employees and management. What is lacking at this point is a more intrinsic, individualistic approach to enlisting the worker's body *and* mind in the effort to reach the firm's goals. This requires an understanding of rewards and how best to motivate both employees and management personnel. *Motivation* can be defined as instilling a desire in employees to perform tasks because it serves their own purposes. *Rewards* are tangible and intangible benefits received when goals or objectives are met. As a rule, the sooner the reward is received after the performance that initiated it, the happier the worker, and the more likely he/she will be to repeat the performance.

The company must find out what motivates each employee and manager to act. It obviously cannot have 200 different reward or motivational programs, but it may at least need different programs for various levels of the organization, and perhaps some optional rewards or benefits for each level. A male worker whose wife has an excellent insurance plan at her job may not be motivated by insurance benefits. Instead, being allowed to select from a menu of benefits, such as college tuition reimbursement, seminars, or increased retirement funding, might be preferred. The type of monetary bonuses desired by employees or managers may depend on their level in the organizational structure. Some may prefer bonuses in the form of cash or increased pension funding; others may prefer stock. A combination of various bonuses would be another option. Symbolic rewards (trophies, plaques, certificates, T-shirts with an imprint of achievement) are an additional consideration.

Frequently, firms consider the fact that they offer a secure job, good working conditions, quality supervision, decent wages and benefits, and interpersonal relationships to be sufficient motivators. But according to Frederick Herzburg, these factors will not necessarily motivate employees. It is simply important that they be maintained at a level that does not create dissatisfaction. He referred to them as *dissatisfiers* or *hygiene factors*. A second set of conditions, *satisfiers* or *motivators*, serve as the tools of motivation. They include achievement, recognition, responsibility, advancement, the work itself, and the possibility of growth. The basic difference between hygiene factors and motivators is that hygiene factors allow management to bring employees to the level at which they can be motivated. If the employee or manager is not satisfied with his/her working conditions or dislikes his/her supervisor, that employee or manager will probably not be motivated to perform at an optimal level. Though there have been many academic assaults on Herzburg's two-factor theory, it is still one of the most applied motivational tools. Follow-up research on Herzburg's results have shown that there was a misinterpretation of the categorization of money as a motivator. The absence of money as a motivator was in fact one of the reasons his theory has been so popular with managers. The use of Herzburg's various motivational factors was much less expensive than motivating with money.

There are countless theories as to the effectiveness of money as a motivator, many of which contradict each other. In reality, each person will act differently toward its use as a motivational tool. One plausible theory is that there is a direct relationship between the need for money and its motivating power. If employees cannot pay their bills, or if they are not driving the car they want or living in the house they would like, then money will probably motivate them. Once the bills are paid and their basic wants are satisfied, the effectiveness of money as a motivator is diminished (Reich, 1990).

A method of motivation that is gaining wider acceptance in service businesses is *enfranchisement*. It is the combination of empowerment—allowing employees to make decisions necessary to perform their work at peak levels—and some type of compensation that rewards individuals or groups for performance (Schlesinger & Heskett, 1991). The most notable efforts of the hospitality industry to use enfranchisement have been in the area of restaurant servers who have been compensated primarily by tips from customers. Many restaurants will also include bussers, hosts, and occasionally cooks in a tip pool divided at the end of the night. Managers can be paid a bonus based on various measures of performance, primarily sales and profit, and, with greater frequency, customer satisfaction.

Applications of enfranchisement in the fast-food segment and the hotel industry have been slow in coming. Individual rewards will be more difficult to distribute and possibly more subjective, so group enfranchisement should be considered. The achieving of sales goals or occupancy levels (or REVPAR) along with appropriate empowerment might help.

Sporting events would be less satisfying for both players and spectators if no one kept score (Sandy, 1991). Too often, people go to work for months at a time without knowing how their efforts have impacted the company's results. A primary reason why people participate in sports is that they need to feel good about their abilities. They need to know that they are good at something. If daily targets, or objectives, are developed for each functional department, employees and management will have a better understanding of what is important and how the game should be played and, therefore, will be motivated to win.

CONTROLS

After the strategy has been institutionalized (through the policies and action plans), its achievement must be monitored to keep the firm's actions on course to meet its objectives and to ensure the strategic direction is in harmony with the firm's competitive environment. Without control, there is a natural tendency for group endeavors to lead to chaos.

Controls are the systematic evaluation of the organization's performance to determine whether it is accomplishing its objectives and implementing its strategies in an effective manner. They help assure that all work expended in preparing and writing the strategic plan will be put into action (Bungay & Goold, 1991). Controls also help prevent strategic surprises by setting up a continuous environmental monitoring system. Since the firm will be setting objectives and strategies that will be accomplished over the long and short term, a two-tiered approach is required. The two basic levels of controls are discussed in the following.

Strategic Controls

Strategic controls guide the strategic direction of the company by attempting to assure a continuous and effective match between the present internal abilities of the firm and the opportunities and threats in the environment. In the majority of cases, strategies that are included in the initial plan will be implemented as written. These are referred to as *deliberate strategies*. However, after a strategy is set, there will be changes in the business, in its competitive environment, and in the way the leader interprets their effects on the business. There must be a constant awareness on the part of management to make sure that the strategy as intended is still viable in light of new information. For example, if management or employee performance has improved, there may be new strengths and opportunities, and possibly fewer weaknesses and threats. If there are environmental changes, such as societal trends progressing faster than assumed, then changes in the strategies may be needed. When important events are noticed, decisions will have to be made about whether the firm's objectives or strategies should be changed (Camillus & Datta, 1991). These are referred to as *emergent strategies* because they were not part of the original plan (Mintzberg, 1978). Emergent strategies that are successful and worthy of inclusion in the next plan will become deliberate strategies (see Figure 11.3).

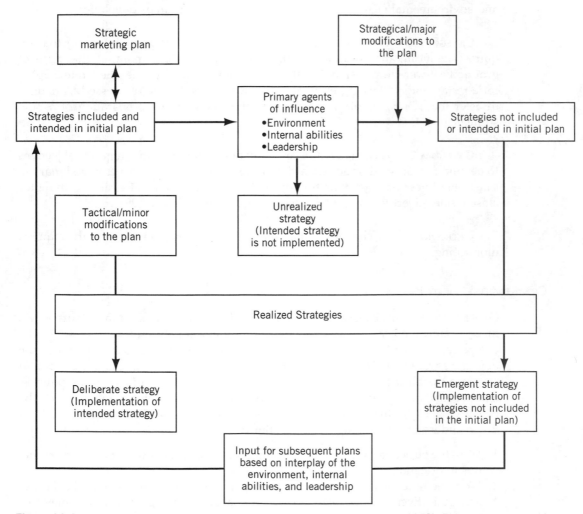

Figure 11.3 Strategy creation sequence. *Source:* Adapted from Mintzberg (1978). Patterns in strategy formation. *Management Science,* 24, 934.

Strategic control is essentially moving through the plan from the mission statement down through long-term objectives and grand strategies to note changes that could cause management to alter its plan. If changes are found that require a new strategic direction, then changes in annual objectives, functional strategies, and supportive policies and action plans may also be required. It should be a routine responsibility of management to consistently monitor the company's abilities and its environment, making sure that the company is on track to reap the greatest competitive advantage from the environment. (For information on compiling a marketing information system see Chapter 3. For assessing the importance or potential impact of an environmental factor see Chapter 5.)

CLASSIFYING CHANGES   To simplify and organize the assessment of internal and environmental factors, a scale such as the following can be developed:

CATEGORY 1   A major change in either the company or environment that requires significant modifications to the company's strategic plan. If the price of ground beef were to rise significantly over a short period of time, the strategic plan for a restaurant specializing in hamburgers would need to be reassessed. A natural disaster that destroyed all or part of a facility requires the preparation of a new strategic plan.

CATEGORY 2   A change in the company or environment that requires objectives to be modified upward or downward. If a competitor moves into a crowded market, sales objectives may need to be adjusted downward. Likewise, if a competitor closed, sales objectives might be increased (Camillus & Datta, 1991).

CATEGORY 3   A change in the company or environment that only requires monitoring.

Operational Controls

Operational controls consist of monitoring each functional area to make sure it will meet its annual objectives. Monthly or quarterly interim objectives can be set so the company will not have to wait until the end of the year to decide whether the objectives were met. The primary purpose of managers' meetings is to discuss and compare the business's level of performance with the standards set in its policies, and to measure its progress toward objectives. If there is a problem with meeting the objectives, or with the execution of functional strategies, the problem can be tracked down and isolated by asking three questions:

1. Were the objectives improperly set, either too high or too low, or based on erroneous information?
2. Were the functional strategies and corresponding policies and action plans properly set? (Even if effectively carried out, a poor strategy will not achieve its objective.)

3. Were the strategies (and policies and action plans) properly institutionalized and implemented? (Effective objectives and strategies do not necesssarily lead to effective execution.)

After management locates the root cause of the problem, it must solve it as fast as reasonably possible. The method of solving any business problem is the same process by which the objective or strategy was set in the first place. A problem with the objective would be looked at based on its compatibility with the environment and the ability of the firm, then appropriately modified. A problem with strategy formulation, policies, action plans, and institutionalization or implementation would ideally be addressed by locating the source of the problem, then developing a solution.

One of the primary reasons for failure is the inability to track performance and recognize deviations from what is needed for success in a particular business. Overall performance will be improved if management will simply monitor each key area of the company, then make corrections as required. This is what management gets paid to do. Too frequently, managers spend so much time physically or mentally putting out fires that they have little or no time to find out what the real problem is. When this occurs, the only result can be increased stress for both management and employees, the subpar performance of the business, and, in most cases, the eventual decline of sales and profits. One of the reasons the strategic marketing process is so valuable is that, if management takes the time necessary to prepare and utilize it, many of the inherent risks of business are either minimized or eliminated.

When in doubt about a means to control any business activity, use the following four-step control process:

1. Establish standards or goals. For example, each housekeeper should be able to clean four rooms per hour.
2. Measure actual performance. For example, 3½ rooms are being cleaned.
3. Identify the deviations. For example, performance is one-half room below the standard.
4. Determine the cause and take corrective action. There are two causes: (1) there is inadequate supervision or attention being paid to the standard, and (2) more training is required for newly hired housekeepers. Corrective action will include addressing the above issues and means of increasing the motivation for housekeepers through bonus programs.

CONTINGENCY PLANS   It is a near-impossibility for a company to successfully implement every one of its strategies. For this reason, each major strategic decision should have an accompanying contingency plan ready to implement if the original strategy is falling short of its intended target. If a strategy calling for lowering prices to attract more customers was not producing results, contingencies of lowering prices further, broadening the items or services included in the reductions, increasing promotion, or improving quality might be necessary. If the contingency plan was prepared and ready to go, valuable time would be saved. Additionally, if desirable, the continuity of the original strategy could be saved.

THE BRYAN HOUSE AND CITY GRILL INSTITUTIONALIZATION AND CONTROLS

The Bryan House

INSTITUTIONALIZATION

Organizational Structure

The marketing department will be expanded to include one or two new sales managers. The kitchen must be monitored closely to determine whether a new chef or outside consultant is needed.

Leadership

The general manager is capable of implementing this plan. She will need the assistance of the management companies' corporate supervisors.

Corporate Culture

There is no problem with The Bryan House's corporate culture. Employees willingly work together and are generally proud of their work and the hotel. Change is always difficult; their professional attitudes will make implementation easier.

Rewards and Motivation

Since our employees' compensation is slightly below that of other competing hotels, each employee should be on some type of incentive program. At departmental meetings, employees with exceptional performance should be recognized with trips, hotel stays, dinners, and annually with a plaque.

CONTROLS

Strategic Controls

All management personnel will play a part in the hotel's marketing information system. Each will be assigned periodicals and journals to review and competitors to monitor. Part of each executive committee meeting will be set aside for a discussion of strategic issues. This information will be accumulated in a database by a secretary in the marketing department.

Operational Controls

Guest comment cards will become the central feature of our new control system. The cards will be available in a display at the front desk for guests to take and complete at their choice. Additionally, each fifth guest that checks out will be asked if they would take a few moments to complete the comment card. (This must be a random selection, otherwise the results will not be reliable.) We must be sure that it does not take longer than two or three minutes to answer the questions. On a weekly basis, each departmental manager must review his/her department's progress toward departmental objectives. It is imperative that each employee know how his/her performance affects the hotel's financial performance and image, and that we want employee input into all major decisions.

City Grill

INSTITUTIONALIZATION

We will not have any problems institutionalizing our strategy because we have excellent managers and our culture is geared toward doing everything within our power to please the customers. Management has been doing a good job, but, with additional training, hopefully performance can improve. We have a simple structure and can therefore implement policies quickly. Rewards will be offered to all employees for meeting objectives.

CONTROLS

Strategic Controls

We will institute a marketing information system to keep track of changes in the external environment. It will include subscribing to several restaurant magazines, national business magazines (*BusinessWeek, Forbes, Fortune,* and *Inc.*), and both Houston newspapers. Each manager will be assigned one or more periodicals to review for pertinent information and articles. At each weekly manager's meeting, we will spend five minutes discussing important events that could affect the restaurant's current strategies or provide us with new opportunities.

Operational Controls

Progress toward annual objectives will be closely monitored and reviewed on a weekly basis at each manager's meeting. Additionally, implementation of all policies (both existing and incremental) and marketing action plans will be the full responsibility of the applicable supervisor. Our key concerns are that we continue to achieve a 4.2 CSI (customer satisfaction index) and an average monthly profit of 15%.

Contingency Plan

We will monitor our progress toward our objectives on a weekly basis and make appropriate changes as necessary.

If we are not meeting our objective of a 20% increase in takeout business, we will increase our use of point-of-purchase displays and offer a temporary discount for to-go orders.

QUESTIONS AND PROJECTS

Institutionalization

1. What is the difference between institutionalization and implementation?
2. Discuss the following terms, and describe why each is important to the implementation of policies and action plans:
   (a) Organizational structure
   (b) Management
   (c) Corporate culture
   (d) Rewards and motivation
3. Why is delegation of authority critical in service industries?
4. Discuss the abilities of a manager for whom you have worked, based on his/her managerial skills.
5. Discuss the corporate culture of various businesses for which you have worked. How has their culture helped or hindered the company's performance?
6. Do you feel it is too expensive to offer all employees financial incentives? What do you think is the ideal benefits package for salaried and for hourly personnel, for each type of hospitality firm?

Controls

1. What is the basic purpose of controls?
2. Define strategic and operational controls.
3. What are the basic questions to ask if a company is not meeting its annual objectives?
4. Discuss controls used by companies for which you have worked.

Leadership Skills of Famous Athletic Coaches

In "Effective Management Techniques in Business: Lessons from Famous Athletic Coaches," Wookey and Kleiner (1991) discussed the following traits possessed by some of the most successful coaches and how they applied to business:

1. They all had an intimate knowledge of the game. This allowed them to be innovators, to take chances, and possibly to fail. When they did fail, they learned something positive from it.
2. The great coaches trained their teams to be masters of the fundamentals of their sport. Inexcusable mistakes were minimized.
3. Hard work was expected. Since physical conditioning is one of the most critical points of differentiation for a sports team, the coaches made sure that their teams could outlast their opponents.
4. The success of any one player was secondary to the success of the team.
5. Every great coach was an outstanding motivator. Although their styles and methods of motivation differed, each was able to get the maximum talent out of their players. Billy Martin, former coach of the New York Yankees professional baseball team, would on occasion intimidate or threaten players. John Wooden, coach of the most successful college basketball team of all time, the UCLA Bruins, was a father figure to his players. Business managers must generally focus on positive styles of motivation.
6. All of the great coaches were respected. This was generally earned because of their mutual respect for their players. Players come from a variety of backgrounds, so it was important that coaches not impose their own value judgments on them.
7. Great coaches had a high level of confidence in themselves and in their abilities. This confidence manifested itself in the players.

Sample Strategic Marketing Plan (Annotated)

The following is an annotated strategic marketing plan concerning nutrition considerations for foodservice establishments (Reich, 1995).

STRATEGIC IMPLEMENTATION OF NUTRITIONAL PROGRAMS FOR FOODSERVICE ESTABLISHMENTS: GUIDELINES, RECOMMENDATIONS, AND EXAMPLES

The process by which effective nutrition programs are implemented will commit far more of the staff's time and energy than most people assume. Frequently, kitchen personnel are the only concern when making nutritional or any changes to a menu. The reality is that virtually every department within a foodservice facility will be impacted if the changes are to be successfully carried out. Effective nutritional upgrades of menus consist basically of three key processes. First, one must have the ability to decide what nutritional changes will be important and significant, as perceived by the customer. Obviously, there are currently people whose consumption patterns are based primarily on a concern for nutrition, and year by year this market is growing larger. Consumer demand for nutrition in foodservice facilities will likely follow this curve. However, for most foodservice operations, this consumer segment is still too small for radical nutritional upgrades. Second, management must acknowledge other environmental issues such as the economy, technology, competitors, suppliers, and political regulations. As the pace of environmental change quickens, monitoring, forecasting, and recognizing the importance of various issues will become critical skills. Third, one must assess the abilities of the firm to execute the nutritional strategy. This will entail educating and training internal and external stakeholders affected by menu decisions. Addressing the needs and concerns of management, chefs, kitchen workers, servers, customers, suppliers, and the local community will be an essential element of nutritional as well as any other strategic change. If management or employees with the appropriate knowledge are not available to assess factors related to the decision, then outside help from a registered dietitian may be needed.

Strategic Market Management

This often used, but generally misunderstood, term can be defined as the joint preparation of a long-term strategic plan and annual functional plans to assure a long-term compatible fit between the organization's capabilities and goals and its competitive environment (Kotler, 1991; Reich, 1995). Its objective is essentially to simplify and increase the effectiveness of strategic (long-term, critically important) decision-making through the utilization of a tested comprehensive process (Lele, 1992). The process consists primarily of six basic tasks—the mission statement (or company mission), a situational analysis, objectives, strategies, implementation, and controls, all interrelated and interdependent (Thompson & Strickland, 1992). Because of the misconceptions of strategic planning—primarily those of being time-consuming and overly complicated; reserved for larger firms; not capable of producing short-term results; and generally not worth the effort—many firms have rejected its use (Aram & Cowen, 1990). Consequently, its application for nutrition has generally been limited to hospitals and larger foodservice organizations with corporate planning departments. This absence of strategic planning has led to a lack of focus on important environmental issues, especially threats posed by competitors who may be more accurately tracking consumer desires and other environmental changes (Fombrun, 1992). Even in larger firms, the degree of focus on nutritional planning has been questioned (Scarpa, 1991). Change is a natural function of business (Olsen, Tse, & West, 1992), but few realize its significance (Morris & Brandon, 1993). Unfortunately, the importance of strategic planning is often realized only after a crisis (Aram & Cowen, 1990). There will always be debates over the importance of strategic planning (Campbell, 1991), but for the vast majority of firms, critical thinking will win out over intuition.

BROAD IMPACT   Nutritional decisions will have a much broader impact on a facility than minor menu changes will.

1. Various levels of customer-contact employees will be required to know enough about the changes to converse with customers and answer their questions. As an organization's focus on nutrition increases, employees will need to help educate as well as feed its patrons (Gill, 1990).

2. The kitchen staff will obviously need to be trained in nutritionally sound procedures. There are still many kitchens where the vegetables are not considered "done" until they have been boiling for several hours.

3. The human resources department will need to prepare training manuals focusing on nutrition in language that will be understood by all employees.

4. Job descriptions will possibly need to be modified to reflect a higher level of necessary skills.

5. The marketing department will need to know how customers perceive nutrition, what they will actually purchase, and how to communicate the facility's new offering without offending present customers. What is the legal or moral responsibility of the foodservice industry regarding nutrition? What emphasis should it place on nutrition? Should its role be that of changing customers' dining habits or responding to them? Will there be a legal nutritional requirement in the future? These and many more questions must be pondered as nutritional issues take their much-deserved front-and-center role in the nation's social and physical consciousness (Bernstein, 1991; Quinton & Weinstein, 1991). Additionally, because of the increased cultural diversity of diners in hotel restaurants, it is becoming critically important to know what they will and will not eat.

Tracking of nutritional attitudes can be accomplished through survey questionnaires and monitoring product sales (Gindin & King, 1990). As time passes, more and more research is being published on consumer attitudes toward nutrition. For example, Medaugh-Abernathy and Fanelli-Kuczmarski (1994) found that nutrition programs are more effective when based on a comprehensive needs assessment, including socioeconomic factors, food consumption patterns, and nutrition knowledge and attitudes. Moorman and Matulich (1993) found supporting evidence for their hypothesis that the greater an individual's education, behavior control, and perceived health status, the more inclined the individual is to perform health-oriented behaviors (McDonnell, 1993). As businesses increase their focus on employee wellness programs, corporate markets will open up for foodservice organizations that cater to their corporate nutrition philosophies. Other markets such as fitness clubs and athletic teams can also be targeted (Priori, 1993).

6. The menu development department (whether a chef or a registered dietitian) will need to be competent in nutritional principles and imaginative enough to create or locate recipes that are compatible with the kitchen's equipment and the skills of its employees, and that allow for a reasonable degree of cross-utilization with current product inventories. At some point in the future, nutritionally focused food additives, such as fiber concentrates, will be combined with existing menu items to improve the overall nutritional content (Wisker, Daniel, & Feldheim, 1994). This will require more than just a passing knowledge of nutrition.

7. Changes must take into account present and possible future laws governing presentation and availability of nutritional information.

8. Strategic decisions, such as nutrition, that have a major impact on people must be considered from an ethical standpoint (Divine, 1992).

9. The finance department will be required to consider the importance of expenditures for new equipment and smallwares and for promotional budgets.

10. Management must coordinate these changes within the current organizational structure and corporate culture, without allowing costs to escalate or morale to decline.

LEARNING CURVE   The strategic planning process cannot be learned in the 15 minutes it will take to read this appendix. Effective utilization and realization of its benefits will require study and practice. The goal or mission of this appendix is to help those involved in nutritional decisions in the foodservice industry to develop a reasonably competent grasp of strategic planning and to be able to apply it to their particular circumstances. (The process can be applied in a similar manner to any important decision.)

Historically, menu planners assumed that whatever occurred in the past would continue in the future. Society's limited knowledge of nutrition significantly reduced the need for analysis of future trends. Sweeping changes related to nutrition were rare, if not totally absent. Also, until the 1960s, most companies promoted their products or services to mass markets (Kotler, 1991). As knowledge about different types of food and concern for what people were eating grew, market segments become smaller. This segmentation of consumer markets has subsequently caused competition to intensify, requiring foodservice organizations to develop the ability to adapt to serve the smaller target groups. Strategic refocusing (Crabens, 1991), or adaptation to these changes, requires the ability to forecast future wants and demands of targeted markets. Managing in today's environment means management of rapid change (Hahn, 1991), and leaders in the foodservice industry can stay ahead of their competition only by observing, forecasting, and adapting to these changes. Noticing significant trends in the environment before they represent either a lost opportunity or a threat to the firm is possibly modern management's most important skill. Good management requires good strategic planning skills (Thompson & Strickland, 1992). Therefore, it is essential that those responsible for nutrition develop the adaptive skills necessary to compete in today's market. The following quote is offered to highlight the importance of information in modern competitive environments:

> A relatively small number and amount of ingredients can spell the difference between a highly satisfying entree and a mediocre meal. (Aram & Cowen, 1991)

A NUTRITIONALLY BASED STRATEGIC PLAN

The following is a hypothetical example of the nutritionally related information that would be included in the plan. Those not schooled in strategic planning must recognize that there will be some redundancy. This is a necessary and purposeful part of strategic planning. The concept is to identify strategic issues, to set long- and short-term objectives as benchmarks, to develop long- and short-term strategies to show how the objectives will be achieved, and then to set policies and an action plan to assign specific responsibility for those strategies. (To differentiate between the descriptions of the plan and the actual plan, the City Grill Strategic Plan will be set in *italic type*.)

THE CITY GRILL

The City Grill is a casual dining restaurant in a middle- to upper-middle-class suburb. The menu consists of traditional American cuisine prepared mainly from fresh ingredients. Its focus on nutrition has been minimal. The check average is $7.00 for lunch and $14.00 for dinner, including alcoholic beverages. The restaurant has a 36% food cost, 30% labor cost, and an 8% return on sales. The employee turnover percentage is 100%. (The situational analysis below will contain the balance of information normally included in a standard case study.)

Mission Statement

The mission statement is a broad statement of the company's characteristics, goals, and philosophies or, more specifically, its products, services, markets served, focus on profit and growth, and philosophies for dealing with stakeholders, such as personnel, customers, and the society in which it operates. The focal point of the mission statement is the decision of which products and markets the firm will focus on in the future. Peter Drucker (1974) states that this can be determined by asking three questions: "What is our business?", "What will our business be?", and "What should our business be?" This series of questions helps the firm focus on how customers think of the firm now, how the industry will change in the future, and how the business should move to align itself with expected changes. The general view of the mission statement is that it should allow for maximum flexibility so the firm can adapt to rapidly changing internal and environment factors.

We will serve the upper-midscale market quality, nutritionally balanced meals. All foods will be prepared in a clean and sanitary manner, be appealing to the eye and the palate, and represent a good value. Employees will be trained in the principles of good nutrition. With an understanding of what we are and what we represent will come a unity of purpose that will benefit employees, the business, our customers, and our local community.

Situational Analysis

The situational analysis is a thorough study of all situational factors that must be considered before strategic decisions are made. The situational analysis is composed of the internal analysis and environmental analysis.

INTERNAL ANALYSIS   The internal analysis is a detailed review of the establishment's performance in all functional areas. (A functional area is any unit or department of a business that performs a unique task. Depending on management's desires, this categorization could be as narrow as a prep area or as broad as the kitchen.) Any time changes are being considered, it is necessary to have a realistic appraisal of the firm's strengths and weaknesses. The determination of strengths and weaknesses can be made according to several standards: customers' or management's opinion, achievement of last year's objectives, trends in performance, or the matching of present abilities with projected future environmental trends. Because of the speed with which the concern for nutrition is changing foodservice strategies, the matching up of present abilities with future trends would be an important standard of measurement when considering the firm's nutritionally related strengths and weaknesses.

With this information, management will know what the firm is capable of doing, and whether there are critical areas that may need to be improved. Since changes in one area will generally require compatible changes to be made in other areas, the entire organization must be analyzed. With this comprehensive view will come a more conceptual understanding of the tasks necessary to implement nutritional changes.

OPERATIONS   *The kitchen staff is currently preparing all food according to our recipes. Compliments about our food and service far outweigh complaints. The chef is the only kitchen employee who has a basic knowledge of nutrition, and this is minimal. He and two assistants have been responsible for designing menus and writing recipes. Only the chef and two assistants have taken a sanitation course. Twenty percent of the staff is not fluent in English. The kitchen facilities are clean, but sanitation practices could be improved. The can opener blade was not cleaned after being used to open a can of ham. Only the most basic of equipment is available.*

None of the job descriptions contain information about nutrition. Likewise, there are no training manuals detailing specific nutritional requirements or policies to facilitate operational changes. The human resources department does not currently address the applicant's knowledge of nutrition when interviewing prospective kitchen workers. The employee turnover percentage is 100%.

MARKETING   *There is currently no marketing information system that tracks the frequency of foods that customers are ordering.*

The product mix has been quite popular, though not as nutritionally sound as it should be. Many items consist of over 40% fat.

No customers have complained about the prices.

The atmosphere is somewhat plain and could use some upgrading. The only promotional effort was the successful participation in a fundraiser for the United Way.

FINANCE/ACCOUNTING   *Since it is part of a major corporation, the company is financially sound. Finance officers have said that if prudent changes are made, any reasonable requests for funds should be granted. The restaurant currently has a 36% food cost, a 30% labor cost, and an 8% return on sales.*

ADMINISTRATIVE MANAGEMENT   *The overall management of the facility has been very good. Employees willingly help out wherever they are needed. Food and service are a constant focus. All costs have been controlled successfully. For these reasons, if changes are made, no major administrative problems are foreseen. Success has probably been due more to hard work than to effective policies and training.*

ENVIRONMENTAL ANALYSIS   The environmental analysis is an in-depth study of trends and factors that might represent opportunities or threats to the firm. Opportunities can be defined as factors that, if taken advantage of, have the potential to help the business increase sales, profit, or competitive position. Threats are essentially the opposite, being anything that could hurt sales, profit, or competitive position (Reich, 1995). The environmental analysis is divided into two sections—the remote and operating environments. The remote environment consists of political regulations, the economy, societal shifts and trends, and technology. The firm will have little control over these factors. The operating environment consists of personnel, ecology, customers, competitors, suppliers, and creditors. The firm will exert varying degrees of control over these factors.

The key trends we are concerned about, in this particular analysis, are issues related to nutrition, but all areas of the environment must be examined to expose possible factors that could impact the selection of a strategy. For example, we know the economy moves in cycles. During inevitable downturns, will customers be more concerned with reducing their expenditures on dining out? Will the trend toward an increased focus on nutrition in their lives continue?

REMOTE ENVIRONMENTAL FACTORS

Political Regulations   *There are new federal labeling laws that will increase the restaurant's need to focus on nutritional issues. At some point in the future, a law could be passed requiring that all foodservice establishments have the ingredients and nutritional contents of their menu items available to the public (Quinton & Weinstein, 1991). Presently, the primary legal requirement is that foods must be prepared under safe and sanitary conditions.*

Economy   *The economy has been in a recession for several years and is just now shaking free of it. Sales are increasing, but not drastically. If we are going to add more healthful foods to the menu, we must be sure not to significantly increase the price.*

Societal Trends   *The current trend is toward better nutrition. People of most demographic groups are learning more and are increasing their requests for foods that are low in fat, sodium, and sugar. Beef consumption has dropped significantly in the last 20 years and shows no sign of picking up. Among the other trends that will influence nutritional awareness and demand are increases in two-income families, the aging of the population, increased demand for ethnic foods, increased demand for quality and flavor, the physical exercise orientation of most consumer segments, women's increasing role in all purchasing decisions, and the desire for a better quality of life.*

Technology   *Computer systems are available to analyze a person's nutritional requirements. Modern equipment such as convection steamers, Impinger ovens, and slow-cook and microwave ovens have vastly improved nutrient retention. One new register system will print the nutritional content of foods on the consumer's guest check.*

OPERATING ENVIRONMENTAL FACTORS

Personnel   *Few of the available personnel for employee or management positions have much knowledge about nutrition.*

Ecology   *As the City Grill becomes more nutritionally oriented, reliance on animal protein will diminish, improving the restaurant's image in the eyes of our target customers. A recent book targeted beef as one of the most destructive forces on our planet. As this feeling spreads, being known for offering primarily fish, poultry, and vegetables will become a strength and will allow us to take advantage of many opportunities.*

Customers   The first step in customer analysis is to segment the market into groups with similar personal characteristics and buying habits. This is accomplished by identifying groups according to the four bases of segmentation—geographics, demographics, psychographics, and buyer behavior (Kotler, 1991). The purpose of segmentation is to identify the personal characteristics of the various customer groups in the business's trade area. Subsequently, management must select or target on which of these segments it will focus its strategies (primarily, those that the business can most profitably pursue). The general focus will be customer groups that have the potential to make up the largest percentage of the establishment's business. There will also be groups that, though of secondary or perhaps tertiary importance, must be considered as viable target markets. Since each customer market has a different opinion of the importance of nutrition, there will probably be several smaller groups that, when combined, could provide the business with a potentially valuable market. If these smaller markets have been ignored by other competitors, then they may represent the opportunity to develop a niche—a small market that is not currently being satisfied, and one in which few competitors are expressing a major interest. These groups will become the company's target customer segments.

For brevity, the following analysis is a compilation of the restaurant's various segments.

Geographics. (Where customers live or work.) *According to our last survey, 70% of our customers either live or work within 5 miles of the restaurant (its trade area).*

Demographics. (A statistical representation of the target customer.) *The target customers are between 25 and 35 years old; 25% are single; 15% are divorced; 60% are married; 80% have children; married couples average 2.5 children—50% under 8 years old; and household income is between $35,000 and $45,000 per year. Eighty-five percent have professional jobs, both spouses work in 75% of married households, the average home costs $95,000, and the average car is valued at $20,000.*

Psychographics. (Characteristics of customers not specifically related to purchase behavior.) *Customers' life-styles, general personality profiles, and social class are somewhat homogeneous. Most are active in some type of outdoor sport; very few are sedentary. Running, tennis, and golf rank as very popular. Seventy percent belong to a religious organization of some type. Politically, very few are conservative. The majority are moderate to liberal.*

Buyer Behavior. (Characteristics of customers specifically related to purchase behavior.) A variety of personal preference factors were found to be important. The average customer:

- *Wants a reasonable amount of good wholesome food at a fair price.*
- *Is definitely concerned about nutrition.*
- *Frequents the restaurant once a week.*
- *Wants homemade bread. (The restaurant does not serve homemade bread.)*
- *Has been requesting more fresh fish selections.*

Almost 30% have requested nutritional information about menu items. Lunch customers, though from the same demographic group, are not dinner customers, and vice versa.

Competitors   *We have only one primary competitor in our trade area, Anthony's Italian Restaurant. Its food is excellent. Most items are prepared by skilled chefs, from fresh ingredients. Prices are high, averaging about $5.00 per person above that of the City Grill. (Because of its higher prices, our target customers will only eat at Anthony's half as often as they dine at our restaurant.) Its service quality is below what its customers expect. Overall, nutrition was not a major consideration when Anthony's developed its recipes. Protein, carbohydrate, and vitamin content are balanced for most meals. Its primary nutrition-related problems are that the chefs use too much fat (olive oil and butter) and salt for most entrees and vegetables. (Since many of these deficiencies would be relatively simple to solve, we should carefully monitor Anthony's actions. Hopefully, by increasing our nutritional focus now, we can preempt some of Anthony's potential improvements.)*

There are several secondary competitors in the trade area. These include McDonald's, Burger King, Wendy's, Taco Bell, Pizza Hut, and Long John Silver's. All of these restaurants are popular, primarily because of their attraction to children.

Suppliers   *Because of the proximity to Dallas, there are no problems getting any type of food and beverage products desired. There is always an abundant selection of fresh fish, and Dallas is a major distribution point for fresh vegetables and fruits. The restaurant's relationship with its suppliers is very good.*

Creditors   *Since the business is part of a larger firm, there should be no problems obtaining funds for worthwhile projects.*

SWOT Analysis

The SWOT analysis is the detailed search for factors that could impact the business or should be considered when preparing its strategies. SWOT is an acronym that represents the "strengths and weaknesses" from the internal analysis, and the "opportunities and threats" from the environmental analysis. Its primary purpose is to develop a summary of the firm's strengths, weaknesses, opportunities, and threats that will serve as a menu to guide the selection of strategic alternatives. Theoretically, the firm's opportunities are matched with its strengths. Threats are analyzed to determine whether it is necessary to defend against them—such as when a competitor lowers its price. Weaknesses are judged to be either detrimental to the business, and therefore requiring attempts at improvement, or neutral. Those judged as neutral will require monitoring and could possibly be placed on a low-priority task list. A key indicator of whether or not a weakness must be corrected is if it affects the ability of the firm to pursue a potentially profitable opportunity.

Strengths

- *The chef has some knowledge of and concern for nutrition.*
- *Current menu mix is popular.*
- *Customers think prices are fair.*
- *This year's promotion with the United Way was successful.*
- *Since we are part of a major corporation, we have access to capital.*
- *We have good management.*
- *Most costs are in line. (Minor improvements could be made.)*

Weaknesses

- *Only one member of the staff knows anything about nutrition.*
- *No one in management has an adequate knowlege of nutrition.*
- *Twenty percent of the staff are not fluent in English.*
- *Sanitation practices could be improved. Many utensils are not regularly sanitized.*
- *Job descriptions and training manuals do not contain information about nutrition.*
- *Employee turnover is 100%.*
- *No marketing information system exists.*
- *The menu mix does not include many nutritionally balanced meals.*
- *Fat content is somewhat excessive for some entrees.*

Opportunities

- *A law may be passed requiring foodservice establishments to have nutritional information available. (Since we will place a strong focus on nutrition before our competitors, we would hopefully be recognized as a leader in this area.)*
- *The country has been in a long recession; therefore, people are looking for value.*
- *People in general are becoming more concerned about nutrition.*

GEOGRAPHICS

- *Seventy percent of customers are within 5 miles of the restaurant.*

DEMOGRAPHICS

- *Average household income is approximately $40,000; 60% of the households consist of married couples; 80% of households have children; 85% have professional jobs; the average home costs $95,000; and the average car is valued at $20,000.*

PSYCHOGRAPHICS

- *Most people are either runners or play tennis or golf; 70% are members of religious organizations; and most are moderates or liberals.*

BUYER BEHAVIOR

- *Consumers are very concerned about nutrition, frequent restaurant about once a week, want homemade bread, and are requesting fresh fish and nutritionally balanced meals.*
- *Target customers eat at Anthony's once a month.*

- *There are plenty of quality suppliers for any nutritional upgrades.*
- *Price resistance is reasonably low, though value is critical.*

THREATS

- *The country is just coming out of an economic downturn. Consumer confidence is not extremely high.*
- *Few available cooks know anything about nutrition.*
- *Many fast-food restaurants lure away couples with children.*
- *The word* nutritious *is a turnoff to some customers.*

Strategic Analysis and Selection

Management will now review the SWOT analysis for key factors that will impact decisions relating to the degree of the additional focus on nutrition. The most important factors should be analyzed by asking a series of questions that elicit, as much as reasonably possible, all major influences of the factors. The goal of the process is to develop strategic thrusts that will guide the remainder of the strategic planning session. (For brevity, only the key opportunity, "Customers want more nutritional menu items," will be addressed.)

SWOT FACTOR TO BE ANALYZED

Opportunity: Customers want more nutritional menu items.

GUIDELINES FOR SWOT ANALYSIS

1. What is the firm's current market position in relation to customer demand?

Because of our use of fresh ingredients, we are viewed as having reasonably nutritious food. Unfortunately, because of our lack of focus on nutrition, the reality of the situation is that our menu is high in fat.

2. What are the key SWOT factors that must be evaluated in the plan?

Lack of nutritionally balanced menu offerings
Customers' concerns about nutrition
High household incomes (averaging around $40,000)

3. What are the implications of this opportunity (or strength, weakness, or threat)?

More nutritional menu items would help differentiate the City Grill from other restaurants in the trade area.

Many groups, such as the Sierra Club and the Vegetarian Society, could be on a mailing list for coupons when the new menu is implemented.

Competitors may not be as proactive and therefore might not focus on nutrition for several years.

If we focus too much on nutrition and became known as a health food restaurant, we could lose some regular customers.

If we were careful to offer nutritious items without pushing nutrition, we could attract those who are concerned about nutrition, without offending those who do not care.

4. Have existing strategies related to the SWOT factor been effective?

The restaurant has not focused on nutrition but has recognized its importance by making some marginal attempts at getting away from beef, fat, sodium, and sugar.

5. What alternative or optional strategies should be considered?

- *We could add six new entrees, two each of chicken, fish, and vegetarian.*
- *One or two of our four beef entrees could be dropped.*
- *A convection steamer would be a nice addition to the kitchen.*
- *It would be beneficial to have a registered dietitian as a consultant for the restaurant.*
- *We should consider integrating nutrition into our existing promotions, without promoting the image of being a health food restaurant.*
- *Policies and procedures will need to be written or rewritten.*

6. Is the strategy compatible with the competitive environment?

A frequent problem in implementing nutrition programs is assuming that the public wants nutrition in every aspect of their dining habits—now. A strange occurence is that while some people are saying that they are concerned about nutrition, they are nevertheless buying richer desserts and still eating steaks. Timing is critical. The pendulum is swinging toward an increased concern for nutrition, but not all customers view this with the same interest.

Yes, the majority of our customers have requested more nutritious menu items. We need to make sure that we do not focus so much on nutrition that we lose customers who are not overly concerned about it.

7. Does the strategy place realistic demands on the abilities of the firm?

In most cases this will not present a problem. Often, the key to overcoming a skills-related hurdle is effective training and supervision—for example, written, detailed directions; communication of the directions and their importance; and enforcement of deviations.

The restaurant's employees have the ability to follow recipes, but a registered dietitian will need to be retained to help oversee the development of the new menu items.

8. Is the strategy worth pursuing?

This is viewed from the perspective of each key functional area. For example, the marketing department is concerned with sales and image. Management (operations, human resources, and purchasing) judges viability based on quality improvements and productivity. Financially related departments view potential strategies from the perspective of how they affect the bottom line, debt, and future cash flows.

Another important consideration is that many changes will influence the business over the long term. For this reason, management must be concerned about the monetary and image-related effect of potential strategies in both the short and long term. If it increases the bottom line temporarily but hurts the long-term image, the strategies being analyzed might require modification.

It should increase sales, as long as the changes are not viewed as a radical departure. Implementational costs should be kept to a reasonable minimum. Food costs for nutritional items must not be more than 2% over the restaurant's current food cost percentage.

9. How will competitors react?

Some industry segments react quickly to competitive moves, while others respond more slowly, if at all (Porter, 1980). Most foodservice companies have increased their focus on nutrition, but few have been aggressive in their approach. A bold move in the area of nutrition will generally bring only a measured response. When competitors see that the public has accepted or rejected the strategy, a greater effort may follow.

Since most of our competitors are fast-food restaurants, their ability to upgrade their offerings is up to the franchisor. Currently, all fast-food concepts are doing something to promote their version of nutritious foods.

Anthony's would be our biggest concern, but it would need to make a radical change to its menu to bring it in line with our proposed new menu mix.

10. What should be the primary strategic thrusts for the next planning period?
Focus on upgrading the nutritional content of our menu.
Improve our image related to supplying nutritionally balanced meals.

Long-Term and Annual Objectives

LONG-TERM OBJECTIVES   Long-term objectives are the desired results over a specified period of time, generally more than one year in the future. The period of time will vary for each long-term objective. The long-term objectives will generally be more ambitious than annual objectives. For example, if the current food cost was 36%, the long-term objective might be 32%, but the first step to reach that objective—the annual objective—might be 34%. The key qualities of objectives are that they be measurable as a number or time (dollars, percentage, amount/quantity, or date) and be motivating to those who must attempt to achieve them.

ANNUAL OBJECTIVES   Annual objectives are the desired results during the first year of the plan. The annual objectives are based on and supportive of the long-term objectives. The annual objectives may contain additional supportive objectives that help achieve the long-term objectives. (See the discussion on Competitive Position below for an example.)

Objectives can be set in any number of desired areas. The practice of categorizing objectives forces management to consider a variety of alternative optional objectives. The following seven objectives were adapted from Pearce and Robinson (1991):

SOCIAL RESPONSIBILITY   Anything that improves the firm's image as a responsible member of its community, such as helping charitable organizations, and recycling.
- *Long-Term Objective. Help an organization that focuses on nutritional programs for young children.*
- *Annual Objective. Help the "Nutrition Project" by donating $500, and asking employees to volunteer for a minimum of four hours per year.*

PROFITABILITY   The level of desired profit.
- *Long-Term Objective. Increase the average annual return on sales to 15%.*
- *Annual Objective. Achieve a 10% return on sales this year.*

PRODUCTIVITY   The ratio of input to output, basically any percentage figure on a statement of income (profit and loss statement), from food cost to linen cost.

- *Long-Term Objective. Lower food cost to 32% and labor cost to 25%.*
- *Annual Objective. Lower food cost to 34% and labor cost to 28%.*

EMPLOYEE DEVELOPMENT   Training and hiring of employees and management, both as an ongoing effort and to upgrade specific and general career skills.

- *Long-Term Objectives. (1) Train all employees in the importance and principles of good nutrition. (2) Develop comprehensive training programs for all positions and send managers to seminars. (3) Increase employees' overall knowledge of nutrition.*
- *Annual Objectives. (1) By August 15, 19xx, begin three monthly, two-hour nutritional training classes. (2) Develop basic training programs for all positions by June 15, 19xx. Send each manager to one seminar this year. (3) Hire a registered dietitian by January 15, 19xx.*

EMPLOYEE RELATIONS   Actions of management that focus on improvements in the working environment, such as working conditions, benefits, and the quality of supervision. The primary measure of the success of the firm's efforts in this realm is its turnover percentage. Morale and productivity are additional considerations.

- *Long-Term Objectives. (1) Add insurance benefits. (2) Lower employee turnover percentage to 60%.*
- *Annual Objectives. (1) Add insurance benefits by the end of the year. These should include both medical and dental coverage. (2) Lower employee turnover percentage to 80%.*

COMPETITIVE POSITION   Anything that represents an improvement in competitive performance—market share, sales, customer count, market segment goals, growth in units, customer satisfaction index (CSI), adding products or services.

- *Long-Term Objectives. (1) Add entrees that differentiate our restaurant from competitors. Be known by 50% of our community as a restaurant that offers nutritious foods. (2) Reach sales of $1,300,000 for 19xx.*
- *Annual Objectives. (1) Add six nutritionally oriented entrees by August 5, 19xx. Be known by 30% of our community as a restaurant that offers nutritious foods. (2) Reach sales of $1,100,000 this year. Increase percentage of family diners by 20%, singles and couples by 10%.*

TECHNOLOGY   Equipment or changes in layout or design that increase speed of service, productivity, or quality.

- *Long-Term Objective. Replace most outdated pieces of equipment with items that produce a more nutritious product.*
- *Annual Objective. Purchase a convection steamer for the kitchen by April 10, 19xx.*

Grand Strategies

Grand strategies are the basic actions the company will pursue in reaping the greatest benefit from internal and environmental factors. The grand strategies are generally divided into two broad areas: product and market strategies, and business strategies. Since business strategies deal with expanding outside the concept, divestment, and solving serious problems, they will not be discussed in this appendix.

PRODUCT AND MARKET GRAND STRATEGIES   Product and market strategies can be divided into four categories. At this point in the plan, only general recommendations are made. For example, the restaurant will add more nutritious items, but the specific items will be named in the functional strategies later in the plan. In this particular case, the actual strategy is product development, and nutrition is being considered because this is what customers are demanding. West and Olsen (1990) termed this strategy "innovation and development" and found this to be an indicator of high-performing firms. Product and market strategies include concentration, market development, product development, and diversification.

CONCENTRATION   This consists of attempting to increase sales by focusing on the firm's current market (target customers) with its current product/service mix. This could include pricing or promotional strategies, decor modifications, or opening new locations in the same city or geographic area.

We will continue to serve high-quality, high-value foods and beverages with first-rate service. We hope to attract more customers by improving our word-of-mouth advertising from current customers.

PRODUCT (AND/OR SERVICE) DEVELOPMENT   This entails offering new products for existing customers. "Existing customers" are generally viewed in a broad context, for example, fast-food customers or fine dining customers. This is more of a theoretical ideal, because when any new product is added, new customers will usually be attracted. When Wendy's Old Fashioned Hamburgers added its salad bars, it attracted many customers who had previously not patronized fast-food restaurants. It is acceptable to use the term "product development" to cover any new product additions or modifications of existing products. Some planners prefer the term "diversification" for substantial menu changes.

Our staff and a registered dietitian will develop new menu items that will focus on improving the nutritional value of our menu. We want the menu to have plenty of nutritious selections without presenting the image of being a health food restaurant.

MARKET DEVELOPMENT   This refers to adding new market segments with existing products, or opening locations in new geographic markets—generally in other cities.

We will not focus on adding new market segments this year, but in the future, as nutrition becomes more important, we must stay attuned to changes in our current target customer and potential target groups in our trade area.

DIVERSIFICATION   This is adding new products for new markets. There are two ways of viewing this strategy: either a restaurant adds nutritional items (a new product) to attract nutrition-conscious customers (new customer segments), or the company opens a new type of restaurant that focuses on a new market segment. Either definition is acceptable as long as people within the firm understand what is implied. The author's personal preference is to classify adding any product or service to a concept as "product development," and opening a new concept as "diversification."

(Since the new products are focused on existing target customers, and there will be no new concept, nothing will be considered for diversification.)

Functional Strategies

These are the strategies necessary to achieve the restaurant's annual objectives and grand strategies. They are set for each key functional area or department of the business. Since the majority of current operating policies are included in the company's operations manual, it is necessary to include only the new or upgraded strategies in the strategic plan. Marketing strategies, because of the need to keep up with changes in the environment, will change more than other functional strategies.

MANAGEMENT STRATEGIES

OPERATIONS   *Complete daily labor and food reports. Purchase convection steamer.*

PERSONNEL   *Hire a registered dietitian, on a part-time, contractual basis, to help develop recipes and the nutrition class. This should be accomplished by the end of this month.*
Develop a six-hour nutrition class and a basic training program for each position in the restaurant.
Find a reasonably priced carrier for medical and dental insurance.

FINANCE/ACCOUNTING STRATEGIES

BUDGETING

$500 for "Nutrition Project"
$500 for promotion
$1800 for convection steamer
$5000 for nutritional consultant

MARKETING STRATEGIES

PRODUCT   Add six new entrees, two each of fish, chicken, and vegetarian, by August 5, 19xx.

PRICE   The prices must stay within our current structure, though it is acceptable to price fish according to market price. The goal of a 34% food cost must be kept in mind.

PLACE   Place refers to a new location, and to the facility and its atmosphere. *There will be no changes related to place.*

PROMOTION   *Help citywide "Nutrition Project." Solicit employee volunteers. Suggest a minimum of four hours of work for each employee.*
Promote new entrees with flyers mailed to regular customers.

Policies

Standardized or relatively permanent activities are undertaken to support strategic decisions.

MANAGEMENT POLICIES

OPERATIONS   *The general manager or manager on duty will complete a daily labor and food report each morning. The objective for these cost areas will be 28% and 34%, respectively.*

PERSONNEL   *The owner will hire a registered dietitian, on a consulting basis, to help develop recipes and the nutrition class. This should be accomplished by the end of this month. The registered dietitian will work with the chef to create the new recipes and will be solely responsible for the development of the six-hour nutrition class.*
The general manager will assign to department supervisors the task of writing basic training programs for each position in the restaurant.

FINANCE/ACCOUNTING POLICIES   *Set aside $500 for "Nutrition Project," $500 for promotion, $1800 for a convection steamer, and $5000 for nutritional consultant. Money is to be disbursed according to existing company policies.*

MARKETING POLICIES   *All menus must include information about nutrition.*
Promotions should feature good, healthy, nutritious foods.
There will be monthly meetings between the registered dietitian and the marketing department to make sure that the program is being implemented as effectively as possible, and to ensure its ongoing success.

Action Plans

Temporary actions are taken to help accomplish strategies and objectives.

MANAGEMENT ACTION PLAN   *The general manager will be responsible for purchasing a convection steamer by April 10, 19xx.*
The owner will find a reasonably priced carrier for medical and dental insurance and have the plan ready to implement by the end of the year.

FINANCIAL ACTION PLAN   *To help make sure that all productivity and profit goals are met, the restaurant's accountant will meet with management once a month, or as needed, to review causes of any variances.*

MARKETING ACTION PLAN

PRODUCT   *The registered dietitian and chef will be responsible for creating six new entrees, two each of fish, chicken, and vegetarian, by August 5, 19xx.*

PRICE   *The prices must stay within our current structure, though it is acceptable to price fish according to the market price. The goal of a 34% food cost must be kept in mind.*

PLACE   *Since no changes will be made for the restaurant's location or atmosphere, there will be nothing for "place" in the marketing action plan.*

PROMOTION   *The general manager will be responsible for soliciting employee volunteers for the "Nutrition Project." This should begin no later than August 15, 19xx. Volunteers will be given a dinner-for-two at the restaurant.*
The assistant manager and owner will work together to create a flyer to advertise the new entrees. The cost for this should be kept below $500.

Institutionalization

Institutionalization refers to the task of effectively ingraining the new policies and action plans into the business. There are four primary factors to acknowledge when implementing changes—organizational structure, management, corporate culture, and rewards (Pearce & Robinson, 1991).

ORGANIZATIONAL STRUCTURE   Organizational structure is the division of tasks for the most effective and efficient accomplishment of goals. For most businesses, there is a normal progression from a simple structure with an owner or manager and employees, to a functional structure with a manager, one or more staff functions, such as marketing and accounting, and one or more line functions such as operations or dining room and kitchen.
The City Grill will require no structural changes, other than hiring a nutritional consultant.

MANAGEMENT   Any new strategy will live or die by the support it receives from the manager or supervisor of the organization or department. There are many skills required of managers, but the most important related to strategy execution are the ability to communicate effectively and the determination and ability to uphold standards.
No major changes are necessary, except that since the restaurant will be placing an increased emphasis on nutrition, it would be beneficial if all managers were to begin a personal exercise program.

CORPORATE CULTURE   Corporate culture determines what employees and management feel is important to themselves and the business. Some employee groups are very loyal and do their best to support organizational policies, while others do only what is minimally required. One of the greatest advantages of the hospitality business is that a good leader can make radical changes in corporate culture very quickly. Simply call a meeting and communicate new policies in whatever tone necessary to assure understanding and compliance. In some businesses with deeply ingrained corporate cultures, the ability to change or institute new policies may be complicated by factors such as union suppoort, support from employees with tenure, bureaucratic routines, and hidden agendas (Reich, 1995).

Through nutritional training sessions, training, and employee meetings, the new strategy of offering nutritionally balanced food should not present any problems. It will be important to make sure that the chef and cooks follow the new recipes; otherwise, the strategy could fail.

REWARDS   Quality leadership and a positive corporate culture by themselves will go a long way to instilling a sense of loyalty in employees and management. What is lacking at this point is a more intrinsic, individualistic approach to enlisting the worker's body and mind in the effort to reach the firm's goals. This requires an understanding of rewards and how to best motivate both employees and management personnel. Motivation can be defined as getting employees to want to do what management wants them to do. Rewards are tangible and intangible benefits that are valued by employees.

When employees successfully complete nutritional training, they will be presented with a framed certificate and a T-shirt specifying that they are official members of the City Grill Heart-Healthy Warriors. After successful implementation of the nutrition program, all employees will receive a complimentary dinner for two at the restaurant.

(These rewards reflect only on those aligned with the nutritional program. There would obviously be a greater need for overall reward systems for the restaurant.)

Controls

Control is monitoring and evaluating the business's performance to make sure that it is accomplishing its objectives. There are two levels of control for strategic market management.

STRATEGIC CONTROLS   These ensure that the premise on which the strategy was set has not changed. They entail monitoring the performance of the business to make sure that it has the same or improved strengths and weaknesses as those used in setting the strategy, and monitoring the environment to determine whether there have been any changes that would affect the new strategy.

To help us monitor the environment, the owner and each manager will be assigned different periodicals to read, such as magazines, newspapers, and journals, and each will have specific competitors to evaluate. At the weekly manager's meetings this information will be discussed and analyzed for its potential impact. Customer surveys will be completed twice per year. Comment cards will be provided to guests during the introduction of the new menu and will also be available throughout the year.

OPERATIONAL CONTROLS   These entail monitoring the company's performance to make sure it is on course to meet its objectives. The basic approach for locating and solving a planning-related problem is to backtrack through the plan until the problem is found. Common problem areas are that objectives have been set too high, the wrong strategy has been adopted, or the strategy is not implemented properly. Interim objectives can be set as necessary.

Progress toward annual objectives will be monitored and reviewed at each manager's meeting. The performance of each functional department related to the new strategy will also be discussed.

Conclusion

The strategic marketing process is not a simple, one-two-three answer to the planning and execution of nutritional programs. The process will generally take several weeks with perhaps twenty to fifty work-hours of time. This is certainly a small price to pay for exponentially increasing the chance of success for nutritional changes, and for that of the business itself. The primary benefit of strategic marketing is that it acknowledges all major factors of the business and its competitive environment. This leads to a greater understanding of how various factors will affect strategic decisions. The information gathered in the process will also be used as an integral component of the business's marketing and management information systems. The nature of today's dynamic business climate mandates that nutritional programs can no longer be based primarily on intuition but must be developed through strategic thinking based on the strategic marketing process.

REFERENCES FOR APPENDIX

Aram, J. D., & Cowen, S. S. (1991). Strategic planning for increased profit in the small business. *Long Range Planning, 23(6),* 63–70.

Bernstein, C. (1991). Healthy-foods stampede poses dilemma for fast-food chains. *Restaurant & Institutions, 101(25),* 32.

Campbell, A. (1994). Brief case: strategy and intuition—a conversation with Henry Mintzberg. *Long Range Planning, 24(2),* 108–111.

Cravens, D. W. (1991). *Strategic Marketing,* 4th ed. Homewood, IL: Irwin.

Divine, H. A. (1992). Ethical concerns in food and beverage management. In: S. S. J. Hall (Ed.), *Ethics in Hospitality Management: A Book of Readings.* East Lansing, MI: Educational Institute of the American Hotel & Motel Association.

Drucker, P. (1974). *Management: Task, Responsibilities, Practices.* New York: Harper & Row.

Fombrun, C. J. (1992). *Turning Points: Creating Strategic Change in Corporations.* New York: McGraw-Hill.

Gill, K. F. (1990). Communicating a healthful message: school foodservices must develop strategies for promoting sound health & nutrition. *Food Management, 25(4),* 48.

Gindin, R., & King, P. (1990). Advertising, promotions & merchandising. *Food Management,* **25(2),** 28.

Hahn, D. (1991). Strategic management—tasks and challenges in the 1990s. *Long Range Planning,* **24(1),** 26–39.

Kotler, P. (1991). *Marketing Management: Analysis, Planning, Implementation, & Control,* 7th ed. Englewood Cliffs, NJ: Prentice-Hall.

Lele, M. M. (1992). *Creating Strategic Leverage.* New York: Wiley.

McDonnell, S. (1993). Chefs catering to today's quirkier tastes. *Crain's New York Business,* **9(32),** 21.

Medaugh-Abernathy, M., & Fanelli-Kuczmarski, M. T. (1994). Food intake and food-related attitudes of older women: implications for nutrition education. *Journal of Nutrition Education,* **26(1),** 3–9.

Moorman, C., & Matulich, E. (1993). A model of consumers' preventative health behaviors: the role of health motivation and health ability. *Journal of Consumer Behavior,* **20(2),** 208–228.

Morris, D., & Brandon, J. (1993). *Re-engineering Your Business.* New York: McGraw-Hill.

Olsen, M. D., Tse, E. C., & West J. J. (1992). *Strategic Management in the Hospitality Industry.* New York: Van Nostrand Reinhold.

Pearce, J. II, & Robinson, R. B. Jr. (1991). *Formulation, Implementation, and Control of a Competitive Strategy,* 4th ed. Homewood, IL: Irwin.

Porter, M. E. (1980). *Competitive Strategy: Techniques for Analyzing Industries and Competitors.* New York: Free Press.

Priori, J. T. (1993). NJ firms feature fitness. *New Jersey Business,* **39(2),** 14.

Quinton, B., & Weinstein, J. (1991). Should you care what your customers eat? *Restaurant & Institutions,* **101(9),** 40–41.

Reich, A. Z. (1995). Strategic implementation of nutritional programs for foodservice establishments: guidelines, recommendations, and examples. *The Journal of Nutrition in Menu & Recipe Development,* **1(2),** 3–30.

Scarpa, J. (1991). McDonald's menu mission. *Restaurant Business,* **90(10),** 109–111.

Thompson, A. A., & Strickland, A. J. III (1992). *Strategic Management: Concepts and Cases.* Homewood, IL: Irwin.

West, J. J., & Olsen, M. D. (1990). Grand strategy: Making your restaurant a winner. *Cornell Hotel and Restaurant Administration Quarterly,* **31(2),** 72–77.

Wisker, E., Daniel, M., & Feldheim, W. (1994). Effects of a fiber concentrate from citrus fruits in humans. *Nutrition Research,* **14(3),** 361–372.

References

Aaker, D. A. (1988). *Strategic Market Management*, 2nd ed. New York: Wiley.

Aaker, D. A., Kumar, V., & Day, G. S. (1995). *Marketing Research.* New York: Wiley.

Alm, R. (1992). World to pay for excesses during '80s. *The Dallas Morning News*, Dec. 27, pp. 1-H, 17-H.

Andreoli, T. (1992). Murder on the menu: whodunit doing boffo biz at Stern's restaurant. *Stores*, **74(1)** 130, 132.

Aram, J. D., & Cowen, S. S. (1991). Strategic planning for increased profit in the small business. *Long Range Planning*, **23(6),** 63–70.

Barich, H., & Kotler, P. (1991). A framework for marketing image management. *Sloan Management Review*, **32(2),** 94–104.

Beck, R. C. (1990). *Motivation Theories and Principles*, 3rd ed. Englewood Cliffs, NJ: Prentice-Hall.

Belch, G. E., & Belch, M. A. (1990). *Introduction to Advertising and Promotional Management.* Homewood, IL: Irwin.

Bell, C. (1992). How to invent service. *The Journal of Services Marketing*, **6(1),** 37–39.

Bennett, P. D., ed. (1988). *Dictionary of Marketing terms.* Chicago: American Marketing Association, 117–118.

Berkowitz, H. (1994). Marketing gets lost in translation/international ad subject to gaffes. *The Houston Chronicle*, June 21, p. 1.

Bertagnoli, L., & Chaudhry, R. (1994). The big picture: R&I's 1994 foodservice industry forecast. *Restaurants & Institutions*, **104(1),** 50–92.

Bhargava, S. W. (1993). Gimme a double shake and a lard on white. *BusinessWeek*, Mar. 1, p. 59.

Bliss, W. K. (1994). *Dealing with Different Personality Types.* Lecture at the Conrad Hilton College of Hotel and Restaurant Management, University of Houston, April.

Bly, R. W. (1993). *Advertising Manager's Handbook.* Englewood Cliffs, NJ: Prentice-Hall.

Bogner W. C., & Thomas, H. (1993). The role of competitive groups in strategy formulation: a dynamic integration of two competing models. *Journal of Management Studies*, **30(1),** 51–67.

Boone, L. E., & Kurtz, D. L. (1987). *Contemporary Business*, 5th ed. Chicago: Dryden Press.

Boyd, H. W. Jr., & Walker, O. C. Jr. (1990). *Marketing Management: A Strategic Approach.* Homewood, IL: Irwin.

Brooker, R. E. Jr. (1991). Orchestrating the planning process. *The Journal of Business Strategy*, **July/August,** 4–8.

Brown, J. S. (1991). Research that reinvents the corporation. *Harvard Business Review*, **69(1),** 102–111.

Brown, J., Huang, E., Majors, P., & Reich, A. (1994). *The Bluzz Room.* A marketing plan prepared for Priscilla Majors.

Bungay, S., & Goold, M. (1991). Creating a strategic control system. *Long Range Planning,* **24(3),** 32–39.

Burack, E. H. (1991). Changing the company culture—the role of human resource development. *Long Range Planning,* **24(1),** 88–95.

Byars, L. L. (1984). *Strategic Management: Planning and Implementation.* New York: Harper & Row.

Byrne, J. A. (1993). The horizontal corporation, it's about managing across, not up and down. *BusinessWeek,* Dec. 20, pp. 76–81.

Cadotte, E. R., & Turgeon, N. (1988). Key factors in guest satisfaction. *The Cornell Hotel and Restaurant Administration Quarterly,* **28(4),** 45–51.

Callan, R. J. (1994). Development of a framework for the determination of attributes used for hotel selection—indications from focus group and in-depth interviews. *Hospitality Research Journal,* **18(2),** 53–74.

Callan, R. J. (1995). Hotel classification and grading schemes, a paradigm of utilization and user characteristics. *International Journal of Hospitality Management,* **14(3/4),** 271–284.

Camillus, J. C., & Datta, D. K. (1991). Managing strategic issues in a turbulent environment. *Long Range Planning,* **24(2),** 67–74.

Campbell, A. (1991). Brief case: strategy and intuition—a conversation with Henry Mintzberg. *Long Range Planning,* **24(2),** 108–111.

Campbell, A., & Yeung, S. (1991). Creating a sense of mission. *Long Range Planning,* **24(4),** 10–20.

Carpenter, G. S., Glazer, R., & Nakamoto, K. (1994). Meaningful brands from meaningless differentiation: the dependence on irrelevant attributes. *Journal of Marketing Research,* **31(3),** 339–350.

Chajet, C. (1991). The benefits of strategic naming. *The Journal of Business Strategy,* **September,** 61–64.

Covin, J. G. (1991). Entrepreneurial versus conservative firms: a comparison of strategies and performance. *Journal of Management Studies,* **28(5),** 442–462.

Cravens, D. W. (1991). *Strategic Marketing.* Homewood, IL: Irwin.

Cronin, J. J. Jr., & Taylor, S. A. (1992). Measuring service quality: a reexamination and extension. *Journal of Marketing,* **56(3),** 55–68.

Day, G. S. (1994). The capabilities of market-driven organizations. *Journal of Marketing,* **58(4),** 37–52.

Dean, J. W. Jr., & Sharfman, M. P. (1993). Procedural rationality in the strategic decision-making process. *Journal of Management Studies,* **30(4),** 589–609.

DeFranco, A. L., & Reich, A. Z. (1995). Building a foundation for better learning through integrative instructional modeling. CHRIE *Hospitality and Tourism Educator,* **7 (1),** 13–16, 66.

Deighton, J., Henderson, C. M., Neslin, S. A. (1994). The effects of advertising on brand switching and repeat purchasing. *Journal of Marketing Research,* **31(1),** 28–43.

DeLa Cruz, T. (1994). Harley-Leonard: Hyatt's big push into technology. *Hotel Business,* **3(12),** 1, 52.

Dillon, W. R., Madden, T. J., & Firtle, N. H. (1987). *Marketing Research in a Marketing Environment,* 2nd ed. Homewood, IL: Irwin.

DiMingo, E. (1988). The fine art of positioning. *The Journal of Business Strategy,* **9(2),** 34–38.

Dodge, R. (1992). Don't bet ranch on full-blown expansion yet. *The Dallas Morning News,* Dec. 27, pp. 1-H, 18-H.

Dodson, J. (1991). Strategic repositioning through the customer connection. *The Journal of Business Strategy,* **12(3),** 34–38.

Donham, W. B. (1922). Essential groundwork for a broad executive theory. *Harvard Business Review,* **1(1),** 1–10.

Drucker, P. (1954). *The Practice of Management.* New York: Harper & Row.

Drucker, P. (1974). *Management: Task, Responsibilities, Practices.* New York: Harper & Row.

Drucker, P. F. (1985). The discipline of innovation. *Harvard Business Review,* **85(3),** 67–72.

Dunn, S. W., & Barban, A. M. (1978). *Advertising: Its Role in Modern Marketing,* 4th ed. Chicago: Dryden Press.

Dutton, J. E. (1993). Interpretations on automatic: a different view of strategic issue diagnosis. *Journal of Management Studies,* **30(3),** 339–357.

Emory, C. W., & Cooper, D. R. (1991). *Business Research Methods.* Homewood, IL: Irwin.

Feltenstein, T. (1986). New-product development in food service: a structured approach. *The Cornell Hotel and Restaurant Administration Quarterly,* **27(3),** 63–71.

Feltenstein, T. (1992). Strategic planning for the 1990's: "exploiting the inevitable." *The Cornell Hotel and Restaurant Administration Quarterly,* **33(3),** 50–54.

Fitzsimmons, J. A., & Maurer, G. B. (1991). A walk-through audit to improve restaurant performance. *The Cornell Hotel and Restaurant Administration Quarterly,* **31(4),** 94–99.

Fuld, L. (1991). A recipe for business intelligence success. *The Journal of Business Strategy,* **January/February,** 12–17.

Gemmell, A. J. (1991). Planning the Japanese way in the United States. *The Journal of Business Strategy,* **March/April,** 4–7.

Getty, J. M., & Thompson, K. N. (1994). A procedure for scaling perceptions of lodging quality. *Hospitality Research Journal,* **18(2),** 75–96.

Gibson, J. L., Ivancevich, J. M., & Donnelly, J. H. Jr. (1991). *Organizations: Behavior, Structure, Process,* 7th ed. Homewood, IL: Irwin.

Grant, R. M. (1991). The resource-based theory of competitive advantage: implications for strategy formulation. *California Management Review,* **Spring,** 114–134.

Green, D. H., Barclay, D. W., & Ryans, A. B. (1995). Entry strategy and long-term performance: conceptualization and empirical examination. *Journal of Marketing,* **59(4),** 1–16.

Guralnik, D. B. (1986). *Webster's New World Dictionary of the American Language.* New York: Prentice-Hall.

Hahn, D. (1991). Strategic management—tasks and challenges in the 1990's. *Long Range Planning,* **24(1),** 26–39.

Hart, C. W. L., & Troy, D. A. (1986). *Strategic Hotel/Motel Marketing.* East Lansing, MI: Educational Institute of the American Hotel & Motel Association.

Hayes, L. (1994). *Creativity in the Business Organization.* Speech at the University of Houston College of Business, Houston, Texas.

Haywood, K. M. (1986). Scouting the competition for survival and success. *The Cornell Hotel and Restaurant Administration Quarterly,* **27(3),** 81–87.

Headley, D. E., & Choi, B. (1992). Achieving service quality through gap analysis and a basic statistical approach. *The Journal of Services Marketing,* **6(1),** 5–14.

Herring, J. P. (1991). Senior management must champion business intelligence programs. *The Journal of Business Strategy,* **September,** 48–52.

Heskett, J. L., Sasser, W. E., & Schlesinger, L. A. (1993). Achieving breakthrough service. *Harvard Business School Management Programs.*

Heyer, S. J., & Van Lee, R. (1991). Rewiring the corporation. *The Journal of Business Strategy,* **July/August,** 40–45.

Hiam, A., & Schewe, C. D. (1992). *The Portable MBA in Marketing.* New York: Wiley.

Hilton, C. N. (1957). *Be My Guest.* New York: Prentice-Hall.

Hinterhuber, H. H., & Popp, W. (1992). Are you a strategist or just a manager? *Harvard Business Review,* **January/February,** 105–113.

Hooper, T. L., & Rocca, B. T. (1991). Environmental affairs: now on the strategic agenda. *The Journal of Business Strategy,* **June,** 26–30.

Houghton, J. R. (1992). Leadership's challenge: the new agenda for the '90's. *Planning Review,* **20(5),** 8–9.

Hurley, J. A. (1990). Highway hotel: anatomy of a turnaround. *The Cornell Hotel and Restaurant Administration Quarterly,* **31(2),** 36–44.

Ireland, R. D., Hitt, M. A., Bettis, R. A., & Auld De Porras, D. (1987). Strategy formulation processes: differences in perceptions of strength and weakness indicators and environmental uncertainty by managerial level. *Strategic Management Journal,* **8(5),** 469–485.

Jago, A. (1994). *Organizational Behavior.* Lecture at the University of Houston.

Jain, S. C. (1990). *Marketing Planning & Strategy,* 3rd ed. Cincinnati: South-Western Publishing.

Javidan, M. (1991). Leading a high-commitment, high-performance organization. *Long Range Planning,* **24(2),** 28–36.

Judson, A. S. (1991). Invest in a high-yield strategic plan. *The Journal of Business Strategy,* **12(4),** 34–39.

Juran, J. M. (1992). *Juran on Quality by Design.* New York: Free Press, p. 300.

Kara, A., Kaynak, E., & Kucukemiroglu, O. (1995). Marketing strategies for fast-food restaurants: a customer view. *International Journal of Contemporary Hospitality Management,* **7(4),** 16–22.

Kasavana, M. L., & Smith, D. L. (1982). *Menu Engineering: A Practical Guide to Menu Analysis.* Lansing, MI: Hospitality Publications.

Katz, K. L., Larson, B. M., & Larson, R. C. (1991). Prescription for the waiting-in-line blues: entertain, enlighten, and engage. *Sloan Management Review,* **Winter,** 45–53.

Kinnear, T. C., & Taylor, J. R. (1987). *Marketing Research,* 3rd ed. New York: McGraw-Hill.

Klemm, M., Sanderson, S., & Luffman, G. (1991). Mission statements: selling corporate values to employees. *Long Range Planning,* **24(3),** 73–78.

Knorr, R. O., & Theide, E. F. Jr. (1991). Making new technologies work. *The Journal of Business Strategy,* **January/February,** 46–49.

Koss, L. (1994). New year rings in era of real change. *Hotel & Motel Management,* **209(1),** 20–21.

Kotler, P. (1991). *Marketing Management: Analysis, Planning, Implementation, & Control,* 7th ed. Englewood Cliffs, NJ: Prentice-Hall.

Kotler, P., & Armstrong, G. (1990). *Marketing, An Introduction,* 2nd ed. Englewood Cliffs, NJ: Prentice-Hall, 229.

Kotler, P., & Stonich, P. J. (1991). Turbo marketing through time compression. *The Journal of Business Strategy,* **September/October,** 24–29.

Labovitz, G. H., & Chang, Y. S. (1987). *Quality Costs: "The Good, The Bad and The Ugly."* Boston, MA: Organizational Dynamics.

Lee, L. L., & Hing, N. (1995). Measuring quality in restaurant operations: an application of the SERVQUAL instrument. *International Journal of Hospitality Management,* **14(3/4),** 293–310.

Lele, M. M. (1992). *Creating Strategic Leverage.* New York: Wiley.

Levitt, T. (1980). Marketing success through differentiation—of anything. *Harvard Business Review,* **58(1),** 83–91.

Lewis, R. C. (1985). The market position: mapping guest's perceptions of hotel operations. *The Cornell Hotel and Restaurant Administration Quarterly,* **26(2),** 84–91.

Lovelock, C. H. (1991). *Services Marketing.* Englewood Cliffs, NJ: Prentice-Hall.

Luck, D. J., & Rubin, R. S. (1987). *Marketing Research,* 7th ed. Englewood Cliffs, NJ: Prentice-Hall.

Makens, J. C. (1988). Building your customer base with key accounts. *The Cornell Hotel and Restaurant Administration Quarterly,* **29(2),** 24–29.

Makridakis, S. (1991). What can we learn from corporate failure? *Long Range Planning,* **24(4),** 115–126.

Malcomb Baldrige National Quality Award (1996). U.S. Department of Commerce, National Institute of Standards and Technology, Gaithersburg, MD 20899.

Mansfield, E. (1980). Technology and productivity in the United States. In: M. Feldstein (Ed.), *The American Economy in Transition.* Chicago: University of Chicago Press, pp. 563–582.

Marcom, J. Jr. (1990). Three-star brands. *Forbes,* **146(12),** 251, 254.

Martin, W. B. (1986a). Defining what quality service is for you. *The Cornell Hotel and Restaurant Administration Quarterly,* **26(4),** 32–38.

Martin, W. B. (1986b). Measuring and improving your service quality. *The Cornell Hotel and Restaurant Administration Quarterly,* **27(1),** 80–87.

Mayersohn, H. (1994). That dog won't hunt: why what you've always done won't work anymore. *The Cornell Hotel and Restaurant Administration Quarterly,* **35(5),** 82–87.

McCann, J. R. (1995). *Hotel Marketing Strategies.* Lecture at the Conrad Hilton College of Hotel and Restaurant Management, University of Houston.

McCarthy, E. J., & Perreault, W. D. Jr. (1993). *Basic Marketing, A Global-Managerial Approach.* Homewood, IL: Irwin.

McClave, J. T., & Benson, G. (1994). *Statistics for Business and Economics.* New York: Macmillan.

McCleary, K. W., & Weaver, P. A. (1992). Simple & safe. *Hotel & Motel Management,* July 6, pp. 23, 28–29.

McDaniel, S. W., & Burnett, J. J. (1990). Consumer religiosity and retail store evaluative criteria. *Journal of the Academy of Marketing Science,* **18(2),** 101–112.

McDaniel, S. W., & Rylander, D. H. (1993). Strategic green marketing. *Journal of Consumer Marketing,* **10(3),** 4–10.

McDonald, M., & Leppard, J. W. (1992). *Marketing by Matrix.* Oxford: Butterworth–Heinemann Ltd.

McDowell, B. (1995). America's favorite chains. *Restaurants & Institutions,* **105(3),** 52–72.

McKee, D. O., Varadarajan, P. R., & Pride, W. M., (1989). Strategic adaptability and firm performance: a market-contingent perspective. *Journal of Marketing,* **53(3),** 21–35.

McLeod, R., Jr. (1993). *Management Information Systems.* New York: Macmillan, p. 458.

Miller, D. (1994). What happens after success: the perils of excellence. *Journal of Management Studies,* **31(3),** 326–358.

Mintzberg, H. (1972). Research on strategy making. *Proceedings of the Academy of Management,* Minneapolis.

Mintzberg, H. (1978). Patterns in strategy formation. *Management Science,* **24(9),** 934–948.

Mintzberg, H. (1991). The effective organization: forces and forms. *Sloan Management Review,* **32(2),** 54–67.

Mintzberg, H., & Waters, J. A. (1985). Of strategies, deliberate and emergent. *Strategic Management Journal,* **6(3),** 257–272.

Mirabile, R. J. (1991). Identifying the employee of the future. *The Journal of Business Strategy,* **May/June,** 32–36.

Morgan, D. (1992). Think locally, win globally: Harvard's Porter pushes regional clusters as the key to industrial competitiveness. *The Washington Post,* Apr. 5, p. 1.

Myers, D. (1993). How to use local census data. *American Demographics,* **15(6),** 52–54.

Norris, M. (1992). Warren Bennis on rebuilding leadership. *Planning Review,* **20(5),** 13–15.

Olson, E. M., Walker, O. C. Jr., & Ruekert, R. W. (1995). Organizing for effective new product development: the moderating role of product innovativeness. *Journal of Marketing,* **59(1),** 48–62.

Organization for Economic Cooperation and Development (1992). The world economy in 1993: gaining momentum. *The Dallas Morning News,* Dec. 27, p. 1-H.

O'Rourke-Hayes, L. (1993). Quality is worth $11,000 in the bank. *Restaurant Hospitality,* **March,** 68.

Ozol, C. (1991). The surrogate wage function and capital: theory with measurement. *Canadian Journal of Economics,* **24(1),** 175–189.

Parasuraman, A., Zeithaml, V., & Berry, L. (1988). SERVQUAL: A multiple-item scale for measuring consumer perceptions of service quality. *Journal of Retailing, 64* (Spring), 12–40.

Parasuraman, A., Zeithaml, V. A., & Berry, L. L. Cited in Headley, D. E., & Choi B. (1992) Achieving service quality through gap analysis and a basic statistical approach. *The Journal of Services Marketing,* **6(1),** 5–14.

Patterson, W. C. (1993). First-mover advantage: the opportunity curve. *Journal of Management Studies,* **30(5),** 759–777.

Pearce, J. II, & Robinson, R. B. Jr. (1988). *Formulation and Implementation of a Competitive Strategy,* 3rd ed. Homewood, IL: Irwin.

Pearce, J. II, & Robinson, R. B. Jr. (1991). *Formulation, Implementation, and Control of a Competitive Strategy,* 4th ed. Homewood, IL: Irwin.

Perry, L. T. (1991). Strategic improvising: how to formulate and implement competitive strategies in concert. *Organization Dynamics,* **19(4),** 51–64.

Peter, J. P., & Donnelly, J. H. Jr. (1991). *A Preface to Marketing Management,* 5th ed. Homewood, IL: Irwin, p. 86.

Peter, J. P., & Donnelly, J. H. Jr. (1992). *Marketing Management: Knowledge and Skills.* Homewood, IL: Irwin.

Peters, T., & Townsend, R. (1986). *Winning Management Strategies for the Real World.* Chicago, IL: Nightingale-Conant.

Piercy, N., & Morgan, N. (1991). Internal marketing—the missing half of the marketing programme. *Long Range Planning,* **24(2),** 82–93.

Piner, P. (1993). *Hotel Marketing Strategies.* Lecture at the Conrad Hilton College of Hotel and Restaurant Management, University of Houston, April.

Pomice, E. (1991). Shaping up services. *U.S. News & World Report,* July 22, pp. 42–44.

Porter, M. E. (1980). *Competitive Strategy: Techniques for Analyzing Industries and Competitors.* New York: Free Press, pp. 89, 149.

Porter, M. E. (1991). Towards a dynamic theory of strategy. *Strategic Management Journal,* **12,** 95–117.

Powers, T. (1990). *Marketing Hospitality.* New York: Wiley, p. 304.

Price, L. L., Arnould, E. J., & Tierney, P. (1995). Going to extremes: managing service encounters and assessing provider performance. *Journal of Marketing,* **59(2),** 83–97.

Priori, J. T. (1993). NJ firms feature fitness. *New Jersey Business,* **39(2),** 14.

Quinn, J. B. (1985). Managing innovation: controlled chaos. *Harvard Business Review,* **85(3),** 73–84.

Rapp, S., & Collins, T. L. (1987). *Maximarketing, The New Direction in Advertising, Promotion, & Marketing Strategy.* New York: McGraw-Hill.

Reich, A. Z. (1990). *The Restaurant Operator's Manual.* New York: Van Nostrand Reinhold.

Reich, A. Z. (1991). An interactive plan for teaching hospitality marketing: conceptual misconceptions in hospitality marketing instruction. *CHRIE Hospitality and Tourism Educator,* **4(1),** 67–70.

Reich, A. Z. (1992). How well do you pitch? improving your classroom delivery skills, *CHRIE Hospitality and Tourism Educator,* **4(3),** 67–68.

Reich, A. Z. (1993). Applied economics of hospitality production: reducing costs and improving the quality of decisions through economic analysis. *International Journal of Hospitality Management,* **12(4),** 337–352.

Reich, A. Z. (1994a). Comprehensive strategic planning as a capstone course in hospitality education. *CHRIE Hospitality and Tourism Educator,* **6(2),** 67–70.

Reich, A. Z. (1994b). Carol Robinette vs. Hamburger Hamlet of Chevy Chase, Inc. (Deposition as expert witness). *The Superior Court of the District of Columbia,* Civil Action No. 92CA014709, May 26, 1994b Rockville, Maryland.

Reich, A. Z. (1995). Strategic implementation of nutritional programs for foodservice establishments: guidelines, recommendations, and examples. *The Journal of Nutrition in Menu & Recipe Development,* **1(2),** 3–30.

Reid, R. D. (1989). *Hospitality Marketing Management,* 2nd ed. New York: Van Nostrand Reinhold, pp. 141, 152.

Reimann, B. C., & Ramanujam, V. (1992). Acting versus thinking: a debate between Tom Peters and Michael Porter. *Planning Review,* **March/April,** 36–43.

Relihan, W. J. III (1989). The yield-management approach to hotel-room pricing. *The Cornell Hotel and Restaurant Administration Quarterly,* **May,** 40–45.

Robbins, S. P. (1991). *Management.* Englewood Cliffs, NJ: Prentice-Hall, pp. 459–479.

Robert, M. M. (1991). Attack competitors by changing the game rules. *The Journal of Business Strategy,* **September/October,** 53–56.

Robertson, T. S., Eliashberg, J., & Rymon, T. (1995). New product announcement signals and incumbent reactions. *Journal of Marketing,* **59(3),** 1–15.

Ross, E. B. (1985). Making money with proactive pricing. *Harvard Business Review,* **84(6),** 145–155.

Ross, J. (1993). *Total Quality Management: Text, Cases and Readings.* Delray Beach, FL: St. Lucie Press.

Sandy, W. (1991). Avoid the breakdowns between planning and implementation. *The Journal of Business Strategy,* **September/October,** 30–33.

Schall, L. D., & Haley, C. W. (1986). *Introduction to Financial Management,* 4th ed. New York: McGraw-Hill, p. 9.

Schlentrich, U. (1993). The World of hospitality. *Hospitality,* **January,** 14–16.

Schlesinger, L. A., & Heskett, J. L. (1991). Enfranchisement of service workers. *California Management Review,* **Summer,** 83–99.

Schmitt, B. H., Simonson, A., & Marcus, J. (1995). Managing corporate image and identity. *Long Range Planning,* **28(5),** 82–92.

Seal, K. (1991). Hotels tuning into "L.A. Law." *Hotel & Motel Management,* **206(20),** 3,29.

Senn, J. A. (1990). *Information Systems in Management,* 4th ed. Belmont, CA: Wadsworth.

Sharp, J. (1993). *Hotel Occupancy Tax Accounts: Period Ending September 30, 1993.* Austin: State of Texas.

Sisk, H. L. (1969). *Principles of Management.* Cincinnati: South-Western Publishing, pp. 6–14.

Smith, W. R. (1956). Product differentiation and market segmentation as alternative marketing strategies. *Journal of Marketing,* **21(1, July),** 3–8.

Snow, C. C., & Hrebiniak, L. G. (1980). Strategy, distinctive competence, and organizational performance. *Administrative Science Quarterly, 25,* 317–337.

Source Strategies, Inc. (1991). *The Texas Hotel Performance Factbook.* San Antonio: Source Strategies.

Spender, J. C. (1993). Some frontier activities around strategy theorizing. *Journal of Management Studies, 30(1),* 11–30.

Staff (1995). On-line options. *Restaurants USA, 15(6),* 21.

Staff of Sandelman & Associates (1994). Tracks . . . foodservice news and views. *Sandelman & Associates, Inc.,* **Spring,** 1–2.

Staff of *Skills Update* (1994). Re-engineering the workplace, what does it mean for the hospitality and tourism industry? *Skills Update,* **Winter,** 1–2.

Stalk, G., Evans, P., & Shulman, L. E. (1992). Competing on capabilities: the new rules of corporate strategy. *Harvard Business Review, 70(2),* 57–69.

Steinle, J. (1992). Making your decisions the right ones. *Hotel & Resort Industry,* **May.**

Stone, A. (1994). Hotels with corporate room service. *BusinessWeek,* Jan. 24, p. 110.

Sutherland, M. (1993). *Advertising and the Mind of the Consumer: What Works, What Doesn't and Why.* City, Australia: Allen & Unwin.

Swinyard, W. R., & Struman, K. D. (1986). Market segmentation: finding the heart of your restaurant's market. *The Cornell Hotel and Restaurant Administration Quarterly, 27(1),* 88–96.

Therrien, L. (1993). The hunger pangs let up a little. *BusinessWeek,* Jan. 11, p. 97.

Thomas, H., & Pruett, M. (1993). Perspectives on theory building in strategic management. *Journal of Management Studies, 30* (1), 3–9.

Thomas, R. (1993). The valuation of brands. *Marketing & Research Today, 21(2),* 80–90.

Thompson, A. A., & Strickland, A. J. III (1992). *Strategic Management: Concepts and Cases.* Homewood, IL: Irwin.

Thurow, L. C. (1992). To whom will world belong in the 21st century? *Houston Chronicle,* Apr. 26, pp. 1E, 4E.

Topfer, A. (1995). New products—cutting the time to market. *Long Range Planning, 28(2),* 61–78.

Traveling can be a big headache. (1992). *Houston Chronicle,* Nov. 29, p. A-14.

Tse, E. C. (1988). Defining corporate strengths and weaknesses: is it essential for successful strategy implementation? *Hospitality Education and Research Journal, 12(2),* 57–63.

Tse, E. C., & West, J. J. (1992). Development strategies for international hospitality markets. In: R. Teare & M. D. Olsen (Eds.), *International Hospitality Management.* New York: Wiley.

U.S. Bureau of the Census (1990). *Statistical Abstract of the United States: 1990,* 110th ed. Washington, DC: U.S. Government Printing Office.

Vajta, P. G. (1991). A vision to look beyond cost control. *The Journal of Business Strategy,* **January,** 54–57.

West, J. J., & Olsen, M. D. (1990). Grand strategy: making your restaurant a winner. *The Cornell Hotel and Restaurant Administration Quarterly, 31(2),* 72–77.

Whiteley, R. C. (1991). Why customer focus strategies often fail. *The Journal of Business Strategy,* **September/October,** 34–37.

Wookey, G., & Kleiner, B. H. (1991). Effective management techniques in business: lessons from famous athletic coaches. *Industrial Management, 33(4),* 17–19.

Zeigler, S. K., & Howard, H. H. (1991). *Broadcast Advertising,* 3rd ed. Ames: Iowa State University Press.

Zeithaml, V. A., Parasuraman, A., & Berry, L. L. (1990). *Delivering Quality Service: Balancing Customer Perceptions and Expectations.* New York: The Free Press.

Index